M000289924

About the Author

As a young teen I spent each waking hour being creative in any way I could. I had big dreams of becoming a writer, or a reporter, or maybe even a singer or an actress. Dreaming took me into another world. A world full of joy, that I wanted to live in forever.

As I grew and became a mother, those earlier dreams were hidden away and I devoted my life and all my pride in raising my children. They grew and had families of their own, and the empty nest syndrome was and still is too hard to bear.

My focus became my work in the caring profession. My career as a Healthcare Assistant for the NHS, at the Royal Bolton Hospital became my life. It allowed me to provide support and comfort to the vulnerable. The pride of wearing the uniform and the care and compassion within my role was overflowing. It also provides a stark contrast the way it was within my childhood and my vulnerable youth.

We are truly blessed with some wonderful countryside in Bolton. I must have walked over most of it at some point in my life. Being close to nature has always been part of my everyday routine, if not the in countryside, I'm at home in my lovely garden. I am blessed too, to be able to be close to nature and some wonderful wildlife that visit my garden every day.

My story is hard but it also represents a journey from chaos to peace and fulfilment. I am in my Happy place.

Invisible Scars

Maggie Gallagher

Invisible Scars

Olympia Publishers
London

www.olympiapublishers.com
OLYMPIA PAPERBACK EDITION

Copyright © Maggie Gallagher 2022

The right of Maggie Gallagher to be identified as author of this work has been asserted in accordance with sections 77 and 78 of the Copyright, Designs and Patents Act 1988.

All Rights Reserved

No reproduction, copy or transmission of this publication may be made without written permission.
No paragraph of this publication may be reproduced, copied or transmitted save with the written permission of the publisher, or in accordance with the provisions of the Copyright Act 1956 (as amended).

Any person who commits any unauthorised act in relation to this publication may be liable to criminal prosecution and civil claims for damage.

A CIP catalogue record for this title is available from the British Library.

ISBN: 978-1-80074-394-6

This is a work of non-fiction.

First Published in 2022

Olympia Publishers
Tallis House
2 Tallis Street
London
EC4Y 0AB

Printed in Great Britain

Acknowledgements

This book is a memoir of the early part of my life and the things that made me who I am today. Telling the story meant I had to include events of other people's lives. I had no wish to bring back unhappy memories of those involved so names and certain events have been changed. I thank the family and friends who have offered their support, and who have been constantly on hand to remind me of small details, incidents and conversations, without them this book would never have been possible. You know who you are, and what you mean to me. Massive heartfelt thanks go to my children. My love for them goes deep inside my soul. I am so proud of you all, Debbie, Nikki, Stuart and Dean. Writing this book took me into the place where all the bad memories were hidden. I felt I was reliving those memories all over again. I apologise to them if, at times, I was impossible to live with. I love you all with all my heart. Also, I would like to thank Simon Maguire for his help, understanding, patience, and never-ending encouragement. He has been a constant support and has become a dear and valued friend throughout. I also give thanks and gratitude to Olympia for believing in me.

INTRODUCTION

I am trembling at the thought of putting pen to paper after all this time. Some people say things should be left in the past. As if they think it's that easy to forget it and pretend it didn't happen.

"Get on with your life!" they tell me. Even a family member had said that too. Is that just an excuse so they don't have to listen to me? Do they think that it has not had such a devastating effect on their lives, as it has it has on mine and my children? Surely it must have had an impact. I know it must have had, their family is my family, I am part of the family too, and the trail of devastation that has been left behind has torn our whole family apart at every seam. Surely, they can see this can't they? They should open their eyes to this. Instead, they turn a blind eye and pretend nothing has happened within the family. They should be more understanding if nothing else. Shouldn't they? Do they even care?

Our family's lives were destroyed in ways which we all were never to recover from. Each family member tried to convince themselves that it should be forgotten. I've tried that too; I've tried so hard to forget but it doesn't work. Life goes on, of course it does. It's got to. I've got on with my own life, as we all have to. I've carried on, been happy with my lot in life, and yes, I've had a lot of good times. I accepted the way things were a long time ago, and I just made the most of everything that came my way.

Still, deep in the pit of my stomach, the pain has been there waiting to rear its ugly head again and again. As it has done so many times in the past.

At times, the traumas of our childhood are too difficult to deal with for all of us.

The past has had an effect on who I am today, however, I've not forgotten what was done to us, or swept it under the carpet as if it did not happen.

I hurt deeply for my brother's sake and in my mind, I still see the bruises on his face. I can still hear the screams of my mother and of my sisters when they were beaten with that 'stick'.

Still hearing those screams are partly the reason to write this, if I can, and try as hard as I might to rid myself of the nightmares, and try to deal with what has happened, and those traumas of the past will be buried once and for all.

We were only children; with little we could do about the situation. Despite it all we survived and eventually went on to live our lives away from the home of our dramatic and disturbing childhood.

We all left, in turn, and went off in different directions to lead our own lives and find some sort of happiness — something that we had been denied growing up! None of us really knew how to be happy or what it really felt like to be loved.

We left the place of our childhood behind to find our own niche in the world. A place that we all believed would be better. A place where we could find some sort of peace or even love… if it existed.

I knew what I wanted in my life from a very early age and that was to fall in love. I would disappear into all the romantic pictures in the magazines and see into a world where love existed and celebrated on television. Those pictures took me into a magical world where everyone looked so happy, their eyes were sparkling at being 'in love'. They seemed to be so close to one another.

I don't ever remember seeing that same sparkle in my mother's eyes. I remember the fear in her eyes.

I thought then that it would be wonderful to know how romance, love and tenderness could feel. Maybe I would even have my own family one day; children of my own. I always believed that I would be a great mother.

My big brother Paul, (two years older than me) hasn't forgotten his childhood and the terrible beatings he was given. He is now a loving family man. I believe he is still affected by what he went through when he was a little boy. They didn't end at all for him not until he had the courage to leave home with the rest of us.

When he got the courage to walk out that door, I knew he would never walk back through it again. What happened to Paul still gives him nightmares to this day.

Sometimes, his hands shake uncontrollably even though he is his own man, in his own house.

At times he freely talks about his past. At other times, I'm sure he has a constant battle to come to terms with the years of beatings inflicted on him by his own father. Maybe he too, needs his own answers as to the reason why he was put through all the torments he endured from such an early age. Still, somehow, he has learned to be a loving family man to his wife and his five children. How?

I still have horrible flashbacks of the past that keep coming to the surface of my mind as I'm sure the rest of them must do too.

Surely the rest of the family must realise and understand that it's not that easy to forget things and leave them in the past. I know we all have to get on with life and learn to cope with the way things are, and I know I've tried so hard to forget those times but there's always something that stirs up an ugly reminder as I go through my life.

Ann is my big sister — just over a year older than me. She has been my rock. She has always been my 'big sister' and we all looked upon her as being a mother figure, when our mum wasn't around. Now she is a mother herself to a beautiful daughter. She left the family as soon as she was old enough and made a better life for herself. Training to be a nurse from the age of seventeen and stepped on the ladder of success to become a paediatrician in a faraway country. I wonder how it has been so easy for her to forget the traumas of those early years, or has she?

Maureen, is my younger sister, eighteen months younger than me. Maureen and I were close as children for many years. We shared a secret that kept us close at that time. The closeness we shared disintegrated as we reached our teenage years. It was never to return. I have to hope that in writing this book, I might be able to find answers to certain questions that have always troubled me. However, as the years roll on and as we all grow older and greyer, some say that we should keep the widening distance between us because that is the only way there will ever be any peace in each of our lives.

My younger sister Andrea was also continuously affected by the beatings she suffered as a child. She still hasn't got over the way she was treated. Later as she grew, her psychiatrist told her that she had blocked most of the traumas out of her mind. Maybe that's a good thing for her not to be able to remember what had happened to her, and in a way I'm glad that she can't remember. However, I can remember everything that happened to her and sometimes wish that I couldn't. I still cry at the memories of what was done to her, and the immense feeling of guilt has built up over the years because I could not protect her. I was just a kid.

My baby sister Jane was also beaten terribly, from a very early age. She would say that even to this day she has had a terrible life. She has suffered many personal tragedies since her disturbing childhood, making life too difficult to cope with. Jane was such a beautiful child. As a child she didn't resemble the rest of us. She had fair hair which would turn even lighter in the summer sun, hanging in natural ringlets down her back.

I can remember Jane and Andrea being so full of mischief as youngsters and both having trouble talking properly. There were certain words that neither could pronounce. The word 'bed' would be pronounced 'bad' and 'said' would become 'sad'. For years, the daily ritual that they both had to suffer was to be flicked around the head with the back of our father's hand every time they said the words incorrectly. Neither would shed a tear to avoid being hit again.

Although we three — Ann, Maureen and myself were not beaten as Paul, Andrea and Jane were, we still were part of it and witnessed the entire trauma that took place in our home. A childhood full of cruelty and violence endured by our siblings and our mother. Later, another lady, Mary, she was also beaten. She came into our home and became our step-mother. Little did she know of the traumas that she had walked into.

Most of my earliest memories are of our mum being beaten or knocked around the house by our father. Broken furniture and shattered glass. Mum had some really bad beatings from Dad, until she was black and blue and at times had to be admitted into hospital after yet another savage beating from him. We never found out why he kept beating her. She left him many times, always returning. Each time she came back, before long, she was pregnant again.

Dad was this big aggressive man who seemed to be very charming (if you didn't know him.) He had a look of Engelbart Humperdinck and he could sing too. We were told that he had been a big hit with the ladies especially when he was singing in the local pubs, the Tempest and the Colliers.

12

Dad was in the Schooner public house singing when our mum first met him. She fell head over heels in love with him, as so many other women did too at that time. When he saw our mum, a young and beautiful dark-haired girl, who looked a lot like Sophia Loren, he was hooked. The story goes that from then on when he sang, he sang to her. It wasn't long before they were married. Mum's family liked Dad at first, but after a very short while they found out what he was really like. Another man in the Schooner had tried to chat Mum up and Dad knocked him out right in the middle of the pub. When he got home with Mum, he beat her up too, saying that it was her fault.

Understandably Mum's parents didn't like Dad from then on. They tried to stop the wedding and tried to keep them both apart. They felt so strongly against the wedding that Grandad and Dad fought several times and on one occasion Dad bit the end of grandad's finger clean off. Somehow Mum's parents knew what sort of life Mum was going to have with him. Mum turned against all her family and was soon pregnant, so they ran away and got married with only a couple of witnesses, dragged in off the street outside the registry office.

Soon their first child, Paul was born on the 13th November 1956 at Haslam's nursing home in Bolton. Soon after Dad got a job on the waterways in Shardlow, Derbyshire. They left Bolton to start a new life.

Just eleven months after Paul was born, along came Ann, on the 30th October 1957. I was born on the 3rd November 1958. We were all born in a big hospital called Babington Hospital in the village called Belper, in Derbyshire.

We lived in a caravan in Long Eaton, near where Dad worked but eventually moved into a little stone cottage with a green wooden door in a little village called Shardlow. It was right by the side of a river that would flood the kitchen every time it rained. I remember the cobbled courtyard in front of the cottage, with high stonewalls all around and huge noisy turkeys running around the grounds. Green fields and hedgerows surrounded the cottage.

Mum would have to run across these fields, knee deep in mud, to try to escape another beating from Dad if his toast was too cold or she hadn't done what was expected of her. Shortly after I was born, after Dad had beaten her up on yet another occasion, Mum had a miscarriage.

13

She was told not to have any more children by the doctors at the hospital, because she also suffered from asthma and her chest was really chronic all the time. She was told she just wasn't strong enough to cope with another pregnancy. However, against all the advice from the doctor's Mum was pregnant again soon with Maureen, born 2nd July 1960, followed closely by the arrival of Andrea on the 17th September 1961.

One morning after Dad had gone to work, Mum was found, collapsed on the floor, at the cottage by the local shopkeeper and his lovely wife, who had stopped at our cottage to drop off some groceries. She was battered and bruised. This kind old lady from the village shop gave Mum some money and helped her on the first bus back to Bolton with us all. Mum had finally escaped from Dad while he was at work. Derbyshire and Dad were left behind! Mum cried behind the dark glasses that were to conceal her black eyes, for most of the journey back to her hometown. Her tears stung her sore eyes. She wiped them away on the baby's shawl as she held her tiny fifth child, Andrea so tightly in her arms.

It didn't take Dad long to find us though. He found out where we were living, which was a pokey little one roomed flat on Seymour Road, in Bolton. He had left the job in Derbyshire and it wasn't long before she was made to go back to him. Once again Mum became pregnant, with Jane born on the 8th November 1962.

Although some people at first thought our dad was charming, we didn't at all. We were all scared stiff of him and so were a lot of other people who knew him and knew what he was capable of. I can still remember how afraid of him we all were and how he seemed to enjoy making us all feel that way continuously. Yes, he was a good-looking man, and he could sing, and turn the ladies' heads. Everyone loved him until they found out what he was really like, and it didn't take long for them to find out. Mum was stunning and glamorous. She could have had anybody, we were told, why did she have to fall for him?

Mum finally left Dad in that cold winter of 1962 and settled in Bolton and thought that she had seen the last of him. She tried to rebuild all our lives. She didn't expect Dad to ever leave Derbyshire and come in search of us. That's where my earliest memories of those early days start. I must have been around four years old.

As my childhood ended and I grew into adulthood my strong hopes for a better future putting all the nightmares of my past behind me forever, faded. I walked into an even bigger nightmare that was almost impossible to wake up from.

Another nightmare for me began and one that took me away from the only family I knew. That nightmare was to last for over twenty-five years! How could this happen? How could it be that something that had disturbed me throughout my childhood allow me to walk into another traumatic situation? Why?

What was stopping me from moving on with my life? Was it our upbringing? Would the past forever dictate the future?

CHAPTER ONE
Mum's Escape

Paul and I were playing in the garden of the tiny flat in Seymour Road that Mum had moved into when she had left Dad back in Derbyshire. It was a relatively large stone-built house in Bolton, that had been converted into flats. We all lived in just the one room.

I clearly recall one sunny day when Paul and I were running around in the overgrown back garden of this big house. There was a stone wall that had tumbled down at the top of the garden and over the wall was a dark wooded area. We were just tall enough to be able to peer over and see bluebells everywhere, all the way through the trees.

Paul took my hand and we clambered over the old stonewall and wandered into the wooded area beyond. There were tall trees with footpaths leading through. We raced together to play amongst the trees, bluebells and other wild flowers, having such a good time, we were so happy. I remember the birds singing. I could see them high up in the trees. We were skipping and running through the long grass laughing as we chased each other. Paul would hide behind a tree and I would race to find him.

We hadn't gone very far away from the house when Paul knelt down at the side of the footpath to pick some bluebells for Mum. As I wandered further up the path, something caught my eye; a horrible, gooey mess in the dirt in front of me. It looked like a big puddle of 'snot' (that is the only way of describing it.) It was disgusting! At the side of the mess there was a child's shoe! One black shoe, just like Paul's gym shoe. After studying this and poking it with a stick I shouted to my brother. With a handful of bluebells and a few dandelions he ran across to me and stared. I asked him what it was. With wide eyes like saucers, he looked at me and told me that, that's what happens to you when you put a plastic bag on your head. He ran off giggling down the path in front of me and lumbered back over the wall to take the flowers back to Mum.

I stared into the horrible mess on the ground prodding with the stick again, so horrified at hearing what my brother had told me. It really frightened me. I had the scary thought of someone putting a plastic bag on their head and then 'melting' into this horrible gooey mess. I believed everything that my big brother said, it must be true.

I also remember the quietness of that little room we shared in Seymour Road. Dad wasn't there. There was no shouting. Mum seemed to be smiling behind her dark glasses. The glasses to cover the black eyes that Mum always had. She wasn't crying any more. Before long Mum's bruises began to fade and she removed the glasses, placing them in a drawer at the side of her bed. She began to smile again.

The happiness was short lived! Dad found us and it wasn't long before Mum and Dad were back together again. We all went to live with our grandma and granddad in the house that Mum was brought up in, 20 Shackleton Grove in Bolton. She had lived there all her life with all her sisters and a brother. Grandma and grandad were moving out into a smaller place, a bungalow, just big enough for the two of them. All their children had now grown and had homes and children of their own. After a few months Grandma and Grandad found their bungalow and moved out. Mum and Dad and us children stayed behind in the house when they left.

The council were not impressed with Dad taking over the house like that and said that we all had to leave; they tried to evict us all. Mum phoned the local newspaper and they sent a reporter up and we all had our photograph in the paper. The photo was on the front page of the Bolton Evening News and showed our brother Paul playing happily in the front garden in the snow. Not long after this we were told we could stay.

The house was a three-bedroomed council house with three rooms downstairs; living room, kitchen and bathroom. It had a large back garden; which Granddad had made lovely. There were nice lawns, which were always cut short with borders at either side. In summer they were full of flowers and shrubs. The front garden wasn't as big as the back garden but was just as well kept. There were privet bushes all round; tall ones at the sides and smaller ones at the front. There was a tree that Granddad had planted when Mum was a youngster in the front garden near the front privet bushes. The house was one of four houses in a row.

In between our house and the Baron's house next door there was a ginnel, with a huge arched entrance, which led through to the back gardens. The ginnel was a lot of fun. There was a tiny, wooden doorway half way down the ginnel that was our coal shed. The coalmen would carry the coal in huge, black, dirty sacks on their shoulders. They would open the little doorway and tip the coal inside the coal shed. Inside the kitchen was another small hatchway to the coal shed also and Mum would open and fill the coal bucket from there.

Later, Dad fitted in a gas fire and blocked the old fireplace up with a big sheet of shiny blue Formica that was held in place with shiny, silver studs. Paul and I watched him work trying not to get in his way. We didn't need coal delivered any more when we got the new gas fire, so we gave it a good clearing out and started to play inside it. It was a mucky job and we got filthy but we liked our pokey, dark, secret room in the middle of our ginnel.

We pretended that it was our home away from Dad. We didn't have a dad when we played there. It was our escape! Sometimes Mum's escape from Dad too when he was in a bad mood!

When the weather was bad, we still wanted to get out of the house — out of the way of Dad — so we played in our secret house or out in the ginnel or the 'tunnel' as we would call it then. We would run wild, racing up and down the ginnel, especially when we had our clogs on and Dad wasn't in to give us a good hiding for making too much noise! We enjoyed making the noises and hearing the echoes.

The Baron's, our neighbours next door, would soon come out and tell us off. I wore my clogs all the time. They had a hard-wooden base and black stiff leather uppers nailed and studded onto the wood, fastened with thick strong shoelaces. We all had them. My brother and sister's clogs were black, the same as mine, but Jane, my youngest sister, wore little red ones. I would have liked my clogs to have been red too. I liked red. Jane's were very tiny clogs, maybe they only made the small ones in red and the larger ones in black. We wore them for school too although I didn't remember any other children wearing them. Some girls in my class laughed at them but I tried to show I didn't care.

I remember Dad fixing rubber soles on the bottom, so they wouldn't make as much noise when we ran in them. He sat them upside down on a metal thing he called an anvil and hammered away at them and fixed on the new rubber soles, which he cut from an old rubber tyre. They weren't the same after this as they weren't much fun now that they didn't make the echoing noises up our ginnel. I think the Barons were pleased though.

The Barons were lovely people, Mr and Mrs Baron and their son, Derek. They must have been quite old because their hair was as white as snow. Derek was all grown up, very tall and thin. He always wore a grey suit. According to Mrs Baron he was going blind. He could see, at the time, through glasses with thick-lenses but he would eventually become totally blind. They didn't know how long it was going to take for his sight to go but they were told it was just a matter of time. Sometimes Derek would pop his head round the ginnel and peer at us through his thick glasses and shout at us to go and play elsewhere or not make as much noise. Usually, startled by his loud, gruff voice we would hurry away and play around the front.

Mrs Baron was always baking; she would come to our house with pies and cakes she had baked for us. She never forgot us when it was baking day. They were good too! They didn't have any grandchildren of their own, so we were treated as if we were their grandchildren at times. When we played in the garden she would come to the fence and give us biscuits.

I remember one hot summers day I was playing in the street outside our house, with my doll and pram. Dad was doing something in the front garden and Mum was standing wearing her sunglasses as usual chatting to Mrs Baron over the fence. I reached forward to lift my doll up onto the pillow and I felt a sharp pain in my wrist. I dropped my doll back into the pram. To my horror there was a huge bee attached to me. I let out a big screech and instinctively tried to brush it away with my arm to try to knock it off me. My wrist hurt and I was screaming, jumping up and down uncontrollably. Dad came over to see what the matter was, followed by Mrs Baron. They soon realised what had happened. I was picked up and taken inside to Mrs Baron's house and sat on a cupboard in her kitchen. She put, what she said was, magic white paste, on it. I could see where the bee had stung me on my wrist as it was red, swollen and very sore. Mrs Baron spread the magic white paste on my wrist and soon the pain stopped. My tears soon stopped too. It really was magic paste, or was it the chocolate biscuit that Mrs Baron placed in my hand?

A few days later Dad burned my dolls pram on a bonfire in the garden, saying that the bees had built a nest in the back of it and he didn't want them to sting me again, so it had to be burned.

The Barons had a telephone — the only house in our street with one. A big black one that made a loud ringing noise that filled the house. Mum had to use that telephone at Mrs Baron's house to call for the doctor one day because my nose was bleeding. It wouldn't stop. Mum tried everything to get it to stop and had to hold a bowl in front of me. It was filling up with the blood from my nose. My nose bled for such a long time. I didn't know why. I couldn't remember why it was bleeding. I must have fallen over... again. I remember that Mum's hands were shaking and she was crying. The doctor arrived and managed to staunch the bleeding. Dad was up a ladder, at the time, painting the wall in the kitchen too busy to be disturbed. The doctor told Dad that the fumes from the paint weren't doing us any good. Dad grunted and carried on painting. When the doctor left Mum was pushed over into a chair and was shouted at.

Mrs Baron could hear Mum's screams crashing through the walls when they fought. She heard the shouting and the door slamming as Dad left. She heard Mum's cries.

When Mum and Dad didn't come home one night, Mrs Baron looked after us and made us sandwiches until we were all taken away by two ladies and a man.

CHAPTER TWO
Mum's Gone

One night as we were all asleep in our beds, I was awakened by shouting coming from downstairs. It was Dad raising his voice at Mum again. I couldn't get back to sleep so I lay there listening to his thundering voice. The noise was getting louder as Mum came running up the stairs. She was crying as he chased after her.

By the time they had reached the top of the stairs Andrea's crying, from her cot in the other room, added to the racket. I pretended to be asleep, as I always did. I knew I would have got into trouble if Dad knew I was awake. I could see Dad through the small opening of our bedroom door. The landing light was on, and I could see Mum crying. The sleeve of her flowery blouse was ripped at the shoulder. Andrea was still screaming in her cot as Mum and Dad were arguing and shouting at each other. I saw Dad reach for his belt, undo the big silver buckle and pull it off from around his waist, I took a big gasp of breath. I knew he was going to hit Mum with the belt. I heard Mum shout, "No!" to him as he charged by her knocking her to the floor. He went into the bedroom to where Andrea was screaming in her cot. I remember panicking, thinking he was going to hit the baby. Mum was screaming and screaming at Dad, pleading with him to stop. Dad took the belt and fastened Andrea down in the cot so that she couldn't get up. Mum was still crying as she was pushed backwards out of the bedroom and she fell back onto the landing and banged her head on the banister. Dad slammed the bedroom door shut behind him. I could still hear the screams of Andrea. They both made their way downstairs and I heard Mum falling again. Suddenly there was silence.

I remember wetting my bed that night. I got out of bed quietly so as not to be heard by my dad. Ann, who also had been woken by Mum and Dad fighting, saw me; she couldn't sleep either with all the shouting. She got out of her bed and quietly asked me what the matter was. Sobbing gently, I told her that I'd wet my bed. She tiptoed over to the cupboard where we kept all the sheets, opened the door gently and reached high up inside for a clean sheet. She folded it and covered the wet patch in my bed and then looked at me and put her finger on her lips. Quietly, she told me to get back into bed and go to sleep. Ann looked after me that night so that I wouldn't get into trouble.

That night Mum had been beaten, as she had been on so many other nights before. It was the way of life in our house; most nights we were disturbed by these fights. We were getting used to hearing them all the time and seeing our beautiful Mum battered and bruised the next day. The things we heard terrified us each time as we lay trembling in our beds, pretending to be asleep. We all learned to live with the broken furniture and the blood on the walls.

Next morning Mum stood at the garden gate looking for the rag and bone man coming down the street. We could hear his shouts in the distance. We knew he would be in our street next. Mum always had a few old rags for him to collect each time he came and in return she was given what was called a donkey stone. It was a square block of grey chalk. It was used to clean the doorsteps. Everybody used them to clean their doorsteps. The routine was that one house had a white doorstep and the next one had a grey coloured step. Mum used to say, "Cleanliness is next to godliness". I knew that meant everything had to be nice and clean and our mum was always busy cleaning around the house. Dad liked the house to be clean, so I could never understand why he threw his dinner all over the place. Sometimes it would be right up the walls. Mum was always made to clean it all up.

While Mum stood waiting for the rag and bone man, his voice getting louder and louder as he made his way up Moss Bank Way, I stood with her, climbing up on the gate as I wasn't big enough yet to see over the top. I liked to see the rag and bone man. He would give us brightly coloured balloons or pieces of chalk to draw with on the pavement. It kept us busy, drawing pictures in the street for hours and out of the house away from Dad.

While we were waiting, Ian Anderson, one of Paul's friends, came over to ask if Paul was playing out, but before he spoke, he looked at Mum's face. Puzzled he asked her why she was wearing sunglasses, as the sun was not shining. I looked up at Mum and she looked at me. She knew that I knew why she had the glasses on. It was to cover the black eyes that she had. She didn't say anything back to Ian, she just smiled at him and opened the gate wide enough to let him through to play with Paul who was in the back garden.

Mum had always got black eyes or some bruising to her face and body. Sometimes she couldn't hide the bruises. They were visible for all to see. I couldn't understand why Mum was being hit like this.

Sometimes Paul would have similar marks on his face. I began to think it was the way things were done; that's what happened when you got married and had a husband or wife. It was happening every day. As with all the other everyday routines I thought Mum had no choice but to put up with it.

Sometimes Dad would take Mum off for a ride on his shiny black motorbike. Mum would sit in the sidecar that was attached. I could never understand why she was bleeding into her handkerchief and shaking like a leaf when she came back.

One day I walked into my brother's bedroom and saw Mum knelt on the bedroom floor. She had moved Paul's bed and was lifting up the lino in the corner of the room, hiding a five-pound note underneath. She saw me watching and put her finger to her lips and whispered to me, 'Don't tell your dad!' Although I didn't understand why Mum was hiding money under the lino, I knew that Dad would have lost his temper with her again if he knew. I did what I was told. I never did tell Dad. She would have had another beating from Dad if I had told him and I didn't want that! I had a secret and I wasn't going to tell.

Without any warning Mum disappeared. I didn't know where she'd gone or what had happened to her. One day she was there, the next she was gone. She had left before and come back again but this time it soon became evident she had gone for good.

As the days turned into weeks, we realised she was never coming back. Nobody told us what had happened. We didn't dare ask or else we would have got a slap for sure. It was as if we had to keep our mouths shut and not talk about her again. I don't remember any of us asking about Mum or ever being told anything about her. She just wasn't there any more and that was that. She had disappeared. We wouldn't see Dad hurt her any more. She had gone but what about us? We asked ourselves if we would ever see Mum again? I remember wondering if she had taken the money that I saw her hiding underneath the lino.

After Mum had disappeared, I secretly went to look in Mum's hiding place, but the money was gone. I still kept Mum's secret just in case she ever came back. Somehow, I knew that this time she wouldn't be coming back like she had so many times before.

As the weeks and months went on, I could still remember Mum singing as she washed the dishes in the sink, 'I see the church, I see the steeple'. The song was something about a lady who was getting married. She sang the song over and over. Sometimes she sang 'Ava Maria', at the top of her voice, especially when Dad wasn't in. I would sometimes sing along with her as I watched her wash the dishes. The song would go round and round in my head when I thought of her. Occasionally, I would have fantasies that Mum had become this big film star and had been whisked away by the television people. She was very glamorous and I believed that something special had happened to her, such as becoming a movie star, just like the ones that we used to see on the TV. I thought that was the reason she couldn't be with us any more. I used to hope that when she had made a lot of money, she would come back for us all. I dreamed often that this would be true, but deep down I knew the real reason why she had gone.

We were left with Dad — Mum was gone. Jane and Andrea went soon after too. I didn't know why or where they went or whether we would see them again. Later we found out that they had to stay at Aunty Jean's house for some time and then go to stay at Aunty Nora's. Eventually, they were back at home and a strange fat woman was in our house looking after us until Dad came home from work each night.

When Dad got a job as a bin man, driving a big yellow bin wagon, this huge woman would come in our house and look after us until we went to school and until Dad came home after work. She was there when we got up in the morning and when we came home from school too. I didn't like her very much. She seemed so big and more importantly she wasn't our mum. I would stand in the corner of the living room, open the sideboard cupboard door wide and hide behind it to dress for school each morning. I didn't like the way she would stare at me when I was dressing. She would also shout loudly just like Dad. I wanted my mum, not her!

Sometimes Dad would pick us up from school in his yellow bin wagon. We thought it was very exciting to have a ride home in this vehicle as we loved it. I remember Dad being so happy and smiling as he drove us all home. We would wind the window down and wave at all our friends along the way.

Soon Dad didn't have that wagon any more and we walked home from school each night. The fat woman would be waiting at our house when we got home. She would stay with us until he got home. She would sit in dads chair like a fat blob smoking her cigarettes, one after the other, looking through the window. As soon as Dad was back, she would put her coat on, pick up her handbag and leave. I'd stick my tongue out at her through the window as she walked down the path. I hoped that she wouldn't come back but each morning she was always there when we came downstairs.

CHAPTER THREE
The Accident

Our school, Johnson Fold C.P. School, wasn't that far away from our house on Shackleton Grove. I loved going to school. Most days we would all walk there together.

I remember my first day at school and being shown around. The toilets were the first thing I remember as they were so small, just the right size for us kids. There were lots of toys in our classroom. My favourite thing to play on was a seesaw with a green metal frame and a canvas seat that two could sit in, one at either end. It was great fun. My teacher was very pleasant and talked quietly to us, not shouting at all. She was nothing like Dad. I was in the first class and made lots of new friends.

One of my new school friends was called Gwen and five years old, just like me. We both sat and played together.

One day she was gone. I never saw her again. I found out that she had died. My new school friend was gone. Everybody was very sad, and we had a special assembly in school to pray for her. I liked her a lot; she was my best friend in my class. I really missed her and have never forgot her. Her hair was dark brown, the same colour as mine and she had the largest big brown eyes I had ever seen.

I've always remembered the time when we were going on a school trip to visit a farm to see the new baby lambs. I held Gwen's hand as we all waited in a line to leave school and get on the bus that was waiting for us all in the car park. As we were about to leave the building, it started to rain heavily. We were told not to worry by one of our teachers who said that it was just an April shower. It did stop, just like she'd said it would. In fact, the rain stopped, the sun started to shine and the sky turned blue again. I looked at Gwen's little face. Her eyes were sparkling. She was smiling and so excited as she pulled me out through the door and onto the bus.

The farm was only a short bus ride away and we were soon there. We were taken on a tour around the farm, looking at all the animals. The big farmer showed us the horses and the cows. They were so big. I had never been so close to any animals before. He also took us all to see the baby lambs. We all waited quietly as he went inside a huge wooden barn. Soon he appeared holding a baby lamb. It was so cute we all said, "Ahh" as he brought it near to us. It was so white and fluffy and so tiny. The farmer then explained to us that the lamb couldn't feed from its mother and had to be fed by hand, by the farmer, from a baby's bottle. He showed us the strange shaped bottle with a teat at each end. It was full of milk ready for the lamb to feed. He asked us if we would like to feed the lamb. We all excitedly raised our hands in the air saying, "Yes! Yes! Yes!" The farmer chose me! He knelt down in front of me and asked me to kneel down and hold the lamb on my knee. He passed me the bottle and I placed one end into the lamb's mouth. He was making such a noise. I looked up at Gwen and she was smiling back at me. She came to the side of me, to stroke the baby lamb as he was being fed. He was so sweet.

Before long the school trip was over and we were back at school. It was a good day, a day that I would never forget, just like I will never forget my friend, Gwen.

Mr Beeton was our headmaster. He was a tall, large, balding man. He was always smartly dressed in a suit and always wore a different coloured tie every day. He had big black boots, which were always so shiny. He always told the children of our school to polish their shoes until they could see their faces in them.

Every day in assembly all the children would be lined up for the headmaster's inspection. He would inspect the shoes of the boys and girls, and if they weren't shiny enough the children would be in trouble. My shoes were always polished. It's something that we had to do at home as a chore, every Sunday night, ready for school the next day. Dad made us polish our shoes and they had to be done properly as he would be inspecting them too. We got a clout if they weren't done properly, or if we got some shoe polish on the floor.

When I was seven years old, my younger sister Maureen joined our school. I was in the third class then and she was in the first class. Paul, our brother was nine and one day he had to take some words home and learn how to spell them for the spelling test the next day. When he got home, he showed them to Dad. Dad then sat him on the floor in front of him and told him to spell the words. Paul didn't know them all. Dad shouted at him louder and louder, "Spell this!" "Spell that," he yelled. If he got the word wrong, he would hit him right across the face. Paul struggled with every word. Each word that he got wrong meant that he was clouted across the face, again and again. I went upstairs to play with my dolls and it wasn't long before Paul was sent to his room without any tea.

We had been at school for most of the year and we were coming up to the school holidays. It was a lovely day and we set off for school as usual. Dad was still in bed but had given us some money to spend at the shop. Maureen and I were so excited and couldn't wait to get to the shop for some sweets before school.

When we reached the shop, we realised it was Wednesday and the Co-op was closed. We were so disappointed that we couldn't spend our pennies. But then we remembered the other shop was open across the main road, Moss Bank Way. We weren't allowed to cross this road, but we wanted some toffees, so we just had to go. We knew Dad would kill us for doing this so we decided not to tell him. We sneaked across the top of our street and kept out of sight of anyone who knew us and rushed down the alleyway that led on to the main road. I was holding Maureen's hand all the way and we stopped at the edge of the main road. The shop was in front of us and we were glad to see that it was open. I could see people waiting to be served by the lady behind the counter. I knew how to cross a road; I had done it so many times before. So, still holding Maureen's hand I remembered to look left and right and then look left again. I knew that it was all clear and to keep looking and listening while we crossed. With that in mind off we went. We must have managed to get halfway across the road when a big white van hit us. I can remember seeing the pennies that I was holding in my hand, rolling across the road and into the edge of the kerb. This was the last memory from that day.

There were lots of witnesses that saw the accident and came down to try to help. We had both been knocked down. When the van hit us, we were thrown several feet into the air and we were told later that we were still holding hands when we hit the ground again. Someone rushed to tell Dad that we had been knocked down and he dashed out of the house to get to us. Dad had run down to the road to see what had happened and he grabbed the driver of the van and punched him, knocking him over in the middle of the road. Dad broke one of his fingers when he hit him.

We were both unconscious and taken in an ambulance to hospital. We went to Bolton Royal Infirmary. Maureen had received a broken leg and other cuts and bruises and was placed on the children's ward. I was unconscious for about three days, I was told. Dad and Aunty Nora later told me they thought that I wouldn't wake up. They both thought I was going to die from my injuries. Like my sister, I too had a broken leg, but had also lost a lot of blood from an injury to my foot, which needed stitches. I had other broken bones too, specifically in my chest, my nose and face. I also had scratches all over my face and my legs which were very painful.

When I finally came round, I woke up in bed with white, crisp sheets over me. I really didn't know where I was. I remember feeling scared and wondering what had happened to me. I could see green screens all around my bed. I lay there very still, as I couldn't really move. I slowly moved my head and looked around. I saw the screen move in front of me, and the face of a wrinkly, old lady was peeping through the screen. When she saw me looking at her, she smiled, then quickly disappeared. I couldn't move. I wanted to cry. I lay there wondering what was happening and thinking that I must be in hospital. Although I had never been in a hospital before. I didn't know why I was lying in that bed. I was trying to remember what had happened to me. I tried to move, but I couldn't move my arms and legs at all. My face was sore. My eyes were beginning to fill with tears. I remember hearing footsteps, getting louder as they approached my bed. I felt really scared as a tear slowly fell down my cheek. I couldn't understand where I was and what I was doing there.

The screens were hurriedly pushed to one side of the bed, which startled me, I was met with nurses busily fussing around me and writing notes on a clipboard at the end of the bed. The doctors were wearing white coats with lots of pens in their top pockets. One doctor said, "Hello," and smiled at me and said nice things to me about my big brown eyes. They told me what had happened to me and that my sister was doing fine and she was on the children's ward waiting for me. I tried to talk but couldn't. The doctor took this thing from around his neck and put one end of it in each of his ears and the other end he put on my chest. He told me it was to listen to my chest. I was told it was a stethoscope. This happened a lot over the next few days.

I had seen one of those stethoscopes before and I was reminded of the first time that I saw one. It was before our mum went away. I had come home from school and I had to stretch up and look through our front window to see if anyone was in. I could see Mum and Doctor McKenna. He was using one of those to listen to Mum's chest. She was always coughing and sometimes she couldn't even breathe properly and had to have some special medicine to make her better. I still missed her.

A few days later I was wheeled, still laying in my bed, down a long corridor and into a huge noisy lift that was just big enough for my bed and the nurses. A nurse pressed the red button on the side of the door and the lift went down. Once out of the lift we went along another corridor and through two heavy wooden doors to the children's ward. There were lots of windows and at the end of the ward there was a huge bay window with lots of brilliant sunlight shining through. I propped myself up on my elbows and looked around the big room for Maureen. The nurse pointed her out to me at the side of the ward and she wheeled my bed right next to hers. I was really pleased to see her. She was lying down in her bed sucking her thumb. Her eyes widened when she saw me. We both reached out our arms to each other and held hands. Her leg was in plaster like mine and neither of us were allowed out of bed. Both of us had a wire cage underneath the bedclothes to lift the bedding off our legs. I was bandaged on my other leg which also hurt. I didn't know what exactly I had done to that leg. I was just told I had cuts and bruises.

The ward was full of children all with different things wrong with them. Some of them were not allowed out of bed, as was the case with us, because they had their legs in traction to stretch them. It sounded strange that someone would want to have their leg stretched; maybe they had one leg longer than the other, who knows?

Soon we were allowed visitors. Dad came to see us all the time and I remember Aunty Nora coming to see us. Mum never came. I was too scared to ask Dad if Mum would be coming to see us, or to ask for her. I just hoped that she would come but she never did. We were in hospital for months but no visits from Mum or any of her family. I couldn't understand why.

There were lots of visits from Aunty Nora. She would bring us lots of presents, sweets and toys to play with. She bought me a doll, which had a lovely outfit on. It had a white all-in-one stretchy suit and a brown pinafore dress over the top and another outfit that came with it — a pair of dungarees. I could undress it and change its clothes. I played with this doll all the time. It was the nicest doll I'd ever seen. For some reason the nurses took this doll from me and wouldn't let me have it back. I remember crying and asking for it back, but it was never returned. I was too scared to tell Dad just in case I got in trouble for being selfish as well as being in trouble with the nurses. Our visitors bought sweets and chocolate for us too, but the nurses took them from us when our visitors had gone. They said they were to be shared with the rest of the ward, but they never were, we never saw them again.

After a while we started to get a bit clever and began hiding our treasures in our beds and in our cupboards amongst our other things, but the nurses found most of our chocolates and we were told off. The nurses were strict and really liked to tell us off when things were found hidden in our bed or under our pillow, but we still tried to get away with things. Most of our presents from our families were well hidden. When the nurses didn't find our stashes of sweets, we would have lots of fun at night when the nurses thought that they had tucked us all up. They would turn off all the lights, wish us goodnight and go to their office. When they disappeared, we would whisper to each other from across the ward to see who was awake and who had got sweets to share. We would throw sweets to each other from across the ward. None of us could get out of bed, so we'd miss each other's beds most of the time and the sweets would land on the floor and we couldn't get them.

Early the next morning when the nurses came back into the ward, there would be Liquorice Allsorts scattered all over the floor. We were all asked questions as to where they had come from. Of course, nobody had a clue where they had come from at all! The nurses got very clever and soon found all our hiding places. They amazed me with their ability to find out everything. They even knew whether we had washed behind our ears or not. They knew everything, we had to be very careful.

As the weeks went on, I got better and stronger and the time came to remove the stitches from my leg. The nurses told me that they had to attend to my foot and I must be very brave. I held the hand of one of the nurses very tightly. I hadn't seen my foot and what I had done to it. The nurses were gentle and kept asking me if I was all right and whether they were hurting me. They weren't at all; it wasn't painful at all. I expected it to hurt a lot, but it didn't. The nurses said I was very brave and soon they were done and all the stitches were out. There was a long scar across my ankle and I knew I would have that for the rest of my life. I thought the scar was cool, it was in the shape of a cross. I used to think that it was the mark of Jesus' cross on my ankle and that he had put his mark on me to protect me in some way.

The next day it was Maureen who was to have something done, but that wasn't pleasant at all. She had developed a huge and very painful boil on her bottom.

This was the day when the nurses had to lance the boil. Maureen was screaming her head off as she didn't want them to touch it. It was too painful, but it had to be done. A few nurses held her down on the bed as she was kicking and screaming for them to get off. All the children on the ward were staring and the other nurses stood around watching.

I couldn't stand to hear her loud and piercing screaming any longer so I reached for my headphones from behind my bed and put them on my head. The music was quite loud from the headphones, but I could still hear her screaming, so I held the headphones tightly to my ears to try to block out her screams. As I held them tightly Maureen let out this almighty scream and I got an electric shock, from the headphones, which made me jump and my hands tingle. I took them off my head quickly and threw them down onto the floor. Maureen quietened down then, as the nurses' job was done. She rolled over, put her thumb in her mouth and went off to sleep.

After seventeen long weeks in hospital, I was allowed home. Maureen had gone home a few weeks before me, so I was glad when finally, I was allowed home after so long. My favourite doll, the present from Aunty Nora, was never returned to me when I was going home. It was never seen again after it was taken from me on that ward. I never forgot that doll. When we were leaving the hospital, Dad was handed a big plastic bag. Inside it were our clothes, the ones that we were wearing on the day of our accident. The doctors had needed to cut the clothes off us because we were so badly injured when we first arrived at the hospital. We couldn't wear them any more, so they were thrown away.

We were in hospital for such a long time, but our mum never came, not once. I waited and waited. I looked for her every day. I hoped every day that she would come. Every day at visiting times I would sit and stare at the blue wooden doors at the top of the ward wishing that she would walk through. The other children in that ward had their mums sitting by their beds every day, but our mum never came.

When I finally got home, I had to sleep downstairs with Maureen, in a single bed. We both still had our legs in plaster and we were both still on crutches and couldn't go upstairs. The single bed was in the front room downstairs and we had to sleep top to tail, which wasn't very easy and neither of us had much room to move around. Maureen still had a sore bottom from the boil that she had in the hospital and it wasn't long before I accidentally banged into it with my plastered leg while getting into bed. She screamed loudly in pain.

After a few weeks we were allowed to go back to school. I had missed school a lot and although we had to have a few lessons in hospital, I would have rather been at my own school. We were still both in plaster, so we had to use our crutches to get around. We had both become experts with our crutches by then. We had no trouble at all getting to and from school, in fact it was fun. We had to put our pot legs up on chairs while we were sitting at our desks. I couldn't wait to get the plaster off, so that I would be able to run around with the others in the playground.

After a few more weeks the plaster was taken off at the hospital. It felt strange at first not to have the weight of the plaster on my leg after so long, but I was soon running around with the others once again. Later, after Maureen had her plaster removed, she still experienced quite a few problems with her leg. It would lock and stiffen at the knee when she was sitting down or kneeling on the floor. She would scream out loudly in pain until Dad would knock her knee with his hand to release it. This would happen quite often when she wasn't expecting it This went on for years afterwards. We were both awarded £365 by the courts, as compensation from the man in that van who knocked us down. It was put in a trust until we were older but by the time, we were fourteen there was nothing left because Dad had made withdrawals on our behalf for school uniforms and other things.

CHAPTER FOUR
The Stick

As the years went on, we were all pupils at Johnson Fold School. There was a member of our family in every class at our school. All the teachers knew our family. We all walked to school together each morning and walked home together when school was finished for the day. One day after school we were walking home together and Andrea caught her dress on the bushes at the side of the path that led out through the school gates. She looked down and the hem to her dress had ripped quite badly.

When we got home, Dad saw what she had done to her dress and went absolutely crazy. He was shouting and bawling his head off, you could hear him all the way down the street. We sobbed our hearts out assuming we were all going to have a good hiding. We were all standing at the back of the living room and watching Andrea looking up at him, her eyes widened in terror as he was shouting at her. It was difficult to hear what he was saying as he was shouting so loudly. I was crying and needed to go to the toilet. Frozen to the spot I stood watching Dad, wondering what he was going to do with her. She was six years old. I'd seen what he used to do with Mum. Now he was about to start on Andrea.

Dad was always very strict, and we knew that if we were naughty, he would really punish us, but this time it seemed different. He was really angry. Dad turned to Paul, shouting to him to go outside to find something to hit Andrea with.

We were all shaking in horror and sobbing, trying not to cry so Dad wouldn't turn on us. He didn't like any of us crying. We were always told not to cry or else we would get something to cry for, which usually meant a back-hander around the face.

Dad sat down in his chair waiting for Paul to come back with something that he could hit our little sister Andrea with. I couldn't believe that he would really do such a thing to her. We all stood behind the settee silent, watching. The sound was broken several times by the sound of Andrea's sobs as she stood waiting for what was about to happen.

Next, the back door opened and in walked Paul. Dad stood up from his chair and stood in front of sobbing, trembling Andrea. Paul entered the living room and looked at Dad. His eyes were red with crying and he had a scratch on his face which was bleeding slightly. He held out his shaking hand to Dad which held a little twig that he had broken from a tree. I guess he must have caught his face when he snapped the twig from the tree. Dad turned to Paul and snatched the twig from his hand and threw it down. With his face reddened and screwed up he said, "That's no bloody good!" He raised his arm and Paul cowered. Dad clouted Paul around the head and pushed past him. Paul dropped to the floor banging his head on the sideboard as he fell. Dad went outside to the back garden to look for something to hit Andrea with. We were all still watching our tiny sister Andrea sobbing and visibly shaking for what seemed like hours waiting for Dad to return. I really wanted to go to the toilet, but we were all frozen on the spot watching Andrea from behind the settee. We knew we all had to stay put. There was nothing we could do.

After a few minutes, I could hear Dad coming back through the back door, Andrea started to cry a bit louder. She knew what was going to happen. We all did. Dad barged through the door and it banged against the sideboard, making us all jump and tremble even more.

In his hand was a stick, long and about two inches thick. He had ripped it off an old door that we had in the back garden. We all stared at this stick and gasped. I was shaking uncontrollably. Andrea's cries grew louder at the sight of the stick he was about to hit her with. Andrea was pleading with him not to hit her, saying she was sorry over and over. She dropped to her knees. We all looked on, rigid with fear at what we were seeing.

Dad grabbed Andrea by her thick, curly black hair on the top of her head and pulled her up and started to hit her on the behind with the stick. We felt every blow too! I couldn't hold myself any longer and wet myself. I just couldn't help it. Blow after blow, they went on and on and on. Knocking her around and around. I could see blood running down her chin from the corner of her mouth. When he was done, he threw the stick to the floor releasing Andrea from his grasp. Andrea fell to the floor on her knees, crying and wincing from the pain. Dad then turned to us all and told us to get out of his sight. We all ran as fast as we could up those stairs and into our beds. Andrea was sobbing for most of the evening until Dad came upstairs and told her to shut up or she would get some more. As quietly as she could, she sobbed and sobbed until she was finally asleep.

We couldn't console her at all. We just had to leave our little six-year-old sister alone and stay in our beds not making any noise at all, in fear of him coming upstairs again. I lay in our dark bedroom listening to Andrea's sobs. Our stomachs were empty. There was no tea for any of us that night. My stomach rumbled as I wiped the tears from my face with my sheet and drifted off to sleep.

That was the first time he had used that stick to hit any of us with. Usually, he'd take his belt off and have us bend over the settee. One after another, we were all belted like that. He used his hands also everyday but mostly that was only done when we hadn't done anything wrong. He would just clout us across the head when we had to pass him or if we became too close to him. He used to say, 'That's before you do anything'. We soon learned not to get too close to him.

The stick became a regular feature in our house. It was used on several other occasions after that and was always available and near at hand for him to use it when he wanted to. When it was not in use, it was propped up at the side of his chair within his reach.

On Saturday nights, when the football results were on television, we all had to sit in silence while he watched and listened to them. If any of us made a noise or we started to squabble between ourselves, he would quickly lunge forward and reach for the stick. We'd all disappear in a flash upstairs and not come down again for the rest of the night.

There were many nights like this when we were sent to bed without having anything to eat at all. Each time I would listen to my tummy rumbling before finally drifting off to sleep.

Most nights all of us would sit in the front room huddled together on the settee or sat close to the fire, keeping warm. The front room was the warmest room in the house. We would sit on the rug in front of the fire, drawing pictures on scrap paper. We were always very quiet so as not to disturb Dad until we were all sent to bed at eight pm. On very rare occasions we were allowed a biscuit or a slice of toast before bed and I would eat mine slowly, so I wouldn't be sent to bed until we had finished. Sometimes it worked and we did manage to stay up a bit longer.

Dad found another use for that stick, as well as hitting us with It. He used it to dunk the washing in the washing machine. We had a twin tub; a washtub on one side and a spin tub on the other side. The water would get very hot when the heater was put on and steam would fill the kitchen. When we were younger and smaller, I remember that Mum would bathe us all in it. It was just big enough to fit us in and give us a good bath.

When we grew too big to fit in the washing machine Dad brought home a big, grey tin bath. It had to be hung up on the back of the door. We all had a bath in it. Paul took his bath first, then the rest of us, one after another. We had to be quick to bathe before the water went cold.

Sooner or later we all had a 'taste' of that stick. When Jane was about six, she started to bring reading books home from school to practice. One night we were all ready for bed and sat in the living room waiting for bedtime. Jane was knelt down on the floor at the side of Dad trying to read her book. He was sitting on the edge off his chair listening to her as she struggled with the words. He reached out for the stick and laid it down on the floor in front of him. Jane paused and looked up at him and tried to edge away from him in fear of getting hit with the stick. Again, we all sat rigidly, we knew now that Jane was going to get it. She looked so tiny knelt down on the floor at the side of him. She was told to carry on reading. She trembled and got stuck on a word so Dad reached for the stick and whacked her with it across her arms. The more she struggled with the words the more Dad lashed out at her. She sat trying not to cry and trying with all her might to get the words right but the more he hurt her the more frightened she became until she couldn't say any of the words from the book that was in front of her. Dad struck her again with the stick across her arms and asked her what the word was again. She whimpered. She didn't know. She was shaking with fear and couldn't say anything by this time. The more he hit her, the more she was blinded by the words until she couldn't see them any more. With silent tears she was sent to bed.

The next morning, I got up early and I could hear voices downstairs. When I went into the living room, Jane was sitting on Dad's knee, as the doctor had come to examine her. The doctor was talking to Dad about

Jane and suggesting that he give her medicine and keep her off school for the rest of the week. The doctor told Dad that Jane had a very high temperature and tonsillitis. When the doctor had gone Jane was put back to bed. That was the first and only time I had seen Jane sitting on Dad's knee. Dad had never sat any of us on his knee, ever. I always thought it was strange that the doctor never mentioned the bruises on her arms.

Before long Dad had found another use for that stick!

CHAPTER FIVE
Memories of Shackleton Grove

After chores were done in our house we were allowed to play out. Sometimes when the weather was bad, we had to stay home and find something to do. I was always knitting or making something out of cardboard boxes.

One afternoon I was sitting on our brand-new settee that Dad had just bought a few weeks earlier. I had my sewing box, needles, cotton and scissors. I spent most of the afternoon making some clothes for my Sindy dolls. When I finished, I put everything back away in the box and stood up to take everything back upstairs. As I was leaving the room Ann looked down at where I had just been sitting and there was a tear in the vinyl on the arm of the settee. I was horrified. It was about an inch long. I looked down and couldn't believe it. My stomach churned! I felt sick.

Jane looked on, then rushed out to tell Dad what had happened. Dad had been at a neighbour's house, and was so angry when he came in. His eyes widened as he inspected the damage and started to shout at us.

We were all stood, shaking and silent with fear, at the back of the settee looking at the damage. I managed to stutter to Dad that I was sitting there with the scissors but I didn't do it. The others were saying, "It wasn't me, Dad! It wasn't me!" At this point he went out of the room, I'm not sure why, but we all assumed he might have gone to find something to hit us with. As he was walking out of the room, he said that whoever had done it had better own up or that we would ALL get a good hiding when he came back. I was almost wetting myself again as I stood there waiting for him to come back. I was the one who must have done it; I was the one with the scissors. I turned to Andrea and said, "Say it was you and you can have my china tea set." Of course, she said no.

After a few seconds Dad came back into the room. His big, thick black belt with the silver buckle was ready in his hand. I remember thinking to myself at that time, why is he using his belt and not the stick? It was there in its usual place at the side of his chair. He folded his belt in half. It was now ready to be used to hit us. I looked at Andrea. I could tell by the look on her face that she was going to tell Dad what I had said to her while he was out of the room. She was just about to tell him what I had asked her, so I shouted out, "I did it! It was me. I'm sorry! I'm sorry!" He looked at me, and said, "Right get over!" I knew those words so well. We all did. With the belt in his hand, he pointed to the settee. I did as I was told. I was already in tears as my dress was lifted up and I was belted on the behind several times. I had already wet my knickers as I silently sobbed with my face buried deep into the cushion on the settee.

When it was over, I went upstairs and changed myself. My bottom stung but I was relieved that I hadn't been hit with that stick. I'd managed to avoid it so far and I wanted it to stay that way. My bottom was stinging, and I couldn't sit down but I thought it would have been a lot worse if he had used the stick. I was still not sure whether I had done that to the settee, but it was me who had had the scissors. There was no other reason for the settee getting damaged though. It must have been an accident; I wouldn't have done it on purpose.

I didn't use my sewing box again and I wasn't allowed to touch the scissors ever again. Dad put some glue and black tape over the tear in the arm of the settee, but as the months went by the rip got bigger and bigger until finally the settee was thrown on to the bonfire.

After that day, after all our chores were done, I would make sure that I went outside even if the weather was bad. We all would rather have been outside rain or shine, rather than inside with Dad. He was always in a bad mood and was always shouting at one of us as, in his eyes, we could never do anything right. We never ever knew why. We just knew it was best to stay out of his way as much as possible.

Our garden wasn't as nice as it was when grandad was looking after it, when he lived there. Maybe this was due to us kids running about all over it. Sometimes Dad would make a start and do some digging in the garden. He would use his big spade and dig at the bottom of the garden. He had already dug up lots of flowers and rose bushes. There were weeds growing there now — dandelions and buttercups. I liked buttercups. If you held the buttercup under your chin, you could tell whether you liked butter or not. The yellow from the flower would shine under your chin and that meant you liked butter. I didn't like dandelions much because

Ann told me that if you picked them you would wet the bed, so I never went near them.

One sunny day when I was sitting on the stones at the bottom of the garden, I was playing in the dried-up soil trying to dig with an old spoon that had been left in the garden all winter and had rusted. The soil was dry and crumbly almost like powder. The hole I was digging was getting deeper and deeper. I didn't really know why or what I was digging for. I think I was just bored and didn't want to go indoors out of the sun. I sat happily digging away at the soil when the spoon suddenly hit against something hard. My eyes widened as I tried to see what I had found. Excitedly, I began to dig faster; it was something big and hard and looked like some sort of pot. I removed the soil gently from around the pot and tried to lift it carefully out of the earth, but it wouldn't budge. I could see that there was writing and some sort of picture on the side of it, but I still couldn't tell what it was. After removing more soil from around the pot and from inside it, it began to move. It had a handle at one side and I tried to hold it and pull gently and lift it from the ground. It must have been in there for years, I thought to myself, as I finally released it from the ground. It was very dirty, but it did appear to be whole. It was a large cup. I wiped away the soil from the front and underneath was a picture and the words "British Railway Company" over the top of the picture. I didn't understand why it was buried in our garden. I took it indoors and washed it in the kitchen sink. It was a bright yellow colour and not damaged at all. I thought it might have belonged to our granddad and he had lost it in the garden when he was digging. Dad said he didn't think he worked on the railways, so it couldn't have been his. I kept it in a safe place and thought if I ever saw Granddad again, I would ask him if it was his and he could have it back.

I had watched Dad do some digging at the bottom of the garden and one day I decided to have a go myself with the garden fork, when Dad wasn't looking. The fork was heavy, so heavy I could hardly lift it, as it was nearly as big as me. I stood at the bottom of the garden, and after checking that Dad wasn't watching from the window, I lifted the fork up high and dropped it in the ground but instead it went in my foot. I felt a sharp pain and let go of the fork. I could see blood seeping through my sock. I wanted to let out a scream, but I couldn't let Dad find out that I was playing with his garden fork. I knew that I would have been in trouble. I could hardly walk and tears were streaming down my face.

I hobbled around through the ginnel to the front of the house, went in through the front door and sat on the stairs. I slowly took my shoe off and then my sock. The fork had made a hole in the top of my foot. I wiped the blood away with my sock. The house was empty, so I went through to the bathroom to wash away all the blood. The wound was deep and bleeding a lot and it hurt so badly but I just couldn't tell anyone. Dad wasn't around. I think he had nipped to one of the neighbour's houses. I never did tell him what I had done; it was my own fault for messing about with his garden tools. He did tell me not too. My foot was sore for ages and when it healed, I was left with a scar on the top of my foot.

One time Dad gave us a tent to play with in our back garden. He said he had owned it since he was in the army. We all tried to put this tent up in the garden. It was made of a thick heavy canvas material so we could hardly lift it. We would get one side up and bang the pegs into the ground and then go to the other side, to get that end up too and the first side would fall down. It was really hard work. It was far too heavy to lift for us girls, so Paul went for a couple of his mates to come and help. Eventually, after all their hard work it was up and we could play inside it. The ground sheet was put down inside the tent and we all went inside and played camping out. We thought that it would be good to camp out all night in this tent, but I didn't think Dad would have let us. The tent was really big. We could all stand up inside it. Soon we had a garden full of kids playing in our tent. We weren't allowed to sleep in it of course but we kept it up for days and days.

I moved all my dolls in there, after a while and I used to imagine that this was my house and my dolls were my children. I was busy playing in the tent one day, talking to myself and my dolls when all at once the tent collapsed right on the top of me and my dolls. I was really scared. My heart was beating so fast and I couldn't breathe. I thought I would never get out of there. The weight of the tent was too heavy for me to lift and I was scrambling underneath to try and find a way out. I was beginning to panic a little bit and started to scream for someone to get me out. Thankfully, Paul appeared and lifted the tent off me. I told him I was scared stiff and I thought that I was going to suffocate. He started to laugh his head off and told me not to be so soft. The tent was put up again and Paul and the others played in it quite a lot after that with all their mates, but I never went in it again after that day. I think Dad sold it to a man up the street a few weeks later.

All the children in our street used to play together — all ages, all sizes. We all used to look after each other. We would play with skipping ropes and roller skates. The boys would help us to make go-karts out of wheels that were off old prams that had been thrown out and left on the waste land at the back of the houses on our street. We would attach the wheels to planks of wood. The front wheels were attached with a nut and bolt to the wood. A hole had to be drilled through so that the wheels would pivot. We attached a long piece of rope to one side near the wheel and then to the other side. When the go-kart was ready, we would have races down the street and down small hills in the park. It was fantastic! Sometimes there would be a few accidents and someone would fall off and have a few bumps and scratches, but we'd still get right back on again and have another go.

I remember when Paul made his go-kart and went to the top of Sabden Brew. He came hurtling down on it really quickly; he crashed it right into the Taylor's house at the bottom and broke their fence. The go-kart was intact but Mr Taylor came out and gave Paul a good telling off. Thank goodness he didn't tell our dad!

When the buckles on our roller skates were broken and could no longer be worn, we would make a new plaything out of them. We made what we would call a book-skate. We just had the wheels and the metal that they were attached to and we would put an old Beano annual on top and sit on it. It was great fun riding and going down Sabden Brew speeding fast. We entered into competitions to see who could stay on the longest and particularly to see who could stay on to the bottom of the hill. I was quite good at it as I could stay on the book-skate all the way down the hill.

One day we had been playing with our 'book-skate' most of the day and I was on my way down the hill with the wind blowing through my hair. As I reached the bottom of the hill the coal wagon went flying by, right in front of me. Just a second later and I would have gone straight underneath that wagon. I could have been squashed by one of those big wheels. It really frightened me so I didn't play that game on the hill again after that. Maybe I wouldn't have been so lucky the next time.

Summertime in Shackleton Grove was great fun. Dad and some of the other neighbours would play football in the street. Paul would join in too; he would laugh and run around kicking the ball towards Dad and seemed to enjoy Dad playing with him. One day Paul fell over and cut his lip; it was pouring with blood. His tooth had gone straight through his lip. He lay sobbing on the ground. Dad yanked at his arm and shouted at him to get up and clipped him around the head and told him to stop being so soft. I don't remember our Paul playing football with him again.

There used to be an empty house at the top of our street and all the local children would gather at this house to play in the garden. The house had been emptied for a long time. All the kids in our street would say that this house used to have a witch living in it. She died, and her body was found in the house weeks after. It was said to have been a horrible sight with flies everywhere and the maggots had eaten her. The house was all boarded up and there was a horrible smell around the house, but we all still played in the garden. There was a tall, brick built shed at the side of the house with a flat roof. We loved to clamber up and jump off onto a couple of old mattresses that had been dumped in the garden. It was great fun. We lined up on the roof of the shed and took our turns. Each of us had a different jump every time. Someone would jump off backwards and some would do somersaults. I wasn't all that brave to do all those acrobatic jumps but it was still great fun jumping through the air and landing with a bump at the bottom. No one got hurt. It was fun and quite safe. We were happy.

On one occasion we had been having so much fun playing at our game, when Maureen had a disagreement with one of the other kids. I think she missed her jumping turn or someone pushed in before her, so she raced home and said that she was going to tell Dad what we were doing. We hadn't been told not to play on this shed, so we carried on playing.

Maureen came back saying that Dad wanted us all in right now. We all came out of the garden and headed home. When we got in Dad was standing there with his belt in his hand. He asked us what we had been doing. We said we were only playing up the street in the garden. He said,

"Right bend over." He waved his belt towards the settee for each of us to lean over. Paul went first, then Ann and each one of us in turn. We had to go round again for a second belt, then a third. We were all hit apart from Maureen; she stood at the corner of the room watching as we were all punished. As I was belted, I looked at her standing there watching and there was a wicked smirk on her face. She was smirking because she had got us all in trouble.

As we got older, we managed to wander further and further away from home. We would all play together, us and other friends from our street and we would go to different places exploring. We would go to Moss Bank Park, Barrow Bridge and to Doffcocker Lodge.

Doffcocker Lodge was a lovely place. It was a huge lodge in the middle of fields. There were swans on the lake, which I really liked, but you couldn't go near them because they would attack you. We used to sit on the bank of the lake and watch them flying and landing on the lake. Sometimes they would come up really close to you and make you think they were coming to say hello, but they weren't. They were just checking us out to see if we had some food for them (which we never had) and would have eaten ourselves if we had as we were always hungry.

It was a lovely walk all the way around the lodge with always lots of other people out jogging or walking their dogs. The best time was in summer when we could paddle our feet in the water. There was a little stream leading off away from the lodge and this wasn't very deep, but the water ran on cobbles which were really slippery, so it was difficult to walk on them, if we had taken our shoes and socks off. Maureen did slip on them one day and got wet through. Although she was upset and started to cry, it was so funny we all laughed our heads off. We had to stay out until she had dried off in the summer sun, so we wouldn't be in trouble when we got home.

There was another occasion that wasn't funny at all. When we opened our front door that morning, the snow had piled up behind it and it came tumbling in the house. We had to get the shovel and move it back outside. We had had a lot of snow during the night but despite the freezing temperature Ann, Paul and I went down to the lodge. Everything had frozen up.

Doffcocker Lodge looked as pretty as a picture, all white and frosty.

It was just like the pictures on the Christmas cards on display in Bastows; our local newsagents and toffee shop. As the lodge was frozen solid, we could stand on it. We were having great fun sliding on the ice pretending we were ice skaters. Ann and I decided to skate out on the ice to see if we could get right out to the middle of the lodge to where the little island was; we wanted to look to see if the swans were hiding amongst the reeds. We hadn't seen them for ages. We had gone quite a long way out onto the ice and we could hardly hear Paul shouting to us from the edge of the lodge. We couldn't hear what he was saying so we just waved at him. Suddenly we stopped because we could hear the noise of the ice cracking under our feet. Frozen with fear we both held our breath. We grabbed each other tightly and started to scream our heads off. We were both really scared. We thought that the ice was going to break underneath us and we would drown in the deep water. Neither of us could swim. Neither of us could move. We were too scared to move as the ice cracked loudly. Tears were streaming down our faces. We pleaded for someone to help us; we screamed and screamed. We were sure Paul was still on the bank of the lodge. Would he come and get us? Without knowing how, we got back to the bank. We dried our tears and made our way back home. Still to this day I can never remember how we got off that ice that day. We learned a lesson though, that day. The lodge could have swallowed us up forever. We would never do that again. There must have been a guardian angel watching over us that day.

Barrow Bridge was a lovely wooded area with a stream running through it and footpaths that led through the trees and up the hills to green fields with miles and miles of countryside. There were old stone steps that used to lead to an old factory which had been knocked down years ago. We would run up and down the steps and try and count them all. We always came to a different number each time as we lost count on the way down, but I think there were sixty-three steps altogether!

The houses at Barrow Bridge were beautiful, just like the ones you see on a jigsaw puzzle box. The stream ran all the way through the little village, with little waterfalls at places where the water level dropped. We could go paddling in the water as it wasn't all that deep. The pebbles were a bit slippery though and sometimes we would slip and end up wet through. We didn't dare go home until we had dried off. The stream was full of little tiny silver coloured fish. Paul told me they were called

Tiddlers or Sticklebacks because they had spikes on their backs.

One day we went to the stream with our jam jars and caught some of these fish to take home. Once our jam jars were full of fish we set off for home, excited that we were going to make a fishpond in our garden.

At home we looked around to find something to make our pond with. All we could find was an old washing bowl. We thought that that would do so we filled it up with water and put our fish in. We put stones at the bottom and Paul chopped up a worm, so they had something to eat. We stayed and watched them swimming around until it was time to go in. They seemed so happy in their new pond.

The next day, we went to see our fish. To our horror they were all dead and floating on top of the water. We couldn't understand why they had died. We decided to go back to Barrow Bridge and get some more. We thought it could have been the worm that had killed them. Maybe fish don't like worms, we thought. We collected more Tiddlers and placed them in our washbowl, acting as a fishpond.

The next day the fish were dead again. We had made a lovely fishpond for them and this time we didn't put a worm in there. We soon got tired of going fishing only to have the fish die, so we didn't bring them home any more. We would still go fishing but after we had caught them, we would let them all go again back into the water when we were ready to go home.

Moss Bank Park was another favourite place we would like to go exploring. There were lots of things to do; swings, roundabouts and the sand pit. At the far side of the park near the wooded area, there was a very old tree trunk that had been there for years and years. It had fallen down ages ago and it was just left where it fell, maybe for the children to play on. Each summer this tree trunk would be covered in ladybirds and we all used to collect them, take them home and put them in our garden.

We would also collect caterpillars off the trees in the park. They were mainly yellow ones with black dots all the way down their backs. There used to be hundreds of them. The trees were covered with caterpillars. If you were lucky you would come across an unusual type of caterpillar. I found one once that was quite unusual as it had a long, brown body covered in spiky hairs and about half way down its body there was a little black raised lump sticking out. I put this caterpillar into a matchbox and took it home. I kept it in the garden for ages until one day it went missing.

I thought it might have escaped into the garden. I searched for my little friend for ages, but I never did find him.

There were animals in the park as well; rabbits, guinea pigs, goats and chickens. They were kept in the old stone building at the side of the rock gardens. The gamekeeper was called Jimmy and became a really good friend to us. We all used to go and talk to him and he would tell us all about the animals and how to look after them. The rabbits had lots of babies and Jimmy said that we could have one if we wanted to. I would have liked a rabbit of my own, but I wasn't sure that Dad would let me have one. I was told to go and ask him and if he said that I could, to go back to Jimmy and I could pick my own. I knew what Dad would say before I asked him, so it took a while for me to ask.

When I thought he was in a good mood I asked him. To my surprise he said yes. Then the others asked if they could have a rabbit as well, and he said that we could only have two rabbits. We couldn't believe that Dad had said yes. We all felt really happy and raced down to the park to tell Jimmy. Jimmy took us into a shed where the rabbits were. We chose two fluffy white ones with the pink eyes. They were so cute. They were placed in a box and we made our way back home.

When we got home, Dad had already made us a rabbit hutch out of an old cupboard that had been thrown in the outside shed. It had wire mesh on one side and a door on the other side. It looked really good and I thought it was a very nice house for our rabbits. Ann and I named them Snowy and Queenie. They were only about two months old and still so tiny. Jimmy gave us straw and sawdust for the rabbit hutch and some food for them to eat. We had to buy some more from Mittens pet shop in town when we needed it.

The rabbits soon grew bigger, but had to be separated because my rabbit was having babies! Dad told me she was pregnant and I was so excited. I just couldn't believe they were going to have some babies. I just thought she was fat. She started to bite the fur away from her neck and take it into her bed. She would also collect the straw in her mouth with it sticking out at each side and take it into the nest box. It was amazing to watch. This activity carried on for ages until the nest box was full of straw and fur.

The next day I went to her to feed her. She was still in the nest box. She peeped her head out and looked at me as if to say hello, but she didn't seem to want to come out of the nest box. I put some food in her dish and left her alone to have her babies.

I told Jimmy, our friend from the park that my rabbit had had babies and he told me that I shouldn't try to look into the nest box because she might get scared that the babies were in danger and she could eat them. This horrified me. I made sure Queenie was not disturbed by any of the others at all.

After about a week she was coming out of the nest box more and more and I was allowed to take a little peep in at the babies when she was busy eating. Oh, they were so cute, there seemed to be lots of them. I couldn't count how many there were as they were all curled up together in their nest. They looked so warm and snug.

After a couple more weeks, the babies were peeping their heads out from the nest box. There were eight of them. They were all white with pink eyes like their mum and dad. They were like little fluff balls. We weren't allowed to keep any of them, so when they were old enough, they were taken to Mittens pet shop down town, so they could sell them. We were all sorry to see them go, but it wasn't the last lot of babies we had with those two — they had another three lots after that! Dad decided at this point that we weren't allowed to put them together any more.

Queenie was really tame; she wouldn't bite at all. She would come straight to me when I called her name. She would even follow me around the garden. When I picked her up, she would nestle her head under my arm and go to sleep. She was so sweet, I really loved her. We were always together, Queenie and me. Some days I would take her for a walk up the street. I would tie a piece of pink ribbon around her neck as a collar and another long piece of ribbon as a lead and off we would go up and down the street. I think she enjoyed all the attention from all of the other children.

One day, after I had been outside for most of the day, playing with my friends, I went home. I walked through to the kitchen from the living room. Dad was in the kitchen standing at the kitchen table with Queenie sitting on the table. I was just about to ask Dad what was up with her when he picked up the stick that was lying on the table at the side of her. I stood rigid watching him strike her on the back of the neck. She twitched and lay down. She was killed right in front of me. Dad had killed her. He went outside and came back with Snowy. My rabbit was left lying there on the table in front of me. She wasn't breathing. She just lay there not moving but her eyes were still open. I went closer to her to touch her, but Dad came in through the door, which startled me, and I jumped and stood back as he put Snowy on the table next to Queenie. Snowy looked at Queenie and sniffed at her. Dad had the stick in his hand again and soon Snowy too, was dead. Tears were in my eyes and I just had to turn away as he twitched just as Queenie did. Snowy and Queenie were both dead.

By now the others had come back inside and were standing watching what was happening to our pet rabbits. Dad said he was going to cook them for dinner. I stood in silence shaking. I just felt sick to my stomach, there was no way I would be eating our rabbits. I couldn't believe what I had just seen.

Dad hung our rabbit's upside down and tied them to the window frame with their back legs. He got a sharp knife from the drawer and put the knife into the mouths of the rabbits and twisted it round. There was a lot of blood coming from their mouths and it was dripping all down the window and down into the kitchen sink below. I was stunned and frozen to the spot as I watched all this happening. I didn't cry or protest in any way. I would have probably got a good hiding if I had done that. It would have been worth it though if only he hadn't killed our rabbits.

After I just wanted to go to the bedroom to cry but Dad put his hand in his pocket and gave us all a threepenny bit each. He had never given us so much money before. It was such a lot of money; we could buy a lot of sweets with that. We all raced out of the door and off to the shop. I think Dad gave us that money to make up for killing our rabbits but it didn't. I will never be able to have another rabbit again after that. Dad cooked dinner that night and he told us that it was chicken, but I knew he was telling lies. There was no way I was going to eat them. That was Queenie and Snowy on our plates and I just couldn't eat them. I think I was ill that night and went to bed with no tea. But for once I didn't mind going hungry. I closed my eyes in bed that night and many nights afterwards and I could see my Queenie lying there lifeless on our kitchen table with her pink eyes staring out into space.

I had watched my sisters being hit with that stick and now my rabbits had been killed with it. What or who would be next?

CHAPTER SIX
Playtime and Johnson Fold Primary

Dad arrived home one day with a big white dog called Petra. She was beautiful. Nearly as big as me and so fluffy like a teddy bear. Petra was pure white with pointed ears and I remember trying to climb up on her back but she would always sit down as she didn't like me climbing on her. We didn't have her very long. We got up one morning and she wasn't there any more. I think Dad sold her.

A few weeks after our rabbits were killed, Dad came home with another dog, a puppy that looked just like Petra. He was pure white too and had pointed ears and we called him Snowy because he reminded us of Snowy, one of our pet rabbits. I spent a lot of time with Snowy, playing with him all the time and taking him for walks around the street. He was my dog and I loved him loads.

One day Dad sent me to the shop for a packet of Disprin tablets as he must have had a headache. After leaving the shop I saw Jimmy, my friend from the park, who had given us our pet rabbits, Queenie and Snowy. I hadn't seen him for a while, not since Dad killed our rabbits and I hadn't told Jimmy what had happened to them either. I hadn't been down to the park at all since they had been killed nor had I seen any of the other rabbits down there. I still cried sometimes when I was on my own, thinking of my rabbits. I didn't have time to talk to Jimmy, Dad had told me to hurry, so I just waved and shouted to him. I said 'hello' and that I would see him soon and then I raced home.

As I turned to wave goodbye to him again before he disappeared around the corner, I fell over tripping on the pavement and then fell over a wall, which had a drop of about 10 feet on the other side of it. I lay on the pavement below. I didn't know what had happened for a moment. I was stunned. A lady came over to me and helped me to my feet. She had seen me fall off the high wall. I was dizzy and felt sick. I was bleeding from a cut above my left eye. She gave me her hanky to wipe my face. I couldn't talk. My eye was hurting but I didn't cry at all. I picked up Dad's tablets and all the change that was scattered around on the ground in front of me. I couldn't lose any of the change from Dad's money, he would have gone mad. The lady asked if I was OKAY. I nodded to her, still holding the hanky she gave me against my eye and then I rushed off home.

When I walked in, I told Dad what had happened and he sent me off to clean myself up. After tea my eye was really swollen. I was getting a black eye, just like those that Mum used to have. It was almost shut with the swelling. I was sitting on the settee that evening and I called for Snowy to come to me while he was in the garden. I watched him as he walked towards me and it looked as if he was walking in mid-air. I could hardly see through my damaged eye, as the night went on as it was so swollen.

The next day I was up early and ready for school. My black eye was a real mess and there was blood on my pillow, but off I went to school. I had to go and call for my friend Belinda. She lived in the street at the top of our street called Johnson Fold Avenue. We always walked to school together. As we were setting off to go to school, I could hear Dad shouting for me. I looked towards my house and Dad was at the gate waving to me to come home. I tried to run home, but my eye hurt when I ran, so I walked down the street with Belinda beside me to my house. As I reached Dad, he said that I wasn't allowed to go to school with my black eye. I was to have the day off school and I knew it was not going to be enjoyable being at home.

I loved everything about school. I never got into any trouble. I would have been at school every day and all day if I could. I was always the one that volunteered for everything; milk duty, 'tidy up monitor' anything that they wanted I would do. I would even volunteer for every play that was put on each year for the parents and teachers. I would go to every audition and I would get a part in most of the plays that were put on in our school.

The best play I ever appeared in was called "Egg for His Majesty." Three of us auditioned for the part of the witch and as I had long black hair, I thought I would make a good witch. I brushed my hair forwards over my face and when it was time for my audition, I hunched my back and cackled just like the witch in the Wizard of Oz. The other girls were really good and I thought one of them would get the part. I was so pleased when I was told that I had been awarded the part as the witch. It was me they wanted to play the witch who wanted to steal the king's magic hen. I went to every rehearsal; which seemed to go on for months.

I would even practise my witch's voice at home. I scared Jane once. She thought I was a real witch when I dressed up in the witch's costume and jumped out from behind the bedroom door. She screamed loudly! I thought I was going to be good as a witch in that play. I loved every minute of all the rehearsals. The makeup, the dress rehearsal and all the other characters too. The story was great and so funny. I knew all my lines and most of everyone else's lines off by heart. We played for the school and all the teachers first and then the school sold tickets for the parents and anybody else who wanted to see the play.

On opening night, I was nervous and nearly forgot my lines in some places and had to be prompted by one of the other players. The makeup and the costumes were fantastic. I had a tatty old black dress, which was tattered and torn and I had long false fingernails and a horrible stick-on spot at the end of my nose. I really did look like a scary old witch. I nearly frightened myself when I looked in the mirror, after all the makeup was done. I'm not surprised that I scared Jane so much. It was a good play and we all had lots of fun taking part and everybody enjoyed it. It was about a king who lived in a huge castle and he had a hen that laid him an egg every morning for his breakfast. Suddenly the hen started laying golden eggs and was then stolen by a wicked old witch. Everybody was trying to get the hen back for the king so that he could lay the golden eggs for him, as he needed the money to get himself a wife and live happily ever after. It was a happy ending and the play was a huge success. It was shown every night for a full week. Lots of tickets were sold for the show and the school hall was full every night. Every seat was taken and some people without a seat had to stand up for the whole show.

During the performance, I would peer out from behind the scenery and look around in the audience that consisted of all the other mums and dads, to see if my dad had come to see me in the play but he was never there. All the other parents were there except my dad. I was to act in other plays at my school but this one was always my favourite. Dad was never there in the audience to see any of them.

Mrs Mellor was our drama teacher. She wrote all the plays herself. She was so nice to everybody and she never shouted at anybody. The kids in her class loved her and were sad when they had to move from her class to the next. She always had more new ideas for plays, so all the kids would be queuing up at the auditions.

When I was in the top class my teacher was called Mr Rhyl. I thought he was the bees' knees; he was my favourite teacher of the whole school. I was really sad to leave Johnson Fold Primary School. I will always hold happy memories of that school.

I particularly remember playing leapfrog all the way round the playground with just my friends until we were joined by most of the other children on the playground.

The school meals were best though. There always seemed to be plenty to eat and we got a pudding afterwards too. I always joined the queue for seconds.

At home we weren't fed all that much. We seemed to be always hungry. We were hungry in our beds some nights. I remember listening to the noises in my tummy while I tried to get to sleep. There were odd occasions when we would go home from school and there would be a really nice smell. It would fill the house and we just knew it was Dad's hotpot. This was our favourite meal that Dad cooked for us. I remember the fullness in my tummy after eating a big bowlful of hotpot. He made a lot of stews as well. They weren't as nice as his bacon hotpots though. He put everything in the stews. We didn't like them but sometimes we were so hungry, we would guzzle it down without even tasting it.

Sometimes before we'd go to school, if Dad was out of his bed, he would make porridge in a big pan and he would put salt in it. It was horrible but we were made to eat it. It didn't look nice; it didn't smell nice and it tasted absolutely disgusting! None of us liked it but we must have pretended that we did because he thought that we loved it so he kept on making it for us. Really, we were all too scared to tell him that we didn't like it. We didn't dare tell him that we hated it. I think we just ate it most of the time because we were hungry and because there was nothing else for breakfast. There was food in the house but we were never allowed to go in the larder or to help ourselves to anything from the cupboards. If we were caught, we would have been in trouble.

Ann and I were in the Juno's. We had a green uniform with badges on, which we had to earn. I remember being awarded a badge for making a cup of tea and another for making a bed. We would go to our church, which was St Andrew's, in the evenings, about twice a week to take part in the adventures there. Each week we would learn a new task to earn a badge. We all had to attend church on Sunday morning every week. We were all dressed up in our Sunday best and sent on our way to church for Sunday school.

One week it was 'bob a job' week. All the children from the church took part in this. We were to go knocking on people's doors and ask them if they had any jobs for us to do for them. This could be anything from going to the shop for them, sweeping leaves, helping tidy their garden or any job at all. In return, they were to pay a 'bob', which was a shilling. I loved every part of this and I was always out there, every spare minute, knocking on doors and saying, "'Bob a job week', do you want any help at all?" Every door I knocked on, presented a person that needed a little job doing, either nipping to the shops on an errand or taking their dog for a walk around the block. Most days I was doing little jobs all day. I kept very busy and loved every minute. It made me happy being outside and helping people and I raised lots of money for 'bob a job' week.

The money was all handed in to the church and there was to be a prize for the one who had collected the most money. When everybody had handed in all the money that they had collected, it was counted. After a couple of weeks, at the Sunday morning service, we found out who the winner was. As we all sat in our pews with a hymn book in front of us, the name of the winner was read out. To my surprise, it was my name. I had won! I couldn't believe it. I thought one of the big boys might have won the prize. I didn't think it would have been me at all. I was asked to walk out in front of everybody in church to be awarded with my prize, everyone started to clap their hands. I was so excited and happy. My prize was a reading book all about the birth of Jesus. It was signed inside by the vicar who had written, 'This book is awarded to Margaret Gallagher'. I read it over and over. I treasured it and kept it for years.

CHAPTER SEVEN
Home Alone

Some evenings Dad would sneak out to the pub at night, when he thought we were all fast asleep in our beds. The younger ones would be asleep but Paul, Ann and I would be wide awake. When we thought it was all clear and Dad had walked off up the street, we would slowly creep out of bed, being careful not to wake any of the young ones. They would surely tell Dad that we had been getting out of bed. We would sneak downstairs in the dark and steal some food to eat because we were always hungry. Paul would put the fire on, and Ann would go into the kitchen to get some bread and a fork so we could make toast in front of the fire. Ann stuck the fork into the bread and held it in front of the fire until it was toasted. We would all sit huddled around the fire until the bread was toasted and was ready to eat. That toast sure did taste delicious. We would stay up for ages, until we thought that it was time to go back to bed before Dad came home and found us out of our beds.

One night when Dad was out, we were all awake and chasing each other around the bedroom. We were jumping on the beds and jumping from one bed to another and playing tipple overs and somersaults over the beds. It was great fun. Suddenly, the big bed broke in two and we were sent flying landing on the floor. We just lay there stunned and shocked at what had just happened. We all started to cry hysterically. We just didn't know what to do. Paul got up off the floor and went to lift the bed up to see if he could fix it. The sweat dripped from his forehead and the tears fell down his cheeks as he tried to lift it up with all his might. He cried and was shaking as he collapsed into a heap on the floor — he couldn't fix it. We all thought that we would be in for it when Dad came home from the pub. We were all sobbing and looking at each other with the same fear on our faces.

After we had been sitting there for what seemed an age, Paul had a good idea. He went next door to ask Mr Baron if he could help. Soon he came back with Derek and came straight into the bedroom to see what was wrong. We were looking at him, as if to plead with him and we were hoping that he would be able to fix it. He took one close look at the damage that we had done. He looked underneath the bed then went home saying that he would be back in a minute. He soon returned with a long piece of thick rope. Derek sent us all round to his house to see Mrs Baron, while he was fixing our bed. We were all still in tears, as we walked into our neighbours' house. We were then asked to sit down. Mrs Baron was kind to us and gave us all a biscuit to cheer us up a bit as we were all still very upset at what we had done. Mrs Baron told us not to worry but we knew we would be in trouble when Dad returned. Soon Derek was back from our house. He had fixed the bed. Mrs Baron said that we should all go straight to bed when we got back in and go straight to sleep, as our dad would soon be home. We thanked them both and went home. We went straight upstairs, got into our beds and soon fell fast asleep.

The next morning, we didn't tell Dad about the bed, but he noticed the repair a few days later. He asked Paul what had happened to the bed. Nervously, Paul with a red face told him that the bed broke and he asked Derek to fix it. To our amazement we didn't get told off at all. We couldn't believe it. He must have been in a good mood that day.

On another one of the many occasions when we had been left on our own, Paul and I were wide awake, as the others slept. We decided to go downstairs for something to eat as usual. We sneaked down the stairs slowly in the dark and as we almost reached the bottom of the stairs, there was a really strong bright light that shone through the window of our front door. We had to cover our eyes, as the light was too bright. It really scared us because we didn't know what could have caused such a blinding light. We raced back upstairs and didn't go down again that evening. Paul kept saying that it was a spaceship landing in our front garden, but I was too scared to think about it and went off to sleep.

The next morning Paul and I were still talking about the bright light, when we were having our breakfast. I finished my breakfast and went outside to play. I opened the front door and as I went to shut the door behind me, I looked at the lawn in our front garden. It was all brown, blackened and burned. I shouted to Paul inside to come and have a look at it. He came out and said, 'I told you that a spaceship had landed in our front garden'. I think he was right. We both raced in to tell Dad what had happened. He came outside to see what we were talking about. He looked at the lawn and stood there with his pipe sticking out of his mouth, but he shrugged his shoulders, made a grunting noise, and just went inside to read his paper again. There was no reason at all why the grass was all scorched like that. There was nothing else for it. A spaceship really must have landed on our front lawn. It must have done. That's what had caused the blinding light last night. Paul said that the spaceship had landed because the Martians wanted to come to visit. The little green men wanted to come to our house. We decided that if they were to come again, we would let them in to talk to them. We waited night after night for them to come back to visit us again, but they never did.

I was sure that our house was haunted. There were lots of strange noises and mysterious things happening. Things disappeared and then reappeared again later in places that we had previously looked for them. We would hear the whistle of the kettle coming from the kitchen but when we looked the kettle hadn't been put on the stove at all. There were noises upstairs when we were all downstairs. Sometimes, Dad would hear them too and think that there was somebody upstairs. He would go up and check but there was never anyone there.

My friend Belinda and I would swap ghost stories when we were at school, during playtimes. She told me of a ghost that lived in her house. Her ghost had even left its footprint on the carpet in their hallway. She took me to see this after school. She opened the front door of her house and there it was in the place where she had said. I put my foot at the side of the footprint to compare the size and it was a lot bigger than mine. Belinda told me that it didn't match any of her family's feet. I believed her and everything she used to tell me at school about this ghost, who she thought was the ghost of a man because the footprint was even bigger than her dads' foot.

One night, while we were all in bed fast asleep, I suddenly woke up, I didn't know what had woken me as it wasn't morning yet — it was still dark outside. My sisters were all asleep. My three younger sisters were in bed at the side of me and Ann had her own bed at the other side of the bedroom. Paul had his own bed in his own room.

As I lay there listening to the silence of the night, I turned my head to the side and tried to fall back to sleep. I looked across towards Ann's bed, I saw a figure standing there very still, at her side, as if looking down upon her. I thought it looked like a woman because it seemed to have been dressed in a long black gown, like a long dress that a nun would wear. I blinked my eyes to see if I was seeing things, but she really was there. She wasn't moving at all, she just stood there.

It was dark in the room, but I could make out the edge of the door and the dressing gowns hanging on the back of the door. The dark figure stood there, away from the door. Her outline was so clear. I believed she really was there. I thought for a moment that it could be our mum; I thought that she had come back to us. I wanted to call out to her but as I stared at her I was getting more and more frightened. I realised that she wasn't Mum. She must be a ghost! I hid my head under the bedclothes and didn't come out again! I must have drifted back to sleep.

The next morning, I asked Dad if he had been into our room last night, but he hadn't. I knew that it wasn't Dad. It was a lady. I just knew it was a ghost. We had a real ghost living with us. I couldn't wait to see Belinda at school to tell her about our spooky visitor. I had seen a ghost. I wondered who she was. I asked myself if she had lived in our house before she died? Did she die in Ann's bed? What was her name? I wasn't scared any more of what I saw that night. As my imagination grew, the fear went from me and I hoped I would see her again. I imagined that she would come back another night and tell me who she was, but she was never to be seen again.

CHAPTER EIGHT
Dad's Girlfriends

We were getting quite used to being left on our own at night when Dad went out. We hadn't dared to do anything else naughty since we broke our bed that night. We would still sneak downstairs and try to get something to eat because we were always hungry, but mostly we would just stay upstairs in our beds reading and whispering to each other. Sometimes, when I lay there unable to sleep, I hoped that I would see our ghost again. Strange things still happened now and again but I never saw this lady again after that first time.

Dad had quite a few ladies calling at the house, but no one stuck around very long. There was one lady who used to come to visit Dad quite a lot, although I was never really sure if she was a girlfriend of Dad's, she was really nice to us. She was called Margaret. She had black hair and black rimmed glasses. I would think of her often, after her visits stopped. As I grew older, a long time after first meeting this nice lady, I saw a lady on the television, who looked just like Margaret, I had a flashback of a memory when Ann and I had spent some time with her. It was Nana Mouskouri, she was singing on a television show; she was from Greece. I realised that it wasn't the same lady, but she looked a lot like her. Seeing this lady on the television reminded me of the nice time we had with her and of the happy memory she made for us.

I remember Margaret came to visit Dad one day and asked if she could take Ann and I out. He said we could go with her and we were both dressed up in our best Sunday dresses and our shoes were polished until they shone. Our hair was brushed and put into ponytails and off we went. I had my best coat on. I must have been around five years old. Excitedly, we waved to Dad as we were leaving. As we all walked up the street I held on tight to Margaret's hand. Although she had her gloves on, I could still feel the warmth of her hand wrapped around mine so tightly. I looked up at her as we walked, she was so beautiful, I wished she was our mum. That day, I would secretly pretend that this lady was our mum.

We got on a bus first to the railway station, then we went to buy tickets at the little window of the ticket office. Our train wasn't due immediately, so we went into a waiting room and took a seat at a table near the window, so we could watch the trains. Margaret bought both of us a drink of orange juice and had a cup of coffee herself as we waited for the train to arrive. It wasn't long before our train came and we waited at the side of the platform until it stopped.

There were lots of people getting off the train and rushing up the steps at the end of the platform. There were lots of people getting on the train as well and we had to hold on to Margaret's hand so tightly as we climbed up the high step onto the train. We had to try and find somewhere to sit, so we walked down the centre of the train, passing rows of seats with people sitting reading newspapers. Some people were fast asleep in their seats as well. As we made our way down the train, we soon saw four empty seats and rushed to them to sit down. I was sitting next to a window, so I could see the outside. The train was very noisy and made loud rattling noises as it went along. Margaret told us that it was the wheels on the railway line underneath the train that were making all the noise. I liked it on the train, but sometimes it went so dark that it scared me. Margaret put her arm around my shoulders and held me close towards her and told me that the train had gone through a long tunnel, and not to be scared.

It was a long way to Manchester, but soon we were there, and everybody stood up and rushed to the doors as the train came to a stop at the station. We got off the train and made our way out of the station towards the market. I felt really good at the side of Margaret as she was holding our hands tightly. I was pretending Ann and I were her children. We both had all her attention for the whole day. It felt wonderful. I remember being so happy that day. I wished that I could have stayed with her forever.

When we reached the market, it looked like a very big place. There were lots of people rushing around everywhere. Margaret led us through the market, never letting go of our hands, for what seemed like hours, from one stall to another. Eventually, she led us to another huge stall that was full of all sorts of different kinds of sweets; chocolate ones, fruity ones, coloured ones and minty ones. There was everything on that stall.

Margaret looked at us as we were looking at all those sweets with our eyes wide open and our mouths watering. We looked up at her and she smiled at us and said, "Pick anything that you want off this stall". There were too many options to choose from. We just couldn't decide. We had never seen so many different sorts of sweets before. After a long time trying to decide I saw what I wanted. Ann had made her choice, and I picked what I was going to have. I chose a bag of chocolate crunchy. It was cinder toffee coated in chocolate. The bag was full of big chunks of chocolate crunch. Soon our trip to Manchester was over and we said goodbye to the market and made our way back to the railway station to catch a train back home. I didn't want to go home. I wanted to stay with Margaret forever.

During the train ride, I bit into the huge crunchy rock shaped pieces that seemed to last forever and tasted delicious. I still had a lot left when we got home. Ann and I had to hide our treasure from the others because we didn't want to share any of it with them. It was a lovely day in Manchester; I didn't want the day to end at all. We had all had such a good time.

After a while, Margaret didn't come to our house again. We didn't know why but we didn't see her again. I really missed her. I never forgot the great day in Manchester we spent with her. I wasn't sure whether she was a girlfriend of dads, but I did wish she was, at that time. I thought of her often and hoped she would come back one day, but she never did.

Soon there was another lady in Dad's life. She was called Marianne. This lady seemed to be around quite a lot although she didn't talk to us much. We were always sent out to play when she came to the house. She didn't seem to stop very long. She was very pretty and looked like Marilyn Monroe, a lady off the television. We used to pretend to our friends that she was this film star.

One night, we had all been put to bed, because Marianne was coming over to see Dad. I heard the front door open and Dad was talking to Marianne at the door. The door was closed behind them and they both went into the front room to talk.

We had all been told to stay in bed and go to sleep. The little ones were asleep already but I just couldn't get to sleep at all. I needed to go to the toilet, which was downstairs, through the living room and through the kitchen. I couldn't go downstairs now that Marianne was there. I shut my eyes and tried to go to sleep. I lay there for ages and ages and I couldn't wait any longer. I slowly stepped out of bed and tiptoed to the bedroom door and opened it slowly. I crept downstairs slowly trying not to be heard. I could hear the faint voices of Dad and Marianne coming from the front room. As I stood at the bottom of the stairs, I was so scared I was going to be in trouble, my heart was pounding in my chest but I really needed to go to the toilet. I put my head closer to the door to listen for a moment, to try and decide whether to go in or to go back upstairs to bed. I could hear them talking and laughing inside the room. I must have stood there for about five minutes and then all at once I pumped! It was a loud one! I was really scared now. Dad must have heard that. The voices and laughter stopped and it was silent. Dad shouted from inside the living room, "Who's there?" My hands were shaking as I told Dad that it was me and that I needed the toilet. I reached up to the door handle and slowly opened the door. I peeped around the door and was told to hurry up. I rushed through the living room to the toilet. Dad was sat with Marianne on the settee. Dad was at one end and Marianne was at the other end. They had a blanket over their legs and Marianne was only wearing a bra. I didn't know why. I wondered where she had put her clothes. Why had she taken them off? After using the bathroom, I rushed back through the living room and went up the stairs to bed.

Soon Marianne didn't come to the house any more either. I didn't like her as much as Margaret; the lady who took us to Manchester. I wished that we could have seen Margaret again as we really liked her. Now Marianne was gone as well. I would wonder all the time where they all disappeared to; just like our mum. We were never told and we certainly weren't allowed to ask any questions about any of them.

It wasn't long before Dad had another girlfriend. This one was really nice too and she seemed to like us as well.

CHAPTER NINE
Mary: Welcome to the Family.

Mary was a lady who spoke differently from us in Bolton. She had blond hair and was so pretty. She told us that she was from a place called Kent, which was down south near London. We had heard about London. She told us that the Queen lived there. We already knew where London was. We had an aunt that lived there. Dad's sister, our Aunty Lena, she was a children's nanny who lived in London. We didn't see much of her as she lived so far away. However, she did send us parcels of second-hand clothes from the family that she was working for.

Mary was lovely and we all liked her. We liked the way she spoke. We thought she was so posh. She had a nice smile and she was very kind to us. Mary had a little girl called Lorraine. She was eight years old, the same age as Maureen. Mary and Lorraine soon came to live in our house, along with their pet dog, a black mongrel called Sam. Sam had to stay in the garden because Dad didn't like him. At this point, we had Dad, Mary, seven kids and a dog called Sam in the house.

The huge big bed that we all had slept in; three at the top and three at the bottom, which had broken in two when we were jumping on it a few years ago, had now been moved. It had been moved to Dad's bedroom so that they could both sleep in it. We all had new beds side by side, in what was now a very cramped bedroom.

Lorraine was so pretty. She looked just like her mum. She had long blonde hair and deep blue eyes and she had dimples in her cheeks when she smiled. She was very shy when we first met her. She soon fitted into our family, just like her mum did. Mary was to be our new mum.

In the mornings, she would always be up before us to send us off to school. Lorraine changed schools and now went to our school. She was in the same class as Maureen. Mary brushed our hair before we went to school and each day, we had a different hairstyle. One day we would have bunches, then we would have plaits and some days, pigtails. We all had long hair, which looked so much better after she had brushed it for us in the mornings. She said it made us all look prettier and she was right, it did.

It felt good to have a mum, just like the other kids at school. We didn't call her Mum yet though but we told everybody that Lorraine was our new sister, although she didn't look like any of us. We all had dark eyes and dark hair and she had blue eyes and was fair but that didn't matter to us, she was still our new sister. Everybody was fascinated by the way she talked. She was very posh too and we used to try and talk the same way as her, so we would sound posh too.

Mary seemed to accept six extra children in her life. We certainly had accepted her. It was as if she had been there for ages and ages and we were all her real kids. She was a better cook than Dad. She made some nice things for us to eat. We loved her shepherd's pie! We had a proper family now; a mum and a dad. The house seemed so happy.

After a few months there were little arguments between Dad and Mary. Mary would make Dad's tea and 'serve' it to him, while he sat watching the television in his armchair by the fire (just like he did with my real Mum). He would take one look at it and it would go straight in the bin at the side of him. Sometimes, the meal would be thrown straight at the wall. Mary cooked, what looked and smelt like lovely meals, and he would either bin them or throw them around the room. I could never understand the reason why he did that. Mary would be shouted at and be required to get on her hands and knees and clean it up off the floor, just like our mum had done previously. At first Mary would ask him why he had thrown his dinner or what was wrong with it. Dad would then shout loudly and an almighty argument would start. We were all told to get out, so we would 'fly' upstairs. We would hear Dad shouting at Mary. I noticed Mary started to cry a lot. Soon, she stopped asking for a reason why and just cleaned up the mess when she was told.

I can still remember the times when Mum lived with us and Dad would do this to her, when she had cooked for him. I can still remember her knelt on the cold floor, in tears as she scrubbed it.

We were all still hungry after we had eaten our tea each evening. We would have eaten the meals that Dad used to throw away. We could have shared them out between all of us. We wouldn't have wasted them. I couldn't ever understand why he wasted the food like that. We were never allowed the same meal as Dad. During the week, we would have beans on toast, or egg on toast, or sandwiches after school for our tea. Dad always had a huge cooked meal. We would come home from school to the smells of Dad's tea cooking and wonder whether it tasted as good as it smelt. We never got to find out. The bin had it all! He would just toss the food away without even tasting it at all sometimes. I always knew that this was the sign of yet another argument.

The arguments that Dad and our real Mum would have would come flashing back to my mind. I could hear Mum's screams once again but she had left us and had not come back. I hoped that Mary wouldn't leave us as well. She didn't. She stayed. It was nice to have Mary around. She didn't treat us any differently from one another or her own child. There was nothing I didn't like about her; she was just perfect. I hated Dad treating her this way. I felt she would leave too just like our mum had left.

After Mary and Lorraine had been living at our house for quite a while, we found out that Dad and Mary were going to get married. I was so pleased. Mary might stay with us forever after all.

On the day of the wedding, we had all been sent to school. We were not allowed to go to the wedding. After school, I raced home as fast as I could as I knew that they would have been married by the time school had ended that day and they would be at home. Dad had a shiny purple Zephyr, which had shiny silver handles on the doors. It was parked outside our house and was covered with bits of confetti all over the bonnet. I ran in through the door, very excited and was closely followed by all the others. Dad and Mary were standing in the living room hugging each other. They were all dressed up. Dad wore a grey suit and Mary wore a pretty, blue floral dress with flowers in her hair. They had got married. We were all so pleased. They both looked so happy.

If only we could have had a day off school to be at the wedding. Maybe children weren't allowed at weddings, I didn't know. There wasn't a big party afterwards, as there had been for one of our cousin's weddings; at the Co-op Hall in Bolton.

After the wedding day we were to call Mary, "mum," I was delighted. It's what I had hoped for, for such a long time. Life seemed great! We had a mum and a dad again. Now we were a proper family. We had a step-mother. At first the thought of a step-mother scared me. I had read the fairy stories about the wicked old step-mothers; as in Snow White and Hansel and Gretel. But Mary wasn't like that at all.

We all seemed so happy that day. I watched Dad and Mary hugging each other. They were so 'in love' and happy.

But the arguments soon started again. Little niggles at first which were soon forgotten about but the arguing soon got worse. Dad was shouting at Mary and she was crying once again. I didn't want Mary to go away just like Mum had done. Soon Mary started to have black eyes and other bruises just like Mum had.

Dad was thumping her too. We would see her bruised and beaten just like Mum. Her lips would be cut and swollen, but still she stayed.

She didn't sing as much any more, as she had done when she first came to live at our house. At the beginning, she would sing constantly when she was sweeping, 'there's a place for us, somewhere a place for us.' I remember our mum singing too. I will never forget that. I often wondered why she stayed. She saw what Dad was like with us. She knew how strict he was with us all. Everything seemed easier when Mary was around because she would try to keep us all out of his way most of the time. She knew how afraid of him we all were.

Before long, Mary was going to have a baby. We were going to have another brother or sister; we were all excited and looking forward to having a new baby in the house. When Mary was five months pregnant, Dad was shouting at her again. We were all sent to bed as usual. We all raced up the stairs and shut ourselves into our bedroom. No matter how hard we tried to block out the sounds from downstairs, we could not. I had my head under my pillow so tightly, but I could still hear the screams, the shouting, the smashing and the banging. Lorraine was crying uncontrollably, crying for her Mum. Ann was crying too and wrapped her arms around Lorraine to comfort her. The noises went on for ages. We could hear Mary crying and pleading with Dad to stop. It sounded like the furniture was being tossed around the living room. Then everything went quiet.

The next morning, we all got up expecting that we would see Mary as usual making a cup of tea or getting breakfast ready. I expected to see her in the same state that Mum had been in, with a cut face and black eyes, before she left. I thought we would see Mary now wearing those same sunglasses, as Mum had done, to cover up her black eyes. But Mary wasn't there. She wasn't in bed either. We didn't know where she was. Dad shouted to us all and told us to get ready for school. We didn't ask any questions. We got ready for school in silence and went on our way. Lorraine was confused and shaken and wondered where her mum had gone. She stayed silent and didn't ask any questions. She was now afraid of Dad too. I was really worried at school all day and prayed in assembly that she hadn't left us.

After school had finished for the day, we all rushed home, hoping to see Mary waiting for us. But she wasn't there. Dad still didn't tell us anything at all about her and we just had to carry on and not ask questions. We could tell Dad was in a bad mood by the look on his face. We all tried to keep out of his way as much as possible by playing outside. Later, Dad shouted for our Paul and told him he had to go to Barstow's for some St. Bruno tobacco. Dad put the money in his trembling hand and told him to hurry up. When he came back from the shop Dad took the tobacco from him and checked the change. Dad then walloped Paul right across the face, knocking him flying and shouting that there was a penny missing from the change. Dad said that Paul had spent it but Paul kept saying he hadn't.

Dad then told Paul that he had better go and find it and sent him back up to the shop. He shouted after him, as he tore through the door, that if he didn't come back with it, he would be in for it. Paul searched the streets all the way up to Barstow's but he couldn't find the penny. He knew he hadn't spent it. He knew he couldn't go home without it. He looked outside the shops and in every gutter. He was distraught.

He climbed on a number one bus that was parked up at the bus stop at the top of Chorley Old Road. He was hysterical, as he tried to explain to the bus driver that he had lost a penny and his dad was going to kill him if he went home without it. The bus driver listened to Paul's cries, reached in his pocket and gave him a penny. Paul tearfully thanked the driver and hurried home. When he went in, Dad was sitting talking to cousin Julie. He was smiling and seemed to be in a better mood, so Paul put the penny on the mantelpiece and Dad shouted to him "See I told you you'd lost it." Paul knew he hadn't lost or spent any of that money. If it wasn't for the kindness of the bus driver he would have been battered again for sure.

It was days before we saw Mary again. We were so pleased to see her, but there was something wrong. She looked tired and drained. She had a cut above her eye that had been stitched and her lip was swollen. I noticed that she didn't have a fat tummy any more. Mary wasn't pregnant! With eyes like saucers, I thought that's where she had been, in hospital to have the baby. For a moment a smile came to my face, thinking that we had got a new sister or brother. Then the smile disappeared. I asked if she had had the baby and I was told that she had lost it. No baby, the baby must have been dead. That was that, from then on it wasn't mentioned again. The house seemed quiet.

After a few months Mary was pregnant again. I was really worried for her and scared that this baby would die just like the other had done. I overheard her talking with a relative that she had been told by a doctor that she shouldn't have any more babies, as it could be dangerous for her to do so. As Mary got bigger and bigger, she passed the five-month stage, where she had been when she lost the other baby. She was getting bigger every day. One night when the football was on the television, Mary went into labour. We were all in bed but we were woken up when the ambulance came for Mary to take her to hospital. Secretly, we peered through Paul's bedroom window, pressed our faces against the cold glass and watched as she was helped into the back of the ambulance. Dad didn't go because he was watching the football.

On 3rd of May 1970 Mary gave birth to our baby sister. It was a long time before Mary came home from the hospital. On the day that Mary and the new baby finally came home, the sun was really hot and we all raced to see our new sister. As we rushed through the door, we were told to be quiet! We were not to wake her. We all peered over into the carry-cot to see her. She was so tiny lying there sleeping, so cute with loads of jet-black hair. We all asked what she was called at the same time, which made us all laugh quietly together. Dad and Mary smiled at each other and said "Laura, she's called Laura." There were eight of us now. Eight kids, and a mum and dad!

CHAPTER TEN
A Christmas Remembered

Mary was always knitting. She had knitted all Laura's little cardigans, bootees, hats and jackets. Mary's bag with her wools of many different colours and her long knitting needles were always at the side of her favourite chair within her reach.

One specific Christmas in our house was very special for me and my sisters. A really big surprise was waiting for us when we got up that Christmas morning. We were not expecting the day to be any different from the Christmases before. However, as we walked into the living room, there in front of us, were six pretty new dolls. Each one was sitting on a little pile of presents. I couldn't ever remember having a Christmas tree to decorate or presents that were wrapped or even Christmas stockings as you would see on the television. I have never ever forgotten this first Christmas after Dad had got married to Mary.

We came downstairs together and walked into the living room on this special Christmas morning, which was so magical, it was like a dream. We weren't given much, as there were so many of us and our presents weren't wrapped with fancy paper but that didn't matter to us that morning, as we all stared at our very own baby dolls. Somehow, we all knew which doll belonged to each of us and went closer to touch them. Each doll's knitted outfit was a different colour. We all lifted our own doll off the small pile of presents in order to hold them closely. We studied their outfits realising that Mary must have knitted all those dolls' clothes and done this lovely surprise for us all.

Each doll was dressed in a knitted hat and coat, with a dress underneath and even knitted knickers and vests. The dolls also had socks and shoes. They were all so lovely. It was such a complete surprise! I had no idea that she was doing all this for us. She was always knitting, but I didn't see her knit anything like these dolls' clothes. It must have taken her such a long time to do all this. I played with my doll all the time and the clothes lasted for years and years.

I never forgot that Christmas or another Christmas time when I had wanted a china tea set. I had wanted one for ages, after seeing one in a picture book. That was all I wanted to play with and to pretend to have tea parties with all my dolls. The night before Christmas, I sneaked down before any of the others were awake, just to see if I was to get my china tea set. I knew exactly what the tea set box would look like.

I looked around at the piles of presents in the living room. There was a pile for each of us. I looked for my pile and looked for the tea set. Somehow, I knew which pile mine was but the small china tea set that I really wanted so badly was not amongst the small selection of presents on my pile. I looked round at the other piles and then to my horror I saw it. I recognised the box! I carefully took it from that pile and put it on my pile. I took something off my pile and exchanged it for the tea set and went quietly back to bed. When Christmas morning came, I knew I had got what I wanted because I had made sure of it!

I had that tea set for ages and ages and played with it all the time. I wouldn't let the younger ones play with it because it was so delicate. When I wasn't playing with it, it was carefully put back in its box of soft straw and stored in a safe place.

After school one day, I came home to find Andrea and Jane playing with my china tea set. They sat on the doorstep outside the house playing. I was horrified! I rushed to them to take it away and I realised most of the tiny pieces were broken. I was heartbroken. With tears in my eyes, I left them to play with it and walked away devastated. I cried into my pillow for ages. I couldn't show how upset I was really feeling because inside I felt the guilt of that cold Christmas morning sneaking downstairs and swapping those presents over. I knew it shouldn't have been mine, so it served me right. It was my treasure for a while though and I did look after it for such a long time.

Mary took the place of our real mum. She had been accepted by all of us. It was as if she had always been our mum. The memories of our real mum were slowly fading when I looked at her. I did feel that Mary loved us and cared for us; a love that I never felt or saw from Dad at all. Mary had been around for ages now and had seen the various types of punishment that our dad was capable of inflicting to all of us and especially to Paul. Paul was punched with Dad's fists most of the time.

He was constantly slapped around the head for no reason at all or just because he got too close to his hand. All those flicks across the head made Paul develop a twitch. It had become a habit and the more Paul twitched his head; the more Dad would hit him. Paul avoided him as much as possible. At first Mary would disagree with the way he would discipline us and objected, but she soon knew that she must not interfere or else she would get a thump as well and she did get thumped at times when she tried to stop him.

We were always good and well behaved for Mary. All she needed to do was to say that she would tell our dad if we didn't behave or we were squabbling. She never did tell Dad though on the odd occasions that any of us misbehaved for her.

However, we all still believed every time that she would tell. She had to be seen to be very strict with us all and to make us all think that she was the boss and I think she had to show Dad that she could keep us under control. This was probably so that he didn't have to give us the punishment his way if any of us dared to step out of line.

I was in trouble one day but I can't remember what I had done wrong. Mary had to pick up Dad's stick and hit me with it. She knew she had to do it and so did I. I was made to lie over the arm of the settee and I was struck on the behind twice. To my amazement it didn't hurt at all. I looked at Mary and she was looking at me with tears in her eyes, as if it broke her heart to have to do this. For a moment, I looked at her and then I pretended that it hurt because all the others were watching. I pretended to cry. She knew instinctively that I understood why she did it. I knew in my heart that she didn't really want to lift up that stick and hurt me with it.

I grew very close to Mary after that, in many ways. I would watch her cook and knit and admire her a lot. Although it remained unspoken, we understood that we liked each other. She knew that I understood what she was going through with Dad and that I also remembered our real mum and what she went through too.

I was still only about eleven years old and although I believed Mary and I were close at that time, there were no kisses or cuddles from her at all, not to any of us. I never knew what it was like to be kissed or cuddled at all. There was no show of affection to any of us. I didn't know what it felt like because it was never there. None of us ever saw anything like that in our house. I knew it was missing from our family because I would see other mums kiss their kids at the school gate. I would wonder why they did it and why it never happened to any of us. Was it because we were all too naughty or too ugly or maybe there were just too many of us?

I remember seeing Dad cuddling Mary at times especially after they had a row. He would beat her and then he would buy her flowers and she would sit on his knee. Mary left Dad a few times but was soon back and everything was rosy again for a short time.

One evening, we all sat downstairs watching television, Mary was folding Laura's nappies and putting them away in the cupboard at the side, where Dad was sitting in his chair. Dad and Mary were talking to each other, but Dad's voice was getting louder. He kept tutting every time that Mary had to pass him to put the nappies away. She was in his way of the television. I could feel that something was going to happen. I was used to the tensions. I knew what was going to happen and also, he had put his tea straight into the bin that night, so we all knew he was in a bad mood. I think Mary must have lost her temper with Dad because she picked up a knife and went for Dad with it. Dad jumped up and knocked the knife from her hand and started to thump her over and over again. We all rushed upstairs out of the way, just in case we got hit as well, as the punches went on.

We could hear Mary screaming for Dad to stop hitting her, but it went on and on and things were getting broken downstairs. We could hear the noise of furniture being knocked over and ornaments were being smashed. The noise went on and on. We didn't go back downstairs that evening. Anne sat on her bed cuddling Laura trying to hide the sounds.

Mary wasn't around when we got up the next morning, but she was back a few days later. There must have been a good reason for Mary to have attacked Dad in that way. I didn't hate her for it at all. I felt sorry for her. She was going through the same thing our mum had done. I was sure that she would leave and not come back next time.

Mary always left Lorraine and Laura behind. Dad didn't let her take them with her. That's probably why she came back to him time and time again. I think she knew that she had no choice but to put up with the way things were. Mum had been beaten up in the same way Mary was beaten up. On one occasion my mum had been hospitalised and almost blinded by Dad. In the end she had to leave all her children behind to escape from the beatings and probably from being killed by him. I could never understand why she had left all her children behind, with him! Mary knew that there was a reason for our real mum leaving — she found out the hard way. Dad was never going to change the way that he was, but I think she stayed because of Laura and the rest of us. She knew that if she had left our dad, he would have taken things out on us and maybe things would have been worse. She stayed to protect us all, but things were not to get any better. In fact, they got worse as the years went on. We all had been living in a nightmare that we thought was normal life and Mary, Lorraine and Laura were now in that same nightmare with us.

Dad would never let Sam, Mary's dog, into the house. He was usually tied up in the shed or the garden. It was often my job to take him for a walk. He was usually very good on the lead. On this one particular day it had been raining none stop so Sam had been tied up in the shed all day. When I got my coat on and he saw the lead he started to jump up and down, excited at the prospect of going out. When we were in Johnson Fold Avenue, the next street to ours, the dog walked really well not pulling on his lead at all. All at once he saw another dog further up the street and started to bark at it. I had the lead wrapped around my hand tightly as he started to pull me up the street towards the other dog. He was so strong. He was running really fast and I couldn't keep up. I fell over and Sam pulled me along up the street on my tummy. I was screaming for him to stop but he pulled me right across a muddy grass verge. I was in a mess. I was covered in mud all down the front of my new green coat. I couldn't let go of the lead, as Sam would then have run off and I would have found myself in serious trouble for letting him run away. Now I was going to be in more trouble for getting my coat dirty. Sam stopped pulling when the other dog ran off out of sight. I came to a stop and lay there covered in mud off the grass. I started to cry as I looked down at my coat.

My favourite green coat with a fur collar was in a dismal state. I hadn't had it long. It was given to me by my Aunty Lena. Whatever was Dad going to say? I knew I was going to be in serious trouble. As I stood on my feet, Sam was still trying to pull me again, so I pulled the lead as hard as I could and shouted at him to sit, which to my surprise he did! When I turned around, to go back home, I saw a lady coming towards me. It was Aunty Renee; she had seen what had happened from her window and came out to help me. Aunty Renee used to be our mum's friend.

I remember Mum telling us that she went to school with Renee when she was a little girl. She said that Renee, another girl called Sally and herself, became ill while attending school, with a disease called diphtheria. Mum and Renee got better but Sally sadly died. I remember Renee used to visit our house sometimes and look after us all while Mum and Dad were at work. When Mum lived with us, she visited a lot but she stopped coming when Mum left. We would call her 'aunty' but we knew that she wasn't our real aunty. I looked at her familiar face as she came towards me and remembered her as being our mum's friend from long ago. She could see the state that I was in, so she took me to her house to clean me up. The dog lead was tight around my hand and was beginning to make my fingers go purple. She loosened the lead and tied it to her gate and took me inside.

I had never been inside her house before as it always looked dark and scary from the outside, with the overgrown trees and bushes around the house. Aunty Renee didn't come out of her house much. Dad didn't ever like us going into anybody else's house. We always knew that this was Mum's friend's house, but Dad told us we weren't allowed to talk to her. We didn't know why that was. I was still sobbing at the thought of going home and Dad seeing the state of my coat and I think Aunty Renee knew that as well. In her sweet soft voice, she told me not to worry, and that she would take me home and tell my dad what had happened. She gave me her handkerchief and wiped my coat with a cloth to try and take off most of the mud. She noticed my knees were bleeding. I had scuffed them on the pavement as the dog had pulled me along. She sat me down in a big chair in the kitchen and bathed my knees with antiseptic and cotton wool. When I was cleaned up, she untied the dog from the gate and walked with me down the street to my house.

Dad stood listening to her at our door, smoking his pipe. She explained to him what had happened outside her house. She then went back to her house up the street and I thanked her as she left. Dad put Sam in the back garden and attached a thick piece of rope to his collar, so he wouldn't run off from the garden. He told me that I wasn't allowed to take Sam out again. Sam was just left tied up in the back garden but he managed to escape many times and ran away from home. He would bite through his lead or snap the rope that he was tied up with and he would be gone. At first, he would come back on his own, but then Dad would beat him with the stick that he used to hit us with or he would hit him with his belt. I could hear him striking him with that stick; Sam would howl and howl as he hit him time after time. Sam would still try to run away whenever he got the opportunity. If we left the gate open, he would be off. Every time he was found and returned to the house he was beaten again. Soon Sam was gone too.

CHAPTER ELEVEN
Finding Mum

I remember the death of my Uncle Jim. It was a very sad time for all the family. The children were kept out of the way as usual after he had died. We were obviously not allowed to attend the funeral. He was dads' brother and had died of stomach cancer.

There was a lot of rushing around for everyone, for weeks before he died. All Dad's brothers arrived in Bolton, to spend time with Jim and to say goodbye to him. I can remember Mum and Dad rushing around with pillows and sheets all the time, then everyone crying when he finally died.

Uncle Jim was married to aunty Barbara and they had four children: Gillian was the eldest, Stuart, who was about nine, Matthew who was about eight and then Anita just five years old. They lived in a house on Montserrat Road, not that far from us.

Barbara and the children moved away soon after Uncle Jim died. They went to live far away in another town and we didn't get to see our cousins for a long time. After some time, they moved back to our estate. They lived closer to us this time; in fact, they lived in the next street. Aunty Barbara had remarried by this time to a man named Colin with whom she'd had another baby. They called this baby Darren Colin, after his dad.

We were all cousins and became good friends again, in fact we used to play together all the time. Anita was always round at our house playing with my sister Maureen and myself. If she wasn't calling for us, we were calling for her. We'd go to the park and play on the swings; we would explore many of the places that we had previously loved going to.

One sunny day we had been to the park for the afternoon and we were on our way home. Instead of crossing the field, leading on to Moss Bank Way, which was usually the quickest way home, we went another way home up a long narrow road at the side of the rock gardens that eventually led to Lightbounds Road. This was the longest way home but we liked to go this way because it was dark and spooky, even during the middle of the day. There was a tall chimney at the top of this road and we liked to stand at the bottom and look up right to the top as it seemed to be touching the sky. The chimney had been there for hundreds of years. I didn't know what it was used for. I think it was something to do with the big old mill that was a little further down the lane which by now was just an empty, old stone building. We didn't go to play down there as it was far too scary and we believed it to be haunted.

This road also had huge conker trees on either side. The trees would drop their conkers every year and we would collect the big ones. We would pierce a hole through the middle and thread the string through the centre. This enabled us to have conker fights. The conker that didn't break was the winner.

There were cobbles on the surface of the road and high stone walls on either side of it. The road wasn't used much by cars but there were always many people around. This included people riding bikes and occasionally we would even see people riding horses or ponies up and down the lane. We had to keep to the sides, most of the time as we walked all the way up to the top. There was no pavement at all to walk on, just the cobbles but there was a little gap between the wall and the edge of the cobbles of about five inches. This gap was like a gutter that would get full of dead leaves, mud and sludge that collected there.

As I walked along the side of the road not really watching where I was walking, my foot slipped into a large gap in the gutter. It was like sinking-sand and my foot went deeper and deeper into the sludge. I was stuck up to my knee in the thick sludgy mud. I couldn't get my foot out. I pulled and pulled at my leg. When I finally got free, my foot came out, but the sludge had kept tight hold of my shoe. There was no way I was going to put my arm in that mud to try and get it back. It had disappeared forever. I had to walk home wearing only one shoe and my other leg covered in mud and sludge.

When I got home, I was in tears and petrified. I knew I had to tell Dad what had happened. I walked in at the back door of the house and Dad was standing at the sink looking out of the window. He turned and noticed I had only one shoe on and that I was covered in mud, so I told him what had happened. He stared down at me, as I sat on the doorstep, taking my muddy socks off and trying to wipe all the mud from my legs. I thought he was going to shout at me and give me a good hiding, but Dad didn't shout at me or get the stick out. He just glared at me and shook his head. He never said a word.

I didn't have any other shoes to wear for school, so I had to wear my gym shoes, which were already too tight and had a hole through the rubber on the bottom. I kept putting cardboard inside, so my socks wouldn't keep getting dirty on the bottom. The cardboard would get soggy when it was raining. I wore those gym shoes in that state for ages but it didn't bother me. I didn't complain, I couldn't do that. I was just glad not to get a good hiding for losing my other shoe.

During that hot summer, we spent quite a lot of time with our cousins after school and at weekends. However, when I moved up to big school — Smithills High School, I didn't seem to see as much of cousin Anita as I did during that hot summer holiday. She was still at the primary school and I had made some new friends of my own age at my new school. I didn't want to leave Johnson Fold School at all. It broke my heart when I left but I was still excited to be starting a new school and I hoped that I would enjoy it as much as Johnson Fold School. Paul was already at the new secondary school; however, Ann had passed her eleven plus, so she went straight to the grammar school, which made Dad really proud of her. I remember sensing that at the time.

I adapted to life at Smithills very well, making lots of new friends. I liked the new school uniform that I had to wear, and I managed to tie the tie properly each morning. Dad gave me a grey mackintosh that I had to wear every day. It was a free one from welfare and I hated it! Nobody else had one at school. It seemed old fashioned to me. It was too big and seemed to drown me. I didn't like wearing it at all. Most days I would come out of the house wearing it and then when I was out of sight of home, I would take it off and drape it over my arm while I walked to school.

I would walk to school every morning rain or shine, it was quite a long way, but it was a nice walk when it wasn't raining. I would walk down the dark lane through to Barrow Bridge and every time I passed the place where I lost my shoe I would wonder where it was. I would look up at the tall chimney and walk past the old spooky mill, past the aluminium works and down onto the road that led to my school. Some days I would walk through Moss Bank Park and then down Smithills Dean Road, which took me a bit longer to walk to school, especially if I called for my friend on the way.

I'd heard that if you bathed your face in the dew each morning, it would make you beautiful. I wanted to be beautiful — just like Lorraine. Crossing the field in Moss Bank Park one morning on my way to school I could see the dew on the grass glistening in the sunshine. I reached down, soaked my hands in the dew and rubbed it all over my face. I wanted it to work and make me pretty just like her. She was born beautiful and would never have to rub her face in the morning dew.

This 'ritual' went on for ages, until one day I walked into school and a teacher glared at me and told me to go and wash my face. Puzzled, I left the classroom and went to the toilets. As I looked up into the mirror, I was shocked to see that there were dirty, black, streaky marks down my face. I was so embarrassed that I had walked all the way to school looking like that and didn't realise. I washed my face quickly and went back to the classroom with a face now reddened with embarrassment. I didn't bathe my face in the morning dew ever again after that.

The first year at this new school went quickly. I was very interested in art and spent a lot of time drawing and sketching different things, although I still wanted to become an actress. Ever since my primary school days I had been interested in drama and writing little plays that we would act out on the playground.

I also enjoyed 'entertaining' my friends with impersonations of different people, including the headmaster. I could do a good impersonation of both Frank Spencer and Kermit the frog. My best though was singing, 'Gimmi' the Moonlight,' by Frankie Vaughn. I would be surrounded with all my classmates watching. Most of whom would be roaring with laughter by the end of playtime. I would love making them all laugh. I made a lot of friends because of the stories of our 'ghost' and with the impersonations. I would try out new ones I had seen on television, such as the songs that Morecambe and Wise always sung on their show. I could pick up one of their catchy songs quite quickly and copy their dance and then act the fool on the playground with my friends. It was fun.

At the end of my first year, having never been interested in boys at all, I had my first kiss with a boy called David H. We shared a kiss at the edge of the woods near our playground. We had just come back to school after cross-country running. I remember not being all that impressed at all. I needed a brace on my teeth, so our teeth banged together as he kissed me. School was great but hard work, so at the weekends and school holidays, we made sure we enjoyed ourselves as much as we could.

During the summer school holidays, of 1971, we would make a packed lunch for our dinner consisting of two sugar butties wrapped up in a brown paper bag. We would stay in the park all day until teatime. Of course, I was trying to keep out of Dad's way for most of the time. Sometimes, Anita, our cousin, would come along with us all to the park and we were totally shocked when one day she started talking to Maureen and me about our real mum. We had never heard anybody talking about our mum, at least not for a long time. We didn't mention her at all in the house as we were never allowed too, and because we all liked our new 'mum'. We didn't want to upset Mary at all and we thought we would be in trouble if we spoke about our real mum. So, it was strange to hear Anita start talking about her like this. She talked about her as if she saw her all the time. She was saying all sorts of things about her, where she lived and what she was like. She told us that her mum went to see my mum all the time and she had been to my mum's wedding that July. Our mum had married again. How could this be? How had this happened? We couldn't believe what we were hearing. I couldn't understand why our cousin went to see our mum and we couldn't. I wanted to hear more and more. We knew we had to keep all this news concerning our mum a secret. Dad couldn't find out that we were talking about Mum as he would have gone mad. We promised each other not to say a word about this to anyone — it was to be our secret. I was shocked to hear Mum had married again. I wondered if she would have had some more children and forgotten about all of us. Anita's stories were fascinating, I just wanted to hear more. Each time we met up together, we would talk. One day I asked her if she would take us to go and see her.

I could still remember Mum and the song she sang. I was longing to see her again, and dreaming that one day, I would. I felt I must go and see her before she had forgotten about us altogether. Anita said that she would take us to see her but we were scared, too scared that Dad would find out. How could we do this without Dad finding out? There was a lady on Coronation Street, who I really thought was my mum. She was called Elsie Tanner. When I first saw this programme on our little black and white television set, I really thought that this woman was our mum. Despite this, Anita never mentioned anything about our mum starring in Coronation Street.

The memories I have of Mum seemed so clear. The memories of her and what Dad had done to her before she left us. I thought at that time that she had gone off to make a lot of money in the television industry. The woman on television looked just like our mum. It must be her. That is what I let myself believe and where I thought she had gone all those years ago. I simply believed she had gone to star in Coronation Street but with everything that Anita said it made me think that this was not true. While Anita talked and talked about our mum, I soon realised that this was not where she had gone at all. She was in fact only in the next town and getting married to someone else!

After a few weeks of trying to plan a way of getting to see our mum, Maureen and I finally decided that we were definitely going to go. We were to leave the next weekend on the Saturday and we were to walk all the way to Horwich, which is where Mum had moved to live. We had never heard of this place but Anita told us that it was not a long way and we would have to walk the distance. It shouldn't take more than an hour to get there if we walked fast. If we set off in the morning, we could get there before dinnertime. We never told anyone of our secret and we couldn't wait for the week to pass. Eventually Saturday arrived! We had managed to keep it a secret from all the others. I felt sure that they would have told Dad if they had known what we were going to do.

After breakfast and when our chores were done Maureen and I went to call for Anita. We made sure that none of the others were following us before we went off up the street. We raced to Anita's house, very excited, but still really scared that we were going to be found out. We were too excited to back out now so as we knocked on Anita's door, we prayed that she could still take us to Mum's house today. We hoped that she hadn't said anything to her Mum about our secret, as she would surely stop us going.

The door opened slowly and one of Anita's brothers came to answer it. We asked him if Anita was playing out and he went to get her. After a few minutes Anita came out. She hadn't forgotten what we were doing that day and she also hadn't told anybody where we were going. Excitedly, we all set off.

We had soon left our estate and were on Chorley Old Road heading towards Horwich and away from Bolton. We had to walk up a big hill, past the Old Links Golf course. When we were at the top, we stopped to look at the view — we could see for miles. It felt like we were on top of the world. We could see all of Bolton and the town hall clock in the distance. It was a lovely sunny warm day and we were all getting a bit warm as we were rushing on towards Mum's house. I was looking at everything as we travelled on our way because I wanted to make sure I could find my way for the next time; just in case we had to come on our own the next time.

Soon we came to a zigzag in the road and then to a church with a large graveyard and Anita said that we were nearly there. We could see lots of houses in the distance, along this long straight road, heading slightly downhill. Anita pointed out that this was Horwich, as we all rushed down the hill. I was getting more and more excited as we were walking, but at the same time I did wonder what would happen if Mum was not in. Even worse, what if she didn't want to see us and sent us away.

I shuddered at the thought of her turning us away, but then shook my head. She'd never do that I thought, she was our mummy. We just had to find her, so off we went trying not to think about things like that. If she wasn't in, we would simply have to go back on another day. We were trying to decide what we were going to say to her when we did see her. We were trying to remember her voice and what she was like before she left us.

The journey to Horwich seemed to take no time at all. It was a lovely walk, the scenery and the houses along the way were beautiful. There were lots of sheep and cows grazing in the fields, which we were amazed to see. We hadn't seen many cows before or been so close to them. We passed a huge building that Anita told us was the swimming baths. She told us that she went there regularly with her brothers and there were two swimming pools. She said it was fun and she could swim already. Anita also recognised a pub where Mum had held her wedding party. At that point, she told us that we were nearly there, it was just down this street and around the corner.

We turned onto Wright Street, where Mum lived. There were houses joined together in a row, on one side of the road all the way up the street. There were cobbles on the road and each house had a tiny garden at the front surrounded by a knee-high brick wall with a wooden gate at the edge of the path, which led up to the front door. We came up to the house that Anita said was where our mum was staying. I looked at Maureen; we couldn't believe we were really there. We both stood there for a moment just looking at the huge red door, then I decided to go and knock. There was a big, round, black knocker on it, so I reached up and knocked it hard. My heart was racing and thumping hard in my chest. Mum was going to answer this door any minute now. We waited and waited but there was no answer, so I banged hard again. I couldn't believe we had come all this way and she wasn't in after all. As we were leaving the garden, there were tears in my eyes as I shut the gate behind me. I wiped my eyes on my sleeve. Anita said we should go back to the pub that we had passed previously, up the road, because Mum might be working there. We agreed with her and were about to set off again when a door opened at the house next door to Mum's house. A little old lady asked who we were looking for. Anita told her that we were looking for a lady called Maria. Mum's first name is Margaret, the same as mine, but now she calls herself Maria, which is her middle name. The old lady then told us that she knew her and that she had moved into the next street. She pointed to the street across the road and we quickly headed off, saying thank you to the lady. We headed down the back street, as the lady had told us we should knock at the back door of the house. We walked about halfway down the back street and then looked back towards the top of the street. The old lady was standing pointing to us to show us which one it was. She shouted that it was a green gate and that it would be open. As we reached the gate we turned to the lady and she was nodding her head as if to say that's the one.

I slowly lifted the catch and opened the gate. We walked into a small yard. There was a green wooden door to our right as we walked through the gate. I opened it slowly and there was a toilet in there. The houses were just like the ones on Coronation Street; they had outside toilets too. I shut the door and we went further up the yard to where there was another door. There was a window at the side of the door, but we couldn't see through to the inside. The curtains were slightly open, but it was too dark to see in and there were plants on the windowsill. There was washing pegged out on the line in the yard, so I had a feeling that she was going to be in. I knocked on the door lightly. I was even more nervous now, as we stood waiting for her to answer. There was no answer, so I turned the doorknob and to my amazement the door opened.

As I opened the door there was yet another door in front of us that was already open a little. I pushed on the door to open it a bit wider to see if I could see inside. The door opened with the noise of the hinges creaking, which sounded really spooky. My heart was racing. I could see a staircase leading up at the right and I couldn't wait any more. She must be in. I just shouted, "Mum!!" at the top of my voice. The house was silent. I shouted again. I was trembling and almost in tears. She must be in because all the doors were open. But there was only silence. Was she here? Did she live here? Where could she be? Would we see our mum today after all this time? Will we ever see her again?

I shouted again as a tear fell onto my cheek and slowly ran down my face. Suddenly we heard footsteps on the old creaking floorboards upstairs. We held our breath as we heard them reach the top of the stairs. Still there was no sound of her voice. Was that our mum upstairs? Were those the footsteps of our mum? The footsteps were getting closer. I looked up towards the sounds and I could see her feet in a pair of bright blue, fluffy slippers. Then she was there, right in front of us. She looked at us in amazement. I don't think she believed what she was seeing. I was overcome with emotion at that point and burst into tears as I reached out to her. I took hold of her around her waist and hugged and hugged her. I didn't want to let go. Her arms were wrapped around me as I cried and then she reached out to Maureen to hug her too. We all held each other so tightly in the doorway. Then she spoke. She said that she thought that she was dreaming when she heard us calling to her. At that point we were all in tears as we were led inside.

At last, my dream had come true, I was twelve years old and I was here with our mum at last. I wanted to stay with her and never leave but I knew that this couldn't happen. She was just as I remembered and she was so beautiful and glamorous. I couldn't speak as I was sobbing that much. We were taken through to the front room. Mum was still holding us so tight as we all fell on to the sofa. Mum wiped the tears away from my face and she stroked my hair. She reached up her sleeve for her hanky and wiped the tears from her eyes. She couldn't believe that we were there. She caught her breath and went on to ask how we had found her and how we had got there. There were so many questions that she wanted to know the answers to but it took us a while to stop crying and tell her of the journey that we had just taken. We were talking for ages, still hugging each other on the sofa. She asked if we were hungry and we all said yes, as we were always hungry. Anita had been sitting very quietly on a chair at the side of the settee, it was as if we had forgotten her. Mum got up from the settee and went over to Anita and gave her a big hug and a kiss and thanked her for bringing her babies to her. She nearly started to cry again. She said she would make us all something nice to eat and disappeared into the kitchen.

The three of us sat together silently and still in shock. We were still thinking that we were all dreaming. We looked at each other and then looked around the room. It was lovely. We were sitting on the sofa in front of a wooden coffee table. It had a glass bowl full of apples and oranges and the biggest bunch of purple grapes I had ever seen. I couldn't take my eyes off those oranges. I had only ever seen fruit in the shop at the top of the street, sometimes we would have a piece of fruit at school with our dinner, but we never had fruit at home. There was a huge coal fire, similar to the one at our house before Dad replaced it with a new gas fire. There were little ornaments on the fireplace, some made of brass. There was also a companion set next to the fire; it consisted of a little shovel, a poker and a little brush, that were used to clean the area around the fireplace. There were pictures on the wall of flowers and cottages. Lots of green plants were on the windowsill and on tables in the corner of the room. There was a fluffy rug in front of the fire and there were fluffy pink cushions on the settee that were soft and comfortable. A small television stood in the corner of the room with a framed wedding photograph on the top. It was a nice warm room and I liked it a lot.

Mum was soon back from the kitchen, holding knives and forks. She laid the table and asked us to come and sit there to have some dinner. Mum had made us a piece of 'fish in batter' as she called it. We had never had anything like that before, but it was good. She also made us some bread and butter to go with it. Bread, with butter on it! We were all so full when we had finished. She then gave us all a slice of malt loaf, also with butter on it — we hadn't had that before either! Mum told us about David, the man she had just married and she showed us the photograph of the wedding. It was lovely! Mum had her hair up in a bun with curls hanging down at the side of her face and she wore a long, lacy white dress. David had worn a very smart, dark blue suit. Mum told us that he was at work and that he wouldn't be home until late. I told her that we had to be home for around tea time but we could come again tomorrow if she wanted us too. She said she would be sorry to see us leave today but said she would give us the bus fare home and for us to come back tomorrow. That way it may be possible for us to meet David.

All too soon, it was time for us to leave. Mum walked with us to the bus stop on the lane and waited with us. Once again, we were hugging each other and crying, we just didn't want to go but we knew we had to. We weren't waiting long before the bus came. It pulled up in front of us, the door opened and we climbed on. We raced to the back of the bus, so we could wave at Mum through the back window. The bus slowly pulled away from the bus stop and we were waving at Mum until the bus went around a corner and Mum was out of sight. We turned to sit on the seat as the conductor came towards us for the fare. We all sat quietly on the bus not quite believing what a day we had had. I couldn't believe that we had spent the whole day with our mum and it was to be our secret. Mum was just as I had remembered her, she hadn't changed much at all, and we were going to see her again tomorrow. We couldn't wait. One thing I realised that day at Mum's house, was that she was not the woman on the television that I thought she was. She just looked like her. This is where Mum had been. Not all that far away from us all.

Soon the bus neared our estate and we got off. We were very nervous as we arrived home, after seeing Anita home and making sure she wasn't going to tell anybody where we had been. Mum had given us the bus fare for the journey the following day and I had hidden it down my sock. As we walked in, Dad asked us where we had been all day and we told him we had been in the park playing. We rushed off upstairs out of sight as quickly as we could, not believing we had got away with it. I was praying that we would be able to get to see Mum again the following day and that night we were in bed nice and early.

We had a wonderful secret and we were keeping it from all the others. We had to; we had no choice. Jane and Andrea were too young, they would have told Dad because they probably wouldn't remember our mum, so they wouldn't understand. We also thought that Anne and Paul would have told Dad, but we weren't sure, so we didn't tell them, just to be on the safe side.

The next day the sun was shining, just like the previous day, so we knew it was going to be another lovely day. We had chores to do in the morning, as always, so we couldn't leave the house until we had done what we had to do. It was getting on for dinner time when we were allowed out. I was beginning to think that we would never get to Mum's house. She might be thinking that we weren't coming.

When we finally got out of our house, we raced to the bus stop. I had already put our bus fare that Mum gave to us, down my sock again ready for when we got on the bus. In our rush to get to the bus, we both forgot about Anita, and we left without calling for her. We were already on the bus when we realised that we had left her behind. The conductor collected our money and we were on our way. We sat on the upper deck of the bus so that we wouldn't be seen. If we saw someone we knew, we could hide between the seats out of sight. We had it all worked out, but we didn't expect to forget Anita, but it was too late now, we were nearly there.

It didn't take the bus very long, not nearly as long as it had taken us to walk. The bus pulled up at the bus stop that we needed and we got off. We raced down Beatrice Street to number 19, where Mum lived. We banged on the door hoping that she would still be in. The door opened and Mum was there. We were so relieved to see her, as we stood there out of breath with our running. Mum gave us a big hug and a kiss and said that she thought that we weren't coming. She beckoned us to come in and said, "Look who's here?" As we walked in, there was a lady sitting on the settee. She looked really familiar; I was sure that I had seen her before. "Do you know who this lady is?" Mum said. I looked at her and thought hard. Then I remembered, I was sure it was Aunty Flo. "Yes, that's right," Mum said and Aunty Flo stood up and came over to us and gave us another hug. "Do you remember me then?" she asked.

I did remember her, but it was a long time ago, I must have been very young. I remembered being at Aunty Flo's house on Union Road, with Dad. We were standing at her back door watching the trains going past high up on a bridge. The bridge had arches underneath and Dad had to lift me up so that I could see. Dad was pointing at the trains and they were all lit up against the darkness. She was Mum's sister and she did look a bit like Mum. I told Aunty Flo my memory of her and she said that she had remembered that day when we had visited her house.

Mum told us that she had telephoned Flo the previous day following our visit. Our mum had explained to Flo that we were coming back so Flo would have the opportunity to see us as well. Aunty Flo said that Mum shouldn't have let us go back and that we should have stayed. Mum made a pot of tea and some sandwiches and we all sat around the table. Drinking tea was a treat as we were not allowed to drink tea at home.

I remember Mum asking us if we wanted to stay. We both said we wanted to stay but we both got scared and excited at the same time. We didn't know how it would be possible to stay with Mum and we knew that Dad would go mad. Mum said we weren't to worry about that and that she and David would sort it all out. We hadn't met David yet but Mum said that he would be home soon as he worked in the local pub on Sundays.

After spending the day with Aunty Flo, it was time for her to go home, so we all walked her to the bus stop and waved at her as she left. She wished Mum and us good luck before she left and hoped that everything would be sorted. Soon the bus was gone and I hoped that we would see her again soon.

Mum then took us to the pub where David worked to see if he was ready to finish work. As we walked in through the pub door there where men stood leaning on the bar drinking beer and David was standing behind the counter in a pink shirt. He looked at us as we walked up to the bar with Mum. "Hello," he said. "You must be Margaret, and you must be Maureen." We both nodded and stood there very shyly. We had never been in a pub before and we were glad to meet David after all this time. Mum sat us on a tall stool at the side of the bar and asked if we wanted a drink of pop. We both nodded again and I thought this was brilliant.

Soon it was time to go back to Mum's house. Mum was talking to David about what Aunty Flo had said. Mum told David that Aunty Flo had stated that we should not be sent back home. David agreed and said that we could stop if we wanted to. We both were sure we didn't want to go home at all. We had made our minds up already. It was decided; we were staying. We were so excited. We couldn't believe it. I remember jumping around the room in excitement.

David suggested that we should be introduced to his family, so off we went to David's parents' house. The house wasn't far from Mum's house. As we walked in their house, I remember feeling very wary and a little scared as there was quite a lot of noise from children shouting and they had raised voices. The house was quite dark and gloomy and as we were led through the hallway of this very untidy house, David shouted "Hello!" as we entered a room off the hall. All at once a girl came charging over to David and jumped right into his arms flinging her arms around his neck. He fell onto the settee with her and told us that she was his crazy little sister, Carol. She became very shy then and got off David's knee and went to hide in the other room. The house was huge! There was room after room and there were people all over the place. Slowly, we were introduced to them one by one, then we were asked to stay in the other room with all the other kids, so we could get to know each other.

There was an old piano in that room, so we were both trying to play something on it and getting to know the others at the same time. While this was going on Mum and David were talking to the grown-ups. They must have been talking about us and that they had decided to keep us. We were getting on really well with the other kids. There was Carol, Colin, Maureen and Anne. Anne was about fourteen or fifteen. Colin was about the same age as Maureen. There were others in the other room who were all brothers and sisters of David. There were loads of them all living in that house! I thought there were a lot of us at our house but there were more in this family. It was no wonder it was untidy and so noisy.

They were all asking questions. They asked where we lived and whether or not we were staying with our mum now. There were so many questions! Carol was so funny, she made me laugh a lot. She acted more like a boy than a girl! While we were playing, a car pulled up alongside the house outside. We couldn't see who it was as the windows were too high to see through but Mum came into the room where we were playing. She had a very worried look on her face. I knew something was wrong, I had seen that look on her face before. She put her finger to her lips and said, "Ssh! Your dad is outside. He has come to get you to take you back home." Maureen and I started to cry as I wondered how he knew where we were. Mum said that Anita had been to Dad's house and told him that we had come to see Mum. She had split on us.

Mum told us to keep quiet and not to come out of the room as she was going to try to talk to him. I couldn't hear any shouting at all but Mum came back in the room with tears in her eyes. She said that he had got a policeman with him and he was talking to him but she thought that we might have to go home with him as he had a special paper to say that we should stay with him.

I cried so hard for what seemed like ages. I didn't want to go home with Dad, I knew that he would get us back and give us a good hiding. I knew there would be trouble if we were to go with him. I tried to explain this to Mum and begged her not to let us go back with him, but she said there was nothing she could do. She was crying and sobbing with us as she held us so tight. David came into the room and said that we had to go. Mum didn't want to let us go. I hung on to her pleading with her not to let him take us. When we were separated Mum fell in a heap on the floor with her arms outstretched crying for us as we were taken through the front door to where Dad was waiting in his car.

Dad looked at us both as we came out of the house and neared the car. His face looked so angry as he stared at us. The tears froze on my cheeks as the car door was opened and Dad shouted to us to get in. We sat on the back seat of the car and I lowered my head and wiped my face on my sleeve as Dad started the engine and we were driven away. Dad didn't say another word all the way home. We were both sitting silently huddled together on the back seat shaking with fear as to what he was going to do to us when we got home.

It was a long drive home and as we approached our street I began to shake even more. I sat rigid, so scared, I couldn't move at all.

Dad pulled up outside our house and got out of the car. He opened the back door and told us to get in the house and out of his sight. We raced inside the house and up the stairs as fast as we could. I got undressed and got into my bed and stayed there for the rest of that evening. We weren't allowed downstairs, not even for something to eat. I wanted to cry and cry but I couldn't. I was afraid that if Dad heard us, he would be up and we would be in serious trouble. I couldn't believe that he had not taken his belt to us but we thought he would be upstairs any minute to do it, or maybe he was going to save it until the morning!

CHAPTER TWELVE
The New House

I woke up the next morning feeling lucky that we hadn't been beaten the night before, although I did feel that he wouldn't forget what we had done in a hurry and we could still be punished at any time. Dad told us that morning, that we were not to leave the street at any time, unless he knew where we were going. I didn't think Dad wanted us to run off to mums again. We would not have dared to; we were too scared at the time and just felt lucky that we hadn't had a good hiding. I did wonder to myself, why did he not want us to stay with our mum when he doesn't like us anyway?

After the beating that Andrea received, for ripping her dress on a bush, I thought that, what we had done was far worse and that we would be in trouble for sure.

As the next few weeks went by, we weren't allowed to talk about what we had done to any of our siblings. We were dying to tell them that we had seen Mum and she had said that she loved us all but I dared not. Ann and Paul assumed that we had been in serious trouble with the police.

One night Paul was in trouble with the police, when he was down in the park and he was brought home by an officer. Paul was thirteen at the time, so he was allowed to play out for longer than we were. We were all in our beds by the time he was brought home. I heard the loud knock at the front door. Dad answered the door and began to speak to the policeman. When I heard the door close, Dad started shouting at Paul. I could hear Paul being knocked about downstairs in the kitchen, which was directly underneath our bedroom. I knew what sort of noise the stick made when Dad used it. It was a sound that I would never forget. Paul was being hit with the stick and I could hear every strike. I lay in bed and I counted more than twelve beats of the stick. I didn't know what Paul had done but this seemed to be the worst beating he had ever had. It seemed to go on and on for most of the night. Paul was always beaten very badly, it was usually done with Dad's fist and not the stick, as had been the case on this occasion. Never once did I hear Paul cry or shout out in any pain, it would have been worse for him if he had, but he must have been in a great deal of pain.

Paul later told us that he was down in the park with his friends and he had let the tyres' down on a car. A man had seen him and phoned the police. Paul pleaded and begged the man not to phone the police but the man took no notice of the fear on his face. Paul knew what Dad would do to him when he returned home. That was the reason for the vicious assault on him that day. I had seen Paul punched to the floor and then kicked around like a football, but not once did I see him cry. After it was all over, he limped off to his room holding his tummy tightly and he wasn't seen until the next day. It was very clear that he had suffered. His face was bruised and his eyes were swollen. There were even times when we noticed that he had teeth missing.

We did have group photographs taken on the odd occasion, but Paul was never on many of them as he always had some bruising to his face or a black eye, just like our mum.

Later that summer Dad got a letter from the council to say that we could move into a bigger house. The new house wasn't very far away from where we lived but it was a nicer, more modern house with four bedrooms and a bathroom upstairs. It was on Montserrat Road, number 47. This was a main road, with lots of traffic. The bus from Bolton town centre also ran along this road, turning around at the terminus at the bottom of Lightbounds Road. It would then come back past our house to go back into town. It was a nice house; we all liked it and liked the area. It seemed posher than Shackleton Grove.

Shackleton Grove was a very old house but I knew that I would still miss it a lot. I didn't have many good memories from there, they were mostly bad memories, but still, I would miss the friends and neighbours, such as Mrs Baron and the Andersons.

I knew that I would never forget the memories of Mum in that house. I didn't know whether we would ever get to see her again as she would not now know where we lived. What if she ever wanted to try to find us? Then, I instinctively knew that I would try to get to see her again if I got the chance — perhaps when I became older.

The new house was great. There was lots of space and it was so much bigger than the other house. Just like Shackleton Grove, this house also had a ginnel, which led through to the back garden. Round the back there were brick sheds built on to the back of the house, like outhouses. One of the sheds was once used as a coal store, when the house had an open fire. Now, new modern gas fires had been installed by the council. The walls of this shed still had black soot showing the signs that coal had once been stored there. There was an outside toilet too, which reminded me of the outside toilet in Mum's back yard, though this one looked as if it hadn't been used in a long time. It certainly needed a good clean as it smelt awful.

The other shed was really spacious and had a small window at one side, which let the light in. I thought this would be great for us to play in with our friends on rainy days or maybe Dad would let us have some more rabbits. We could keep them in hutches inside the shed, where they would be warm and dry.

There was a boy called Alan, living next door, who went to the same school as I did. He was also the same age as me. Within a few months of moving Alan had stolen a kiss from me in the shed in our back garden. When he tried to steal another, we were disturbed by my younger sister Andrea, who thought it was hilarious that I should want to kiss the boy next door.

Ann and I were to share a bedroom. Paul was to have his own bedroom, as he did at the old house, because of course, he was the only boy. The other four were to share the largest bedroom at the front of the house. Baby Laura was to sleep in a cot at night, so she shared Dad and Mary's bedroom. It was strange having a bathroom upstairs and took a lot of getting used to. Downstairs there was a long hallway, which led to three rooms. The living room, which was the largest room at the front of the house, had a long window on one side which let lots of light in. There was a dining room, which led to the kitchen, at the back of the house. There was also a little pantry at the side of the kitchen, which had shelves along each wall for groceries. There was a shiny new sink unit under the window, with a cupboard underneath it and there were cupboards on the wall, with drawers underneath them. It was all so different to the old house. We'd had an old, white, square pot sink with a wooden draining board at the old house and Mary had put a piece of material round it as a curtain to hide the pots and pans.

Most of the house didn't need to be decorated, but Dad wallpapered the living room and painted the hall and landing. He didn't like the flowery wallpaper, so it had to come off. We knew that we had to keep out of Dad's way when he was working on the house, doing jobs such as decorating, as he lost his temper if any of us got in his way. We had new carpets put down in our bedrooms for the first time. We thought this was great as we could sit on the floor of our rooms and not get cold bums. We had lino down in the old house, which was really cold to walk on with bare feet, especially in winter.

The carpet in the living room was lovely. It had a green flowery pattern on it and we got a new yellow striped three-piece suite. It had a long settee and two chairs and one of the chairs was bigger than the other. This was Dad's chair. It could rock and swivel around. None of us were allowed to sit in it, but sometimes when Dad wasn't in, we would 'have a go' when no one was looking. We weren't allowed into the living room with our shoes on and if we put our feet up onto the settee, we would really be in for it. I thought we were really posh now. I liked our new house and I hoped that we could all be happy here. This was going to be the start of our new life; in a new house, in a new area. All the bad memories were left behind, at Shackleton Grove. Although all those memories would probably never ever be forgotten.

The old house was left behind now but we were hoping that something else would have been left behind too, but it wasn't. The stick that Dad used to hit us with, dunk the washing in the washing machine with and used to kill our pet rabbits was still with us! It moved into our new house with us, as if it was part of the family. It would always be available and in full view of all us kids just in case it was needed if any of us stepped out of line or our chores weren't done properly. It was brought to the new house and was given a new 'pride of place'. This was at the side of the new swivel chair that Dad sat in each night as he watched TV. He was waiting for the time when it would be used again. This was a lovely house, could it really be possible that things could be any worse here than at the old house?

It was great that Ann and I had our own room, away from the

younger ones. It meant that we could look after our own things and have a lot more privacy. We could do our homework in peace.

We had our meals (if that's what you could call them) in the dining room or the back room as we named it. All of us sat round a big, old, heavy table. We had a record player that someone had given to us and some old LPs. We all liked the Mary Poppins album and knew all the songs off by heart. There was also a Top of the Pops album with various pop songs on it. Ann and I used to dance to them in the dining room, showing off, in front of the others. Dancing was something that we had learned at the Palais. Every time we made too much noise Dad would shout to us to stop and shut up.

Ann and I liked dancing, so every Saturday morning, we were allowed to go downtown to the Bolton Palais, for the dancing session for kids. It was brilliant, we loved it. We'd dance on this really big, wooden, bouncy dance floor learning different dances. My favourite was the March of the Mods. We would all be in lines and go round and round the dance floor until the music ended — it was great fun! We both loved the time away from the others as we felt really grown up to be going on buses and walking around town on our own. I was almost thirteen and Ann was a year older.

Every Saturday, after dancing, we had to go to the Market Hall to see Aunty Nora and Uncle John. They had a butcher's stall in there. We always went to collect sausages for Saturday's tea and meat for Sunday's tea. Aunty Nora was Dad's sister and my favourite auntie. We didn't see her a lot, but we enjoyed our little visits to her on Saturdays. She would always give us a big hug, just like our mum did. But best of all she always had some sweets waiting for us behind the counter. She looked a bit like our dad. She only had one daughter, our cousin Linda. I was given her name as my middle name when I was born. Every weekend was the same; dancing first, on to buy the meat from Aunty Nora's market stall and then take it home.

Now and again, we had to go to the Co-op and exchange the green shield stamps for money. Mary had collected the stamps for weeks and when she had a full book of them, they were swapped for goods or money in the big Co-op store in town. One Saturday we had been dancing at the Palais and we'd had a really good time. After picking the meat up from

Aunty Nora, we set off for home. We were quite tired after dancing to every piece of music played at the dance hall, so we couldn't wait to get home. We left the Market Hall and went down the wide steps at the side, which led to our bus stop. We caught the bus outside the Market Hall and sat down exhausted.

When we arrived home, we went to put the meat in the kitchen. Looking in our bag, we couldn't find it. We searched our coat pockets and the bag again, but it was no use, we had definitely lost the meat.

We were standing in the kitchen panicking and blaming each other for losing it. My heart was beating fast in my chest; we were in for it now. We searched again but it was no use. We must have lost it on the way home, or left it on the bus, we just didn't know. My hands were shaking as I looked up through the window into the back garden. All at once Dad appeared from behind the shed. He had been digging in the garden. The sight of him made me jump and tremble even more. I looked at Ann and she too was looking through the window at Dad. My hands were shaking uncontrollably now as tears were swelling in my eyes. Dad was going to kill us and I could see Ann was trembling too. What were we going to do? We stared at Dad through the window and I could hear the beating of my heart in my chest.

We both jumped as Mary walked through the kitchen door. We turned to look at her. She asked us what we were up to. I stared at her as the tears fell down my cheek. I crossed my legs as tight as I could, as I really needed the toilet. Mary asked what the matter was and why I was crying. We told Mary what had happened. She stood looking at us. I could tell by the look on her face that she knew we would be in big trouble for this.

When Dad walked through the back door, I looked at him and froze. I was shaking from head to toe and I needed the toilet so badly now. Dad was bent down taking his boots off at the door and raised his head to look at us. He asked what was going on and Mary turned to him and told him that we had lost the meat. I could see by Dad's face that he was not very pleased. He shouted to us to get in the other room. We both ran into the living room waiting for him to follow us. When he came in, he was shouting at us and reached for his belt that was hanging over the back of his chair. Doubling it over in his hand he lashed out with it as he shouted out so loud at us that we were stupid and we weren't going to eat that weekend because we had lost the meat. The belt was directed at me and then Ann in turn. We were both hit on our backs and legs as we tried to cover our faces from the lashes. We were hit several times and then sent to our room. There was no meal for us that weekend. We were made to feel so incompetent and stupid; Dad didn't speak to either of us for days. We were made to keep out of his way. We always looked forward to our meals on the weekends, as we ate the same as Dad and Mary, although not at the same table. Dad always had his meals on his knee, sat in his chair in front of the TV. It was always a hot cooked dinner on a big plate, just like the meals at school and we were always full afterwards. We always cleared our plates. There were never any leftovers.

School meals were the best and we always had plenty to eat. We would queue up for second helpings to make sure of it because we knew that when we got home, there would not be much on our dinner table. We knew it would be something on toast; egg, beans or spaghetti. One tin of spaghetti would be shared between us all. It was always the same. Sometimes we would be made to eat sardines or pilchards that were taken from this tiny tin can and mixed up with a fork and spread onto toast. It tasted disgusting. None of us liked it but we had to eat it as there was nothing else.

One night after school we were all given a boiled egg with a slice of toast. I cracked mine open and scooped the egg out of the shell and started to eat. It tasted awful and the white of the egg was a yellowy colour, it just didn't seem right. I called Mary and told her that my egg tasted funny and she came over and picked it up to look at it. She held it to her nose and pulled it away quickly. She told me it had gone off and turned to put it in the bin. I sat there as the others tucked into their eggs and waited to be given something else to eat instead but nothing came. I finished my toast and left the table feeling very hungry. There was no point in asking. We had learned at an early age never to ask because we were always told there was nothing else.

Most weekends we were lucky if we got breakfast at all, but when we did it was a small bowl of cereal or a piece of toast. For dinner it was always two slices of bread with jam, sugar or banana spread on it. If we were really lucky, sometimes we got crisps on the bread. Mary would make one packet of crisps stretch for all our sandwiches. I never knew how she managed it! Mary would buy a large jar of peanut butter which would last for ages, when we didn't stick our finger in it and lick it straight from the jar! We would get a clout around the head if we were caught doing that. We would spread the peanut butter on two slices of bread for our dinner.

I remember playing in the ginnel one day. It was pouring with rain. I was with my friends from Knott Lane — Lyn and Lorraine Allan. I had made some peanut butter sandwiches so we could have a little picnic in the ginnel. They'd never eaten peanut butter before. We tucked in and watched the rain pouring down.

Usually, Saturday teatime was sausage, mash and beans and for Sunday tea, which was the best, we had meat, potatoes and vegetables with gravy. Our plates were full but there was never anything left on any of them afterwards. On Sundays we also had a dessert of jelly and ice-cream or rice pudding. We would look forward to Sundays. From one week to another, the meals were the same. We were all used to the feeling of hunger especially at night time when we lay in our beds. The only exception to this was on Sunday nights.

Although we liked our new house, Paul, Ann and I were not too pleased that we had more chores to do. We never complained though — we didn't dare! We just got on with whatever we had to do. We weren't allowed to complain or we would have been given more work to do. Paul had to keep the garden tidy at all times. Litter constantly blew in our garden from the main road, so every day Paul had to clear it all up. Ann had the polishing and hoovering to do as well as keeping us all in check when Mary or Dad wasn't around.

Ann was more than a big sister to baby Laura; she was like another mother to her. I loved Laura. She was so cute with her big brown eyes that were like saucers, and chubby rosy cheeks. She was becoming quite a handful for Mary now as she was crawling around and getting into everything. We all had to look after Laura at some time which wasn't difficult because we all loved her and loved to play with her. We all just had to keep her happy and out of Dad's way when he was busy or watching football. He didn't like us being noisy. It was better playing with Laura upstairs or in the garden on a nice day than doing our other jobs around the house.

I had to peel potatoes for Dad's tea every night, which I hated doing because there were many times Dad would stand over me and inspect my job to make sure the peelings were not too thick. I would be clouted if they were! I was very careful not to have them too thick because I always knew that he would check them afterwards. After tea, Maureen and I had the kitchen to clean. The kitchen had to be spotless. The pots had to be washed, dried and put away in their right place. The cooker had to be cleaned, worktops had to be wiped down and the floor had to be mopped. It was my job to do the ironing on Sunday afternoons, which would take hours. We all had to make our own beds and polish our shoes every Sunday night for school on Mondays.

The older we got, the more jobs we were to do around the house. Sometimes, we didn't get out to play at all because Dad wasn't happy with the way we had done things, so we were made to stay in until we had done it properly. Sometimes it took all day.

Usually, the house smelt of this awful foodstuff Dad used to cook for the chickens that we had at the bottom of the garden. He kept about a dozen chickens in large sheds that he had built from wood and wire netting. They were fed on potato peelings, old tea bags and other food waste that he would cook in a large pan every day, which stunk the place out. The smell was awful!

There were always fresh eggs every day, though I wasn't sure what was done with them all. We kids didn't eat any of them. The baby chickens were cute, but I didn't like the big ones. They were smelly, noisy creatures and I stayed away from them as much as I could.

Dad was in the sheds with those smelly chickens for hours some days. He was always hammering nails into wood making chicken runs and boxes for them.

Sometimes he would just sit down on an old milk crate watching them clucking away in their pens. I heard him singing in there one day. He was singing that old song of Engelbart Humperdinck's "I had the last dance with you, two lonely people together." Dad sung in the pubs but I hardly ever heard him sing in the house as he always seemed to be in a bad mood most days, so it surprised me to hear him singing in there with the chickens that day.

Dad allowed me to get some more rabbits shortly after moving into the new house and I kept them in the shed in hutches that I built myself. I had about six. They were all different. I had this fascination for rabbits and would always be reading up about them from books from the school library. I learned quite a lot about them that way.

After a few months of tending to these rabbits, they started dying and I didn't know why. I tried to find out from the books that I was reading and I also asked the shopkeeper at Mitten's Pet Shop in Bolton town centre. Nobody could tell me what I was doing wrong or why my rabbits were dying. The back legs of the rabbits would go stiff and the rabbits wouldn't be able to walk. After a few days they were dead. They all died that way one after another. When the last one died, I was devastated.

I never forgot the rabbits that I had had at Shackleton Grove, — Queenie and Snowy, and how devastated I was when they were killed. That experience would stay with me forever. I just couldn't explain why these rabbits had just died this way and it really upset me at the time. Dad thought that they caught a disease from each other that spread through them all and killed them. I couldn't understand it. I kept them all clean and well fed and I brushed their coats every day. I looked after them so well but they all still died. I couldn't bear to keep any more rabbits, so their hutches were all destroyed and thrown on the tip. When the chores were done, I was always with my rabbits but after they all died, I would play out with friends from school most of the time. I could wander off again now like I used to before our visit to Mum's.

It had been over a year since our visits to Mum but I had made my mind up that I was going to try to see her again soon. I was planning to go on my own and keep it a secret, not telling anyone at all this time. I was really missing her and really wanted to see her. I was still very scared to try and get to see her at that time because I felt as though Dad was watching my every move. Even when I was a long way from home — across the other side of the park, catching frogs on Doffcocker Lodge or underneath the Kingdom Hall of Jehovah Witness Church — I always sensed that Dad could see what I was doing and what I was getting up to.

One day Paul was playing with his friends in Craven Place (the next street from us). He didn't see Dad walking across the top of the street behind him. Paul was using swear words while talking to his friends and Dad heard him. Paul was grabbed around the neck and dragged home. He was taken into the dining room and battered.

No matter where I was at any time, I was always looking over my shoulder, to see if Dad was around watching us. We all felt that way. All of us had the same feelings that he would always know or get to find out what we were getting up to.

During that summer of 1971 we all went on holiday to Rhyl. We stayed at a campsite called Sunnyvale Campsite. There were caravans and chalets on this site and it was close to a lovely sandy beach. It was the first time we had been to the seaside, so we were really looking forward to playing on the beach and splashing about in the sea. We stayed in a brown, wooden chalet that was right on the edge of the beach. We were fascinated with the big bed that pulled down from the wall and the other little beds that turned into settees during the day. It was only a small chalet but there was room for all of us and it even had a tiny kitchen as well. We had lots of fun and made loads of new friends during our week's stay at Sunnyvale. There were lots of things to do, from playing bingo, which we all did most days, to playing in the amusement arcades. We liked the beach best though. Although none of us could swim, we enjoyed splashing about in the water in our swimming costumes and building sandcastles with our buckets and spades. We would see who could build the biggest and the best sandcastle.

Paul was always the winner. His sandcastles were the best. We would stay on the beach all day and when the tide came in, we would watch as the seawater swept away our castles one by one.

The next day we would build them up again bigger and better. We were there for a week and even when the weather wasn't all that warm, we would still be on that beach in our costumes splashing around in the salty water or sat in the huge striped deckchairs. We all looked a sight in our costumes, most of which were too big for our thin frames so when they got wet, they hung down past our hips and we had to keep pulling them up. We were so skinny there was nothing for the costume to cling to. You could almost see our ribs poking through our skin. We would be dripping wet through and freezing if the wind was blowing in from the sea but still, we would be sitting building sandcastles or catching crabs with our hands and collecting them all in our buckets. The crabs would snap out at us with their claws and give us a nasty nip if we got too close to them. Dad wouldn't allow us to take them into the chalet though. We were made to take them back to the beach and let them go. I felt this wasn't fair as I wanted to take them home and keep them. I decided to collect seashells instead. We all had a wonderful holiday, even Dad seemed to have a good time and none of us got shouted at for that whole week, until the last morning.

We were packing our bags for the journey home and tidying the chalet for the next holiday makers. Ann was trying to lift the bed back into the wall when all of a sudden it fell from her hands and right onto her toe. Ann screamed and there was blood everywhere. Mary wrapped her foot up in a towel and Dad was really angry. He shouted loudly that she had spoiled the holiday. She was sobbing and in quite a lot of pain so she was taken to the hospital. Dad and Mary took her and we all had to stay and look after the others while they were away. Ann had to have an x-ray of her foot to see if anything was broken. Fortunately, there wasn't but she had to have several stitches in her big toe. When they arrived back from the hospital with her foot all bandaged up, we set off on our journey back home.

The journey home lasted a few hours. We had all enjoyed ourselves at Sunnyvale and hadn't wanted to go home. It had been good to get away from home for a week and all our chores. Even Dad had had a good time! Leaning on each other's shoulders we slept most of the way home, dreaming of the next time we could go back to Sunnyvale.

CHAPTER THIRTEEN
Laura's Fall

When Laura found her feet and started to walk, she was all over the place. I would say that she learned to run before she could walk, and she was so fast! We had to take her out with us when we went outside to play, and at times we would have to push her up and down the street in her pushchair until she fell asleep, then take her back home. We were always warned that if anything was to happen to Laura, while we were out with her, we would be in serious trouble. We had no choice but to take her with us, when we were told to. We were always so very scared of anything bad happening to her. I tended to keep her in her pram most of the time, despite all her protests, except when we were in the park, she loved to play in the sandpit. She would play for ages until she got tired then fall asleep in her pram on the way home. I was petrified that something would happen to her when she was with me. I was the one who looked after her most of the time, especially at weekends. My eyes would be on her all the time. I would watch her like a hawk.

Ann had a part time job on Saturdays and Sundays. She was working with our Aunty Nora. Aunty Nora had bought a little café on Chorley Old Road, near Bolton Royal Infirmary. It was called The Copper Kettle. Ann liked to work there. Soon, when old enough, I hoped that I would be able to work there as well. This left me as the one who took care of Laura if Mary wasn't there or she was busy doing other things. Sometimes she had to go to town to do some shopping. I loved to be with Laura, I loved her little face and loved to make her laugh. I would pretend that I was her mum but I was still scared that something awful would happen to her.

One day, to my horror, it did, and it would be a day that I would never forget!

I was looking forward to playing out as I was going to visit Brenda Anderson. Brenda was one of Mrs Anderson's daughters. Mrs Anderson lived opposite to where we had lived in Shackleton Grove. Brenda now lived at number 18 Shackleton Grove, next door to where we used to live.

When we lived at number 20, an old man called Mr Barns used to live in what was now Brenda's home but he had died months ago. The council had given the house to her and her family. Brenda used to live in Singapore with her husband and children because her husband was out there with the army. They were stationed out there. When he left the army, they came back to live in Bolton. I loved going to her house as she talked all the time, telling stories of their life in Singapore. She talked about the people out there and of the things that happened to them. Brenda taught Ann and I how to play a game called Mah-jong. This was a game that people in Singapore played all the time.

After our chores were done, I asked Dad if I could play out. He said that I could but that I had to take Laura with me. Mary had gone to the shops, so I got Laura ready and put her in the pram. I fastened her in with her pink leather reins which had a picture of a fluffy white lamb on the front and set off to Brenda's house. Jane tagged along with us as well. She was going to play with Brenda's daughter who was about the same age as her.

Brenda was waiting for us when we arrived at her house and let us in. Jane went round the back to play in the garden with her friend. I followed Brenda into the kitchen with Laura, who was still sitting in her pram. Brenda unclipped her reins and lifted her out and she then began to toddle about in the kitchen.

After about an hour and a half Laura was getting a bit tired so I called Jane and told her it was time to go back home. I wheeled the pram to the front door and went back in the kitchen for Laura. I lifted her up into my arms and went through to the front garden. Laura was quite heavy, so I decided to put her down for a second while I got her pram ready. The next thing I knew she had run off down the path towards the road. I quickly ran after her and tried to grab her before she reached the garden gate but she tripped and fell over banging her head on the ground. She lay there screaming. Rushing to her I lifted her up onto my knee to see what she had done. There was an injury to her forehead, which was bleeding quite badly. I couldn't console Laura at all. Brenda came over, lifted her from my arms and took her into the kitchen to clean her up. I was crying and shaking with the shock at what had happened to Laura and the fear of what was going to happen to me when I got home. Laura

106

was still crying while Brenda was bathing her forehead. There was blood dripping down her face and onto her dress. Dad would kill me for sure after this.

Jane came in through the back door to see why Laura was crying. She took one look at Laura and her eyes widened as she gasped in horror. She turned and raced off shouting that she was going to tell Dad what had happened. I knew she would get home before I did. I would be in trouble when I got home.

Laura had a bad graze on her forehead, which thankfully stopped bleeding after Brenda had cleaned it up. I thought that it would never stop bleeding. It still looked bad though. Soon Laura stopped crying and I lifted her up to put her in her pram. This time I didn't put her down on the ground. I put on her reins and fastened them at the back of her and clipped her into her pram heading off for home.

We waved goodbye to Brenda as we left. I was so scared. I was still crying and wiping away the tears from my face with my sleeve as I walked home. Laura seemed happy chattering away in her pram. I didn't want to go home at all. I wanted to run away! I really wanted my mum right at that moment. I missed her a lot. I knew what Dad was going to do to me when I got home.

There were tears streaming down my face as I turned the corner of our street. Slowly, I reached our front gate. I couldn't see or hear anybody around but the front door was open. I slowly pushed the pram up the path to the front door and lifted it up over the two steps into the house. As I pushed the pram along the hallway, I looked up and Dad was standing at the end of the hall. I jumped at the sight of him and then froze staring at him. I wet my knickers there and then. I couldn't help it. At the age of thirteen1 I had wet myself. I was petrified. Dad shouted at me and Laura started to cry in her pram. He wanted to know what the hell had happened. I tried to tell him, but the words wouldn't come out of my mouth. I just stared at him. I was shaking all over. Mary came through from the living room and lifted Laura from the pram taking her into the kitchen to check her over. Dad knocked the pram out of his way and charged towards me. He lifted his hand and struck me across the head sending me crashing into the wall. I banged my head against the wall biting my tongue. I was hit again and again until I managed to scramble up the stairs and into my room.

After changing my underwear, I lay on my bed and cried. My head was sore and I really wanted my mum. I hated Dad. I wanted to run away and never come back.

I hadn't intended for this to happen to my baby sister. I loved her so much. It was a terrible accident, but I was made to feel totally irresponsible for not looking after her properly.

Worst of all, the wound on her forehead didn't heal as it should over the next few days, so she had to be taken to see the doctor. She was given some cream because it had become badly infected and caused scabs to spread over to other parts of her face.

After a couple of weeks Laura's head cleared up and the wound didn't leave any scars. The guilt I felt went on forever.

CHAPTER FOURTEEN
Summer of 1971: Carol: Our double life.

Later that year of 1971 I was back at school. I was now a second-year student at Smithills High School. Everyone at school seemed to have grown so much taller during the holidays. I hadn't seen most of them through the summer and they all seemed to have changed a lot. We were all mixed up into different classes for the second year. This meant we had to get used to our new classmates all over again. Although I was still friendly with the girls from the first year, I made a new friend from my second-year class. She was called Carol. She was so funny. She liked to make people laugh, just like I did.

After a few weeks at school, we got to know each other and found that we were so very much alike in many ways. We lived near each other and she also came from a big family. There were eight kids in our family but there were nine kids in hers. Carol had the most amazing bright, red hair and big brown eyes. We really got on well and talked all the time, mostly about boys and who was the best-looking lad in our class.

Gary O'Connor was the girls' favourite in our year; all the girls liked him. He had long, blond, wavy hair. He was quite nice looking but I still secretly quite liked David, who I had kissed when I was a first year. I didn't think any boy would ever like me because I was too much like a tomboy. Most of the time I was ignored in favour of the prettier girls like Vanda and Tonia. They were stunning and all the boys would flock around them. Carol fancied a boy called Keith. He wasn't as tall as most of the boys in his year and he had red hair like Carol's. I didn't think he was interested in girls at all. He liked playing football and seemed to be very shy; he didn't seem to talk to any of the girls. His face would turn as red as his hair when any girl tried to speak to him. Carol enjoyed the drama classes in the same way I did and she loved being part of the activities that our teacher Mrs Edwards gave us to take part in. We would be the class clowns and always find something to be giggling about.

There was a fancy-dress competition every year at our school. All our class had to dress up in fancy costumes and the winner got a prize at the end. There was a boy who dressed up like 'Cousin It' from the 'Addams Family'. He had made a long woollen wig, going from his head down to his feet. It covered his whole body and he wore a pair of sunglasses to complete the outfit. The winner was in fact our classmate Gillian who had dressed up as a French girl. She had worn a striped navy and white tee-shirt and a black beret. She rode on stage on an old bicycle with a string of onions draped over the handlebars with croissants and baguettes in the basket at the front. This was in support of the Common Market. Our country joined the Common Market later in 1973, although I didn't really understand at that time what it meant for England. She deserved to win although there were many other well-designed costumes. The competition was shown at night to a full house of parents and other pupils. It was a good show, with lots of money raised for a good cause. I enjoyed acting and the drama classes, in fact anything to do with the theatre and stage. Carol did too and we took part in most of the plays and drama groups. Sometimes it was as if we were a double act; just like Morecambe and Wise. Our drama class took part in a scary event at the Octagon Theatre in Bolton town centre. We were all supposed to be watching a play held at the Octagon Theatre that was supposed to be performed by the resident actors and actresses. We were all so excited at the idea of spending a full afternoon at the theatre, instead of being in a classroom. When we got there, instead of being led through the main entrance and shown to our seats we were led in through a side entrance and asked to proceed along a narrow, darkened passageway. We all stopped chattering and giggling as we all felt a little scared and wondered where we were going. As we followed our teacher along the narrow corridors, which seemed to go on forever, one of the men leading us said that some of the actors were missing and had been poisoned. He said that they had been poisoned by brown, horrible, mouldy things that were scattered around the floor and under no circumstances should we touch them. We all looked towards the floor and saw the items scattered around. I clung onto Carol; my heart beating so fast in my chest. Some of my class thought that they looked like old tea bags. I hadn't ever seen teabags before, as we used tea leaves at home.

Suddenly, there was the noise of banging and of people wailing and shouting for help. At that point we began to get really scared. It seemed to go on for ages. The class and teachers were told that we had to find and rescue all the actors and actresses, from somewhere in this place, before any more were poisoned to death. We really did think it was all true. We believed what we had been told. It was very scary. One of our classmates, Vanda, became really upset and started to cry and had to be comforted by the teacher. The lads in our class were trying to be macho and brave and trying to comfort the girls who were upset. They told them not to worry and that nothing bad would happen to them. Somehow, we had to find out who had poisoned the actors. We then had to find them all, rescue them and lead them all to safety, out of the building, as fast as we could. We were all to be like the detectives but we all thought that we were in danger too. We thought that whatever had happened to them was going to happen to us. We, as a class, managed to find all the poisoned actors. They looked terrible as if they really had been poisoned. We all had to help them up off the floor and lead them outside to safety in the car park at the back of the theatre. Miraculously they all made a complete recovery and started to clap their hands right in front of us all. We didn't know what was going on and stood around shocked and stunned at what had just happened in there. We were all so relieved when we were told that we had just taken part in some sort of hoax; that it was all an act — a pretence. The actors were not really poisoned at all. They were acting. The old, mouldy, brown things scattered around the floor in the theatre were actually old, mouldy tea bags just as some of the girls had thought; they were not poisonous at all.

We were children and scared. We thought it was real. We did become the detectives and it did appear as if we had rescued everyone. However, no one was poisoned and no one really needed rescuing by a bunch of children. So really it was us doing acting and putting on a show for them — mystery solved! My first acting role, in the Octagon Theatre, gave me nightmares for a very long time afterwards.

My new friend Carol and I spent most of our school days together. We were best friends now. We would talk all the time, always getting told off by our teachers and given D merits for talking in class. If we got a certain number of D merits, there was automatic detention. Neither of us minded the detentions because we would still find ways to chatter. I would have stayed at school all day if I could. I didn't like going home. After meeting each other at school, we later found out that we lived close to each other as well. Carol lived on the same estate as we did, so we called for each other most weekends. On school nights we would do our homework together. Carol and I got really close that year and told each other everything. She knew about my dad and how scared I was of him and how he treated us. She even knew how scared I was to be telling her about him, just in case Dad would find out that I was talking about him, but I knew that I could trust Carol, she kept all my secrets. She was a true friend, I loved her as if she was my sister. I used to wish that I lived with her instead. She didn't get hit by her parents, as we did. That confused me a lot at that time because I thought that all kids were treated the way we were.

I would think to myself that we must have been very naughty children to be treated this way and that no other family had children who were as naughty as we were. I would see the bruises on my mum and then on Mary, but I never saw them on anybody else's mum. I saw bruises on my brother and sisters. I never saw any bruises or marks like those on any of my school friends' brothers or sisters. Carol was afraid of my dad too; she didn't like to call for me at our house. She would wait at the gate until I was allowed out.

One lovely hot sunny day, I called for Carol with some of my sisters. We were going for a walk up to the 'cigarette tunnel' and I asked if she would like to come along with us. Carol brought along her little sister Tina in her pram. We all had two sugar butties wrapped up in the wrapper of a Rathbone loaf. The butties were for our dinner when we got there. It was quite a long walk and hard work pushing the pram up the hill on Chorley Old Road, past the golf course.

When we reached the top of Chorley Old Road, we arrived at a pub called The Bob Smithy. We turned right onto Scout Road, and further up Scout Road was 'cigarette tunnel'. It was a lovely walk in the hot sunshine and we were glad when we got there so we could paddle our feet in the cool stream.

It was called 'cigarette tunnel' because it was shaped like a long cigarette. It went right underneath Scout Road. We could stand up in the tunnel and could almost touch the top. It had a shallow stream running all the way through it. It was a great place for us to play and explore. We would spend hours there. We would all take our shoes and socks off and go paddling in the water, splashing each other and collecting the shiny pebbles from the stream. Sometimes we would just sit on the bank and bathe our feet in the cool water and tell stories to each other or just lie there in the sunshine, looking up at the sky and making pictures out of the clouds. We just loved to run up and down the tunnel shouting to each other. Our voices would echo along the tunnel. It was great fun in the warm sunshine.

Many times, during summer, we would go up there and really enjoy ourselves. We would laugh and play as if we hadn't a care in the world. We would forget all the shouting and screaming and the traumatic sounds of home for just a short time. If only we could have stayed there forever away from all that. Nothing would ever spoil the fun we had on our days at 'cigarette tunnel'.

After what seemed like the longest and hottest day of summer, we made our way back home. We reached the end of Scout Road and headed back downwards towards home, along Chorley Old Road, as it was a lot easier to push Tina's pram down the hill this time. Tina had finally fallen asleep, after her hectic afternoon in the sunshine.

As we walked further down the hill towards home, I could see a brown car pull over on the opposite side of the road in front of us. The driver of the car seemed to be staring at us as we walked along. I watched this strange man and wondered why he had stopped at the side of the road. It didn't seem as if he had broken down. As we all got nearer, the man shouted over to us through the open window of his car. We all faced towards him. At first, we didn't hear what he said and ignored him because he was a stranger but then he shouted to us again and this time I heard every word he said. He asked if we wanted a 'wank'. I was horrified at hearing this and knew very well what it meant and that it was a swear word. It meant something very rude. He shouldn't have been shouting things like that to us, we were only children.

Mary had told me what it meant a few weeks ago, when I was writing a poem at home and trying to get some words to rhyme. When I had said this word, she told me that I couldn't use it as it was a swear word. It was a good job that she told me because I would have never known that otherwise.

My sister Jane then shouted, "Yeh," to him and quickly rushed to the edge of the pavement ready to cross the road to go to him. I pulled her back quickly with the hood of her anorak. Jane was too young to realise what that word meant.

I then picked up a little stone and quickly tried to scribble the registration number of his car on the inside of my coat. When I thought that I had got the right number I called to him to go away and quickly gathered us all together and started running down the hill towards home. I turned to shout to him that I had got his registration number as we started running. With this he sped off quickly out of sight towards Horwich.

We rushed home as fast as we could. I knew that this was a naughty man and he shouldn't have said those things to us. When we got home, we told Mary what had happened and she said that we had to tell Dad when he came home from work. She wasn't pleased about what had happened to us and said that we had done the right thing by taking down the number of the car.

When Dad got home, we told him what had happened. He took us in his car to the police station in Bolton town centre. We were all taken, one by one, into a room and had to tell a policewoman exactly what had happened that day. I was really scared to be talking to this police lady. I had to describe everything about the man; what colour hair he had, what colour car, what he was wearing. I had to tell them everything that I could remember about the naughty man. There were times, while I was talking to the policewoman, she shouted at me and made me jump when she banged on the table. She made me cry and I thought that she didn't believe me.

After we had all spoken to this policewoman we were allowed to go home. Nothing was mentioned about this again at home and I wasn't sure that they had believed us that it had really happened. I felt as though we had done something wrong.

A few months later a policeman called at our house to speak to Dad. He was told that the registration number, which I had scribbled down inside my coat, now belonged to another car. I didn't know how and why but the events of that day were never talked about again. I never forgot what happened that day. I didn't understand why the man had said those things to us.

I was aware from then on that there were these types of naughty men around. We all used to wander around sometimes, a long way from home and never thought that anything like this could happen. We were only children and I couldn't understand why it had happened. I certainly didn't want it to happen to us again. We were always careful from then on, looking out for strange looking men who might say rude things to us again. If we thought we saw somebody that looked a bit strange, we would run away in the opposite direction, as fast as we could. Most of the time we were being silly and letting our imaginations run away with us. Mary said to us, when we used to tell her, it was good that we were being careful.

As the months went on, Carol and I became close friends. It was still scary talking to her about my dad and the way he was with us all. I felt I could tell her anything as she was my best friend but when I used to talk about my mum, it seemed to be exciting. She knew that I couldn't wait to see Mum again. We would talk about her for hours and I think that she was looking forward to meeting her as well. Carol said that she would come with me if I wanted to go back and see her. She knew that it all had to be kept a secret and she hadn't to tell a soul. I knew she wouldn't tell anyone.

We would talk for hours and plan when we would go and how we were to do it. I trusted her a lot and knew that our secret would be safe. I didn't even want to tell Maureen or any of the others because I was sure Dad would find out just like he did before. It was just kept between us.

Finally, the time arrived to visit my mum again! All week long I got more and more excited as we were going to see Mum again on Saturday. On Wednesday night I was dying to tell Maureen where we were going that weekend, especially as her leg had 'locked', when she was curled up on the settee watching television. She screamed her head off in pain and Dad had to rush across to her and straighten her leg out in front of her. Her screams made us all jump out of our skins. She was in agony. Dad yelled at her to shut up and her screams stopped suddenly. She held her breath. Dad pulled at her leg and she screamed out again. Soon the pain was gone and with her thumb in her mouth once again she continued to watch the television.

I really wanted to tell her where we were going at the weekend to make her feel better but I bit my tongue and decided to wait a bit longer before letting her into our secret.

Carol and I didn't have any money, so we decided to walk all the way to Horwich once more, just as we had done so long ago, when Maureen and I bravely went to see our mum. Last time at Mum's, we met Aunty Flo. She'd asked us how we'd got to Mum's house. We told her that we had walked all the way from Bolton. She told us that when she was a little girl and she had a long way to walk, she would run between one lamppost and then walk between the next one and so on, until she got where she was going. She said that it was much more fun and it felt like you got there a lot quicker. I never forgot what she told us on that day at Mum's house. It seemed such a long time ago but I still remembered.

When we set off this time, we did exactly what Aunty Flo had told me she did when walking a long way. We ran to the first lamppost and then walked to the next one and so on and before long we were in Horwich. The journey didn't take as long this time as it had the first time when we walked all the way — Aunty Flo was right! I was thrilled when at last we were there.

"We are here!" I told Carol, as we approached Mum's front door.

I knocked on the door very excitedly. After a few seconds, I looked through the window to see if she was coming to answer the door. I could see the back door was open and thought she may have been in the backyard. I knocked again at the door. Looking through the window again I saw her coming in through the back door. She had clothes pegs sticking out of her mouth and an arm full of clean washing that she had just brought in off the line. Carol knocked at the door this time and I could see Mum empty her arms to rush towards us. As she did, she glanced towards the window and caught sight of me peering through. Her eyes widened and her face lit up as she saw me. I knew she was glad to see me again. She opened the door quickly and came to hug me again as she had the first time that we had visited.

"I knew you'd come back!" she said as she took us inside.

We all sat down on the settee and she started with lots of questions again. How had we got there and how were the others? I told her about our new house and everything about school and how all the others were. Mum liked my friend Carol and gave her a hug, for being such a good friend and for coming with me to see her. Mum told me that she was welcome anytime. We were both starving as we hadn't eaten since the morning, so we were soon sitting at the table tucking into chips, egg and beans. It was delicious.! We even had bread and butter; only Dad was allowed bread and butter with his dinner, in our house. Our plates were soon wiped clean with the bread and our tummies were full. A full stomach was a great feeling that I wasn't used to.

The day came to an end far too quickly and soon it was time to go home. Mum gave us some money for the bus fare, so we could go up to see her again the next day. We didn't know whether we would be able to risk going up again that weekend. We had to be careful but we said that we would try. We couldn't risk being found out, this had to be our secret. Dad would surely kill me this time, if he ever found out that we were seeing Mum again.

We got on the bus to go home and when it approached our estate, we hid ourselves down between the seats so that we couldn't be seen by anyone. We made sure that nobody saw us getting off the bus. We ran the short distance to Carol's house. She had thought of a good hiding place for the money that we had got from Mum. We wrapped it in a plastic bag and secretly placed it under the bushes and dried leaves in her front garden. It was a great hiding place. No one was looking when we hid it, so we knew that it wouldn't be found. That was the money for our bus fare back to Mum's house. We couldn't lose it.

When I got back home, after the secret reunion with Mum, Maureen was curled up on the settee, sucking her thumb watching television. She would be in trouble if Dad saw her sucking her thumb. Still sucking her thumb, she turned her head away from the television and momentarily glanced at me before continuing to watch with more interest. If only she knew where I had been that day. I stared at her for a moment wondering what she would have said if I told her. Would she be too scared to keep the secret? Would she tell? I wanted to tell her but I was sure she would tell Dad. There was no way that she could keep this a secret from anyone. I watched her over the dinner table that night while we ate our sausages and mash potatoes. I wanted to tell her about the chips, egg and beans that we ate at Mum's house that day. I wanted to tell her how Mum was and that she missed her too, but I couldn't.

We weren't able to go up again the following day because Carol had to do something with her family and I didn't want to go alone without her. It was, however, the start of weeks of secret visits to Mum's, that we made most weekends. I would tell Dad that I was at Carol's house and Carol told her parents that she was at my house with me. This secret was kept from everyone.

Mum would have lots of things for us to do during our visits. Even when we helped her to do the cleaning it didn't seem as if it was such a chore as it was at Dad's house. Everything seemed so much more fun at Mum's house. She taught us a lot. I would watch her cooking and help her do little jobs around the house such as polishing all her brasses, which took hours. Carol and I would sit in front of Mum's roasting open fire and we would polish away at the brasses until they gleamed. We would have very rosy cheeks when we had finished from the warm glow of the fire.

Mum didn't have a twin tub washing machine like ours, so she would do most of her laundry by hand in the big, white pot sink that she had in her kitchen. She had a mangle that she would push outside into the back yard and she used it to squeeze all the water out of the clothes that she had washed. I loved using the mangle. It was great fun. I would turn the long handle at the side of the mangle that turned the rollers. Mum would push dripping clothes between the rollers and all the water would be squeezed out and drain away down the grid. I had seen mangles on the television before, but I had never used one. It was old fashioned, from the olden days, but I enjoyed it.

As the weeks went on, Maureen found out that we were seeing Mum again. It had slipped out one day, when we were arguing in the park over something and of course like many times before she said she was going to tell Dad. She said that if we didn't take her, she would tell him. We had no choice but to take her next time. We had to promise to take her along with us. Also, we made her swear that she wouldn't tell anyone. We knew that she would have told Dad if we hadn't let her come with us. She had gotten us in trouble with Dad before, when she hadn't got her own way, so we had to trust her this time and just hope she wouldn't blab.

The next weekend, Carol and I caught the bus to Mum's house again.

We had planned to take Maureen with us that morning but she had disappeared. She had gone playing out somewhere and we couldn't find her. When we got to Mum's we were surprised to find Maureen sat there already at our Mum's house. She had got there before we did. She had walked it all the way on her own, to surprise our mum herself. It was a nice surprise for Mum to see Maureen again after so long.

As the weeks followed, the three of us enjoyed time with my mum. We would go all over the place with her. She would take us for long walks up to Rivington Pike and to the Japanese Gardens. We would take picnics that Mum had prepared for us. She was always saying how delicate Maureen was and that she was too thin and had to be fattened up so there was always plenty to eat at Mum's house. On some nice days, we would walk for miles and miles until it was time to go home again.

We even had a trip to Blackpool. Mum and Aunty Flo took us on the bus. It was a long way and very hot on the bus but we enjoyed every minute. We walked along the pier from one end to the other and we ate fish and chips sitting on the beach. The seagulls were hungry too and they wasted no time at all finishing the chips off that we left. Mum and Aunty Flo took us all to see the laughing clown. It was a big clown puppet dressed in a brightly coloured outfit, sat on a huge chair, in a round glass cabinet. He would mechanically roll around in this rocking chair laughing hysterically. He was so funny; everyone surrounded him and would be laughing out loud as they stood to watch him. He had been there for years and years and Aunty Flo said that she remembered him from when she was a little girl. Dad never did find out that Mum took us there.

On cold or wet days, we would stay indoors at Mum's house and we would sit for hours with Mum and she would teach us to crochet. We both picked it up easily. I took some crocheting home and sat on the settee in front of Dad and worked on making a bobble hat. I would make lots of things like jackets and scarves for our dolls. Ann liked the bobble hat that I made and asked me to make one for her.

Sometimes we would undo old woolly jumpers and use the wool again for the things we wanted to make. Soon all our friends wanted us to make them bobble hats just like ours. One day, Dad asked who had shown us how to do this and I lied to him and told him it was Carol's Mum who taught us.

He must have remembered Mum doing crocheting when she lived with us. Mum made lots of things by crocheting. She made some lovely things for a new baby that belonged to one of the neighbours in her street. The fancy stitches were too hard for us to learn, we could only do the simple stitches but Mum was an expert. The little dress that she made for the new baby down the street was beautiful. She had also made a promise to Maureen that she would make a dress for her soon.

Mum also had a trick with a large coat button. She threaded a long piece of wool through the buttonholes and spun it around quickly between her hands and then gently pulled her hands apart so that the wool would stretch out slightly and the button would spin around and around and make a really cool sound. It would spin one way and then the other way making this unusual sort of musical sound. We were amazed with the sound and didn't really understand how it was being made.

Mum would also fold paper into different shapes to make different animals. She taught us how to make a bird that flapped its wings. We made these all the time out of different sizes of paper and then we would spend ages colouring them in to look like real birds with feathers. Laura was fascinated when I made one for her; though it didn't last very long. She would tear it and then come running back to me pleading with me to make her another one.

Carol was sometimes not allowed to come with us to see my mum on some weekends but she still kept our secret safe and continued to hide the money for the bus fares that Mum gave us, in her garden. She was a true friend and I loved her and never ever forgot her.

Maureen and I had a regular routine now of going to see our mum. We were quite pleased with ourselves that we could keep our secret from the rest of the family. We hadn't told a soul for months and months. It was as if we were living a sort of double life. During the week time our life was at Dad's house and school, at the weekend we were at Mum's. We were in two different worlds. There was the horrible scary world that was living at Dad's house. In this world we could hear the constant screams from Mary when Dad hit her. We could hear the shouting and banging that kept us awake at night. The other world was at our mum's, where we were well looked after and well fed. We were loved, kissed, cuddled and treated as if we belonged there.

Although we were only at mums for a few hours each weekend, I would pretend that we lived in this world all the time. Even when we were back at Dad's house I would lie on my bed and close my eyes and wish I was back there instead of being at dads. I would try to close my mind to the loud voice's downstairs and to Mary's cries and just imagine the other world not so far away, where I wanted to be all the time. We were getting to know Mum more and more and the other family that Mum belonged to, since she had married Dave.

Dave's family, the Crawfords, were a large family and lived in Horwich quite near to Mum. There were about thirteen kids, all living in a big house not far from where Mum and Dave lived. Most of them were grown up but still lived at home with their mum and dad in this huge house. On our visits to see Mum we would visit them all the time. They were always pleased to see us and always very friendly. We'd spend lots of time there playing hide and seek in their big house. The family seemed to enjoy having a house full of noisy kids running all over the place. It was fun, we loved it, it was so different from the life we had at dads. We hadn't to run about, or make a noise, or argue with one another in Dad's house. It was a case of get your chores done and get out of his sight as fast as you could, not going back until it was teatime and chores time again.

At the Crawford's, the kids had a large room at the front of the house to play in. The grown-ups seemed to spend their time in a foggy smoky room at the back of the house. Here they watched television while drinking cups of tea and smoking cigarettes. The big men in the house were drinking beer from brown bottles, smoking cigarettes and reading their newspapers. The front room belonged to the kids — they could do anything in there. It was quite dark and untidy of course but they seemed to like it that way and so did we. There was an old piano that the kids were always trying to get some sort of tune from and two huge, old, tatty leather sofas and lots of books on high shelves. At one end of the room there was a large fireplace with a high mantelpiece above it, with a large mirror hung high up on the wall above. There was an old record player sitting on a long dusty sideboard playing Neil Sedaka records. The youngest child, Carol, around eight or nine, would hide behind the sofa and cover her ears every time he sang 'Oh Carol'. She didn't like it at all. We loved it there. We couldn't wait to be around this family forever.

CHAPTER FIFTEEN
Jane's Beating

After spending a busy night over at Uncle Don's house babysitting, he drove Ann and I home the next day and dropped us off outside our house. He waved to us and said that he would see us again next time. I really didn't want to baby-sit for them on the weekends. We had to sleep over which meant that I couldn't go to see Mum on that weekend. This meant that Maureen would go to see Mum on her own.

Of course, I could never tell them the real reason why I didn't want to baby-sit — no one could find out our secret, ever! So, I just had to baby-sit and keep my mouth shut.

Uncle Don was Dad's brother, he looked just like Dad as well, except that Uncle Don was losing his hair on the top of his head. Uncle Don was married to Aunty Andrea and they had five children; Steven, Sarah, Susan, Sharon and Selena. Everyone could tell that we were cousins. We were all very much alike, with our dark eyes and dark hair. Steven was the same age as I was. He was the eldest and the big brother. We hardly saw him around as he was always playing out somewhere with his mates.

We liked Aunty Andrea and Uncle Don and didn't really mind about babysitting, once we got there. The kids weren't all that much trouble and we would spend most of the day playing on Astley Bridge Park and exploring Astley Bridge with our cousins, until Uncle Don was ready to take us home after tea.

After being dropped off at home by Uncle Don, we raced inside. Jane was standing at the end of the hallway when we went through the front door. It wasn't her bedtime but already she was dressed in her nightdress. She was standing in the doorway smiling at us as we walked in, dressed in a dark red bry-nylon nightdress. With the bright sun shining through the window behind her I could see the outline of her tiny thin body through it. As I got closer to Jane, it seemed as if she still had her underwear on underneath her nightdress, which we were always told that we weren't allowed to wear in bed. The underwear that we wore then

122

was thick cotton navy-blue knickers with thick tight elastic around the legs and around the waist. We all had to wear them. Dad got them all from a welfare place in town, all for free along with vests and long white knee length socks. I got a new school coat from there too, that horrible grey mackintosh that I hated to wear with my new school uniform. It was quite funny when we wore those knickers, sometimes the elastic would snap when we were out playing in the street. The knickers would fall straight down around our ankles. We would grab at them and pull them up quickly and run off home to change them. It seemed to happen a lot when we were playing out. We would have to thread the elastic back through the waistband with a safety pin then we were able to wear them again. All the other kids in the street would laugh and call us names for wearing welfare knickers. I never did know anyone else in our school that wore them. I thought at that time it was because we were poor and couldn't afford to buy certain things.

It did appear as if Jane still had her horrible navy-blue underwear with the tight elastic, on underneath. She would have been told off for sure if Dad knew, so I quietly told her to go and take her knickers off, before Dad noticed. I walked into the dining room and put my bag down on the floor. Jane told me that she hadn't got her knickers on. Jane sometimes told lies, so I turned to her sharply and frowned at her. I really didn't want her to be in any trouble. Although, I thought she must have already been in some kind of trouble with Dad to be dressed in her nightdress at that time. I told Jane that I could see that she had her underwear on so she should go and take it off right now. I stared at her sternly as I was getting quite cross with her. I just knew I could see the dark knickers through her nightdress, so why was she lying to me? She would be in serious trouble. Jane looked up at me with her large, sparkling, hazel eyes, which were shining brightly as they were slowly filling up with tears, as she tried to assure me that she hadn't got any knickers on at all. She turned her back to me and lifted up her nightdress above her waist. Ann and I looked on as she raised her nightdress. Jane was right; she didn't have any knickers on. She wasn't lying to me at all. How could I have been so sharp with her? Her tiny body was black and blue. She had been battered again. She had huge purple bruises across her bottom, across her legs and up her back. The bruises were so dark it appeared as if she really was wearing her dark underwear underneath her nightdress. It was the bruises that we saw, not the underwear. I quickly pulled down her nightdress. I didn't want to see any more. I felt sick in my stomach. Jane winced and jumped in pain as I straightened down her nightdress. I had caught her little arm. I thought that I had scratched her accidentally but as I looked at her arm, I could see that she had bruises on her hands and up her little arms. She must have been trying to protect herself when Dad was hitting her. Dad had beaten her with that stick again. I wanted to ask her what she had done but we could hear Dad coming in through the back door from the garden. Jane ran off upstairs and Ann and I made ourselves busy putting our overnight things away. Dad looked at us as he walked past, grunted and went into the living room.

The house was so quiet. There was just the sound of the television in the living room. Dad was watching the snooker and Mary was bringing the washing in off the line. I sat in the dining room polishing my shoes for school and pondering the reason why Jane had been beaten so badly. Why did Dad take the stick to our little seven-year-old sister and beat her so badly?

With it being so quiet we could hear the faint humming sound produced by the electric pumps in the fish tanks that were against the wall in front of me. Dad had four large tanks, each on an iron stand, full of brightly coloured tropical fish. Dad would sit in front of them for hours, smoking his pipe and watching all the fish swimming around. They would have lots of babies sometimes, but some of the bigger fish would eat most of them.

Later that evening Ann and I found out why Dad had beaten Jane that day. Dad had noticed that some of his fish were missing and knew that Jane and Andrea had been messing with them. They were both beaten with the stick until one of them admitted who it was who had taken some fish out of one of the tanks with the little net and put them in the other tank, where the bigger fish had then eaten the smaller fish. That was the reason behind the beating. Dad carried on beating Jane with the stick until she was black and blue.

The next day Jane went to school as usual like the rest of us. Each time Paul was beaten by Dad, he always had to tell the teachers that he had fallen over playing football or he had been fighting with a boy in the street. The school teachers always seemed to believe him.

When Jane arrived at her classroom she couldn't sit down on her hard chair at her desk. She was in quite a lot of pain. The teacher looked at her closely and noticed the bruises that were clearly visible on her hands and on the backs of her legs. She was immediately taken from her classroom and taken to see the school nurse. That day she was taken away from school and didn't come back.

When I got home after school there were two ladies talking to Dad in the living room. We were all told to get upstairs. We could hear Dad shouting. The ladies didn't stay long.

After they had left, I noticed that Jane wasn't home from school. She was usually home before me. I quickly realised that those two ladies who were in our front room, must have been social workers and that they had taken Jane away. I knew why she had been taken. It was because of the bruises and the beating that she had been given by Dad that weekend. Were we ever going to see Jane again?

As the days passed, we weren't told anything about Jane. We weren't told where she was or whether she would be coming back home. As always, we were too scared to ask Dad anything about her, just as we were when Mum had left. This time it was Jane who had gone, and like Mum she had been beaten too. The beating and the bruises she suffered, that weekend, while Ann and I were babysitting at Uncle Don's house, haunted my mind. If only we had been at home that day, we would have been looking after Jane and she wouldn't have got into all that trouble. She would still be at home with us all now. Jane was only seven years old and I loved her. I should have been looking after her that day. I wanted her home. I missed her. The social workers called at our house on several occasions during the next few weeks but Dad refused to speak to them and wouldn't even answer the door to them.

The following weekend after Jane was taken away, Maureen and I rushed to Mum's house as fast as we could. We couldn't wait to tell her what had happened to Jane. When we reached Horwich we jumped from the bus and ran down the cobbled street to Mum's house.

We ran in and we both exploded into floods of tears as we started to tell Mum what had happened to Jane. We hadn't cried at all at home, we weren't allowed to but as soon as we saw Mum and started to tell her, we just couldn't stop crying. Mum was trying to comfort us in the best way she could but she was just as upset as we were that her little baby girl had been treated this way. Mum couldn't do anything at all except listen to us. She couldn't allow anyone to find out about our visits. She couldn't make any enquiries with the social services as to where Jane was or whether she was ever going to be allowed home. She couldn't risk Dad finding out about our secret visits or else we would be in trouble too and we would have probably ended up in the same place as Jane, wherever that was. Dad would have gone mad if he knew that we were at Mum's house.

It was three weeks before Jane was brought back home again. All her bruises had healed and we were all really pleased to see her and to have her home with us where she belonged. Secretly, we asked Jane lots of questions as to where she had been, what it was like and what had been happening to her.

There were more visits from the social workers, over the next few weeks but Dad would ignore them. We would watch from our bedroom window as they got back in their car and drove away without seeing anyone. Before long, their visits stopped.

CHAPTER SIXTEEN
Abandoned

Suddenly, we heard Dad shouting up the stairs at all of us. I wondered what was going on. We were all startled and jumped up out of our beds. I looked over at the clock and could see it was too early to get up for school. It was only ten to seven but we all had to get up, get dressed and go downstairs. Someone was in trouble I thought, as Ann jumped out of her bed and rushed into the bathroom. What could we have done wrong? Dad didn't sound too pleased. Someone was in for it, whatever it was.

I got out of bed and went into the next bedroom where the others were just getting out of their beds. The house was quiet except for our whisperings. We wondered who was in trouble. I whispered to the younger ones to ask if any of them had done anything wrong but they all looked at me with the same fear in their eyes that I had seen so many times before. They shook their heads. My stomach was turning over and over and I felt sick.

I heard Ann coming out from the bathroom so I walked along the landing back to my room following her. As she was getting dressed, I looked at her and she had tears in her eyes and looked as if she had been crying a lot. I asked her what the matter was and I could see her eyes were red and swollen as she looked back at me.

I couldn't believe it was Ann who was in trouble. She was the apple of Dad's eye. She never got into any trouble. What had she done that had been so terrible? I pleaded with her to tell me. She sat down on the bed and told me that she had run away in the middle of the night to find Mum. I couldn't believe what she was saying. Dad would now know that we had been seeing Mum. Our secret was out. Dad knew. We were all in serious trouble now. Why did she have to run away? Couldn't she have waited until the weekend as we had planned?

I had been so pleased the previous week that we had confided in Ann about Mum. We had told her everything. We trusted her not to tell but I didn't expect her to be brave enough to run away in the middle of the night and try to find her all by herself and on a school night too. I couldn't have done that. I wasn't that brave. I didn't know she had guts. I wish I was more like her. Since we had told Ann, she had been asking all sorts of questions about our mum and we were happy to tell her everything. She assured us that she would never tell. We had planned to take her with us that next weekend. It was going to be a lovely surprise for Mum as well.

When we all started back at school, I was in the third year in class 3C, which was supposed to have been an exciting time but my mind was on the secret meeting that weekend between Ann and our mum, I just couldn't wait. Now this has happened. It was only the second day of the new school term. I was enjoying my new class. The form teacher was great. Why couldn't she have waited just another few days? I didn't know why she had decided to go off in the middle of the night. She shouldn't have done that.

I was trembling with fear as I sat down on the bed and put my head in my hands. Ann was ready to go downstairs but I didn't want to go down there. I started to cry. We were going to get battered for sure. I could just imagine Dad waiting for us downstairs with the stick in his hand.

I could hear the others making their way downstairs, unaware of what was about to happen. Ann blew her nose and pulled at my arm and said that we had to go down. I stood up and wiped my face on my sleeve. I had to go to the toilet first, as I always did when I knew we were going to get in trouble so Ann waited for me. I came out of the toilet and looked at Ann.

"Dad is going to kill us!" I whispered to her and I needed the toilet once again. I could hear Laura chattering away to herself downstairs. The others were already there waiting for us to come down. We couldn't hang on any longer. We had to go down now.

"Come on," Ann said. I wiped my face again with my sleeve. My legs were trembling as we made our way down the stairs. We held hands as we slowly opened the door into the living room. As we stepped inside, Dad was sitting in his chair. I expected him to have the stick across his lap, ready to use on us but he was just sitting there looking into space. I looked at the stick propped up against the wall at the side of him.

Mary was sitting on the edge of the settee with Laura on her knee who was gurgling away to the others sitting beside her and pulling at Lorraine's hair. They all sat in silence and waited. Ann and I walked in and stood by the fireplace, rigid with fear. I wanted the toilet again badly but stood stiffly waiting. Jane and Andrea were sitting in the chair at the other side of the room, wondering what was going on. Maureen hadn't been told that our secret was out and didn't know anything of Ann's midnight escape to Mum's. Paul made us both jump as he walked in and stood at the side of us. Dad then sat on the edge of his chair and leaned on his arms across his knees. My heart was beating so fast I could almost hear it. With his eyes facing the floor, Dad said to us all.

"Where do you all want to live, here or at your mother's?" I was shocked. Was he really saying that we could choose?

There was not a sound at all in that room. Jane and Andrea sat together in the chair with their mouths open, wondering what was happening and probably confused as to who Dad was talking about. We had never told them that they had another Mum who lived in Horwich. I wanted to shout out, "At mums! At mums!" but the words wouldn't come out. I was still shaking. I looked at Mary.

Tears were streaming down her face as Lorraine went to sit closer to her side. I was sure that she wouldn't have wanted any of us to go.

Laura had now come down from her Mum's lap and was pulling at my legs to be lifted up. I looked down into her big brown eyes and brushed her fringe that was falling across her face. I didn't know what to do. I was going to miss my little sister. Dad repeated himself again. We all jumped as he raised his voice at us.

Jane and Andrea were the first to speak up and say that they wanted to go to live at mums. They couldn't possibly know who Dad was talking about or who he meant when he said 'mother's'. They had always called Mary "Mum". They were both babies when our real Mum left so they couldn't possibly remember her. They were too young to know who she was. Lorraine was crying too now.

Slowly, one by one we all told Dad that we wanted to live at mums. Dad sat in his chair stiffly as we waited for his reaction to what we had all just said. I really didn't expect what came next. He sat back in his chair and said that we had better go and pack our things then. Mary gasped, "No!" as she realised that all of us, except Paul, were leaving. For some unknown reason, he had decided to stay at Dad's house. I knew he would have been too scared to tell Dad that he wanted to leave as well, just in case Dad gave him another beating. I knew he did want to leave really. He didn't want to be left behind, after all that Dad had done to him. We were all scared but still we managed to tell him that we wanted to leave.

I watched Mary as the tears fell from her eyes. She had been so good to us all; she didn't deserve this. Lorraine was still crying uncontrollably as she held onto her Mum tightly. Was this really happening? Was Dad going to change his mind? Was this a dream? Was it some sort of game to test us all? Would we all be getting a good hiding now for providing the wrong answers? Jane and Andrea rushed past us and ran upstairs, followed by Maureen. Ann and I left the room and went upstairs too. Could we really be leaving?

Ann started to collect all her belongings. She seemed to be in a hurry, so I quickly gathered my things together as fast as I could. We didn't have many clothes, so it didn't take long. The house was so quiet except for the sound of cupboards opening and drawers closing as the others packed.

When we were all ready, we went downstairs with our things. Paul stayed in his room out of the way. We stood in silence holding all our belongings in the middle of the front room. Dad made us all jump as he sprang out of his chair and left the room.

After a few seconds he came back with a pink sheet from out of the bedding cupboard upstairs. Without saying one word he laid it on the living-room floor. He snatched each of our little bundles off us and placed them inside the sheet and tied it into a large knot at the top to make one large bundle. He lifted it up and took it outside to the car. He opened the boot with his key and placed the bundle inside and slammed the boot shut. I watched his every move from the window while Mary and Lorraine were still visibly upset but not saying anything to us at all. I couldn't believe that we were actually going. I was going to miss Laura and Lorraine.

Mary had taught me a lot and I would never forget her. I loved her from the beginning, and I always would. I didn't know whether we would see each other again but I would always remember all three of them. Dad returned from outside and told us all get in the car. I looked down at Laura, who was sitting on the floor, playing with her toys. Was I ever going to see my baby sister again? Tears swelled up in my eyes. I wanted to kiss her goodbye but I stood staring at her, rigid with the fear of losing her forever. As a tear fell from my eye, it froze as Laura looked up at me, with her rosy cheeks and big brown sparkling eyes. She waved her tiny hand at me and said, "Tata tata."

Mary stood up and went into the hallway to put her coat on. Dad turned to her and said that she was not coming but Mary shook her head and said that she was. With a look of determination on her face she raised her voice at him as she spoke. It was the first time that I had heard Mary speak to Dad like that. I thought that there was going to be another row or that she was going to be punched again, but instead Dad just looked at her and turned to walk out to the car. We all followed and climbed into the back seat of the car as he started the engine.

As we set off, I turned to look through the car window. I wanted one last look at our house. Lorraine was standing at the window holding Laura closely. She was on the windowsill with her little face pressed so tightly up against the glass. They were both crying. I could see their tears. I could almost hear their wails. Tears were falling from my eyes too. I lifted my hand to wave to them. At that moment I didn't want to go. I didn't want to leave Laura. How could I ever not see her again? She was my sister and I loved her. Would I ever be able to come to visit her?

The journey took about half an hour but it seemed a lot longer. No one spoke. When we arrived at Mum's house Dad pulled up outside. I still couldn't believe that he was letting us all live at mums. I thought it was some sort of dream that I hadn't woken up from. He got out of the car and went to open the boot lifting our bundles throwing them on the ground by the side of Mum's front door. He opened the back door of the car and told us all to get out.

As we stood on the pavement outside Mum's house, I wiped the tears from my face with my sleeve as we all stood watching Dad as he got back inside his blue car and drove off quickly down the cobbled street. For what seemed like ages, we stood and waited. We waited, believing he would come back. I thought that he might change his mind, turn the car around and come back for us but he didn't. He was gone.

With my hand shaking, I turned to knock at Mum's door, as tears were swelling up again in my eyes. The street was deserted. There was nobody around at all. No sound, except for a few birds chattering in the early morning sunshine. I knocked at the door again. I turned to look at the others.

"She'll be in bed," I told them.

Jane and Andrea sat down on the edge of the kerb and stretched their legs out in front of them. The sun's rays were shining on the cobbles. Everything was glistening as the early morning drizzle began to dry up in the sunshine. It was going to be a lovely day. It seemed like we stood waiting for ages before Mum came to the door but it was in fact only a few minutes. The door opened and there was Mum. She peered around the door with her sleepy head. Her eyes widened as she caught sight of us all standing there on her doorstep. She looked down at the bundle of belongings and knew that we had all been dumped in the street. She opened the door wider and looked out up and down the street. She asked us where Dad was and we told her that he had left us and gone. She seemed to take a big breath when she realised, he wasn't around.

I started to cry again as I saw the complete shock on her face to see us all on her doorstep like that. She looked into the thin scared faces of the children she'd lost so long ago.

Jane and Andrea stood gazing at her, trying to remember that this lady was their Mum. They stood quietly watching her every move. Mum looked at them and said, "My babies! My babies!" She hugged and kissed them on the doorstep. Mum was crying now as she took us all inside. Ann lifted the bundle from the pavement and took it inside.

We were all talking at once as we all tried to explain to Mum what had happened that morning and how we all had come to be there at her door. Mum was shocked and couldn't believe what had happened. She listened to Ann, while she told her of how she had run away in the middle of the night to try and find her. She was spotted by the police, walking along the road out of Bolton, on her own, in the early hours of the morning. She must have been very scared and lonely as the police picked her up in their car. She didn't know the address of where she was heading so she had no choice but to be taken back home to Dad's house. As she listened to Ann's story she held tightly to Jane and Andrea and kept stroking their hair and looking into their tiny confused faces, only turning away when she had to wipe the tears from her face with her handkerchief. We were all huddled together on the settee as Mum kissed us all. She kept repeating, "My babies! My babies! I've got my babies back!"

Over the next couple of months, Mum had a terrible time with Jane and Andrea. They were only babies when Mum had had to leave us all and they didn't remember her at all when they had first met her on her doorstep. At just nine and ten years old, they had grown up without any memories of Mum at all. They were both behaving strangely for her. They were becoming strangers, to us older ones too. We tried to help Mum with them and tried to make them behave themselves but they took no notice of us at all. Their behaviour was terrible. We couldn't understand it. They had been so well behaved most of the time at Dad's house, and when they didn't behave, they knew what they would get. With Mum they were cheeky and rude and asked for different things all the time. At first Mum would give in to them to make them happy but when it was impossible to give them what they wanted Mum had to say no so they would cause a scene in the middle of the street.

One night Mum and Dave took us all to the fair. Jane and Andrea had never been to a fairground before. They were so overcome with the loud music and the flashing brightly coloured lights. They wanted to go on every ride. It wasn't long before Dave and Mum had run out of money. When it was time to go home Jane and Andrea both started making a fuss and running off. They had a tantrum again, screaming and shouting that they didn't want to go home, shouting that they wanted to go on more rides. Everyone stared! It didn't matter where they were or who was watching. They would be naughty until they got what they had asked for. They were getting very spoiled. Mum tried to be firm with them but they both ran off and Dave had to look for them for ages and bring them back. Mum was going out of her mind with worry. I didn't remember them ever asking Dad for anything. None of us ever asked him for anything. We had learned not to.

Jane and Andrea had changed school when we all moved to Horwich. Now they attended Lord Street Primary School. At first, they seemed to settle down at school. They enjoyed the fact that Maureen and

I attended the school next door — Albert Street Secondary School. They could see us on the playground through the railings every day. They had also started causing trouble at school too. When Mum managed to get them to school, they would run out of class or cause some sort of trouble. Mum didn't know what to do. She was crying quite a lot too at that time. I didn't like to see her crying. I could still remember the tears that she had cried all those years ago.

A social worker would come to visit and try to talk to them but it didn't make any difference at all. To Jane and Andrea, Mum was a stranger, who said that she was their Mum. They did not remember her. They only remembered the life that they had had with Dad and Mary.

After trying so hard, unsuccessfully, to be a Mum to them both, Mum thought they would be better off if they went back home to Dad's house. The social worker made all the arrangements. Mum had tried her best for them but I think that they were both unable to adjust to all the attention that was paid to them. They had not been used to this previously. They couldn't understand it. I think that they were both used to the way Dad was with them and didn't understand it when someone suddenly started to show them a bit of love and attention. They didn't know what it was. It was too late for our real mum to try and show it to them. Jane and Andrea had caused a lot of trouble and there were a lot of heated telephone calls from Dad about Jane and Andrea going back home.

On the day that they were sent back to his house, Dad phoned and threatened Mum and Dave, saying that he was coming over to Horwich that night to get the rest of us and take us all back home. Mum was petrified and knew that Dad would come if he said he would.

Dave didn't seem worried at all and kept telling Mum it would be all right but she knew what Dad was like. She said that he would come and beat David up and try to take all of us back with him. She was really scared and we were all becoming really upset. Dave reassured her again that it was going to be all right. He had told all his brothers to come down to our street to help and protect us just in case Dad was planning to beat him. Dave was a big man and seemed so tough. He had a scar all around the tip of his nose and once told us that he was in a fight in the pub and someone had tried to bite his nose off. We all knew what Dad was like though. Everyone was scared of our dad on the estate where we lived.

Dave had big tough brothers so I didn't think that Dad would be able to beat them all up. They all came down to Mum's house and tried to comfort her and tell her not to worry but it didn't help Mum at all. She was trembling and crying. We were still very scared and thought that Dad would come and beat everybody up and somehow manage to take us all back home. Everyone was waiting.

The street had gone dark except for the streetlights on the corner. Dave's brothers were waiting at the end of the street in the shadows. I could see the end of their roll-up cigarettes glowing in the darkness. They lit up their faces as they inhaled. Dave was standing in the doorway waiting for Dad.

Dave told us all to go upstairs and lock our bedroom door. We rushed upstairs and sat at the window looking out onto the street below. The neighbours had all been told that there might be trouble in the street that night and I could see that some of them were already peering out from behind their closed curtains, now and again, to try to see what was going on.

All at once, we heard the screeching of tyres in the street. We all gasped, as we knew it was Dad's car. I heard a wail from Mum downstairs as she knew he was here, just like he said he would be. We watched as Dad parked his car in the middle of the street and David stood waiting at the edge of the pavement. Mary was sitting in the passenger seat next to Dad. The curtains of the house opposite were twitching as Dad got out from his car. He slammed the car door and started to run towards Dave.

We all gasped and held our breath as Dad kicked out at Dave trying to knock him down. Dave was punching him as Dad lashed out at Dave once again. Dad tried to get away from Dave but he was holding onto Dad's old, brown cardigan. Dad pulled himself out of it and ran off down the street. Dave then turned and came back to the house, dropping Dad's cardigan to the ground. Dave's brothers came to join him. It was all over so quickly.

We all came away from the window and rushed downstairs to Mum. She was sitting in her armchair crying and still visibly shaking, so we all went to sit beside her hugging her tightly. We were all in tears, but relieved the fight was over and that Dad was not going to take us all back to his house. Mum was still in tears so Dave knelt beside her and placed his arms around her. Suddenly, there was a knock at the door and we all jumped in fright. Dave rushed and opened it.

It was Mary. She had been sitting in the car watching the fight between Dad and Dave. She had seen Dad run off down the street. As she walked in it was clear that she was very upset. She looked straight at Mum, with tears in her eyes and walked across sitting at the side of her, holding her hand tightly. Mum and Mary shared some tears and started talking together. Ann and I went to the kitchen to make a pot of tea.

While we were in the kitchen there was another knock at the front door that made us all jump and rush to Mum's side again. We thought that Dad had come back to get us. A policeman walked in. We were so relieved. He stood in the doorway and spoke to Dave and Mum about the evening's happenings and asked if everyone was all right.

Suddenly, while they were talking, Dad burst in through the front door into the vestibule and tried to barge his way past the policeman. The policeman held him back as we all screamed and started to cry again. We clutched on to our mum as tightly as we could. Mum was shouting to the officer, "Get him out! Get him out!" Dad was holding his arm as if he was injured and said to the officer that he was going to take all the children back home with him. Mum screamed louder at the policeman to get him out of her house while we all sat shaking with fear at the thought of being taken back home with him. The policeman then took Dad by the arm and led him outside closing the front door behind them.

Mary finished her tea and placed the cup on the coffee table. She touched Mum's hand as she left to join Dad outside. We all sat silently as she walked through the door without saying goodbye. We heard Dad's car start up and drive away. It was all over.

Jane and Andrea had stayed back at Dad's house but it wasn't long before they were taken into care by the social services. They were placed in different children's homes. At first, they were in homes that were near to where we lived but after a while Jane was sent to a place in the south of England called Hastings. She was placed in a home that was run by nuns. Andrea was sent to several different homes, as she couldn't settle in any of them. Some of the children's homes were miles away from our dad's house in Bolton. This was the start of them living in and out of different children's homes.

They were allowed to come home to Dad's house sometimes, at weekends or school holidays. At other times they could come to see us at Mum's house when we would spend a little time together, before they had to be sent away again back to their homes. It was always a sad time for everyone to see them leave. Jane and Andrea would get terribly upset and not want to leave us but they had to go back. They were told by everyone that if their behaviour changed, they would be able to stay a bit longer on the next occasion. This didn't happen because they weren't behaving themselves in the children's homes at all so their visits were always short.

Ann was also having a bad time at mums. She went to a grammar school at the other side of Bolton and had to leave the house early every morning to get to school before nine o'clock. She also missed Laura terribly, she (or Ann) was like a second mum to her. We all missed her too and wondered how she was all the time. We hoped that we would be able to see her soon.

I was shocked when Ann had to leave Mum's house and go back to live at dads. I thought that the problems she was having were related to the difficulties travelling to school each day, however they weren't; there were other reasons that seemed to be a secret. Something happened between Mum and her but none of us knew exactly what. She wouldn't say. It did mean, however, that Ann left us and went back to dads. We would see her sometimes and ask how Laura and the others were but she never came back to Mum's house, not even for a visit. I didn't really understand why, maybe I would get to find out the real reason for her leaving later in her life.

CHAPTER SEVENTEEN
The New School, History Lesson

Maureen and I settled down at Mum's house really well. I think we'd had the time to get to know her again with our secret visits over the past year or so. We had made a lot of new friends from around the village, which made it easier for us to settle down at school. I loved Smithills High School and really wished I could have stayed there but it would have been difficult to get there on time each morning. I only spent a couple of days in the third year before I left to live in Horwich. I didn't have the chance to say goodbye to anyone there. One day I was a pupil there and the next I was attending another school. It was really hard to leave.

The teachers were great and I enjoyed every lesson, especially drama with Mrs Edwards and maths with Mr Bradshaw. Even the maths lessons were fun. Mr Bradshaw was so funny. We all learned a lot from Mrs Edwards and got on with her so well. All the class liked her. She looked a bit like a hippy with long, flowing skirts, blouses with baggy sleeves, and suede leather waistcoats. Her long wavy red hair would hang loosely down her back. Sometimes, she would tuck it behind her ears when it fell across her face as she leant over to see someone's work. She didn't act like a teacher. It was as if she was a pupil sometimes, which made her class full of fun most of the time. We always complained that her lessons were not long enough, because they were over far too quickly.

The new school was called Albert Street School. It was a much smaller school than Smithills so I knew that I wouldn't have any trouble finding my way around the place as I did when I first went to Smithills. I remember walking into Albert Street School with our mum on our first day. I was feeling a bit scared and unsure of what to expect as Mum left us in the office with the headmistress. Mrs Watson welcomed us into the new school and then took us to our new classes.

As the door opened to this huge classroom, the whole class fell silent and looked straight at me as I was taken to the front of the class. I was feeling really embarrassed as I was introduced to them and shown to my desk. It was a large classroom with around thirty pupils and although I missed Carol, my best friend from Smithills, it wasn't long before I had made new friends from here.

The same week that I started this school, there was another new girl that joined our class. Her name was Susan and she was really nice. We became good friends. We had both just moved here from another town and another school. We felt we had a few things in common, so we tended to stick together most of the time. We lived near each other as well, so we spent time together after school. I soon settled down to the new routines of this school and enjoyed most of the lessons.

History was becoming a subject that I was finding easy and enjoyable. I liked the teacher and I liked learning about the kings and queens of the olden days, including the different battles of Britain through the ages. History was the first lesson on Wednesday mornings, after registration and I would always rush to the history classroom to get there on time. I didn't want to miss any of the lessons at all. After registration one Wednesday, I was kept behind and told off by the teacher. I was talking during registration, for the second time that week. I was warned that if I did it again, I would be in detention. After this little chat I knew that I would be late for my next lesson which was history. I picked up my school bag and rushed to the history classroom as fast as I could.

I barged through the double doors at the end of the corridor leading to the history classroom, almost falling over as I slid along the polished floor. At the end of the corridor, I could see my class all lined up outside the room and Mr Hampson pacing sternly up and down the row. He looked really angry at the class standing silently in front of him. I got in line with my class wondering what was going on as Mr Hampson looked towards me. He seemed very cross as he came closer to me. I thought I was going to be told off again for being late to class. I looked up at him and said," Hello." He took a big deep breath, his face reddened and his eyes glared back at me. He raised his hand and struck me right across the face. I wobbled a little and bowed my head with embarrassment. My face was smarting as the tears fell down my cheeks. I only said hello to him, what did he hit me for? He was my favourite teacher and he had just hit me. I couldn't believe it. The class still stood there silently as I wept. I was so embarrassed at being hit like that. I didn't expect to be hit like that from a teacher. I had seen enough of that at our dad's. Mr Hampson was shouting at me but I couldn't hear a word he was saying. When he finished shouting, he continued to pace down the class. I still had no idea why he had hit me like that or as to why the class was all lined up outside the classroom. My face was burning. I felt as if I couldn't stand there any longer. I turned and ran as fast as I could back along the corridor, through the double doors and through the main entrance. I was going home. I wanted to tell Mum what he had just done to me. I could hear Mr Hampson shouting after me as I raced from the school. I ran crying. My face was still stinging as I ran through the school gates towards home.

The tears were streaming down my face and my ear was hurting as I pushed open our front door. Mum was sitting at the table in the kitchen with a crossword puzzle and a cup of tea. She jumped up quickly as I burst in. She asked what the matter was, as I tried to speak to her to tell her what had happened. I was sobbing uncontrollably as she sat me down and tried to hear what I was saying. When she realised what had happened, she looked at my face. I had a red handprint across it where he had hit me and my ear was burning hot from the force of the slap. Mum was very angry and went to get her coat. She said we had to go back to school to sort it out and she was going to have a word with the teacher who had hit me.

As we walked through the main entrance to the school, Mum held my hand tightly as we approached the headmistress's office. Mum knocked at the door hard. My face was still burning as we heard Mrs Watson call for us to enter her office. Mum opened the door and we walked in. We were asked to take a seat as Mum explained to the headmistress what had happened. My face still showed the mark indicating where I had been struck hard. Mum and Mrs Watson talked and then Mrs Watson left the room to speak to Mr Hampson. Soon she was back with Mr Hampson. As he came into the room, I glared at him as he began to talk to Mum.

I couldn't believe what I was hearing. He talked about the fact that the class had been told to stand outside for disrupting the lesson and then he said that he hadn't hit me. I stood and glared at him in disbelief. How could he say he hadn't hit me? I still had the mark across my face. It was still stinging. Could they not see that? I couldn't speak. I just stood there.

This was my favourite teacher in the school and he was lying. He had hit me. All the class saw him. Why had he lied? I was embarrassed and angry and felt so humiliated but couldn't speak out to defend myself. I just stood sobbing with my head down in shame. I was sent back to my history class to continue my lesson.

I walked from the office, I closed the door behind me and headed towards the history room. I really didn't want to go back in there. He had hit me in front of the whole class and then he denied it. He was a liar and if he thought that I was going to work in his class again, he was mistaken, because I wasn't. As I walked into the classroom, the class was sitting quietly getting on with the work that Mr Hampson had given them to do. The subject was Henry VIII and his six wives. They all stared at me as I walked to my desk and sat down. My friend asked if I was all right. I said that I was and continued to tell her what had just happened in the office. I sat at my desk and leaned back against my chair. My history book was still in my bag and there it was going to stay. I didn't like this teacher any more. I didn't intend to do any work in his class. I didn't even intend to talk to him ever again. The door opened and in walked Mr Hampson. He looked over at me and I glared at him straight in the eye and folded my arms stubbornly in front of me. I looked at him in disgust as he stood at the blackboard and continued with the lesson. The rest of the class carried on working in their exercise books and I just sat back in my chair, stubbornly staring into space. My exercise book stayed in my bag. I didn't like him any more and I was certainly not going to work in his class again. History was still my favourite subject but not with him teaching it! I had a history lesson twice a week and I didn't intend to do any more work in his class. I ignored him when he tried to speak to me but I didn't care. Soon he stopped talking to me altogether and I was glad. He knew why it was that I was behaving like this. I hated being in his class and he knew it.

CHAPTER EIGHTEEN
David — Puppy Love

In the early 70s, most of the grammar schools were changing into comprehensive schools or secondary modern schools, as they liked to be called. The government said that it would give equal opportunities to all children — rich or poor and despite their abilities. I wasn't exactly sure what it all meant but I was just glad that I was leaving Albert Street High. The new school we were to attend was called Rivington and Blackrod Comprehensive School. This was a lot bigger than Albert Street, and a lot posher I thought. It was a very old school right on the edge of Rivington. It was surrounded with woods, lakes and miles of beautiful countryside that we had already explored with Mum. It was going to be a lovely place to learn. I was really looking forward to attending this school. Mum would take us on long walks all around this area and we would see the big school from the road and couldn't wait to start school there.

It was at this school that I discovered boys. I'd shared a kiss with David at Smithills, in the first year of my old school in Bolton and I remember not being very impressed at all, but the boys in my class suddenly seemed more interesting to have around. I was still quite a tomboy and liked to play football and hang around with the lads from out of my class. I was always dressed in trousers or jeans and baseball boots. I would never wear a dress or girly clothes at all. I had an old khaki green parka coat that I wore until it dropped off my back. I loved that coat. Everybody was wearing parkers at that time. It was the trend of that age. Mum would tell me off sometimes because she was sick of seeing me wearing it.

I was crazy about the new Scottish group called the Bay City Rollers. They were brilliant and their records soon got to the top of the charts. All the girls all over the country were mad about them. I saw them all screaming for them on the television and there were girls fainting in the street, when they managed to get to see them. All the girls in my class wore lots of tartan just like the singers from the band. I too, had sewn a strip of tartan all the way down the side of my jeans. It took me hours to sew that in place. I even wore a tartan scarf around my wrist all the time at school until I was told to take it off, then it just got tied around my waist. I just adored Les McEwan.

When Donny Osmond appeared, he became my heartthrob. I put pictures of him on my wall and I bought a floppy hat just like the one he wore. The Osmond Brothers had been around for a while, but Donny was now in the charts on his own with 'Puppy Love'. All the girls in my class fell madly in love with him. I was sure that I was the one that he would be marrying one day. After school, I would sometimes go to my friend's house to 'rehearse' for our group, as we would call it.

My friends Jackie and Pauline Wright were twins so when we played together, we would call ourselves "Two Plus One." We thought we were the 'bee's knees.' We would sing and dance away to the latest chart hits, just as they did on the television. We would know all the songs off by heart and then record ourselves singing on our old tape recorder. We would sing in front of the mirror using a hairbrush instead of a microphone. We wouldn't allow anyone to listen to us even though we thought we were good. We even believed we were going to be famous one day!

Whenever we got fed up or got kicked out of the house for making too much noise, we would walk around the streets or around the local park. If we had a bit of money we would hang out in the local diner. It was called Ferretti's. All the kids from our school would go there. It was the local meeting place for most of us teenagers. Everyone knew where it was and how to get there. We would have a frothy coffee and sit chatting with all our friends from school. We would chat about who was going out with who and who we would like to go out with from our school. There was always our favourite loud music playing on the jukebox in the diner and we would learn from each other all the dance steps to each record. If the weather was bad, we would stay there for most of the day. No one ever seemed to mind that we would only ever have one drink. We were never in any trouble at all. The ladies behind the counter sometimes would ask us to wipe down the tables or collect the glasses — we would love it. We'd pretend that we were waitresses.

I had only lived in Horwich for a few months and already we knew almost everybody from the village. David B was a boy in my class at school. He was very cheeky in class and always causing some sort of trouble around the school.

I thought he was really good looking and I liked him a lot. He made me blush when he spoke to me but I did seem to do that a lot when anyone spoke to me. He had blond wavy hair that was spiky on the top and he also had deep, blue eyes. When he smiled his whole face would light up and his cheeks would become wrinkly with his laughter lines. Most of the teachers would let him get away with a lot of the things that he got up to in school. He would smile at them with his cheeky face and flash his long eyelashes at them and with that little twinkle in his eye he would get away with anything and everything. He was always getting caught smoking in the woods at the side of the school, at play times but he didn't care, he just kept on doing it and didn't worry about being caught. His parents knew that he smoked and they didn't seem to mind at all. It would never bother him if he got caught. He would just laugh and try to get out of the detentions that he was always given.

David had a mate called Malc; he was gorgeous too. I would stare at him all the time, mostly when he wasn't looking, I really wanted to go out with him. My friend and I would follow these two around school each day, at play time and dinner times and try to get their attention. I fancied Malc a lot. He would get really embarrassed and his face would go red when I couldn't take my eyes off him in class. My heart would beat so fast when I saw him. I was hoping that he would ask me to go out with him but he never did. I don't remember ever seeing Malc with a girl. I think he was too shy to talk to any girls but I still liked him. David and Malc were always together. They were like brothers. They were both very similar. Both had long blond hair and were the same height and build. Malc's hair was long and straight and parted in the middle and just past his shoulders. David's hair was long and fell to his shoulders too, almost wavy, but cut into a feather cut, like Rod Stewart's. That was all the rage at the time.

We all became buddies and would always be together playing football or hiding in the woods smoking. I thought he was sweet. David had loads of girls chasing him, because he was so cute and cheeky. He wasn't bothered about asking any of them out and didn't care if they ever said no. He would just go on to the next one. He was always bragging about all the popular 'good looking' girls that he had snogged from our school, behind the bike sheds, so I was surprised when he started to chase me, because I wasn't 'girlie' like them. I was a tomboy and although I liked Malc, I really didn't think that he, or David, would ever look at me that way. I certainly didn't think of myself as being pretty.

My biology teacher, Miss Jones, once said that I was 'an attractive girl,' during the lesson. I could remember all the class laughing. I laughed too but at the time I couldn't understand why she would think that way because I didn't see myself as pretty or 'girlie' like some of the other girls in our class; the ones with a bust and wearing makeup. I wasn't like that. Despite this, I began to think that David liked me and I was too naïve to know why. Maybe it was because I could play football or I was a faster runner than most of the boys in my class.

David would call for me all the time. He would make some excuse that he was looking for someone else and wanted me to help him find them. We became inseparable. I even had my hair cut to match his. He would come with me when I was delivering my newspapers. He carried my heavy bag and he'd fold the newspapers and post them through the letterboxes. His hands would always be black from the newspaper print. My paper round was a lot easier with him helping and it didn't take as long to finish it. He would also help me to tend to my rabbits and seemed to quite enjoy them just as I did.

We would go swimming down Bob's Brew. This was a small pond in the middle of a field at the top of Crown Lane. It had a large brown iron pipe sticking out from the banking and water would trickle out into the pond from it. We would sit across this pipe and paddle our feet in the water. When we felt brave enough, we would stand on the pipe and jump in the dirty water. The water wasn't all that deep but when it rained the water level would be quite high, deep enough for us to stand up in. The bottom of the pond was muddy and slimy and I didn't like standing up in it. It felt horrible. The water was a filthy brown colour, but we didn't care. We would jump straight in there fully dressed and then swim for ages. We would walk around in the warm sunshine until our clothes were nearly dry, before going home to change. Mum never minded. She liked us having fun and would laugh with us sometimes when we told her the funny things that we had been doing.

I had a babysitting job on Friday nights, looking after two small children, Jonathan and Suzanne. They were so cute. After they were tucked up into their beds, David and I would lie on the sofa together pretending to be grown up and trying to learn how to French kiss, just like they did on the late-night television programmes. I didn't think that we could do it properly at all. We would just end up laughing too much, although I didn't like the smell of the cigarettes on his breath, when we kissed. He was always making me laugh with his fooling around and the corny jokes he would tell.

One night we both tied string to some of the knockers in our street. We then stood at the end of the street and pulled hard with the string. When all the knockers banged on the doors we ran. We could hear our neighbours shouting at us as we ran off laughing our heads off. We always denied it though, if we were confronted.

David and Malc had weekend jobs in a garage as forecourt attendants. Their job was to sweep up the forecourt and to serve customers with petrol. Malc and Dave couldn't help fooling around at work on the forecourt when they didn't have customers to serve and they were a bit bored, particularly when the manager wasn't looking. On one such occasion a really nasty accident happened.

Dave and I had been seeing each other for months. One day, while they were at the garage, they started to fool around flicking lit matches at each other and trying to dodge out of the way of the naked flame. David's trousers had already been splashed with petrol from the petrol pumps, when suddenly a lighted match caught his trousers and they burst into flames. David began to panic as he tried to put the flames out but the flames got through to his skin. Both legs were badly burned.

He was taken to Bolton Royal Infirmary. I wasn't able to see him at all for over a week. When I was allowed to see him, I was shocked with what I saw. Both legs were very badly burned from his ankle right up to the top of his thighs. They were very heavily bandaged. He was lying in his hospital bed in quite a lot of pain and unable to move around. The first time I saw him after his accident, I cried and cried. He looked so sad. He cried too. He wasn't the same cheeky chap from our classroom.

He had to stay in hospital for about six months. Visiting times were only an hour a day and I went to visit him every single day after school. I cried every time I had to leave him. It took months and months before he regained that cheeky smile. As the months went by, he started to get better and was able to get out of his bed. Things started to look a bit brighter for him and the old David started to come back to us.

I missed him dreadfully, while he was in hospital and would listen to music a lot. One song that I played over and over again was an old record called 'A Boy called David' I can't remember who the singer was. I learned that song off by heart.

The words were so special and romantic and meant a lot to me. One line from the song, in particular, was special to me. 'A boy named David, he's so beautiful I can't believe my eyes'. I sang it over and over. I missed him so much.

One day I sat down and wrote down all the words from the song on a sheet of paper and decorated it all around the edges with fancy patterns and 'love hearts' and gave it to him in hospital. He kept it with him at the side of his bed. I would smuggle cigarettes and small cans of pale ale into the ward for him. It was really exciting for him to hide them away from all the nurses because he wasn't allowed to drink alcohol at all, of course, or smoke his cigarettes. He had been doing both for ages. I think he enjoyed being able to be a bit naughty again, for a change. He was never caught with any of the things that I had taken in for him. Unless the nurses turned a blind eye because of his cheeky face, just like the teachers had done at school.

Towards the end of David's stay in hospital, he had all the bandages taken off and we could see the damage that had been caused to his legs. It made my stomach turn over when I saw what he had done. Both legs were scared all the way from the top to the bottom, red raw, very swollen and painfully sore in certain areas. It was months since the accident and he was told that he would have the visible scars for the rest of his life. Now it was time for him to try and walk again. With help from crutches, he was allowed to walk around the ward and watch television in the day room. Although still in a lot of pain, slowly his walking improved and he was allowed to come home. He still needed to visit the hospital several times for check-ups and still needed to wear thick elastic bandages on both legs for ages.

After leaving hospital David became an expert on his crutches and would chase up and down our street on them as if they were his new legs. Soon he could get around without the help from the crutches altogether and was becoming more and more like his old cheeky self.

Although Malc and David weren't allowed to work at the garage any more, they both continued to be the best of friends, as if the accident had never happened. David and I stayed together for fifteen months. I had turned fifteen by this time and realised that I was growing a lot taller than him while he didn't seem to be growing at all. I finished with him because I didn't want to have a boyfriend who was smaller than me. We still stayed very good friends and would still hang around together with the same group of kids. He was so good looking it wasn't long before he had other girls chasing him.

CHAPTER NINETEEN
Maria Colwell

One cold winter's morning, in January 1973, I was up very early to deliver my newspapers as usual. David didn't help me in the early mornings, when I was on my paper round, because he couldn't get up as early as I did. This particular morning, I wished that he had been with me. My newspapers were always ready and, in my bag, waiting for me to deliver them when I arrived at the newsagents.

As I approached the counter, I yawned and wearily said, "Good morning!" to Brian the shopkeeper. I glanced down at the newspapers that he had lying on the counter. What I saw shocked me so much I couldn't move or speak. On the front page of every newspaper was a big photograph of a little girl who looked just like my sister, Andrea. I thought it was her. She had jet-black hair and dark eyes just like Andrea. This tiny little face had the same look in her eyes that Andrea had. I lifted up the paper and started to read. Brian told me off and told me to hurry up and get on with my round. I quickly rushed from the shop, carrying my bag of newspapers. I started to deliver the papers, with the face of this little girl going through my mind. Pulling out a newspaper for number 36 Wright Street, I saw it too had the same photograph of that little girl. I sat on the wall outside the house to read it.

Her name was Maria Colwell; she was seven years old. The story read that her stepfather had battered her to death. He had kicked her and punched her until she was dead. What I was reading made me cry. The memories of the beatings that Jane and Andrea had been subjected to came flooding back.

This tiny little girl had been living with foster parents until she was six years old, then she went back to live with her real mum and stepfather. In less than a year she was dead. She had been starved and weighed less than two and a half stones when she was killed. Her stepfather battered her, then pushed her to a hospital, in an old pram that he used to fetch coal in. She died in hospital soon after from her injuries, which were two black eyes, broken ribs, brain damage and 'extensive bruising' to her face, buttocks, arms and legs. It was a cold morning and I trembled. I cried and cried in the middle of the street, remembering the purple bruises all over Jane's tiny body. I couldn't read any more.

I folded the paper and posted it through the letterbox and carried on delivering all the rest. This little girl was dead. Jane, Andrea and Paul could be dead too considering what Dad was doing to them. When Dad was hitting them with that stick they could die. That stick was still in that house where he lives with Laura and Lorraine. I wondered if he was using it on them. I knew that Dad had repeatedly beaten Paul to the point that he had black eyes too; my brother could be dead. Dad could have killed them all. It could have been their photograph in the newspaper. This little girl had died and my sisters could have died also. I cried so much; I couldn't stop. I couldn't get the picture out of my mind, of this little girl Maria Colwell. The traumatic memories of Paul, Jane and Andrea and of what they had gone through came back, as if it was yesterday.

Paul was still living at Dad's house now. He should have left when we did, but he was too scared, he could be safe now at mums. Dad would still have been beating him up, I just knew he would. He was still seen to have black eyes and swollen lips. Why didn't he escape it all and come to live with us?

Jane and Andrea still went to Dad's house. The social workers took them there in their cars. Did they realise what he had done to them both? They stayed in the children's homes for most of the time, so I didn't think Dad could possibly have the opportunity to hurt them. What if he had started hitting Laura or Lorraine with that stick? A cold shiver ran through me with that thought and I wiped the tears from my eyes. What could I do? I was just a kid. What if he was hitting Laura with it the same way he had done to Jane and Andrea. She was only two and a half. My stomach was in knots. I couldn't breathe. When I returned home after my paper round, I told Mum. I was kept off school that day.

CHAPTER TWENTY
Broken Wing?

During that year my love for animals had grown. I really wanted to be a vet when I grew up. I had managed to persuade Mum to let me have some rabbits. I promised that I would always look after them and keep them clean. I was allowed to keep them outside, in the old shed, in the backyard. I had been devastated when Dad killed our pet rabbits when we were young and I never ever forgot how I felt at that time. I thought that I would never be able to have another pet rabbit after Queenie. I loved her so much. But, when I saw some tiny, baby rabbits, which my friend was giving away, I fell in love with them straight away and offered a new home to two of them. I didn't keep them in hutches as I did with my other rabbits. They were left to run around in the large shed. There was plenty of room for them to run around freely. I had straw and sawdust on the floor and I made sure I gave them bowls of fresh food and water every day. If anyone needed to find me, I could always be found in the shed, with the rabbits, cleaning them out or giving their fur a good brushing. If I was not messing around with my rabbits, I would go exploring in the empty, derelict houses with all my friends.

The row of terraced houses, at the back of our house, was about to be knocked down and we would all go on treasure hunts, to see what we could find in there. We weren't allowed to play there because the houses were dangerous, so we would always get told off if we were caught by any of the neighbours. However, we would still play there; we couldn't sense any danger.

One day when we were 'hunting for treasure', I found an old box with a full set of dominos inside. They looked very old. I kept them and took them home to show Mum. She told me that they were really old and made of half ebony and half ivory, or so she thought. She looked at the set and saw that there was one domino missing from it. I put them away and kept them in a safe place. We never played with them at all but I kept them locked away in a cupboard and intended to keep them forever.

In one of the old houses, which we played in, we found a stray dog. He had obviously been left behind by one of the owners of the house, after they had left. The dog was a little brown mongrel. We all felt sorry for this little dog. He was very skinny, as if it hadn't been eating properly. We would feed the dog with bits that we got from home. I made it a little bed to sleep on and went to visit him every day. I called him Pal.

After a few days, I took him home to show to Mum. Mum liked him and soon she said that he could come and live with us. After a few weeks, Pal had put on weight and settled down as he lived with us. He was a really good dog and never messed in the house ever. I would take him for long walks and taught him to sit and to beg and shake his paw. He was so friendly and such a good dog to have around. He would follow me around everywhere I went and hardly ever needed to be on a lead. He loved it when Mum would take us all on long walks, up to Rivington, although I had to be careful that he didn't wander too far away from me, while off his lead. I thought he might go and chase the sheep in the fields, if he managed to get through any of the fences.

On one of our long walks to Rivington, we had taken a picnic and walked right up to the top of Rivington Pike. At the top were old ruins of a small castle. We could play in and around the old stones that had fallen down ages ago. From the top of the Pike, you could see for miles. You could see the whole of Horwich and the town hall clock in Bolton and even further away than that. Mum said that on a clear day you could see Blackpool Tower.

When we all arrived at the top of the pike, I allowed Pal off his lead. We laid our blanket on the ground and sat down tucking into the picnic that Mum had made. The sun was shining and Mum was attempting to get a suntan while Maureen was off playing in the old ruins. I had just finished eating a sandwich when I realised that Pal had gone. I looked around and couldn't see him anywhere. I called out his name but he was nowhere to be seen. I jumped up from the blanket and stood looking down the hill, hoping I would be able to see him playing around in the grass at the bottom. I called his name, again and again but I couldn't see him anywhere. All at once everything went black. I had fallen backwards on to the ground and I was seeing stars. I didn't know what had happened to me.

After a few seconds, I sat up; my face was sore. My mouth was bleeding badly as I tried to think what had happened to me. There were people running up the hill towards me, and something was lying on the ground in front of me. What had happened? I had been hit by something hard, right in the face. I looked across at Mum, who was still sitting on the blanket; she was laughing her head off. Her arms were folded across her stomach, as if it would split open because she was laughing that much. It must have looked really funny to her, whatever it was that had happened. I sat there without moving at all, trying to figure out what I had been hit by. I rolled over and tried to get to my feet. As I stood up, I felt really dizzy and wobbled a little. I saw two men in front of me. They lifted up an object from the ground, the object that I had just been hit in the face by. One of them asked if I was all right and then carried on inspecting the damage that had been done to what looked like the wing of a plane. It was about three feet in length and had broken off from the rest of the body of the plane. The object was in fact part of a large remote-controlled plane.

There were a few people flying them at the bottom of the hill. The planes looked about six feet long. I couldn't believe that I had been hit in the face by one. I put my hand to my face and tried to feel where it had hit me. The blood was now dripping down my chin, onto my t-shirt and it was hurting. I had been too worried about Pal to notice the group of people at the bottom of the hill flying planes.

Suddenly, Pal came running towards me, wagging his tail excitedly and jumping about around my legs. I bent down to clip his lead to his collar and became dizzy, falling to the ground again. I sat there for a few moments, stunned and watched the men carry the plane and its broken wing back down the hill. They didn't look at all pleased that their plane had been damaged. I managed to get to my feet again and went to join Mum. I couldn't understand why she was laughing so much; I was hurt and in pain, why was she laughing? Was it so hilariously funny for her to see her daughter, hit in the face by a plane? Soon after we made our way back home.

The sun was burning my face as we walked. It was really sore and swelling up by now. I could feel it. It had stopped bleeding but it was throbbing and hurt a lot. I was glad to get back home.

When I looked in the mirror at home, my face was in a state. I was so embarrassed that I had just walked all the way through Horwich looking like that. I was not surprised that everyone we passed was staring at me. I burst into tears; they stung my face. I realised that I had been really lucky. If the plane had hit me, two inches lower or two inches higher, I would have been seriously injured.

CHAPTER TWENTY-ONE
Tomboy Forever

The first two years, living with Mum in Horwich, had been eventful. I had experienced my first boyfriend and gone through his traumatic accident with him. I had made lots of new friends all around Horwich and from school. I was still quite the tomboy, so most of my friends were tomboys too or boys. I had a paper round and a babysitting job. The money I earned came in handy with my pets and was spent wisely. I seemed to be growing up fast and enjoying my life in Horwich.

Most of the girls in my class at school had already started their periods and were wearing bras, but not me. I had little pimples where my bust should be and couldn't even imagine myself wearing a bra, at all. I didn't want to grow up. I just wanted to stay just as I was. I was too busy just being a kid and I couldn't even imagine being a woman. I would have to wear girly clothes — even worse, dresses! The thought of that made me squirm. I liked my baseball boots and jeans and didn't intend to swap them for girly clothes; no way.

We had learned all about 'the changes' that were going to happen to our bodies in class. We had watched films all about 'it'. We all sat giggling in our classroom, as our teachers tried to explain what it was all about. They were trying to teach us everything that we needed to know, about the changes that would take place inside us, soon. I just didn't want to know. It wasn't going to happen to me; no way. I would put it all out of my mind and forget all about it. I was just too busy to think about silly things like that.

Not long after these lessons it was impossible for me not to think about the changes because things were happening to my body that were out of my control. The pimples that I had, where my bust should be, were getting bigger and I soon fitted into the bra that my big sister Ann had passed down to me ages ago. I had stuffed it in the back of the drawer and forgotten that it was there. I certainly had no intention of ever wearing it. I was also getting little hairs under my arms. I could count them! I thought they were horrible and couldn't understand what they were there for. It seemed that my body was changing and I didn't like it at all. I was beginning to realise that it was out of my control. No matter how hard I tried to put it out of my mind, and pretend that it wasn't happening, I couldn't stop it at all. I would think of Ann and wish that she were here, so I could talk to her. She had probably been through all this by now and would probably tell me to stop being stupid. Although I was aware of the changes taking place in my body, I still tried to put it out of my mind and carry on enjoying myself with my friends.

We still spent a lot of time with the Crawfords. They had a big house that we all loved to run around in. On one such occasion we were all happily playing and running around outside in the warm sunshine. I had been thirsty all day, so I had bought a big bottle of Vimto cordial out of my paper round money. I had never had this before, but when I tasted it, I really liked it and couldn't stop drinking it all day. By the end of the day, I had drunk the entire bottle but I had got this awful tummy ache. I thought that I must have drunk too much of this Vimto cordial because I didn't feel very well at all.

As it got dark, I thought that I really should go home. My tummy ache was getting worse. Suddenly I realised that I needed the toilet badly and rushed inside the Crawford's house and up their stairs as fast as I could. I rushed to the toilet. It was all in darkness. I tried the light switch but nothing happened. They had no light at the top of the stairs. I couldn't see a thing. As I reached the bathroom door, I hoped that there was a light in there but when I pressed the light switch in there, nothing happened again. In the darkness I managed to find the toilet with my arms stretched out in front of me and quickly sat on it. I was just in time. I had the 'runs' really badly. My tummy was hurting and tears were in my eyes. I just wanted to go home.

I must have been sitting on that loo for about an hour in the dark. I was too scared to move. I felt poorly. As I sat there trying to look around, my eyes were slowly adjusting to the darkness. I wished that I hadn't drunk so much of that Vimto. I didn't realise it would make me feel so ill. I felt so bad I thought that I just had to get home. I tried to look around in the darkness for a toilet roll. I couldn't see one anywhere but hanging up on the wall, at the back of the toilet, were little square pieces of newspaper hanging up on a piece of string. I was horrified. Could this be what the Crawfords used instead of toilet roll? I couldn't believe that they would use this to wipe their bottoms. I sat there in tears and in pain. I knew I should be getting home so there was nothing else to do but to use this newspaper and get home as fast as I could.

I rushed home feeling very uncomfortable. I rushed down the back street and opened the back gate to our yard. Our toilet was at the end of the yard and I was relieved that the light was working so I could see what I was doing. I sat on the toilet once again, still in quite a lot of pain and feeling dreadful. I was in such a mess. I had soiled my underwear and needed to change. The Vimto had gone straight through me causing me to be in a mess. I wasn't going to drink that again. I was sitting there for ages not feeling any better at all. Suddenly, I realised what had been happening to me. It wasn't the Vimto that had gone straight through me. I had started my periods. I was fifteen; it was finally happening. How could I have been so stupid as to think that it was the Vimto that had caused me to be in such a state? I felt so daft. I sat there as tears filled my eyes once again. I didn't know what to do. I knew Mum would be inside so I opened the toilet door a little and shouted to her, hoping that she would hear me calling for her from the top of the yard. I shouted and shouted to her and hoped that Maureen wasn't around to know what was happening to me.

After a while I could hear the squeaking of the back door opening and Mum answered my calls. She came up the back yard to the toilet door and asked me what the matter was. I opened the door slowly and looked up at her. The tears were streaming down my face; I was sweating and my stomach was hurting. I told her that I thought I had started my periods. A smile came to her face as she looked at me sat on the toilet in such a mess. In a soft and tender voice, she told me to finish off in the toilet, come inside and she would help me to clean up.

When I walked into the kitchen, Mum put her arm round my shoulder and showed me what she had done for me. She had got everything prepared. There was clean underwear with soap and water in the bowl, ready for me to clean myself up. She had even got a packet of sanitary towels and told me that she had bought them ages ago, especially for this moment and explained to me how to wear them. I felt really embarrassed but Mum made me feel special that night and I was so glad that we were sharing that time together.

She left the kitchen and closed the door firmly shut behind her, while I cleaned myself up. I felt a lot better after I got cleaned up, but I still had the tummy ache. I knew now that this was the reason why I had been feeling so bad. It had not been caused by drinking too much Vimto. I had become a woman but I was wondering if it always hurt so badly? I lay on the settee at the side of Mum. She had filled up a hot water bottle and I put it on my tummy. That seemed to ease it a little. I was glad Mum was the only one who knew about this. Maureen was out playing. She would have laughed at me if she knew and I didn't want that. Mum and I talked about this and what I should expect every month. I felt quite close to Mum at that time. Mum and I kept this a secret from Maureen. I didn't want her to find out what had happened to me. It was only spoken about when no one else was around. I spent most of the next week around the house. I didn't want to play out at all. I would make up excuses, that I had other things to do, when my friends called for me. Soon the week was over and I felt more like myself again. I was off again everyday playing out with my friend, without a care in the world.

I couldn't believe what had happened to me that summer and expected to be looking and feeling differently by now, but I wasn't. I didn't look like a woman yet at all. I wasn't ready to be a woman anyway — I was too busy enjoying being a kid! I just looked and felt just like I had always done, with no difference at all. I didn't like the idea that I had to go through this same thing every month for the rest of my life. Why? It wasn't fair! I didn't want to be a woman yet but I knew that there was nothing at all I could do about it!

CHAPTER TWENTY-TWO
Cruel Love

I had started wearing a bra, and I hated it. All the girls in my class knew that I had become a woman. We would all talk together about what it was like. It helped to talk to each other about these things. Some of the girls had started their period's ages ago but there were a couple of girls that hadn't started at that time and it seemed to help them to listen to all our experiences. We would all laugh together, remembering the day we had started. We all had different experiences to tell. It seemed funny to talk about it now but my experience of 'that day' certainly wasn't funny then.

I had to have a few days off school, over the next few months because of the bad tummy aches. I felt absolutely dreadful the whole time. I didn't like to attend physical education (P.E) classes while I was having my period. I was pleased to have that excuse. I hated the P.E classes sometimes, especially the showers afterwards. I hated having to undress in front of the others, let alone shower in front of everyone. Sometimes I just couldn't be bothered to run around a field playing hockey. I didn't know why but I would always be the one who got hit on the shins with the hockey stick, when we were 'bullying off'. I hated it. My shins would be covered in bruises afterwards.

The year 1974 was my last year at school. I would be sixteen years old in November that year. I would be leaving school in April. I knew that I would be taking a number of exams at school but I wasn't really interested in staying on, going to college or any other form of further education. I had had enough of school. I just wanted to go straight into working for a living and getting a wage. I had no idea what sort of work I wanted to do, maybe something to do with animals, or maybe children. I knew I was good with children and I had already passed my child care exam as well as the St. John's first aid course. I had attended that course a couple of weeks ago, which had been great. I really enjoyed it.

I knew that I wanted to have money in my pocket that I had worked hard for. I was full of dreams of what I would be able to buy including living in a place of my own. I was thinking about the possibility of my own flat or even travelling. From where I was then, it all seemed such a long way off until next year but I just couldn't help dreaming of those things, instead of dreaming of marrying Donny Osmond or Les McKeown out of the Bay City Rollers.

I was still quite interested in drama, during my last year at school and auditioned for a part in the school production of 'Oliver'. I managed to get the part of Charlotte. The rehearsals started after school every night. To my horror, in one scene, I had to do a dance with the boy who was playing Oliver Twist. It wasn't a hard dance to learn, it only lasted about five minutes but I was so nervous. The idea of dancing in front of the whole school, on opening night and then in front of the parents terrified me. I didn't mind all the dressing up and the makeup — I just didn't want to do this dance!

All the cast members worked really hard at every rehearsal. After a few months, everyone had learned all their lines and all the scenery was finished. There was only three weeks to opening night and everyone was looking forward to performing but most of them were just as nervous as I was.

During an outdoor games lesson, our class was taking part in sporting activities on the school playing field. Some were doing the long jump; others were throwing the javelin and our group was doing the high jump. When it came to my turn to jump over the pole, I was very confident. I knew I could do it. I had jumped higher than that before, it was easy. I was ready to go. I took a deep breath and off I went. I ran towards the pole and lifted myself up as high as I could, up over the pole, without knocking it off. I was so pleased. As I went over the pole, I hit the ground awkwardly. I heard a crack and twisted my ankle. I lay there for a moment holding my ankle. The teacher came over to me and helped me to my feet and on to a chair at the side of the field. She took my shoe off and looked at my foot and then sent me to see the school nurse.

I hobbled off the field and back into school. I was checked over by the nurse, who said that I had sprained it. She wrapped it up in a bandage and sent me to my next lesson. The bandage helped a little but it was still painful to walk on. When I got home, I showed my foot to my mum and told her that I had sprained it in the games lesson. She took the bandage off to have a look. It was a little swollen and very bruised but it didn't stop me wanting to play out that night with my friends. She wrapped it up again and off I went.

I sat on the swings with some friends, just talking between ourselves about the latest record that was at number one in the charts and who had bought it. We were in the middle of a conversation about what we would do if we ever met Donny Osmond or David Cassidy, when we were all distracted by the sound of Maureen's voice shouting something while heading towards us. We all turned to look at her and tried to make out what she was saying.

As she got closer, it was clear what she was saying. She was shouting at the top of her voice, in front of everyone, "Maggie's started her periods!" She was repeating it over and over. Everybody heard what she was saying and I was so embarrassed I went bright red. I knew that she must have been in my drawer at home and found my 'monthly things and the pain killer tablets that Mum had bought me for the period pains. She now knew! She had found out and I just knew that she would make fun of me in this way and take the opportunity to embarrass and humiliate me in front of all my friends whenever she could. I could see they were looking at me and laughing; even Dave was laughing at me. After all these months of keeping it a secret she now knew. I just knew that she would do this to me. I was so angry with her that I jumped off the swing and started to chase her around the park towards the market place. I had forgotten about my painful ankle; I was so annoyed at her. I couldn't catch her, so I gave up after a while and went home to tell Mum what she had said.

Mum told me not to be bothered because she would certainly be going through the same thing soon. She was right. I remembered what I was like and how scared I was at the time, when I started my periods and realised that she would no doubt go through the same thing. I decided not to let it bother me any more.

The next morning, I was getting ready for school and I noticed that my foot was still really sore. I could hardly walk on it. I took the bandage off and my foot was bruised and swollen. It looked worse than it had done the previous day. I showed Mum and she thought that I should go to the hospital to have an x-ray.

Julie, our cousin, had been staying at our house for a few days, so she took me to the hospital on the bus. Julie was eighteen. I liked her a lot and got on with her well. She had a boyfriend who had a motorbike. Her Mum, who was our Mum's sister, had died when she was small, so she had become very close to our mum and would come to stay at our house often.

I limped into the casualty department of Bolton Royal Infirmary, with Julie. After a short wait, I was sent to see a doctor who sent me to have an x-ray. After another long wait outside in the corridor, I was sent back inside the doctor's room again. The doctor was looking at my x-ray on a machine on the wall. It lit up so he could see the x-ray properly. He turned to me and said that I had broken a bone in my foot and pointed it out to me on the x-ray. I could see the broken bone clearly. I knew it was painful but I didn't think that I had broken it. The doctor told me that I would have to have a plaster cast on my foot, from the knee down for the next six weeks and that I mustn't walk on it at all.

I suddenly remembered the school play. I told the doctor that I was going to be taking part in the school play, in three weeks. I asked him if I would still be able to do so. He didn't recommend that I appeared in the play and said that I shouldn't walk on it, if at all possible.

I was pushed in a wheelchair by one of the hospital porters, to the plaster theatre, to have my leg set in plaster. The nurses then had to teach me how to walk using the crutches that I had been given. I told the nurses that I had had crutches before, after the road accident when I was younger. However, I had forgotten how to use them now and it was quite funny learning how to use them all over again. When I was more confident with the crutches, Julie and I were sent home in an ambulance.

As we arrived outside our house, Mum came to the door and stood watching as I struggled to get out from the back of the ambulance. She took one look at my leg in plaster and started to laugh out loud again, just like she did when I was hit in the face with that plane at Rivington. It did look really funny though, even Julie was laughing now. I had the rest of the week off school, learning how to walk properly on the crutches.

When I went back to school, I had to explain to our drama teacher that I couldn't take part in the school play due to my injury. They had a stand-in, who had been learning all the words and the dance. She now had to take over my part. In a way I was glad. I was too nervous and really didn't want to do the dance in front of everyone, especially with a boy. That's the only thing that put me off doing the play. There was no way I could take part now with a broken foot so I had a good excuse. The play went ahead as usual and my stand-in was brilliant. I thought she was so much better than I would have been.

After a while, having my leg in plaster, really slowed me down and I began to hate it. I couldn't run around as usual with my friends and I wasn't allowed to do my paper round either. By the time I had been in plaster for about three weeks the itching was driving me mad. I would get one of Mum's knitting needles and try to poke it down the plaster in order to try and reach the spot that was itching. I could never reach it and it was driving me crazy. I was getting fed up and couldn't wait until it was taken off. I would spend quite a lot of time out in the back yard with my rabbits in the shed. I would sit in there with them for hours, watching them and trying to clean them out the best I could. I was fed up with not being able to do the things that I used to do and not being able to get around as much.

I think I was getting on Mum's nerves too, by hanging around the house, looking fed up and always being with the rabbits. I wasn't able to help out around the house like I usually did and I think this was annoying Mum too.

One day I was in with the rabbits, changing their drinking water, when Mum came storming out in the backyard and started to shout at me about being in the shed with the rabbits instead of doing things indoors. She told me to pack my bags and go back to live at Dad's house. I was gobsmacked! I couldn't believe it! After all this time she was throwing me out, after everything that we had been through to find her when I was only thirteen years of age. She'd said that she loved me then but I felt she couldn't have loved me at this point and done this to me. She was throwing me out just because I couldn't vacuum for her! I really thought that she loved me but she didn't. I was fifteen, with a broken foot and she was throwing me out! I didn't want to go back to dads. What about all my school friends? What about my rabbits? I would have to leave them behind. I couldn't carry them. What if Dad did not want to take me back? Would I have to go into a children's home like Jane and Andrea? As I packed my things, I cried and cried. Mum must have heard me.

I walked up the street on my crutches, struggling to carry the few belongings that I had put together in a small suitcase and a carrier bag. I got to the end of the street and turned back to see if Mum was coming after me, to say she had changed her mind and that I could stay, but she wasn't. I waited for a moment and then carried on my way to the bus stop to catch a bus to Dad's house. I cried all the way there.

I got off the bus at the end of the road that led to Dad's house. It was a short walk but it seemed to take me such a long time to get to where I was going, as I hobbled on my crutches carrying my few belongings. I was so scared. I didn't know what to expect. Would Dad let me in? Would he turn me away?

I hadn't been back to this house for nearly two years. I was thinking of Laura and how much she must have grown since the last time I saw her. It would be great to see her again after all this time but what would Dad say when I turned up on his doorstep. I was trying not to cry. The memory of when I left this house kept flashing through my mind, when Laura was standing up at the window with Lorraine, crying her eyes out because we were all leaving. It broke my heart to think of her that way and it had always haunted me and made me cry, so many times, just to think of that time. I was on my way back to Dad's. I would be seeing Laura again very soon. Would she remember me?

As I got closer to the house, I stopped, put my bags down on the ground and leaned against someone's gate for a moment. I was so hot and sweaty and out of breath. I wiped my face on my sleeve and thought about what I was going to say. I could see Dad's house in the distance. His car was parked over the road so he was home. The front door was wide open. It would be lovely to see Laura again, and Lorraine and Mary. I had missed them all so much but I thought it would be best not to visit after we had left, as I thought that we wouldn't be allowed to visit or that we would have been turned away. I was too scared to come back to Dad's house after leaving, so long ago. Now I had no choice but to return. Where else could I go? There was nowhere else to go. I wiped my face again and collected my bags from the ground and carried on hobbling towards Dad's house.

By the time I neared the front gate I was shaking like a leaf. I just wanted to cry; I was so nervous. I stood at the gate looking up the path, staring inside the house. I could see Laura sitting cross legged on the floor in the dining room, at the end of the hallway. She was now four years old. She had grown so much. Tears filled my eyes as I watched her chatting away to her dolls and trying to dress them. She could talk, I thought, as I looked at her. She would not remember me. I didn't want to move. I just wanted to look at her and watch.

A tear fell from my eye, as suddenly she looked up from her toys and looked towards me. She quickly got to her feet, dropped her doll and started to run towards me. She was shouting," Hiya! Hiya!" My eyes widened, I thought that she wouldn't have remembered me after all this time. I wiped my eyes on my sleeve as she came closer to me. I still couldn't move. I couldn't get over her face; it hadn't changed at all. Her big brown eyes sparkled as she climbed up on the wooden gate to greet me. Did she really know me? Did she really remember me? I couldn't hold the tears back any longer. Still, with the front gate between us, I swung my arms around her and hugged her so tightly. How could she still remember me? Although she didn't say my name, I knew in my heart that she knew who I was. I couldn't stop looking at her little angelic face and kissing her rosy cheeks. Now the tears were streaming down my face; I had missed her so much. I was trembling uncontrollably. She told me not to cry and squeezed me tightly around my neck. Laura wiped the tears from my cheek with her tiny hand. I kissed her forehead and then wiped my face on my sleeve once more.

I looked away from Laura's face and saw Dad standing at the front door watching us. My stomach turned over and a cold chill ran through me. I didn't know how long he had been standing there watching. Laura then turned to look at him, got down from the gate and ran towards him. Dad asked me what I was doing here so I told him that Mum had thrown me out. He glared at me as I nervously stood back away from the gate, supported by my crutches. I was convinced he was going to turn me away. Dad looked down at the plaster cast on my leg and at the few belongings on the ground beside me. I was so shocked when he turned away and said that I had better come in then. He turned and walked back inside the house. I picked up my belongings, opened the gate and slowly went inside.

I sat on the floor in the dining room, next to Laura, as she carried on playing with her toys. I reached out to her once more, pulled her towards me, hugged her tightly and whispered in her ear 'I LOVE YOU.' Suddenly, Dad shouted from the living room, "Put the kettle on Mags!"

CHAPTER TWENTY-THREE
The Homecoming: Nothing's Changed

The house looked the same as it did when I'd left. As I looked around the dining room, I could hear the fish tanks still making the same sounds from their electric pumps that I remembered so well. Dad looked the same too. The only difference was that Laura had grown so much and could now talk so well. I soon settled down to the everyday routine at Dad's house.

Two weeks after I had arrived at Dad's, it was a relief to have the plaster cast taken off my leg. I was able to get around a lot better without the crutches. I was so ready to be free of the plaster. I'd even tried to cut it off myself weeks earlier with a pair of scissors because I was so fed up with it. I got a good telling off from the hospital for trying to do this. I thought they were going to put another plaster cast back on at one point because I had made a mess of the other one. What a relief it was to walk out of that hospital that day!

I still attended Rivington and Blackrod High School and would travel each day on the bus. I liked this school and with only another ten months left, there was no point in changing school again. I had made lots of good friends at Rivington and I didn't want to leave or forget any of them when I left Horwich, as had been the case when I had left Smithills. I had really missed my friends from Smithills and I didn't want to do that again. Some evenings I would travel on the bus back to Horwich to visit them and stay overnight at their house on weekends when I was allowed to. I made sure I stayed well away from Mum's house though because of the way she had made me leave. I felt rejected badly and didn't want to see her or even visit ever again.

I had a babysitting job after school, a couple of nights a week for a family that lived on Albert Street. I would go to their house after school and look after their two children for two hours until their dad, Jimmy came home at around five o'clock. I did this for a couple of weeks and they would pay me a pound (I only got fifty pence from my babysitting job in Knott Lane.)

One day Jimmy came home from work as usual and asked me if I would make him a cup of tea. While I was in the kitchen making the cup of tea he came and stood at the side of me. He reached over and put his arm around my shoulder and tried to kiss me on my mouth. I was horrified. In an instant, I pulled away from him, ran from the kitchen, picked up my school bag from the front room and ran out of there as fast as I could. I never went back. I couldn't understand why he'd done that; a grown man trying to kiss a schoolgirl. I was scared that this big man, the father of the two children that I had been looking after, had tried to do this to me. I was just a kid. It scared me for a long time. I decided to stay away from the area where he lived. If I ever saw him in the streets of Horwich, while I was on my way to school or coming from school, it would make my stomach turn over and I would turn and run in the opposite direction or run into a shop. I was petrified.

Paul and Ann were still living at Dad's house after leaving school. They both had jobs and were earning money. Paul was working at the local garage as a motor mechanic and also thinking of applying to go into the army. Ann was working as a telephonist, at a catalogue sorting office in Bolton town centre and still had her little job with Aunty Nora in the Copper Kettle Café. She was also going to college because what she really wanted to be was a nurse and she had applied to live in the nurse's home at Bolton General Hospital. I thought it probable that they would both be moving out and starting their own careers. This would be the start of their new life away from home and I imagined that it would be my turn next.

I really didn't know what I wanted to be when I left school. Ann was very clever at school and passed all her exams, but although I did like going to school, I wasn't all that clever and wasn't really bothered about passing exams in the way that Ann was. I was good at Art and English, and at one time thought I would like to be a writer, as I liked to write essays and stories at school. I knew I wanted a job to earn my own money and eventually leave home. I also knew I wanted to get married and have my own family one day. I was good with children and really enjoyed my babysitting jobs. I enjoyed being with the children so much that I thought maybe I would become a nursery nurse. When I was younger, I loved animals and wanted to be a vet, but after all my rabbits died, I totally went off the idea of working with animals, just in case I could never make any of them better. I would have needed a lot of higher qualifications than I was already taking and would also need to pass all of them. I didn't think I would ever be clever enough for that job. There were too many jobs to choose from, I didn't know what I wanted to do. I would have to hurry up and make up my mind in terms of what I wanted to do when I left school. I would be leaving school the following April. I hoped that I would have a job by then.

Lorraine and I spent quite a lot of our time together after I moved back home. She was always very pretty, and as she was growing up; she became even more beautiful. I thought that she could be a model one day. In the years that she had lived in Bolton she had lost her Kentish accent that she had when she first came to live with us. By this stage she talked more like us and had her own Lancashire accent.

Mary, on the other hand, hadn't lost her accent at all; she still spoke in a really posh accent. She would often reprimand us for not pronouncing words properly, or for using words that she didn't understand. I remember her laughing at the way we pronounced certain things. Often, she didn't understand them or they had a different meaning locally from the meaning that they had in Kent. I loved hearing her laugh.

Jane and Andrea were still in children's homes but would sometimes come home for visits at weekends or for a few days during the holidays. It was good to see them but they would still get into trouble quite a lot when they came home. Dad had to go through their suitcases before they went back to the children's homes just in case, they had taken anything that didn't belong to them.

A number of times Dad found things in their cases that they had taken. I remember one occasion, when we were all going to a family wedding, there was an unexpected visitor who called at our house. We were all dressed in our best clothes and ready to go to the party. The shopkeeper of our local newsagents called at the house to speak to Dad. I knew that one of us would be in for it. It could have been any of us, but this time it was Jane. She had been stealing from the local sweet shop, in the same way as we all had at some point. Sweets were never bought for us, so we would sometimes steal them. I stole a bottle of milk from someone's doorstep once on my way to school and I drank it before I got there, as I was so hungry. I didn't get caught though. Jane must have been caught.

Dad went mad and told her to go to her room and she was not allowed to go to the wedding. The rest of us were told to get into the car and Dad drove us to the party at the Co-op Hall in Bolton. He dropped us off then left to go back home to deal with Jane. We all knew what that meant; Jane was in big trouble yet again.

Jane wasn't allowed to return to the house, from the children's home, for a long time after that.

After moving back home and settling in again, it wasn't long before I realised that our family moving into this new house hadn't made any difference at all to the way Dad was. The rows between him and Mary continued. It was Dad who did all the shouting and Mary who sat silently, trying to avoid his blows. There was still furniture getting broken, meals were still thrown against the walls and Mary was still crying a lot.

At times it was Laura that was being shouted at. She would be made to sit still on the floor in between his legs. She was clipped around her head and told to shut up if she was making too much noise, while he was watching the football. She would never cry, she already knew, just as we did, not to cry. I thought things might have been different for Laura because she seemed to get all the attention as she was the smallest. She would be sitting on his knee sometimes and he would play with her on rare occasions. I didn't remember him ever being like that with any of us. At times Laura would be treated in the same way that we were, especially if Dad was watching something on the television. He hadn't changed, not one bit. I wondered if things would change for little Laura? Would things be the same for our baby sister as they had been for us?

CHAPTER TWENTY-FOUR
The 'Rec' Dave. Love at First Sight

After chores had been done the older ones would go outdoors or we would stay in our bedrooms and keep out of Dad's way. We would never sit down in the same room as him.

Ann took me along to the youth club that she went to twice a week. It was called The Bolton Recreation Club. Everybody called it 'The Rec'. It was a fun place to be in the evening and a popular place with teenagers. The grown-ups who ran it were really friendly to us all; they were more like our best friends. They were always ready to help with advice if anyone had problems or difficulties. They would always make sure that we knew that we could go to them if we needed to. Of course, I could never go to them. I was too afraid. I couldn't even talk to any teachers at school about what was going on at home. It wouldn't have done any good.

'The Rec' was an old building, with a huge entrance hall, a staircase leading up to the top floor and under that staircase there was another narrow staircase that led to the cellar area underneath the building. The cellar area was the place where bands would rehearse. There was always a group of young lads, with greasy hair, playing loud music on their electric guitars and banging on drums. Some bands were good, but I thought I would stay with the Bay City Rollers. When they sang 'Bye, Bye Baby,' I could sing along as I knew every word. That was proper music but the music that they played was too loud — it would give me a headache!

There were different rooms leading off from each side of the hallway. A couple of rooms at the right where like store rooms. One room was full of chairs stacked one on top of another; the other room was dark inside with no window and there was no light bulb hanging from the ceiling. Both rooms were very dusty.

The room with the chairs stacked together had a door propped up against the wall. I thought that no one had got around to fixing it back up yet. Courting couples would sit in there, kissing and cuddling each other. That room had two long tatty old settees and a couple of wooden tables against the wall.

To the left of the hall were two huge rooms. One was a lounge area where it was possible to buy coffee and biscuits at a kiosk. The other was a games room with a snooker table, dart board, pool table and a big cupboard at the bottom that stored all sorts of other games and toys that we might have wanted to play with. Upstairs was a basketball court, with a shiny, slippery wooden floor and hooped baskets that were high up at each end. There were other locked rooms accessible from the landing on the stairs and two rooms that were the girl's and boy's toilets. It was great to go there. I would run and play and make as much noise as I wanted and no one would ever tell me off. Here we could all be kids. I felt as if we could do what we wanted to do, which was to have some fun and have a laugh. This was where I first saw Dave — yes, another Dave! What was it about lads called Dave?

There was Dave H, who shared my first ever kiss, when I was eleven, in the woods when we had been doing cross-country. There was Dave B, my first 'boyfriend' and although we were inseparable for about fifteen months, we were more like brother and sister. I was more interested in kicking a football around with him rather than doing all that 'sissy girly stuff.'

I was at 'The Rec' looking at this boy called Dave too! I didn't think he would ever look at me the way that he looked at all those older blonde girls that came here. He was probably about eighteen and I was just a kid. I wouldn't even be able to walk in those high-heeled shoes that those older girls wore and Dad would have killed me if I had worn a skirt as short as they did! Dave made my heart pound and I had butterflies in my tummy when I looked at him. I hoped that he would notice me. He had long, shoulder length jet-black, curly hair and green eyes. He had broad muscular shoulders; he was gorgeous! He made me blush bright red one day when I bumped into him. I ran away quickly in embarrassment hoping he wouldn't notice. I felt like such a clumsy fool.

After a few weeks of him not noticing me at all, he was sent away to a detention centre. He had found himself in some sort of trouble with the police. I was really sad for him and hoped that I would see him again soon. 'The Rec' was full of good-looking lads but none were as nice as Dave, I thought.

After his time in the detention centre, he appeared back at 'The Rec.'

'Oh, flippin' 'eck' look who's there, I said to Nicky, a girl I had befriended. We were both sitting with our feet up on the coffee table, drinking frothy coffee in the lounge (I wasn't allowed to drink that at home.) At that moment, Dave walked past us and into the snooker room. Minutes earlier, we had both been dancing to Abba's 'Waterloo' and pretending that we were the girls from that group. We tried to dance in the same way they did, when they had been on the television and had won the Eurovision Song Contest. I was glad that he hadn't seen us. I hadn't forgotten how he had made me blush and how my heart would beat faster when I saw him. I noticed that my heart was beating again like that but he walked right by us without a glance in our direction at all. Nicky could tell that I liked this boy and she promised not to tell anyone.

In no time at all the older girls surrounded him, flirting with him, as I had done the first time that I saw him. There was no way he would ever look at me. Disheartened, I dragged Nicky up to her feet and decided to ignore them and go and play darts.

Dave was playing snooker with Tony, his mate. While we played darts, I kept glancing at him. I watched him as he leaned across the table with a smouldering cigarette hanging out from the corner of his mouth. He took a shot at those brightly coloured balls. I was hoping that he would catch a glimpse of me looking at him and maybe then, he would notice me.

Time and time again, I would try and get his attention, whenever I went to 'The Rec'. I didn't think I ever would catch his attention. I really liked him and I thought that this might be love. Was this what love felt like? I had never felt anything like it before. I had had a boyfriend before, but I had never felt like this.

One evening Nicky and I arrived at 'The Rec', we were early so there weren't a lot of kids in. Nicky told me that she had pinched a fag out of her mum's fag packet, so we went into the 'dark room' so that she could smoke it. She had never smoked before, she told me. I told her I had smoked before but told her it was horrible and I would never do it again. We laughed together, when I told her of the time I got caught smoking at school. We both collapsed in a heap together on that old tatty settee. There was no light bulb in the ceiling fitment, so we just had the light shining in from the hall through the doorway. Nicky lit up her secret cigarette while I watched as she confidently took a drag, taking all the smoke into her lungs. She turned a funny colour and started to cough her head off. It was so funny; I laughed my head off. When she got her breath back, she laughed too and held the cigarette between her fingers, too frightened to take another drag. We watched it as it smouldered away in her hand. She looked so cool though. The fag was slowly burning away. We watched in fascination as the grey rings of smoke disappeared towards the ceiling, as she tried to get the courage to take another drag. We were being hypnotised by the swirls, when all of a sudden, we were 'awakened' by Dave barging into our secret hideout.

He rudely pushed himself between us and took the cigarette from Nicky's hand. Nicky didn't complain, she let him have it. I think she was relieved that he had taken it. I sat rigid. I couldn't move. I couldn't speak. It was Dave; he was sitting next to me. I watched as he thanked Nicky and put the cigarette to his mouth and took a big drag. His shoulders lifted as he inhaled, then he blew it out with one long exhale. Nicky and I looked at each other and then looked back at Dave. He smoked that fag like it was his last. When it was all gone, he stubbed it out in the ashtray. We all sat in silence for what seemed like ages, then he looked at Nicky, then looked at me. We were both in awe of this lad, who was sitting here between us. He was just about to say something when Nicky blurted out that I fancied him! He turned to look at me and I blushed again, as I had previously, and quickly ran out of the room and upstairs as fast as I could.

I locked myself into a cubicle in the girl's toilet. I was so embarrassed. How could she do that? She'd promised not to tell anyone. How could I face him again after that? My heart was pounding. My hands were shaking. I wanted to cry but I had put some of Ann's mascara on my eyes. I would have looked even more stupid with it running down my face.

After what seemed like ages Nicky came running into the toilet. She banged on the locked cubicle door telling me to come out and that Dave had told her that he fancied me as well. I couldn't believe what I was hearing. I thought she was lying. I unbolted the door and asked her not to lie to me. Still sulking, I sat on the sink cupboard feeling really stupid. She told me that she wasn't telling lies and that he had said that she had to come and get me or else he would come up here himself. It was true, she said and looked at me straight in the eyes. She smiled at me and said that he wanted to go out with me. I jumped down from the cupboard and looked into the mirror. My face was still flushed. She told me that I looked fine as she pulled at my arm and dragged me back downstairs.

Dave was still sitting in the 'dark room' waiting. He was smoking another cigarette when we walked in and he stared at me with those beautiful, piercing green eyes and smiled. My heart-melted right there and then with that smile. His smiling eyes wrinkled up almost to the point of being shut when he smiled at me. We both sat down on the settee beside him. He was talking to me but I couldn't hear a word he was saying. I just couldn't believe that he was sitting next to me and he had said what he had said. I was watching his lips move but I couldn't hear the words that were coming out of his mouth. I was just imagining being kissed by those lips and what it would feel like. I felt so stupid, I didn't know what to do or say. I felt just like a child. He reached out and took hold of my hand. I held my breath as he smiled at me again and I melted. I watched his hand wrapped around mine. His thumb was gently stroking the top of my hand. I looked over at Nicky but she had disappeared. She had left the room and we hadn't noticed.

"Your skin is so soft," he said, as he leaned towards me and whispered in my ear. 'Can I kiss you?' He kissed my cheek and leaned his head on my shoulder. This was a dream, I thought, as he kissed my neck tenderly. His arm slid around me and I was in his embrace. My heart was beating so fast and so loudly that I was sure that he could hear it. His lips were so warm and tender. Was this the moment that I had dreamed of? Was I falling in love? If this was a dream, I hoped I would never wake up from it. We kissed and kissed for such a long time. It was better than I had ever been kissed before.

We had been kissing and talking for ages. I glanced at my watch and jumped up and said, "It's 9:30! My dad told me to be in by 10:00! He'll kill me if I'm late!" I put my coat on and waved at Nicky as I rushed through the double doors to make my way home. I forgot to say goodbye to Dave as I was too busy panicking that I was going to be late home.

As I raced to the bus stop, I heard someone shouting my name. I looked back and Dave was chasing after me and struggling to put on his jacket as he ran. I stopped and waited for him.

'Did you think that I would let you walk home on your own?' he asked me, as he put his arm around my shoulders. I smiled as he kissed my cheek. Laughing, I told him that I caught a bus so he said that he would wait with me until it arrived, if I didn't mind and held me tighter towards him. Of course, it was all right with me. This was so nice. I couldn't believe it was happening. I felt as if it was all a dream. He was so nice and seemed such a gentleman.

We both stood at the bus stop, outside 'Sally-up-steps' public house. We could hear the loud voices of the beer drinkers inside. Dave held me so tightly and kept kissing me. I felt so safe and warm inside. I didn't want to go home. I wanted to stay with him forever. We noticed the bus approaching, from the town centre. He kissed me again so tenderly, for the last time, as the bus neared the stop. We had arranged to meet again at 'The Rec' a few days later.

I jumped on to the bus, paid the fare and raced upstairs. I sat at the back of the bus on the long seat and waved to him through the window, until I couldn't see him any more.

It was a little before ten when I got home. Dad was sitting in his chair smoking his pipe. The smell of that tobacco filled the house. Morecambe and Wise were on the television and Mary was smiling at the pair as they sung their funny songs. Both sat silently, with their eyes glued to the television as I looked around the door and said that I was going to bed. There was no response as usual as I went upstairs.

Ann was sitting on her bed reading. I was so happy that night but I couldn't tell anyone; I wanted to keep it to myself. It took me ages to drift off to sleep. I was wondering whether Dave would be the one that I would marry one day.

Over the next few weeks Dave and I saw each other at 'The Rec' regularly. I went to his house to meet his mum and his sister but I didn't take him home to meet my dad. I didn't think Dad would approve of me having a boyfriend. He would have stopped me seeing him for sure.

I didn't tell anyone at home that we were seeing each other — not even Ann. I knew she had a boyfriend too but I wouldn't say anything about Dave, not even to her. Dad had stopped Ann from seeing her boyfriend. He was one of the Kaleen's and Dad didn't like the family, so she was told not to see him any more. Dave was my secret and I wasn't going to stop seeing him.

As the weeks went by and the friendship between Dave and I grew, I started noticing that another girl at the 'The Rec' was hanging around Dave too much. She was older than me; seventeen like Dave. She was called Mo. She smoked cigarettes and pushed her way around 'The Rec' as if she was the boss. She was a big girl but she looked like a lad. I didn't like her at all. She was scary. The way she would hang around Dave would make me think that they used to be girlfriend and boyfriend. I began to feel jealous. When I asked Dave about her, he said that he had been out with her and they had finished a long time ago but she still wanted to go out with him again. I was scared of this girl and didn't want to talk to her at all. She would always be hanging around Dave and me. It was impossible to get away from her at 'The Rec'. I didn't want to be her friend.

Mo had a friend called Kath, the same age as her. They had been friends for a long time and were always at 'The Rec' together. One day they weren't together. Kath was sitting all on her own and Mo was at the other side of the room. Kath came to join Nicky and I in the lounge and started to talk to us. Dave was upstairs playing basketball with his mates. Kath started asking questions about him. She asked where he was and how long we had been seeing each other. Kath continued to tell us that Mo used to go out with him but that it was all over now. She also said that she had fallen out with Mo because she wouldn't leave Dave alone. Kath said that I should tell Mo to keep away from Dave because although she appeared to be hard, she wasn't. I told her that I couldn't do that because she was bigger than me and that I felt threatened by her. Kath started to laugh and told me that she wasn't that tough. I laughed her comments off, not believing any of what she had said and went off with Nicky to play darts. I wasn't aggressive and wouldn't hurt anybody.

Kath followed us again and joined in the game of darts. She was trying to be friendly with us and as her conversation drifted away from Dave, we found it easier to talk to her and to be her friend. We had been playing darts for around an hour when she suddenly announced she needed the toilet and asked me to go with her.

We went upstairs to the girls' toilets. I glanced at Dave playing basketball as I passed the room. He waved and smiled. I commented to Kath that I thought I was in love with him. She looked down at the floor and laughed strangely. The smile quickly left my face when suddenly she pushed me into one of the cubicles. The door slammed shut behind me. I couldn't understand why she had done that.

I turned and saw big Mo standing behind me. She had bolted the door. I was really scared. She started to push me around in the cubicle, saying that I had to finish with Dave and that she wanted to go out with him. She told me he belonged to her and that I was to leave him alone. Mo started hitting me on my face and around my head. I cowered into the corner of the cubicle but there was no escape from her; she was so big. I couldn't talk or shout out. Dave was in the next room and would have heard me if I had shouted to him. But I couldn't. Mo grabbed my hair, pulled me down and kneed me in the face. Next the door was opened and Kath pulled at her telling her I had had enough. They both left. I could hear them going down the stairs laughing. I sat down on the floor resting my head in my arms. I ached where she had punched me and my face was sore. I could feel my eye swelling and couldn't stop the tears from falling. I knew I had to stop seeing Dave or this would happen again.

As I sat there, I realised that I had been tricked into believing that they weren't friends. It had been a trick to get me in there, so she could beat me up because of my friendship with Dave. I stood slowly to my feet and brushed myself down. My blouse was torn where she had pulled at me.

I looked in the mirror as I left. My eye was swollen and I was flushed. My head was throbbing. I didn't want to stay there any more. I had to get home. I rinsed my face under the tap and dried it with the paper towel. I walked quietly down the stairs and out of the building. I didn't say anything to anyone as I left, not even Dave. He would be wondering where I had gone to.

I walked to the bus stop, trying to think of what I was going to say to Dad when I got home. I wondered how I would explain my swollen eye if he noticed it. I thought that I could just say that I fell off the bus or something like that, he knew how clumsy I was.

When I got home, he didn't notice. He didn't even look at me. I went to bed and silently cried myself to sleep. If I didn't want this to happen again, I knew I had to finish with Dave but I didn't want to. I didn't want to go to the 'The Rec' again either.

The next day I got ready for school. My black eye was hardly noticeable. The swelling had gone down and there was only a slight bruise at the corner of my eye. It wasn't as bad as I thought it would have been. No one in the house noticed so hopefully no one at school would notice.

After school that night I would normally have got ready to go to the 'The Rec'. It was Friday night and I would always go there Friday nights, however I was not going to go because of the events of the previous night. After chores, I stayed in my room and did some work on a project I had to do for school.

Around eight o'clock, there was a knock at the front door. Dad answered it and shouted up the stairs to me that there was someone at the door for me. I stopped what I was doing and went downstairs. It was Dave. I couldn't believe it. How did he know where I lived? I hadn't told him. I was so shocked that he was at my door. I grabbed my jacket off the hook and went outside with him. As we walked around, he told me that he knew what had happened at the 'The Rec' and what Mo and Kath had done. It had got around the club and the staff had also found out about it. It was expected that Mo and Kath would be barred. Dave had asked Nicky where I lived and thought he should come and see if I was all right. I was pleased that he had.

As we walked around, for what seemed like hours, we held hands and cuddled each other. I didn't want to finish with this boy and I told him what Mo had said to me, specifically that she wanted to go out with him. He laughed and said that she had no chance. He told me that he loved me and we kissed. He said that he wanted to stay with me forever. How could I finish with him? I loved him so much. We walked all the way over to Moss Bank Park as we talked. I saw the swings in the distance and said to Dave, "Race you to the swings!" With that, I set off running as fast as I could, with Dave chasing after me. He ran past me and beat me to the swings. We both swung high, laughing. We went higher and higher until we couldn't go any further. My stomach ached with laughing so much. I felt so happy!

As it was getting late, it was time for us to start making our way back home. This time I walked Dave to the top of Moss Bank Way, so he could catch his bus back into Bolton. We arranged to meet again the next day in the town centre at seven-thirty. As he got on his bus and waved goodbye, I couldn't wait to see him again the following day. I went home feeling such a lot happier than I had been the previous day.

The next day I waited at the town hall steps, as we had arranged. I waited and waited. I looked up at the big clock, it said seven forty-five. Where was he? I paced up and down and walked across to the fountains just in case he was at the other side of the precinct but he was nowhere to be seen. I waited until eight-thirty, then I decided to have a walk over to 'The Rec' to see if he had gone there instead.

As I walked past the fire station, I saw Tony, Dave's mate and shouted across the road to him. He ran across the road to me and I asked him if he had seen Dave. Tony began to tell me that Dave had been arrested that morning and was now in prison. I was so shocked I couldn't believe it. The previous night we had been so happy together, in the park, but now he was in a prison somewhere. I thought that I may never see him again. I didn't know what to say. I walked away from Tony with tears in my eyes. I walked all the way home from town in tears. I couldn't understand what had happened and why he hadn't told me any of this. I knew that he had been to a detention centre for getting in trouble with the police before but I thought that was in the past. I thought that we would be together forever.

My birthday passed by a few weeks later. There was no party and no celebration. I don't even think I got any cards. I thought of Dave all the time. I missed him so much.

A few days after my birthday, there was a letter delivered to the house. I picked it up off the mat and it had my name on the envelope. I had never received a letter before. In the corner of the envelope was printed, 'H.M. Prison. I knew straight away that it was from Dave. With my heart racing, I quickly put the letter into my pocket and ran upstairs. I had to hide it quickly. If Dad saw it, he would go mad. What would he say if he knew that I had got a letter from someone who was in prison? I didn't think he would be very pleased. I hid that letter, until I could find a safe time to read it in private and maybe write back to him.

When I went to school, the letter was put in my satchel and I read it while I was there. His letter was full of sweet words telling me that he loved me and of how much he was missing me. He said that he would be in prison for about six months and that he had stolen a car and had been caught by the police. He hoped that I would be able to go and visit him in prison. I didn't think I would ever be able to as it was too far away. I wrote a letter back to him, while I was at school and I had to buy a postage stamp from the secretary in the office at school. I posted the letter on my way home.

I received quite a few letters from Dave, while he was in prison and was able to keep it a secret from the household for quite a while that I was receiving them and writing letters back to him. Unfortunately, one day Dad got to the mail first when a letter had arrived from him to me. He knew it was a prison letter and straight away he said that he hoped that I was not writing to anyone in prison. He said that such people were 'jail-birds.' I knew what he meant. I had to stop writing to him. I had one other letter from Dave that I didn't reply to and then there were no more. Dad would never have approved of a friendship between Dave and me.

CHAPTER TWENTY-FIVE
Growing Up

That first Christmas, after moving back home, was the best ever. Dad gave us money to spend on whatever we wanted. He gave Ann, Lorraine and I £50 each. It seemed such a lot of money! We felt so rich! We all had a great time spending it down town. I felt really grown up spending the money on myself for the first time. I bought myself lots of new clothes. I couldn't remember the last time I had had new clothes. I always had Ann's old clothes passed down to me when she had grown out of them. After I grew out of them, they were handed down to the next one and so on down the family. I didn't seem to mind at the time, it was how things were done in our house. Ann had some nice clothes; I would look forward to her growing out of them so I would get to wear them. We were all used to having 'hand me downs' and extra special to be able buy the new clothes that no one else had worn before me.

Also, that Christmas, Mary's mum, who we called Nan, had bought us all a present. Ann got some perfume in a nice bottle and I got a gift-box set of 'Mum' deodorant that smelt lovely. I loved it. I hadn't started using deodorant until then as I never had the money to buy any. I didn't want to ask for it just in case I was told 'NO!' After starting to use it, I used it all the time. It was something that I never ever wanted to be without.

I felt as if I was changing and finally growing up; the tomboy in me was disappearing. The baseball boots were hanging up by the laces in my cupboard and were never worn again. I even started to wear tights for school, just like some of my school friends, who I had told just a couple of weeks earlier that I would never be seen wearing. 'American tan' was the most popular shade in our form, 5R. As soon as someone wore a different colour, we would all change to that same colour.

Although they felt strange to wear them at first, I soon got used to them and after a while I wouldn't wear anything else. I was shocked and surprised, one day, when Dad said that I had a nice pair of legs, after he noticed that I was wearing tights. This made me feel good. I had never heard Dad make a remark like that before, not even to Mary. I must have nice legs, if Dad said that I had. It made me more confident to wear them even more often. I believed Dad when he gave me that compliment. I tended to wear more skirts from then on and hardly wore jeans. I was becoming a 'lady' and was beginning to like the idea!

Although this seemed to be the best Christmas that I had ever had, just after Paul left home. This was sooner than we expected him to do. I thought he would leave to join the army but it was not to be.

Dad had gone to the pub one night and taken the car. He had too much to drink, so he had to tell Paul to drive the car home. He only had to drive the car around the corner to be at home. Paul had already had quite a few driving lessons and Dad was sure he would be able to drive the car the short distance home.

Paul had a couple of his mates with him and instead of going straight home in the car, they all decided to go on a little jaunt in the car around Bolton. Somehow Dad got to find out about this and Paul was beaten up quite badly again, by Dad. He was kicked and punched around the living room. His face was such a mess. He had black eyes, cut lips and bruises all over his body. His face was so swollen we couldn't recognise him.

He left home shortly after that and went to stay at Mum's house. From there, when he was old enough, he applied to join the army and was soon accepted. From then on, he had his army career. First was training at the army base in Sutton Coldfield. I was so proud of him joining the army and so was Mum. He had a photograph taken of him in his army uniform and he looked so smart. It had pride of place in Mum's living room, on top of the television. "This is my son," she would tell all her friends when they visited the house.

Paul soon got the chance to travel to different countries and even learned how to drive properly. He even drove tanks. We were all very proud of him and we would look forward to all the letters he sent, telling us about all the adventures he was having.

Ann was accepted by the nursing home and she too moved out from home to start her nurse's training at the hospital. She studied really hard, as always. She had lots of exams that she had to pass to complete her training. It was as if she was meant to be a nurse. She already looked like a nurse, when we saw her for the first time in her uniform. She wore a blue pinafore dress, which had a gold watch clipped on upside down to the front right-hand side of the lapel and a wide elasticated belt with a shiny silver buckle at the front. She had to wear a white hat that she had to make by folding stiff paper. This hat had a blue line across it to say that she had done one year's training. The lines across the hats would correspond with the number of years she had trained. The hat would be held on her head with lots of hair clips. Ann also wore a long black cape with a red lining and straps that would cross over her chest. She looked so dedicated. She reminded me of the project I had done at primary school about a woman called Florence Nightingale. She was the first woman who cared for the sick and wounded in the Crimean War many years ago and was known as 'The Lady with the Lamp' She was the first ever nurse.

It would take years of hard work for Ann before she would be fully qualified. I knew she would make a good nurse. I was going to miss her a lot.

CHAPTER TWENTY-SIX
Halbros Sportswear

In just three months' time I would be leaving school. I had no job to go to and I really didn't have a clue what I wanted to do. I didn't like the idea of leaving school without having a job to go to. I could always stay on at school for the sixth form but I didn't like that idea either. I was, however, beginning to think that staying on at school was what I would have to do.

I got off the bus before the school stop and decided to walk the rest of the way. I had plenty of time and knew that I wouldn't be late. On the way to school, I passed a factory called Halbros Sportswear. I knew it was a sewing factory and that they made sport-shirts and other sportswear. I was always good at sewing at school and I had even made myself a skirt once. I decided there and then to walk in and ask for a job.

I was nervous as I walked down a narrow, dark corridor towards a door, which had the word 'Office' on it. Further down the corridor, I could see lots of women sitting at large machines busily sewing. There was lots of noise and activity; people were rushing around carrying big bundles. To the right of where I was standing was a room with large machines, which were making the materials that the shirts were going to be made from. They were big round machines with lots of reels of cotton thread at the top. They were weaving the fabric. The fabric was coming out of the bottom of the machines. There were all sorts of different coloured fabrics; plain colours and striped. It was fascinating to watch and I could really see myself working there.

Excitedly, but still very nervous, I knocked on the office door. When I heard a man say, "Come in," I timidly, opened the door and popped my head around the door.

I could see a gentleman dressed in a suit, sitting behind his desk looking at some papers in front of him. I gently closed the door behind me. He peered up from above his spectacles and looked at me. I stepped closer to his desk. He asked me what he could do for me. With a shaky voice, I asked if there were any jobs going at his factory. I told him that I was about to leave school in a couple of months and would be interested in learning how to sew. He jumped up from behind his desk, smiled at me and said that his name was Mr John Mather. He asked me to follow him down the factory to see what he could do.

I was taken on a sort of tour around the factory and introduced to a lady that was the supervisor and would be the one to show me how to sew, if I was lucky enough to get a job. I felt strange walking around the factory, in front of all those busy workers, dressed in my school uniform but after the tour and to my amazement, I was offered a job there and then. I couldn't believe it!

I was taken back to the office and taken to see another lady, who worked in the office as a secretary, and I told her the date that I would be leaving school. She filled in some other forms and I had to sign my name on each one. She also told me the date I was to start work in the factory. I would be starting work just one week after leaving school in April.

I would just be fifteen and a half years' old and I would be working, earning my own money, just like Paul and Ann. I was so excited. I couldn't believe it. I was so happy. I felt on 'cloud nine' as I left the factory that day and rushed to school. I knew I was going to be late now, but I didn't care. I was so happy to have finally got a job. I couldn't believe that I had walked straight in there, all by myself and had the courage to ask for a job just like that. I was so pleased and so proud of myself.

When I arrived at school, I was quite a bit late and I had missed part of the maths lesson with Mr Wright. After first reporting to the office, to let them know why I was late, I hurried off to the maths lesson. I walked into the classroom and went over to the teacher's desk. Mr Wright was standing at the blackboard writing some maths questions. He turned to look at me arriving late for his lesson. He peered at me through his glasses and rubbed his chalk-dusted hands together as I told him I was sorry to be late. He told me to go and sit down and catch up with the work that they had been doing. He didn't look very pleased that I was late, and carried on by saying, as I sat down at my desk, "God help you when or if you ever get a job girl." He placed an emphasis on the 'if you ever.' I stood up and turned to him and smiled. I told him that I had just got a job and placed an emphasis on the 'sir'. I must have looked pretty pleased with myself as I sat back down at my desk. I know that I felt it.

After the lesson Mr Wright dismissed the class and asked me to stay to have a word with him. I thought that he was going to tell me off again for being late, but he didn't. He wanted me to tell him all about the job. I told him that I just walked into the factory and asked for a job. He seemed pleased that I had got it and wished me luck. I couldn't wait to get home and tell Dad and Mary all about my day.

A few weeks later, I was again told off at school. There was always some reason why I was being told off. I was told off at least once a day. Mostly it was for being too cheeky and answering back or talking in class. I was always doing that and running through the corridors in school. I was always rushing around; I couldn't help it. I was always late for lessons too. This time though, it was for something serious.

I had been caught smoking in the girl's toilets, with a bunch of other girls. I wasn't really a smoker, but I would try it when my friends did it and I smoked a few with Dave in the woods when we hung out there together. I was showing off and keeping in with the 'in' crowd at that time. Everyone did it. There were about six of us girls, all crammed into this small cubicle in the girl's toilets at break time. We were all having a laugh and a giggle and talking about boys as usual. We were also comparing the tattoos that some of us had done a few weeks before. We had all gathered outside the typing room at the top of the stairs with Indian ink and a compass. We dipped the tip of the compass into the ink and started to stick it into parts of our skin. I stuck it into my hand making a small black dot on the palm and then into my knee making another small blue dot; wiping away the blood afterwards. I didn't think that they would work but after a week, the wounds had healed, and I had two tattoos.

At home, I wore a plaster on my knee for ages, to cover the tattoo, so Dad wouldn't see it as he would have gone crazy. He commented one day that I seemed to be falling a lot on that knee. I just agreed with him and said how clumsy I was.

Lesley, one of the girls huddled in the toilet with us, lit up a cigarette. It was passed around to all of us. We all watched each other take a drag of the cigarette in turn.

Outside our locked cubicle, there was a lot of noise from other girls going in and out, noisily chatting away to each other. All at once the huge heavy toilet door opened and we could hear a teacher's voice shouting. It was Mrs Smalley. We were all horrified and tried to waft all the smoke from the cigarette away, with our hands. She knocked at our cubicle door and told us all to come out. Gingerly, we all appeared from the cubicle and stood in front of her. She asked us if we had been smoking and we told her that we hadn't. She didn't believe us, so she smelt our breath and sent us straight to the headmaster's office. We all had to wait outside his office for ages and then we were sent in one by one to speak to him.

As I waited outside the head's office, I was getting more and more scared of what was going to happen in there. Would he tell Dad? If Dad found out that I had been smoking, he would kill me. I sat there shaking. The other girls were coming out of his office, looking really worried at the thought of their parents finding out what they had been up to. I couldn't let my dad find out. I would be slaughtered. Soon it became my turn to speak to the head.

With tears in my eyes at the thought of what Dad would do to me when he found out, I walked into the office. Mr Hamer, the headmaster, was a very tall, stern looking man, with a loud deep voice, though not as loud as Dad's, but it still made people jump sometimes, when he shouted down the corridors as he caught people running instead of walking. He looked up from his desk and asked me for an explanation as to why I had been sent to his office. I admitted to him that I had been caught smoking in the toilets with the other girls. I told him I was only trying it, that it had made me cough and I would never do it again. I started to cry and begged him not to tell my dad. I couldn't stop crying and got really upset.

Mr Hamer stood up, came towards me and sat me down on a chair. I told him what Dad would do to me, if he found out that I had been smoking. I was becoming more and more upset at the thought. He was looking very concerned for me and then assured me that he wouldn't tell my dad. Instead, I had other duties to do around the school as a punishment. Litter duty for the whole week wasn't so bad really. It was better than Dad's punishment would have been, if he had found out.

The day I was leaving school was brilliant! All the school leavers from our year had one big party. We brought food and cola into school.

We prepared our own lunch in our classroom.

There were lots of tears and everyone was hugging each other. We all wrote messages of best wishes on each other's school shirts and signed our names. We also tore up all our school books. I didn't want to see another schoolbook, ever. We were all going our separate ways and didn't know whether we would see each other again, although there were lots of promises made that we would all meet up soon. We had taken our exams and had to report back to school in two months to see what our results were. I wasn't really bothered about collecting my results. I wasn't that confident that I had done well in them at all. It would have been an excuse for Dad to go mad at me if I hadn't done well, or as well as Ann had done. I had a job to go to and that was all that mattered to me at that time. This was the start of the rest of my life. I knew what I wanted to do. To work and earn a living and maybe get a flat of my own. Maybe I would meet someone, get married and start a family. That was my aim in life. My dream! My future.

CHAPTER TWENTY-SEVEN
Nan

The first time I ever met Nan, I wasn't sure that I liked her. It was when Dad married Mary. She was a stern looking woman, with short, black, tightly curled hair, that was going silver around the edges. She wore a pair of small round spectacles that rested on the end of her nose as she glared at people. I was scared stiff of her and wouldn't go near her for ages, but she was Mary's mum and Lorraine's grandma. They seemed to like her. I didn't think she liked us all that much. When we first met her, it was as if she only wanted to speak to Mary and Lorraine, when she visited as all the rest of us were made to go out and play out of her way.

I knew we had our own grandparents out there somewhere; I could still remember them. I used to love going to visit Mum's mum and dad. We would see quite a lot of them when we were all younger, but when Mum left us all, we didn't get to see them any more. In fact, we didn't get to see any of Mum's family again after she left. Dad's Dad had died a long time ago. He was never ever talked about by anyone. Dad's Mum was blind and deaf and living in a hospital. I met her a few times while she was there.

On one occasion we had all been taken to the hospital to visit her. All she could do was sit in an armchair for most of the day. She couldn't do much at all. She was sitting in an armchair, in a large room, with other old ladies, sitting in their chairs around the edge of the room. She was dressed in a floral dress that hung over her knees and showed the tops of her stocking that were rolled down just below her bony knees. She had a red wrinkled cardigan over her shoulders and an old pair of pink slippers on her feet that were dirty and stained. Her feet would shuffle backwards and forwards on the floor as she spoke to us. I could still remember the smell of the ward. There was no other smell like it. I couldn't describe it. It was horrible. I had never smelt that smell before. I didn't like it and wanted to leave. I didn't understand whether this old lady would know who we were or if she would remember us. I didn't have any other memories of her in any other place other than that hospital ward and I was always scared when we had to visit her there. She seemed so loud and frightening. We would all be taken one by one to her side. She would put her large arm around us and feel our faces with her fingers and squeeze us tightly. She smelt like the room — it was awful! We would kiss her on her cheek as she dribbled from the corner of her toothless mouth and we would try to tell her who we were. We had to write the letters of our names on her thin trembling hand. This was the only way to communicate with her. I felt sorry for her. She couldn't hear us or see what we looked like or see anyone else around her. She wouldn't and couldn't have known if there was someone else in the same room as her, unless they were sitting with her and touching her. She wouldn't have been able to see all the other ladies in that room, all sitting in their armchairs just like her. It was as if they were all waiting for something, staring into space and waiting, but not really knowing what they were waiting for. Maybe they were all waiting to die. She must have been so lonely.

Our grandma died a few years later, without ever leaving that hospital ward. This meant we now had no grandparents that we had contact with, so when Nan came into our lives it was as if she became our grandma as well as Lorraine's Nan. We now had a grandma, again. We had to call her nanna. I had not heard anyone called nanna before. It reminded me of a nanny goat.

I had to have regular visits to the dentist to have teeth taken out and have a brace fitted to straighten some of my teeth. Sometimes, I would have to have the whole day off school, if I was to be put to sleep to have teeth taken out.

On one occasion, after I had been put to sleep in the dentist chair, I was laughing as I woke up from the anaesthetic. The dentist asked me what I was laughing at, and I told him of the dream that I had just had, about a clown with a big red nose that came to visit our school and gave all the children large red rosy apples. I remember the dentist laughing with me.

A few weeks later, a clown, with a big red nose, did come to our school and gave all the children apples. I couldn't believe it; my dream had come true.

We would have to go to the dentist at Halliwell Health Centre, which was near to where Nan lived. We would always call in to visit her. Dad would have a cup of tea before taking me back to school. She used to look after her grandson, Andrew. He was a cute little boy with blond hair and very unusual eyes; one eye was deep blue and the other one was brown. I had never seen that before. I was fascinated and asked Nan why are his eyes different colours. She abruptly informed me, 'because they are!' He was only about two years old. On this visit he was sitting in a highchair and Nan was feeding him his dinner. Nan had been looking after Andrew since he was a baby, but when he was a bit older, he went back to live with his parents.

Nan was then on her own in that large house, which became too much for her, so she decided to move into a small flat on Park Road near the town centre. When she settled down in the flat, we all had to take it in turns to stay with her at her flat. This was at the weekend or during the holidays from school to try to make sure she wouldn't be so lonely.

When it was my turn, I hated it. I didn't want to go at all. She had no television, just a radio to listen to. She said she didn't like the television. It was too quiet and I had nothing to do there. I spent most of the time sitting on the front gate, swinging my legs in front of me, and watching the traffic driving past. The couple of days I spent there seemed like forever, I was so bored. Maybe I missed all the others or the routine and noise of our house, I didn't know, but I couldn't wait to get home.

When Nan finally took me home, she told Dad and Mary that I wasn't to stay at her flat any more because I was too moody. I wasn't moody. I was bored, that's all. I thought I was going to be in trouble, but Dad just looked at me and tutted. I lowered my head, embarrassed and left the room closing the door behind me. I secretly gave her the 'V' sign and pulled my tongue out at her from behind the door. I didn't care what she thought. I was glad that I was not going to be made to stop at her flat again. I didn't think that she liked me very much and I certainly didn't much like her either.

After Paul and Ann had moved out from our home, to my horror, Nan came to live with us. I had to move out of the bedroom that I had once shared with my big sister Ann and sleep in Lorraine's bedroom while Nan moved into mine. I didn't like that at all! I had to make her cups of tea with a spoonful of honey in. I always forgot to put the honey in.

One thing I liked about her was the war stories that she would tell. Now and again, usually when Dad was at the pub, Nan would tell us tales of the air raid shelters that she and her family had to hide in, to escape the bombs during the war. We would sit cosily in our nightdresses and dressing gowns, listening intensely until it was bedtime. If Dad came home drunk, we had to rush upstairs out of his way.

One night, Lorraine and I were woken up by a scratching sound. We didn't know what it was. It seemed to be coming from different areas around the bedroom. We spoke to Dad about it, but he hadn't heard anything that night and said that we were imagining it. We knew we weren't dreaming and for the next few nights the same scratching was heard in our room. Eventually, Mary heard the same scratching. It had disturbed her sleep too. She instantly knew what it was.

The next day she informed us that it was a mouse! Horrified, we listened as Dad told us that we had to find it and catch it. Nervous and excited at the same time, Lorraine and I raced upstairs and went in search of the mouse that had kept us awake for days. We searched cupboards, drawers, under beds and behind the wardrobe but we couldn't find that mouse.

Dad told us to search in the airing cupboard that was in his room because it was more likely to be in there where it was warm. The airing cupboard was full of sheets and towels, all folded and piled up at the side of a big round water tank. It was nice and warm in there. Cautiously, we began to take the bedding slowly out of the cupboard. We knew the little mouse would be hiding in there. Lorraine had a box ready and waiting to put it in when we caught it. As we neared the bottom of the cupboard, we heard a scuffling, which made us both scream and jump back. It was the mouse! We knew we had to catch it, so we moved nearer and removed another pile of bedding from the cupboard; we saw it. It was a small brown mouse with a long tail. It was so tiny and cute. I couldn't believe that this little thing had made all that noise in our bedroom for the last few nights. It was scurrying around in the cupboard trying to escape. Soon we had it cornered and caught it in the box.

"We've got it!" we called to Dad, securing the lid of the box tightly.

We rushed downstairs to show him. Mary screamed and rushed away from us as we appeared with the captured mouse. She screamed to us to keep it away from her, and Nan just took one look at me with those eyes of hers as if to say, 'Come near me with that if you dare!' Dad was laughing at Mary and slowly he lifted the lid slightly and peered inside. He told us that it was a field mouse from the farmland at the back of our house. To our horror he told us to put it in a plastic bag, take it in the garden and throw a brick on it. He said that it would come back if we let it go outside and there were millions of mice in the fields, so they wouldn't miss this one. We knew that we had to do what Dad said, so off we both went to the garden to do the deed. I thought Dad was right, but really all I wanted to do was to let that mouse loose in Nan's room instead. Whatever would she have thought of that? It would serve her right for taking my room.

CHAPTER TWENTY-EIGHT
Schooldays Over

The alarm clock was ringing waking me from my sleep. It was Monday morning and the first day of work for me. The clock said 6.30 am and I started work at eight am. Excitedly I jumped out of bed. I knew that today was going to be a day like no other. I was going to work. I couldn't wait. I looked into the bathroom mirror. The same face as the day before stared back at me. I still looked the same. I still felt the same, but I knew that things would never be the same again. I was not a schoolgirl any more. No more school uniform. No more homework. No more teachers telling me what to do!

The house was so quiet, and peaceful, as everyone was still in bed. At seven fifteen am, I was out through the front door, quietly pulling it shut behind me. I waited for the bus and looked down at myself. I was going to work! I even looked like a worker, in my pink overall, as I smiled to myself.

Last week I was wearing a school uniform and catching this bus to go to school, but today, only a week later I was in my working overall and catching the bus to go to work. The bag that once carried my school books and pencil case, was now carrying my lunch. I felt so proud and smiled to myself again as the bus pulled up in front of me. I was nervous and excited. I was now entering the big wide world. I had my dreams of where I wanted to be and this was just the beginning. This was to be the start of the rest of my life.

I jumped off the bus outside the factory, where I was about to start work as a sewing machinist. The factory-made rugby shirts and other sportswear for teams all over the country, and when I had been trained, I would be making them too.

I could hear the noises of the machines as I approached the entrance. There were two ladies standing in the doorway smoking cigarettes. I felt nervous and clumsy as I passed them and walked into the building. I made my way to the secretary's office who then showed me how to 'clock on' and 'off' at the start and end of each day. My card had already been prepared for me, with my name on the top. I had only ever seen my name at the top of my school books; this was so exciting! I had to place my card into a machine with a clock on the front, press a lever, pull the card out and place it in a slot at the side, with all the rest of the workers in the factory. This told the secretary the times that each worker had started and finished work, whenever anyone was late or had worked overtime. Somehow, I didn't think that there would be detentions if I was late for this job, I would probably just get sacked, so I shouldn't ever be late.

I was taken down a long thin corridor to see the supervisor. I had been introduced to her on the day that I had walked into the factory to ask for the job. Today, she would be training me on the sewing machine. When we were introduced again, she told me her name was Mary. I knew that I wouldn't forget that name, as it was my step-mothers name. She smiled as she showed me to the machine that I was to be working on. It was a lot bigger than the machines at school, which I was used to. There were rows of tables and benches in the long wide room, with ladies, who were all strangers to me, sitting at each machine working hard at what they were doing. Soon, I would be working alongside them all and they would no longer be strangers. The room was full of all the different sounds from the machines but above all that racket, the radio could still be heard playing the latest chart music. It was Radio One, I thought, as I tried to listen to Mary as she spoke about what I would have to do on the machine.

It was, of course, 'Bye, Bye Baby,' by the Bay City Rollers. I was distracted for a moment when the DJ said that it was still at number one, after three weeks.

Mary sat down at the machine and reached down by her side and pressed a red button. The machine began to make a whirring noise just like the other machines. It was scary at first; it was so much noisier than the machines I'd used at school. Mary began to show me how to use it and pointed to parts of the machine telling me what they were called and what they did. This included the lever that made the machine go backwards and the knee pad, which when you moved your leg to the side, lifted the foot up. It was so different from the machines I'd seen before and it seemed frightening to be learning it all. I didn't feel confident at all and wondered whether I would be able to do it. Mary picked up a scrap piece of material from the side, lifted the foot with her knee and placed the material underneath. She lowered the foot to hold the cloth and started to sew along the edge. Mary guided the fabric underneath the foot of the machine, with her thin fingers, with shiny nails. She then stitched straight to the end, turned it round and stitched it back to the other end. It looked so easy. She was talking to me all the time as she sewed, patiently explaining how the machine worked. She told me to keep the edge of the cloth in my mind's eye as I sewed as this would keep the stitching straight. I was watching and listening to her every word. It began to look a lot easier and I was beginning to feel a bit more confident.

Mary told me it was my turn to have a go. Nervous but confident, I sat down at the machine. I tried to remember everything that she had told me. I placed my feet on the treadle underneath the machine, lifted the foot with my knee and placed the material under the needle. I moved my knee away from the kneepad and let the foot lower onto the material to hold it in place. My feet were placed on the treadle in the way that she had shown me so I pressed down. The material then seemed to run off at a speed in front of me. It scared me and I jumped back in my chair. I moved my fingers away quickly from the vicious looking sharp needle. I didn't know what I had done wrong but Mary then said that I had pressed down too hard on the treadle with my feet. I was shaking as I rethreaded the needle. I tried again but it wasn't as easy as it had looked when Mary had done it.

After a few minutes, Mary left me to practise on my own for a while. I soon got used to the speed of the machine and got more and more confident. Every so often Mary would come back to me to see how I was doing. As my stitching got better and was in a straight line, Mary gave me different things to sew.

By ten am I was beginning to learn how to sew a rugby shirt, starting with the collar. A loud bell suddenly rang out over the factory and all the machines went silent. Mary came to me and switched my machine off and said that it was break time. All the ladies moved from behind their machines and went through the door at the other end of the building into the canteen. I followed Mary and joined the others for a cup of tea. We all sat around long tables. I was one of the workers now and it felt great.

Everyone was chattering between themselves and I was sitting listening to all their different conversations. I had been given a cup of tea with two sugars, by the lady in the kitchen. I didn't have to pay for it. I hadn't drunk tea before as we weren't allowed to drink it in our house. Dad would say that we weren't allowed tea or coffee, until we were fetching a wage into the house. I knew that in two weeks' time I would be fetching that wage into the house. After fifteen minutes, the bell rang again, and all the women got up and went back to their machines. The noise of the machines filled the room as they were all switched on again.

During the rest of the morning, my sewing improved more and more. I was making full collars, and I was getting faster and faster at completing them. I was beginning to enjoy myself and felt at ease with the work. I knew I could do it.

At 1pm the bell rang again, and all the women left their machines once more. Some women left the building; some went into the canteen. I switched off my machine and joined the others in the canteen. I had made sandwiches at home that morning, for my lunch, so I sat at the table with the others again. I smiled at some of the girls, who sat down with me but I was too shy and nervous to speak to any of them. Most of them seemed a lot older than I was. One girl looked really familiar, as if I had seen her before. I kept looking at her and at times she would be looking at me. I smiled, blushed and she smiled back. I was sure I had seen her before. She asked me if I had gone to Rivington. I nodded and she said that was where she knew me from. She began to tell me that she used to go to that school but was in the class above me and left school the year before I did. She said that she remembered me from school because I was always being told off by one of the teachers. I laughed, as I thought, yes, she was probably right, I was told off all the time at school as I was a bit cheeky sometimes. She looked familiar, but I didn't remember her name. She told me she was called Mandy so I told her I was called Maggie. We talked and talked as we ate our sandwiches, until the bell rang out again, after the hour-long lunchtime was over. She was lovely I thought and I was glad that I had made a friend at work. I liked her. She had curly blonde hair and green eyes and I hoped that we would become good friends.

Soon, my first day at work was over. I clocked off, at five o'clock and set off home. Although I was feeling exhausted (and my bottom ached from sitting down on that hard chair all day,) it had been a great day. I had really enjoyed it. I was looking forward to working again the next day, but I thought I would take a cushion to sit on, so that my bottom would not ache so much.

During the next few days, at work, Mandy and I spent a lot of time together. We found we had a lot in common. We were the same age, had gone to the same school and she had only just started at Halbros too. She had only started two months previously and had found it hard to use the machines at the beginning. She told me that she had been hopeless and couldn't do it at all. After only a few months though, she was making her own money. That was the term used to describe a worker that sewed beyond their target and earned extra money. She told me that she got paid more than me because she had finished her basic training and by then was making extra wages. I would be on a basic wage until I had finished my training. I had a couple of weeks to learn the job, before I started making my own money. I was worried about not being good enough to earn more than my basic wage, when I had finished my training. I knew though, that I would work hard and try to get my speed up on the machine. I was sure that I would be able to achieve the same as Mandy, and all the other ladies in the factory, with time.

The first week went by so quickly. I wasn't paid at the end of that week, as I had to work 'a week in hand'. At the end of my second week at work, which went by just as quickly, I was still enjoying it and learning very quickly. I was by then a lot faster on the machine and I knew exactly how many rugby shirts I had to make each day or each week to earn a decent wage. I was almost making enough, after only a couple of weeks, so I knew that I would be able to earn a good wage each week. At the end of the working day on Friday, Mary came around the factory with a plastic tray in her hands and gave everybody their wage for that week. I was very excited, as I watched her getting closer and closer to me. She arrived at my machine and placed the little brown envelope on the edge of my machine. I looked at her and smiled excitedly and then stared at my wage packet I had earned my first week's wage! Everybody rushed to open their wage packets, but I didn't dare to. I had to take that wage home unopened. Dad had already told me not to open it, so I didn't dare.

I was so excited as I travelled home on the bus that night, with this little brown envelope, which was my unopened wage packet. All the way home, I kept pulling it in and out of my pocket, just to look at it. I jumped off the bus and ran all the way home.

Excitedly, I rushed inside to where Dad was waiting, sitting in his armchair. He looked up at me and smiled like a Cheshire cat as I handed him my wages. I had never seen him smile like that before. He quickly opened it, pulled out the contents and placed it on the newspaper on his lap. He seemed to be as excited as I was. Dad picked up the piece of paper from my wage packet, which he told me was my wage slip. It showed the hours that I had worked and the amount of wage I had been paid. I had been paid a basic wage of £19.50. He told me to keep all the wage slips because I would need them. After certain deductions of tax and national insurance, whatever that was, I came home with £15.18. I had never had that sort of money before. I had earned every penny!

Dad looked at the wage slip and then put everything back into the packet. He passed it back to me. I looked at him and wondered what he was doing. He said that I could keep every penny of my first wage packet. My eyes widened and the big smile on my face grew bigger as I was wondering what to spend it all on. It was all mine; I was to keep all of it. Dad carried on explaining that next week's wage had to be tipped up and told me to be careful with the money and make it last. He also told me that I had to pay for my own dinners and bus fares for the following week. I assured him that I would be careful and looked across at Mary and smiled at her. She was smiling too and pleased for me that Dad had given me back my wage that I had worked so hard for. Dad was explaining that I should also save some, but as his words were drifting through my head, I was drifting into a dream world and already it was being spent.

All I could think about was that it would be Laura's fifth birthday in the next two weeks and I had never been able to buy her anything for her birthday before. I knew that I would be able to buy her something nice, for the first time, and I also knew just what she would want.

CHAPTER TWENTY-NINE
Laura's Birthday

"Happy birthday Laura!" I called to my little baby sister, as she rushed to me. She wasn't a baby any more. It was her fifth birthday. The last five years, since her birth on that bright sunny day of the third day of May 1970, had flown by.

Quite a lot had happened since then. I had grown up a lot. We all had. Jane and Andrea were still separated from the family, in children's homes; separated too, from each other in different parts of the country. They would not be with us to see Laura's birthday. Maureen still lived at Mum's house and hadn't come back since we all left two years ago. She would not be there that day either, nor would Paul, as he was in the army.

Ann was there as always. She would never miss the day. She hadn't missed any of Laura's birthdays, as I had while I lived at Mum's house, but this time I was back home again and could be with her on her birthday. Lorraine, Mary and Nan were there and Dad, of course.

I was holding Laura's present in my arms and was so excited because I knew I had bought what she had wanted for such a long time. I had the big box in my arms, all wrapped up in fancy, brightly coloured paper, waiting for her to rip it all off to reveal her present. I couldn't wait! "Happy birthday!" I said again as I handed her the gift.

The box was huge; almost too big for her to hold. Her eye's widened as she looked up at me. They were like two huge, shining saucers. Eagerly, falling to her knees on the floor, with the weight of the heavy parcel, she started to unwrap the surprise.

I had walked all through town, in and out of every toy store, until my feet ached, in search of that toy. I knew what she wanted and I had been determined to get it. I had been all over the market hall, the Co-op and in the other big department stores. They had all sold out of the toy.

Finally, I walked into Woolworth's, beginning to feel down and so tired when I saw what I wanted, displayed high on the shelf in front of me. All at once it was there. There were lots of them, all in a row on the top shelf. The store was packed. I was hot and my feet hurt as I queued up to pay for the gift. I was relieved and excited that I had bought this for her. I couldn't wait for her to see it.

Laura ripped at the wrapping paper quickly and discarded it behind her. There, in front of her sitting in the box was a 'Tiny Tears Doll'. She was dressed in a little, pink, cotton dress and matching pink, frilly socks. The doll had big blue eyes, with long eyelashes; they stared out at her from the box. Laura gasped in amazement and tried to lift the doll from the box, however the doll wouldn't budge. The doll was all fastened in with ties that had to be cut away with scissors.

Mary watched as the doll was released from the box and taken into Laura's arms. The doll also came with accessories; a dummy, a feeding bottle and another set of clothes. Laura climbed on the settee and started to feed her baby. She had loads of other dolls; big ones, small ones, all different sizes, but they were left in the toy box and never played with any more. This was her real baby doll; a 'Tiny Tears' that she named Betsy.

Betsy was special. She looked and felt like a real baby, and she was real to Laura. She had floppy arms and legs and when she was fed, with the bottle, she 'weed,' when you squeezed her leg. None of her other dolls could do that. Betsy went everywhere with Laura. She was sitting beside her at the dinner table while she ate and in her bed beside her while she slept. They were inseparable.

Mary had found some of Laura's old baby clothes in the attic and had given them to her for her baby. The doll was dressed and undressed and played with all day long. This was the first present I had bought for Laura. I felt good to have been able to do that for her with my own money. She loved that doll. She had lots of presents on her fifth birthday that year, but none as special as Betsy, her 'Tiny Tears Doll'.

CHAPTER THIRTY
A Brush with the Law

Over the next few months my time at work flew by. I was spending more time at work than at home. I was now a competent machinist and learning everything there was to know about the work that had to be done at Halbros. I loved to be at work and earning some money, although I didn't see much of it.

My wage packet, each week, was handed over to Dad, unopened of course. I was given fifty pence each day for bus fare to and from work and enough for a pasty from the pie shop. As I was now bringing money into the house, I was allowed a cooked meal at teatime, cooked for me by Mary, and a cup of tea to go with it, just like Dad.

I still had the usual chores to do around the house every day. This was hard at times, because I was so tired after a day at work, but it all had to be done without any complaining. We were used to it now and knew what had to be done each day, so we just got on with it. Inside I was longing and dreaming of the day that I would leave, move out and get a flat with my friend Mandy. I was tired from working but enjoyed every minute spent away from home. I was sick of all the chores with no appreciation. I was sick of the constant atmosphere at home; sick of the arguments and fights, most of all I was sick of the fear.

Mandy and I would sit on a wall outside work at dinner times, eating our pasties and custard tart. We would talk about what it would be like when we had our own place. We were planning everything from the furniture to who was going to do all the cooking. We already knew the colours we were going to have on the walls. I knew, deep inside, I would never be able to save up enough money to move into a flat on the small amount that Dad gave me.

He took most of my wages. I had babysitting jobs that paid me a little bit of extra money each week but that was always spent down at the 'The Rec' or for other little things that I needed, like deodorant and toiletries. There were things that I would buy myself, rather than embarrass myself by asking Dad or Mary to buy them for me. There wasn't much left to save at the end of the week. It was frustrating to me that I had to hand my wages over and didn't have anything to show for it, except a cooked meal each day instead of the 'usual on toast' and the fact that I was now allowed to drink a cup of tea at home.

If I had my own place, I would be able to do what I wanted with my wage. I knew I could earn more money at work, by putting more hours in if needed, but at that time there was just no point. Dad took it all, no matter how much I earned and brought home each week, in my unopened wage packet. I was hoping he would be saving some of it for when I was older, just as he advised me to do when he allowed me to keep my first wage packet.

Dad went down to the pub most nights and took Mary with him to the Tempest on Saturday nights. Lorraine and I were left to look after Laura. Previously, they had not gone out as often as they did at this time. Mary always dressed up. She wore makeup and had her hair done. She would smell of talcum powder and hair lacquer and Dad would put on a shirt and tie and splash his face with the 'Old Spice' cologne, from the funny shaped white bottle, with a picture of a ship on the front. They always looked happy to be going out together but within a few hours they would come home arguing. Lorraine and I would always make sure we were out of the way and in our beds by the time they got home.

Mandy and I talked a lot. She knew of the difficulties I had at home but still we dreamed of the future and hoped that one day our dreams might come true. Mandy had a boyfriend called Gary and would talk about what he was like. She had been seeing him for a few weeks. Her parents would not have approved of her seeing any boy, so she kept it a secret. She was always being told by her parents that she was far too young for any of that 'carry on' and she had to concentrate on her work. Mandy's parents were strict, but they had never hit her or her older sister Karen throughout their childhood. Why was our dad so cruel?

I was hoping that I would find another boyfriend soon. I was wondering if I would ever find anyone as nice as Dave, my first love. It had been ages since I'd last seen him. I would always remember his smile and the feeling I felt deep inside when I looked at him. I didn't know if it was 'true love' if that's the way 'it' should feel, I only knew that it felt so special at that time.

I had introduced Mandy to the 'The Rec', where Dave and I first met. We went twice a week and she loved it. Dave didn't seem to go any more; maybe he was still in prison. Mo and Kath didn't go any more either which was great. I didn't want to come into contact with them ever again.

Mandy and I joined the darts team at the club, as did most of the kids there. Neither of us had played before but it was fun. There were two teams; boys and girls mixed. Surprisingly, Mandy's team, along with my team, got into the semi-finals and then into the final. Our teams had to play each other to see who would win the trophy at the end. I couldn't believe that after beating everyone in the team there was only Mandy and I left. We had to play one another. We had three games each and played in front of the whole club. I was so nervous my hands were shaking as I threw each dart, but it was so exciting, playing in front of everyone. It was all on the last double score.

I threw shot after shot at that double but my darts just wouldn't go in. Mandy was soon ready to throw for her double, to win the match, as she had caught up to me so quickly. We were both on double one. The darts just wouldn't go in. To the cheers of everyone watching and to the relief of both Mandy and I, I got it. My dart went in double one. We were both getting a bit fed up of playing by this stage and thought we'd be there all night. We both hugged each other and cheered being glad it was all over. The trophy was mine. It was the second thing that I had won in my life. First, the book about Jesus, that I had won at Sunday school and now a dart's trophy. I was ecstatic.

While sitting on the wall outside our factory, having our usual chats during dinnertime, Mandy and I would get whistled at, by some of the lads that worked at the plastics factory next door. We would both blush, but I was sure it was Mandy that they were whistling at. She was so pretty with her blue eyes and blonde hair. I was just too plain. One lad from the plastic factory would walk by each day and say 'Hello.' We would giggle and turn away. One day we said hello back to him. It was he who blushed then. We thought this was hilarious and giggled even more.

After a while he joined us on the wall while he ate his dinner. I thought he fancied Mandy, but she thought that he fancied me. He told us his name was Robert and that he was nineteen. He was nice to talk to, but after a while neither of us thought that he was chatting us up and was sure that he was just being friendly. He talked about his girlfriend and his plans for marrying her one day. He was so sweet.

One sunny morning I met Mandy from her bus on Chorley New Road and we walked up Julia Street towards our factory. It was only seven-thirty am. We didn't have to clock on until eight am. Mandy couldn't wait to tell me about the events of the night before, when she was babysitting. Her boyfriend had 'tried it on' with her and she threw him out of the house and finished with him. She was so angry that he could think that she would do things like that when she had only known him a few weeks. She said she wouldn't go out with him again.

Suddenly, Robert drove past us, on his noisy motorbike, beeped his horn and made us both jump out of our skins. We screamed and shouted after him. He drove to the top of the street, turned around and came back down to us. He laughed at us and asked if we wanted a lift. We said no but then I changed my mind and asked him if I could have a 'backy.'

There was a back street at the top of the road and he told me that I could have a ride down there away from the main road. Nervous but excited at the same time, I jumped on the back and held on tightly around his waist. Mandy was waiting at the side of the pavement for her turn. With the wind blowing through my long dark hair, he sped off all the way down the back street and back again to where Mandy waited. It was all over in a second.

To our horror a policeman appeared from nowhere and stood there in front of us. I knew we were in deep trouble. The officer, all dressed in dark blue and wearing his helmet was standing right in front of us. He pointed his finger at Rob indicating that he should switch off the engine. Robert turned the key and we both got off the bike. The officer asked if I knew that it was illegal to ride on a motorcycle without a helmet. I said that I did and said I was sorry but as we were only in the back street, we didn't think it mattered. He raised his voice and started going on about how falling off the bike and getting injured would be just as easy down a back street as on the main roads. I wasn't worried about falling off, I just wanted a 'backy'.

After asking Robert all sorts of questions, the officer took out his notepad from his pocket, wrote down Robert's name and address and told him he was in big trouble. I could see the look of worry on his face. The policeman turned to me and asked for my name and address and told me that I would be hearing from the police station because it was an offence to travel any distance on a motor vehicle without a helmet. Robert was in trouble too for allowing me to get on the bike without a helmet. I was so scared. What would Dad say? I was about to get in trouble with the police. Dad would go mad. I didn't think we would get in trouble that early in the morning. Mandy looked on; she was looking just as scared as I was.

After the policeman had left, Robert put his helmet back on and drove to work. Mandy and I arrived at work a bit late that morning and had to explain ourselves to Mary, our supervisor, when we arrived. I was worried all day as to what I could possibly say to Dad when I got home.

At dinnertime, Robert told us how worried he was and that he could probably lose his licence and he wouldn't be able to drive. I told him how sorry I was that I had pestered him so much. How were we to know that the police were lurking around the corner? When I got home that night after work, Mary was in the kitchen preparing a shepherd's pie for tea. I stood at the side of her, as I always liked to do when she was cooking. I watched as she spooned the mashed potatoes on top of the mince, then with a fork, she made a pattern on the top. Her eyes never left the dish, until the top was finished while I informed her of the events of that morning. She seemed to be listening to what I was saying to her but after I'd finished, she just raised her eyebrows and made an 'ohm' noise from her mouth. She lit the grill and placed the pie dish under it to toast.

After a few minutes with no more response, she handed me the knives and forks for the table. I wasn't sure whether she would be telling Dad or even if she cared. I left the room, laid the table and went up to my room. Mary didn't tell Dad that evening as I had expected her to. It wasn't spoken about again from that day.

As the weeks went by, I forgot about the police officer and my brush with the law. Nothing else was mentioned. However, a couple of weeks later the postman delivered a letter addressed to me. In the top corner of the envelope was the word 'Police.' I was so lucky to be the first up out of bed that morning and got to see the letter before anyone else. I knew what it was about straight away. I quickly opened it. The letter spoke of the offence that was committed on that certain day, time and place. It continued…

'No more proceedings will be taken against you regarding this offence, but if your name comes to the attention of this police station again, this offence will be taken into consideration.'

It frightened the life out of me, but I was relieved that it wasn't being taken any further and I wasn't going to court. I had to read it over and over to make it sink in that I wasn't going to court. I was hoping that Robert would get a letter like that as well. I tried to convince myself that he would get the same letter too. I really hoped that he wouldn't lose his driving licence. I hid that letter in my purse and didn't tell Dad or Mary about it. I didn't really feel that they needed to know about it.

At work I showed the letter to Mandy; she was pleased. We hadn't seen Robert for a few days, so we weren't sure whether he had received a letter like mine or not. That same afternoon we found out that Robert had left the plastics factory to work somewhere else, so we never saw him again. I never knew what happened to him. I had no intention of having my name come before any police station ever again — I knew that for a fact! That would be my one and only brush with the law. To think that once upon a time I had wanted to be a policewoman but the black tights that all the police women wore had put me off. I couldn't ever see myself wearing black tights. Having that officer approach, as he did that morning really frightened me forever.

CHAPTER THIRTY-ONE
Silences and Cruel Stares

Oh no not again! I was suddenly awakened by the loud bang from the heavy wooden front door slamming shut. Every weekend was the same. Dad's drinking was getting worse. The fights were getting worse. Mary was getting really hurt.

After the rows, they would always make up. There may be no speaking or snipes for a few days. Sometimes we would hate to be around them because the atmosphere would be horrible. Dad would shout at us more when they were fighting. We would all try to stay out of their way until the argument was over and they had made up once again. When they had made up, Mary would sit on Dad's knee. They'd be kissing and cuddling each other. They'd be laughing together for a few days and Dad would buy Mary flowers and the house would seem a happy place to be. It didn't seem to last though.

After a few weeks' things would go back to the same way that it had always been and the fights would start again. Just recently though, when they fought, the making up afterwards, the kisses and cuddles and the laughter just didn't happen any more. Dad had smashed the glass vase that used to sit on the window sill, so there were no more flowers either. The house was quiet. No one talked. Not even Laura. She played with her toys, but she didn't speak. The house had a bad atmosphere all the time, full of tension. Dad seemed angry and ready to start a fight again at any time.

When Jane and Andrea visited at weekends, after the chores had been completed in silence, we all got out of the way either playing in the park or in the sheds outside. Jane and Andrea came home, from the children's homes most weekends, to spend some time with all of us together. Most of their time at home they rarely saw Dad or Mary. Dad would be out at work or just out and Mary would be shopping in the market hall on Saturdays. They spent most of their time with Laura and I down at the park just to keep out of Dad's way, especially if there had been some argument that weekend. Dad's voice was so loud when they argued. I would lie in my bed and cover my ears, but I would still hear him screaming at her. He would call her awful names. Mary would moan and scream, asking him to stop.

He was saying that Mary had looked at another man. He called her a 'liar' and a 'tart.' She cried. I heard another thud as he thumped her again. Bang! went the living-room door and smash went a beer bottle hitting the wall. Would it ever stop? I lay in my bed and put the pillow over my head; I could not stand to listen any more. It was going on and on. I was trembling. I could feel my heart beating so fast in my chest. He was going to kill her one day. Why did she stay?

I could hear Nan in the next room. She too had been woken again from yet another argument. She was up out of her bed. I hoped she wouldn't go down the stairs, as Dad would turn on her. She was an old lady. This time the row was getting louder and louder. It sounded like her daughter was getting really hurt this time. I was sure he would have woken the entire house.

I looked over to Lorraine's bed. I knew that she would have woken just like me and be listening to her mummy being beaten downstairs. Nan left her bedroom and went into the bathroom. Laura would have been awake too, but she had learned at an early age that she had to stay in bed and 'be' asleep, just as we all had. Nan left the bathroom and went back to her room. She slammed the door behind her in the hope that the arguing pair downstairs would hear her and quieten down but the row got louder and louder.

Another smash was heard as a picture fell from the wall. I could hear the struggle as Mary was pushed out of the living room and onto the stairs. It sounded like she stumbled as she was pushed. He was dragging her and pushing her. He was swearing and shouting at her to get up and get upstairs. I heard the fear in her voice as she pleaded with him to stop. She was at the top of the stairs by then and being punched and pushed towards their bedroom. With her cries ignored she was punched and bashed along the landing and into their bedroom. We could hear Mary, but we could do nothing. Some of his punches missed and he hit the door. He slammed the bedroom door shut and bolted it. Mary got punched again. I heard the thud and she pleaded with him once again to let her go.

There was a sound of breaking glass. That must have been the dressing table knocked over, breaking the mirror. Nan was up again now. She left her room and went to the door of Dad's bedroom. She couldn't stand to listen any more. She felt she must try and help her daughter. She tried the handle. She could hear the punches. She shouted, 'Terry let her go! Let her go! Leave her alone. She's had enough. Let her out!' She banged on the door but the slaps and punches to her daughter went on. She heard her daughter's cries, but he wouldn't let her go. Mary shouted to her mum and told her to go back to bed. She said that she was all right. We knew that she wasn't!

Reluctantly, after a few minutes, Nan went back to her bedroom. There was nothing she could do. There was nothing anyone could do. The fight went on. Dad was still swearing at Mary and calling her rude, disgusting names. He slapped her again and pushed her on to the bed. I could hear Mary pleading with him to get off her and let her go. The large wooden headboard banged against the wall loudly. She screamed, 'Let go! Let go! Stop!

Eventually, all went quiet. All we could hear was Mary's sobs. Had Dad fallen asleep… ? But it wasn't over. Dad started arguing with Mary again and wouldn't let her out of the bedroom. Mary shouted that she would get out of the window. He replied saying, "Oh you can, can you? Well go on then, get out of the window!' I heard him jump off the bed and drag her to the window.

The sash window was pulled down. I could hear the struggle. I couldn't believe it. What was he doing to her now? It sounded as if Dad was pushing Mary out of the window. Mary screamed, 'No Terry! No Terry, please!' My heart was thumping so loudly in my chest that I could almost hear it. Then silence. I couldn't hear Mary any more. Had he really pushed Mary through the window? I sat up in bed straining my ears. Where was she? I couldn't hear her any more? I was trembling. Lorraine was quiet, but I knew she would be lying awake listening in her bed next to mine. There were no whispers between us that may have been heard by him as they fought. We knew that we would all be awake and listening to every sound as soon as the front door was slammed when they came home from the pub. No one could possibly sleep through what was going on. We knew the signs. We knew each and every horrible sound.

Afterwards as always was the silence. We lay there and listened. Laura didn't come out of her room. She made no sound. No cry for her mummy. No whimper. Her mummy was being beaten in the room next to hers and she lay in her bed without making a single sound. I knew she must have been woken by the commotion, just as we always were. At five years old she had learned not to 'interfere' during their arguments, just as we had learned not to, at an early age, when Dad was beating our real mum.

I have always remembered it. I have forgotten nothing. It had never gone away. Would Laura always have these memories just as we had? Would Laura always have to listen to this for the rest of her childhood, just like we had done through ours? In the silent darkness of my room, I lay back on my pillow. Still with the echoes of her screams in my head I drifted off back to sleep.

I awoke the next morning with the sound of the door creaking as Laura tiptoed into our room. She slowly opened the door quietly and peered in. I quickly hid my head under the blankets, so she couldn't see me when she looked around the door. I heard her tiny familiar footsteps on the lino as she came closer to my bed. She tugged at my bedclothes softly whispering my name. Suddenly, I appeared from under the covers making her jump. 'Boo!' I whispered to her, trying not to wake Dad in the next room. She giggled oh so quietly as I lifted her up and across my bed and hugged her tightly. We snuggled together and I kissed her forehead gently. She giggled as I squeezed her tighter and tighter. The thoughts of last night flashed through my head. Did this little girl know what had happened to her mummy last night? The house was so quiet.

Lorraine stirred in her bed. She opened her beautiful blue eyes and looked over to us from across the room. She asked what the time was. I reached over for my alarm clock and told her that it was ten past eight. Laura jumped down from my bed, sat on the rug and reached under the bed for Lorraine's pencil box. She tipped the entire contents on to the rug as Lorraine jumped from her bed and collected them all up again. She told Laura that she was not allowed to play with the pens as they were for school. Handing her little sister, a sheet of paper, torn from her exercise book and a pencil, Lorraine climbed back into her bed. Laura continued contentedly scribbling while Nan left her bedroom next door and went downstairs.

The kettle whistling on the stove downstairs interrupted the silence of the house. There was a knock at the front door and Nan answered it. Whoever could that be that early on a Sunday morning, I thought? I tried to listen to who it might be, but all was quiet downstairs. It was too quiet. I got out of bed and after dressing I slowly made my way downstairs. I was hoping and praying that Dad hadn't really pushed Mary from the bedroom window. Hopefully it had just been a horrible dream. I hoped that they would have just drifted off to sleep while they argued.

I neared the bottom of the stairs and I could hear slightly muffled voices coming from inside the living room. With my ear to the door, I listened. I could hear Nan's voice and another person, but I couldn't tell who it was. I slowly opened the living-room door and popped my head around. I was just about to ask Nan if she wanted a cup of tea, when the shock of what I saw made me freeze.

Nan and Mary were standing in the corner of the room at the side of the window. Mary, startled, was rushing to pull down her nightdress. It was too late! I saw what she had been revealing to her mum. She was showing her what Dad had done to her the previous night. My eyes widened with shock as I looked at her as she straightened her nightdress. I saw the huge purple bruises and the deep scratches covering her back. I saw her face was swollen and discoloured and I saw the cuts on her lips. Our dad did all that. Tears filled my eyes. I was shaking. How could he do that to her? How could he keep doing that to her? Mary slowly bent holding onto the arm of the sofa and took a cigarette from the packet on the floor. With her hands visibly trembling she lit it with a match and rushed past me through to the kitchen.

Dad really had thrown her from the window. She was pushed out and on to one of the outbuildings. Luckily, that had saved her fall otherwise she would have landed on the concrete below. I was so relieved that Dad hadn't killed her.

Later that day I overheard Mary talking to Nan saying that the police had picked her up walking in the street late that night and took her to some refuge place for the night and had brought her back early that morning.

It was a quiet Sunday that day. Silence, as Mary cooked the Sunday dinner. Silence as the meal was eaten. Silence as Dad slept in his chair with his stomach full. I watched him sleep. His thick, shiny, black hair always combed back and held with Brylcreem. His head resting on the back of his armchair, very slowly sliding and dropping downwards and then jerking back again as he slept undisturbed. There had been apologies, gifts and bouquets from Dad on occasions when they had argued and times when Mary had forgiven him for his beatings upon her and they laughed together again for a short while, but not any more. There were no more apologies or flowers, just silences and cruel stares.

A few days later I came home after work and Mary, Nan and Lorraine had gone. All their clothes from their wardrobes had gone. Nan's room was bare. Her photographs from around her room were gone. These included photographs of the family she had left behind in Kent, when she moved to Bolton with Mary and Lorraine, all those years ago. They were all gone. Lorraine's toys were gone and her pencil box, that she kept under her bed was gone. She had gone just like our mum had gone.

Again, someone had been left behind and that someone was Laura. She had left her baby behind. Why had she left Laura behind with him? She loved her, why did she leave her — with him? Would she ever come back for her? She must. She couldn't leave her baby, could she? Maybe she would come back in a few days. She had left before and come back after a while. She must come back. She must come back... for Laura.

This time it felt different though. I didn't think Mary would come back. Not this time. She had had enough. I saw the state of her when he pushed her from that bedroom window. She couldn't take much more of that. He would have killed her one day.

Our real mum had left time and time again and didn't take any of her six children with her. She would always come back to him and to us. The day eventually came though when she didn't come back at all. She didn't come back to him or for any of us kids. Why? I couldn't understand.

As the days turned into weeks Mary didn't come back. She was gone forever. Dad was quiet. No questions were asked as usual. They were gone. Mary wouldn't suffer any more. Dad wouldn't make her cry any more. Dad would not hurt her any more. I would not hear her cries any more. She would still be crying though; I knew she would. She would be crying for her little baby girl.

The house was so empty.

CHAPTER THIRTY-TWO
Mary: My Hero

Over the next few weeks, it became clear that Mary wasn't coming back. I would probably never see her again. I missed her greatly and would cry myself to sleep some nights thinking of her. I was glad she was away from the terrible life she had with my dad, but I was sure she would still be living with the torture of not being with Laura. Laura was quiet. Dad was quiet. The house was too quiet.

Laura never asked any questions like 'Where's mummy?' or 'Will my mummy be coming back?' She was just too quiet; she played in her room all on her own or sat in front of the television watching 'Tom and Jerry 'cartoons.

Dad stayed off work to look after Laura for a long time after Mary left. There was no one else to look after her when she came home from school until Mrs D offered to take care of her whenever there was a need. Ann would come back home from the nurse's home as often as she could. Jane and Andrea would be home from their children's home most weekends, if they had behaved themselves throughout the week. They all helped to look after Laura when they could.

Andrea had put loads of weight on since she had been in care. She must have been fed properly in the children's home. At this time, she was thirteen years old and her boobs were enormous. She was wearing bras already, and they were almost as big as Mary's. I was so skinny, so I didn't think my boobs would ever grow that big. I wasn't wearing a bra at her age, and I really didn't think I needed one at that time either. They had changed from being like pimples to being like fried eggs, but I didn't care much really. I didn't want them at all. I hadn't forgotten that tomboy in me.

After a while, our house was full again at weekends. Jane and Andrea were allowed to come home from the children's home most weekends and they behaved themselves at our house too. They knew that they hadn't to put a foot wrong while Dad was around, knowing that the stick was still in the house. It was propped up in the kitchen at the side of the washing machine. Dad still used it when he used the washing machine, to push the clothes down into the scolding hot water. I wouldn't touch that thing when I did the washing. When I pulled the washing machine out to use it, I would let the stick fall to the floor and I'd kick it to one side out of sight with my foot. I hated to touch it. I would rather burn my hands in the scolding water than to touch that stick. It would make my stomach turn just to look at it, remembering all the damage and trauma that it had caused in Dad's hands. Dad never let my sisters forget that the stick was there, waiting, ready to use if they ever stepped out of line. For some strange reason, Jane and Andrea hoped that one day they would be allowed back home for good. Maybe they thought that Dad wouldn't hit them again with that stick if they left the children's home. I knew they would be very wrong to think that.

During the week the house was empty; Dad would be at work; Ann would be back at the nurse's home and I would spend as much time as I could at work. Some days I didn't want to go home at all. I would have preferred to stay at work all the time if I could. I was now making my own money, which meant that the more work I completed, the more I got paid, so my wages were growing every week. I didn't think I was a fully qualified machinist at that time though.

Mary, our supervisor, always said that if the needle went through your finger while you were working you were 'a fully qualified machinist'. We had seen a lot of the machinists damage their fingers in that way. Sometimes there would be blood everywhere. I laughed at her comment but was horrified at the thought of it. I would hate that to happen to me. I thought I would faint at the sight of blood. While we concentrated on our work in the factory one day, with Radio One broadcasting through the speakers, we all got distracted. We could hear a sound like a cat crying. It was so loud we thought that a cat was trapped in the factory somewhere. We all stopped working and listened carefully to try and hear where the sound was coming from. At the far end of the factory and on the bottom row of the machinists sat Janet, she'd only been working at the factory for a short time. She was sitting with her head leaning against her machine. The noise was coming from her direction. As Mary got nearer, she could tell that something was wrong.

Instinctively she knew what the matter was. Janet had caught her finger under the needle of the machine. It had gone straight through. It was her making the noises. Mary knew what to do and quickly released her finger from the machine. All of a sudden Janet slumped back in her chair and fainted. Mary tapped her face gently and she came around. Janet was carried off to the staff room to recover. She was now, I supposed, a fully qualified machinist. We all laughed about it for weeks until each of us in turn caught our finger under the machine. It wasn't so funny then!

At home, although I missed Mary and Lorraine a lot, I never missed Nan. I couldn't remember a time when I'd liked her. She always seemed to scare me, from the very first time I met her, at her house in Halliwell. When I went to stay for a week, during the school holidays, with her in her pokey little one roomed flat on Park Road, I hated every minute and sulked the whole time. I spent most of the week sitting on her front gate swinging backwards and forwards and missing my sisters. When she said that I wasn't allowed to stay with her again I was so glad. Most of all, I always thought that she disliked me. I could tell by the way she looked at me sometimes. I could feel it. The feeling was mutual; I didn't like her, and she didn't like me. I was glad that she had gone. I would not miss her.

Mary was never like her. She was nice, beautiful and kind and I learned so much from her, I would always have respect for her. It was just a pleasure to know her. Everything about her I would remember forever. I hoped that we would meet again one day. She was and always would be my hero. I would never understand why Dad treated her the way that he did or the fact that he treated our real mum in the same way until she too eventually left him. What did they do that made him do what he did to them both? When I was younger, I thought that all children were treated in the same way that we were. I also thought that all dads behaved like our dad towards mums. As I got older, I realised that I was wrong and realised that he was wrong too. As I grew up, I became more confused as to why it was happening, to us. We weren't all that badly behaved. Were we not wanted? I would never be able to understand the reason WHY. I wanted Mary to be my real mum. I loved her so much.

One day, Mandy and I were in the pie shop, during our dinner break from work, and while we were being served there was a tap on my shoulder. I turned around and it was my mum. My stomach turned over. I hadn't seen her in months. Not since I'd left her home on crutches. I felt awkward at first talking to her, but she was smiling and friendly as if she'd forgotten what had happened a few months before.

We stood outside the shop, after being served, and talked for a while. I told Mum I was working, that Mary had left and how things were at home. She was so shocked to hear what Dad had done to Mary and said that she had tried to warn her time and time again that Dad would never change. Mum was working in the local pub as a barmaid, so we couldn't talk for long. Mandy and I also had to rush back to work. She invited me to go to her house for tea that evening so I accepted.

After work that night I went down to Mum's house for tea as promised. I walked in through the back door, knocking on the door as I went in. The house had the smell of something good cooking on the stove and Mum was setting the table in the living room. I hung my coat up on a hook at the back of the door and walked into the kitchen.

Maureen was standing leaning against the kitchen door, sucking her thumb, and dressed only in a flimsy nightdress. Her thin frame showed through. She asked me what I was doing there but I ignored her and walked straight passed her into the lounge.

Mum said that she hadn't been to school as she hadn't been well. Mum always said that Maureen was 'delicate' or 'not well'. She had always been thin because she wasn't fed properly at Dad's; none of us were fed properly. All of us were always hungry. Presently she was at mums, eating more, but she was still not getting any fatter, so she really must have been ill or 'delicate' as Mum described it. She must have been too ill to go to school that day or to get dressed that day either. She didn't look ill to me. She looked how she had always looked except that presently she had broken one of her front teeth clean in half. She told me that she had fallen over in the swimming baths a few weeks previously. She had always been clumsy, like me.

During the meal, Mum and I talked, and she told me that they were all moving soon because the house was going to be knocked down. All the old terraced houses around the area had already been demolished. The old empty houses, at the back of our house, that we used to play in a year or so ago, had all gone. There was nothing left now except flat wasteland. The following year or possibly even sooner, Mum's house would go too. Mum also told me that Julie, our cousin, and her boyfriend Roy were having a baby. Mum was so excited with the news, when she was told and had already started to crochet something for the baby. Julie and Roy would surely have to get married soon with a baby on the way.

After tea, Mum brought out some photographs that she had taken of Julie and Roy. They appeared to be a really nice couple. Julie seemed so happy. Roy had a big, black, shiny motorbike. There was one photo taken outside, at the front of the house with Maureen sitting on Roy's bike. She was wearing a peach-coloured crocheted dress that Mum had made for her on her fifteenth birthday that July. The dress was beautiful. Maureen suited it really well. Mum had promised to make Maureen a crocheted dress ages ago and she'd kept that promise.

It was nice to see Mum again; I had missed her. I thought she hadn't cared about me when she threw me out of the house last year, but she was telling me that she loved me and she always had. She said she wanted me to come back home and live with her again. Why did she throw me out, if she cared so much? Was it because I was working at that time? Was that the reason why she wanted me to go back to live with her? She hugged me, kissed my cheek and made me promise that I would go back and see her again soon. I liked being hugged by her.

CHAPTER THIRTY-THREE
The Navada

Ann was spending more and more time at home, and Dad seemed to be spending most of his time away from the house, since Mary had left. We did not know where he went off to, but he went most days and did not tell us anything. We all preferred him not to be around really. We would have preferred it if he had never come back home at all. He could stay away forever if he wanted to, we wouldn't have minded at all. We could manage by ourselves and we certainly wouldn't miss him. It was down to Ann and me, most of the time, to look after things around the house, when Dad was away. Ann seemed to have taken Mary's role around the place. She tended to Laura as if she were her own. She did most of the cooking, which wasn't bad. She gave the orders for us to obey. She was very bossy! I didn't realise just how bossy she was until Mary left.

At the weekends, I did most of the laundry, in the old twin tub washing machine. I also did the ironing, as well as my normal chores, plus my full-time day job at the factory. The house had to be kept clean and tidy at all times. If there was anything out of place, Ann would tell us to shift it before Dad came home or else, we would be in for it. We were always reminded. We didn't need to be reminded; we already knew. How could we ever forget? We had experienced this all our lives.

Ann was busy studying too when she was at home. She had either got her head in a book or she was scribbling something down on paper in a folder. She was in her second year of training, to be a state registered nurse but she had lots of exams to pass before she would be fully qualified, so she was working very hard. I watched her sometimes and wished that I was as clever as her. You could tell just by looking at her that she was really intelligent. She had always been clever ever since primary school days. All her school reports were good. She had top marks in everything and always achieved a very high standard in behaviour.

In contrast, I was afraid to take my school reports home. Some of

Jane and Andrea's school reports were really bad and they got a good hiding when Dad saw them. So, every time I got my reports, I would read through them and I would tear out the pages with all the bad comments from the teachers. Comments like, "Could try harder!" (there were plenty of them) or comments such as, "I find Margaret to be a disruptive influence in class at times," and "Margaret is the class clown!" Dad never got to see any of those. I would hand him the, sometimes thin, school report and hope he didn't find out what I had done. He never did. I did try hard at school and enjoyed going. I had lots of homework from school, but it was always done at school during break times. I never took it home just in case Dad saw me doing it and wanted to see my work to see if it was done correctly. The memories of the beatings Jane suffered, when she was trying to read to him, flashed through my mind constantly, every day. I would never be as clever as Ann. I liked having some fun and making people laugh in class too, but that was never allowed. Ann was clever enough to pass her eleven plus exam and go to grammar school. I thought I had done well in the eleven plus exam and even though it was easy at the time, I really thought that I had passed but I hadn't.

I felt the disappointment from Dad that he never had with Ann. It was obvious to the rest of us that Dad was very proud of Ann. We even thought that she was his favourite. She never seemed to get told off or get into any trouble at home or punished in any way, unlike the rest of us and especially in the way Jane, Andrea and Paul were punished. I still looked up to her in many ways. Although she was only twelve months older than me, she seemed more grown up than me. She was more like a lady. She wore really nice clothes that she bought herself and she also had a proper boyfriend by this time. He would come to the house to pick her up and drop her off at home in his car. Lorraine and I would race to the window to try and catch a glimpse of him, but we were never quick enough so he remained a mystery. He took her on a date to the Navada, which was a skating rink in Bolton town centre. A pop group called 'Sweet Sensation' were appearing there on stage. I had never heard of them before but one of their records, 'Sad Sweet Dreamer,' got in the charts and was soon at number one and they were also on 'Top of the Pops'. When Ann saw 'Sweet Sensation' on our television, she screamed in delight that she had seen them at the Navada. She also told me she had a great time and what a really nice place the Navada was when she had been there. She explained that you had to swap your shoes for rollers skates and skate around a big dance floor with all sorts of dance music playing. She told me the skates weren't like the roller skates that we had when we were kids, they were white lace up boots with wheels attached to the bottom. I thought the place sounded wonderful and I really wished I could go there sometime.

A few weeks later, on a damp drizzly Saturday morning, my friend June and I were really excited to be waiting in the long queue outside the Navada Skating Rink on Spa Road. The queue went all the way up the road towards Queen's Park. Everyone in the queue seemed as excited as we were. I couldn't wait to get inside. There were people of all ages waiting to be admitted. There were little children from the age of about five and lots of adults. Some of them had brought their own skates. There were skates of all sorts of different sizes and colours, with bells and fancy brightly coloured ribbons attached. They had them tied together and hung over their shoulders. They weren't like the roller skates that we had at home. The old rusting ones that we would position an old Beano annual on top of, as a seat and have hours of fun riding down Sabden Brew, until I was almost squashed under the big wheels of the coal wagon, when it drove past the bottom of the hill right in front of me.

I remember everyone cheered as the long queue started to slowly move. The front doors had opened at last and the people were being admitted. June had been there before, so she knew what to do and where to go, when we went through the double glass doors and up to the little kiosk window to pay our admittance fee. We were given a coloured ticket for our skates and followed the others through another set of glass doors, into a corridor which led to the room where we could exchange our shoes for skates.

The loud pop music filled the place. Along the corridor were open doorways, which led through to a huge ballroom with a shiny wooden floor, as big as the one at the Palais. The floor was filling with the people from the queue, now wearing their skates and confidently skating around the floor to the music. I leaned against the wall and watched them all for a moment, mesmerized. They seemed to be skating so fast. Tiny little kids, of Laura's age, skating just as easily as the grown-ups. I thought that Laura would love it here. I would bring her next time. There were bright lights of many different colours, shining down from the very high ceiling. There were also large, spinning, silver mirrored balls, with lights shining on them, reflecting thousands of tiny lights onto the skaters below and all around the enormous hall. I looked on with a sense of awe at the vast place. June pulled at my coat and rushed me off to collect our skates.

After swapping our shoes for skates, we sat on the floor threading the laces through all the many eyelets of each boot. June was already up on her feet, skating around the carpeted area and ready to join the other skaters on the dance floor, before I'd even fastened up one boot. She held out her hand and pulled me to my feet. I was wobbling and very unsteady. I thought I was going to fall straight onto my bottom as soon as I got onto that floor. It wasn't as easy as it looked, it was far more difficult than skating at home. I practiced skating up and down the corridor, holding June's hand, for a while and after a short time, I was skating.

We slowly made our way through the swinging double doors that led into the ballroom. We stood behind the barriers and watched all the skaters. I held on tightly to the barrier and June left my side and joined the other skaters on the floor. She glided round the floor with ease. She made it look so easy. I watched her skate all the way around the floor. She then came to a stop right in front of me and she urged me onto the dance floor with her. I took hold of her hand and off we went. It was so scary because some skaters were going so fast past us and then there were the clumsy ones, that fell over right in front of us that we had to skate around without falling over them.

They never seemed to hurt themselves when they fell. They would just roll around on the floor laughing, until one of the skaters, wearing the red blazers, would go to help them to their feet. I was still a little unsteady, but it was great fun. Before long I was able to skate without holding onto June's hand and without falling over on to my behind. Just when I was feeling quite confident, the music faded, and everyone had to leave the dance floor.

The DJ stopped the music and told everyone to take their partners for the 'quickstep.' I remembered that the 'quickstep' was one of the dances that we were taught at school. However, I didn't think that it could be danced wearing roller skates. I stood by the barrier and watched as a few couples skated onto the floor and got into their positions. All the red blazer wearers were choosing their partners from the skaters behind the barriers and getting ready to skate. The skaters took their positions and the music began. The couples danced arm in arm and the spotlight shone around the room, looking for the best couple. The men spun their ladies around and danced with ease, at times skating backwards on one leg. It looked so romantic. It was just like watching Fred Astaire and Ginger Rodgers on television. The music stopped and the spotlight chose the best skaters. The spot light shone down on the chosen skaters, then a lady carrying a tray full of prizes, skated towards them. They were each awarded different prizes from the tray. The pop music would then continue and we joined all the other skaters on the floor once more and skated round to the latest pop chart records.

All too soon the skating session was over and it was time to leave the Navada. The time had gone by so quickly. I had enjoyed my first time at the 'Nav' and looked forward to the next time. It was great fun. I hoped that one day I would learn how to do the quick step like those skaters and skate really well like the red coats. Maybe I would even learn how to skate backwards. I would come again soon. Next time I would take Laura; I knew she would love it.

Over the next few weeks, I couldn't keep away from the Navada. I would even go there on my own sometimes, because there was always someone that I knew inside, so I was never on my own for long. The 'Nav' was open at night too, but not open for the younger children. There were more teenagers at the night sessions and the upstairs bar was open and served alcohol. The sessions lasted longer than the morning or afternoon sessions. Friday evening sessions were really good.

On Friday nights the Navada was full of good-looking boys, all showing off on their skates. Mandy and Janet from work, and I started going on Friday nights, if I wasn't babysitting, assuming I had managed to save enough money during the week. We were getting more and more confident on the skates every time we went. We were getting just as cocky as the boys were. We could speed around that floor. The three of us would always skate in a row with our arms linked together. We were even learning how to do the dances too. We would watch and try to follow each step of the other skaters. It wasn't long before we had picked it up.

During the evening session, the DJ would ask the lads to find a partner to skate with them. The floor would empty and gradually fill with skating couples. If you didn't have a partner you couldn't go on the floor. Mandy, Janet and I would stand at the barrier hoping someone would ask us to take part in the spotlight dance. After each slow romantic record stopped, the spotlight would be shone around the skaters and then settled to shine on one couple. A red coat would skate up to them and award them a prize. The DJ would play about five slow records and we would be watching and waiting to be chosen.

Mandy would always be picked first, then Janet, but I was never chosen. I would be sad for a while. Eventually, the slow music would stop, the 'best couples' would be picked and we would all join the skaters on the floor again.

When the DJ played the next record, it was one of the Bay City Roller's hits, so I soon cheered up. Still secretly I hoped that one day I would be chosen.

I met Janette Walsh in the 'Nav' one afternoon. I knew Janette from Smithills High School. I hadn't seen her for about three years, not since I was about thirteen. I had left Smithills to go and live with Mum in Horwich. We used to play together all the time at school. I remembered that we both disliked our Christian names that our parents had given us, so we decided to change them, and use our middle names while we were at school. Hers was Christine and mine was Linda and we wouldn't answer to anything else. She was still the same Janette, her face just the same, but she had grown up a lot. She said that I just looked exactly the same as I did when I was at school, except out of school uniform, of course. I knew I had grown up a bit on the inside, since school, but it wasn't all that noticeable on the outside, as it was on some other girls of my age. The tomboy in me had not completely gone.

Janette and I had a long chat over a cup of coffee in the café area. I told her I was working as a machinist and she informed me that she actually worked at the Navada. In fact, she continued to tell me that her parents owned it. I didn't believe her at first, but she told me it was a family business run by the Walsh family. All her family worked there;

her dad Graham, her mum, brother Chris and other family members. She pointed out some of her family, including her brother Chris, who was a red coat and skating around the floor. He was very good looking and a little older than Janette. I remembered him from school because all the girls used to fancy him. It seemed that the girls were still chasing him around by the way he was surrounded by them on that dance floor.

Janette's dad was wandering around in the corridors, as if he was patrolling. I often saw him standing on the balcony watching the skaters below. I had never seen him with any skates on his feet.

After our coffee we both went for a skate down on the floor. Janette was a really good skater. She tried to teach me how to skate backwards. She made it look so easy, but I still couldn't do it properly. I had no trouble at all at going forwards. We arranged to meet again at the 'Nav' the following Saturday morning when I intended to bring Laura. I had promised to bring her for weeks, but I needed to get more confident on the skates first, before I took her on the floor.

When Saturday morning arrived, Laura was so excited. Her little face was beaming when we went in. We went up to the counter, where we were to exchange our shoes for the skates. Laura was so tiny that she couldn't see over the top of the counter. I placed her tiny size three shoes on the counter and asked for the size of skates that she would need. The lady behind the counter looked at the small pair of shoes in front of her and said that the skates did not come in that small size.

My heart sank. I was really disappointed as I thought Laura wouldn't be able to skate that day. I was really looking forward to taking Laura skating. The lady looked over the counter down at Laura, smiled at her and said that she would have to wear her shoes inside the skates and fasten the laces up quite tight, so they would stay on her feet. To my relief, I could take Laura skating! The lady handed over the smallest pair of roller skates on the shelf; a size fives. I had never seen any so small.

We went over to the seating area to put them on. I put Laura's shoes back on her feet and placed the roller skates over the top. After lacing them up tightly, I stood her up. I held her steady for a moment to see if she could stand up straight in them. Her feet seemed so heavy. She pulled away from me and said that she could do it by herself. I watched her trying to skate across the carpeted area of the changing room. She was doing fine. Her skates looked so enormous on her tiny feet, but she hadn't fallen over. She was laughing and giggling at herself as she bumped into the walls as she came to a stop.

I decided to take her into the corridor to see if she was able to skate on the tiled floor. This was more of a struggle for her. She was sliding all over the place and couldn't keep upright at first. I held her hand tightly and told her to lean forward a little, as she skated, so that if she fell over, she wouldn't fall on to her bottom. This seemed to help her and she was soon skating up and down the corridor on her own. She learned a lot more quickly than I did on my first time here. She was eager to get on the dance floor with the other skaters, so holding her hand tightly we set off. Laura had the time of her life. She fell down a couple of times but didn't hurt herself at all. She would topple over and then just get right back on her feet again, giggling her head off carrying on trying to skate. I watched her like a hawk. She was having so much fun. Inside I was thinking of the time I took her out to a friend's house, when she was smaller and she fell over and bumped her head badly. That nightmare still haunted me. I should have looked after her better on that occasion. I should have held on to her hand more tightly. I felt it was my fault. I watched Laura and wouldn't let her leave my side. If she fell, I would catch her and keep her safe. I would have died if she had hurt herself again. We had our photographs taken in the little photograph kiosk, but when the strip of four little black and white photographs came out, from the front of the machine, I could only see the top of Laura's head, on a couple of them. She was so small. When she sat on the stool with me and looked through the little window, where the flash comes from, she had to stretch up. On one photograph I had lifted up her leg to show the size of the roller skate that she had to wear over the top of her shoe. It was a good photograph of the skate and in one corner of that photograph, part of Laura's tiny face could be seen. She was smiling. I loved to be with her and make her smile. I loved her so much!

CHAPTER THIRTY-FOUR
The First Date

We were getting really busy in the factory. There was a big demand for all the sportswear that we made. There were orders coming in from all over the world and we were all asked to do some overtime to cover them. As the demand grew more machinists had to be taken on. The work was harder at this time because the management had the 'time and motion' people in. There were men and women walking around with clipboards watching the work. They were timing people and then writing things down. Every part of the work that was done in the factory, from the weaving to the finished garment, was timed. They would know just how long it had taken to do a certain task. They then decided just how many garments had to be made in one day. It was a nervous time for everyone, as the mistakes made when sewing weren't timed. During the time that it took to do all the alterations there would be no payment. The basic wage was out, and we were only paid for the correct number of items done in each day. We had a target to work to and couldn't go below it. If we went over it, it was fine.

My wage packet was different every week. Some weeks I was below the target, and the supervisor had a word with me about my performance.

Over the next few weeks, there was to be a big change in the factory. The management had just purchased an old church building, that had stood next to our factory, disused for years. Builders had been brought in to start working on the alterations and the old church building was joined onto our factory. The toilets were modernised and redecorated. Above them on the second floor was the new ironing and packing area. Along a newly built corridor, joining the factory to the church, was to be our new canteen and a new kitchen area. At the other side of the factory, the thin partitioned walls, of the old existing kitchen and small canteen area, were taken down to extend the weaving room and the cutting rooms.

As the work on the factory got underway, I was becoming more aware of one of the builders. He was a tall, dark-haired lad of about nineteen. He was so good looking, I suppose, but I didn't really notice until all the other girls in the factory noticed that he was watching me all the time. He was a plumber working on the toilet and kitchen area. Every time I looked up from my machine, he seemed to be there looking across at me. He would be sitting in the canteen, at brew times too, and always staring. He seemed to be watching me all the time. It was becoming embarrassing. I would blush every time our eyes met. He would smile and wink at me all the time. All the other girls that noticed his looks and stares would giggle and tell me that he fancied me, which only made me blush even more. I couldn't understand why he was being so nice to me when there were so many other girls in the factory nicer than me.

Each tea break he would sit at our table and chat to us. I would sit listening to him talking but I was always too shy to speak to him. I'd blush every time he tried to talk to me. I didn't think he fancied me at all. I did secretly like him though. I thought he looked a bit too old for me. I was nearly seventeen and he looked about nineteen. He was called Kev.

After about a week of Kev trying to talk to me, one of his work mates came up to me in the factory, told me that Kev really did fancy me and wanted to take me out on a date. I just blushed again and laughed. I didn't believe him. Kev then asked one of my friends to ask me if I would have a night out with him.

At lunch times, in the canteen, Kev and I started to talk to each other. I soon agreed that I would have a night out with him. He seemed both delighted and shocked that I had said yes. It was as if he thought that I would have said no. I was so nervous. It was the first time anyone had asked me out on a proper date like this. I started to get a nice warm feeling inside. He was quite a pleasant person to talk to. He made me feel good.

I began to imagine what he would be dressed like on our date and how different he would look outside those baggy blue overalls. I wasn't sure about going to meet him on my own, because I still didn't know him all that well. We arranged that I would take my best friend Mandy along too and he would bring along one of his mates, Alan. The four of us would all go on the date together that Friday night. I called for Mandy that Friday night and together we both went off to meet them. We told ourselves that if they weren't there, we would go to the Nav instead, as we usually did on a Friday night. We had arranged to meet them at eight o'clock outside the factory. I was secretly hoping that they would be there, but I felt nervous and a little excited, as we got closer and closer to our rendezvous. This was all new to me. Although I had had boyfriends before, it had never been like this. I hadn't ever been asked out on a real date like this before. Yes, there had been Dave at school. That school girl thing and Dave from the Rec, who was now slowly disappearing from my mind. They didn't seem to matter right now. That schoolgirl part of my life had gone forever. This was real. It was happening. I wondered if this was the way things should be done? Had I really grown up, finally?

We arrived in Horwich at seven-thirty and decided to go to Ferretti's for a coffee, to kill a little time and try to steady our nerves, before we walked around to the factory to meet them. Mandy was feeling just as apprehensive as I was.

After the coffee, we made our way around to the front of the factory where we had arranged to meet up with them. In the distance, we could see two dark figures standing there. It was them. Neither of us could believe it. They had turned up. I was clutching on to Mandy's arm tightly, whispering to her that I could see them. With nervous giggles, we hugged each other as we neared them.

Kev looked so handsome. I couldn't believe it. This was not a dream it was real. I couldn't take my eyes off him. He looked so tall and handsome, just like a prince. So different from the scruffy overalls he wore at work. He wore black trousers and an open necked white checked shirt with the collar resting on the collar of his black leather jacket. I didn't even notice the friend that he had brought along to be Mandy's date for the evening. Kev introduced him to Mandy but at that moment for me there was a silence, except for the sound of my heart beating so fast. Everything around me disappeared. All I could see were Kev's dark eyes. I was brought back to reality as Kev touched my arm, leaned forward and said, "You look lovely!" and he kissed me gently on the cheek. There was a strange sensation in my stomach, as he whispered, "Shall we go?"

We walked aimlessly, not really knowing where we were going or what we were doing. I didn't care. I was arm in arm with Kev who seemed so charming and at that moment I felt so safe and so warm. I had never felt that before. I looked at Mandy and smiled. She had her arm linked through Alan's as they walked, deep in conversation. We walked and walked the length of Horwich, eventually returning to the factory where we had started. There was a pub called' The Old Original Bay Horse,' on the corner next door to our factory. Kev suggested that we went in for a drink. Mandy and I looked at each other and told him that we were too young to go in pubs and we'd probably get into trouble. He assured us that no one would know and said that we'd be all right. Feeling so safe, being with him, we went in.

There was a strong smell of beer as we walked through the door and lots of large men leaning against the bar drinking from large glasses. Unnoticed, we were guided to a corner table and sat down. Kev and Alan went to the bar for drinks and while they were gone, Mandy and I huddled together discussing our dates. Mandy quite liked Alan and I told her what I thought of Kev. Kev turned to look at us, winked at me and smiled as he waited for the drinks to be served. My stomach did a somersault. I thought that he was lovely. We were having such a good time, but felt a little uneasy about being in the pub. Neither of us had been in a pub drinking before. They soon arrived back with the drinks, two pints of beer and two half pint glasses of lager and lime and took their seats at the table next to us. Mandy and I had never drunk lager and lime before but remembered some of the girls at work say they drink it when they are on a night out. It was the only one we knew. It was a tasty drink, but we still felt increasingly uneasy with being in the pub. We had heard stories of the police raiding these pubs, looking for underage drinkers. We were underage and drinking in the pub. We really shouldn't have been there. I was fidgeting and looking towards the door every five minutes waiting and expecting a policeman to walk in. I felt uncomfortable. Kev sensed I was feeling this way. He took my hand and tried to reassure me, but after we had finished our drinks, we left. It was nine-thirty already. I had to be home by ten thirty, so we didn't have long before I had to be on that ten o'clock bus back to Bolton.

As we left the pub, Kev put his arm around my shoulder. Once again, I felt so secure in his arms. He apologised for taking us into the pub and said that the next time that he took me out he would take me somewhere nicer instead. I felt so happy. He wanted to take me out again. I was absolutely ecstatic. We carried on walking around together until it was time for Mandy and me to get our buses home and we found ourselves walking down the side street of the factory towards Chorley New Road. It was quite a dark street at night, but we both felt safe to be with our dates. Kev held me more tightly towards him as we were walking. He stopped and looked at me and said that he had had a lovely time. He kissed me on the lips. I pulled away for a moment and held my breath. Was this really happening? He kissed me again so tenderly. I just couldn't move. I didn't want him to stop. Kev said that he had wanted to kiss me all night. We leaned against a wall in the dark back street and held each other, kissing so passionately. I put my arms up inside his warm leather jacket and held him and didn't want to let him go. I looked for Mandy and Alan in the darkness and it seemed that they had the same idea as us, because they were right next to us in each other's arms too. We held each other and kissed until it was time to go home.

I was on cloud nine all that weekend! I just couldn't wait until Monday morning when I would get to see him again. I would close my eyes and see his dark eyes looking back at me, and feel the sensation in my stomach, when he had kissed me repeatedly.

The weekend seemed to last forever. At last, it was over and I was on my way to work. My stomach was turning over and over. I sat down at my machine and started work, awaiting his arrival. I heard the familiar whistle coming down the corridor. It was him. I looked up from my sewing and watched him. He had not brushed his hair and didn't look as if he had shaved that morning. One of his jacket pockets was torn but I thought he still looked handsome. He was holding on to some copper pipes balancing on his shoulder, and in his other hand was his large tatty toolbox. He looked tired and deep in thought. When his eyes met mine, his face seemed to light up. He smiled and winked at me just as he had done in the pub. I blushed and smiled back at him and was content to have seen him.

I continued my work. Did he really like me as much as he appeared to? I was beginning to like him a lot. Every break time and dinnertime were spent with Kev in the canteen. Both Mandy and I enjoyed his company. He made us laugh with all his corny jokes and the stories about his early plumbing days when he was training. We chatted about anything and everything. Kev told us that the work on the factory would soon be over and they would be moving on to their next job. I would miss him at work when their job was finished. I hoped to be seeing him again, as I expected him to ask me out again on another date.

I didn't have to wait long for another invitation, because during the week, on a dinner break in the canteen, he asked me out again on that Friday night.

Obviously, I said yes. We arranged to meet at the bus stop at the bottom of my street at eight o'clock. He got the bus from the town centre and was waiting to meet me. I got on the bus and he came to the front and paid my fare. It was so romantic. I felt so special. I was beginning to think that this lad liked me.

We had a lovely night in Horwich. He didn't take me in the pub, as he had promised not to, instead we sat in a café holding hands talking. Soon the night was over. We kissed all the way home on the bus. I thought that this might be the boy I would be taking home to meet Dad soon.

At work, the following week, Kev asked me out again; I agreed. Their job was to be over at the end of the week. The factory extension was completed, and it was time for them to move on to their next job. I wouldn't be seeing Kev again at work, but I was confident that we would still be seeing each other. It had been great to be at work the last couple of weeks. Seeing the factory change and especially seeing Kev every day.

We arranged to meet again at the bus stop, the same time as we had done the previous week. As always, I was so nervous. I was wearing a pale blue three-piece trouser suit that belonged to our Ann. It suited me and I looked so much more grown up, I thought. I hoped that Kev would think so too. I had told Ann all about Kev, when she was visiting at the weekend and she suggested that I borrow her suit — the same one that she had worn when she went on a date with one of her boyfriends. She looked beautiful wearing it. I was absolutely thrilled when she offered. I never thought she would though because she had got some really nice clothes and had paid a lot of money for them. I was always waiting for her to pass things down to me like she used to. She had her own money to spend on lots of nice things, but I still had to hand my wage over to Dad. I didn't see much of it, not enough to go out and spend on nice clothes.

I was waiting at the bus stop as usual just before seven forty-five pm. I was wondering whether he would like what I was wearing and beginning to panic a little thinking that he might not. He always said that I looked nice whenever we had met because he was so charming. What if one day he didn't like what I was wearing? I was beginning to get really nervous. The bus was slowly nearing the stop and I held my arm out for the bus to stop, expecting to see Kev sitting at the front of the bus as usual. He wasn't there! The doors opened. I looked inside at every seat, then stood back from the bus. The doors closed and the bus pulled away from the stop. The driver gave me a strange look when I didn't get on. I looked at my watch. Maybe the bus was early, I thought. Maybe he missed that one and would be on the next one.

I waited and waited for what seemed forever for that next bus to arrive but he wasn't on that one either. I stayed at that bus stop for two hours. Many buses passed by me and I felt more tearful after each one. I couldn't understand why he wasn't on any of them. I was cold. My legs ached. It was dark now and I was still standing there waiting for him. It was clear by then that he was not going to show up. What did I do wrong? With tears slowly filling my eyes I made my way back home. I thought he liked me. It was a miserable weekend and I was happy to be back at work in the factory on Monday. The work of the builders was done. They were gone. I never saw Kev again.

Mandy and I soon forgot about Kev and Alan. Our lives were too full to sit dreaming about what might have been. We were busy having fun, before he came into our lives, so we could do that again. Inside I hurt a little, wondering what went wrong between us. I didn't let it show at work in front of the other girls. Only Mandy knew how much I liked him. She was my best friend. She thought that, maybe, he was too old for me. I never knew his age. I didn't ask him how old he was. I thought he must have been about nineteen. Maybe she was right.

Mandy and I were very busy at work learning the different jobs and earning as much as we could each week. We saw each other most evenings after work. On Friday nights we would go to the Navada. If we didn't have much money, which was most of the time during the week, we would go to each other's houses or just simply wander around. I liked Mandy's family. She lived with her mum and dad in a really nice house. She had a bedroom of her own, that was filled with all her very own things. She had a wardrobe of her own; full of her own clothes. None of them had been passed down from her sister, as most of my things had. She used to share that room with her older sister, but she got married and had two children and moved across the road from the family home. They were a close, quiet family and I liked to visit Mandy's house more than she liked to visit mine.

Mandy fell in love with my baby sister Laura but she didn't like my dad at all as he scared her. They didn't say much to each other, she just wanted to keep out of his way. Dad didn't really say much to any of us any more, not since Mary left, he seemed to have become very quiet. He still didn't let us forget that we had chores to do every day, but sometimes it was days before I would hear him say something. Even then all he would say was "Do this!" or "Do that!"

Mandy listened to the stories of my family and the way things had been for us all. Sometimes she cried with me and just hated what we had been through. She had experienced a very different life than mine. I was beginning to realise that not all families were like mine and there were in fact, good and nice parents, who brought up their children without violence. Families who had shown their children love and kindness who had also laughed and played with them. I hadn't experienced this in my family. It was too late for our family. Childhood was over for us, but I knew that when I had children they would not live as we had lived. I knew that I had love within me, I could feel it. I loved Laura with all my heart and more. I loved my sisters and my brother. I loved my friends and I loved all animals, as indeed I still do. I knew that it was there, and I knew that I would never hurt another human being. Where had that love come from, I thought to myself? It hadn't been shown to me, so how could I feel all that love inside me, when all I had been raised on was violence and hatred?

One Friday night we returned to the Navada. We were becoming experts on our skates. For weeks I had skated around the floor, while the loud pop records were playing from the stage. In addition, I would stand behind the barrier watching the couples dancing to the slow, romantic, spotlight music. I waited in anticipation, for someone to choose me to dance with them, but week after week I would just stand and watch.

One night, I was standing in my usual place, just behind the barriers, in a dream world and watching all the skaters going round and round the floor. Dreaming, as usual, of this fine handsome prince that had chosen me. I imagined he was spinning me around and around on the floor. All of a sudden there right in front of me was Dave, with just the barriers between us. I hadn't seen Dave for ages, not since he stood me up in Bolton town centre.

I had found out that he had gone to prison. I also found out that he had made a girl pregnant. What was he doing here? He grabbed my arm and dragged me onto the dance floor. I couldn't believe it, after all this time of waiting to have a partner to dance with for the spotlight dance, someone had chosen me. When I had finally been chosen it was by him, my first love. My heart skipped a beat. I couldn't speak. I just looked at him. He smiled back at me and said that he had spotted me earlier, lost me and then found me again. He put his arm around my shoulder and we danced close together to the music. He took my hand and spun me around and under his arm. He held me tightly against him and we giggled. I couldn't believe I didn't fall over. He was such a good skater and he led me round and round the dance floor until the music stopped.

We stopped dancing and stood still while the spotlight shone around the room, looking for that winning couple. I looked up at Dave and he kissed me. We laughed and hugged each other. I couldn't believe that he was there. The spotlight chose a winner; it was us! We had been chosen. It made us both giggle even more as we went up to collect our prize.

As the rest of the spotlight dances continued, we went off the floor and sat at one of the tables to have a chat. It was really good to see him again after all this time. We sat holding hands and looking into each other's faces from across the table. He told me that he had been in prison for stealing a car. He told me that he was presently living with his sister Pat. I remembered the time when we babysat for Pat and her husband. She lived in Tonge Moor, with her husband Bill, and she had twin baby boys.

I recalled that I had asked Dad if I could stay at Mandy's house for the night. His reply was the usual grunt, as he continued to smoke his pipe. I actually stayed with Dave at his sister Pat's house. We babysat while they had a night out. When they got home it was late, they were quite tipsy and went straight up to their bed. Dave got undressed and got under the blanket on the settee, but I was too shy to get undressed. I switched off the light and took my skirt off, so it wouldn't get creased up. I lay down at the side of him, still dressed in my tights and a tee-shirt. There was no way I was taking anything else off.

As we snuggled up together it was clear what Dave wanted from me that night. He wanted us to have sex, but I was only just sixteen and so very shy. I told him no. I was not ready to lose my virginity at that point. I wasn't ready for anything else to happen between us. We kissed and giggled together then we fell asleep in each other's arms. I didn't think that Dave would have respected me if I had done 'it' with him. I knew that he had dated many other girls and one who was supposed to have had his baby. There was no way I wanted to get pregnant by him. Dad would have killed me. I didn't think Dad would have liked Dave. He had tattoos and I didn't think he had a job.

Shortly after, I heard that he had found himself in more trouble with the police. Dad wouldn't have liked us seeing each other if he had known that. He would have killed me if he had known that I had a boyfriend that had been in prison.

Back at the Nav, I asked Dave about the girl who had had his baby. He said that an old girlfriend had had a baby girl and called her Tracey. Apparently, they had moved away and he didn't see them any more. We chatted for some time, then Mandy came off the floor with her partner, to join us. Dave bought us all a coffee and we stayed chatting, altogether until closing time. After kissing me goodnight, Dave went his own way and Mandy and I went ours.

Each time we went back to the 'Nav,' I would look for Dave and expect him to jump out and surprise me again, like he had on that night, but we never saw him again. After a while, there was no more waiting alone behind the barriers for someone to dance with. There was always someone there that would drag us on the floor for the slow dances. However, there wasn't anyone who was as special as Dave. No one surprised me as much as he did on that night, we won the spotlight dance at the Navada. It was a special time that I would remember forever. I didn't expect to see him again.

It seemed such a happy time for Mandy and me. It seemed that when we weren't at work or at home, we would spread our wings and fly. We were free. We had fun. Having a partner for the slow spotlight dances didn't matter to us any more. If we didn't have a partner we would get on that floor, have a laugh and skate together. It was against the rules, but we didn't care. It soon started a trend because lots of other girls did it too. We would get fed up sometimes of being dragged on the floor by stupid annoying people who had had too much to drink, or who just couldn't skate. Also, the spotty ones with sweaty hands would insist on holding hands all the way through to the end of the record and then they would follow us around like lap dogs, as if they owned us, just because they had danced with us. Sometimes we had to run away and hide from lads, when they got too possessive and wouldn't leave us alone.

One night we had to hide away from two lads upstairs on the balcony area. Alcohol was being served up there in the bar, strictly to the over eighteens, so we shouldn't have been there. We sat at a corner table, giggling away and hiding from the two lads. When we peered over the balcony, we could see them below looking around trying to find us. It was so funny. We noticed that two red coats had spotted us, and they were heading up the stairs to shift us out of the bar. We jumped up and made our escape, still wearing our skates, and down the back-narrow stairway we went. There was a table across the doorway, blocking the exit to the staircase, so I swiftly climbed over it and scurried down the stairs.

When I had reached the bottom of the stairs I turned to see if Mandy was in hot pursuit behind me. What I saw made me roar with laughter, I nearly wet myself. Mandy was running down the stairs on her tiptoes looking like a ballet dancer in roller skates. She was coming down so fast that she nearly lost her balance and almost fell head over heels.

We both skated off and got lost in the crowds, relieved that we hadn't got caught and we were pleased that we had not broken our necks. The two lads never caught us either, but they must have soon forgotten us because later that evening we saw them trying to pester other people. We just giggled!

CHAPTER THIRTY-FIVE
Andrea's 'Accident'

One Saturday afternoon Dad got a telephone call from the children's home that Andrea was staying in. We hadn't been allowed to see her for a while. Both Jane and Andrea had been moved from one home to another not staying long at any of the homes. Now they had been separated and moved to different homes far away from each other. They weren't allowed home on weekend visits for a while. As usual, I was too afraid to ask any questions about them both. Dad never told us anything about them. I just presumed that they'd been naughty and weren't allowed any home leave.

After the phone call, I overheard Dad talking to Mrs Wainwright, next door, saying that Andrea was in hospital. Something had happened to her. The last time I had seen Andrea, I noticed that she had put on loads of weight and her bust was enormous. I remember thinking how lucky she was that she was being fed properly. I was nearly seventeen years old, working and still I went hungry sometimes. I was still too scared to ask if I could make something to eat. I was so skinny. Dad had been asked if he could go to see her as soon as he could. I presumed I would be looking after Laura while he went to see Andrea but instead Dad said I could go with him. Mrs Wainwright offered to look after Laura while we went over to the hospital.

Dad was quiet as he drove over there. I sat wondering what the matter with her was and what could have happened to cause her to be taken into Townley's Hospital in Farnworth, from the children's home miles away. He parked the car and we went into the hospital.

He seemed to know where he was going, so I followed closely behind along the long, wide corridors. There were lots of people walking around and through one open doorway I could see a woman sitting in a large leather chair, looking out of the window She was rocking backwards and forwards and she looked very strange. It reminded me of the ward that our grandmother was in.

We walked through two heavy double doors, which had the words 'Russell Ward' over the top of the doors and there she was, right in front of us. I was so shocked at what I saw. Andrea was so thin. I hardly recognised her. It was only a few months since I'd last seen her. She had put loads of weight on then; she was quite tubby. Now she had lost so much weight. How could this be? She also had a big gash on her forehead that had been stitched. Was this really our Andrea? I looked at her closely and it was as if she didn't recognise us. She was sitting on a bed with her head hanging forward and her arms hanging limp by her side. Her eyes were very heavy, as if she was trying to fall asleep.

A nurse in a dark blue uniform was holding her up trying to dress her. It was as if she would fall over if the nurse let go of her. She was dressed in a pink tee-shirt, a grey pleated skirt and white knee length socks. Dad and I stood watching her. She didn't even know we were there right in front of her. The nurse held on to Andrea, on the bed and was putting her thin, bandaged arms into a baggy woollen cardigan, fastening up the buttons. Andrea didn't look at us at all, she just stared at the floor. The nurse laid her down on the bed and she closed her eyes. I went over to her, sat on the edge of her bed and held her hand. I tried to talk to her and tell her to wake up, but it was as if she was fast asleep. Was she listening? She was bandaged all the way up her arms. Whatever had she done? Why was she here? She was only fourteen. What had they done to her? I had never seen her like this before. I wanted to cry. What had happened to her?

The nurse was quietly talking to Dad and telling him that our Andrea had been transferred to the hospital because she hadn't been eating properly and had collapsed several times. She told him that the injury to her head happened at the hospital that morning. She had got out of bed, fallen over and banged her head on the wooden cupboard. The nurse then told Dad that Andrea was under sedation. I overheard what the nurse was saying to Dad, but I was puzzled. I didn't really understand what it all meant.

Dad was taken outside the room to talk privately to the nurse, in the corridor. I couldn't hear what they were saying. I looked at Andrea sleeping. She looked like an angel. She was so pretty. Her jet-black curly hair had grown so long since I'd last seen her. It was shining with the ray of sunlight from the window as she lay sleeping. I stroked her warm forehead and tried to talk to her, but it seemed she just wanted to sleep. I didn't think that she knew I was there.

Dad came back into the room and we were asked by the nurse not to stay too long, as she was sedated and would be asleep for most of the day. We both sat looking at her sleeping for a while and then Dad said that we should go home. It didn't seem as if it was my sister there in that bed. I couldn't understand why she was sleeping in the afternoon. I wanted to ask Dad what 'sedation' meant and why the nurses wanted Andrea to sleep in the middle of the day.

On the way home in the car, I asked him what it all meant, and he told me that it was medicine that makes you go to sleep. He didn't shout. The rest of the journey home was silent. Andrea had been given medicine to make her go to sleep. Why? Why did they want her to go to sleep? It was only two o'clock in the afternoon. Why did she have those bandages on her arms? I didn't understand.

We saw her again at the hospital, when she seemed to be a bit better. She seemed quiet and didn't really want to say much to us. She just seemed as if she was going to burst into tears all the time. Her arms were bandaged but I still didn't know what she had done.

A few weeks later, when she was better, she was taken back to another children's home, so we didn't get to see her for a while. It was ages before she was allowed back home at weekends for visits.

There was something different about Andrea. She didn't seem the same Andrea. Something had happened to her and I was not sure what it was. She seemed quiet and withdrawn. Her arms were badly scarred all the way up. I asked her what had happened to her arms and she just said that she had cut herself, then pulled at her sleeve to cover the scars and ran off.

Each time I saw Mum, I would tell her how Andrea was and that she was getting better, although I still didn't really understand what had happened to her, when she was at the hospital. Mum hadn't seen Andrea for ages, not since she left and was put in the first of many children's homes all that time ago.

I saw Mum quite often during my dinner breaks from work or when she invited me for tea. She worked at the pub on most nights. After tea she would take her curlers out and back comb her hair and put some mascara on. She would get dressed up and go to work behind the bar at 'The Bay Horse.' She looked really nice, as she walked up the street arm in arm with Dave. They didn't go home until after twelve o'clock.

Every time I came to visit, the street looked more and more deserted as one by one the neighbours moved out and their houses got boarded up. The whole street had to be demolished along with all the other terraced houses in the surrounding area. Half of Julia Street and Wright Street had already been flattened. The derelict houses, that we used to play in when we were younger, were all gone.

Mum's neighbours and friends had moved out of their houses, the houses that had been their homes for years and years. Mum said it was so very sad to watch them all drive away never to be seen again. Mum had been happy there, but by that stage she had started packing getting ready for their move.

The council had offered Mum a house on Whitehall Lane in Blackrod and after looking at it, Mum accepted it. She was just waiting for the day when the council would send her a letter to say she could move into it. Mum was excited about the move and was looking forward to it. She was so excited that it had a big garden at the front and at the back. Mum liked her plants; she had a house full of them. She couldn't wait to start work in the gardens.

Excitedly, she told me that it had a proper bathroom upstairs, with a real bath. She said that it had been years since she had had a bath. She'd had to make do with the kitchen sink and the small shower cubicle, behind the kitchen door under the stairs.

A few weeks later, Mum's move went ahead. It didn't take her long to settle in to their new house. This was number 75 Whitehall Lane in Blackrod. It sounded so nice. I was looking forward to seeing it. I missed Mum. I didn't think I would miss her as much as I did, but I didn't get to see as much of her when she moved.

Before she moved, I would bump into her sometimes on the Lane in Horwich, when she was shopping, but I thought that in future she would shop in Blackrod.

I might not ever see her again, unless I went to find the new house and visit her. I didn't know whether she was still working at the pub or whether she would get another job in a Blackrod pub. Although I had Mum's new address, I still felt a little abandoned once again and sad that she had moved further away from me.

On the bus, going to work one morning, I didn't feel well at all. I was hot and my back ached. I knew it was just my 'monthlies' again. Every month was the same. I would have really bad stomach-ache, backache and bad headaches sometimes. When I was at home, I would just go to bed with a hot water bottle and go to sleep but when I was at work, I couldn't do that. I had to work through the agony. Usually, I could handle the pain and get through the day, but as the morning went on the pains got worse. I couldn't do my work properly and was running to the toilet every five minutes. I felt so unwell.

By eleven o'clock, I had turned a horrible shade of green. I couldn't keep out of the toilet. Mandy noticed I was missing from my machine and came to see if everything was all right. She knew I hadn't been feeling very well. She took one look at me and said that I looked awful. Mandy suggested that I go home. I was leaning over the sink being terribly sick. I didn't know where it was all coming from. I didn't seem to be getting any better. I felt absolutely awful and I was feeling worse every minute. I had never been as ill as this before and I had never had to have any time off work either. I thought I was going to pass out.

Mary the supervisor came into the toilets to see what we were doing. She had noticed that neither of us were at our machines and came in search of us, thinking that we would be messing about in the loos. She realised, as soon as she saw me that I was ill. She said that I was too ill to work and I must go home.

I was a bit unsteady on my feet, so she helped me out of toilets and back to my machine. I felt really embarrassed being so ill and having to walk through the factory in front of all the workers. They were all looking at me and saying that I looked bad. I hated being ill. I collected my bag and coat and left the building. I so wished Mum only lived around the corner again. I could have gone to her house. She would have made me better.

As I walked along Lee Lane towards the bus stop, I wasn't feeling any better. I felt that I couldn't get on a bus just in case I was sick again all over the bus. I didn't know what to do. I felt as if I was going to pass out. I realised that I had to ring Dad. We'd had a telephone installed at our house a few weeks previously and we had been given stern warnings as to what would happen if we were caught using it. I tried to remember the number but wasn't sure if I'd got it right. I remembered that there was a phone box outside the Bay Horse pub. Struggling to walk properly I made my way along the lane to the phone box. I was praying that he would be in and that I dialled the right number.

Letting out a sigh of relief, at hearing his voice, for the first time in my life I was so pleased that he was there. By this time, I was crying with the pain. I asked Dad if he would come to get me. I told him where I was. He told me to stay where I was and put the phone down.

I was hot and clammy. I felt so dizzy. I was sure I was going to faint. My head was throbbing. I leaned my aching head against the window of the telephone box. The glass was cold against my hot forehead. I watched and waited for Dad's car to come up the lane. I got a sharp pain in my stomach again and was sick all over the phone box. It wasn't long before Dad came to my 'rescue' and drove me home.

When we got home, I ran upstairs to the bathroom. I started to take my clothes off. I was so hot and sweaty. I sat on the toilet in just my bra and knickers and leaned over to be sick in the sink. I asked myself when it would stop? I couldn't stand it any more. Tears were streaming down my face as Dad pushed open the door and came into the bathroom. He handed me two white tablets and a glass of milk. I took the tablets with the milk and handed the glass back to him. What he said next shocked me. As he walked out of the bathroom he said, 'I hope you're not bloody pregnant!' Embarrassed that he had seen me in just my underwear and being so ill, I was then so shocked that he would ever think such a thing. I turned to him and straightforwardly stated, 'No, I'm still a virgin'. How could he possibly think that I could be pregnant? Could being so ill like this mean that you could be? Is that what it feels like when you are pregnant? If so, I didn't really think that I ever wanted to get pregnant. Worn out and so drained I left the bathroom and went across the hall to my bed and slept for the whole day.

The next day I was feeling much better and went back to work as usual. It's funny how women say that they are cursed each month. I didn't understand what they meant before but after that episode I did. I felt that we had all been cursed with having to put up with that every month. My monthlies were never again quite as bad as they were that day. I learned how to recognise the signs early enough and then take some medication before it got too bad. That way worked for me and I didn't have to take any more valuable time off work.

CHAPTER THIRTY-SIX
My Birthday

It was the 3rd of November 1975 and it was my seventeenth birthday. There were no birthday cards to open when I got up that morning, there never were. I didn't remember ever receiving any cards from anyone for any of my birthdays. None of us did, except Laura of course. She would get cards from her mum and Nan when they lived at our house, but since they had left there hadn't been any word from Laura's mum at all. We didn't know where she was or what had happened to her. I did hope she wouldn't forget Laura and that she would still send her birthday cards, as she grew older, so she wouldn't ever forget her mummy.

It had been Ann's eighteenth birthday last week and Dad had bought her a car. She had been having driving lessons, so when she passed her test there was a car waiting for her. An eighteenth birthday is supposed to be a special one I've heard, and it certainly was for Ann. The car must have cost a lot of money. She was so thrilled.

Dad shouted at her the other day because he was taking her for a drive, in her new car, and she pulled out without looking, in her mirrors. Another car nearly hit her.

I didn't have driving lessons as they seemed too scary to me. Ann must have been so brave. I was too scared to drive, particularly so if Dad was sitting in the passenger seat. That would have made me a nervous wreck and I wouldn't have been able to do it.

Even though it was my birthday that day I went off to work as usual. It was pouring down with rain and I was freezing. I didn't feel any older, I didn't look any older. As I took the bus to work, I sat looking out of the window at the cold, damp, miserable day. My mind wandered. I wondered what my seventeenth year would hold for me. I wondered whether I would get a proper boyfriend or whether Mandy and I would finally move out of our homes and get that brilliant flat that we had been dreaming of. The same old dreams ran through my mind but still seemed so far out of reach.

How would Dad be if I left home? There would be just him and Laura left in that big four bedroomed house. I didn't think that Jane and Andrea would ever be allowed to leave the children's homes and live back at home permanently. Ann came home now and again but I knew she was happy staying at the nurses' home.

I knew I would miss Laura, but she could always come and stay for tea, or even overnight, at our new flat so that I wouldn't miss any more of her growing up.

I smiled to myself as the daydream disappeared and I jumped back into the real world and went into the factory.

Mandy and Janet met me in the cloakroom. To my surprise they wished me 'Happy Birthday' and handed me birthday cards. I didn't expect that. I didn't think anyone would remember.

Leonard and Dorothy came over to me and gave me a card. They were married to each other and they had worked at the factory for years. Leonard worked in the cutting room and Dorothy worked in the ironing room. They were both lovely people and had been so friendly since I had worked there. I didn't expect so many cards. Everyone had been so nice.

Ida and Andrea, on the buttoning machines, also had birthday cards for me. They were big Shirley Bassey fans, and talked all the time of when they saw her in concert. Mum had one of her albums and I played it all the time at home.

We all went off to the pub for lunch, to celebrate my birthday — non-alcoholic drinks of course. We were still not old enough to drink alcohol and we would have been sacked if we had gone back to work smelling of beer. It was the best birthday that I had ever had.

Surprisingly, Dad later gave me some money and at the weekend Mandy and I went to the market hall and treated ourselves to some new clothes. That Saturday night we arranged to have a night out at the Navada skating rink, dressed up in our new clothes. I was wearing a new, striped green, cheesecloth blouse that tied in a knot at the waist and new corduroy jeans. Cheesecloth material was popular at the time. I felt really good dressed in the new clothes for a change and not in some of the clothes that Ann had passed down.

That night, at about seven o'clock, I was ready for our big night out. I was so excited. I had to pass Dad in the doorway as I left the house. I always hated doing that, as I expected a clip around the head as I passed by. By that stage, I would duck automatically. This time there wasn't the usual clip around the head. I turned back to him to say, 'See ya,' as I walked down the garden path. He was leaning in the doorway with his hands in his pockets. His smouldering pipe perched at the side of his mouth. He had a strange look on his face when I passed him. It was a look that I had not seen before, it was like a smile, which was unusual. I looked at him puzzled and asked him what was up. I then looked down over myself thinking that I had forgotten to fasten a button or that I had spilled something down my front. Taking one hand from his pocket and removing the pipe from his mouth as he spoke. He told me that nothing was wrong. A mouthful of tobacco smoke escaped above his head. He replaced his pipe between his lips and grinned that same strange grin again. I thought I liked that look. I hadn't seen it before. It made me think that he liked me. I smiled back.

I went across the road and waited for a number nineteen bus that would take me into town. I didn't have long to wait. I sat down and paid the conductor and when I looked out through the window, back towards our house, Dad was still standing there, leaning in the doorway, watching me with that same strange look on his face. He raised his arm and waved at me. I waved back. I couldn't believe it. He had never done that before. I had never seen him like that before. I liked it. I had a strange feeling inside, a nice feeling. I held my head up high. I felt special. Did he like me after all? Mandy and I had a great time that night.

Laura still loved going skating at the 'Nav' on Saturday mornings, although her tiny feet still didn't fit into the roller skates. As we were coming to the end of another year, I had saved up most of my babysitting money and bought her a pair of her very own brightly coloured Fisher Price roller skates. The skates were to be her Christmas present for 1975. They would extend as her tiny feet grew. She loved them. I was hoping that she would be able to wear them when we went to the 'Nav' in the new year, but we were told she wasn't allowed to wear them because they weren't the lace up boot type. She still had fun wearing them around the house. She would skate up and down our garden path really well. Her feet soon grew, and within the next year, she was able to wear the grown-up skates, as she called them.

CHAPTER THIRTY-SEVEN
1976

Throughout the December of 1975, every time I turned on the radio, all I heard was 'Bohemian Rhapsody' by Queen. I knew it word for word, but I was getting a bit fed up with it after a while. For a period of nine weeks, it had been at the top of the charts. I taped the top twenty from the radio every Sunday night, on my portable cassette tape recorder. I switched the tape off before Queen came on. I had it taped too many times by then. I didn't know how it had stayed at number one for so long.

The Bay City Rollers only had six weeks at the number one spot, with 'Bye, Bye Baby'. This had been released earlier that year and I believed it to be a far better record than 'Bohemian Rhapsody'. Everyone liked the 'Rollers' and everywhere you went the teenagers would be dressed like them. They would have tartan scarves tied around their wrists or sewn down the side of their jeans, just like I did. Every time their music would play everyone danced. I thought there was a possibility that their next release would stay at the top of the charts for a longer time. I was glad, when finally, Abba's 'Mamma Mia' knocked Queen off the top spot.

Back at our house, Dad had been having a big sort out. The bed with the big wooden headboard that he shared with Mary, and my mum before her, and all us six kids when we were smaller, was finally thrown out into the back garden. I was sure that old bed had belonged to Grandma and Granddad in the distant past. It had been around for years. Dad got the big axe from the shed, cut it up and burned it, along with its old mattress, on a big bonfire. Dad swapped all the bedrooms around. He had moved all his clothes and things into the largest front bedroom. It had been empty, since Lorraine left. Just four empty beds that used to be filled by Jane, Andrea, Maureen and Lorraine.

After Jane, Andrea and Maureen left, it became Lorraine and Laura's room. Filling the empty beds was Laura's collection of dolls. Jane and Andrea hadn't slept there for a long time. Andrea was still having some problems in the children's home and was not allowed to come back home. It seemed such a long time ago since we were all under one roof and we filled all those beds.

Dad said that I was to move all my things into his old room, so that Laura could have the room that I used to share with Ann. After Lorraine left, Laura wouldn't sleep in her own bedroom any more, she preferred to sleep in Ann's bed instead.

I hated Dad's old room. I didn't want to change. I didn't want to sleep in there. I could still hear the screams of Mary, from the night when Dad pushed her out of the window. How could I sleep in there with the nightmare of that night still haunting me? I had no choice. After moving my bed and things in there, I stood at the window looking out. The sound of the sash window being opened that night echoed through my mind. Tears were falling down my cheek. I was remembering that horrible night over and over again. I stared out at the shed roof below. The shed roof had stopped Mary from falling and probably from being killed on the concrete below. I thought of Mary, and I hoped that she was safe. More tears filled my eyes and I pulled the old tatty thin cotton curtains together. They were never opened again while I slept in that room. Even when Dad had agreed that I could redecorate the room, with some new brightly coloured yellow floral wallpaper and I had pinned up my entire collection of my favourite pop star posters, the nightmares didn't ever leave me.

I played my music with Donny Osmond smiling down at me from the wall and I drifted off into my own little dream world. The dream world of when I would leave this place for good. I would meet Mary again someday and invite her to my own house for tea. Wherever she was, I still cried for her.

Later that year, Dad bought a new television set. It was a colour television. We'd had the old one for years and it was black and white. The picture on the old one kept rolling around and Dad would bang it on the top sometimes. Dad had to put money in a black box at the back of the new television, to be able to watch the programmes.

It was so funny, when one day, he was watching football and the money ran out. He jumped up from his chair, his trousers falling down, almost showing his bottom, as he wrestled in his pockets for a coin before he missed any goals. He was muttering some swear words under his breath. The television eventually came back on and he went back to his chair clutching his trousers. He never saw me laughing at him from behind my 'Jackie' magazine. He looked so funny.

After the football had finished, the news came on. It was all about Harold Wilson resigning as Prime Minister. Everyone had been talking about it at work and the newspapers were full of it. He had been the leader of the Labour party for thirteen years. He had resigned; I didn't really care why. That seemed to be grown up stuff that I couldn't understand. James Callahan was to be the new Prime Minister.

I was eighteen in November 1976 and I would be old enough to vote, but I didn't really understand why we should or what all those politicians were supposed to be doing down there in London. I found it all so boring and I couldn't understand what they were going on about most of the time. I asked Dad if he went to vote and he said that he didn't. I thought I probably wouldn't either. All I knew about voting was that it was a secret. If you vote you haven't to tell anyone else who you voted for. I didn't know why. It seemed daft to me. I was too busy having fun. I didn't have enough time to sit and watch television. I hated being indoors. I would rather be hanging around with my friends than staying in.

Mandy came to my house quite a lot and we walked around the estate, chatting and messing about, with our friends. A lad called James and some of his mates, from Johnson Fold Avenue, had been hanging around with us on some nights. James kept asking me to go out with him and tried to put his arm around my shoulders, whenever we were walking around. I felt really embarrassed and didn't like it at all in front of all my friends. I told him to get off me and leave me alone. This happened all the time. I had known him most of my life. He had been in the same class at primary school. He left to go to Whitecroft and I went to Smithills. We had grown up together. It felt weird that he should be like this now. He was nice enough to talk to and we had a laugh together, but he had no chance if he thought I would go out with him. I just didn't fancy him at all. He had got blond curly hair that needed cutting and he was very chubby, in fact some people called him 'Billy Bunter' and he was a bit scruffy.

I remembered the way Dave made me feel when I used to see him, and James certainly didn't make me feel the same way that Dave did.

This was a boy I had known all my life. He used to chase all the girls around the playground and pull their hair. When I looked at James, I didn't have any of those feelings that were there for Dave.

One night he called for me. I was babysitting for Laura. Dad had gone to the pub again. The money had run out on the television, so I was sitting listening to my music, on my tape recorder and reading Ann's 'Jackie' magazine. She had brought this round the previous week. James and I chatted for a while on the doorstep. I was getting cold standing there on the doorstep on that chilly night, so I invited him in. Really, I shouldn't have done so, Dad would have gone mad if he had known. However, Laura was in bed fast asleep and James looked a bit lonely. He assured me that he wouldn't stay long. I made him a cup of coffee then we sat on the settee talking and listening to some music that I had taped from the radio. We had been chatting for a while, when he looked at me strangely and quickly lunged forward and tried to kiss me. I pulled away. There were tears in his eyes and he started to cry saying he was sorry. I couldn't understand this, a boy crying like that. I had never seen a boy crying before. Not even my brother Paul cried after one of Dad's beatings.

With red bloodshot eyes, James was saying that he loved me and wanted to be my boyfriend. It was strange to watch and quite funny, but I tried my hardest not to laugh because I could tell he was really embarrassed and serious at what he was saying. He was holding my hands tightly. I put my arms around him and held him to try and comfort him. We kissed. He kissed my face and my neck, and we held each other tightly. He was so sweet I never imagined that he could have been the gentleman that he proved to be that evening. I was beginning to think that he could be my boyfriend. He had been there all my life, just around the corner. I looked at the clock, it was getting a bit late, so I began to panic. I didn't want Dad to come home from the pub and find James there, so I said that he had to leave. He left after a long kiss goodbye on the doorstep. However, there were no butterflies dancing around in my tummy as there had been when Dave kissed me.

That weekend, Jane and Andrea had returned from the children's homes for a visit. We hadn't seen them for a few weeks, with all the problems that they had been causing at their homes. It was great to see them again. While we all sat and talked about how we all were and what we had been doing, in the weeks we had been apart, my mind was elsewhere. I was confused about James. I let him kiss me, but I didn't fancy him. He was not ugly, but I just didn't fancy him. I couldn't understand why I kissed him or why I let him kiss me. I couldn't understand why he cried.

I had done most of my chores that Saturday morning when Mandy called for me. I was doing the laundry in the kitchen when she arrived, so when I was pegging out the washing, in the back garden, I began to tell her what had happened the night before with James. She had an excited look on her face as she listened to all the 'goss.' She said that she thought he was cute, but she knew I didn't fancy him at all, not like I did with Dave. Her face changed, and she grabbed me and pulled at the collar of my blouse. Her eyes widened, and a look of shock came on her face. "Did he do that?" she asked looking at my neck. I didn't understand what she was going on about and I went back inside to look in the mirror that was leant against the window frame in the kitchen. What was it that had shocked her so much? To my horror there was a massive "love bite," as Mandy called it, on my neck. James must have done that last night I told her. I didn't know how. I have seen some girls at school with them and there was a woman at work who had always got them on her neck. I didn't really understand how or why they got there, but I had never had one of those before. How did he do that? It looked disgusting. Why did he do that? Did it mean that because they are called "love bites" you had to be "in love" before you could have one on your neck? I was not "in love" so why had I got one?

Mandy told me that she once had one and got told off by her mum. She said that if you put toothpaste on them, they go away. I hurried upstairs before Dad could see it and plastered the toothpaste on it and covered it up completely. It was a good job that Mandy saw it before anyone else did.

Later that day, after peanut butter butties for dinner, Mandy and I suggested we all go for a walk down the park. I asked if Andrea and Jane wanted to come with us. They said yes, and as always, we would be taking Laura, as she loved it in the park.

Dad was sitting in his armchair smoking his pipe and watching the television. He took one look at me, threw his pipe in the ashtray that was on the floor and shot out of his chair like a bullet. He made me jump. I ran and cowered at the other side of the room, wondering what I had done wrong. He grabbed hold of my clothes and shook me so hard. He lifted me right up off the floor and banged the back of my head on the wall. I could hear my blouse ripping under my arm. I didn't know what I had done wrong. He pinned me against the wall and shouted at me. I couldn't understand what he was saying to me, but remember the smell of the stale tobacco on his breath. I remembered; he must have noticed the 'love bite'. I thought he wouldn't be able to see it under all that toothpaste, but it must have rubbed off on my collar.

Jane and Andrea both looked on. Mandy was standing in the doorway in disbelief at what she was seeing. She knew what Dad was like, having heard the scary stories, but now she had seen what he was like with her own eyes. He tossed me across the room like a rag doll. I went sailing into Mandy, almost knocking her over. I was too frightened to hear what he was shouting. I scrambled to my feet and ran outside with Mandy.

Walking down the street I cried and cried, "I hate him! I hate him!" I didn't want to be there any more. I wanted to leave. Mandy tried her best to comfort me. She held my hand tightly. I was shaking. She was shaking. Dad had scared her too. She cried with me. She told me she would never, ever come to my house again. I didn't want to live there any more. But where could I go? Mandy and I didn't have the money necessary to find a place of our own. I was going to leave. I would not stay there. I had to get out.

We both sat on a park bench for hours. I didn't want to go home. After Mandy went home, I wandered around thinking of what I could do and where I could go. My mind was blank. I didn't know what to do or where to go. I thought of Mary. I would have gone to her if I knew where she was. I really wanted to run away and never come back. It was getting darker and darker and I had no choice but to go back home that night. I walked in through the back door and went straight upstairs to my bed crying myself to sleep. Dad never spoke to me at all the next day, which was fine by me, I didn't want to speak to him either. I did the family's ironing in my room that day and stayed there for most of the time just to keep out of his way. I knew that Mary would have let me live with her, I knew that she would. I couldn't stay there any longer. I had to go.

It was a relief to get back to work that Monday morning. All weekend I had been thinking of how I could leave home, then Mandy suggested that I go back to live with my real mum. That thought hadn't crossed my mind because of the way she was when she threw me out last time. I didn't think I would be able to go back there. Mum had hinted to me several times that she wanted me to go back living with her. I still thought it was just because I was working at that time and she could do with my wages. I wanted to keep my own wages as I had worked hard for them, not give them away to someone else.

That week flew by. Mandy and I kept busy during our lunch hours. We would buy a pasty from the local pie shop for our lunch and tuck into it as we walked around the main streets of Horwich. We would enquire in all the local shops for anyone who knew of a flat to rent. We didn't have much luck and grew more and more disappointed every day. Everyone we spoke to wanted to rent flats to over eighteen-year-olds. We both had a few more months to wait before we were eighteen. Even when we turned eighteen it was possible that we would not find a flat to rent in this area. We wanted to be close to work but we had been told that all the flats in the area had been occupied. I felt as if our dreams of finding our own place were being deflated. I couldn't stay at Dad's any longer; I had to get out of there. I decided I would go to Blackrod, at the weekend and talk to Mum and ask her if I could go back to live with her.

CHAPTER THIRTY-EIGHT
Mum's Recalled Nightmares

"...That was when he was having an affair with a woman called Marianne." Mum said with tears in her eyes and her hands visibly shaking as she took a drag on her cigarette, recalling the time when she found out about another one of Dad's secret affairs. At the time she had realised what had been going on with them both. Mum bravely confronted Dad, after she had seen their reflection in the mirror on the kitchen wall, they were kissing each other in the kitchen.

Mum said, Dad was like a maniac. There was a terrible fight in the house. Things got broken as he pushed her around. He dragged her outside into the sidecar of his beloved motorbike and drove off with her. She recalled that he drove her around Bolton for what seemed like hours on his black shiny motorbike, speeding around every bend in the road. Where he was driving her, she didn't know. She was sitting petrified in the sidecar of his pride and joy listening to him shouting at her until her ears hurt. He told her about the nasty horrible things he was going to do to her when they returned home.

She remembered how she was sitting frightened to death while he drove really fast round and round the roundabout at the top of Moss Bank Way. He did this time and time again until she was sick. He would continue the fight when they arrived home. I remembered those noises, then, after the fight was over there was awful silences. I could still remember the times when I was a lot younger when we all lived at Shackleton Grove. Dad would often take Mum for a long drive, on his big black motorbike and she would always be sitting in the sidecar.

Mum always wore her brightly coloured headscarf so that her hair wouldn't blow too much in the wind. She would sometimes be bleeding, and I could tell that she had been crying behind her dark glasses when she came back from those motorbike rides. I could never understand why.

Dad would spend hours in the garden polishing the chrome until it shone and sparkled in the sunshine. We would have been in serious trouble if any of us had gone near that bike after he had polished it.

Mum and I were sitting in the garden of her new house in Blackrod. It was the end of April and the sun was already belting down. The sky was so blue. It was a gorgeous day. Mum had planted lots of flowers in her new garden and she knew the names of every flower and plant she had planted. It was only early spring and already it looked beautiful in the warm sunshine.

I had finally left Dad's house a few days previously and moved in with Mum again in Blackrod. I just packed my small bag of belongings together and left. I never wanted to go back there ever again. I would go back to see Laura of course when Dad was not around, but if it wasn't for her, I would never go back. I was too scared to tell him I was leaving. I never even left him a note. I didn't think he would care though. He probably wouldn't even notice that I had gone. Someone else would have to do the ironing on Sundays. Mum and I were sitting on a tartan blanket, relaxing in the warm sunshine, with the small transistor radio blasting out. Maureen was out somewhere with her boyfriend so Mum and I talked over bacon butties and a nice cup of tea from a teapot. Mum's cups of tea from the teapot were so nice. Mum had never really talked to me before about why she had left Dad. She had told us bits and pieces, but she said that now I was old enough to know what had really happened.

All morning she had been telling me the stories of when she lived with Dad and the things that he used to do to her. Most of them I could remember. When I was younger, I couldn't understand why she would come back home in such a state when she had been on a bike ride with Dad. As Mum explained it, it all became clear. It was because Dad had hit her. They would have a fight about one thing or another, Mum said. They would argue and he would punch her.

I could remember everything from the time when I was only about four years old. I was lying in my bed listening when Dad threw our mum down the stairs. Whenever this happened, Mum would be gone the following morning, only to return a few days when the bruises had faded. Even before I was born there were so many more nightmares for Mum that happened long before then that I clearly had no memory of. Even before they got married, there were big arguments and horrific fights. Mum recalled another nightmare of the past.

After I was born, she soon fell pregnant again. On one occasion Dad's morning toast wasn't warm enough, so she was beaten. Later that day while Dad was at work, I was just a baby sitting in my pram at the end of the yard. My brother and sister played happily around the cobbled yard unaware of what was happening to their mummy in that cold damp toilet further down the yard. She was losing her baby. When Dad saw what had happened, she was beaten again and again and repeatedly made to look at the 'dead baby' in the potty.

Mary had lost her baby after Dad had beaten her and before long, she was pregnant again. Mum and Mary both had a terrible life with Dad and I couldn't understand why he was this way with both of them and all of us. The more horror stories I heard from Mum added to the nightmarish memories that I had of him and only made me feel more hatred and fear for him. I didn't understand why they had both stayed with him for so long.

The word 'divorce' seemed to have been associated with scandal in those days and wasn't much talked about. I walked out on him and I didn't ever want to go back.

I knew that in my future I would never love a man who hit me. It cannot be love when someone hits you surely? I would be out of that relationship as soon as I could. There would be no way I would stay. I wanted to marry a good man; a prince, a knight in shining armour, just like the one who woke Sleeping Beauty from her slumber or the one who fell in love with Cinderella. They all lived happily ever after in the story books that I had read. I wanted to be rescued and live happily ever after too. I didn't think all men were like Dad. In fact, I was beginning to think that most men were good guys and it was Dad that was just a bully and a bad guy. Mandy's dad didn't hit her mum. Mandy's sister Karen was married to a nice guy and had two little boys. He didn't hit her either. Mum was married to Dave at that time and he didn't treat her badly. I didn't think I had ever heard him even shout at her. Mum wasn't scared of him as she had been of Dad. I saw no fear in her eyes when she looked at Dave. The fear in her eyes, when she had lived with Dad still haunted me. I had seen fear in Mary's eyes too, every time she looked at Dad. He must have known how scared we all were of him. Couldn't he tell? Could he not see it? I was just a kid and I could see it. I knew what fear looked like. I saw it in Mum's eyes, Mary's eyes, our Peter's eyes — swollen from the beatings most of the time. I'd even seen the fear in Jane and Andrea's eyes and in our baby sister Laura's eyes, when Dad had been shouting at her for making too much noise when the football was on television.

I hated the fact that I had left Laura again. It broke my heart. I knew that Ann would look after her, so I knew she would be okay, and I knew I would see her again. She wouldn't forget me, and I wouldn't forget her. Dad was not home most of the time, so I would get to visit her. I would try and see her when he was not there. That way I would not have to look at him. He wouldn't ever see the fear in my eyes again. I knew that it would be Laura's sixth birthday in a few days, so I would have to see her then. I would just have to. It would break my heart not to be able to see her.

The sun had slowly moved across the garden while we had been talking the afternoon away. Mum was clearing the tea tray away when Maureen came into the garden. She was smoking a cigarette. I was really shocked. I hadn't seen her smoking before. I asked her if Mum didn't mind her smoking and she said that she had been smoking for ages and Mum let her. Mum came back out from the house and saw Maureen, sitting on the garden wall smoking. She didn't seem to mind at all.

Maureen would not be seventeen until July, but she seemed to have grown up a lot since moving there. She was wearing makeup and had a boyfriend. I never thought she would be a smoker, particularly with her bad chest and being so 'delicate' as Mum used to call it. I watched her as she cleverly flicked the cigarette stub over the fence.

CHAPTER THIRTY-NINE
Tony

I found it to be great living at mums. I had more freedom, more money in my pocket and fewer chores to do. Mum allowed me to keep most of the money that I had earned in the factory, for myself. She simply took enough for my 'board and lodgings', as she called it and said the rest was for me. This was a big change for me and meant that Mandy and I could go shopping for new clothes, most weekends, whenever we needed them. I didn't have many clothes and nice things. Most of what I had, had been passed down from our Ann, so it was good to be able to buy what I needed with my own money.

I managed to save a little each week for our future. Mandy and I were still planning to have that place of our own as soon as possible. We didn't intend to live with our parents for long. I noticed that I had been eating a lot better while I had been staying at mums. She was a really good cook and she was trying to feed me up. She always used to say that I was too skinny. We had fruit in a bowl on the table and we could help ourselves to it. We hadn't had fruit at dads ever.

When I was small, I saw fruit in the shops, but Mary never bought any of it. At mums I was even allowed to go into the fridge and have a drink of milk if I wanted to. If any of us did that at dads' house, we would have been battered for sure. Mum cooked us things that I had never previously experienced before like fish in batter, steak and onions and dumplings. I had never heard of dumplings before, but they were delicious. Even Mum's sandwiches were delicious, instead of the sugar butties or the crisp butties, it was bacon or ham and salad. Salad with tomatoes, cucumber and lettuce was great; I'd never tasted anything like that before.

I remember Mary giving Dad a salad for his tea once. Dad took one look at it and threw it across the living room. Mary was battered so she never gave him salad again. I never understood why he did that.

As children, we never had anything like that sort of food, while we were at Dad's house. Dad and Mary would have nice big meals; food that looked just like the food that Mum provided. We kids would only be allowed to sniff the aroma coming from the kitchen. There was always a big pan of mushy peas on Mum's stove, but I wasn't keen on them, but Maureen loved them. I put loads of weight on at mums.

Mum and Dave both worked at a pub in Horwich called 'The Bay Horse,' so sometimes when they came home late at night, they were tipsy and could make some funny noises with their laughing and giggling, at the funny jokes they had heard in the pub that night. Mum always started clattering around in the kitchen when they returned home and started cooking a curry for him. The delicious smell would fill the house and come right upstairs to our bedroom and wake Maureen and I up. We would rush downstairs for a helping before Dave devoured it all. The smell of the curry would always wake me up, even though by now I slept much more peacefully. Previously I had been kept awake with the sounds of Dad's loud angry voice and doors slamming. Sometimes even the rumbling of my tummy would keep me awake. The ghosts of yesterday still haunted me.

From time to time, I would wake from a nightmare relating to my experiences at Dad's house. Lying in the darkness, I would still believe for a moment that I was still there reliving it all. I would see Mary's face as clearly as the day, before me. In my nightmare, she would be battered and bruised and crying again. I would hear her voice echoing in my mind, begging him to stop over and over again. I would quickly realise that I was not there any more. Mary was safe, I was safe. We were both in a better place now. I would soon fall fast asleep again. Would these nightmares ever end?

When Mum and Dave were working in the pub, I was sometimes allowed to go with them. Mum always looked so glamorous behind that bar and everybody thought she was beautiful. She did look so much like Elsie Tanner. It was good to see her smiling and having a good time. She was enjoying her life. I would sit at the corner of the bar on a tall stool and I would look over to her and watch her. It was sometimes hard to believe that she had ever had all those bad times, which were in fact not so long ago. I thought Mum's bad times were over at last.

With Dave by her side, her bad times were over, he would look after her always, I was sure.

Some of the customers in the pub would ask Mum who I was, so she would tell them that I was her daughter. She smiled proudly when she introduced me. I felt so proud too.

One time when I was there, I noticed a lad walk in. He went behind the bar, said something to Mum and then ran off quickly upstairs missing every other step on the way. I thought that he must live there at the pub. Mum glanced at me and smiled, continuing to pull a pint for a customer. I sipped my lager and lime and wondered what it would be like to live above a pub. I didn't think I would like it. I thought it would be too noisy and I thought that I would probably not get much sleep with the music blasting out from the jukebox all night.

After a while, the lad came back downstairs, all smartly dressed in a clean tee-shirt and jeans. Once again, he went behind the bar and started pulling pints for the men at the bar. Mum picked up her cigarette packet and lighter and came to sit on a stool next to me. She said that it was her break time as she sipped her gin and tonic and lit her cigarette. She flicked her ash in a large ashtray in front of her. She told me that the lad's name was 'Tony' and he worked there at the pub. She said that he had been staying at the pub in the rooms upstairs, while the landlord was away on his holidays.

The pub got so busy with all the customers wanting their beer that Mum had to get down from her stool and go back behind the bar to give him a hand.

When it was Tony's break, he came to sit on Mum's stool at the side of me and he too lit a cigarette. To my surprise he started to talk to me. I blushed shyly. He asked my name and loads of questions; I thought he was so nosey. He was funny too and made me laugh. I wasn't sure if I liked him or not. He reminded me of the Artful Dodger in 'Oliver Twist.' He looked just like Jack Wild, but a bit older. He then went back behind the bar and pulled himself a pint and got me a half a lager and lime. He had bought me a drink. I looked at Mum for reassurance, she looked at me and smiled. She had been watching him 'chatting me up' as she called it. Shortly after last orders had been served, at the bar, it was time for all the customers to go home. Tony was shouting, "Can I have your glasses please gents?" One by one the men finished their beer and staggered out of the pub. It was so funny watching some of them almost falling over chairs and stools as they wobbled their way to the door.

Tony then said to me that it was his night off the next evening and would I like to go out with him for a drink. I quickly said that I would and arranged to meet him in the pub the following evening.

After helping to clean all the tables and empty the ashtrays, it was time to wash all the glasses before we could go home. The glasses were cleaned in a large sink of hot soapy water with a spinning scrubbing brush sticking up through the suds. You had to place the glasses over the spinning brushes to clean them inside; it was fun.

On the way home, in the taxi, Dave and Mum were telling me what a nice lad Tony was. Dave said he had known him a long time and he had always thought of him as being a nice enough lad. I was looking forward to seeing him the next night.

The next day, Tony was waiting for us when we walked into the pub. Mum and Dave were working that night, so I was able to stay with them in the pub. Tony was sitting on his usual stool at the bar, so I sat at the side of him. He asked if he could buy me a drink and I agreed.

This was the first of many nights out that I had with Tony. He was twenty-one and seemed a lot older than me. He was a really nice guy who made me laugh all the time, with the funny stories he told. He talked all the time. We got on really well and I liked to go into the pub with him and watch him working. I was not eighteen at that point and shouldn't have been going into the pub, but he made me feel so grown up. I liked the noise and the music and the different smells of the beers and the cigar smoke, from the little old wrinkly man who sat all alone in the corner.

Tony lived with his mum and dad right at the top of a long steep road, Longworth Road in Horwich. He wrote poems for me and little love letters all the time. He was always telling me that he loved me and that he was going to marry me one day. He made me feel as if I was special and the feelings I had for David, my first love, were slowly disappearing. I was beginning to feel the same way for Tony. While his parents were away, I stayed with him alone at his house. We had arranged that I was to stay the night in his room with him. He knew that I was still a virgin and still so very shy with him and not ready to take our relationship any further at that point. I felt that one day it would happen and maybe Tony was that special person that I would lose my virginity to. Maybe I would marry him one day!

The thought of all that grown-up stuff still scared me. I was still quite the 'tom boy' and not ready for all that seriousness. What if things changed when I got married and he was just the same as Dad was to his wives? What if Tony was just the same as Dad? What if I ended up having the same sort of life as my mum? How would I know? Tony had told me that he had only been with a couple of girls before and he wasn't all that 'experienced' as he put it. He would wait until the time was right and when I was ready, before anything would happen between us. We drank some cider and had some chips from the chippy, while listening to music and then we went upstairs to his room. His room was full of posters of wildlife and owls. He could name every wild bird in the countryside. He was so clever. I was so impressed and so proud that he was my boyfriend. Maybe one day we really would get married to each other.

He went to the bathroom and I took my jeans off and climbed into his small single bed and covered myself with his sheets. I was feeling so nervous and wondering whether that night would be 'the night'. Tony came in from the bathroom and sat on the edge of the bed, he leant across and kissed me on my forehead as he unbuttoned his shirt. He took his shirt off and reached across to turn his radio on. There was some soft sweet love song that I didn't recognise, and the disc jockey was saying that it was requested by Tim who had dedicated it to his girlfriend whom he loved very much. He said, "… and this is the new one from Rod Stewart, 'Tonight's the Night.'

As the music started, I was remembering that Rod Stewart was the one who sang 'Maggie May.' Rod began to sing and we both lay there together and listened. It was so strange to hear those words while Tony and I were lying there silently side by side in his bed. Rod Stewart was singing about two other lovers who were spending their first night together just like we were. It was as if he was singing that song just for us:

'Tonight's the night, Gonna' be all right,

Coz I love ya girl,

Ain't nobody gonna stop us now,

Don't say a word my virgin child…'

263

I felt as if that was a sign that I was to lose my virginity that night with Tony. We kissed and held each other. Tony was saying that he loved me, over and over. We were getting closer and closer. Tony asked, "Shall we do it?" I started to tremble as I nodded my head. We lay side by side kissing for what seemed such a long time then Tony got out of bed and went to the bathroom. I was so scared. This was the night that I was going to lose my virginity.

It seemed like he had been gone for such a long time. I lay there wondering whether I wanted to do it that night. I was so scared; I could get pregnant, then we would have to get married. I was too young to get married and I didn't want babies yet.

When Tony came back from the bathroom, he turned off the light and climbed back into bed. My whole body was shaking, but as his cold body touched mine, I could feel he was trembling too. He held me so tight in his arms and we started to kiss. Suddenly he jumped out of bed and rushed back to the bathroom again. I lay there listening for him, wondering what the matter was.

After a while he came back into the bedroom, saying sorry over and over again. He climbed back into bed and told me that he was nervous too. We nestled in each other's arms and before long we both fell fast asleep. It had crossed my mind that night that he could be a virgin too, although he had told me he had had lots of other girlfriends. Was it his first time too? That night was not the night for us — thank God! My virginity was still intact.

The next morning Tony was so embarrassed about the night before. I could see it in his face, but I didn't know how to tell him that I was relieved that we hadn't 'done it.' I felt that it was the wrong time and the wrong place, and I was just not ready at that point. If it was the first time for him, maybe inside, he felt the same way.

Later, over a coffee in the canteen at work, I spoke to Mandy about it and told her how embarrassed we both felt. She agreed with me that it probably wasn't the right time for either of us, and not to be so bothered about it.

Later, Tony and I talked, and both agreed to stay just the way we were until we were both sure of what we wanted. We carried on seeing each other most evenings and agreed not to rush with taking things further and just let things happen naturally. It was never that easy to take our relationship further, even if we wanted to, because every time he would call for me or we saw each other, over the next few weeks, we were never able to be alone.

At home there was always a house full, so it felt as if we were brother and sister sometimes, instead of boyfriend and girlfriend. Maureen always seemed to be around and followed us most of the time. Sometimes it got a little annoying. She would make fun of us and try to embarrass us, if she caught us kissing. I wished that she would grow up.

Uncle Ted, cousin Julie's dad, lived with us as well, so we did have a house full. Uncle Ted was such a funny man. He had a tanned, wrinkled face, a gruff voice and jet-black curly hair. He looked just like Sidney James. He worked on the buses as a bus driver. He was married to Mum's sister Doris, who was our cousin Julie's Mum. She had died of cancer when Julie was only seven years old. Uncle Ted told us that Julie had just had a baby boy who they had called Mark. We had not seen him at that point, but Uncle Ted had said that he was lovely with chubby cheeks, blue eyes and blond hair.

Tony got on so well with our comical Uncle Ted. They were always laughing together, sharing jokes while they smoked their roll-up cigarettes and drunk beer, down the garden.

One night, while Tony and I were sitting in the garden trying to be alone with each other, and as the evening sunshine slowly left the night sky, Tony looked at me and said, "How about going away for the weekend to Southport? We could stay at a 'posh' hotel and be on our own for a change. We will have to pretend we are married though." It sounded so romantic but sharing a hotel room when you were not married, wasn't the done thing; it would be shameful.

I was a bit shocked by his suggestion at first. I didn't think Mum would ever let me go to a hotel with him, but I intended to ask her anyway. Inside I was hoping Mum would agree to us going. I really wanted to go with Tony; he was so romantic! I thought we were going to stay together forever. It could be the right time for us to spend the night together.

Maybe after this weekend, if we got to go, neither of us would be virgins, besides, lots of girls of my age were having sex before marriage.

On the outside I wanted things to happen between us but on the inside, I still wasn't sure what I wanted to do or whether Tony was 'the one.' He told me that he loved me, and I felt as if he really did. However, I still felt too young and too tom-boyish for all that. I knew what he wanted to take me away for, but he had assured me that we would wait for the right time, the right time for both of us. Still, I had the memories of what Mum and Mary went through, flashing through my mind, trying to spoil my dreams. Tony was so sweet. He had never raised his voice to me or lost his temper in any way. He was not like my dad. He had listened to me and knew what my childhood had been like. He had promised me that he would never hurt me, and I didn't believe he ever would.

CHAPTER FORTY
Southport

On a warm and sunny Saturday morning in June, we were on our way to Southport. Mum had given us her blessing. I thought maybe she had had a feeling that Tony would make a good son-in-law one day. I knew she liked Tony a lot. She hugged us and said that we had to be careful. Tony looked at me and giggled. He put his arm around my shoulder and pulled me towards him tightly saying that we would try our best. I blushed and giggled with him, but not really sure why.

I had packed a few items of clothing and my toothbrush, into a small vanity case. We were both just as nervous and excited as each other about the trip. Tony's boss, John, landlord of the Bay Horse pub, drove us all the way to Southport in his car. Along the way, I was sitting on the back seat of John's car, with Tony at my side, holding my hand. I gazed through the car window, at the green fields, filled with what looked like dark green cabbages. I also noticed farmlands filled with sheep, cows and horses grazing in the warm sunshine. I had never been to Southport before, or seen views quite like the views I experienced at that time. They stretched for miles and miles. I was trying to imagine how I would be feeling the following day, when we would be on our way home. I probably would not be a virgin any more. I stared at his face as he spoke to me. His words fell on deaf ears as I was daydreaming. Would I be different? Would I look different?

I began to feel scared again, just like I did before. My stomach was turning over.

Was I ready this time? I just didn't know. I looked down at the loose 'wedding ring' on the third finger of my left hand. I had borrowed it, so we could pretend that we were a real married couple. I wondered if I would ever wear his ring for real one day. Was this lad the prince that would rescue me? Would there be a happy ending for us?

We had only been travelling for about an hour or so when we finally arrived in Southport. John dropped us off, on a long tree lined street, with shops and big old grand houses on either side. Tony hadn't booked us into a hotel. He said that we would have no problem getting a room at whatever hotel we wanted as they were never fully booked at this time of the year. We walked along the road, looking at the buildings, until we came to the first hotel. I was embarrassed and couldn't walk in with him. I was sure that they would be able to tell that we weren't married and not let us have a room, so I waited outside while he went inside to see if they had a vacancy. I sat on a bench, outside, watching all the people walking by. He was soon back, telling me that the hotel was too dear, and we would try another.

At each hotel we came to we did the same; I waited outside while he went inside but with each one, they were either fully booked or too expensive. We were both beginning to feel a little tired and hungry and wondered whether we would ever find somewhere to stay today or have to go back home.

We arrived at a hotel called the Scarlsbrick. I looked up at the huge grand stone building and thought that the place looked really expensive too. I thought there wouldn't be room for us there either. Tony went inside to ask about a room. Soon he was back with a huge smile on his face and told me that they had got a room, but it was directly over the disco and a bit noisy. It was only £15 for the night, so he had booked it. Relieved that he had finally found somewhere to stay, I picked up my bag and followed him inside.

We both had to sign our names in a big book that lay on the wide polished counter. We signed our names as Mr and Mrs Norris. Tony was handed a key and glancing at each other and smirking we said, "Thank you," and quickly dashed up the staircase to our room.

Our room was on the second floor, some distance down a long wide corridor. Tony looked at each door, along the corridor, looking for room number 125. Our room was half way down the hallway.

Tony placed the key in the lock and slowly pushed open the huge creaky door. We both peered inside. Tony dropped his bag to his side and whisked me up into his arms and carried me into the room and dropped me onto this huge double bed in the centre of the room. I shrieked and giggled as he climbed up on the high bed next to me. We lay there for a moment looking around the room.

There were two very high sash windows in front of the bed, which overlooked the shops of Lord Street below. Dark red, velvet curtains hung from them gracefully, tied back at each side. There was a dark wooden wardrobe at the far end of the room, at the side of a white porcelain sink with an oval mirror hanging on the wall above it. Tony jumped down off the bed, picked his bag up and brought it into the room. He then climbed back onto the bed and nestled at my side. I couldn't believe we were all alone at last. He must have heard my stomach rumbling because he asked if I was hungry. I told him I was absolutely starving, so we decided to go out for something to eat.

We left the room, locking the door behind us, and went to the nearest café. We didn't realise just how hungry we were. Neither of us had eaten since that morning. We ordered beans on toast and a huge mug of tea. After we had eaten, we went for a walk and came across a boating lake not far from the hotel.

People were sailing around in little brightly coloured rowing boats. The big yellow pedal boats, parked up at the side, caught Tony's eye. He dragged me over to them, paid the attendant, who then pushed our pedal boat onto the water. We nervously climbed inside and began to peddle, trying our best not to crash into another boat. Every time we peddled near another boat, or the boat wobbled too much, Tony panicked and shrieked and tried to steer the boat away. He was looking nervous, but I could only laugh at him because he was so funny. He kept trying to look over the edge, to see how deep the water was. It was too dark, so we couldn't see the bottom, but I didn't think it would have been that deep. Tony was looking more and more nervous and I was trying not to laugh at him. I asked him if he was all right and if he wanted to go back to the edge. Braving a smile, as the sweat slowly dripped down from his forehead, he told me that he was fine. He then announced to me that he couldn't swim, but felt so proud of himself, because he had been able to get into one of these boats. He told me that he was just showing off and trying to impress me. He was so sweet. I laughed with him but was secretly a little relieved when our time on the lake came to an end. We were both safe and sound back on dry land. I didn't know that he couldn't swim.

After the excitement on the lake, we walked slowly in the warm sunshine back to the hotel. We talked, while tucking into a bag of the most delicious chips that I had ever tasted; we had been tempted by the smell coming from a chip shop along the way. We'd had a beautiful day so far; it was so good to be with Tony. He could talk for ages about anything and everything. I would look intently into his face as he spoke. He seemed to know lots about lots of things. He was so clever. He would impress me all the time with the things he talked about, so he really didn't need to try so hard to impress me, as he had done on the lake earlier in the day.

Back at the hotel, the disco was already underway, in the room directly underneath our room. The music was so loud. We could hear it from our room, but it didn't bother us. We were soon washed and changed and heading in the direction of the music and looking forward to passing the night away dancing on the dance floor.

The disco was huge. I didn't expect it to be as big as it was. Bright coloured lights were flashing in time to the loud music. Tony found us a place to sit, in a darkened corner, facing the dance floor. I settled down on the padded seat that circled the table. Tony went to the bar to collect some drinks. I watched Tony as he leaned against the bar to order the drinks. I felt so happy to be there, I felt so happy to be there with him. He was so handsome and such a gentleman. We had had a beautiful day. I wished that time could have stood still and that we could have stayed there forever. I imagined that all the bad things hadn't happened, and we could have stayed that way forever.

The dance floor was slowly filling as the disc jockey played the latest disco records. I watched as couples took their places on the dance floor and danced away in each other's arms to the music. Ladies danced together around their handbags, which were all together in a pile on the floor in front of them. My feet were tapping. I wanted to dance too. Tony returned from the bar just as the disc jockey started to play "You to Me Are Everything" by "The Real Thing." He placed our drinks on the table in front of us, then took my hand and led me to the dance floor. He held me so tightly as we started to dance together on the floor. He was singing the song in my ears as we danced. He was so romantic. He looked into my eyes and repeated every word as if the song was meant just for me. "That is our special song," he told me, as we sat down between dances.

There were lots of records played by the disc jockey that night. We danced to most of them together. The whole evening was so special. It was our first real night together. Could this be it, I thought to myself?

The waiters asked us if we were on our honeymoon as they served us with our drinks. We must have looked so close, as we smooched on that dance floor. It felt really strange but as we danced it was as if there was no one else around except Tony and I and the music. We told the waiters that it was our honeymoon and giggled to ourselves, getting tipsy and dancing the night away. The disco went on until the early hours, but we decided it was time to go back to our room.

We were both exhausted from the day but we'd had a wonderful time. We staggered back to our room arm in arm. My head was spinning. I felt so dizzy. I must have drunk too many port and lemons. It was a relief when Tony found our room and opened the door. I took off my shoes and threw myself on the bed before I fell over. The room was spinning too by that time. Tony shut the door and came to join me on the bed. He lay down at the side of me, kissed my cheek and put his arm around me. We lay side by side looking at the ceiling for a moment hoping for the room to stop spinning somehow. The music still played on downstairs.

Tony sat up and said, "Let's order room service. I'm starving, are you?" He jumped to the edge of the bed and picked up the phone. I sat up and leaned against the large wooden headboard as the room didn't spin as much that way. Tony eloquently ordered sandwiches and coffee for two.

Room service soon delivered a plate of chicken sandwiches cut into triangles and garnished with salad, accompanied by two cups of milky coffee. We lazed across the bed and tucked in to them; they were delicious. We didn't realise how hungry we were. I sat up to drink my coffee. The room didn't seem to be spinning as much now.

Placing the pillows behind me I leaned against the headboard and sipped the hot coffee while we chatted. Tony was lying across the bed, resting on his stomach and then he stopped talking and stared at me for a second. He stretched across me and placed his empty cup on the bedside cabinet. I watched him, and his eyes never left mine. He moved closer to me and gently took the half empty cup from my hand and placed it down next to his. He leaned forward and kissed me gently on the lips. I held my breath; my heart was beating so fast. He paused and looked into my eyes.

"I love you," he said, so softly. His lips met mine again and I was in his warm embrace. I could almost hear every beat of my heart as he held me so tightly. We snuggled together side by side on the bed still fully dressed. Tony reached across and turned off the light and took off his shirt. The night was hot and so quiet by then, as we kissed so tenderly once more. I was hot and still a little dizzy. My stomach was turning over and over. I couldn't breathe in Tony's arms. I had strange sensations deep inside. I'd never felt them before. Tony's warm hands slowly slipped under my t-shirt and he pulled me closer towards him as he stroked my back. His touch was so soft. My t-shirt was lifted up over my head and he was caressing my neck and shoulders. He held me tightly, yet so tenderly. His lips met mine again so passionately. The room seemed to be illuminated by the moonlight in the late-night sky. I was so relaxed. I closed my eyes and began to melt into his embrace. The thoughts of the past were disappearing and all that mattered at this moment was Tony and I, and the night.

When I stretched and opened my eyes it was light again. The morning sun was beating down from the sky through the windows in front of us. Tony was lying fast asleep, at the side of me, and looking so peaceful. I was still half dressed and had been covered with a blanket. I kissed Tony on his forehead and he stirred.

"What happened to the night?" I asked him. He smiled and suggested that I had fallen fast asleep in his arms. I was still a virgin. Tony stretched and rolled onto his back and put his arm around me, pulling me closer to him. I lay with my head against his chest listening to the steady beat of his heart. I couldn't believe it. Nothing had happened. I had fallen asleep in Tony's arms and he had covered me with a blanket while I slept. This was supposed to be "the night," I was not supposed to be a virgin by the morning when I woke up. Tony raised my chin and kissed me and then said that it didn't matter, and that it would happen in its own good time. He was so sweet. I was beginning to wonder whether it would ever happen between us. We've been together for months now. I thought, maybe the time is still not right. Just like the time before. Or maybe I just don't want it to happen. He's brought me to this posh hotel, so we could finally be together, but it hadn't happened.

We lay in each other's arms and drifted off to sleep again. When we woke, Tony realised that we were going to be late for breakfast. We were both starving, so I rushed to the bathroom, along the corridor, with my bag and got ready, leaving Tony to get ready in our room. Looking in that large mirror, above a white ceramic sink with brass taps, I wondered if I would have looked any different that morning if I had lost my virginity with Tony that night. I was sure I would look and feel so different. I wondered what it would have been like to feel him so close to me in that way.

We held hands and ran down the stairs to the dining room. It was almost 10 o'clock and the kitchen staff stopped serving breakfast at 10 am so we were nearly late. The waitresses, wearing their very clean white pinafores, had cleared most of the tables. Most of the guests had eaten breakfast already and had left the hotel. Tony went over to one of the waitresses to ask if we were too late to have breakfast. We were shown to a table and soon served with our meals.

Breakfast consisted of bacon, eggs, sausage and beans with bread, toast and a cup of tea. Both of us were quite hungry, so we tucked into the served dishes. Despite this neither of us cleared our plates. Neither of us enjoyed the breakfast; it was so greasy and not very warm. Shortly after that, not so nice fry up, we left the dining room and went back to our hotel room to get ready to leave and go back home.

I wished that we could have stayed another night but it was back to work for us both the following day. Having handed in the room keys, at the reception desk, we left the hotel. As we left, Tony checked the bill and grabbed my hand, he giggled out loud.

"Come on quick!" he said, pulling me down the steps from the hotel. "We should have paid for those sandwiches that we had last night. Hurry before they realise and come after us." Clutching his hand tightly, my tiny vanity case under my arm, we shot off down the road giggling and heading towards the bus station.

We waited nearly an hour for the bus to take us back home. We had had such a good time. I just wished that we could have stayed a bit longer. If we had stayed longer, I might not have been going back home as a virgin.

We boarded the bus back to Horwich and sat on the top deck on the back seat. All the windows were open and a cool breeze was blowing through the bus. We were still very hot and sweaty though.

It was another gorgeous hot and sunny day. Tony held my hand, but I got more and more irritated by how sweaty it was, so I pulled my hand from his. We were both quiet and didn't really talk much to each other along the way. We were both looking out through the windows at the same familiar countryside that we'd seen the previous day. We should have been different people that day. We were not supposed to be the same as we had been.

I looked at Tony as he stared through the window. I wondered what he was thinking. Was this lad my love, I thought? Would he be my husband one day?

When the bus pulled into Chorley Bus Station, we were both too hot even to sit next to each other. The bus was like a mobile greenhouse. Tony noticed a vending machine on the station and rushed down from the bus to buy us both a carton of refreshing ice-cold milk, before the bus pulled away from the station to continue its journey. It seemed as if we were on that bus for hours!

Eventually, the bus pulled up outside Horwich Town Hall and we were so relieved to get off. The Bay Horse pub was just up the street; Tony suggested we call in for a cold beer.

Mum was working behind the bar when we got in there. She seemed so glad to see us. She asked if we had had a good time. I lowered my head and felt a little embarrassed with her question. I felt like telling her that I was still the same person that I had been the previous day. I was still a virgin. I just couldn't talk to Mum about that. I sat at the bar drinking a refreshing cold glass of orange juice and told her all about our lovely time in Southport.

It was good to get back home and carry on with our normal lives. We were hoping to come back as different people, with both our lives changed in a way that would have certainly changed us forever. Once again it was not to be.

CHAPTER FORTY-ONE
The Bolton Palais

The summer of 1976 was just the best; the weather was gorgeous. The sun shone most days. I still lived at Mum's in Blackrod and I was still seeing Tony.

Tony and I were still very close and talked a lot and had a lot of laughs, but we rarely spent enough time together, to further the relationship that we had. We were becoming more like sister and brother. I felt I must have preferred it to be that way. We had times when we were alone, such as, when we stayed in the hotel in Southport, I just wasn't ready to lose my virginity to him. I was scared. I didn't want to change. I just wanted to stay as I was.

He was busy working at the pub. He worked most evenings, and Mandy and I were always together. We spent time together at work and on weekends we were out on the town. Usually on Friday nights, we would be at the Navada. We would be skating while Tony was busy pulling pints in the Bay Horse. I felt as if we were drifting apart at times.

After we had finished at the Navada, we would carry on our night of dancing at the Bolton Palais De Danse. It was the place to be on Friday and Saturday nights in Bolton.

The Palais was a huge dancehall that I had been to as a young child on Saturday mornings. Ann and I would dance to 'March of the Mods' on that huge dance floor. Now I was here as a teenager dancing to all the disco sounds from the charts. The Bolton Palais now had a totally different and exciting atmosphere. There were no children running around wild on the dancefloor or dancing around to the March of the Mods. There was beer being served from those bars and cigarette smoke filling the air. We were in the world of the grown-ups.

After our night was over, Mandy would either stay the night at my house or I would stay at her house. We always had a taxi home and it was always very late when we got back. I would not have been able to stay out so late if I had still lived at Dad's house. We worked all week and would look forward to enjoying ourselves at the weekend.

I had more money in my pocket. Dad used to take most my wages each week, whereas, now, Mum didn't take much for board and lodgings.

I felt I was living and enjoying my life. I now had the money that I had worked hard for in the factory, to spend how I wanted. I enjoyed working by then and had something to show for it at the end of the week.

All the factory girls were saving up for a 'work's do' that had been planned for later that coming August. We were all going to go to Batley Variety Club to see the Stylistics. Mandy and I couldn't wait. We were both into the Stylistics in a big way, as we were with the 'Bay City Rollers'. The Stylistics records were always played wherever we went. They'd been around in the charts for ages and they had gone to number one for three weeks with 'Can't Give You Anything (But My Love)'. This had been in August of the previous year.

The whole of the factory was going to the club. We were travelling there by coach, having a meal there and watching the full show. We were all so excited! Mandy and I had never been to a concert or anything like that before.

After work on Fridays, Mandy and I would go shopping at Talibs in Horwich. It was a really cheap ladies' fashion store. We loved everything they sold and we always found something new to wear for that evening. Usually, we chose matching outfits; our tastes were just the same. I was buying my own clothes now, instead of having the cast-offs from Ann; it was great! I also had a wardrobe of my own to put them all in. I was getting a good selection of nice new clothes of my very own and it felt good.

It was quite scary for Mandy and I being in Bolton Palais on Friday nights, as both of us were still only seventeen. There were big muscular men called bouncers that threw people out if they thought that people weren't old enough to be in there. They looked so frightening; all dressed in black and so huge. They must have thought we looked old enough to be in there because we were never asked how old we were nor were we ever thrown out.

Sometimes, all the lights would go on in the club and we'd see all the bouncers running across the dance floor to an area where a fight had just broken out. There was usually a lot of noise and hustle and bustle as glasses were smashed. These incidents were quickly over and the drunken men, who had been fighting, were thrown out. These experiences were so scary when they happened. We'd be terrified if it was ever near to us. I would remember the times when Dad would attack Paul and Mary; the noise of these horrors was the same as the fighting in the Palais. The fear was the same.

One night we saw two men fighting on the balcony above the dance floor. They were wrestling with each other as the bouncers raced to them. All of a sudden, they fell right over the railings and onto the dance floor below. They just got up again and carried on fighting. It was a wonder they didn't fall onto any of the people who were dancing. Everyone scattered and left the bouncers to do their job. The culprits were soon thrown out; this was really the scary part of the Palais, despite its many attractions. Both of us found these experiences scary, we would be aware that these things happened in there and we tried to keep out of the way of any commotion, having a good time and forgetting about the bad things.

The Palais was a huge place. Mandy and I stayed together all the time. We danced together, went to the bar together, although we only drank the odd lager and lime, and even went to the toilets together. We didn't want to lose each other in that place. If either of us were asked to dance by some guy, which did happen all the time, he would have to have a mate with him then we could both dance with them at the same time. It was great fun for us to be asked to dance. We were good dancers and liked to show off a bit on the dance floor. Sometimes we would be asked if we wanted a drink. We would chat with them for a while, and then make an excuse that we both wanted to go to the toilet. We'd then disappear to another part of the club and avoid them for the rest of the evening. Neither of us wanted to be with any of those lads. We were free. We were having fun. We didn't want to be tied to anyone. This was our night out and we didn't want anyone else to spoil it. This was our routine every Friday night.

Maureen had her sixteenth birthday that July and we all went to the Palais for a night out together. There was Mum and a friend of hers, called Arthur, Paul, Maureen, Mandy and me. Mum wore a lovely long, blue dress, which had a frill around the bottom; she looked a picture wearing it. Mum's friend Arthur was a really nice man and he seemed to like Mum quite a lot. He danced with her the whole night. He knew that she was married to Dave, but they both seemed to be having a good time. Mum was smiling. It was a good night, except for this scruffy old drunken man that kept grabbing Mum and trying to dance with her right in the middle of the dance floor. Mum was getting a bit annoyed with him, but he just wouldn't go away. Paul ended up punching him right on the nose and he went flying across the floor. It was so funny! The big scary bouncers surrounded us. They grabbed hold of Paul and almost threw us out. After explaining to them what had happened, they threw the scruffy drunk out instead.

On sunny Saturday mornings, Mandy and I would be off to Blackpool. I loved Blackpool, ever since Mum had taken us there when we were younger. We would go most weekends. A train would leave Bolton train station first thing on a Saturday morning and we would be on it. Always hoping for window seats, as sometimes the train would get really packed; we would have a bet on who would spot Blackpool Tower first.

Within an hour or so we would be walking down through the town centre window-shopping in all the shops we passed. We would be heading for the beach. Some weekends we just spent the day at the beach when we hadn't taken much money with us. When Mandy and I had both done a bit of overtime and earned a little bit more at work in the factory, we'd be at the fun fair.

The sun was so hot one afternoon on the fair that the tarmac on the roads and walkways was almost melting. We could feel the heat from the ground through our sandals. It was a bit cooler to walk in the shade from the stalls. Undressed down to just our bras and shorts, we didn't care what we looked like. We didn't have a care in the world. Everyone was walking around scantily dressed and they didn't seem to bother either. Getting more and more pink by the sun every minute we'd have ride after ride on the log flumes and become soaking wet every time! At least it cooled us down a bit. We soon dried off in the sunshine. We were free and enjoyed every minute, and it showed. I'd never had so much fun before, not ever.

Sometimes we would take along the little girl who lived next door to us in Whitehall Lane. She was called Michelle. She was five years old and so cute and so well behaved. She reminded us so much of Laura. Michelle was about the same age as her. I became very fond of Michelle and spent quite a bit of time with her. It was just like being with Laura. Michelle would often come knocking on our door to show me paintings that she'd done at school that day. When she gave me one of her paintings, I put it in my bedroom next to Donny Osmond.

I wished that I could have spent some more time with Laura, my baby sister; I did miss her so much. It seemed ages since I had last seen her. I thought to myself, at that time, that I could not wait to have children of my own. I'd like a little girl and I'd call her Michelle.

From time to time my mind was free from all the bad memories from home; they got buried somewhere deep in my mind. Since leaving Dad's house I had been too busy to think about how things were at his house. I had been too busy having fun with my friends, growing up, trying to be happy and venturing out into the big wide world. I felt free. I wasn't constantly looking over my shoulder any more. I knew that Dad was not there to show his disapproval of me so I could relax and have a good time with my friends. I was still just a kid and there wasn't much I could do about those other things now. I had to keep busy and try to get on with my life and grow up. There were things I had to do. I had dreams for the future to fulfil. The world was my oyster, as people had told me.

Sometimes things happen along the way that we have absolutely no control over, but they can have such a dramatic and sometimes traumatic effect on the rest of your life, forever. I realised that I had to start my life as a woman and make the most of things and try to put my childhood nightmares behind me, if I ever could. I was free.

We made quite a few friends in Blackpool during our visits and on many occasions, we would see them when we walked along the beach or the promenade. I wished I lived in Blackpool. I would have loved to wake up each morning and go for a walk along the beach. When Mum left our dad for the last time, and never came back to us again, she had gone to live in Blackpool with some friends of hers and during the visits that Mandy and I made to Blackpool we would sometimes call at their house to see how they all were and just to say 'hello' from our Mum.

We called her 'Aunty Pauline' although we knew she wasn't our real

'Aunty.' She had two daughters; Catherine and Maria. Catherine had a baby boy and lived in her own house with her husband and Maria was fifteen and still at home with her mum and the two black Scotch Terrier dogs called 'Whiskey' and 'Scottie'.

Maria had been very friendly when we first met her a couple of weeks ago. She gave us tours around Blackpool showing us all the best places that she went to. She went to pubs, drank beer and smoked cigarettes. She seemed so much more grown up than we are. She had a boyfriend too who looked about twenty. We both liked spending time with her and we all got on really well.

One day we went into her living room and found her sitting on her boyfriend's knee. She wasn't dressed properly and they were doing something that they shouldn't have been doing, especially at her age. I was concerned that neither of them appeared to mind us walking into the room and 'disturbing them'. They didn't stop to cover up; they just carried on regardless. Mandy and I couldn't believe it. We'd never seen anything like that before. We were both so embarrassed and shocked that she could do things like that at her age. It was horrible. That bothered us a lot and we quickly left the room.

We ended our day in Blackpool and never went to her house again. The following weekend we saw Maria again at the beach. She told us she wasn't seeing that boyfriend any more. After what we had seen the previous week, we didn't feel comfortable to be friends with her any more and made some excuse that we couldn't spend the day with her. Our visits to Blackpool each weekend stopped for a while soon afterwards.

Back at the Bolton Palais on Friday nights, Mandy and I were getting to know everyone who worked there. We got to know all the staff behind the bar and the lady behind the kiosk counter in the foyer. We would stand and chat to her and watch her sewing with a needle and thread making dolls, when she wasn't busy serving everyone. Everyone got to know us too. They would ask if we were twins or sisters because we both wore matching outfits. We were regular visitors now and still loved it.

The DJ was very good. He played the records that were popular with everyone in there; the dance floor would be packed with people dancing every time he was on stage. He was called Danny Sinclair and he was very friendly and liked people going to him on stage, requesting their favourite records for him to play. Mandy and I were always asking for a Bay City Rollers hit or a hit by the Stylistics of course. It was brilliant when he played our records and mentioned us by name. It made us giggle and feel important; he made everyone feel that way.

As soon as Mandy and I were up dancing, on that bouncy dance floor, we wouldn't be able to sit down all evening because every record he played was good to dance to. We would stand in front of the stage and dance. Our handbags would be either on the floor in front of us or left on the front of the stage, where we could see them. All the girls would dance around their handbags. It was so funny to see this at first. Mandy had had her bag stolen from under her nose the previous week, so we watched our bags at all times from that point on.

Mandy's eighteenth birthday was Friday 6th August. She had received lots of cards from the girls in the factory and we took her out to the nearby pub for lunch that day. Whenever it was anyone's birthday at work, that's what we did. We were celebrating at the Bolton Palais that night of course. Some girls from work were coming too and meeting us there. We couldn't miss the Palais!

In the Palais I secretly told the DJ that it was Mandy's birthday and asked if he could mention her and present her with a surprise present that I'd bought for her. It would be great for her to receive the present on the stage in front of everyone, just to surprise her. I'd bought her a fancy bedside lamp for her bedroom.

We all drank and danced the night away as usual and Mandy didn't suspect a thing. She was getting quite tipsy from all the drinks that had been bought for her.

The Dennis Langfield Band had ended their spot and the stage started to rotate with the introduction music for the DJ. With each record played, I was getting more and more excited waiting for the DJ to mention Mandy's name. I was beginning to think he'd forgotten about her, when all at once he came out to the front of the stage and asked for Mandy. We were sitting down talking to a bunch of lads.

With the sound of her name filling the vast hall, we all turned towards her and cheered. Mandy sat in a state of embarrassment; she slid down in her chair and tried to hide her face in her jacket. Despite her shyness and embarrassment, the DJ managed to get her up on the stage and present her with the gift in front of everyone and then made her stand there, while all the people at the Palais sang 'Happy Birthday' to her. He asked her how old she was and then after a few other questions he presented her with the gift that I had bought for her. Still giggling with embarrassment, when she came back to our table, she said that she'd never forgive me for that. She would probably get me back on my eighteenth birthday a few months later. She opened her present at our table and said that it was just what she needed. We danced and danced away the rest of the night. We were both quite tipsy by the time we got home that night.

The next evening Mandy's mum and dad took us to the Olympus Restaurant. It was right next door to a huge hotel in Bolton town centre called The Swan Hotel. It was Mandy's birthday treat from them. I'd never been to a fancy restaurant before. I can fondly remember going into this posh, warmly lit restaurant. I was so nervously excited about the food and what to order. I'd never even looked at a menu before. I was starving and hungry and hadn't eaten anything since the packet of crisps at dinner. I expected that the food would be posh too.

All the tables were set waiting for the customers. In the far corner, there was a couple seated at a table with a lit candle flickering and a small red rose, in a tiny vase in the middle of the table. They were leaning towards each other and holding each other's hands. They looked so romantic together and so much 'in love'. There was also a party of about ten people, sitting at the far end of the room, having such a good time laughing and joking between themselves. They were all drinking beer and getting quite noisy. I thought that this was probably a 'works do' like the one we were going to have, from Halbros, in a few weeks.

The foreign looking waiter approached us as we walked in. Mandy's dad told him our name and at that point we were shown to a table for six people; this was half way down the room. I nervously sat down in my place and Mandy was seated next to me. The silver knives and forks sparkled against the crisp white tablecloth in front of me. We were all given menus to look at and we decided what we were going to eat. I had never seen tables looking so nice as these before. It was so posh. There was soft music being played through speakers around the room.

Mandy and I fidgeted in our seats and couldn't stop giggling at the waiter. He was dressed in tight black trousers and a crisp white shirt, almost as white as the tablecloths, and a red bow tie. We were expecting the bow tie to spin around like the one that Eric Morecambe wore on the television. He had a little white folded cloth over his arm. We didn't know what that was for. Maybe it was to flick us with if he knew that we were giggling at him. Whispering to each other and chuckling away to ourselves, Mandy and I hid our slowly reddening faces behind the menus, so he wouldn't see.

Everyone chose their meals from the menu, but I was unsure of what to order so I decided to have the same as Mandy. Mandy had ordered something called scampi. It sounded nice, but I hadn't got a clue as to what it was. I'd never heard of it before. I was too shy to ask anyone and I certainly was too embarrassed to ask the waiter what it was because I would just be giggling at him too much. We were served with drinks while we waited for our meals.

Our food soon arrived, and it looked and smelled delicious. The waiter placed warmed plates in front of each of us, wiping each one of them beforehand with the white cloth that was over his arm. Each dish that we'd ordered was served onto the plates. I looked at my plate and then at Mandy. I'd never had scampi before; they just looked like little orange crispy meatballs. They were served with chips and salad. It looked good but smelled a bit fishy. I wasn't sure whether I was going to like them, but I was far too hungry so I would try them anyway.

Our table went quiet as we all started to eat. I'd started on the chips, then the salad and then decided to try the scampi. They were just mouthful size, so I picked up my fork and tried to stick it into the scampi ready to devour. To my horror the scampi shot off my plate, across the table between Karen and Geoff and rolled right across the floor, underneath the table of the couple in the corner. Mandy roared with laughter. In turn Mandy's parents, Karen and Geoff saw the funny side. I had never seen Mandy's dad smile. He always had such a stern look on his face, but he too giggled as he watched the scampi disappearing across the restaurant. I, however, could have died of embarrassment. I went bright red and sunk into my chair.

I lowered my fork to the table and picked the next one up with my fingers and bit into it. It was horrible! I didn't like it at all. It tasted too fishy. I had to spit it out into the paper serviette; I couldn't eat it. Dessert was much better — apple pie and custard. I knew I liked that. I also knew not to order scampi, if I was ever to go again.

Later that evening, after the restaurant, we all went to a club in Farnworth. Recalling the flying scampi made us all laugh again and again throughout the evening.

A few weeks later, the night of our factory's 'works do' had arrived. As usual, Mandy and I had bought matching outfits from our favourite shop, Talibs. A long-sleeved blouse with a shiny black and gold tiger skin design and we both wore black trousers too. Mandy and I didn't really wear much makeup, but that night we made an exception and wore eye shadow, mascara and hairspray in order to keep our hair in place, especially for the Stylistics!

It was weird seeing the girls from the factory all 'dolled up'. We were only used to seeing each other wearing tabards and overalls but that night everyone looked so different. Everyone was wearing new clothes and makeup. They had all had their hair done. I hardly recognised some of the same women I had been working with for the past year. We could sense the excitement as we boarded the coach outside the factory.

Before long we were on our way to 'The Batley Variety Club' in Yorkshire. There were butterflies in my tummy and my hands were shaking. I couldn't believe we were on our way to see the famous Stylistics. They were on the telly and on the radio all the time. I had bought their records. I had never seen anyone famous before and now here we were, on the coach travelling to see them. We would soon be there. I was so excited. I didn't think we would miss the Bolton Palais tonight.

The previous week at the Palais, we had asked Danny the DJ if he would play some of the Stylistics records for us and throughout the evening the records were played. I thought the DJ was quite nice. He always talked to us and played the records that we requested. He was courting a girl called Roberta. I thought that she would feel lucky going out with him. He was like a superstar, up there on that stage every night. We had danced all night as usual to the music he played and especially to the Stylistics records that he played for us.

On this night, however, we would see 'The Stylistics' in the flesh! Real people, famous people; the group that we listened to all the time would be there on the stage right before our eyes. We would be dancing all night for them too.

At last, the coach stopped, outside a huge car park, at the side of the club. The car park was filling up with cars and coaches trying to park. There was a traffic jam, as each vehicle waited their turn to park. We could all see the big, bright, yellow sign on the front of the club. It read, 'Variety Club'. The sign was in huge yellow letters and surrounded by little yellow stars. There were different coloured flashing neon lights all around the entrance as we walked in. The place didn't look as nice as the Palais or the Navada from the outside. It looked more like a 'working man's' club, the sort of place that only men were allowed in, to smoke maybe, and to play snooker.

In the bright orange, turquoise and green painted foyer, there were photographs and posters on the walls of various television stars that had appeared there at the Variety Club. Mandy and I looked around at the familiar faces that we'd seen on the television: Tony Jones, Ken Dodd, the Bachelors, Cliff Richard and Roy Orbison. There were only a few faces and cabaret acts that we didn't know.

I spotted a photo of Shirley Bassey. I loved Shirley Bassey. I had a couple of her LPs and I would sing along with her sometimes using a hairbrush as a microphone and I was very conscious that my mum looked just like her. I was amazed that such a big star like her had been on the stage here too. I wished I could have come to see her.

Through the double doors at the end of the foyer we could hear music playing. My stomach still had butterflies, jumping around inside and my heart was beating so fast with all the excitement. I couldn't wait to get inside. The club was so much bigger on the inside than it seemed on the outside. It was far bigger than the Palais.

All our eyes were fixed firmly towards the stage as we walked through the doors into this vast space. There must have been about one hundred or so Formica topped tables surrounding the stage. Before long every table was filled with partygoers. There were probably over one thousand people there that night. Our groups were directed to tables with very good views of the stage. Each table would seat four. There was

Mandy and I at one side of our table; Janet and her sister Sandra at the other side. We were all just as nervous and excited as each other.

There was food available to buy at the kiosk. Things like scampi in a basket. No thank you, I thought to myself after my previous experience of scampi. I would never eat that again after the embarrassing meal at the restaurant on Mandy's birthday.

Mandy and I ordered a drink called barley wine. This was a really strong beer that one of our friends at the Palais had introduced to us. We had drunk it once before at the Palais and it got us both quite tipsy after just one glass. We saved ourselves some money that night because we didn't want another drink after drinking that. It didn't taste all that pleasant though; I didn't really like the taste of any beer; however, it was cheap and I could sip it slowly throughout the evening becoming quite 'tiddly'.

When the Stylistics finally came on stage, it was absolutely amazing! There were supporting acts on before the Stylistics came on but nothing compared to the main event. The applause they got was nothing compared to the reception that the Stylistics received. Everyone was up out of their seat and cheering and applauding.

The lighting was amazing; the familiar music was so loud. One of the Stylistics' singers had a broken leg and he came on stage with his leg in plaster. He had to sit propped against a stool as he performed. He had a spotlight shining down on him throughout the show. They sang all their greatest soul classics that we knew and some that we hadn't heard before. We were all singing along with them.

Russell, the lead singer, had such a good voice. He sang in such a high pitch that I didn't know how he reached all those high notes, for a man! They were dressed in their white matching suits. They were like the suits they wore on the cover of one of their albums that I had bought a few weeks earlier. They looked so elegant and sophisticated. They were sensational. To the never-ending (it seemed) cheers and applause, after a few hours, their show came to an end. It seemed to be over far too quickly. I could have stayed and listened to them all night.

The disco started after the Sylistics had finished; as usual Mandy and I were up dancing. Mandy and I were half way through our second glass of barley wine by this time, so we were quite merry. As we danced, we noticed a build-up of people queuing at the stage doors. They all were queuing for autographs from the band. We thought about joining the queue to see if we could get their autographs, but we thought they're so famous, they probably wouldn't give them out. Besides, we were having too much fun dancing to the disco music. Once we were up on that floor nothing could drag us away. We didn't want to waste our time in a queue.

Later, when the queues had dispersed, we noticed that some of the band members were coming through the stage door and towards the dance floor. They stood around talking to one another and looking around the club. Mandy and I walked straight over to them and asked if they were with the Stylistics and could we have their autographs. To our surprise they reached over to one of the tables and picked up a paper serviette and scribbled down their autographs, then they passed the serviette to Mandy. We both unfolded the serviette and looked at it. It was just squiggles; we couldn't make out what it said at all. We knew they weren't the Stylistics, so we started to bombard them with questions one after the other about the band. Eventually they told us that the Stylistics had left the building and that they were their roadies. They had American accents. We had never spoken to any Americans before.

As we talked, the club was emptying. The night was over, and everyone was going home. The roadies asked if we wanted to go to a party with them. Mandy and I looked at each other and then simultaneously asked if the Stylistics would be there. The roadies said that it was an 'after the show' party especially for them. Mandy and I giggled to each other. We couldn't believe that they'd ask us to go with them. We couldn't accept their surprisingly tempting offer. We had to go home. There was no way we could or would go with them. Anything could have happened! We would have been so far away from home. How would we have made our way home from who knows where? We couldn't possibly even think about it.

We turned towards the exit and saw that we were being beckoned by our friends, from our factory, to hurry. We would have missed the coach if we hadn't left right away. We said our goodbyes to the Americans and waved as we walked away.

There was a balcony above the exit of the hall and as we left, I looked up. Two beautiful black women caught my eye. Their outfits were very sparkly and they had feather boas wrapped around their necks. They looked like Americans too. They must have been something to do with the Stylistics I thought. Maybe they were their wives. They looked so familiar. I thought I'd seen them somewhere before, but I just couldn't think, where.

When we finally got on the coach, everyone cheered and clapped their hands. We got really embarrassed at being the last two to get on the coach. They had been sitting there, waiting for us for ages. We were almost left behind.

On the journey home I felt sick. My head was spinning. I shouldn't have drunk that second glass of barley wine. Thankfully, I fell asleep on Mandy's shoulder.

The following week at work everyone spoke about the Stylistics and the brilliant 'works do' at Batley Variety Club. It was such a great night.

CHAPTER FORTY-TWO
The DJ

It was Friday night again and Mandy and I were off for a night out at the Palais. We had brought Maureen along too this week, she had just turned sixteen so was too young to go into the Palais but we took her along anyway. Despite this, she liked it there just as much as we did. We had had a great night out at Batley Variety Club the previous week, but it was good to be walking through the doors of the Bolton Palais once again. I was sure that we would have been missed the previous week. We were always the first ones on the dance floor each week.

At the start of a good record, we were up dancing together in the middle of the dance floor and before the record had finished the dance floor was full. We were always the ones who encouraged everyone else to get up dancing.

While having a break from dancing, we sat at our usual table by the dance floor. The DJ came over to us, before he went on stage, and asked where we had been the previous week. He must have missed us too. He sat down at our table and listened to us recalling the events of our Friday night, watching the live performance of the Stylistics at Batley Variety Club. I asked him where his girlfriend Roberta was. He told us that he had finished with her a couple of weeks previously. We all chatted for a while until it was time for his DJ spot on the stage. We all felt quite honoured to have been talking to the DJ, Mr Danny Sinclair. It was the first time that we had spoken to him off the stage. We knew he talked to all the girls in the club. He was very popular, and a very good DJ. However, he must have missed us the previous week.

It was a strange sort of night after that. The DJ talked over the microphone about the Stylistics and mentioned that Mandy and I had been to see them the previous week. He played lots of their hits during the evening. It seemed weird the whole night. It felt that he was playing the records just for us. He certainly seemed to be watching us the whole time. It made us both feel special.

A lad came up to me and asked if I wanted to dance. While we were dancing, Danny took off the record that he was playing and changed it. He played "You Make Me Feel Brand New," another one of the Stylistics. I thought at the time that it was strange for him to do that; he had never done that before. The lad and I carried on dancing and chatting regardless and unaware of what was about to happen.

The DJ jumped from the stage and strolled over to us and interrupted our dance. He tapped the lad on his shoulder and said, "Excuse me!" He pulled me into his arms and started to dance with me! I looked across at Mandy and she was smiling like a Cheshire cat. He held me so close. I had never danced with anyone that closely before. I hadn't seen Danny dance with anyone, or ever seen him jumping off the front of the stage and dance with anyone else that way before. Not even when he was seeing Roberta. I didn't think I'd ever seen him dancing with her. I was shy and embarrassed but as we danced, he was so tender and he made me feel so comfortable in his arms. I liked that feeling. I felt so special. Just as the record was finishing, he asked if he could have the last dance with me and I nodded nervously. He jumped back on the stage and cued in the next record.

When I sat back down with Mandy I was trembling with the experience. I couldn't believe that I had been dancing with the DJ. Mandy was chatting to a lad called Ray. He had been chatting her up for a few weeks by then. I didn't think she liked him because he had just come out of Borstal.

At the end of the evening, Danny jumped off the stage and danced with me again just as he had done before. The record was 'When you're Young and in Love' by The Marvelettes. This was always the last record he played at the end of the evening. It was a slow, smoochy record that seemed to get everyone up on the dance floor dancing closely with their loved one, probably getting them all in the mood for going home. Mandy was up for the last dance too with Ray.

We were all just about to leave the club when Danny rushed over to me and asked if I would like to go for a meal with him. He told me that after he finished work, he and all the bouncers would go to a restaurant in Farnworth. He assured me that he would get me home safely afterwards. I was a bit scared, but I liked him. I really wanted to go with him, but I didn't want to leave Mandy and Maureen. I didn't want to go with him alone. They didn't want to go home without me, so it was agreed that they would both come along too so that we could all go home together after the meal. Danny asked us to wait while he went for his car.

After about five minutes he walked back in the foyer and escorted us out to his car which was parked outside. His car was a little green coloured Mini. There was a narrow sticker across the top of the windscreen saying, 'BOLTON EVENING NEWS.' I had no idea what the significance of this sign was at the time. Danny opened the door and pulled back one of the seats. We all climbed in and sat huddled tightly together on the back seat. One of the bouncers came along too and sat in the passenger seat. We had seen him around the club before but hadn't spoken to him until now. He was a big man with a large tummy, black wavy hair and a black bushy beard. The man didn't say a word as Danny drove. He just grunted to us when Danny had introduced us. Danny said, 'This is Colin, and he's my cousin.' Danny hadn't been driving long when he pulled up in a side street and turned off the engine.

He asked Mandy and Maureen to stay in the car, as agreed, and he assured them that we wouldn't be long. He held the seat forward while I got out of the car. I was feeling a bit scared. Not the same scared feeling I had had when I lived at Dad's house. I had endured that particular fear for most of my life so far; I knew what that felt like. This scared feeling was different. I wasn't frightened like I had been at dads. It was just that I was nervous, and it was all so strange to me. At the same time, I didn't want to embarrass myself again as I had in the other restaurant.

I liked Danny, but I didn't really know him, other than he was the DJ from the Palais. He was like a stranger. Danny took my hand and told me not to worry, that it would all be fine. He must have seen the worried look on my face. He slipped his arm around my waist and pulled me nearer to him. We walked a little way and then came to the restaurant. Danny pulled open the heavy door and I walked in. I took a deep breath and looked at him as he followed me in. No one had ever opened a door for me before. I smiled at him. I liked him. He was a gentleman. I felt like a real lady.

Tony had never opened a door for me. He was always at the pub working these days. We never seemed to have any time together. He had never made me feel like a lady. I had never been able to feel more than a friend to him. I hadn't experienced anything like this before; it had allowed me to know what it was like to be treated like a lady. I liked that feeling.

The restaurant was called 'The Kohinoor'. I could smell the strong aroma of spices, like the ones Mum used when she was making one of her curries. The Kohinoor was an Indian restaurant but nothing like the one we went to for Mandy's birthday. I didn't think they would serve scampi here!

The room was warm and inviting and decorated with bright red and gold colours. There were also beautiful Indian designs hanging on the walls. Fancy folded napkins had been put on every table. All the tables were laid out with clean white tablecloths and cutlery. I was surprised that the place was empty except for the bouncers, seated at a long oblong table in front of the window; they were waiting for us to join them.

When we sat down, Danny introduced everyone to me, as the Indian waiter gave out the menus. The bouncers ordered curries, but Danny said that he didn't fancy a curry, so he ordered a well-done steak. I felt too uncomfortable and shy to say what I wanted so Danny ordered a steak for me too. I hardly spoke throughout the meal. I sat listening to the others talk about their night's work in the Palais and the trouble that they'd had during the night.

Danny was trying to make conversation, but every time he talked to me, I blushed. I was so shy it was embarrassing. I was finding it so hard to cut the steak that I kept making the table wobble. Chewing the steak was difficult too; I had never had steak before. I was glad when the meal was over and it was time to leave.

It was nearly three o'clock in the morning. When we got back to the car, Danny asked if we wanted to go to his house for a drink. He said that it was just around the corner. I hesitated but agreed saying that we wouldn't be able to stay long.

Danny pulled up in front of a row of terraced houses, on a main road not far from the restaurant; the five of us went in. We were led through the front door and through a small vestibule with a Georgian glazed door; this led into the front room. The first thing I noticed in that room was the bright orange shiny walls. I'd never seen walls painted that colour before.

It was a bit dazzling. I also noticed a sort of musty smell. The room was tidy with just the odd ornament on a wall unit in the alcove. There were also ornaments on the mantle of the old tiled fireplace. The house felt cold and damp.

Hung on the wall of the chimney breast was a large framed picture of a lovely little dark-haired girl; she was holding a Labrador puppy. It was a beautiful picture. I stared into the picture and drifted off somewhere in a daydream, wondering if I would have a child like that one day. Mandy, Maureen and I sat together on the settee and Danny went into the back room to get us a drink.

Colin sat in one of the chairs opposite us and never said a word. I looked at him and thought that he didn't look as if he was related to Danny. I wasn't sure whether they were telling the truth about being related or not. All the members of my family looked similar: brown hair and brown eyes being a common factor. It was easy to tell that we were related when we were together.

A moment later Danny came back with a brown bottle and told us it was a wine called Blue Nun. None of us had tried wine before and I wasn't sure about accepting anything from him. I'd heard stories before, about how some men get girls drunk just so they can have their wicked way with them. That wasn't going to happen to me! He poured the wine into glasses and gave one to each of us. He turned the gas fire on full to warm the place as it was chilly. Colin sipped his wine and so did Danny. But we just sat there sniffing it. It smelt like vinegar.

I turned to Mandy and frowned. I decided not to drink any of it! Of course, Maureen was always braver than me, she drank all of hers. Danny started to talk about his house and mentioned that he was going to try and rent it out to someone to help pay the bills. He told us that it was too big for him to live there on his own. He spoke of his recent marriage break-up. This meant that in due course he would have to sell it and give half the house value to his wife. It was a shock to hear that he was married.

When he mentioned 'rent' Mandy and I looked at each other and became very interested. We had been looking for somewhere to rent for ages. Mandy was eighteen and I would be eighteen in November; both of us were desperate to leave home and find our own place to live. We'd been dreaming of it for ages. We asked Danny if he would consider renting it out to us. We told him we were both working and had full-time jobs and could pay him rent. We were delighted and amazed when he said that he would think about it.

It was nearly three thirty in the morning, so we knew we should go home. We gave Danny the directions to our house and while he was driving us home, we spoke about renting his house as we were so enthusiastic about that possibility. Mandy and I were so excited. We couldn't believe our luck. We hoped we would soon be moving into our own place.

Mandy had also mentioned to Danny that she'd had a couple of driving lessons. When we were parked up on the lay-by at the side of our estate, he suggested that he picked us both up at ten o'clock so we could go for a drive to Rivington so Mandy could practice her driving on the quiet roads. It sounded like a great idea.

Mandy and Maureen started to walk up the footpath to our house, without me, because Danny had taken my arm gently and brought the two of us close together.

He kissed me. The kiss was amazing! My heart was beating so fast, but I wasn't scared any more. He looked into my eyes and said that he had wanted to kiss me all night. He said he wanted to see me again and I blushed lowering my head. I wasn't sure what I was doing. I was seeing Tony and here I was kissing another man. I wasn't thinking straight. This man was also married. I couldn't start seeing a married man even if he was estranged from his wife. Danny assured me that he would be at that place, on the bye-pass, at ten o'clock, later that same morning. I left and followed the others home. I turned for a moment to watch him drive away. Not thinking for one minute that he would show up later that morning.

To our surprise, at ten o'clock that morning, he was parked up in the lay-by. Mandy and I were so shocked. We didn't think he would be there. Danny got out of the car and opened the car door for us. He drove us to Rivington.

While he was driving, he asked if we thought he wouldn't turn up. We giggled and nodded. He turned to me and said that he told me that he wanted to see me again and was shocked that I hadn't believed him. I smiled back at him. I felt sort of warm inside. Could this man really like me? I wasn't anybody special. I didn't even think that I was pretty. There were loads of other girls around in the Palais that I thought were prettier than me. Why me?

It was a beautiful day and great to be up Rivington Pike in such lovely weather. All through my teenage years I had spent a lot of time around here and always loved the walks with my mum. This was also a setting for my cross-country runs with school. Unfortunately, as I was now working, I had not been up here for ages. The same applied to Mandy for the same reason.

Danny drove around, looking for a safe quiet road, away from the traffic for Mandy to practice her driving. He found a suitable spot and pulled up on a long narrow lane and got out of the car. Mandy then got in the driving seat and Danny sat in the passenger seat beside her. I was nervously sitting in the back seat. I'd never seen Mandy drive before. I did hope that she would not crash his car. There were no other cars around, only trees and a long stretch of road in front of us, so I started to feel better. He told her not to worry, as the car didn't belong to him, it was a company car belonging to 'The Bolton Evening News'. He explained that he worked for the newspaper as a reporter and his job as a DJ was just part-time. I was learning more and more about this man and I liked what I was hearing apart from the fact of him being married. He seemed perfect apart from that and I was beginning to like him more and more. I was concerned that I had been seeing Tony for a while now, but he was always in the pub and he was always drinking. I didn't like it when Tony got drunk. Still, we remained good friends. How could I tell him that I had started seeing another man?

Dad used to be in the pub all the time and then come home and beat Mum up. Could Tony turn out like my dad? Danny told us he didn't drink except for the odd glass of wine now and again. Mandy drove us slowly up and down the lane with Danny talking to her all the time and reassuring her as to how well she was doing. He talked her through reversing the car and turning it around. It was good. We all enjoyed ourselves. I was impressed with Mandy's driving; she did really well! She would be a good driver, I thought, when she had taken and passed her test as I was sure she would. Danny was making her feel so confident and at ease, while she was driving. I hoped to have driving lessons one day, but I thought I might be too scared to drive a car.

After Mandy had been driving for about an hour or so she said that she'd had enough driving so they swapped seats again and Danny continued to drive us around the quiet lanes of Rivington. The sun was shining. It was such a lovely day and we didn't want it to end. Danny told us that he didn't want to take us home as he would like to spend the rest of the day with us. We were having such a good time and definitely had no objections; we didn't want to go home at that point either.

He parked the car and we all went for a walk through the ruins of an old castle at the side of a reservoir. There were old rusty railings surrounding the water, obviously to keep people away from it. However, the railings didn't deter Mandy and me; we found a gap in the railings and climbed through. We walked along the edge of the water, throwing pebbles, and watching them skip across the top of the water's surface. We sat on big rocks at the water's edge and talked and laughed together. Danny spoke of lots of things including his marriage and the separation. He told us that they hadn't been married long. She was just sixteen and he was nineteen; they had married on Valentine's Day, which sounded so romantic. One problem that he found significant was that his wife would never stay at the house they'd bought together, after they'd married. She had complained that it was damp and too far away from her parent's house. Eventually she had gone off with another man.

The sun shone down on the still water making the gentle ripples sparkle and flicker. It looked magical. I could have stayed there forever. All the rest of the world had disappeared. It was so calm and peaceful with just the birds singing, I felt so relaxed. Every past nightmare vanished from my mind. All the fear disappeared, just for a while.

We all started to get a bit hungry, so we decided to go to Rivington Barn to see if the café was open. I climbed back over the railings and Danny held my hand and helped me over. I thought this was really sweet of him. To my horror my trousers split all the way up the back. I just couldn't believe it! I had embarrassed myself yet again. Danny and Mandy laughed their heads off, but I could have cried. I didn't think it was funny at all. They were my favourite trousers and there I was with my bottom hanging out of them! I went bright red. The last thing I wanted to do was to embarrass myself in front of Danny. I quickly took my cardigan off and tied it around my waist to hide the split. We were having such a good day, but now I just wanted to go home. I couldn't walk around with a huge tear up my backside.

Danny dropped us off at home and he arranged to pick us up that same evening and take us to the Palais. We had never been to the Palais on a Saturday before because you had to be twenty-one. Danny assured us this wouldn't be a problem if he was with us.

The day had been cut short after I tore my trousers but we both looked forward to seeing him again that night. I was in fact supposed to be seeing Tony at the pub that night, but I would have to tell him that I was going to the Palais instead. Mum made it clear that she didn't approve of me seeing a married man and didn't want me seeing him. She wanted me to stay with Tony.

By the following weekend someone had told Tony that I had been seeing Danny. I think it was Maureen who had told him as she had always fancied Tony. One night after he'd finished working at the pub, he came around to the house. It was very late and he'd been drinking. I answered the door and stood in the doorway. Tony looked at me and asked if we could talk. He started to cry and I cried too. I hated to see him crying. I had never seen him cry before. He begged me not to leave him. He tried to hug me, but I just pushed him away. He smelled of beer.

There was nothing I could say to him. I'd already lied to him, saying there was nothing going on with Danny. I had started seeing Danny and Tony was hurting, I was hurting him. All I could think of was Danny. Danny was the one that I wanted to be with. It was over for Tony and me. There was nothing else to be said. As I watched him walk away down the path, I wondered to myself if I'd done the right thing. I had hurt him and I hadn't wanted to do that. However, what I felt for Danny was different to the way I had ever felt about Tony. I was thinking that maybe I was falling in love with Danny and maybe Danny would be 'the first'. Maybe we would get married after he had received his divorce.

A few days later, I received a letter from Tony. It said on the envelope, "not to be opened until 25th December." It was nowhere near Christmas. I knew by the handwriting that it was from Tony, so I quickly opened it. Inside there were two sheets of paper. It read

... *"Dear Darling, Delovely, Daft Maggie,*

You can't do anything you're told can you? I said on the 25th Dec, but being as nosy as you are, you just had to open it didn't you? God! Can't you do anything you're told? I have just watched Crossroads and I'm feeling sort of eh, well. I'm happy and mad, mad, MAD! Please find enclosed a poem; I hope you like it, coz I do, and I like the poem as well! Sorry, there are two men in white jackets driving a yellow van. Now they're coming down my path! Oh no! Help me, Maggie! I'm not mad! Honest I'm not."

On the next sheet was a poem, it read:

"So, I Returned" by Quentin Crisp (Alias Tony who's not mad).

So, I returned, I just had to see you

I had to see if we were really through. I wanted to know what was so wrong

After all this time yet not so very long. So, I returned, ignoring my pride

God! How I must have cried

The tears welling up in my reddened eyes

At the thought of losing you, and no more Goodbyes. The tears on my lips, they taste of salt

And now I realise it was all my fault.

These stupid silly things we do

So, I returned, to tell you I need you.

So, I returned, a thing I've never done before. And I dry my face, standing outside your door. The light is on and you are not in bed.

My eyes are smarting, and my heart is like lead. So, I returned, with a lump deep in my throat

And my shaky trembling hand comes out of my coat. Then I tap on your door ever so light.

Oh, my dear Maggie, why did we fight? So, I returned, and we stood face to face.

And then you are looking at me and I felt in disgrace. I tried to find the words to say I apologise

And then again, the tears they filled my face.

So, I returned, and I snatched you in my embrace I didn't want you to see the wetness on my face

I held you in my arms, I held you so tight

*I told you I was sorry, and it would be all right. So, I returned, you
began to shudder and cry*

I was so sorry you know I would rather die

*So, you cried, and I cried, and we cried together. But never again,
no more fights, no tears never."*

I cried when I read it. I couldn't believe he had written this for me
and he was that upset. I didn't want to hurt him. I was confused. Tony
had always respected me, and we'd always been very good friends. He
hadn't ever pressured me into having sex with him, ever. He had treated
me so nicely on all occasions. He had never shouted, in the way that Dad
had, nor did he have a bad temper like Dad had. We just hardly ever had
time for each other any more. We had just grown apart. He also drank all
the time and I didn't like it when he was drunk. When in a drunken stupor
he scared me. It would remind me of when Dad would go to the pub and
come home and beat my mum, and Mary. Tony could change and turn
out to be just like my dad. I couldn't bear the thought of that and spending
the rest of my life the way Mum and Mary had done. Besides, Tony didn't
have a car like Danny did. Whether these were good enough reasons to
end our relationship, I just didn't know. I put the letter away in a safe and
secret place and didn't show it to anyone else. I was going to keep it
forever.

I never spoke to or saw Tony again. It wasn't long before I learned
that he had got another girlfriend and was happy. I also found out that
Maureen had been out with him too the following week after we had split
up. I was glad that we had split up, when I heard that.

The relationship with Danny developed. He made me feel safe and
somehow protected. We spent a lot of time together. I loved every minute
we spent together. When he wasn't working, and sometimes after he'd
finished work at the Palais, he would take me out for long drives in his
car.

We would drive along the long motorways just talking together and
listening to music. I gave him a tape of 'The Stylistics Greatest Hits' and
we listened to it all the time. I knew it all off by heart. Some nights I
wanted to stay with him instead of going home but I knew Mum wouldn't
have liked that at all. When Danny and I were apart I couldn't get him
out of my mind. I would mope around the house waiting for him to call

round. I knew that I was falling in love with him.

When we were together, he was always saying that he loved me and wanted to be with me. I talked to him for hours and hours about my dad and Mum and what Dad was like with Mum and Mary and also what he was like with us as kids. He listened and cried. I cried until I couldn't cry any more. He would wrap his arms around me so tightly. He said that he would never, ever hurt me, and everything would be all right and he was going to take me away from all that life and help me to forget it. The memories of all those yesterdays were still so vivid and still inside haunting me.

I still wasn't sure of Danny's love for me; it had only been a few weeks. I couldn't tell him how I was beginning to feel about him. I couldn't tell him how much I loved him. I was too scared and didn't want to feel embarrassed. I did feel so safe when I was with him and he was holding me. I just knew he could never hurt me as Dad had done. Mum still did not approve of Danny. She did not want me to see him at all, but he respected me so much. I tried to tell her and explain that things were great with us, but she didn't listen.

Mandy and I had stayed at his house, occasionally at weekends. Danny and I were together all night but he didn't try anything on with me. He would say he could wait and he wanted to prove his love for me. At that time, I was still too scared to go 'further' with him. He told me over and over again how much he cared about me. However, I wanted to make sure that he was not saying all that just to get me into his bed. My mum constantly told me that men would say anything to get you into their bed! Eventually, as time went on, Mum allowed him to come into the house, when he was picking me up. At first, he didn't really feel welcomed by her, but she seemed to warm to him a little, but still kept warning me behind his back that he was a 'sweet talking guy' and he would hurt me one day. She would say that he had the 'gift of the gab' and that he would only use me. I didn't believe her. What could he use me for? He could have anyone he chose from the Palais, but he wanted to stay with me. It didn't matter what she said to me, I wanted to stay with him as long as he wanted me too. I could see, that one day, Danny and I would share more than friendship. In time we would be together forever.

Danny would sometimes pick me up from work and give me a lift home in his car; this was always a surprise and a very pleasant one. He always wore a shirt and tie and a three-piece suit, for his work with the newspaper. He looked so smart and amazing; he looked just like the bosses of our factory, when they had one of their business meetings. I felt so overwhelmed and proud to be collected from work by him. He would sometimes walk straight into the factory, in front of all the other women, and say, 'Your carriage awaits madam—' something that I would imagine Bret Butler would have said in 'Gone with the Wind'. I would blush, as I was escorted out of the factory, to his car. His car was now a flashy red Ford Cortina GTI, with black leather seats.

One Sunday afternoon I found myself missing him so much. Mum and I had had one of our usual little arguments about Danny. I had been with Danny most of the weekend and Mum had hardly seen me. She had said that I might as well be living with him because I spent most of my time with him. I spend a lot of time with Mandy too, but she never said anything like that about Mandy. Why was she saying these things about Danny? Couldn't she see that he liked me and wanted to be with me? I felt that she was pushing me out of my home again; just like she did before. I had just started to feel safe at home, and I thought she wanted me to stay this time, so I couldn't understand why she would want me to leave; does she not love me any more? I wasn't ready to live with Danny; I didn't know him well enough for that yet. We shouldn't even have been thinking about moving in together at that stage. It was not the right time. Unfortunately, the arguments with Mum got worse and she was also falling out with Dave, her husband, over his drinking. He kept coming home drunk all the time; I just had to talk to Danny about the situation at home with my mum. He would make me feel better; he always did.

Mandy and I stormed out of the house and went to the telephone box to ring Danny. I was in tears again as we spoke. I just couldn't understand why Mum was giving me such a hard time over Danny. I knew that he was a married man, but he had no intention of ever going back to his wife. He had started to see a solicitor to get a divorce from her. I felt my mum was not giving us a chance and not being very fair. Danny did have the words to make me feel better. He was saying over and over again that he loved me. He told me that he wanted me to move in with him as soon as possible. The tears stopped and the thought of us being together forever made me so happy. I told him I loved him so much and the thought of losing him would break my heart. I had never said those words to him before. I was too scared to tell him how I really felt about him, but I so wanted to be with him. Suddenly, the phone went dead. I tried and tried to ring him back, but the phone was engaged all the time. Oh, what had I said? Had I upset him? I should never have said those words. Maybe he wasn't ready to hear those words from me yet. What had I done? Had I lost him forever? The words I had spoken were cascading through my mind. I tried the number again. It was still engaged. Maybe he had another call and he would phone me back.

I waited and waited but the phone didn't ring. I tried his number again and again but still got the engaged tone. I was getting so distraught. I called the operator to see if there was a fault on the line. Mandy and I were huddled together in the phone box, both of us confused as to what had happened to Danny. The operator eventually came back on the line and told us that Danny's phone was off the hook.

All at once there was a knock on the window of the phone box; it was Danny! We both screamed out in surprise to see him. I burst into tears when I saw his smiling face peering through the window. He opened the door and hugged me so tightly.

I still had the telephone receiver in my hand and I could hear the operator saying something. I lifted the receiver to my ear and spoke to her. 'He's here! He's here! Thank you, operator.' I was 'gobsmacked.'

Replacing the receiver, I reached out to him. Danny was holding me so tightly. I couldn't believe he had driven here to me. I was so worried that something had happened to him, while we talked on the phone.

He held me so tightly and kept saying, 'Tell me again. Say it again!'

It dawned on me that what I had said to him on the phone before it went dead made him drive all the way here to where I was in that telephone box. I had told him that I loved him. It was the first time he'd heard those words from me and I told him again then, to his face. I did love him and he told me, it was what he wanted so much to hear. He said that he was so overwhelmed at what I had said to him over the phone, that he just had to come to me and hold me.

We drove around that night in his car until it had gone dark and after taking Mandy home, he drove me back to my house. My house was in darkness. Everyone had gone to bed. Danny came in with me and I made him a cup of coffee. We sat on the sofa together, talking quietly, so as not to wake any of my sleeping family upstairs. I wanted to be with Danny and didn't want him to go. We snuggled into each other's arms and kissed. The night felt special and so right. Danny reached over and switched off the table lamp at the side of us. In the darkness we laid together side by side on the sofa caressing. My clothes were being loosened and I was being touched. I didn't want him to stop. I was shaking, so he asked me if I was okay. He asked me if I wanted him to stop. I was silent but didn't want him to stop. I kissed him and told him I loved him. I was afraid and breathless, but I didn't want it to end. I had to be with him that night.

The words of my mother were raging through my head, 'He will use you for what he wants and then he will leave you. He's no good.' I didn't care what she said. He loved me and I knew he did.

He held me so close and tenderly as he entered me. His softly spoken words of love were now replacing the echoes of my mother's voice in my head. His body moved slowly, and I held him. It hurt; I was burning. I felt his warm caress on my neck. I held him tighter. With his reassuring voice in my ear and the love I felt for him I didn't want the night to end. This was the moment I had been waiting for. I was losing my virginity. I was with the man I loved and with the man who I knew loved me. I was not afraid any more.

The moment was lost as I heard the creaking floorboards upstairs. Someone was coming downstairs! Danny and I held our breath and closed our eyes, lying very still and pretending to be asleep. He was still inside me. We froze in the darkness and nestled together under the thick, heavy, tartan blanket that had covered our worn-out sofa. The door to the living room slowly opened and Uncle Ted staggered in. He coughed and bumped into the back of the sofa as he passed and walked through the kitchen to the toilet. Soon he was back and went upstairs without another sound. Danny and I pulled the blanket over our heads. We couldn't stop giggling. We thought that we were going to be discovered together under that blanket. On that special night, we lay together in each other's arms and made love for the first time. We then drifted off to sleep.

The sun peeping through the window woke us from our sleep. I jumped up and went into the kitchen to wash and get ready for work. I looked in the mirror that was propped up against the kitchen window, to see if I looked somehow different from the night before. I was sure that I should have looked so unlike the girl that I was yesterday. In fact, I looked just the same. I smiled to the face smiling back at me. I felt so happy. I didn't feel like I felt yesterday. I felt so different. I ached inside. I was not a virgin any more. That feeling is what I had been waiting for, for so long; now it had happened. It wasn't what I expected. I thought that it would feel different than it did. It hurt and felt uncomfortable. Is that only because it was the first time?

I thought of my mum and what she would be saying to me now if she knew what had happened to me last night. Her words started to echo again in my mind. Danny walked into the kitchen and held me again. Her words disappeared.

Danny drove me to work, kissed me and promised to be there to pick me up after work that night. I couldn't wait to tell Mandy my good news, in the canteen that morning. In fact, I was sure she would have been able to tell by the look on my face that I wasn't a virgin any more. Later that day, as I worked at my machine, I was presented with a huge bouquet of flowers that had been delivered to the factory. They were from Danny. The card inside read:

'To Maggie…

I Love You… Always Yours Danny.'

I cried inside when I was given them, they were beautiful, yellow roses, lilies, chrysanthemums and some I didn't know the names of. They were all held together with a big yellow ribbon tied in a bow. I was so embarrassed but so proud. No one had ever sent me flowers before. It was a real shock but such a lovely surprise. When we had made love the previous night, it felt so right, but my mum's words made me doubt his love for me. He did love me. I knew he did.

He was outside waiting for me, when I finished work that night. Mum was so wrong, I thought. He had had what he wanted, but he still wanted to be with me. He was here, just as he said he would be.

Within the next few weeks, we spent all our spare time together. He was now a regular visitor at our house and seemed to have been made welcome by everyone. Everyone seemed to like him. Mum also seemed to accept our relationship but when we were at home it was difficult to be alone. My younger sister hung around us like a bad smell at times and the house was always so full.

Mum and Dave's relationship was in trouble. They bickered all the time and argued about his drinking. She wanted him to leave, I knew she did. I longed to be out of there and have my own place. I didn't like the arguments. I didn't like the bad atmosphere.

My weekends were now spent with Danny at his house, so it seemed the most natural thing to do when Danny suggested that I should move in with him.

I commuted to work, from Farnworth to Horwich every day. I set off at seven o'clock, to catch a bus into Bolton, and then another to take me to Horwich. I got to work for eight o'clock every morning.

Every night after work Danny was outside waiting to drive me home. I was growing up fast now. I was now so far away from all the horrors of my childhood. I was learning how to cook, just the way Mary taught me. I was now looking after the man I loved. I couldn't wait to get home each evening and prepare the meal I had planned for him throughout the day. I had asked my friends at work for suggestions, as to what to cook for him. They would always come up with different recipes for me to follow. I would watch Danny's face, as he ate the special meals I had so lovingly prepared. I would be so nervously excited, waiting for a glance of approval from him, indicating that he liked the meal. When I received this approval, I would tuck into mine. My life was full of love at that time. I hadn't known such love as this existed before.

Sometimes it was hard to take in all the love that he was showing me. We didn't fight. We didn't argue. We laughed and giggled. He listened to me. I listened to him. I didn't think such happiness was possible, especially for me. I would cry sometimes, to think of Mum and Mary and the lives they had with Dad. I was aware that for some time at least Dad was the man who they too, thought they loved. Why was it not like this for them?

Danny somehow could sense that sometimes I was down and deep in the dark world of old memories. He would come to me and ask me what the matter was. We would talk away the nights in each other's arms and I would cry on his shoulder and all my bad thoughts would soon melt away.

Wednesday the 3rd November 1976 was the occasion of my eighteenth birthday. I woke up with Danny beside me, who had been sleeping soundly. I kissed him gently. He slept undisturbed. I wanted to wake him up to see if he had remembered that it was my birthday. I kissed him again. Again, there was no response. I whispered, "I love you," in his ear and left his side to get ready for work. On the way to work that morning I was filled with dread hoping he hadn't forgotten my birthday. I tried to convince myself that he wouldn't forget and that there would be something special that he would do for me when I returned home that night.

All my friends at work wished me a 'Happy birthday' and gave me cards. Despite this, I ached inside and felt a bit sad. All I wanted was Danny to call me at work and reassure me that he had not forgotten my eighteenth birthday. There was no phone call. No surprise floral delivery. No surprise visit during my dinner hour with a card as I expected. I just had to face it; he had forgotten.

I talked to Mandy and told her Danny had forgotten my birthday and my eyes filled with tears. It was the first time Danny had made me cry. I thought he didn't love me any more. She put her arms around me and told me that I should have woken him to remind him. That day at work should have been a good day; it was my eighteenth birthday but I felt so sad. The day went so slowly.

When I left the factory, Danny was waiting for me outside. I was so glad to see him and hoped there was a gift in the car waiting for me. When I got in the car, he kissed me as usual but there was no gift. No mention of my birthday. My heart sank. He was quiet. I knew in my heart that something was wrong. I could feel it. I tried to make conversation about my day at work, still not mentioning to him that it was my birthday. I didn't want to remind him. Now I just wanted to forget it myself too.

When we got home, he casually suggested that we go out for a meal that night instead of cooking. My spirits began to lift a little and I went upstairs to get ready. I was slowly forgetting my disappointing birthday. At this point I was really worrying about what was the matter with Danny. I wanted to cheer him up, so going out for a meal just might do the trick. We both got ready and then left the house. Danny told me that he had to call at the Palais, to see someone that he worked with, before we went to the restaurant. The thought that he could be picking up my surprise birthday present flickered through my mind; then slowly faded away fast. The Palais was empty when we walked in. There were a couple of bar staff getting the place ready for opening up later. Danny disappeared, leaving me sitting at the bar, drinking orange juice. He was gone for ages and my stomach began to rumble. I was starving. After about half an hour, he came back to me with an apology, saying that the guy he wanted to see was on his way and he wouldn't be long. With that he disappeared again. The place was so quiet. No music playing. The clatter of the beer glasses, being prepared for that evening's drinkers, echoed through the empty building. I looked down into my glass and began to feel sad once again. This had turned into a horrible birthday. I sat there so alone; did he still love me? I couldn't imagine my life without him. What if he wanted to leave me? A secret teardrop fell from my eye onto the bar in front of me, beside the now empty glass of orange juice.

I looked up at the clock above the bar and it read eight-thirty, my birthday was nearly over. There were butterflies in my stomach and I was filled with the fear of losing Danny. He appeared behind me stirring me from my nightmare thoughts. He apologised to me again and kissed me and seemed to be back to his normal self.

"We can go now," he said. He drove back through Bolton and then through Farnworth towards the restaurant. He turned off the usual road to the restaurant and said that he had to call back home to pick up some more money, then we could go and eat. I was starving and beginning to get a little irritated by his strange behaviour and thought that we'd never get to eat as things were. This behaviour didn't seem like Danny at all. It was all beginning to feel a bit sinister.

We pulled up outside the home we shared together, and he asked me to come in and wait while he got the money because he didn't want me waiting outside in the car on the main road in the dark. I accepted his silly worries and went into the house with him. When we walked into our dark living room the kitchen door in front of us opened suddenly. I jumped back and screamed. I thought we had burglars. Maureen was standing there smiling, holding a birthday cake with candles flickering lighting up her face. The lights came on and the room was filled with people. Mandy was there and Alan, who had been our new lodger for a few weeks by then. Colin was there too and some friends from work, and some people from the Palais. It was amazing. I didn't expect this. I was shocked and a little scared. I pushed my way through the singing group and into the kitchen. I couldn't take it all in. I didn't really know what was going on.

Danny grabbed me from behind and held me. He was laughing. "Did you really think I'd forgotten?" I cried and hugged him. He looked so happy. Despite this, the thoughts of the horrible day, I had just gone through, clouded my mind. Thinking all day that he didn't love me any more and he wanted to leave me. In fact, there he was planning this big surprise behind my back instead. I couldn't believe it. All the messing about and leaving me sitting alone at the bar in the Palais was just to waste some time while everyone was preparing for this lovely surprise party for me. Well, it all worked. I didn't expect this at all. It was a surprise.

Danny shouted down to me, from the top of the stairs, and said, "Maggie!! Come and have a look at all this mess, who's done this?" I ran up to him, as he stood at the top of the stairs, looking into the bedroom we shared; the room that I had cleaned and polished the night before. I had made it so nice for us both, hoping all my hard work was not in vain.

I looked into the bedroom and it all looked just the way I'd left it that evening. I looked at Danny confused. His eyes were smiling. He was acting strangely again, I thought. He looked down and took my hand and kissed it. He gave me a large, white, flat box with my name on the front. I looked at him as I opened it. It was a birthday card. On the front it read:

'To my Fiancé'

I stared at the words 'to my fiancé.' I repeated the words over and over in my mind. I knew what they meant. I looked at him puzzled. "But I'm not your fiancé." He smiled back at me. I was shaking all over. He had tears in his eyes to match mine. "You are now," he said. In his hand, which had been concealed by the birthday card, he produced a small, black velvet box. He opened it slowly. I peered inside. It was a beautiful diamond ring. I just couldn't stop staring into the box. It was just as I had imagined my engagement ring would be. It was my dream coming true.

I couldn't speak. My knees were trembling so hard I thought I was going to fall. Danny took the ring from the box and placed it on the third finger of my left hand. "I love you so much," he said," we were now engaged; engaged to be married."

The music downstairs was filling the house. He kissed me as the tears were falling down my cheek. They were tears of joy. We walked slowly down the stairs, hand in hand to join the others. The guest's downstairs were overjoyed by our news. With Danny by my side, we showed off the ring to everyone and I couldn't stop looking at it on my finger for the whole of the night.

The room was now filled with birthday cards and engagement cards too. Everyone knew what Danny was planning and they were all in on the surprise. This had turned out to be the best day of my life. I could see our future. I could see my life in front of me with Danny. I could see our wedding day. I could see the love. I could see the happiness. I could see our children. I decided then and there that we would have four children: two girls and two boys. There would be no more nightmares. My traumatic childhood was behind me. I had a whole new life starting. A whole new life with Danny was beginning. This was my home from this point on. Our home would be filled with the love that Danny had shown to me every day since we had met just a few months earlier. I had seen the love, I had felt his love, and we shared our love together. A love that I had never felt, or seen, from anyone else in my life before. I could almost hear the sound of the laughter around our home from our children. There was never love and laughter and joy in my childhood. The tears filled my eyes once again as my mind drifted back to those times. Hearing the screams from our mum and listening to the sobs of my sisters. This was the start of the rest of my life and I hoped that one day all those nightmares would disappear. Hopefully, the memories that have haunted me for so long would dissolve. In their place would be our new memories and the dreams of our future together.

We made love that night, with such passion, and lay together in each other's arms, wishing the night would never end. We cried. We were making our own memories now.

The words of my mother still rang through my head. I thought to myself, 'You are wrong, Mum, you are so wrong'. We will show you just how wrong you are.

It was my eighteenth birthday and you are not at my party Mum!

I just wished that you were there with us Mum, so you could have seen just how happy we were.

He may not have been tall and dark, and some say not all that handsome, or what some might expect a prince to look like, but he was my Prince Charming, my knight in shining armour. He had rescued me. This was the happy ending I had so desired all my life.

At that moment, I thought that my happiness was going to last forever. I really thought that all of my dreams were coming true. I had my future mapped out in front of me. I knew where I wanted to be, which was right there in his arms forever for the rest of my life.

However, in just twenty-three days later, another nightmare was on its way... That nightmare would devastate and destroy my dreams forever!

CHAPTER FORTY-THREE
Shattered Dreams

On the morning after our engagement party, I travelled to work on the bus. I couldn't wait to get to work and show off my engagement ring, just like Susan had done a few weeks earlier. Susan was a pretty, shy girl who sat on the next row of machinists from me. She had worked at our factory since leaving school and was about twenty-two. She had been courting with her boyfriend for years and was so shocked when he finally popped the question and gave her an engagement ring. Everyone in the factory was pleased and excited for her when she went round flashing off the diamond on her finger. When I get to work, that will be me I thought to myself!

I was sitting on the upstairs of the bus and gazing at my hand and the ring that had been placed on my finger the previous night. The sun was making the diamond sparkle. I felt so happy. I didn't know if it was a real diamond, as was the case in Susan's ring, but I didn't care. Danny gave it to me and I didn't care if it was just an old brass curtain ring, it would still have been special to me.

When I got to work, everyone had heard my news already from Mandy. She always got to work before me. They were all waiting to see the ring and were just as excited for me as they had been for Susan. I was thrilled. Susan and I compared our diamonds and although her diamond was so much bigger than mine, one of the girls assured me that the diamond in my ring was, in fact a real diamond. She told me that she could tell just by looking at it that it wasn't one of those fake diamonds. There were a few comments from some of the girls enquiring about Danny's divorce. I was so happy and hadn't even thought about his divorce. I knew we had to wait a while to get married and I didn't mind that. I was sharing my life with Danny at that time and that was all that mattered. The engagement ring was firmly on my finger; it was there to stay.

Despite my delight, the ring was very loose. I was horrified when it had slipped off my finger, while I worked that day. After a frantic search, to my relief, I found it between the rugby shirts that I had been working on. It would have broken my heart if I had lost it. I knew that one day it would be joined with a wedding ring; as soon as Danny's divorce came through.

During the weeks that followed, I worked hard at the factory earning all I could. We were planning for our first ever Christmas together.

One Friday night, while we were at the Palais, Danny received a phone call from his ex-wife. She had told him that she needed to talk to him and was coming to the Palais with her parents that night. Danny told me what was happening and told me not to worry about anything. He thought that it was most likely to be associated with divorce arrangements. I didn't worry. His words reassured me, just as they always did. Inside I was secretly hoping that their divorce proceedings would soon be finalized and their marriage would be over. Danny and I could then get married, as we had planned.

Danny was waiting backstage for her to arrive while Mandy and I stayed around the dance floor, trying not to think about them. We carried on just enjoying the evening.

We thought we saw them; an elderly couple and a girl walking through the middle of the dance floor, still wearing their coats. It was unusual to see people still wearing their coats; usually coats were left in the cloakroom as they walked in. That's what made me presume that it was the group of people that Danny was waiting for. I took a second look and thought it couldn't be them as the girl appeared to be pregnant. It couldn't be! Danny hadn't told me that she was pregnant.

They all walked towards the stage door, knocked and waited. Danny came to the door, greeted them and they all went inside. I was shocked at realising that this was his ex-wife and that she was pregnant. I looked at Mandy and almost burst into tears. She was shocked too and we both got up and went into the toilets. I really wanted to go backstage and find out what was happening in there. I knew I couldn't do that but that was my man in there. I couldn't do anything. I just had to wait. I had to wait for them to leave and then find out from Danny what had been said between them. I had a bad feeling in the pit of my stomach. My hands were shaking.

After a short time, and to our surprise, we heard Danny talking over the microphone on stage, so we left the toilets and went back into the hall. As we walked through the foyer, back into the ballroom, I looked around to see if I could see his ex-wife and her parents. Having looked around, it seemed that they had already left. Danny didn't look at me as we sat in our seats at our usual table. I just knew there was something wrong. My stomach was doing somersaults.

After his show on the stage, Danny came to us and asked me to go backstage, as he needed to talk to me. I could tell with the look on his face and the tone in his voice that there was a problem. He was pale as if he had just had a big shock. He looked nervous and edgy. I asked him what was wrong. He looked so sad and close to tears. He looked straight at me and said that he was going back to her. 'She's pregnant with my child, and I can't divorce her.' Danny told me that the scandal would ruin him and he would lose his job at the newspaper. He said that she was six months pregnant and as they were together six months ago, the baby was his.

I couldn't believe what I was hearing. This was my love; my man. He said he would love me forever. We were going to have our own children together one day. Our dreams were shattering, one by one, while we were sitting together in that tiny scruffy backstage room. He told me that he had made her pregnant and that our relationship therefore had to be over!

I was stunned! We were engaged and we lived together. Where was I supposed to go, particularly considering it was two o'clock in the morning?

He then informed me that when he left the Palais, he would have to go back and pick her up from her parent's house. At that point he would bring her back home; back home to the house I shared with Danny. I lived there and Mandy was stopping there too. We couldn't leave. Where could we go at that time of night?

The music had stopped in the Palais ballroom and everyone had started to leave. Danny collected his records and said that he had to go; he was so cold in his approach to me. I was absolutely devastated and in shock. I was trembling, but I couldn't cry. I thought it was some sort of bad dream that I would wake up from at any time. How could he have been so cold to me? After everything he had said to me.

Mandy and I followed him out to his car, which was parked further up the road on Bridge Street. Mandy was just as shocked as I was to hear what was happening. She was also worried, because we had nowhere to stay that night and we couldn't go back to her house and disturb her parents and worry them. It appeared that Danny was just going to dump us both right there in the middle of the street. He didn't seem to care what would happen to us or where we were going to go that night. He was behaving like a stranger. I had never seen him like this before. Up until today all I had seen was love and kindness and so much tenderness.

I loved him with all my heart!

I was beginning to think that I didn't know him at all. He was slipping through my fingers. I was losing him. He placed his records in the boot of his car and got into the driver's seat and started the engine. I was pleading with him not to leave me. He looked at me with such cold, empty eyes and lit up a cigarette. He was sitting there behind the wheel, saying that he was sorry but he had to go.

The passenger door was open so I tried to get into the car but Danny stopped me by leaning over the seat trying to close the door. I hung onto it so tightly and wouldn't let go. I was crying and became hysterical, I pleaded for him not to do this to me. Danny tried to drive the car forward but I just screamed and hung on refusing to let go. I didn't want him to leave me; I loved him. Everything we had shared in the previous few months flashed through my mind. He was leaving me. It was all over.

Driving down the road towards us, on the opposite side of the road was a police car. Danny spotted it and flashed his headlights to attract the attention of the officer inside. The police car pulled up in front of us and the officer got out of his car and came over. Danny told the officer that he was having some trouble and asked the officer if he could remove me from his vehicle so he could get on his way. I could not believe what I was hearing.

How could he do this to me? I couldn't stop my tears. The officer came to me and asked me to let go of the car and let him go on his way. I had no choice, I had to let go. I told the officer that he was my fiancé and that we had only been engaged for twenty -three days.

Danny pulled the passenger door shut and sped off up the street. He was gone, leaving Mandy and I standing there, stranded at the side of the road at nearly three o'clock in the morning. We had nowhere to go. We had no money for a taxi; we usually didn't need a taxi as we were always driven home by the man I loved.

Mandy hugged me and shed a few tears herself too. She had never seen Danny behave in that way before. We were standing there on the deserted street, not really knowing what to do or where to go. It was so cold. I was still trembling and crying hysterically. I began to feel so angry.

Mandy suggested that we should start walking back to the house, which I had shared with Danny, because all our things were there. She said that he would possibly put all our belongings outside in the street and dump them, just as he had with me. She was right, I thought maybe he would do that, so we set off walking, to what I believed would have been my home forever.

I knew that Alan, our lodger, would be at home, tucked up in his bed. He was not going to believe what had happened. Shivering from the cold November wind, we approached St. Peters Way and started walking along it. At the end of that road was Moses Gate, from there we wouldn't be far away from home. We were both tired and exhausted and scared about what might happen when we got home. I hoped that we would get there before Danny and his 'ex' wife. I hoped that when we got there Alan would let us in. I hoped that Danny had not rung him already and asked him not to let us in if we showed up. Where else were we supposed to go?

We then had another fright. A police car pulled up alongside us, and the officers inside asked us what we were doing on the dual carriageway. We told them that we were going home and they told us bluntly that we weren't allowed to walk on that road and we must leave at the next junction. Which we did before we got arrested! We had to go the long way back!

When we reached Moses Gate, we called Alan from a phone box. He would have been in bed but we had to make sure he was awake and that he would let us in when we got there. There was no answer. We carried on our way and before long we had reached home. To our relief Danny's car wasn't outside. The house was in darkness. We banged on the door frantically. We started throwing little stones, from the road, at the front bedroom window, trying to wake Alan before Danny arrived home with her!

We had been trying for about ten minutes when the lights came on and he came to the door to let us in. We explained to him what had happened and we all went upstairs into the front bedroom and stayed there out of the way. We were expecting Danny to arrive any minute… with her!

Within ten minutes Danny's car pulled up outside and he brought her into the house. I could hear their muffled voices downstairs and I could hear him locking the front door. I was trembling. Tears filled my eyes once again. How could he do this? I just couldn't believe it. I could hear them coming up the stairs and going into the back bedroom; the bedroom that I shared with Danny. He was taking her to the same bed that we made love in, just that very morning.

I could hear them whispering and giggling. I wanted to go in there and tell her to go, get out of my bed, and to get out of my house, but I knew I couldn't. Alan was shocked at what we told him and at what had happened. I cried on the pillow and drifted off to sleep, eventually.

The next morning, I woke up feeling still quite exhausted. My eyes felt puffy and swollen from all the tears. Later that day I would have to leave that house. As I lay there listening to the silence, I asked myself, where could I go? I couldn't go back to Dad's house. I wouldn't go back to Mum's house; I couldn't go back there to hear her say, "I told you so." I didn't want to hear those words.

Mandy stirred in the bed opposite and asked if I was all right. I told her that we had better get up and start packing. We left the bedroom quietly and went downstairs. I made a cup of coffee for us both and gathered a few of my belongings from around the house. We sipped our coffee and chatted, sitting on an old electric storage heater in the kitchen. It felt like we had been there for hours. Soon we heard some movement upstairs. The floorboards always creaked in that room.

The bedroom door opened and we heard them making their way down the stairs. Mandy and I sat rigid on the storage heater while they walked into the kitchen. She went straight into the bathroom and Danny went to the kettle to make a drink. He placed two cups on the worktop, made coffee and then took them into the living room without saying a single word or looking at us once. It was as if we were invisible. She left the bathroom and followed him into the front room. I lowered my head when she passed. I couldn't look at her. I didn't want to look at her. I felt humiliated.

Everything we have been through together was all for nothing. It didn't take long to collect the rest of my things from upstairs and afterwards we both drank another cup of coffee, sitting on the storage heater, staring at the two black bin liners in front of us, containing my belongings. I cried again.

The front door opened and we heard Colin's voice. Danny came into the kitchen with Colin, he looked at me and said that he had rung Colin and Colin had arrived to take us wherever we wanted to go. I was gobsmacked. I couldn't believe what he had just said. Danny was throwing us out! Colin picked up both my bags and took them through the front room and out to his car. Mandy and I followed behind him. Danny and his estranged wife were sitting huddled together on the settee, Danny's hand slowly rubbing his wife's swollen pregnant tummy. I felt sick. I wanted to cry and scream so loudly.

The front door, to the house I'd once shared with Danny, was firmly shut behind us as we left. I didn't look back.

I had absolutely no idea what to do or where I was going to go. Mandy asked Colin if he would take us to her house and gave him directions. He drove us to Horwich, where her parents lived. We were both sitting silently in the car as he drove. Colin didn't ask any questions. He dropped us off and drove away; just like my dad had done all those years ago. This awful memory flashed through my mind, as I watched Colin's car disappear round the corner.

Mandy went into her house, to ask her parents if I could stay; she explained the situation and told them that I had nowhere else to go. Luckily, they agreed that I could stay.

I carried my things up to Mandy's room and collapsed on her bed and cried. She sat beside me and hugged me. She was my best friend in the world but even she couldn't stop the pain. At that moment I felt my whole future had been destroyed. My hopes and dreams had been shattered. He had rescued me from my nightmares. He had promised me a better life. A life with him that would be full of love. I believed his every word; I believed in him.

How could I ever possibly start all over again? How would I ever get over him? For the first time in my life, I felt so alone.

CHAPTER FORTY-FOUR
Undying Love?

During the week following that awful weekend, I was so miserable and I cried most of the time. I couldn't sleep. I couldn't eat. I was missing Danny so much. Mandy tried her best to cheer me up and make me smile again. She was so supportive and caring and never stopped trying to halt my tears. I had so much pain inside. It hurt so much. I felt humiliated. I couldn't see any point to my life without him.

Work, the following week, was the hardest; I couldn't let my colleagues know that my relationship with Danny was over. I was still wearing his ring at work. It had tape around it so that it couldn't possibly slip off my finger as it had in the past. The ring was mine and he was not having it back. I intended to keep it forever. At work I was wearing my ring so no one would know that we had split up. I didn't want to be confronted with all sorts of questions. I couldn't bear to be asked any questions about him. I was sure that the tears would start again and I would not be able to stop them.

Outside work though, when Danny's ring was not on my finger, it would be kept safely in Mandy's jewellery box. I now travelled to work with Mandy, on the bus from Horwich instead of Farnworth, so we would always get to work at the same time. I was worried that our colleagues would realise that it was strange for Mandy and I to be on the same bus each morning and start to gossip and ask questions.

I had to put a front on. I didn't want them all to gossip. I didn't want to hear the sort of words that my mum would say if, and when she found out what had happened. It was kept between Mandy and I and we tried to carry on as normal in front of the whole factory. My emotions would get the better of me at times. When I heard certain records being played on the radio, I would be reminded of him and I would quickly disappear into the toilets and have a quiet cry to myself all alone in the cubicle. No one ever suspected that anything was wrong or asked any questions. This week was the hardest I had ever worked too. I would sit down at my machine and sew each day, hardly talking to anyone.

It was as if I was alone in my own little world with my thoughts. I couldn't find any of the answers to the questions that were running through my mind constantly. Each night after work I felt drained and exhausted. At the end of the week all my hard work would show in my wage packet. I was pleased I had managed to earn so much money.

Friday night came, after a very long week, and Mandy and I were ready for a night out. We had gone to the shops again like we used to before Danny came into my life. We bought nice things to wear. It really cheered me up that day to shop with Mandy. We hadn't done it for so long. All my wages would have been taken home with me to Danny's house. It was all spent on the house, either buying things for the house or groceries. I was making a home with him then, but not any more! I didn't have to do that any more. I tried to make myself feel a little better, as if it compensated for the fact that we were no longer together.

Mandy and I tried on our new clothes, in the changing rooms, and I began to smile again. I felt I had got my best friend back and I was slowly beginning to feel free again. Danny was gone and he would not be coming back, so I had to get used to it and get on with my life again. I started to remember all the good times that Mandy and I had had before we met Danny; all the good times at the Palais before he came into our lives.

On our way home from the shops that evening, Mandy and I talked about the Palais, it was the only place we'd got to know. We both enjoyed going there every week. We knew everyone, and everyone knew us. We didn't want to go anywhere else. It was decided that we were going back there that night. Danny wasn't going to stop us. It was a big place and we could get lost in there and we could avoid him. The pain had slowly turned to anger at the thought of him being able to stop us going into our favourite dance hall. He had made his decision to go back to her and I had made the decision to try to forget him and get on with my life. I had to be strong; I knew that it would probably be hard at first to see him again, but I felt it would be the only way I could get over him. It was the beginning of December. I had to face the fact that I wouldn't be with Danny that Christmas.

It was a cold and foggy night as we left the house. We could hardly see what was in front of us. The fog was so thick that we couldn't see the road or the bus stop. We hung onto each other and had to listen out for traffic as we crossed the road. We couldn't see at all; it was so scary; the fog was like pea soup. We could have been killed, as we made our way to the Palais that night.

The Palais was empty when we walked in; it was early and it didn't start filling up until later on. It was free admission before ten o'clock. Thankfully, Danny was nowhere to be seen. It was going to be hard seeing him again and I wasn't quite sure how I would handle it; my best friend in the world would be at my side though. It meant a lot to me. She was my rock and a big support to me.

We decided to go into the Nocturn, which was the smaller dimly lit discothèque under the Palais. There was a staircase at the side of the stage that led down into the disco. We could hide away amongst the crowds in there, until it had filled up a bit upstairs.

Later that evening, when we went back upstairs, Danny was not at his usual place on stage. There was another DJ doing his show! I was relieved that I hadn't seen him around, but part of me still wondered where he was. I thought that maybe 'she' had stopped him doing the discos, just in case he decided to run off with another woman, who knows! If that was what had happened, the Palais would not be the same. He was a very good DJ despite everything. He could play the right records to get the people on the dance floor. If the dance floor emptied, on the rare occasion, that he'd played a certain unpopular record, he would take it off the turntable and snap it in two, right in front of the audience. At the same time, he would already be cueing in the next record. The dance floor would fill again immediately, when he had played one of their favourites. He could work and entertain the audiences; he was well liked by everyone. I couldn't imagine what that place would be like without him.

Mandy and I were sitting at our usual table. I watched and listened to the DJ and looked around at the empty dance floor. The place was filling up; Danny had usually got the people up dancing by this time. I started to miss him again.

Mandy suggested that we went to get a drink from the upstairs bar. I smiled at her and held back my tears as we asked for two lager and limes from across the bar. We were sitting at a table on the balcony overlooking the dance floor. The place was getting quite full now and a few groups of people had ventured onto the dance floor. All the tables were full downstairs and the balcony area was filling up too.

I looked across to the far corner, and through the crowds, I saw them — Danny and 'her'. Danny was smiling at her and they were holding hands across the table, the same table that Mandy and I usually sat at. They looked so happy.

My hands started to shake. My heart was beating so fast. Mandy had seen them too and we got up to leave before we were seen. I couldn't take my eyes off them. Danny turned and looked straight at me. He stared but his eyes were cold and seemed to look straight through me. He turned back to her, leaned towards her and kissed her. It felt like a knife had stabbed at my heart. We rushed off and went into the toilets just to calm down. I couldn't breathe. I couldn't cry. I just felt embarrassed and annoyed that he could have looked at me like that; as if he didn't know me at all. As if the last few months had never happened. As if he hadn't loved me at all, ever. We decided to spend the rest of the night down in the Nocturn disco just so we wouldn't see him again.

We tried our best to enjoy the rest of our night out; we left in a taxi for home at the end of the evening. I didn't want to ever go to the Palais again. It was too difficult to deal with seeing Danny like that. It was going to take a lot more time for me to get over him, maybe it would be best if we found somewhere else to go at the weekend and stay clear of the Palais for a while. I didn't want to go through that again.

During the following week I tried to forget Danny and just get on with my life. At work it was the same as the previous week. I worked hard at my machine and hardly spoke to the girls I worked alongside. The following Friday, Mandy and I went to a new club called 'The Bees Knees' on Crompton Way. We danced the night away and surprisingly really enjoyed the night. However, something deep down told us both that it wasn't quite the same as the Palais.

After creeping in the house again, feeling rather tipsy, we tried our best to stop our giggles so as not to wake up Mandy's parents. We tiptoed up the stairs and went to bed.

The next evening Mandy and I had been babysitting for her sister's two little boys. They were two lovely little boys but still quite a handful and they just would not go to bed when they were told to. When we had finally got to our bed, it was late and we were both exhausted.

Our sleep was soon disturbed by noises at the window. Mandy and I sat up and wondered what it could be. We heard it again. Someone was throwing stones at our bedroom window. It was three o'clock in the morning. I jumped out of bed and went to the window and peeped out to see who it was. To my horror it was Danny.

My heart started to race. I thought I was dreaming. I had to go downstairs and see what he wanted. Mandy and I quietly went down and opened the front door.

Danny was standing there; the glisten of his tears, just waiting to fall to his cheek. He was saying that he loved me and wanted me back.

Mandy's parents had been disturbed too that night, so we had to tell him that he had to go away and he should come back the following morning, if he needed to talk to me. We shut the door in front of him and went back up to bed.

I couldn't believe what he had done. After just two weeks with her, the mother of his unborn child, he was leaving her and wanted me back! Mandy was pleading with me not to go back to him. She said that she couldn't understand how I could even talk to him again after what he had done to me.

It was hard to sleep that night. The thoughts running through my head of the love that I had for him and what our life was like together before that horrible night just two weeks ago.

The next morning, during breakfast, Mandy and I talked about everything, while we waited for Danny to arrive. Mandy was angry at the thought of him just walking back into my life. She didn't ever want me to go back with him and start the relationship again. She kept saying he will hurt me again. I agreed with her. However, I just needed to hear what he had to say.

I couldn't see myself going back to him, despite the fact that I still loved him. I was very aware that 'she' was having his baby!

I wanted to be the one who gave him children! We had dreams of the children we were going to have together. Dreams of us getting married and starting our own family, after his divorce.

Things had changed; she was the one who was carrying his first child. She was the one that he was already married to. How could he possibly leave her to have the baby on her own? What sort of man is he to do a thing like that? Would he do that to me one day, if I was to go back to him? There were so many questions and thoughts running through my head.

When his car pulled up outside, Mandy looked at me, her big blue eyes slowly filling with tears. I knew what she was thinking, I could see it in her eyes, that I shouldn't even be bothering talking to him after what he had done to me. My stomach was doing somersaults, but I felt I needed to talk to him. I wanted to talk to him. I wanted to hear what he had to say.

I have tried to remember what happened next but it remains a blank. I can't remember where we went or what we did that afternoon. Did we just drive around for hours listening to our favourite Stylistics tunes, on the car stereo, as we had done previously, while we talked? Did we go for a long walk over the hills of Rivington, to talk and try to sort things out? I just can't remember.

Before I knew it, I was back at Mandy's collecting my belongings. Most of these were still in the black plastic bag that I had taken there on that dreadful day two weeks previously. I was aware of how her parents had so kindly let me stay with them after I left Danny's house, or should I say, when he kicked me out! Yes! that was exactly what he had done, he had kicked me out! I had not forgotten the tears I'd cried following this. I had not forgotten the day that I had walked out of Danny's house. I could still see them both as clear as day, in my mind, sitting happily huddled together giggling on the sofa. I remember making my way passed them, through the living room and out through the front door with my few belongings. He was sitting with one arm around her back and the other hand placed gently on her swollen belly, waiting to feel their unborn baby kicking.

Mary had allowed me to put my hand on her belly when she was expecting Laura. She would let me feel her kicking inside her. Sometimes I would sit for ages with my hand across her, waiting to feel the gentle kicking of the baby. It was such an amazing feeling, one that I just couldn't wait to experience myself one day.

While Danny waited outside the house, I collected my things from Mandy's bedroom. Her parents had been so good to me, I would never forget their kindness. I didn't know what I would have done without them.

Mandy cried. She couldn't believe I was leaving. She begged me to stay with her. She begged me not to go back to him and wanted me to stay and have that coming Christmas with her and her family. I felt I was losing my best friend all over again.

It had been good to have her back for those two weeks and to have spent all of our time together. She'd tried her best to help me forget Danny and carry on with my life and to make me smile again. Most of the time she succeeded. I would smile on the surface, but inside I cried all the time. I missed him so much but I couldn't let it show.

Mandy had Ray at that time; it seemed that things could get serious between them. I would feel a bit like a gooseberry and in the way, when the three of us went out together. Still, I was happy that she had someone in her life to love, just as I loved Danny. They never made me feel awkward or in the way. However, I could not forget being part of a couple; when it was over. I felt alone and a bit envious of them for being a couple. Maybe I was trying to make excuses as to why I should go back to Danny when the truth seemed clear to me. I loved him and couldn't live without him.

During that afternoon together, Danny and I talked and talked. He cried. I cried. He told me he wanted me and needed me. He said he had never stopped loving me. He said that it had broken his heart to see me walk out the door that day, but there was nothing he could do. He had to go back to her because she was carrying his baby and it could cause a scandal (the talk of 'divorce' was a taboo subject and was kept very 'hush hush,' if it happened in your family), and he would have lost his job at the newspaper. He had told me this on the day he had gone back to her.

I believed him at first, but he certainly didn't look broken hearted the day I left. He looked like he was doing exactly what he wanted to do, and that was to be with her and his unborn baby. I was confused. I asked him why 'she' had gone again this time and he told me that she couldn't stand being in the house alone while he worked, saying she felt lonely and too far away from her parents. She'd also told him that the house was damp and affecting her chest.

That house may have been an old terrace but it wasn't that damp. 'She' had wanted to go back home to her parents and to end their marriage as soon as possible.

Danny then told me that he had got an appointment with his solicitor to start the divorce proceedings against her again. As he had told me so many times before, she had originally left him for another man. He continued to tell me that the child she was carrying could possibly be that other man's child after all, the dates didn't tally with the time they were together. All that he told me had convinced me that we should get back together again. I believed everything he said. I felt so loved again by him, this was the deepest love I had experienced in my life, and once again he seemed so sincere. No one had ever said those words to me before. I felt he was rescuing me all over again and it felt good. I felt wanted and needed by him again. I didn't like to see him cry. I had never seen him cry before. It had broken my heart to leave him that day two weeks previously and he was back again, promising me the world, all over again. I didn't want the world, I just wanted him and to be loved by him. I didn't ask for much.

The last thing I collected from Mandy's bedroom was my engagement ring from her jewellery box. I looked at it, but I just couldn't put it back on my finger, not then. I slipped it in the pocket of my jeans.

I was ready to leave Mandy's house. I picked up my bags and looked at Mandy. A single tear fell from her eye. Dropping my bags to the floor again we hugged tightly. I didn't want to let her go. I didn't want to lose her. I begged her not to cry and tried to reassure her that I would be fine. I told her that I knew Danny would never hurt me like that again and that this time it would work out for us.

It was breaking my heart to leave Mandy this way. I felt I was hurting her! I couldn't possibly stay there indefinitely; we both had dreams of leaving and renting a flat together. That was our dream, before I met Danny, to find a place together and live our lives independently away from our parents.

I had another dream to fulfil, all those months ago, and that was to find someone to love and be loved by and to get married and to have children. I was starting to live that dream again!

I walked through the door of Mandy's house with my two black bin bags holding all of my belongings. I felt sad leaving and saying goodbye to Mandy's parents, they had been so kind. Mandy and I would see each other the next day at work; I didn't ever want to lose my friendship with her, I would just hate that. I was sad to leave and just wanted to cry. I just hoped I was doing the right thing this time. The doubts flicked through my mind again.

As soon as I saw Danny my fears disappeared. He got out of his car and came rushing over to me. He took the bags from me and put them onto the back seat of his car. He was such a gentleman; he then turned to Mandy, who was standing at her front door, watching me leaving. He said in such a sweet voice, "Mandy, don't worry, I will look after her this time."

My heart lifted and I just knew that I really was doing the right thing. I was going to be happy and I was going to make him happy too. He couldn't possibly want to leave me again this time. I sat in the car next to him and he started the engine. We waved at Mandy at the door. Her face was filled with sadness. Danny turned to me and looked at my hand. "Where's your ring? he asked softly. I reached inside my jeans pocket and took it out. He took it from my hand and placed it right back on the third finger of my left hand, just as he had done before, not so long ago.

"That's where it should be," he said, "back where it belongs, no need to take it off again." I was in heaven. In my mind we weren't driving away in a shiny red car; he was my handsome knight and we were riding off into the sunset on a beautiful white stallion.

Walking through that door of Glynne Street was hard. There had been another woman there, living in 'my house'. Would the place be different? Would she have kept it clean? The place did look different at first. Lots of things had been changed around in each of the rooms. There were ornaments arranged differently on the mantelpiece and the furniture had been changed round. It was clean and tidy. She had obviously looked after the place.

Alan, our lodger, was still there living in the front bedroom upstairs. I was so glad to see him and had hoped that she wouldn't have asked him to leave because she might have wanted his room for the baby.

A week after walking back through that door, we had settled back down to the same routine that we had had before I left. I hadn't rearranged the furniture back to the way it was or moved any of 'her' things. I didn't need to; they were fine where they were. I kept thinking of her and how she must be feeling. I felt guilty about the way I felt about 'her' husband. I felt guilty for the way he felt about me. I felt guilty being in 'her' house. It was still technically half hers too. Danny was reassuring me all the time; he wanted me and she wanted the divorce as much as he did and she was never happy with him. I still secretly worried about 'her' and the baby. I hoped that they would be fine.

If it was Danny's baby, I was sure that he would do the best he could for that baby and I wouldn't stand in his way. I could tell Danny didn't like to talk about all this with me so I tried not to mention it at all from then. He would say things like, "It's all in the solicitor's hands now, so let's leave it for them to sort out, and it's not for you to worry about." I was sure it was as upsetting for him talking about that as it was for me living with the fact that 'she' could be having his first child. That's what I wanted to do, if we ever got married. 'Her' child was on the way now and we had to accept it. Danny had told me that 'her' parents were lovely decent people and wouldn't ever see their only daughter go without. She and the baby would probably want for nothing.

Although I had never spoken to 'her,' or knew her at all, except the little things that Danny had told me, I liked the person she was, she seemed nice and I still wished her well and hoped that she would be fine and hoped she didn't feel too bad about me taking her place.

One Thursday night, Danny had gone to work at the Palais, I had decided to stay at 'home' and make some Christmas decorations. Danny had already bought a little tree and we had hung a few baubles on it, but I had wanted to make some decorations and hang them from the ceiling. I was hoping to have them finished and the room decorated as a surprise for him when he walked in that night. I was alone in the house with just the TV as background noise, sitting on the floor surrounded with crepe paper, glue, scissors and tinsel. I was in my element.

I heard someone at the front door. A key was going into the lock. I was startled. I sat up. It couldn't be Danny, it was too early, and it was only nine o'clock. Then 'she' walked in. I looked at her with a sense of horror. She didn't even look at me, she just walked straight through to the kitchen and upstairs without even saying a word. It was as if I wasn't there. I was shocked.

I stopped what I was doing and waited for her to finish what she was doing. I thought that maybe she had come to collect some of her things. I could hear her pottering around the place and left her to it. She came back downstairs and into the lounge carrying a bag that she must have filled with her things. She then went to leave. Again, she didn't look at me at first, but before she walked through the vestibule door to leave, she turned and looked at me and said, "Has all this been planned?" Instinctively and immediately, I said, "No." In fact I didn't know what she meant. Has all this been planned? She walked through the door without saying another word. I wanted to follow her and ask her what she had meant. I wanted her to talk to me. She looked hurt. Danny didn't tell me that she was hurting. He said that she was fine and wanted the divorce. She didn't seem that way to me. I was shaking and couldn't move. She pulled the door shut behind her and I tried to carry on with what I was doing. My hands were shaking so much I couldn't hold the scissors. She was hurting just like I had been a few weeks previously and I didn't want her to be hurting.

I thought that leaving Danny was what she had wanted. I cried uncontrollably; I couldn't stop. The decorations got left for another day.

I fell asleep on the settee and was woken by Danny when he came home. He could tell I had been upset and I explained to him what had happened.

Again, he was there with the right words to make me feel better and the same reassurances that he had always provided. He placed his loving arms around me so tightly that I felt better.

Christmas came and went. Danny was busy working for most of it and the New Year celebrations. It went by so quickly. I didn't want to be left alone in the house at night just in case she came back again, but she never did. We never saw her again or heard from her.

I would go with Danny to most of his disco nights at the Palais. Mandy and I would meet up there and have a really good night out. Some nights Mandy and I would decide not to follow Danny to the disco; we would stay at my house and talk on the CB radio. Danny had set it all up under the stairs; it was connected to a big tall aerial called a 'twig' that he had put up in the backyard. It was so much fun talking to different people over the radio. We would talk away for hours to all sorts of people. Danny would come home sometimes to find us still sitting there in the early hours, talking away. Mandy would always stay over at our house for the night and would be driven back home the next day.

I was happy again and my relationship with Danny was blossoming; I tried to forget 'her' and put her out of my mind. I had Danny and we were happy. I still had Mandy's friendship and we were having fun. I couldn't have been happier. Danny and I had settled down with our routine of running the house and learning more about each other.

One disturbing thing I learned about Danny was that 'Danny Sinclair' was not his real name. I was sitting at 'home,' during a well-earned day off from work, and a lady knocked on the door. She asked if 'Richard' was in. I told her that I didn't know any 'Richard.' She explained that she was called Janine and she was his sister-in-law and she needed to speak to him. This was all news to me; why did he not tell me his real name? He hadn't spoken much about his own family either. We had been too busy with the talk of his divorce and the everyday busy lives we were both living, and enjoying getting to know each other. I didn't think that there was much to talk about his family.

I did know that he had two brothers called Keith and Lee, and there had been a big fall out in the family and he didn't speak to them. He told me also that he didn't talk to his mother either. After Janine's visit, he told me that, that was the reason why he liked to be known as Danny; his name as a DJ. I left it at that.

Over time he was able to speak to me about them and thought that one day the silly argument that they had had with each other would blow over.

We were both so busy, working at our own relationship and being happy, that we didn't seem to have the time to worry about anything else. Life seemed so hectic every day. There didn't seem to be enough hours in the day. We only saw each other for a couple of hours each work day.

At the weekends the house was always full; my younger sister Maureen always seemed to be around and sometimes stayed over at our house. She was having loads of arguments with Mum and didn't want to stay at home with her any more. Mum and Dave had split up and I think Maureen was growing up fast and wanting to move out. Mum didn't like her staying out all night, not knowing where she was. This meant that for

Danny and me it was hard to find any time to be alone. I was still happy and in a strange sort of way I was getting used to our busy weekend routine. At least we were all happy and the house wasn't filled with the bad atmosphere that had been the case in the full house we had grown up in.

During all of this, I was developing my cooking and cleaning skills, and becoming quite a homemaker. I enjoyed working at the factory, but still, every night I would be longing to get home. On the journey home my mind would be filled with ideas of what I was going to cook Danny for tea that night. I would pick up tips from some of the girls at work on how to cook certain foods. When I got home, I would prepare the meal for Danny anticipating his arrival. He was always on time and a meal was usually waiting for him. Our lives were busy but content and there seemed to be nothing at all that could spoil or rock our boat.

In the middle of the night, while we were both fast asleep in bed, the phone rang. It was Colin, Danny's cousin. He was talking to Danny for ages. Danny wasn't saying much, just listening. He hung up the phone and turned to me, as I was dozing, at his side.

"She's had the baby," he said. "It's a boy, they've called him Matthew Luke, and he weighed 4lb 13oz," he continued.

He then sat up on the edge of the bed, with his head in his hands. I sat up and sat closer to him and put my arms around him. We both knew that she was due to give birth any day; we had been waiting for a phone call, informing us of the baby's arrival. It still seemed to be a shock for Danny. He seemed so sad. I was a little confused as to why he looked so saddened. I asked him if everything was all right with them both and he told me that they were both fine. I didn't understand. For me, I was glad to hear the news and even more so that everything was fine with them both. I asked him what was wrong. He got back into bed and held me.

"She won't leave me alone now Maggie," he said quite angrily. I had never seen him like this before. "If he is my son, she will hold him against me and never ever let me see him! She will always be there ready to stick the boot in, just when it pleases her." He told me that he might have to sell the house if she demanded it. He kept repeating that she would never leave him alone, over and over again.

He turned to me and said that he wanted me to have his children one day, his only children. I wanted that too but there was nothing we could do about that now. It was too late for that, but at least we were together, that was all I cared about. I tried to reason with him, but there was the little niggling thought, going through my head, that he could possibly go back to her for the sake of his son and leave me again just like he did before. I kept that horrible thought to myself; he didn't need to hear my fears. He had taken long enough trying to convince me that he wanted me, I had just got to believe that. What he said next shocked me. He said that if we were to have a baby, she wouldn't pester us any more. She would realise that we were staying together and she wouldn't try to get him back. I listened to his every word. I knew that if we had a baby, they still wouldn't be divorced by the time our baby was born so we couldn't get married and our baby would be born 'out of wedlock.' The thought of this scared me! I didn't want an illegitimate child. This was not how my dream was meant to be.

We talked and talked into the early hours of the morning; until he had convinced me that he was right in what he was saying and I was the one he would be standing by forever.

During our relationship, I had been too embarrassed to go to the doctor, for the contraceptive pill. I had in fact never been to see a doctor. We had our own contraception method. Danny would 'get out at Moses Gate' as he called it!

From that night on, he didn't. We were trying for a baby!

I was so scared. Scared of getting pregnant, scared of what people might say because we were not married. Scared of what Dad would say. I would be making mum and dad grandparents! Mum didn't like Danny at all, she was always telling me, behind his back, that he was using me and he would hurt me. Maybe that would change once she knew that I was pregnant with his baby. Dad seemed to like him. I thought they got on really well. I thought that Danny got on well with everyone. This was one of the things I liked about him.

Two weeks later I came on a period. I was devastated. I cried buckets. I thought that we were doing things right. I thought that I would get pregnant straight away, but I didn't. Danny was upset too, but he just turned round and said that we would have to keep trying harder and laughed. Which we did! Every possible moment! The next period didn't show and neither did the next. Was I pregnant? I didn't feel any different, no sickness at all. I didn't know if I was pregnant; I felt exactly the same as I always had. I wasn't getting any fatter! I thought I would have felt in some way different but I didn't. Maybe it was just one of those phantom pregnancies that I had heard so much about. I understood that a phantom pregnancy was when the mind so badly wanted a baby that it believed the person to be pregnant. In response, the body behaves accordingly and stops the monthly cycle. Sadly, in reality there is no baby!

I was still working at the factory, so I hadn't had the time to go to the doctor. I didn't tell anyone at work that I could be pregnant, not even Mandy. I wanted to be sure. I didn't want it to be a false alarm.

When the next scheduled period did not arrive, I thought that I had better go and see a doctor. Danny and I booked an appointment with his doctor, Dr Hunter, at his Stoneclough surgery. I had to take a urine sample to be tested. The doctor greeted us in his office and tested the sample straight away, right in front of us. I was hot and so nervous; my hands were shaking and I could feel my heart beating so fast inside my chest. After what seemed like forever, the doctor looked at us both and said, "Congratulations you're pregnant!"

I couldn't believe it! I was pregnant. I was going to have a baby! I felt the tears welling up in my eyes. The doctor asked me to lie on the couch behind us for an examination. He felt my tummy and told me that I was about ten weeks pregnant. He could feel my baby. It was really there inside my tummy!

He then continued to give me a bit of a lecture about not going to see him sooner. He said that I now had to make regular visits, once a month, to his surgery to see him. Danny listened to all the doctor's words but I just sat there numb, I couldn't listen. I just couldn't believe it. There actually was a little baby growing inside my tummy!

My mind drifted away to when Laura was born. I could see her tiny face and her jet-black hair once again. I could still remember how sweet she smelt when I held her for the first time. I was going to have my own baby soon. I held onto Danny's hand so tightly I was making his fingers go purple. I was still shaking with both fear and excitement at the same time. I was going to be a mummy and I knew I was going to make a great mum.

CHAPTER FORTY-FIVE
A Romantic Break in Paris

It was quite a revelation to be told by the doctor that I was pregnant. To have it confirmed once and for all by him that I was actually going to have a baby, came as a complete shock. I really hadn't accepted it at all beforehand, that I could have a little baby growing inside me, despite the fact that we were trying for a baby. It just seemed too good to be true. To have a baby of my own, was what I had always wanted since I was a teenager. It was like a dream, my dream coming true, although it took me a while to really believe it.

After I was told I felt strange. I couldn't understand why I didn't feel different; or look different. I had no signs at all. No morning sickness, which everyone had told me I would have, and I wasn't getting any fatter either. I thought that I would have felt some symptoms of being pregnant but there was nothing.

Over the next couple of weeks, I got so tired and had to have quite a few days off work due to tiredness. It seemed difficult to get up each morning; I just couldn't get myself out of bed, I felt exhausted all the time. I arrived late most mornings and some mornings I didn't even get there at all. It seemed I didn't have any energy at all. I was sure this was a symptom of the pregnancy that I had been waiting for. I had had a warning from my boss about my timekeeping. The thought of getting sacked scared me, so I tried to make more of an effort each morning. I didn't want to get the sack; we needed the money I was earning, to help with the household bills.

Danny had talked to me about giving up work at the factory, after he realised just how tired I was each morning. He assured me we could manage on his wages and told me to think about leaving the job I loved. I enjoyed my job at Halbros. I would be sorry to leave all the friends I had made there. I would miss them all. However, Danny was persistent, he said I should be thinking of the baby and my health and I needed to rest more. I was convinced that he was right in what he said and I agreed to quit my job.

Danny was good with writing so he wrote a letter of resignation for me. When I arrived at work late again, as usual, on Monday morning, I went into the office to see the boss and hand in my resignation. That following Friday was my last day as a full-time machinist at Halbros and the start of my new life as a full-time 'housewife'.

On my next visit to the doctor's, I was given a prescription for iron tablets. After taking them for just a couple of days I didn't seem as tired and felt I had more energy. I was looking forward to being a mum, but every time I thought about giving birth, in about six months' time, my stomach would do somersaults. I was scared stiff. I would sit and wonder what I would look like with a big fat tummy. Sometimes I would stuff a pillow up my jumper and look in the mirror and imagine that in a few months' time I would look like that for real. I was still so skinny with no sign of my tummy swelling at all, so the thought of being fat made me giggle. I was so skinny that it just didn't seem to be happening.

I was looking forward to spending more time at home with Danny too. After a few days, however, in my new role as a housewife, we had our first tiff. It had been getting me down that we weren't spending enough time together. He always seemed to be working. He worked all day at the Bolton Evening News and each night at his discos. I kept myself busy with chores, however, I did feel desperately alone at times, despite the fact that our weekends were always hectic, and our house was always full of visitors.

We still had our lodger, Alan, and he had a girlfriend called Julie who was at our house most of the time. She was nice and we all got on really well; but I wasn't spending enough time with Danny on our own and it began to bother me. I tried to talk to him one night, when we had a rare occasion to be on our own, but instead of talking, we ended up arguing. I hadn't heard Danny ever say one cross word to me up to that point, but that day he raised his voice, which scared me. I hated hearing anyone shouting or raising their voice, it would always lead to violence in the house that I grew up in. It made me shake with fear that it might be happening in the house I shared with Danny. I wanted to run away.

I ended up in tears and I stormed out of the house. It was dark and chilly. I just wanted to walk and clear my head. I hated to argue with

Danny. I walked all the way to the top of Plodder Lane and sat on an old stone wall thinking things over. I was still in tears and quite angry and I wondered whether it was a good idea to be having a baby with him at all. I felt as if he was putting everything else before me and he just didn't have the time to spend with me. I had lost all my friends at Halbros, when I stopped working there, and all my family. All I seemed to do at that time was to sit at home alone.

The more I sat on that cold stone wall the more I thought that he didn't care. He didn't even bother to come and look for me after I had stormed out of the house. I had been out for ages. Could it be that he didn't care any more? Did he not care for our baby either? Was he regretting getting tied down with me and our unborn baby? Was I going to be left to bring this baby up on my own, just like his ex-wife? Was my mum right when she said he would hurt me? I was becoming more devastated. I cried even more. The bad thoughts were going round and round in my head.

I remembered that nightmare of a night, when he brought his ex-wife back to the house not that long ago, and I had to leave. The thought of that happening to me again and becoming a single parent scared me; I had no idea how I would be able to manage. I loved him so much, I didn't want to leave him, so I decided to head back and have it all out with him once and for all.

I made my way back home. I didn't know what I was going to face when I got there. I didn't know whether Danny would have packed my bags and be telling me to leave again. I just couldn't get it out of my mind that I had lost my engagement ring a few weeks prior to this. Was it a sign or some sort of bad omen? I had been rushing around, due to getting up late. I knew I wasn't going to be on time for work, yet again. I got washed and dressed and put my engagement ring in my apron pocket as usual. When I felt in my pocket, for my ring, it had gone. I searched the bathroom and around the kitchen sink. It was nowhere to be found. Danny was still asleep upstairs, so I left him undisturbed and went to work. I was distraught all the way to work. Whatever was I going to tell him, when I got home that night? I knew I had put the ring in my pocket. I never washed my hands with it on. How could I tell him that I had lost his engagement ring? When I got home from work that day, I searched the house again but the ring was nowhere to be found. My only conclusion was that it had flipped out of the pocket of my apron and fallen unnoticed down the toilet when I was getting dressed.

When Danny came home, he could tell that there was something wrong; for ages I kept telling him that things were fine and that there was nothing wrong. After tea, I broke down and started to cry uncontrollably. I told him that I had lost his ring. Instead of him being angry, as I had expected, he just hugged me so tightly and said don't worry and that he would have to get me another.

The day after, I got home from work as usual and while we were eating our tea, he placed a little black box in front of me and inside was another engagement ring. He told me that it was not as expensive as the first one and it was not a real diamond, but it was similar to the first one so it would have to do until we could afford another. I loved it. I would have worn a curtain ring if it was from him. He placed it on my finger and kissed my hand. He told me never to take it off. From that day I didn't dare take that one off.

I looked at that ring on my finger, as I walked back home all the way down Plodder Lane, on that cold night after our argument and I remembered his words from the day he'd given it to me. Surely, he must love me, why else would he have bought me another ring to wear on my finger. He wasn't cross or angry in any way because I had lost the first one. He didn't shout, like Dad would always do when he was angry.

I was getting cold, and I needed to be home, with Danny. I was sure he loved me. I knew he did. I was so confused. When I walked in, he was sitting on the sofa watching television. I sat down beside him and he instantly reached out and held me. We talked. Danny told me that he had thought that I was going to ask him to stop doing the discos so that we could spend more time with each other. I would have never asked him to do that. The discos were his life and I knew what they meant to him, to entertain the way he did. He was the best DJ in Bolton, in my opinion, plus we needed the money. I spoke to him of my fears of him leaving me again; but as always, my fears dissolved just with one of his hugs. We talked and made love for the rest of the night, falling asleep in each other's arms.

A few days later, Danny surprised me again and told me that we were going to Paris. I was ecstatic. He explained that we would be leaving in a few days and that we were going to stay with a friend of his, called Diane, who used to work in the same office at the Bolton Evening News. She worked as an interpreter and had an apartment in the heart of Paris. He continued and said that she had invited us both over for a few days. Five days in Paris with Danny, I just couldn't wait!

A few days later we were packed and ready to go. Danny already had a passport but I had to fill in a form at the post office and then we were all ready to go. We were to drive all the way there. We set off in the early hours of the morning along the long motorways. We had been driving for hours, listening to our favourite tapes on the cassette player, Gene Pitney, The Drifters and The Stylistics, and of course my favourite Bay City Rollers, over and over again.

Before long, I had fallen asleep in the car. Danny woke me when we were driving through London. He knew I would want to see where our Queen lived. I had only ever seen pictures of London in magazines or on TV. It was four o'clock in the morning and all the streets were virtually deserted. No traffic jams as we saw on the TV. He drove round and around the big roundabout in front of Buckingham Palace. It was a huge, amazing place, I couldn't imagine the Queen living there, it looked too big just for her and her husband. It was to be the Queen's Silver Jubilee later that year and those empty streets would be looking a lot different then, I was sure. We joined the motorway again and headed for Ramsgate. Ramsgate was in Kent and that was near to where Mary lived. My mind drifted away with thoughts of Mary and Lorraine; I wondered how they were. It would have been great to go and see them but I had absolutely no idea where in Kent they were living. It would take forever if we were to try to find them. After a few more hours of driving, we reached Ramsgate. We were to board a hovercraft, and sail across the English Channel to France. I was really excited and a little scared too, as we waited in the queue to drive our car onto it. I had never been on a hovercraft, ferry or a ship, so I was both nervous and excited at the same time. I had never been to another country either. We would be so far away from home and that scared me.

The hovercraft was huge! It was a big red and white boat with two huge spinning propellers at each side. It was sitting on what looked like a big, black, flat, rubber balloon. It just sounded like a very noisy vacuum cleaner. There were about thirty cars waiting to drive onto it. We took our place in the queue and waited. The noise was deafening. We were guided onto the hovercraft and parked our car in the allocated position that we had been directed to. All the cars had to be strapped into place and all the passengers had to leave their cars and were directed up to the decked and seating area above.

We both took our seats with the other passengers on the upper decks. We were quite high up it seemed, and we could see the sea, through all the windows that surrounded us. After a while there was the whirling sound of the big propellers above us and the hovercraft seemed to lift up, as if the big balloon underneath was filling up with air. We started to move along the ground slowly and went straight down from the land and into the sea. The sea splashed on the thick glass windows in front of us. It was scary! I held onto Danny's arm so tightly. It was an amazing journey, across the open sea, but my stomach kept turning over and I felt a little sick for most of the way across the channel. It could have been seasickness, but really, I was hoping that it could be morning sickness. It could be another one of the pregnancy symptoms that I had been waiting to experience.

After a while, through the window, someone spotted land ahead and Danny turned to look and told me that we were nearly there. He pointed to France, across the water in the distance. The hovercraft left the water and went straight up onto the land and the noise of the engines got a lot quieter. I enjoyed the journey on the hovercraft, it was a great experience, but it was also a relief to feel the ground under my feet again.

Soon we were in our car and back on the road driving through France and heading for Paris. It was strange for Danny to get used to driving on the opposite side of the road. He forgot quite a few times. When he was leaving the hovercraft port, he forgot that he should be on the right side and got beeped at a few times from some irate drivers. I just thought it was funny at the time, hearing those other motorists shouting at him in their foreign language. We couldn't understand a word of what they said. He soon adapted, however, and followed all the signs to Paris. It was quite easy, he would say, just one long straight road all the way there, similar to the motorways in England. Danny had all the directions to

Diane's apartment and by mid-afternoon we were parking the car outside her modern apartment block, which was situated on the outskirts of Paris.

The apartment block looked brand new and so unlike the rest of the buildings in Paris. Diane was there to meet us as we pulled up outside. At last, we could stretch our legs. Diane was lovely. She looked radiant and her dark curly hair shone in the Parisian afternoon sunshine. She smiled and shook my hand and gave me a kiss on each cheek, which took me back a little because I had never been kissed like that before. It was customary to greet people like that in France I was told. It was nice. Diane showed us the way to her apartment on the third floor of the building. She led us through the double glass doors and into her apartment. It was smaller than I had expected. It was one square room with a bed at one side and a small sofa against the wall at the other side and a small table and four chairs by the entrance of the kitchen, which was also tiny. There was a door at the side, which led to a bathroom with no bath, just a shower, toilet and a small basin in the corner. The apartment was small and cosy but Diane had got it really nice with cream painted walls and pictures and photos hung on the walls around the room. Diane had prepared some food and had a welcome cup of English tea for our arrival. Diane kept calling Danny, Richard; it seemed weird at first because I had always called him by his DJ name, but she had always known him as Richard.

That evening, she took us to a restaurant to introduce us to some friends of hers. Everyone was so friendly and made us both feel so welcome. We didn't have to pay for the meal in the restaurant either. The food was delicious but I didn't like the liver pate that we ate for the first course. The French chef was a good friend of Diane's; he said that the meal was on the house. I had never met anyone as nice as these people before. We were having such a great time. Diane spoke in French to everyone we met; I had French lessons at school but I still couldn't understand a word she said to them. I was impressed, and we both felt special just being around her and her friends. I wished I had paid more attention to the French lessons at school.

After what had been a long day we headed back to Diane's apartment. Danny and I slept on an inflatable mattress that night in the middle of the living room floor. Diane offered her bed to us and she would have slept on the sofa but we wouldn't hear of it. We were so tired that first evening and as soon as our heads hit the pillow, we were fast asleep.

Diane woke us early the next day as she had to go to work. We got up straight away, in anticipation of our sightseeing tour of Paris. Diane had told us about all the sights and it was only a short walking distance into Paris. With lots to see on the way, Diane suggested that we leave the car in the car park and travel around on foot or on the underground, which was called the Metro. It was a lovely day so as soon as we were ready, we were off on our way. We hadn't gone very far before we just had to stop and have a look in the local shops. There was a little old-fashioned cake shop down an old cobbled side street; the smells radiating from inside were so inviting. We just had to stop and sit at the small round table outside for a while and have a coffee and a croissant.

I looked at Danny, while I sipped the hot coffee, and thought to myself, who would have ever believed that I would be here, in the most romantic city in the world with the one I loved tucking into a croissant? I smiled at Danny and although we were so far away from home and the life we led back in England, I felt so safe and warm inside just by being there with him. He reached out and held my hand, as if he knew exactly what I was thinking. He smiled and said, "I love you," then took a bite from his croissant allowing the crumbs to fall on the table in front of him.

Each day, our time was spent in the centre of Paris; there were so many new sights to see and to experience. Paris was such a beautiful and romantic city. Armed with a map of the Paris underground we could see where all the sights were and the different stations, we needed to go to in order to reach them. It was scary at first to travel underground on the Metro; it was noisy and the trains went so fast. We soon got used to it though and found it to be the easiest way to travel around. We didn't get lost once; however, I still felt a little shaky standing on the edge of the platforms waiting for the trains to arrive to take us to the places we wanted to visit.

The River Seine arcs through the centre of Paris and is spanned by about thirty-seven bridges leading to different places. Danny and I sat on one of the bridges and he asked a tourist who was passing to take our photo. Posing romantically, with the Eiffel Tower in the background,

Danny sat next to me with his arm around my shoulders. I was so happy. There were street sellers and artists displaying second-hand books and works of art on the parapets. We saw the artists sitting with their easels, busy sketching their posing models; we watched them for ages as they concentrated on their sketching.

We walked all the way up the Champs Elysees. That was one of the most popular places to walk for tourists, and according to our brochure it was the most famous street in the world for its cinemas, cafés and boutiques. It was a broad, straight, tree lined avenue with footpaths at each side that led through beautiful parks with fountains, statues and monuments. The school children of Paris were gathered in groups with their teachers all around the park. They were so lucky to be born there in that beautiful city of Paris, with all its rich accumulation of history right on their doorstep. Maybe one day some of these children would possibly become artists when they grew up and would be sitting exhibiting their works of art along the side of the River Seine like the ones there now.

The Arc De Triomphe, was a huge imposing monument that sat at the top of the Champs Elysees. It was built for the French Emperor Napoleon in memory of all the French troops who fought in the war at that time. The names of the battles and the generals were written on the walls of The Arc De Triomphe. The body of an unnamed soldier was also buried there. It was impossible to cross the road around that area because the traffic was terrible. They drove far too fast and were always beeping their horns. It seemed like a free for all with no right of way. We didn't dare try to cross. Diane did say that the traffic in the centre of Paris was horrendous; we became aware of what she meant!

Our trip to Notre Dame was amazing. It is one of the most famous cathedrals in the world and the largest religious building in Europe. It is situated on an island in the middle of the River Seine. On entering that amazing religious building I was filled with a feeling of calm and peacefulness. I had a tingly feeling all over. People were kneeling praying in the silence. There were candles burning all around a big, bronze crucifix. Danny and I said a quiet prayer to ourselves and lit a candle. All around the cathedral were beautiful stained-glass windows, huge crucifixes and tall statues of the Virgin Mother and Child. One tall statue was of Joan of Arc. I had read about her when I was at school.

I stood for ages looking up at a statue called The Pieta. It was of The Virgin Mary; she was holding the corpse of Jesus lying across her knees. She was looking up towards the heavens with such a mournful expression on her face as if she was pleading with the Lord not to take her son away. It was so emotional, my eyes filled with tears as I could feel her pain. We spent most of the afternoon in Notre Dame. It was the most impressive building I had ever seen. The architecture was amazing; I had this overwhelming feeling of serenity just by being there.

On the way out I looked up at the high rose-stained-glass window above the huge entrance; the sun was shining through it and reflected onto the old stone flagged floor. I was in awe of its beauty. Every segment of coloured glass, in the rose shaped window, illuminated and showed biblical scenes from the Old Testament.

We walked out into the sunshine and noticed some visitors were heading to another entrance at the side of the cathedral. Through the old wooden double doors there were narrow spiral concrete steps that led all the way up to the Bell Tower at the top of the cathedral. We followed the others all the way to the top. There were two hundred and fifty-five steps to the chimera gallery; we stopped there and stood on the balcony, overlooking Paris. It was a gorgeous clear day and we could see for miles; we could see the River Seine winding all the way through Paris and the Eiffel Tower, a famous symbol of French civic pride, standing proudly in the distance.

As we leaned on the parapets, gazing at the views, I suddenly thought of a film I had watched on TV when I was younger, it was called 'Quasimodo, The Hunchback of Notre Dame'. He was supposed to have lived there, amongst the ugly gargoyles, that protruded from the sides of the building. Those gargoyles frightened me; they were ugly little monsters that looked like devils. I couldn't understand why they were there; they spoiled that beautiful building. Quasimodo was abandoned by his mother at birth and left in the cathedral. He was found by the priests and lived his life in the cathedral. He was very disfigured with one eye and bandy legs and a hunched back. He would ring the Great Bell in the tower every day, which over the years had made him completely deaf.

Quasimodo would watch out from the Bell Tower, and would notice the beautiful gypsy girl, called Esmeralda, dancing in the square in front of the cathedral and he instantly fell in love with her. She then became the victim of a coward's jealous rage and was convicted of a crime that she didn't commit and sentenced to hang; the man she was supposed to have killed was still alive so she was innocent of the crime that she was accused of. Love struck Quasimodo set out to rescue her. He was so hideously ugly that women would turn their children's faces away and hide from him; but inside he was gentle and kind with a big heart. He rescued Esmeralda from the gallows and gave her sanctuary in the cathedral. Soldiers got the power to invade the church to try to arrest her again but Quasimodo helped her to escape and flee from Paris. He became hunted by the soldiers and in the chase, he fell to his death from the gargoyles. It was such a sad film. I remember crying for Quasimodo at the time.

On the way back to Diane's apartment that night, we strolled hand in hand through the centre of Paris and through the narrow, cobbled streets, feeling quite tired and exhausted, after our visit to Notre Dame. It had been a great day. At that time in the evening, the streets looked very different from the way they did earlier that morning. The bridges and the streets were full of magical glowing amber lights. That morning, the streets had been bustling with people and the horrendous traffic, but as the day turned into night there was hardly anyone around. The roads cleared of all the busy traffic, and the bridges were filled with lights reflecting on the water of the Seine. We could see couples in passionate embraces silhouetted in the dazzling yellowish glow of the street lights. I could see why this was called the most romantic city in the world. Danny and I walked hand in hand and felt as if we belonged there, amongst all the other lovers.

When we finally arrived back at the apartment, Diane was out for the evening with her friends, so we had some time to ourselves to be intimate; we fell asleep in each other's arms.

The next morning, we awoke to another beautiful sunny day. After Diane had gone off to work, Danny and I leaned on the railings, on the balcony, in the sunshine watching the already busy streets below. We planned our day. We planned to visit the Sacre Coeur, which was a former Royal Chapel that sat high on the hill of Montmartre. The Place du Tertre was at the foot of the hill. That was like a market square, with stalls selling souvenirs, which came to life in the afternoons with artist's easels displaying their work for sale. Many famous painters, like Van Gogh and Monet, had lived and worked around that area. They probably liked the quality of the light on the hill while they worked, away from the smoke and grime and noise of the city.

The streets were very steep, winding and narrow and were linked to each other by steep steps. As we strolled slowly up the hill, through the winding streets of old houses, we could see the magnificent Sacre Coeur in the distance. We stood at the foot of the steep steps and gazed up at the stunningly beautiful three white domes of the Chapel. There were hundreds of tourists, with cameras in hand, climbing up the steps to the top.

When we were half way up we noticed a typical old Frenchman, dressed in a black French beret and fawn coloured mackintosh, attracting attention from the visitors and tourists that passed him. We watched him as he stood with little birds feeding out of his hand. It was amazing; I hadn't seen anything like it before. He reached inside his pocket to grab a handful of bird seed and offered it to the hungry birds. It reminded me of the 'Mary Poppins' film, which I had seen when I was younger; particularly the scene where a little old lady was in a park and was feeding all the birds and singing, "Feed the birds Tuppence a bag."

Unfortunately, when we got to the top of the steep steps, we weren't allowed to go inside this impressive white stoned chapel. We were so disappointed. We weren't disappointed with the views from the top though. We sat at the top looking out at the panoramic views of Paris and beyond in every direction, probably extending for about thirty miles. Next to the Eiffel Tower, Sacre Coeur was the second highest point in Paris and its beautiful white domes graced the Parisian skyline from every direction.

When we got back to the apartment that evening, I had been feeling a little uncomfortable and had a slight tummy ache. In the bathroom, I noticed that I had lost a little blood. I told Danny straight away and I started to cry. I worried and thought that I was losing our baby. I felt fine in myself, except for the tummy ache. It was decided that it was either the night of passion we had the night before or the steep steps up to the chapel that might have been a strain. I rested that night and thankfully the following day there was no more bleeding and no tummy ache either; we enjoyed our last day in Paris.

We visited 'The Louvre Museum of Art' on our last day. We wanted to see the Mona Lisa's portrait by Leonardo De Vinci. We took the underground train to the museum and when the train approached the station, we thought that it had pulled up right inside the museum itself. The immaculate marbled walls were lined with exhibits and replicas of artworks. The museum was huge; a vast building formerly a Royal Palace.

Hundreds of years ago, King Henry IV invited hundreds of artists and craftsmen to live and work on the building's lower floors. It was supposed to have housed the French government offices, but then it changed into a huge museum, attracting thousands of visitors from all around the world. They flocked to see the stunning collections of art. The Mona Lisa was the most valuable painting ever to be insured, according to the Guinness Book of Records.

As we looked around these huge rooms, full of sculptures with angelic faces that seemed to be watching us, we explored our way through the museum, noticing masterpieces that filled the full length of every wall. We searched amongst them, but we couldn't find the Mona Lisa. We noticed a tour guide showing visitors around and asked him if he knew where the Mona Lisa was. He pointed us back to a hall that we had just been in and there it was. It was hanging on the wall in a glass box. It was tiny. I didn't expect it to be so small. We were looking for a huge portrait; I was not surprised we had missed it. That tiny portrait was worth over a million pounds. She was sitting behind glass, because she was so valuable, and just as beautiful as we had expected her to be. I focused on her smile and looked deep into her eyes and it looked as if she was looking straight at me. I knew that it would be amazing. When I returned home, I would be able to say that I had actually seen Mona Lisa's portrait in real life.

It was impossible to see everything in the museum in one day; there was just too much to see. It was also quite difficult and a bit confusing to read the plaques. These provided information about the paintings and objects, but they were all written in French and our understanding of the French language was non-existent.

We left the museum and made our way to the Eiffel Tower. We travelled on the Metro to the Palais de Chaillot, which was the location of the naval museums, they were shaped like a banana that had been cut in two. We walked through the centre of the two buildings and on each side and in front of the square was a row of golden statues. These appeared to be like Roman goddesses, adorning the entrances. They glistened in the Parisian sunshine; they looked like giant Oscars.

At the edge of the walled square there were steps that led down to the fountains and the Champ de Mars, stretching out towards the magnificent Eiffel Tower in the distance. At the bottom of the steps, there were children and youths, standing on boards that looked like short wide skis that had four wheels like the wheels from roller skates; these were attached underneath. They were standing confidently, balancing with their arms outstretched and riding around. They looked as if they were riding scooters with no handlebars, doing different stunts in the open spaces. It was fascinating to watch them. We were told that those boards were called skateboards. They reminded me of the toy that we created as children, using an old Beano annual, balanced on top of an old rusted roller skate. We would sit on the book and ride very fast down Sabden Brew; that was so much fun when we were kids.

The Eiffel Tower was first hated by the Parisian people; they said that it dishonoured the country in some way. The French people had gradually got used to it, and would miss it greatly if it disappeared, I was sure. The tourists could take the elevators right to the top to see the whole of Paris. Danny and I strolled hand in hand through the park and right underneath the tower; I went dizzy looking up through the centre of that amazing iron structure. We both agreed that we would take that elevator straight to the top, the next time we visited that beautiful city.

Our time in Paris went by so quickly. We walked our feet off most days and were never bored. We were amazed every day at the sights we saw and only wished that we could have had more time to explore the beautiful romantic and magical city of Paris; there were so many other sights that we just didn't have the time to see.

When we were back at home, we promised ourselves that we would go back there one day. I will never forget our time there and the kindness and generosity of Diane and all the lovely people we met there.

CHAPTER FORTY-SIX.
Rumours

"Frigid!" I gasped. "What does frigid mean?"

Since our romantic break in Paris, a few months ago, Danny and I had been having some bad arguments. We would bicker all the time, mostly about sex. He called me frigid but I didn't know what it meant. He told me that it meant that I didn't like sex! Well, that could be true. I didn't most of the time. I didn't know what I should have been feeling, I just felt glad when it was over most of the time. I didn't really feel comfortable 'doing it'. I hated having to get undressed in front of him. I would rush to turn the light out every night! I was so very shy. Also, I was always too tired and scared most of the time. I was scared to make love with him; I was scared it might harm the baby. I didn't want to bleed again.

Things had changed a lot in just a few months; I had started to call him Richard, which was his real name. When I first met him, I thought his name was Danny, everyone around him in the discos called him Danny and so I did. I would imagine my new name as Maggie Sinclair, if we ever got married. I liked it. When I found out that it wasn't his real name, I was quite disappointed.

At home with him, away from the discos, he was becoming Richard. It felt as if I was getting to know a whole new man. The Richard at home was far different from the Danny at the discos. It seemed as if I had two men wrapped up in one; the fun loving, not a care in the world Danny, at the discos, and the serious, quiet, sometimes withdrawn Richard at home. It was a lot to get used to. With a baby on the way, and stresses with the divorce, things could get quite tense at home sometimes.

My tummy was becoming quite swollen and I had felt little flutters inside me. I thought it was the baby kicking but I was not sure. I was still wearing my normal clothes, although my skirts were getting a bit tight around the waist. I couldn't wait until I would be wearing maternity dresses from the Mothercare store in town.

Richard had become far too busy to be interested in the little cardigans that I had started knitting for our baby; or to take any sort of interest in me any more, it seemed. He still worked full time at the newspaper office; but his work at the Palais ended. This upset him a lot. He had enjoyed his DJ work there. He had some sort of fall out with the manager. I didn't really know why, as he tended not to discuss work or finances with me, saying that it was not for me to worry about, and he would look after everything. He repeated often that he had said he would look after me and he would keep his promise. I felt protected, so I didn't need to worry, I left him to it.

We stayed away from the Palais at that time. I really did miss our good times there.

On the 31st July 1977, shortly after Richard had been sacked from his DJ position, our famous Palais was almost totally destroyed by fire. The roof, the amazing huge chandelier, the revolving stage area, the fantastic bouncy dance floor, were completely wrecked. It was a complete tragedy for Bolton; this wonderful iconic building was in ruins.

Danny Sinclair was a well-known DJ from there, everybody knew him. When he had to leave his work at the Palais, it was said that the place was never the same again, and that was so true. A few people laughed about the idea that he was the one who burned it down, at the time, because of the bad feeling between him and the manager. I was horrified at the thought of Danny being responsible for burning down our fabulous Bolton Palais and I couldn't believe it for a second. He loved the Palais just as much as the whole of Bolton, I was sure about that.

After a massive investigation, it was proven to be some sort of electrical fault. Bolton would miss the Palais. Where would people go to dance now?

My sister Ann had been courting a lad called Malcolm, the lead guitarist from the three-piece band that played there. They had finally got engaged. Maureen had been secretly seeing his friend Carl, the organist, also from the band, but he was supposed to be a married man so I didn't think that would last very long; Maureen would not have welcomed any advice from me about that relationship, she would have thought I would have been interfering and told me to keep my nose out!

The band had all lost their jobs since the fire and had to move away from Bolton to get other work in dance halls elsewhere. Ann and Maureen never saw them again. Ann was totally devastated when Malcolm left. I remember her tears, although she would always say that she was fine and wouldn't be comforted in any way, I knew she was hurting.

Maureen was a free spirit and didn't seem to care at all, although I was sure she was going to miss the Palais just as much as us, despite spending most of her time in the Nocturn nightclub, downstairs under the Palais, she wasn't old enough to get into the Palais ballroom on certain nights. That little nightclub too, underneath the Palais was also damaged by the fire.

Maureen would look much older when she wore makeup and was very attractive with huge dark brown eyes, long legs and she could dance really well, like the 'Go-Go' dancers on 'Top of The Pops.' She would get quite a lot of attention from lads. The boys would buzz around her like bees around the proverbial honey pot.

We missed the extra money coming into the house from his DJ work, at the Palais, especially with me not working any more. It became a strain on him trying to pay all the household bills. He soon cheered up when he was offered a job at two venues. One was at the Happy Pig, on the A6 in Blackrod, which was a restaurant and club, the other was at the King's Head Pub, in Atherton.

Within a few weeks, Danny had these places buzzing. They were packed every night, when he was there.

Mum and Maureen still lived in Blackrod, quite near to the Happy Pig. Mum and Dave had split up and were going through a divorce. Mum was seeing another man, called Jack. Jack was also getting a divorce from his wife. Mum at that time, worked behind the bar at the Red Lion pub in Blackrod; the pub was very near to where she had lived in Whitehall Lane. It was also Jack's local so he went in regularly. He would always say that he fell in love with my mum, the very first time he saw her. I thought he was such a lovely man: very tall, dark and handsome. He was a true prince, just what Mum wanted. Mum adored him, so it was understandable that the romance blossomed between them both. It wasn't long before they moved in together and started their new lives.

He was a coal miner, working underground in the pit. It would make me chuckle sometimes when I would be at Mum and Jack's house and he would come home from work; it would look as if he had mascara on, despite showering.

Maureen worked at the pub too, behind the bar sometimes, she would smile and tell me it was only because she fancied the landlord. I could see why, as he was good looking, but again a married man. It shocked me that she seemed to be attracted to men that were married, when it was clear to me that she could have had anybody she wanted, with her looks and figure. There were plenty of single lads after her.

I didn't see Mum and Maureen as often as I had done previously; we all seemed so busy building our own lives away from each other. I was getting fatter and wanted to spend more time at home getting things ready for our baby's arrival and keeping our home clean and tidy. Richard always let me know whenever he had seen them, when they went to his shows at the Happy Pig. He told me of the new boyfriends that Maureen had. I wasn't surprised that she had plenty of admirers. I was glad and hoped that she was keeping away from the married ones.

One night Richard came home to tell me that Maureen had told him that she was pregnant, which came as a shock because she had only just turned seventeen. I was to be an aunty, which made me smile and I became quite excited. Unfortunately, the next time he saw her she told him that she had had a miscarriage. I felt so sorry for her and a little disappointed that I wasn't going to become an aunty. Our children would have been close in age, and as cousins, they would be growing up together, just like we did with all our cousins. Maureen's boyfriends didn't seem to stick around long. I felt at that time, she should be free and find a lad that would stick around and not get tied down with a baby, when she wasn't even in a stable relationship, but she never appeared to want any advice from her older sisters at all. She was a free spirit doing exactly what she wanted and seemed happy.

Everything was changing, our lives were changing. I was starting my own life with Richard. Our new baby was on the way and I seemed to be drifting away from my old life with my family.

My best friend Mandy was busy courting Ray. She still worked at the factory as a machinist. I didn't get to see her as often as I would have liked any more. My life revolved around Richard and my home. I spent my days at home and I was becoming quite a homemaker. I cleaned the house, washed and ironed and shopped for groceries. I was ironing his many shirts and this could get a bit tedious. The striped ones would make me go dizzy, when I was ironing them, however, I loved every minute.

The worst thing about being with Richard was his sweaty socks! He would take them off and leave them in the corner of the bedroom waiting for me to shift them! They smelled of rotten cheese and stank the place out! They made me feel sick; the stench was horrendous. I would plead with him to shift them, so I wouldn't have to handle them but he would laugh and take no notice at all.

Most afternoons I cooked and waited for him to come home from work. His meal would be ready on the table. Over dinner he talked and I listened intently to the story of his day at work and the advertisements he had sold for the newspaper.

After showering, he dressed in his very smart black velvet DJ's suit, he would soon be off again at one of his venues. He was working so hard.

When I felt like a night out, or when Richard asked me to go along to see his show, I would go. I would sit at the side of the club, with a full view of his DJ's stand, and I would watch his show. I would smile to myself at the way he performed up there on that tiny stage with his headphones on, cueing in the next record. He did look like a star. I loved him so much. I was so proud; he was my man.   All the girls were up on their feet, dancing and jumping up on the stage, asking him to play their favourite songs. His skills as a DJ, in his new locations, were just as impressive as they had been in the Bolton Palais. It was such a tiny dance floor at the Happy Pig, compared to the huge one that he used to fill with dancers at the Palais. I was sure my man was meant for bigger and better venues than these tiny pubs. I would never tire of watching him work, although, as I was pregnant, I would get so tired as the evening progressed into late night. I would in fact have preferred to be at home knitting. I would usually be tucked up in bed, fast asleep, when he came home. He would come home after his late night as a DJ and get into bed and wake me up. He would want to make love every time. I was exhausted most of the time with all my household duties and trying to be the 'perfect wife'. I just couldn't be bothered with it all, it would irritate me, being woken up every night for sex. It still scared me too, since our time in Paris, when I had started to bleed. My doctor said that I should take it easy and rest. I didn't want to make love with him just in case I started to bleed again and lose our baby. When I tried to explain to him how I felt, he would sulk and call me frigid and tell me to stop being silly. I would get really upset about it most of the time but eventually I would give in and he would get his way as usual. I didn't like him calling me that name; he made me feel as if there was something wrong with me. I didn't like us to fall out at all. I was happy and loved him so much. His divorce proceedings were causing him some stress too. He knew how I felt about wanting to get married, before the baby came along, and he said he felt the same way but it was taking so long and I didn't think it would ever happen. His ex-wife had asked for a blood test, to prove that her baby was his. She was demanding half the house and maintenance too. In the many solicitors' letters, which Richard had received, she said that she wouldn't divorce him until all those matters were settled. Richard told me that it could take years to finally be divorced from her. Our baby would be born before his divorce came through. This upset me all the time because it was not respectable. It was not what I wanted my life to be like, it was not how I wanted my dream to be. Richard had assured me previously that she would not pester us if I became pregnant. He said she would leave us alone in those circumstances. It seemed as if she would never leave us alone. It seemed as if it was going to carry on forever and she would never divorce him.

In the beginning it didn't bother me living with him, lots of people were living with their boyfriends at that time. However, since I had become pregnant, I felt it was wrong, and we were in fact 'living in sin'. It was not the way I wanted things to be, but there was nothing I could do about it. We were together, despite all our problems, and that was all that mattered; it was going to be a long waiting game until the day came when we could get married. I didn't know what we would do if we had to sell the house. I loved living there in that house.

Our lodger, Alan and his girlfriend Julie, were about to leave. They were talking about getting a place together and moving out before our baby came along. I didn't want them to go, I would miss them so much. I had got close to Julie. She had been great. She looked after me when I had a bad nose bleed at the King's Head Pub. This was when Richard was working there as the DJ one evening. I didn't feel very well at all. She brought me safely home and sat on the edge of my bed chatting about the baby and our dreams of the future. She stayed with me for hours, until Richard came home.

Over the next few weeks, the relationship between Alan and Julie broke up and she left. I was devastated. I missed our cosy chats. It broke my heart to know that she wouldn't be around when I had my baby. I was hoping that she would always be around and hoped she would be a Godmother to our baby. Life went on and Alan soon moved on with his life and seemed happy enough. We didn't hear from Julie again.

Richard and I were learning to live with the little niggles that seemed to be interfering with our relationship. We managed to tolerate them most days, but the constant everyday niggles about finances and the problems with the divorce proceedings, had taken their toll on us both. We were still happy together and I knew, despite everything, that I loved him and still wanted to be with him forever. I never doubted my feelings for him but over the coming weeks, I grew increasingly fearful that he wasn't feeling the same way about me any more. I was getting fatter and our sex life was still going downhill because of my fears with my pregnancy. Richard became distant and didn't seem himself most days.

One morning, Richard was leaving for work and I went to him to kiss him goodbye. I kissed him and straightened his tie as usual, just as I did every morning. I noticed a piece of paper with writing on it, sticking out of his shirt pocket. I pulled it out and asked him what it was. I had noticed the handwriting was just like Maureen's. Richard suddenly snatched it from my hand and stuffed it into the pocket of his trousers. He said that it was nothing and rushed through the door like a whirlwind saying that he was going to be late for work. I couldn't understand why Maureen would write Richard a letter. What was going on? Why was Richard so secretive? If she had written him a letter, why had he not told me about it? Why had she, my sister, not told me? I worried all day and grew more and more suspicious. I just couldn't think of any possible reason why my sister would write to him and for him to keep it a secret from me. Why did he snatch it out of my hand before I had a chance to read it?

He didn't come home for his dinner that lunchtime, as he usually did and when I phoned his office he wasn't there. He always tried to call to see how I was throughout the day if he wasn't able to come home for dinner; but that day he hadn't. I thought that he must have been avoiding me. My suspicions were growing, I just couldn't understand. By the end of that afternoon, I was distraught and in tears, imagining all sorts. I was convinced that he was going to end our relationship and throw me out all over again. Was he having an affair? I knew that there were always plenty of pretty girls chasing him when he was working as a DJ. Or, could it be that he was going back to his ex-wife again, just as before? All the problems we were having at that time were probably just too much for him to deal with, I feared that maybe he wanted to leave me.

When he finally came home, it was late afternoon and I had fallen asleep on the settee. I was exhausted with my thoughts. I sat up and faced him; he could see I had been in a state. I had questions that needed answering. I wanted to know why my sister had written to him and what was the reason for all the secrecy.

He sat down beside me and started to explain that she had written to him to ask him if he could lend her some money. She was saying that she was skint after losing her job at the sandwich shop. He said that she had been having some problems at home with her mum and that she didn't want me to know or find out that she had asked him for money. He didn't show me the letter, he said that he had thrown it away. I accepted his explanation for the letter. I trusted him, and his words assured me as they always did. My fears disappeared. He said that I was silly to be so upset and to be thinking in this way. He told me that he would never leave me again or hurt me in any way. He also said that he was so sorry to have kept it from me and promised not to keep anything else from me again. He said that I was being paranoid to think that he could ever be having an affair! He was so shocked and quite angry that I could have thought such a thing. He blamed my pregnancy hormones for making me think those awful things about him. He would say, 'How could I possibly have an affair? I am either with you or at work, I haven't got the time to have an affair!' I believed his every word and it was all forgotten about.

Richard and I became a lot closer after that day; he became more loving and attentive and tried to be at home more. He had started to teach Alan the 'art' of the DJ and he had become quite a good DJ as a result of this. So good in fact that he was able to take over some of the DJ spots at the pub. This left Richard to spend a bit more time at home with me.

We would sit in front of the fire, watching a video on our new Betamax video player, or go for long drives out in the car some evenings. We even drove all the way to Blackpool one night, just for a bag of chips. We would 'cruise' for hours along the motorways, talking and listening to the tapes playing on the car stereo. On occasions, we would stop at the motorway service stations for a cup of coffee. It just felt like it did when we first met; so romantic!

We were driving along a country road, one dark night, and Richard ran over a rabbit. It was just sitting there in the middle of the road; he couldn't avoid it. The headlights shone into its eyes and it seemed to freeze. We felt the bump on the car when he hit it. We stopped to see how it was but it was lying at the side of the road dead. It made me cry. I cried all the way back home.

A couple of weeks later Richard bought a big orange caravanette. His idea was that we would spend most weekends travelling around the country. He it was 'our home away from home'. It had a little cooker, a sink with a tap and settees that turned into a bed. There was also a table and a fridge, it was perfect. Our little love nest, I thought. Richard loved it and drove us all the way to Scotland one weekend; that journey was such a beautiful and scenic drive all the way. I loved seeing the hills and mountains. We drove through Gretna Green and then on to Glasgow. Richard told me that couples got married in Gretna Green. Usually, lovers who had eloped. They hadn't got their parents' consent to get married but could just walk in and get married at a younger age than was allowed in England. It seemed like such a beautiful, romantic place to get married. How could anyone want to get married without their family watching? I would definitely want my mum and my sisters there to see me get married to Richard one day.

On the journey home, I started to daydream about getting married to Richard at Gretna Green. I thought that it was a great idea for us to get married there one day; without any of the fuss and the huge expense. Richard had already been married in a church, so we definitely wouldn't be able to; it was not allowed. Our wedding would have to be in a registry office and I didn't like that idea. Gretna Green was such a beautiful place to be married. I imagined Richard and I standing in front of that anvil exchanging our wedding vows. Richard and I talked about it and he thought that it would be a good idea too; we could just get in the caravanette and drive up there and 'just do it.' I thought that when the day finally came, when he was free, that we could do this. Afterwards we would come back and have a big party with everyone. From then on that was our intention; another dream for our future together. The thought of eloping with Richard and marrying him, without any of my family there to see us, didn't seem to bother me at all after I had seen Gretna Green. I thought it would be so wonderfully romantic, I was in dreamland yet again.

I hadn't felt close to my mum over the last few months. We were barely talking. She still didn't seem to accept Richard and I being together, despite me being pregnant with his baby. She told me that she didn't approve of me being with him at all. She would call him a 'sweet talking guy' behind his back. She never came to see us at our home, so I couldn't see how she knew how we were together and what a lovely home he was providing for me. To his face she could be quite pleasant and that made me think that she was beginning to like him. I would hate it when she then became two faced and said horrible things about him behind his back. She even tried to tell me that he was seeing other women behind my back when he was working as a DJ at the Happy Pig. I would tell Richard what my mum was saying. He would get upset and deny everything she had said about him. He couldn't understand why she kept saying those awful things. He told me that she could be trying to split us up, because he wasn't divorced, or maybe she thought that he was not good enough for her daughter. He said that the best thing I could do was to keep away from her and not to listen to any more of her shit stirring and not to get myself upset while I was pregnant. Richard was right, I should not allow myself to get upset while I was pregnant. I didn't know why Mum was being so horrible like that; could she not see that it was upsetting us both? Did she even care? Why was she trying to break up our relationship?

Richard and I tried to put it all out of our minds; it was causing us to bicker when we shouldn't have been bickering. We had to concentrate on living happily together and maybe one day in time she would realise just how happy we were and leave us alone. Our relationship had its problems but at least Richard didn't shout and bawl at me or beat me up as Dad had done to her. I knew that Richard had different women chasing him at the discos, that was part of the job. I had seen what they were like when I had been there. It was part of his job to talk to them and play their records, he assured me that it was all left at the discos and nothing else went on with them. I believed him. He was home on time each night and he was always trying to show me just how much he loved and cared for me, so I accepted Richard's every word and thought that Mum should go and 'shit stir' about someone else. I had no reason at all not to believe him.

Things soon settled down between us at home and we decided to keep our distance from Mum and my family for a while until Mum was willing to accept our relationship and stop calling Richard names. I was hoping that in time she would begin to realise how much in love we were and that one day accept him as a son-in-law.

There was another thing that was puzzling me at that time, this concerned Richard's family. I was beginning to wonder why he hadn't spoken to his mother for months or seen his little brother Lee. I would ask questions about them but Richard never wanted to talk about them at all. I had already met his mother's sister Gloria. This was Colin's mum and she was really nice. However, I got the impression that she didn't get along with his mother at all. After a while, I was to find out the reason for their troubles. I was introduced to his elder brother Keith. "This is my brother Keith," Richard told me one day, when he had knocked at our back door. Keith was the image of Richard, only with dark thinning hair; you could certainly tell they were brothers. He had parked his posh car in the back street and then come down the yard and knocked at our back door. Richard was surprised to see him and even more surprised to see his brand-new posh car parked in our back street. He instantly took us out to look at it. It was a white Lotus sports car. Richard's eyes were huge; it was a gorgeous car. It wasn't long before Richard was sitting behind the wheel and begging for a test drive. When they came back from their drive, we all sat down in the living room and had a cup of tea.

Keith and Richard talked about different things; mostly about cars and business. Richard showed off his new car to Keith. At that time, he had a shiny navy-blue Wolseley. It was an old car but in really good condition. He had part-exchanged it for the caravanette. The caravanette had been too expensive to keep on the road. Keith also told Richard that his marriage to Barbara was over and they too were getting divorced and then the subject of their mother came up. Keith was talking about their fall out openly and even laughed about her with Richard.

It came to light that Richard had conned his mother out of some money and she had taken him to court and won the case. Bizarrely, she ultimately found herself paying the court fine for Richard too. I couldn't believe that Richard had conned his own mother. That was the reason that they had fallen out. How could he have done that? Apparently, the story was that Richard got two family members, who worked at the town hall, to send him a document to say that he had been fined for a driving offence. His mother gave him the money to pay for the false fine instantly. After a while she found out that he had lied to her; there was no driving offence fine, he had conned her. She instantly phoned the police and all of the participants in the con were arrested and taken to court. They were all found guilty of the offence, and all family members involved, lost their jobs at the town hall. At the end of the trial Richard's mother, for some strange reason, offered to pay all the court costs on Richard's behalf. Keith and Richard thought this quite funny and laughed about it. I didn't think it was funny at all; no wonder she didn't speak to Richard. I kept quiet; I didn't understand how he could have conned his own mother. I had been hoping to meet her one day but they had not spoken for over a year, so I thought she might never forgive him for what he had done to her. I was carrying her grandchild and I really hoped that she would want to see the baby when it was born.

When Keith had left, I briefly spoke to Richard about what had happened. He told me that he had regretted doing that to his mother and for getting his cousins in trouble, but he had needed the money at the time. It was before I had met him, and at the time when he was married to his ex-wife, so I wasn't to worry about it. He was visibly upset when he spoke. He did say that he hoped his mother would forgive him in time and we would all be friends again. I could see that he meant what he said. We didn't speak of that again.

Earlier that year, in June 1977 the Queen celebrated her Silver

Jubilee; she had been on the throne for twenty-five years. There was red, white and blue bunting, union flags and banners hanging across every street. Schools were closed for the day, and most people were given the day off work to celebrate, in order to have street parties with their families.

The scenes of London, on the television, were spectacular, with thousands of people old and young, lining the streets waiting to see the Queen ride by in her horse drawn carriage. Everyone was waving union flags high in the air and smiling. The atmosphere must have been amazing.

I was almost six months pregnant and getting fatter, I seemed to be quickly growing out of all my clothes. Maternity dresses, on sale at Mothercare, were quite expensive. I would comment to Richard that with my skills as a machinist I could make a dress if I had a sewing machine and save a lot of money. To my surprise, Richard came home from work, carrying a large box.

"I have bought you a present," he said. Excitedly, I opened the box. Inside was a lovely sewing machine I was so thrilled! I kissed and hugged him so tightly.

I began looking for dress patterns in a dress shop in town and found the perfect design. It was a Simplicity pattern, which had various designs on the front, for the perfect pinafores and smocks that I could make. There was plenty of different material to choose from on Bolton Market; I set to work with the material and the pattern. Before long, and with all the machinist skills that I had learned at Halbros, I had made my first maternity smock top and pinafore dress too. My work as a machinist at the factory hadn't been forgotten.

I went on to make lots of things for the baby with that sewing machine. To save some more money I made my own terry nappies, towels, cot sheets and pram sheets. I was quite proud of myself and the sewing kept me busy on the nights when Richard was out being a DJ. I would feel quite lonely sometimes, when I was home at night on my own; the time would drag as I waited for Richard to come home, so I tried to keep myself busy most of the time by making things for our baby.

At home Richard got interested in Citizen Band Radios. He set one up in the kitchen under the stairs. We had to have a very tall aerial called a 'twig,' which was attached to the wall in the backyard. He could talk to people on the radio. He would talk through the handset saying "1 9 for a copy good buddy," which meant he wanted to talk to someone. Before long there was someone on the other end talking back to him; usually this would be lorry drivers, driving along motorways in different parts of the country. It was interesting listening to the different conversations that people were having. It was supposed to be illegal to have a CB radio in the house, but Richard didn't seem to care and it didn't stop him using it. When he was working at night, I would go on it too; my handle was Purdy: off the Avengers. It was great fun, it passed a lot of time, talking to other CB users that were out there. The nights didn't seem so lonely as a result of the CB Radio.

I found myself spending a lot more time with Mandy, my best friend. I had missed her so much over the last few months. She had been dating Ray for ages; however, her parents had never approved of him because he was a heavy drinker and he had been in Borstal; they knew he wasn't good enough for their daughter. As it turned out they were right not to trust him; because when Mandy became pregnant by him, they had saved some money to buy a pram for the baby but he took it and spent it all down in the pub. Mandy's mum and dad told her that she was to choose him or them. She chose to finish with him and have the support of her parents instead. From then on, I got to spend a lot of time with her. She would come to stay with Richard and me, at Glynne Street, most weekends. We would be on the CB radio passing the nights away. It was a giggle.

It was great fun being pregnant together; we would compare our 'bumps' although I was due at the end of September and she was due in the following February she was already a lot bigger than I was. It looked like she was carrying twins compared to my little 'bump'. We had been looking forward to a night out for Mandy's nineteenth birthday in August so we decided to go shopping at the market. We bought matching pinafore dresses to wear on the night; her dress was beige and mine was blue. While we were shopping, it brought back the lovely memories of our 'girly shops' each Friday when we had got paid from the factory. We would buy matching clothes then too for our nights out at the Palais. I began to wonder if we would be getting our babies matching baby clothes too!

CHAPTER FORTY-SEVEN
Maureen

Over the next few weeks, Richard would say that he had seen Maureen at the disco when he was working. He told me that she would talk to him about the problems she was having at home with her Mum. He said he would listen and try to advise her what she should do. She ended up leaving home, staying with different friends of hers.

She would turn up at my house at times and speak of the places she had stayed. Shockingly, she would speak openly of sleeping with lads in the back of cars. She thought that it was really hilarious and would giggle about it. Her words seemed far-fetched and unbelievable; I was beginning to doubt her every word.

I thought she was a silly spoiled little girl who needed to grow up! If it was true, I was shocked and worried for her safety. I wanted to advise her to stop behaving in that way and to go back home and work things out with Mum, but she would have aggressively told me that she would do what she liked and to keep my nose out of her business. I was sure of that. She would say that she was having fun and that she wanted a baby. I would keep my mouth shut and try to ignore her.

As the weeks went on, she would tell us that she was actually pregnant, and then inform us later on, it was a false alarm or a miscarriage.

Richard and I would sit and listen to her whenever she called. We would look at each other in disbelief. It was hard to believe she would want to do those things. She was only seventeen and the way she was behaving wasn't right and we tried to encourage her to go back home to her Mum's. Richard and I thought that she was making up these stories for attention so we would become worried about her and invite her to come to live with us, but the thought of that horrified me. We weren't close as sisters, not as close as I was to Ann, not ever. I didn't like the way she behaved; she had been smoking and drinking from a very early age. She was spoiled. There was no way that she would have settled down for anyone. I didn't want her to come and live with us; there was no room for her in our house!

It did cross my mind at the time, that she was beginning to feel envious of my relationship with Richard, and of what we had together. I thought that she wanted to have what we had; trying to get pregnant with somebody, anybody, so she could have the same. She was far too young and immature to start a family of her own. She should have been having fun with her friends and not wasting her life in that way. We could see she would get pregnant one day, if she carried on the way she was going. It would be a big mistake for her if she had to raise a child alone. Each time she told us of her pregnancies, I secretly had a dream of becoming an aunty. A child that would call me Aunty Maggie; I smiled to myself and thought how lovely that would be.

I remembered our Aunty Lily. I loved her and hoped that when I became an aunty, I would be loved just as much as my Aunty Lily.

Richard would come home, after the discos, and whenever he had seen her, he would say that she was getting a bad reputation. However, if all that she was telling him was true, there would have been nothing we could have done about it. She was a free spirit and she was doing exactly what she wanted to do. She didn't seem to worry about her own reputation or who she hurt in the process.

She had also begun a strange and horrible habit involving eating toilet roll. She would pull sheets of it out of her handbag or pocket, tear bits off and chew it. I couldn't understand it, no matter where she was or who she was with, tissue was always available for her to chew and swallow. I was puzzled. I didn't know why she did it. When I asked, she just said that she liked it. We all thought it was an attention seeking childish phase but it became irritating and embarrassing to watch sometimes. It seemed to me that she didn't seem to mind everyone being surprised and shocked at what she was doing.

She seemed to visit often in those early days. She would plonk herself on my settee with an ashtray nearby and would wait to be offered a cigarette by Richard. I would get more and more irritated with the way she acted around Richard. Over a period of time, she started to flirt with him and follow him around my house like a lap dog. It didn't bother me at first. I was happy at first with the way she got on with him, and I liked the way she seemed to like him, unlike my mum. However, her games began to get worse and were played out right in front of me. At times, if he walked out of the front room to go to the toilet, she would get up and follow him. After a few minutes she would come back to the front room to where I was sitting and she would be adjusting her jeans or buttoning up her blouse making it appear as if they had been fooling around in my back kitchen. I would initially think it was my imagination, or my hormones playing up again, but it began to happen nearly every time she visited.

Sometimes, I would get up and follow her, a few seconds after she had followed Richard, in the hope of catching them 'at it.' Each time I sneaked in behind her she was only ever at the sink having a drink of water or just standing there alone in the kitchen. Richard, unaware of her little game, wouldn't be anywhere near her. I never did catch them together. I would be angry at myself for thinking those wicked thoughts about my sister, who I thought at that time, was possibly just being friendly. I convinced myself it was just my hormones making me paranoid and suspicious, to be thinking like that. I tried not to think those thoughts about her and certainly didn't ever mention them to Richard. She was my sister; she wouldn't do that to me. She had got all those lads chasing her, as she had been telling us. Why would she ever want to play games with my man? Surely, she must have known how much I loved him. My silly paranoid thoughts left my mind as quickly as they came. However, each time she visited, those little antics of hers started to get worse; I started to think that she was doing it on purpose, just to hurt me and make me think that something was happening between them in my kitchen, when there clearly wasn't.

Why would she do that? I would ask this question of myself. I knew she didn't really like me. Was that the reason why she would come into my home and hurt me like that while I was pregnant? Why was she trying to make me jealous? I was beginning to suspect she was causing trouble for Richard and me on purpose. Were those silly games of hers just another phase, like the chewing of the toilet roll? It happened that often, I was convinced, she was doing it on purpose. How could she be so cruel and heartless? Was she fantasising of fooling around behind my back with Richard while I was carrying his baby?

I decided I didn't want her in the house any more, because of what she was doing. It was upsetting me inside. Her silly little games worked, she did make me think that she was fooling around with my man, right under my nose, and she did make me feel jealous. He was my man; she shouldn't have been doing those things. She would smirk her usual smirk, when she knew I was watching her, as she adjusted her clothing.

Eventually, I spoke to Richard about my suspicions and told him what she was doing and how it was upsetting me. He was unaware of any of her little antics; he laughed and told me that she was only jealous of what we had and I was to ignore her. I was not to get so upset about it and once again his assuring words did make me feel better. He told me that once she had her own proper boyfriend and was in her own relationship, she wouldn't interfere with ours so much.

I hadn't wanted to speak to Richard about it.; I hadn't wanted him thinking that I didn't trust him. I did trust him. I loved Richard. He made me happy; and I knew he loved me. I was beginning to be suspicious of my sister though. Was I right to stop trusting my own sister?

For a while I had kept it to myself, we already had enough problems to deal with without all that nonsense from her. I assumed he would have told me off saying that I was mistaken or being paranoid and mental to be thinking that way of my sister. I knew I wasn't being paranoid. She was doing it on purpose to make me think there was something going on between them — I was sure of it. Maybe Richard had been right when he had said that she would leave us alone when she found her own proper boyfriend; I did hope so. However, I didn't trust her one bit, and I didn't like her coming to the house any more. From that point on, we decided to tell her that we were going out each time she called. We tried not to be around her so she couldn't play her disturbed little games with me any more.

I just wished she would hurry up and grow out of all those childish phases.

One night when Richard came home from the King's Head; he woke me to tell me that Maureen had been at the pub and had got very drunk. He told me that she had nowhere to stay that night and had fallen asleep in his car, he couldn't wake her so he left her there in the car.

The next day Richard dropped her off wherever she wanted to go. I couldn't understand why she had gone all that way to Atherton to where he was a DJ. How did she know he was working there that night? What was she playing at? Why would she want to sleep in Richard's car? Why didn't she go home?

Richard and I fell out about that night and had a row. He told me that he couldn't just leave her on the streets. I did agree, but he should have taken her home to Blackrod to Mum's house. He knew the trouble she had been causing with us; why did he let her sleep in his car? I couldn't understand him doing that. Why didn't he bring her indoors to sleep on the settee? There were no reassuring words or excuses from him that time, only sorry that he did it and that it was a mistake.

Maureen eventually went back to live at Dad's house. I thought that was the best place for her and that she would probably calm herself down a bit at dads. She wouldn't be allowed to stay out all night or get drunk and do the things that she did at Mum's house; Dad wouldn't allow it.

It was Dad's birthday the next time we saw her. It was a bright, sunny, warm day on Friday August 5th.1977. We called at Dad's house with a birthday card and to see our Laura. Maureen and Andrea were both in the house with Laura. Dad had gone down to the pub. Andrea was a month away from her sixteenth birthday and had left the children's home and was back living at dads again. She seemed to be more settled at Dad's house, and she appeared glad to finally be back at home. While we were there enjoying our precious time with Laura, playing in the garden in the sunshine, we heard Maureen and Andrea arguing. Maureen was curled up on the settee watching television. Andrea was shouting at her, that she had to do the pots and tidy the kitchen. Maureen was shouting back at her to stop telling her what to do.

I went in to see what all the fuss was about and Andrea was close to tears. She told me that she had done all the bedrooms as Dad had asked and Maureen was supposed to be doing the kitchen before Dad came home. Andrea started to cry and got really upset and started shouting louder. Maureen just refused to get up to go and tidy the kitchen. Andrea was shouting that she would get in trouble when Dad came home if the chores were not all done. She was hysterical, saying that he would send her back to the children's home. Maureen ignored me too, when I asked her to help Andrea and told her she should be helping Andrea around the house. Maureen just sat watching television, sucking her thumb, ignoring

Andrea's cries.

We had to leave to get back home. I didn't like hearing Andrea upset like that. I didn't want to be around in that house when Dad came home to find the chores hadn't been done. Andrea was still shouting and banging around in the kitchen when we shouted to her from the hallway that we were going. We were just about to walk through the front door when Andrea came running out of the kitchen and grabbed hold of me and tried to put her arms around me; she was saying she was sorry over and over again. I was angry with them both for arguing and didn't want to stay listening to them any longer. Although I thought that Maureen had caused the argument, I pushed Andrea away and said that we had to go. Andrea then turned and ran off into the living room crying.

When I turned and faced Richard as we were leaving, a look of complete shock came to his face; his eyes widened and his face went white. He was looking down at my green checked smock top. I looked down and saw it was covered in blood. There was blood all over me. I nearly fainted with the shock. Instantly I thought of Andrea. I ran into the living room; she was standing in the corner of the room sobbing her heart out.

"What have you done?" I frantically shouted to her. I looked at her hand and it was pouring with blood. The blood was spurting out everywhere. I grabbed her and pulled her outside and held her arm up high and pressed her hand against the wall to try to stop the blood. I shouted for someone to phone an ambulance.

"What have you done?" I cried. She told me that she had cut herself. What she had actually done was stuck one of the sharp kitchen knives right the way through her hand on purpose. She had harmed herself in that way before but this was so much worse; there was blood everywhere.

Ann came home just at the right time to see all the commotion. She wrapped Andrea's hand in bandages. Maureen looked on without saying a word. It was her fault that this had happened; if she had tidied the kitchen, as she was supposed to, instead of sitting on her backside watching television, sucking her thumb, none of this would have happened.

An ambulance arrived and took Andrea to hospital. Richard and I left and went home. I was angry and upset at Andrea for doing that to herself again. Maureen had caused the trouble that day for Andrea.

I found out later, from Andrea, that when Dad had eventually come home from the pub and found out what had happened, he drove straight to the hospital. He went to the waiting room of the Accident and Emergency Department of Bolton Royal Infirmary. There he found Ann and Andrea seated; Andrea's hand was padded with bandages and resembled a boxing glove; Dad went over to Andrea and threw a handful of razor blades at her.

"There you are Andrea!" he shouted at her in front of everyone. "You should be able to do a proper job with those!" He turned and left the hospital and went home.

Andrea had done a lot of damage to her hand. She had severed tendons and an artery and had to have an emergency operation. Ann, being nineteen years old, and a student nurse at that hospital, was allowed to sign all the medical papers to give her consent to the operation. Andrea had to stay in hospital for a few days but when she recovered, she wasn't allowed to live at her dad's house. In fact, she was sent to a special ward at Townley's Hospital. From there she went to another hospital, a hospital called St Carls. It was a long way away in Northampton. Shortly after this incident, Maureen left Dad's house as well and went back to live back at Mum's house. I didn't want to speak to her after she had caused all that trouble with Andrea.

CHAPTER FORTY-EIGHT
1977, The Happy Pig

A few weeks after Andrea was taken to hospital, Richard got a phone call from Colin, his cousin, to tell him that his little brother Lee was in hospital. Lee had experienced an accident and an injury to his eye. Richard and I quickly got into the car and drove to the hospital without even thinking of the fact that Richard wasn't speaking to his mother due to their recent argument. He was so worried and just wanted to see how his little brother was.

We walked into the hospital and along the long corridors to the ward where we were told Lee was. We were greeted by the sister of the ward and we asked her if we could see Lee. She took us to the private room where he was. She told us that his mother was with him and she would tell her that we were there.

We waited outside the room while the nurse walked in. The nurse left the door open slightly, so we could see right into the room. Richard's mum was sitting on the bed at the side of her blond-haired little boy who looked so tiny in that huge hospital bed. He had a bandage over his eye. Also sitting on the bed, were two other familiar figures; they were Richard's wife and her mother. His mother started shouting to the nurse, saying that she didn't want him coming into the room and he was to be sent away.

The nurse quickly left the room, shutting the door behind her, and we had to leave the ward. Richard asked the nurse about the injury to Lee's eye and asked her if he would be all right. The nurse told him that there would be no permanent damage and that Lee would be back at home in a few days.

Richard was angry at his mother for not allowing him to see Lee and really upset because his ex-wife was there too. I knew Richard missed his little brother. I got a good look at his mother too that day; she was a stern looking woman with curly auburn hair and black rimmed glasses. I didn't think I would like her if we ever got to meet again.

That weekend Mandy and I decided to go with Richard to the Happy Pig again. I was reminded of an evening out, a few weeks earlier, when we celebrated Mandy's nineteenth birthday. Richard and I had bought Mandy a gold crucifix and chain for her birthday; she loved it. We wanted to enjoy ourselves as much as we could, while we had the opportunity, before our babies were born.

It was the beginning of September; I was due to have my baby in a few weeks later. I knew that I wouldn't want to leave my baby with any babysitter, so we were out for a good time. We really did find ourselves having a good evening. It felt just like the good old days at the Bolton Palais, when we danced the night away, on that bouncy dance floor. The Happy Pig was only a small place, with a tiny dance floor, that didn't bounce. However, Richard's music was just the same and as usual Mandy and I were the first up on the floor dancing away. We were having a lovely time, although we didn't seem to have the same energy that we did back then. It was so tiring trying to dance all night while being pregnant. I wanted the 'loo' more often too!

While we were sitting, recharging our batteries, having a rest, there was a tap on my shoulder. When I looked round, I was surprised to see an old friend standing there behind me. It was David, my first puppy love boyfriend from school. He hadn't changed a bit. He looked exactly the same as he had when he was thirteen years old. His cheeky smile was just the same as it was back then. I had finished with him when I was fifteen because I was growing taller than him and he smoked cigarettes, plus I had secretly liked another boy in my class at school. When I stood up next to him, he was about six foot tall, he had grown up. I couldn't believe how tall he had grown. When he noticed I was pregnant he said, "Ahhh! Why didn't you marry me?" I blushed and laughed at him and told him the reason why I had finished with him, way back then, and how amazed I was that he had grown so tall. We chatted for a while, then he went to the bar with his friends and Mandy and I went off dancing again.

We also noticed Maureen in there that night. She said 'hello' to us when she passed our table but didn't stop to chat to us. We noticed her going over to the DJ stand. She talked to Richard repeatedly and in a provocative way. She was trying to play her silly games again no doubt. Richard would look at me with a reassuring look and it didn't bother me any more. I smiled, as her eyes met mine and with her usual smirk, she left the stage.

I still hadn't forgotten the upset she had caused a few weeks previously, at Dad's house with Andrea. Following that incident, I still didn't want to speak to her.

I did notice that there was another girl hanging around Richard. She was also there far too much and repeatedly. These experiences did not make me feel jealous but they were significant. She seemed very friendly towards him. She was the fifteen-year-old daughter of Dot and Jim who owned the Happy Pig. She was a pretty little girl with long auburn hair who was obviously trying to be more grown up than her years.

On the way home from the disco Richard asked me who the tall guy was that I was speaking to during the evening. I told him all about David my boyfriend from school.

The following week I was at home on my own while Richard was at the Happy Pig working. At around ten o'clock the phone rang. It was Maureen. I was uncomfortable speaking to her, after the trouble at Dad's house, and the hassles she had created in my home. However, I listened to what she had to say. She started to tell me that David was in the Happy Pig again and had been asking about me. So, what, I thought to myself. She continued to tell me that he had said that I was gorgeous, and he wanted me to come down next week and have a drink with him and a chat. I thought it was strange for David to be saying those things to her. He knew that I was with Richard and heavily pregnant! I didn't know what game Maureen was playing but I didn't believe her for one minute that David would have said those things to her. I told Maureen that I would probably go down the following week so I would see him then, if I did. She said that she would tell him.

As I was about to finish our conversation and put the phone down, Richard came onto the phone. He was shouting down the phone and sounded furious with me, he said that he had just heard me arranging to meet David at the Happy Pig the following week. I had never heard him shout like that before. I couldn't get a word in. He slammed the phone down.

He must have been listening in on the conversation that I had been having with Maureen! I didn't know why he would have wanted to do that. Was she trying to set me up? Why? Richard and I had both agreed previously, that Maureen was trying to wind me up with her behaviour.

Was this another way for her to discredit me?

I didn't think there was anything wrong with what I had said to her on the phone. Was she lying to me to try and set me up so she could say that I was cheating on Richard? How could he think that I would do a thing like that when I was about to give birth to his child?

He was late when he came home that night but I was still up waiting for him. He started shouting and bawling as soon as he walked through the door. I couldn't believe he would ever think that I would want to have an affair with David. I hadn't even seen each other since we were fourteen years old. We were just innocent children then.

I thought he knew me better than that. I was heavily pregnant; how could he think such a thing? I couldn't believe he had fallen for her lies, knowing what trouble she had tried to cause between us in the past. I was convinced, even more so, at that stage that she was after Richard and wanted us to split up.

Why did he believe what she had said? Why was he late home that night? Was he with her? Did he believe her every word and had she been consoling him in the back of his car?

I never got answers to any of those questions. I was, once again accused of imagining everything. He was once again accusing me of being paranoid, and my pregnancy hormones were making me behave in an unreasonable way! Were all the rumours that I had been hearing about Richard true? This question dominated my thoughts.

I came right out with it and asked him. I asked him if he was having an affair with my sister; he denied it and looked disgusted at that very thought. I was shooting all these questions at him, however, straight away he denied everything as if he knew what questions I was going to ask him. I was sure that there was something going on between them. I was angry that he should think that I could ever cheat on him.

We argued for hours. I told him that I would find somewhere else to live and bring the baby up on my own if he thought that I would ever cheat on him. I told him that I would leave if he didn't want me to stay with him any more. I cried and he cried and then we held each other and went to bed. He was saying over and over that he loved me and wanted to be with me forever. He was saying that I was the best thing that had ever happened to him. He was saying that he would never cheat on me, and especially not with my own sister. He cried and begged me not to leave him. He held onto me, with his head on my chest, and he wouldn't let go. We talked about everything for days, and the only thing we were both adamant about, was that my sister Maureen was trying to split us up and cause trouble for us.

When things settled down between us again, I felt that I wouldn't speak to Maureen from that point onwards, considering her behaviour. I hated the way that she was behaving and what she was trying to do to us. I would never be able to understand the reason why. She had to grow up and find her own boyfriend, instead of chasing mine. How could she do it when she knew we were having a baby together? She was my sister; she should not be doing this to me. Richard assured me that he would stay away from her and not listen to any more of her 'shit stirring'.

On the 16th August 1977, I was at home on my own, watching television when there was a news flash' ELVIS: THE KING IS DEAD.' I was devastated. I just couldn't believe it. I had been a fan of Elvis since I was at school. I was a member of his fan club and bought all his fan magazines from the newsagents every month with my paper round money. I had sixteen albums and over twenty singles. I played them all the time; singing along with them with my hairbrush in front of the mirror. I cried and cried for what seemed like hours that night. When Richard came home, I was inconsolable.

The next day all the headlines, in every newspaper, said 'ELVIS the King Is Dead.' For the next few days all the television programmes were about Elvis. All the radio stations were playing his music. I was in tears every time I heard his music. I just couldn't believe it.

Richard prepared a special night at the Happy Pig. He had arranged for an Elvis Tribute Act to appear on stage for everyone. The entertainer was dressed up in a white sparkly suit, just like the ones Elvis wore on stage. He did look remarkably like Elvis too, and he sang just like him. The place was electric. Everyone cheered and the girls screamed. It was a fabulous night.

After Elvis died, I was so distraught I couldn't play his albums any more. I would cry every time. When I was offered a great deal of money for my Elvis collection, from a man who we met in the Happy Pig, I sold everything I had to him. I knew they would be well looked after by this man, who seemed to be Elvis's biggest fan. The money came in handy to buy quite a few nice things for the baby.

CHAPTER FORTY-NINE
Deborah: Born 6th October 1977

"How long have you got left?" a neighbour asked me one day, when I was getting out of Richard's car.

We had just come back from the doctor's after attending my antenatal check-up. I was pleased to have been advised that everything was fine.

"Just five weeks left," I told the neighbour.

"Only five weeks left!" she looked surprised and said, "I thought you were going to say five months left! I was the size of a bus when I was pregnant. You hardly look pregnant at all," she continued.

This lovely lady lived three doors down from us and it was the first time I had ever spoken to her. I would often see her cleaning her windows or walking down our street with her little boy in his pushchair; I instantly liked her and hoped we would be friends one day. She seemed to be around the same age as me. She introduced herself as Diane. She was really nice; she had her little blond-haired boy resting on her hip. She told me his name was Stuart and he was eighteen months old. He was the cutest little boy I had ever seen, and he looked just like Diane.

I had only ever spoken to the lovely little old lady, who lived next door to us, over the backyard wall, when I was pegging washing out. Diane and I seemed to hit it off straight away and we became really good friends from that day onwards. We'd chat on the doorstep, when either of us was out cleaning the windows, or sweeping the front. We would also go shopping together for groceries at Farnworth Market. Diane would show me how to spend wisely and where all the bargains were. It was great to have a neighbour my age and for her to have become a friend.

When we were out shopping one afternoon, I walked alongside the pram carrying her little son. I would imagine the time, in the near future, when I would be pushing my baby along in a pram. I could hardly wait. The excitement was growing day by day. Still, my stomach would do somersaults every time I thought of giving birth.

I would sit for hours over endless cups of tea with Diane and she would tell me of her child birth experience, which wasn't very nice at all. It scared me to death. Still, I tried not to think of all the pain I would have to go through, I just couldn't wait to be a mummy and hold my baby in my arms.

My expected date of delivery came and went. Richard had put the cot up in our bedroom and everything was ready. The old pine chest of drawers was full of baby clothes. Soft fluffy white nappies were all washed and folded in a neat pile on top. The steriliser was full of baby bottles and was sitting on the kitchen worktop waiting for the requisite time. I was waiting. The doctor then told me that if I hadn't had this baby by the following Thursday that I would have to be sent to hospital to start the process. I would be two weeks overdue by then. I was beginning to think that this baby didn't want to be born. I had enjoyed being pregnant and knew I would miss my little bump once the time had come. I looked forward to that Thursday and the prospect of going in to hospital to be started off.

On the Wednesday before, I felt tired all day; I had been really busy over the previous few weeks. I had been cleaning the house and making sure everything was ready for our new arrival. I put my tiredness down to all the housework I had been doing. After sitting down relaxing with a cup of tea, I fell fast asleep on the settee and remained asleep there all afternoon. When Richard came home, he woke me up from my deep sleep. Startled, I woke up and sat up quickly. His tea wasn't ready. I tried to get up from the settee, my back ached. I thought I had been lying oddly on the settee and I still felt so exhausted. I couldn't ever remember feeling so tired.

"You stay there and rest," Richard said, "I will cook the tea." I sat watching Crossroads while he cooked our meal. He cooked sausage, egg, chips and beans and it was delicious; I finished off the lot. I didn't like Richard doing the cooking, he always made such a mess in the kitchen. He would use every pan and he would get grease all over the place. However, that night I was so exhausted; I didn't think about the mess that would be waiting for me to clean up afterwards. It was a lovely meal and I was grateful to him.

My dad would have gone mad with Mary, if his tea wasn't ready waiting for him when he had arrived back from work. I was so glad that Richard wasn't like him. After tea, Richard got ready for his work, at the disco, and I cleaned up the messy kitchen.

He had been gone for about an hour when I suddenly felt a little strange and suddenly needed to rush to the toilet. While in the bathroom, I noticed that I had been bleeding in my underwear. I started to panic straight away. I didn't know what to do. I was alone and scared. I started shaking. I started to cry. My back ached. I thought of Diane, my new friend. I knew she would know what to do.

I locked the house up and went to Diane's house and knocked on her door. Thankfully she was in. She opened the door and tearfully I explained to her what had happened. She smiled and happily took me inside. She told me not to worry. I was instantly reassured; she knew what to do. I felt better not being alone. She asked if I was in any pain but I told her that I wasn't in any pain except for the backache, but I had put that down to falling asleep on the settee all that afternoon. Diane explained to me that I could be in labour and the backache that I was experiencing, was in fact labour pain and the blood loss was probably a 'show'. The more she spoke of labour pain, the more scared I was feeling. My stomach was doing somersaults again. I felt sick and dizzy. She spoke calmly and was smiling so sweetly that I was beginning to settle down and I felt so glad that I was with her. She gave me a sanitary towel to wear just in case my waters broke. She then settled me down on her settee and made us both a cup of tea.

I stayed with her all evening. We talked and giggled the night away, excitedly waiting for something else to happen. Throughout the evening Diane kept asking me whether or not I was experiencing pain; the answer was always no. After endless cups of tea and several visits to the loo, I was beginning to think that nothing was ever going to happen at all.

When Richard came home, I told him what had happened and he started to get excited too. He wanted to take me to the hospital but I was scared. I didn't want to go. I wasn't in any pain, so it was pointless going to the hospital. We went to bed as usual. I expected to be awake all night with labour pain. This is what Diane had predicted. In fact, I slept soundly all through the night.

The next morning, I woke up with Richard and went downstairs to make a brew. I still didn't have any pain but I noticed that I had lost a little bit more blood. Richard decided that he should go to work and he told me to phone him as soon as I started to experience pain. As he was leaving, I got up to wave him off at the door and I got a sharp pain in my lower stomach. It wasn't that bad really, but I told Richard. It went as quickly as it had arrived. It was an unusual pain; a strange sort of pain that I hadn't felt before. As soon as it went, I could feel another one was coming; then that one went too. Richard hung on. I didn't know whether I was in labour as the pains weren't that bad.

After I had experienced about four of the same sorts of pains, Richard said that he had better phone the hospital to find out what we should do. He explained to a midwife, over the phone, what had been happening and he was told that I was definitely in labour. He was further advised that I needed to be at the hospital straight away. It was arranged that an ambulance would come and collect me. Richard got my hospital bag ready and we waited for the ambulance. I had a few more short, sharp pains. These were low down in my tummy but when the ambulance came, they had stopped. At the hospital I was taken straight to the delivery room. I was so scared I was shaking like a leaf. I had not had any more pains at all, I felt scared but okay. If these were the labour pains, mentioned by Diane the previous evening, they weren't so bad at all. I began thinking that the labour, if that was what it was, had stopped.

Surprisingly, when I was examined by a nurse, she told me that I was certainly in labour. She said that she would get me ready for delivery and it wouldn't be long before the baby would arrive. I could not believe it; I had no pain at that stage, I thought it would hurt far worse than that. It was nine o'clock when I had last experienced pain and this was at home. It was now nine-thirty in the morning and still nothing seemed to be happening. I had to be shaved down below; this was so embarrassing. I was also given an 'enema,' to loosen my bowels, they said! That was also embarrassing. I was told to hold it as long as I could! It did loosen me too! I had a warm bath afterwards which was lovely. I had all that done to me but I still didn't have any more pain. I lay in that strange bath trying to relax. My back ached. My stomach was doing somersaults all the time. I was going to be a mummy.

At that point, I was thinking to myself, what would I have, a girl or a boy? I was secretly hoping for a little girl. There was a knock at the bathroom door that disturbed me from my daydream. It was one of the nurses asking if I was all right. She came into the bathroom and held a towel out in front of me and I got out of the bath. As I stepped out of the bath I started to bleed. It was dripping on the floor. I got so scared. The nurse said, "Not to worry, we'll get you back to your room and have a look at you." I was examined again and the nurse said that I was fully dilated. That sounded painful. I didn't know what she meant. She showed me a diagram on the wall, and said, "When you came in you had dilated 2cms," and pointed to the diagram, "now you have dilated 10cms… Have you got any pain?" I told her that I didn't have any pain at all, just a little backache that was all. "Well," she said, "it won't be long."

The door opened and a man, wearing a mask and a green overall, came in. He said, "Hiya," and sat on the chair at the side of my bed. I looked at him strangely, wondering who he was; then I realised it was Richard. I didn't recognise him; I thought he was a doctor. That made Richard, me and the nurses laugh out loud. Before he returned, looking like a doctor, I had begun to wonder where he had gone. I then experienced a strong pain, and shortly after I experienced another one. They were strong and came on gradually, got worse, then wore off slowly. They were stronger than the last lot that I'd had. This was it, I thought; I am in labour. The nurse gave me an injection in my leg and asked if I wanted some gas and air to breathe for the pain. She held a mask in front of me and explained how to use it. At that point I could feel another pain coming, I grabbed the gas and air from her hand and breathed it in. All at once I felt an uncontrollable urge to push. I wanted to push so hard. There was no more pain at that point, only the urge to push. Sweat was dripping from my face and I remembered Richard holding me close. He wiped the sweat from my forehead with his mask, a comical gesture involving his chin. Then our baby was born. It was all over.

At 10.05 am on Thursday 6th October 1977, our baby daughter was born. I could hear her crying. She was lying at the bottom of the bed. She was covered in a yellowish waxy substance, with the appearance of melted wax. The substance was all over her. The nurses wiped her face and wrapped her in a soft white towel and handed her to me. She was so tiny and so gorgeous. Richard was crying and kissed me on my forehead. I cried; I couldn't believe that I had done it!

"What are you going to call her?" asked the nurses.

"Deborah Jayne," we both told her together, staring down into the tiny face of our baby, our little bundle of joy. Deborah looked straight at me, as if she was inspecting my face, just as I was inspecting hers. Her tiny hand and long thin fingers were sticking out from underneath the towel. I couldn't believe her fingernails; they were so long. I tucked her hand under the towel before she scratched her face. With tears streaming down my face, and so overcome with love, I said to her, "I'm your mummy!"

The midwife then had to take her away to be cleaned up and weighed. Before long she was being wheeled back in the room. By then, she was nice and clean and fast asleep. She was tucked up in a little glass cot that looked like a fish tank. The nurses told us that she weighed 5 lb and 10ozs and was 21ins long.

One of the nurses then said to me that because the baby was delivered so quickly, I had torn quite badly and hence I had to be stitched. That wasn't a pleasant experience. I stared at my baby, sleeping so contentedly beside me, until it was over. Although the nurses had told us that Deborah was fine, we had to check her out for ourselves. We inspected her fingers and toes, her ears, her little skinny legs; and her feet. We found her feet to be so very long. We tried to see who she looked like the most. Straight away, Richard said that she was the image of me but I couldn't see it. She was so gorgeous. I couldn't believe that she was just so perfect in every way. The whole experience was great; I thought it was going to be far worse than it was. I thought it would be more painful too after all the horror stories I had been listening to before she was born. From start to finish it only lasted an hour or so. The worst thing was the backache the night before and I hadn't really known that I was in labour then. Later that afternoon, I was wheeled up to another ward; my stitches were a little painful so I was helped onto another bed in the maternity ward. Here were three other mums with their babies.

Richard stayed with us for most of the day and we both gave Deborah her first bottle together. He eventually had to leave and go to work.

That night he came back at visiting time to see us again before his disco. His face was a picture every time he looked at Deborah.

Richard told me that he had phoned my mum to tell her that she was a grandma. I expected a visit from her that night but she never came to see her first and only grandchild. I thought that maybe she was too busy and hoped that she would come another day. That night Deborah was wheeled away from me to spend her first night in the nursery. The nurses reassured me that she would be fine and that I needed my sleep. I did sleep that night.

We were all woken early the next morning by the nurses. All the babies were wheeled back to us and placed at the side of our beds.

After breakfast in bed, I was allowed to get out of my bed and have a shower. That first shower was so uplifting I felt so much better afterwards. I still felt weak, and my stitches were tender but to be able to clean myself up and wear my own nightdress was refreshing. The rest of the morning was spent with our babies. We were all shown how to bath the baby. As if I didn't know how to already; I had bathed Laura often enough! We all watched the nurse as she demonstrated. In the afternoon we were all told to rest on our beds, lying on our tummies, while our babies slept after the two o'clock feed. We were told that lying on our tummies would help get the uterus back in place more quickly. We were advised that we would all have nice flat tummies by the time we left.

That day I had no visitors. I watched all the other visitors arriving to see the other ladies in the ward. I was sitting waiting but no one came. The night time visiting came and went but no visitors for me. I would have loved Mum to come and see me and Deborah, her first grandchild, but she didn't. I felt really grown up now and I was a mummy myself, but I still wanted my mum.

My mind drifted back to the time when I was seven years old. I was in the hospital after I had been knocked down by a van on Moss Bank Way. I would always sit up in bed waiting and watching the big double doors, at the end of the ward, at visiting time, to see if my mum would one day walk through them. I was in hospital for several weeks way back then, but not once did she walk through those doors. I could still remember how I felt every day, the feeling of longing for my mum, and for her to put her arms around me. I would wipe away the tears on my bed sheet.

Almost twelve years later, I was sitting there in a hospital bed, with my own new born baby, sleeping peacefully beside me. I was still waiting for my mum to walk through those doors. I felt exactly the same as I did way back then.

I wiped the tears from my eyes before anyone noticed. I picked my baby up from her cot and cuddled her. I kissed her on her cheek as she slept on my shoulder. I looked out through the window at the outside world and a silent tear slipped slowly down my cheek. The love I felt for my child overwhelmed me, my eyes filled with tears; I swore to myself that I would always protect her and never leave her. I would always be there for her. I would protect her and try to give her the happy childhood that she deserved. She would have the happy childhood that I didn't have. I silently promised my daughter that I would never make her feel the way my mum had made me feel on that day. She slept undisturbed against my shoulder; I was slowly rocking from side to side watching the world go by outside. I was content. As well as my mum, Richard didn't visit that night either. I expected that he would have had a show to do.

The next day, at visiting time, Richard walked through the doors and came straight to me and kissed and held me so tightly.

"God it was so lonely without you last night, I missed you so much," I started to cry again. I had felt so weepy since the previous day. The nurses told me that it was the 'baby blues' and it would last for a few days, and that every new mummy gets the 'baby blues'. I knew it wasn't the baby making me 'blue,' I just missed my mum and Richard.

"Where were you yesterday?" I asked Richard. He told me that there had been a big party at the Happy Pig, it had been J's sixteenth birthday. J was the daughter of the owners of the Happy Pig. He told me that the party had started early and he had been offered double pay which was just what we needed at the moment. I was relieved. I knew that he must have had a big show on. We both spent the rest of the visiting hour cooing over Deborah. We watched her and giggled at all her different facial expressions.

At visiting time, the next day, Richard came again, but shortly after he had arrived, Maureen turned up. She had come all the way from

Blackrod just to see us. I thought that was really nice of her. We had hardly spoken since that day at Dad's house but she was my baby's aunty. All the arguments were forgotten and I was glad to see her. She looked into the cot at her little niece and said that her niece was so gorgeous. I asked her if she wanted to hold her but she said that she didn't want to disturb her while she was sleeping. She just stared at her as she smiled.

After visiting, Richard and Maureen left together. That evening, at visiting time, Richard visited again, shortly followed by Maureen. I did wonder whether she would still be playing her silly games with us as she had done before. Those thoughts quickly disappeared. As soon as I saw Richard, and the way he was with Deborah, I knew he would want to be with us forever. I could see the love in his eyes for Deborah, every time he looked at her.

The next day, my stitches were so painful, I cried. The nurses had told me that sitting on the bidet would help, but I was scared of using it. I hadn't ever seen one before and I wasn't sure how to use it and was concerned that I may appear silly if I had asked for assistance. When I made an effort myself, the spray went all over the place and wet me through as soon as I had pressed the button! I was in so much pain that day, that after a little demonstration from another mum, I decided to give it a further go. I sat on it just like a toilet; then pressed the button and the water sprayed upwards. Instantly the warm water was so soothing, it was such a relief and I began to feel a lot better. After I had been sitting there, for what seemed like ages, I went back to my ward experiencing no pain. I walked in through the double doors, closed them behind me and leaned back against them. A sense of relief must have been written all over my face. I said to the other mums, "I've just been on that 'dildo' and I feel absolutely fantastic!" All the other mums roared with laughter and I didn't know why. They then repeated to me, what I had said. I had got the word wrong; then they told me what a 'dildo' was. I was even more embarrassed. It was so funny, we all laughed about that for ages. It did cheer us all up.

At visiting time my word mix up was the topic of conversation and a giggle for everyone. I would blush bright red when it was mentioned in front of all the visitors.

I was in hospital for about five days. Each visiting time, Richard would arrive and then Maureen would follow shortly afterwards. It felt strange, I had a bad feeling about it once again, but I convinced myself, each time, that it was purely a coincidence. On one of Maureen's visits, she told us that she was pregnant. Not again I thought to myself. I didn't believe her at first because she had said it so many times before. This time she said that she was sure and that she had made an appointment with the doctor for that week. She also told me that she hadn't eaten all day. I felt sorry for her, so I emptied the bowl of fruit that my visitors had brought in for me, straight into her bag. "Take them," I told her, "I am going home tomorrow so I probably won't get to eat them."

After visiting, they both left together as usual. At times, when my suspicions got the better of me, I would look out through the window and watch the road that led from the car park to see if I could see her in his car when he was leaving. I saw lots of cars leaving but I never saw his, I must have missed him. Yet again I convinced myself that I was thinking silly thoughts. I tried to clear my mind of all that rubbish. She knew we were happy and there was no way she would spoil our relationship. After all we were a family, I thought to myself. I was sure she was happy being an aunty to my daughter at that time too. Richard would probably take her back home or drop her off somewhere, that would be all. He was generous, and he would always say that she was my sister and he looked out for her only because she was family, that was all. I believed him and trusted him.

The next day, after the doctor's check-up, I was allowed to go home. I was weighed before I left the hospital and I was surprised to hear that I was only eight stones. Richard came for me just after ten am. We said our goodbyes to all the nurses and to the rest of the women on the ward. He drove me and our new baby home. I couldn't wait to get home. I was so excited.

Deborah was dressed in a lovely white frilly dress and cute little white socks, also a tiny white cardigan that I had knitted myself. She had a white pram suit over the top. She was also wrapped in a soft white lacy shawl. I was wearing a pink and white checked blouse and my brown skirt. I hadn't worn it for ages, and I was pleased that I could fit into it again.

On the way home, Richard suggested that we should go and see his

Aunty Glory and Uncle Mypher. They weren't able to come to the hospital and were eager to see the baby. She made us a lovely cup of tea, when we got there. She then spent over an hour cuddling Deborah. Uncle Mypher had his polaroid camera out, taking photos, as usual. When we were leaving Aunty Glory's house, we met Brenda, who was married to Gary, Aunty Glory's son. He was another of Richards's cousins. She said hello and congratulated us and had a quick peep at Deborah. She was heavily pregnant too and hoping for a little girl she told me. She already had a little boy called Gary Jr. I hadn't met her before; however, I was getting eager to get home. It was nearly Deborah's feeding time.

When we finally got home, Deborah was still fast asleep so I placed her in her pram. Richard had prepared this for her, it was in its place in the living room. There were lots of cards waiting to be opened; some from people I didn't even know and neighbours that I hadn't spoken to before. Deborah didn't sleep long and started to cry for her feed. While Richard cuddled our tiny bundle, and gave her the bottle I had prepared, I went upstairs to change the bed before I had a cup of tea. I didn't know why; it was an odd sort of feeling. It was something I just had to do. I had a strange feeling that Richard might have had another woman in my bed, while I was in hospital, and I didn't want to sleep on those same sheets if he had. I didn't say anything to him about what I was feeling, I knew I was just being silly; he would have gone ballistic and called me paranoid again if I had started to accuse him, especially on that day when we were happy to bring our new baby home. We were having a lovely day; I didn't want to spoil it. I wasn't sure whether I felt at that point that I was starting to believe the rumours or if it was my hormones all over the place? I feared I was beginning to lose my trust in him. My head was all over the place. I was feeling all mixed up and emotional.

Richard was happy, I knew he was. He looked so happy and content with our baby in his arms. How could I be thinking those bad thoughts? I shook my head and told myself to pull myself together. I didn't want to think of anything that would spoil the happiness that I was supposed to be feeling. I just wanted to ignore and dismiss all the bad stuff, for as long as I could. However, I just had to change those bed sheets. When I stripped the blankets from the bed and removed the sheets, to my horror, I found a pair of rolled up nylon tights tucked down the edge of the bed.

I also found some hair clips. I knew they weren't mine. What were the items doing in our bed? My stomach rolled over and my hands started to shake. I was suspicious. Tears filled my eyes. Were my fears, right? He was always at the hospital with my sister; had my sister been sleeping here when I was in hospital? I knew she had been after him for ages but I thought she would have given up on all of those childish games, once she saw our baby, despite the fact that she hated to see us happy. Richard always said he wouldn't touch her with a barge pole. I still believed him. I shook my head once more and tried to get those thoughts out of my head. No! I thought; I didn't think she would do that but I had to ask Richard for an explanation as to why those women's tights were in our bed. I shouted downstairs to Richard and he came upstairs.

"Whose are these?" I asked him. Richard glared at the tights with a look of complete surprise on his face.

"Where did you find those?" he asked. I told him where I had found them and he said that Alan, our lodger, must have had a woman in. He did use our bed now and again if we were ever away. Richard told me that Alan had been using our bed because he (Richard) didn't like to sleep in it without me.

I was relieved with his explanation as usual and I got on with making the bed. I still had a little bit of doubt. Although it was true that Alan did use our bed from time to time, preferring our double bed to the single that he slept in, especially if he had a girlfriend, I was still a little bit cynical. I kept my thoughts to myself and got on with being a mum, and a happy wife.

Over the next few weeks our house was busy with visitors turning up all the time to see Deborah. I was enjoying being a mum. It was hard work but I loved every minute. Both Richard and I were up each night for the feeds and coped really well. We got into a good routine quite quickly. We did have valuable help from Diane, my new friend and neighbour; she was a godsend. She would come round most days and help out. She would tell me her way of doing things. She developed a baby routine that worked for her. My housework was done while my daughter slept outside, tucked up nice and warm in her pram. She would sleep for hours outside in the fresh air. I was able to get lots of work done around the house and make sure Richard's lunch was ready for him when he came home at dinnertime.

As the weeks went by it all became so natural; it was as if I was born to be a mum. I managed my new routine of being a mum, the housework duties, and looking after Richard too. I was proud of myself. Deborah was a happy baby and content all the time. I just couldn't believe how lucky I was. I would sit on the floor, in front of her cot, each night watching her when she was sleeping so soundly. Some nights I would sit and watch her for hours; especially if I thought she was getting a cold. I would watch her breathing; she would be sleeping so soundly that sometimes I couldn't see her breathing and I would start to panic a little. I would stroke her face or hold her tiny hand just for a little reaction; she would stir and smile in her sleep. I was a bit disappointed to learn that her smile actually reflected the presence of wind. Sometimes her tiny hand would wrap around my finger and I would smile and feel so warm inside. She was my perfect baby and she was going to be just fine.

CHAPTER FIFTY
The Affair

When Deborah was six weeks old, I began to hear rumours about Richard and J, the daughter of the owners of the Happy Pig. I heard that they were seeing each other. What made it worse, at that time, was that Maureen was spreading a rumour that Richard was the father of her unborn baby. How could she possibly want to sleep with my man, knowing that I was with him and we had had a baby together? She was my sister; I didn't believe she would even think about doing that. Those rumours would always find their way back to me by concerned friends or from family members. Maureen herself would speak out to my friends, knowing that her lies would come straight back to me. I believed that it was all pure fabrication on her part. How could Richard possibly be having an affair with both of those girls? It didn't make any sense at all to me. I couldn't believe what was happening. It was like living a nightmare. The phone was ringing all day, every day and in the evening too when Richard wasn't at home. I would have to answer, because it was a business line for Richards's mobile discos. However, there was often silence, or I would hear the receiver being replaced.

Richard was adamant that nothing was going on between him and anybody else but I couldn't understand why people were saying those things. Richard and I had been shocked to hear some of the stories that Maureen had told us previously. These stories concerned the lads that she claimed to have been with. Most of which I didn't believe for a minute. I knew that she had lots of lads chasing her, however, Richard wasn't one of them, despite her fantasies. What she was saying behind my back, about Richard, just couldn't be true. Richard told me he had never been with her and I believed him. Richard would tell me at that time, of the way she would behave in the pubs when he was working. He would call her horrible names like 'tart' and 'scrubber.' He also said that he would not touch her with a bargepole. I believed him, when he said that he wouldn't go with her, however, I thought it was wrong for him to be calling her those names, she was still my sister.

When I heard the rumours about J, Richard told me that he liked her and felt sorry for her. He would say that they were friends and they spent a lot of time together, but he assured me that he was not having an affair with her. I thought that Maureen had heard all the rumours about Richard and J and had become jealous of their friendship. I believed that the outcome of this was to weave a web of lies and to cause consternation. At no point did Maureen ever inform me that she was sleeping with my man or indeed that she was pregnant by him. As far as I was concerned these stories were unsubstantiated rumours and hearsay. What sort of sister would I have been if I was to accuse my own sister of sleeping with my man? I knew she liked him and liked to play her childish games but I knew in my heart she wouldn't do that.

One evening, while Richard was out working, J's parents called me and told me that Richard and J were in fact seeing each other. They also told me that the day after I had given birth to Deborah, it was J's sixteenth birthday and Richard had put on a big party for her in the Happy Pig. I was informed that he had bought her a necklace with "I LOVE YOU" on it. I was further advised that he had given her a diamond and sapphire ring. I didn't like what I was hearing.

How could all that about my Richard be true? Why would J's parents lie to me? They had their daughter to protect. I knew about the big party for her, because Richard had told me about it at the time. However, he didn't tell me that he had held the party for her. He said it was work and he was paid for being the DJ.

Everything came as a big shock. How could he be seeing a sixteen-year-old girl when I had just given birth to his daughter? I believed her parents, but Richard was still denying any involvement except friendship with her. He said that she was just infatuated with him and had a crush on him. I was always crying at this time but Richard was so convincing. He would hug me and tell me that he didn't want anyone else and that he loved me.

"Don't let them spoil what we have," he would say.

I couldn't stand hearing all the rumours and having all those arguments with Richard. The phone would ring all the time, day and night, no one would speak when I said 'Hello.' I couldn't stand it. I thought about leaving Richard all the time. I didn't know what to believe any more; I was confused. I couldn't stay with him if he was fooling around with a sixteen-year-old girl behind my back. But what would I do? Where would I go? I had Deborah to look after, how would I cope on my own with her? I had no money and no savings. I had nowhere else to go. I had made one decision at that time and that was to register Deborah with my last name on her birth certificate. The stresses over the affair with J filled my mind every day, and the dreams of the marriage Richard and I had planned since we first met were slowly dissolving from my mind. I didn't want my baby to have his last name, just in case there was any truth in what had been said about Richard, and we didn't end up getting married. Richard was not at all happy with my decision. The list of all the problems, within our relationship, was growing. I was in despair. However, over the next few weeks, Richard was trying his best to prove his love for me and make me trust him again. He would tell me every day how much he loved me. He was home a lot more and had started to do a lot of work on the house; he had built fitted wardrobes in our bedroom and had built a new kitchen. He made it easy for me to forget what had been said and to love him back. Why would he have said all those things to me if the rumours were true? In fact, why would he be with me at all, if he didn't love me?

We were beginning to feel happy again and decided to have our baby christened. Richard's mum, Lola, was back in contact with Richard and had become friends with him again. She would visit us all the time. She was always asking us when were we going to have Deborah christened? She adored her granddaughter to bits, which was so great for all the family. Deborah had a grandma, at last. My mum still hadn't seen my child. I felt that because of all the rumours, that Maureen was spreading around concerning Richard, that I had to keep away from Mum's house. Maureen was always there; I didn't want any sort of nasty confrontation with her.

Soon Richard and I decided to go to our local church and see the vicar to arrange to have Deborah christened. However, when we saw him, we were told that we couldn't have our baby christened because in the eyes of God we were 'living in sin.' We were not married and Richard wasn't divorced and Deborah was illegitimate. When I left the church, I was devastated and cried all the way home. I was broken hearted.

I had to listen to rumours about Richard from people who were trying to stop us being together, worse still, I had God saying that we shouldn't be together either. I was confused. I didn't think I would ever stop crying. Richard just held me. He didn't have the words of reassurance that time. He couldn't deny God's will. In God's eyes we were committing a sin, living together and having a child out of wedlock, as the vicar had told us. Those words were ringing through my mind until my head hurt and I couldn't cry any more.

When my baby was four months old, and fast asleep in her cot, I was sitting watching television, when the phone rang. It was almost ten o'clock in the evening. There was a woman's voice, that I didn't recognise, on the other end. She said, "Your Danny is here at the Kings Head with another woman!" Then she hung up, without saying who she was. My stomach turned over once again and my hands started to shake. I was so angry at hearing all this again, particularly since things had started to settle down for Richard and me. I thought that we were happy again. I had to go there and see for myself if it was true, or if it was someone else who was causing trouble once again for us.

Deborah was fast asleep in her cot, so I bundled her up, wrapped her in a blanket and took her to Diane's house and asked her to look after her. I wanted to see with my own eyes if it was true, once and for all. I had believed Richard's words for so long. If he was there with another woman, I would know that he had been telling me lies and this would be the point at which I would catch him out.

All the way down to the pub, in the taxi, there was still that little niggle in my brain that kept telling me that I was being silly and I shouldn't believe the troublemakers again. He did love me and he did want to be with me. I was heading straight for the King's Head Pub, praying with all my heart that I wasn't going to find any truth in what the mystery voice had said on the telephone.

When I walked in the pub, the first face I recognised was that of Maureen. My heart sank, I felt sick inside. Was that the 'other woman' that was mentioned on the telephone? My sister? My head was spinning; I couldn't believe it was her. I felt so angry. She was standing at the end of the hallway into the pub, with another girl, and she was smoking and drinking beer when she was supposed to be pregnant, although she didn't look very pregnant to me.

When I passed her, I swore at her and said that she should 'piss off' back home. I was fuming! How could she do that to me? She stood there, leaning against the wall with her friend. She carried on drinking, with a smug look on her face. I couldn't believe she would do that to me.

Richard was standing behind his DJ's stand. He had his headphones on and his head was down as he cued in the next record. He didn't notice me walk in. I walked straight across the packed dance floor and stood at his side. A look of complete shock was all over his face when he saw me. He asked me what I was doing there. I explained what had happened concerning the phone call. He turned and glared at Maureen and said that it would be 'her' causing trouble for us again. I looked at our Maureen and she was smirking. I knew that smirk; I had seen that smirk before when she had caused us all to get into trouble when we were kids. I then noticed that Richard was glancing across to someone sitting at a table near the bar area. I looked in that direction, to the right of the room, and saw another familiar face, it was J from the Happy Pig. I couldn't believe it. The two girls, who were at the centre of all the recent 'shit stirring,' were there in the King's Head at that same time. I was confused and waited for an explanation and some answers to my questions. Why were they both there? Richard turned to me and said that Maureen was causing trouble because he had brought J to the pub and she was jealous.

I stood behind the DJ stand, while the loud music played on. I listened to his explanation but I could not believe what I was hearing. He told me that he had brought J because she had a fall out with her mum and was upset. He felt sorry for her. He continued to tell me that they were just friends and there was nothing going on between them. How could I believe him, the two of them at the same time, with him? It seemed strange to me that he wanted to have that kid tagging along with him while he was working. She was not even old enough to be in the pub! However, I was more convinced that there was actually something going on between them, kid or no kid.

My fear, when I first walked into the pub, was that it was Maureen that he was seeing. I felt strangely relieved that J was the other woman and not her. It was J that he had been seeing all along. All of his words didn't convince me otherwise.

As I stood, watching his show and listening to the music, Richard had his arm around me and was trying to be attentive. He was making me feel as if he was showing the both of them that it was me that he belonged to, the mother of his child. Towards the end of the evening, Richard was playing the slow records and couples started smooching on the dance floor. Richard came closer towards me and told me that he loved me and kissed me on the cheek. All at once a beer glass was thrown over the crowd towards the DJ's stand, it hit me on the chin and smashed on the floor in front of me. I was stunned. It came from the direction of where Maureen and her friend were standing. When I looked up, over in her direction, they had gone. I didn't know if it was her that had thrown the glass, but I thought it must have been her. Richard had told me that she had become jealous because he had brought J to the pub and she probably became even more jealous at seeing the two of us together. I couldn't understand why she would be feeling any form of jealousy towards me or my man.

J made her own way back home, with her friend that night. I made it perfectly clear to Richard that although he had brought her, he would not be taking her home again. I had caught him out on his lies that night, but Richard still denied sleeping with her. I believed he had slept with her. I had just had a baby and I wasn't able to have sex for a while but I was trying to do 'it' for his sake. I still didn't like 'it' really. I was always too tired. I asked myself if that meant that he had to go with other women for sex because he wasn't getting enough at home? I couldn't and wouldn't believe any of the rumours about Maureen and him. I could see that she was flirty and threw herself at him at times. I still believed that she was trying to split us up, I also felt that Mum was trying to do this as well. I started to believe that this was because they both knew he was having an affair with J. I did question this as J was a sixteen-year-old kid, who was infatuated, according to Richard. Why would he want to go with a young girl like her?

Before he went to work that night, I recalled, he had his tea with me, got ready for his work, kissed me and Deborah goodbye and off he went to his disco gig in Atherton. That was what I thought he had done, however, instead he must have gone all the way to Blackrod to pick J up and take her to the King's Head that night. Why? That is not the behaviour of someone who is trying to avoid the attention of a sixteen-year-old girl.

The next few months were quite hard. I had to stay with him, although I believed Richard to be a liar and a cheat. I had nowhere else to go. I had to think of Deborah, I needed to keep her safe. Richard and I carried on with our usual everyday routine and the pretence of being a happy family. At times we would bicker, whenever I tried to speak out about J or Maureen, or when the mysterious phone calls started again in the middle of the night. It did make me suspicious again and I accused Richard of seeing J again. He would get angry and deny ever seeing her at all. I tried to believe him. I tried to put Richard's affair with J behind me and maybe even forgive him in my heart. I wanted to give him one more chance because he was giving me everything I wanted and trying to prove his love for me every day.

I was so relieved that it wasn't Maureen; that would have broken my heart forever. He still wouldn't admit to any of it, or ever say he was sorry for what he had done. He said we should move on and it was in the past. I knew that I still loved him and wanted to be with him so I needed to put those nightmares behind me and move on. Through it all Richard was saying he loved me and buying me flowers. He made it easy for me to forget the past and trust him once again and believe in him again. He was so wonderful with Deborah; he had her giggling away every time he looked at her. She was such a daddy's girl.

On the 9th February 1978, my best friend Mandy gave birth to her baby. She called him Craig. Richard and I went to the hospital to see him; he was gorgeous. He weighed 6lb 14oz and he was the image of Ray, her ex-boyfriend. Mandy told us that she was in 'labour' for hours and she thought that she was going to die, it was so painful. My 'labour' had been great, it hadn't lasted for long, I was so lucky. At that time, Deborah was five months old. We were planning and looking forward to the children both growing up together.

A few weeks later I found myself at the Happy Pig with Richard. Lola had been mithering to baby-sit Deborah for ages. We took her up on her offer and I had a night out. Richard was the DJ there as usual. Both J and Maureen were in that night and I sat at a table near Richard and watched them both. Neither of them looked very happy when they noticed me sitting there. J was working behind the bar, but she took the time to speak to Richard. This caused me some concern as she went behind the stage curtain to speak to him, this seemed strange. At the same time Maureen was dancing in a flirtatious way, right in front of him. Her behaviour made me laugh. I thought she was such a child and should grow up. Considering she was supposed to be pregnant, she didn't look pregnant at all, and she was still drinking beer and smoking cigarettes.

I kept remembering Richards's words and realised I had got to trust the man who was doing his best to prove his love and devotion to me.

Later in the evening, I was coming back from the toilets and bumped straight into J, she was crying. I took her back into the toilets and asked her what was wrong. I was comforting that sweet little girl who had just had an affair with my man! She was actually crying on my shoulder, smudging her face makeup all over my tee-shirt. I felt a little sorry for her. She was heartbroken. I was shocked when she turned round and looked at me, with smudged mascara all down her face, she said that my Richard had just finished with her! Maureen came barging into the toilets and became very concerned for J. I left them both to it and walked out of the toilets. I went to Richard and told him what had just happened in the toilets. All he said was that he had told her to stop mithering him and to leave him alone. He said that she was like a stalker who wouldn't go away.

Once again, another episode of his affair was forgotten about and I believed his lies.

Later, when our telephone bill dropped on the doormat, I opened it to find that two telegrams had been sent out on the 14th of February, Valentine's Day. I knew that one of them came to me, he sent me one every year, but I didn't know who the other one was for. When I showed him the bill, he snatched it from me and said that I wasn't supposed to see it. Eventually after a lot of arguing he told me that it was sent to J. The affair was out in the open, I had caught him out with another one of his lies. I didn't know if I could ever trust him again.

Mum's words were ringing through my head that he was a user and a 'sweet talking guy' who would do me no good. However, he still didn't want me to leave him. Why? He kept saying he loved me. Why?

Over the next few months, Richard and I had been round to Mum's house with Deborah. Maureen and I had started to talk again. She seems as if she's grown up a bit this last few months, maybe that game playing phase was over at last.

She said that she had tried to tell me, at the time, that Richard was seeing J but I wouldn't have believed her. I didn't ever remember a time when she had tried to tell me that. All I could remember was the trouble that Maureen had caused for us and the disturbed little games that she played whenever she was around us.

Maureen talked as if she was concerned about my welfare at that time, but if that was true why was she trying to split us up? Her words went in one ear and out through the other ear. I knew what she was trying to do. I had to put all that behind us, if there was any sort of future for Richard and me.

By now Maureen's belly was growing and it was obvious that she was actually pregnant. She was growing out of all her clothes so I gave her all my maternity wear. It was strange to still be passing down old clothes, just like I had done when we were kids. She had told us that the father of her baby was a boy called Trevor who, worked with her when she briefly worked in a shop called 'Stolen from Ivor' in town. She would brag about 'doing it' with him in the stock room of the shop. The thought of the many rumours, she had spread around about Richard being the father of her baby, ran through my mind and there she was telling us a different story. I wasn't bothered about who the father was, as long as it wasn't Richard. I was going to be an aunty to that baby, and I was so pleased.

On the 1st July 1978, Maureen gave birth to a baby girl. Mum phoned us to let us know. Richard and I went to the hospital during visiting time to see her. I was an aunty, finally, and I couldn't wait to see her. When we saw Maureen, Mum was with her. Maureen told us that her baby was in an incubator because she was so tiny, she only weighed 4lb 13oz. That was the same birth weight as Richard's wife's baby, Matthew. We all walked down to the special care unit to see her. The nurse behind the glass wheeled her over to us and we peered through to see her. She was so tiny, but she only had to stay there for twenty-four hours, then she would be back on the ward with her mum. Maureen called her Louise.

She was so cute. I was secretly looking for a resemblance to my child or any similarity with Richard, there was none. I was glad there wasn't!

When Louise was a few months old, she was christened. Maureen was allowed to have Louise christened in a church with a proper vicar. I was surprised at this as she too was illegitimate, just like my daughter. I couldn't understand it. When I wanted to have Deborah christened, I was made to feel sinful because Richard and I were living together. I was devastated at the time.

After Louise's christening, we all went back to Mum's house for a buffet. It was a warm sunny day, so we were all sitting in and around Mum and Jack's lovely garden. We were enjoying the sausage rolls and sandwiches. Baby Louise was lying on a blanket under a parasol with Mum. She looked so bonnie in her white frilly christening robe. During that afternoon, Maureen decided to go off with Ann's boyfriend, Peter. They were going to collect some records from his house. They were gone ages and the christening guests had started to leave. I was so glad that she didn't suggest going off with Richard, to go through his record collection. Ann finished with Peter shortly afterwards.

CHAPTER FIFTY-ONE
New Beginnings

Richard's work at the Happy Pig was over. The owners had decided to sell the place and it was to be turned into a restaurant. That meant it could be a new beginning for Richard and me. I hoped that in time I would forget his affair with J. I had forgiven him to an extent but he still denied ever having slept with her. Deep inside I knew he was lying to me so I didn't think I would ever be able to forget it. I just wanted to put his whole sordid affair behind me and move on.

After all he had done for me, in our home life, and because he was the father of my child, I thought he deserved another chance. I knew, in time, I would be able to forgive even though I knew that I would never be able to forget.

Our home life was beginning to settle down once again. Every day, Richard continued to show me that he loved me and he loved our little daughter. He was at home more, and so loving towards me and our baby; he was fun to be around, he made me smile every day and it was hard not to feel the love I had for him deep inside. I was content, Richard seemed content, and we loved our routine, we were happy again.

Richard never seemed to stop; he was busy all the time. When at home, he always had a screwdriver or a soldering iron in his hand, fixing things and discovering how electrical things worked. He amazed everyone when he wired the house with 'emergency lighting,' as he called it. At that time there were lots of power cuts all over Bolton and Farnworth, he decided to invent a system where we would have electricity even when the power went down.

One evening, during yet another power cut, everywhere was pitch black, with no street lights. All the houses on our street were in darkness too. Richard was ready to unveil his new system. He switched a switch under the stairs, and our lights were on. We had lights in the lounge, up the stairs, and in the kitchen. Richard had wired up a nine -volt battery to a sequence of little pip bulbs all over the house. I was truly amazed. Our new lights were bright enough to shine through our windows, attracting the attention of people passing by. They were all wondering how we were the only house in the street with electricity. I was so proud of my Richard.

I felt it was right to stay and try to forgive him. I did love him with all my heart, and I was beginning to feel how much he loved me. Richard and I talked a lot more about the problems we had had. He had always told me in the past that the girls in the discos came on to him because he was the DJ. I had seen that for myself at his shows; the girls would flock around the DJ stand trying to get his attention. That didn't bother me at all; I would remember the time when I was once one of those girls too. I did get his attention; he was with me and we were a family. However, the affair with J had still happened, and worst of all, he would still lie about it.

My mum's words echoed through my mind and at times, became so clear. My heart was saying different things though. My heart was telling me that he loved me and he wanted to be with me and our daughter. My heart told me to trust him and believe in him. Richards's words would ring through my head, all the time. His work there, at the place where J and her family lived, was over, so we would try to leave it all in the past where it belonged.

Sometimes, on dark days when I was alone with my thoughts, I would think about those times, although I was certain too that he was trying to make me happy and provide a happy home life for us. I knew Richard was trying to put it all behind him as well.

I was happy and felt secure, despite it all. Our home life did make me happy every day. I was happy being a mum to Deborah and a 'wife' to Richard. As far as I was aware, at that time, he wasn't in contact with J any more after his work at the Happy Pig had finished. We never heard from the owners again either.

For a while, we struggled to cope without the wages he had received there. However, the work from his mobile discos was getting better. Over the next few months, he got bookings from bookings and was really popular. Despite that, he still struggled to pay the bills.

One day there was a knock at the front door. Two gas men wanted to turn the gas off, as they said we hadn't paid the bill. The bills were Richard's concern so I didn't have any knowledge of any unpaid bills.

Luckily, I had a young baby so they didn't turn our supply off, which was a relief. When Richard came home, I told him about the gasmen and I was cross with him for not paying the bill. He assured me that he would sort it out the following day. I also questioned the fact that there were other bills that needed to be attended to. I started to question where all the money from his work was going, when he was not paying any of our household bills. He seemed unconcerned and told me not to worry about all that stuff and he would deal with everything. I couldn't stop worrying about the finances; I was a mother and responsible for my child. I was worried about the roof over our heads.

I began to wonder whether it would be a good idea if I went back to work to help support us. Every time I mentioned it to Richard, he would dismiss the idea, saying that my job was to look after him, our baby and the house. He said that I had enough to do. I did all those things and still had time on my hands and I was bored with the same everyday routine sometimes.

One day I was gazing through the window daydreaming, while washing dishes in the sink, the house was so peaceful. I had left Deborah sitting on the floor in the living room, playing with her toys and watching her favourite Tom and Jerry cartoons on television. She was such an easy baby; it was just a joy to be her mummy. I was daydreaming of going back to work again. I could work again as a machinist. There was a factory called 'Vantona,' down the street, not far away. I could get a job there. I was sure that I could look after things at home and still have time to go out to work. Another wage would come in handy too.

All at once I got an eerie feeling, a feeling as if someone was standing behind me. All the hairs on the back of my neck stood up, I got goosebumps all over. I turned around sharply, Deborah was standing there at the back of me, unsupported in the middle of the kitchen. I instinctively screamed with shock. I startled her and she jumped, falling onto her bottom and started to cry. I rushed to her and picked her up and hugged her so tightly. Had she walked into the kitchen from the living room all by herself? Those were her first steps! She was only nine and a half months old and so dainty. Had she walked across the kitchen and had I missed it while I was engrossed in my daydreams?

The thoughts of me starting work again went through the window, as well as the thoughts of washing up! I sat with Deborah in the living room for the rest of the afternoon. I was watching her playing with her toys and pulling herself up with the settee. I couldn't believe how she had walked all the way into the kitchen, she was too tiny. I wanted to see her walking again. I knelt down in front of her and held out a toy. I wiggled it in front of her so she would come towards it. She turned from the settee and took about four wobbly steps towards me, she then took the toy from my hand, and stood there with it for ages. I slowly moved backwards and held out my arms to her, in order to encourage her to come to me; she did. My baby was walking. I was delighted and clapped my hands for her. She was such a clever girl.

When Richard came home, I held our daughter in front of me and said to her, "Daddy's home," and with eyes as big as saucers, she walked straight across the living room and into his arms. He picked her up and hugged her and looked at me with tears in his eyes and said, "She's walking! She's walking!"

Just after Deborah's first birthday, I got my way and went back to work. Again, I walked straight into the factory on Cawdor Street as I had done with my first job after leaving school and I was offered a job straight away. I started to work at the factory from 6pm each evening and I finished work at 10pm. The work was easy. I was making sheets and pillow cases. It worked out quite well for us both. Richard still wasn't very happy that I was going out to work. He would say that he was the provider and my place was in the house with our baby. Despite this, we decided that I would be home with my daughter all day, and when Richard came home from his work, he would take over looking after her. I always made sure his evening meal was on the table before I left for work each night.

I had been working for about a month and really enjoying my time at the factory, and the extra money, coming into the house, was coming in handy too. I had settled down into the new routine once more. However, one night I came home from work and Richard was not at home. Our child was being looked after by his mother, Lola. I was shocked to find her there and that Richard hadn't said anything about going out that evening. I was annoyed to find that Deborah was still awake too, she should have been in bed. Lola tended to spoil her when she visited. Deborah was her first granddaughter and she loved her; however, we had developed a routine with her and she was usually in bed by the time I got home from work. I didn't think it was right for Lola to be looking after Deborah each night, it would be too much for her. She was our baby and we had both decided that we should look after her ourselves, instead of leaving her with a babysitter. It wasn't right.

When Richard came home, it was very late and we bickered. I told him I wasn't happy that he had left his mum to look after our child. He said he had to go to see the manager of a club in Bolton, because he had been offered work as a DJ at his club. The club was called 'The Bus Inn,' and Richard was offered a job to work there each night, every night! He informed me that he had accepted the job. I was shocked and so upset that he didn't think to discuss that with me first, before he had accepted. What about my job? Had Richard organised Lola to baby-sit Deborah each night too! That was just never going to happen! She would never be in a routine if Lola looked after her each night! I couldn't believe that Richard had done that without even talking to me about it first. I was so angry with him but all he kept saying was, that the money was good and we needed every penny. He continued to inform me that I didn't need to go out to work, I could quit, as he would be making more money than I could earn in the factory. However, I was enjoying working and bringing money into the house. It felt good. He totally dismissed my feelings. He didn't seem to care how I felt, he was so inconsiderate. I had been working really hard. I didn't want to give up my job, but there was nothing I could do, after just six weeks working at the factory, I had to leave. I was devastated.

When I got my last week's wage, I went to town and bought myself a new coat. Usually, all my wages went on the house and I had nothing to show for all my hard work at the factory. I hadn't spent any of the money on myself, but because I was angry about losing my job, I treated myself to a new coat and that felt good for a while too!

In April 1979, Richard had been working at the Bus Inn for a few months. The money was good but it came with a price, Richard and I hardly saw each other. He was out at work all day at the newspaper office, he came home for his tea, then he was straight out again to work as a DJ. His life was hectic. I got used to him not being around. I would do everything around the house myself and look after our child on my own. During the day, I filled my life with caring for her, she was the joy in my life and I loved every minute I spent with her. We would go for walks to the shops or to the park, if we were fed up with sitting indoors. Occasionally, we would just spend the afternoons playing or watching the cartoons on the TV. Sometimes she would just snuggle up beside me, put her head on my lap and fall asleep. I would smile and stroke her hair. I was so content. In the evenings, however, I was beginning to feel increasingly lonelier.

After Deborah was tucked up in bed, the house seemed so quiet. Most evenings were spent ironing Richards many shirts and scrubbing the kitchen floor, which took hours! I wanted the house to be clean, for Richard. I felt like Cinderella sometimes, always on my knees cleaning. I kept busy and thought I was happy but deep down the loneliness, I was feeling, was beginning to get me down. Eventually, this situation made me feel fed up with my tedious everyday routine. There I was, just twenty years of age, I wanted to have some fun, just like the other girls of my age. I didn't seem to smile any more, except to my daughter. She made me smile every day. She was my life. I adored her.

I knew I still wanted to be with Richard and I wanted to marry him one day. I knew that I would have to wait for his divorce to come through, if it ever did come through. The wait was endless. The constant visits to the solicitors didn't seem to be getting us anywhere.

During a rare visit to a friend's house, and while our children played happily together in her sunny garden, I was introduced to my friend's new litter of kittens. They were adorable, also very active and noisy, but one of them caught my eye and I instantly started to fall in love with him. I decided to take him home the following week. I called him Tiggles. He soon settled into our house. Richard seemed to love him too. He was such a clever kitten and as he grew, I taught him to chase a little ball made from rolled up tin foil. He would fetch it back to me and then drop it in front of me.

Colin, Richard's cousin called at our house one day with his new girlfriend Heather; of course, I had to show them Tiggles' new party piece. I rolled the little ball across the room and Tiggles ran over to it, picked it up in his mouth and fetched it back to me to roll it again. Heather was amazed, she said that she had never seen a cat chase a ball before. Playing with my new friend each evening helped pass the long nights away while waiting for Richard to come home. I didn't feel quite as lonely.

During some evenings, and especially at the weekends, Richard would come home so late that I had fallen asleep on the settee or gone to bed without him. I would wake up in the morning and he was always there beside me. I had slept undisturbed while he snuggled next to me.

Richard seemed happy, I had put all the problems of his affair, and the rumours that my sister Maureen had spread around, in a box in my mind. I became able to hide such things away deeply. I was refusing to recall all those bad memories of betrayal. We were settling down and enjoying our life.

We hardly ever saw or heard anything from my mum. Mum was busy with her own life and building a new relationship with her new man. They both loved Southport and spent all their spare time there together. Mum would always say that she wanted to retire to Southport, as she loved the place. We hadn't seen anything of Maureen, so we presumed she was getting on with her own life too and settling down with her baby.

One day, my brother came to visit. Richard was at work. It was nice to have a visit from Paul. He very rarely visited, but it was always lovely to see him. Over a cup of coffee, he was telling me that he went regularly to the Bus Inn to work as a DJ with Richard. He then told me that Maureen went in there too. He told me it was a fun place and it got packed every night. Richard hadn't told me any of this. He rarely talked about his work at the Bus Inn, except to say how exhausted he was when he came home. He told me that it was a scruffy little back street 'dive', full of dole dossers, tarts and alcoholics! He also said he was only there for the money and he wasn't going to work there for long, just until our finances got a bit better.

After all the trouble and hurtful behaviour Maureen had caused for us in the past, I couldn't believe he hadn't told me that she was going into that club. There seemed to me to be a bit of history repeating itself. Previously, she had followed Richard into the Happy Pig, then the King's Head and now the Bus Inn.

In the past, Richard had told me when he had seen Maureen, but it seemed that this inclination had changed, concerning her presence in the Bus Inn.

I knew that my box of stored bad memories, which had been hidden away so deeply in my mind, was about to be revealed once more. I didn't like the thought of this. I must have been living in a dream world, to think that we could ever be happy knowing that she was still hanging around him like a bad smell. I imagined her there, flirting with him again, just like she used to do at the Happy Pig! The more I thought of our past history, the more tearful I became.

When he came home, I questioned him and asked him why he hadn't told me about Paul and Maureen. I was upset. I felt so insecure once again. Richard said that Maureen didn't go in often but when she did, she played her usual games with him, flirting around him, as did all the other girls as well. He said he took no notice of any of them. He was always home every night with me. He told me he didn't want me to worry and cause me any more upset. With his arms holding me so tightly my insecurities disappeared and again I took his word, I had to. Hugging me and our daughter so tightly he went on to reassure me by saying that he would never cheat on me. He told me that he loved us both so much. He looked into our daughter's eyes and all around our lovely home.

"Why would I want to lose all this?" he said. I cried. I loved him so much. I felt his love. I felt so silly and stupid for feeling so insecure when things were going so well between us.

A few weeks later, we learned that Maureen had been kicked out of mother's house. She had left with her baby and was living with one of her friends in Breightmet. I had heard that she was pregnant again. We were always hearing of her being pregnant from members of the family, then of her miscarriages or false alarms.

She was still my sister and Louise is my only niece; no matter how she had behaved in the past, I needed to know that she and Louise were all right. I didn't want anything bad to happen to either of them. I needed to find out that she had a roof over her head and enough food for her baby. I wanted to try and help them if I could. Richard knew where she was living and we drove up there.

The area where Maureen had gone to live was quite a bad and poor area of Bolton. It was rough and run down and had a very bad reputation for lots of drug dealing and lots of violence. The people who lived there were mostly poor and out of work. Maureen was living in the home of a friend of hers who was a single parent, called Josie. When we pulled up outside the house, I looked towards it. The front living-room windows were half closed, they were broken, and the curtains looked tatty and worn. The front door was open and there were children of all ages with dirty knees, running in and out. How could Maureen take her baby in there? It wasn't what she was used to at Mum's house. There was no way I would ever have taken my child there.

When I walked towards the house, Maureen greeted me at the door and invited me in. Reluctantly, I entered and stood at the living-room door and looked around. Louise was crawling around on the floor; her little knees were dirty. Josie, Maureen's friend, was sitting in an armchair at the side of an open fire. Between puffs on her cigarette, and flicking the ash into the open fire, she managed to say 'hello' to me. I told Maureen that we had come to see if they were all right, but it was clear to me that they were not. She confirmed that she was pregnant again, only a few weeks, she informed me. I was asked if I wanted a cup of tea but I refused with a 'thank you!' I didn't know why Mum had thrown them out but that was not the place for them to be. How could Maureen want to stay here? If that was how single parents lived, I just felt so lucky that I was with Richard. I would never want to be a single parent. I looked down at my little niece, crawling around on the floor, her dress was soiled and she didn't have a nappy on. She cannot stay there I thought to myself. I felt so sorry for her. I couldn't offer her any money; we didn't have much ourselves. I did think that there must be something that I could do for them both.

I offered to take Louise for a couple of days so that she could sort herself out. I was surprised when she agreed straight away. Maureen quickly gathered a few things for Louise and we were on our way with her in the car. I couldn't wait to get Louise out of there. Richard didn't seem too pleased when I walked out of that house with her in my arms and got her into the car. I told him that she was my niece and I would look after her.

When we arrived home, I bathed her and dressed her in some of Deborah's clothes that she had grown out of. I also brushed her hair. She looked as pretty as a picture. Deborah and Louise, the cute little cousins, played contentedly and watched cartoons on the television together all afternoon.

Louise was a quiet baby and no trouble at all. After a busy day, Louise fell asleep and I carried her upstairs to sleep in Deborah's pram. Deborah had grown out of it and it had been stored away in the back of a wardrobe. I was exhausted, running around after the two little ones all day. I fell straight to sleep as soon as my head hit the pillow.

When Richard came home from his DJ work, he must have made a noise in the bedroom and Louise woke up. She sat up in the pram and screamed her head off. I got out of bed and lifted her from the pram and held her and tried to comfort her but she just screamed and screamed. She had seemed so content during the day, but at that time in the middle of the night, I just couldn't seem to settle her at all. I tried her with a drink of juice but she knocked it from my hand. I thought that she could be teething so I tried to put some Bonjela on her gums but she didn't seem to like that much either.

She had been screaming for over an hour and I could see Richard was growing more impatient. It was four o'clock in the morning and he was tired and wanted to get some sleep but it was just impossible. He snapped and said that we were taking her home first thing the following morning and that we were not looking after her for another night. I was too tired at that time to disagree with him. I couldn't seem to settle her. Maybe she was simply missing her mum. Eventually Louise fell asleep again and I managed to get a few more hours sleep too.

We woke exhausted the next day and after breakfast Louise was taken back to her mum. I felt guilty for not being able to cope with her any longer. My 'motherly skills' worked so well with Deborah but didn't seem to be of any good for Louise. I didn't think babies could cry like that, so loud and for so long. When I told Maureen of the difficult night that we had had with her, she said that she usually dipped her dummy in glucose which usually helped to pacify her. I was horrified, that poor child was going to have bad teeth if her mum carried on doing that!

One night, I had finally agreed to allow Lola to baby-sit, so I could have a night out with Richard while he was carrying out his DJ job at the Bus Inn. He was always asking me to go with him, but I would always prefer to stay at home with our child.

I was really looking forward to going out with Richard and seeing the place he was working in. My brother had told me so much about the place, however, there was another reason why I wanted to go too. Paul, my brother, had previously told me that one of my old flames went to the club. This was my first love Dave from the youth club from the time when I was fifteen. I had adored him back then. It would be great to see him again after all that time and see how he was.

I remembered the times we had had together when we were at the youth club. I remembered how much I had thought I was in love with him back then. Real love, not like the puppy love that I had for David from school. I had never forgotten those times at the youth club. I had been smitten. I remembered how Dave would say that he loved me and make me feel so special. He was so good looking and reminded me of David Cassidy. We would sit holding hands in the youth club, and when I had to go home, he would walk me to the bus stop on Chorley Old Road, outside the Sally Up Steps pub. He would kiss me so sweetly on my cheek and I would sit on the back seat of the bus waving to him until he disappeared from my view.

I still had all his letters; the ones that he had sent to me when he stole a car and ended up in prison. My dad would have killed me at the time, if he'd known I was seeing a boy who was in prison. We both had quite a lot of growing up to do then.

Over five years later my life had become so different. I wasn't that shy, sweet, innocent schoolgirl any more. I was with a man I loved dearly and a new baby to look after, I had grown up. He probably had a family too, but it would be good to see him. I was curious.

The Bus Inn club was down a dark, cobbled back street in the middle of Bolton. It was an old building and looked quite scary, not at all like the other places that Richard had worked. I didn't know whether I liked it or not. Inside, it was dark and scary too, and the seats were just like the seats on buses, that was why it was called the Bus Inn! It was tatty and grubby, not posh at all. My feet were sticking to the floor in places. Some people called that place a 'dive', however, when Richard got on those decks and the brightly coloured flashing disco lights came on, and the loud music began to play, instantly the atmosphere changed. Before long the place was packed and the dance floor was full. Richard was happy. I began to enjoy myself. I was sitting at the bar, at the other side of the club, opposite the DJ stand. I was watching Richard with pride. I smiled at him. He looked quite funny standing behind the decks, bopping away to the music with his headphones on.

I turned away and ordered another glass of lager and lime from the barman and when I turned back around, there she was, my sister. Maureen was dancing away on the dance floor, on her own, right in front of Richard's DJ stand. She was a great dancer and had always been able to dance like the go-go dancers on Top of the Pops. I smiled and watched and waited for her to notice me. I watched her and wondered who was looking after Louise, while she was here. Where did she get the money from to have a night out? She told us that she had no money at all! She was wearing a tight, trendy mini skirt. Her second pregnancy wasn't at all noticeable at that time; if indeed she was pregnant.

I soon noticed another familiar face at the other side of the bar. It was Dave. I recognised him straight away. He hadn't changed a bit. I turned my face away from him and continued watching Maureen dancing and Richard at the decks. I was pretending not to have noticed Dave. I wanted to see if he noticed me or even whether he would recognise me. My stomach was rolling over, and my heart was pounding so fast with excitement. I remembered our love from what seemed like a different world. My cheeks were becoming warm and rosy. I could see my reflection in the mirrored tiles behind the bar.

From the corner of my eye, I saw him approaching. I turned towards him and appeared shocked and surprised to see him. All I could manage to say was 'Hi!' I was so excited to see him again that I just couldn't think what else to say. My cheeks glowed and I could feel myself trembling and blushing. I wasn't sure if this was raw emotion or the effects of the lager. Maybe both? He said, 'Hi' and asked what was I doing in a place like that? His intimation was that the place was less than salubrious. I told him that I had come with the DJ and that he was my fiancé. At that point, he said, "You're with the DJ?" Sipping my lager and lime, I nodded, and went on to tell him that we had a baby together. His eyebrows lifted and then he frowned. He then said something strange. "I thought he was with her," pointing to Maureen, on the dance floor. "He's always with her," he claimed.

"No! She's my sister, and he was probably just looking out for her," I said, correcting him. He looked towards me and raised his eyebrows once more and said, "Oh right." Dave's comments did make me wonder a little. However, I remembered the words that Richard continually told me and my worries drifted away. I put it down to the games that Maureen played, whenever she was around him. I kept that box of bad memories firmly shut.

Maureen was telling everyone she was pregnant, so obviously she must have another boyfriend somewhere. I imagined he would appear at some point, if he had got her pregnant.

I didn't think anything else concerning Dave's comments. I began to relax in his company and our conversation continued. Dave talked about his life and his family. He said he was seeing a girl named Denise. We talked about the time when we were kids in the youth club. We laughed together as we reminisced. I talked about my life and of my baby. At that point, he asked if I was happy and I smiled and said that I was. Dave said that he could see in my eyes that I wasn't happy, and that there was something wrong. I assured him that I was fine and tried to change the subject.

We were sitting at the bar, talking and drinking lager, for what seemed like hours. Throughout our conversation, I kept looking over to Richard at his decks, he was staring at Dave and me intensely. He was giving me some strange looks! It felt as if he didn't like me talking to Dave. I felt a little uneasy at the way Richard was staring at us. I began to feel that I was doing something wrong by talking to another man. Richard talked to other women, all the time, and I shouldn't say anything about that, or complain in any way because that was his job and he was supposed to be able to talk to other women. That was the way it was, I had accepted that, and expected it too! I was his woman and I was not allowed to speak to another man? I began to feel irritated.

During his break, Richard came over to the bar and sat himself on a stool next to us. I introduced Richard to Dave and they shook hands. I told Richard that Dave was an old flame. I had spoken about Dave to Richard in the past so he knew who he was straight away. Richard offered Dave a cigarette and talked with the two of us for a while until his break was over and he returned back to his DJ stand.

Dave and I continued to chat and giggle over yet another glass of lager and lime. We talked about old times and then the occasion arrived when out of the blue Dave told me that he had missed me and that he had never stopped thinking about me. I blushed again and told him that he shouldn't talk like that. At that point, he looked right into my eyes. He said that all he wanted to do was to hold me and kiss me one more time. I was embarrassed and couldn't believe what I was hearing. I was in love with Richard and shouldn't have been listening to that sort of talk. However, it was a long time since I had last seen him, and the same old feelings, I had had all those years ago, were reoccurring. I was feeling a little tipsy too, so I just giggled at him and shook my head.

I had been feeling so lonely at home, at times, for a long time. It felt good to hear what Dave was saying to me. Despite the fact that I would hear lots of nice words from Richard too, it felt good to have a conversation with another adult and to giggle and smile once again, and to feel tipsy. Dave could sense that things weren't right between Richard and me, I kept telling him I was fine, however, inside I did feel like crying at times.

I didn't like the way some things were between Richard and me. I thought about what I had to put up with all through our relationship. I should have been married, not living in sin! I should not have had to cope with his affair with J, or the problems from his wife, and the endless solicitors' issues. I should not have to live with the constant rumours and comments about his, so called, affair with my own sister. I shouldn't have to spend lonely days and lonely nights on my own. I shouldn't have to listen to the words of my old flame saying that he thought the DJ was with my sister, as they were always together. I shouldn't have to keep defending him when I knew deep down in my heart that there was something going on between them. I was only twenty years old. I should be happy.

The only constant happiness I had in my life was my daughter. Every day she brought joy and happiness; I felt this every time she looked at me. She made it all worthwhile. Without Richard, I wouldn't have her. She was the best thing that had come from our relationship. However, at that time, I was beginning to think that Richard and I would never get married and my life would be that way forever, and that was the only way it was meant to be for us.

There I was, listening to my 'first teenage boyfriend,' telling me all those nice things. I was beginning to like what I was hearing. At that moment, I wanted to be sitting with Richard, listening to all those nice things, instead of having my head filled with the rumours and bad thoughts, the insecurities and the paranoia.

I wanted to cry. My eyes filled with tears as I listened to Dave. He wanted me to go outside with him, he said he just wanted to hold me and then he would leave and go home. My head was in bits as he reached out and touched my hand. It was like electricity. I pulled my hand away from him sharply and told him to stop. My stomach was turning over and my hands were shaking and inside I was crying out for him. I wanted him to hold me, one more time.

I felt like that young naïve teenager once more and remembered the feelings I had for him way back then. Just one more hug. I looked towards Richard at his decks, he was busy taking requests from some girl. Before I knew it, I was outside the entrance of the Bus Inn and Dave had a hold of me. He nestled into my neck and then our lips met. His kiss took my breath away. My heart was thumping. I knew it was wrong but it felt so right. I pulled away and nestled my head on his chest. I could hear his heart beating. Then I heard Richards' voice. He called out my name and asked what I was doing. He had seen the kiss; he must have done. He stood right in front of us smoking a cigarette. I stared at him. I didn't know what to say, I didn't want to say anything. I wanted that kiss, just one last kiss from my old flame.

Richard must have seen us walk out together, then he must have followed us. He then said that we all needed to talk. Dave looked at Richard and stayed silent. I didn't want to talk, I didn't want to explain, I wanted to stay there in Dave's arms just a little bit longer. We parted, and I went back inside the club with Richard.

Dave followed and we both sat at the bar while Richard finished his DJ work. Dave was saying that he loved me and wanted to be with me until my head was spinning. I had just been in another man's arms and it felt good. The thought of J, in the arms of my man, was at the front of my mind. I closed my eyes and I could almost see them. I remember her tears, on my shoulder, after he had ended the affair with her. The affair he continued to deny, still, after all this time.

When the night was over, Richard diplomatically suggested that we all went to our home to have a little chat about what had happened. I was quite surprised that Richard didn't show any anger or any emotion, although he had never shown any sort of bad temper or raised his voice to me at all, at that point. It was one of the things I had always admired about him that he was not like my dad. Dave agreed, and before long we were walking through our front door. Lola was sitting on our settee reading and peered out at us, over her brown rimmed glasses. She was hurried off into her little blue Ford Escort and sent on her way home.

I made coffee and we all sat down for our chat. Dave said that he wasn't sorry for kissing me that night and that he still loved me and if I agreed we would be together. I didn't take my eyes off Richard through the whole conversation. His eyes were filled with tears as he listened to Dave. I felt sorry for Richard. How could I leave him? I loved him. How could I take Deborah away from Richard? How could I leave our home? Richard turned to me and said that he was sorry for everything that he had put me through during our relationship and that he loved me and never wanted to leave me. He promised me that things would get better if I stayed with him. I didn't want to leave Richard. Once again, I believed his words. I wasn't prepared to walk into the unknown with Dave. I was also keen not to upset Deborah and take her away from her daddy. My decision was made, I was to stay with Richard and Dave was sent on his way. We both agreed never to see each other or to try to contact one another again.

Richard and I went to bed and made up. I was sorry for what I had done and realised what a big, huge mistake it was to have kissed Dave. I didn't ever expect that to happen, that I could ever be in the arms of another man. I loved Richard despite everything.

The next morning, Richard and I talked and he told me that I had to burn all the letters from Dave, which I had saved in my suitcase of keepsakes. This was to prove to him that Dave meant nothing to me any more. I didn't want to burn all his letters, or the little photo of the two of us, which was taken in the photo booth at the Navada. I used to have it stuck on my sewing machine, so I could see his face, while I worked.

They were from my past, keepsakes of my life before I met Richard, I wanted to keep them forever. With an ache in my heart, I did what Richard asked. All my letters from Dave and the photos were burned and destroyed, while Richard looked on.

When I had some time alone, I just broke down and cried my eyes out. Nothing left except my memories of him. I would never forget Dave or that last kiss.

During the following week, life went on as normal. Nothing more was mentioned about Dave. It was as if the events of that Saturday night never even happened. I wasn't regretting my decision to stay with Richard, I was glad I had done. He was being so nice to me. He constantly reassured me that he loved me and he brought home a lovely bouquet of flowers too! I knew that Dave had been in prison in the past and Richard took pleasure in reminding me of that fact often. He referred to him as a 'jailbird' many times. I was sure Dave was not the sort of person that could ever give me a better life than the one I had with Richard. It was the unknown that I didn't want to venture into. I had no regrets.

On the Thursday of the following week, I decided to get Deborah ready, I put her in her pram and then we went to the local Kwik Save. I needed quite a few groceries and I wanted to cook a special meal for Richard for when he came home from work. After finishing our shopping, I queued up at the checkout to pay for the groceries. To my horror, further down the store, at another checkout, was Dave and a heavily pregnant girl, busy loading their shopping into carrier bags. I couldn't believe my eyes. I thought I'd never see him again and here we were at the same supermarket at the same time! Instantly my stomach turned over and I felt very hot. I bowed my head in the hope that he hadn't seen me. I watched as they both pushed their trolley, full of shopping, out through the door ahead of me. The girl must have been his girlfriend. He didn't tell me that she was pregnant.

I breathed a sigh of relief that we hadn't been spotted and I left the store. With Deborah's pram loaded up with shopping bags, in the metal tray underneath, we carried on our way home. The traffic was busy as we approached the zebra crossing and waited to cross the road. A car stopped at the crossing and I pushed Deborah's heavy pram across. Deborah was sitting up chattering away as I glanced at the car to nod in appreciation for its stopping. While we crossed, and with shock again, I noticed that it was Dave driving the car that had stopped for us. The very pregnant woman was sitting at his side. My stomach went over again and my hands started to shake and I gripped hold of the pram handle so tightly. Dave looked straight at me. There was no way he didn't see us that time. I pretended not to see him; however, I think he knew I had seen him! I carried on pushing the pram along the pavement, and he drove past me slowly. I watched his car disappear into the distance onto Market Street. I continued our walk home, hoping that it was the last time I would see him. My hands had finally stopped shaking and I chatted to Deborah, who by that stage was trying to fall asleep.

We headed on our way down Market Street. I was thinking of what I was going to do when we got home. I would unload the shopping, make Deborah her dinner, make a cup of coffee and then have a relaxing afternoon. I looked at Deborah as she lay in her pram, suckling her dummy. I thought how lucky I was to have her; she was so content. I just loved being her mummy.

A blue car then pulled up at the side of the road and I heard a familiar voice shout my name. I turned and it was Dave! I stopped and bent down and peered into the car. He jumped out of his car and came around to me and said that he would give me a lift home. I protested and said that I was okay and didn't want a lift home, however, he insisted and before I knew it, the shopping and the pram were on the back seat of his car and we were being driven home. He told me how shocked he was to see me again so soon and that he was doing some shopping with his sister Pat, who lived behind the Black Horse pub at the top of Market Street. That explained to me why he was in that area. It wasn't long before we had reached my house and he had helped us inside with the shopping. We chatted for a while at my front door. When he was leaving, he asked if he could telephone sometime just to see how we were. I told him that it would be okay and good to hear from him now and again.

That night Richard was getting ready for his DJ work at 'The Bus Inn' and the phone rang. He answered it and said, 'Hello' but the caller hung up. About ten minutes later the same thing happened again. Although I didn't think anything of it at first, because we got lots of telephone calls like that, I did assume it could be my sister who was doing it, as part of the routine she played with us. However, when it happened again and again that evening, I had a funny feeling that it could have been Dave, and Richard was giving me suspicious looks as if he thought so too. I thought it was best not to tell Richard that I had seen Dave that day. I didn't want him to be upset. I had made my decision to stay with Richard and I didn't think it mattered that Dave fetched us home from my shopping trip. I hadn't done anything wrong. The phone calls stopped and Richard went off to work. He told me to lock all the doors after he had left. He stayed behind the front door, while I did what he told me to do.

About an hour later there was a knock at the front door. It was Dave. I couldn't believe that he had come back to our home. I answered the door and asked him what he wanted. I also asked if it was him who had been ringing earlier that evening. He confirmed that it was him, and that he just had to see me again. He wanted to talk and asked if he could come in and chat for a while. Deborah was playing in the front room, while I was at the door, so I invited him inside. Dave assured me he would only stay a minute. He sat himself in the armchair and Deborah went straight over to him and he picked her up and sat her on his knee. He said she was so adorable, as she chatted away to him. Although she was only nineteen months old, she was quite a good talker.

Dave had been in my home for about half an hour when I heard Richard's car pull up outside. Dave quickly put Deborah down and jumped up and ran through the kitchen and towards the back door. I followed him and told him he didn't need to run off and we hadn't done anything wrong. As he opened the back door to 'escape,' Lee, Richard's Brother, was standing at the back door, looking very shocked. I was shocked too and wondered what was happening. I couldn't understand why Lee was in my backyard at that time of night or why Richard came home from work at that time too. Dave disappeared down the backyard and out through the back gate. Lee came into the kitchen and Richard stood in front of me shouting his head off at me, saying that he knew something was going on and that he had caught me at it! All at once, he whacked me across the face so hard, that I fell toward the kitchen units at the far side of the kitchen. I was so shocked and stunned that he had hit me. He had always promised me that he would never, ever raise his

414

hand to me. My face stung and ached.

All I could see in my mind was my dad hitting my mum over and over again. I was devastated and hysterical. At that point, Richard came towards me again and I thought he was going to hit me again. I grabbed hold of a knife, from the rack, and pointed it at him. I was screaming at him to get away from me. I was hysterical and tried to tell him I hadn't done anything wrong. The tears were streaming down and stinging my face. I wanted to leave Richard. I wasn't staying with a man who could hit me. That was it. I screamed at him that I was going to leave. He grabbed hold of my wrist tightly and took the knife out of my hand. He kept saying that I wasn't going anywhere and I would never leave. I was screaming hysterically and sobbing. I was going to leave and leave him as soon as I could. Richard then picked up the phone and rang his mother, Lola. I could hear him telling her all about what had happened. He asked her if she would come over and sit with me and Deborah to stop the man coming back into the house. I felt humiliated.

Within ten minutes his mother was knocking at the front door. When Richard let her in, she entered in such an angry manner. She shouted at me calling me a whore and a prostitute! I glared at her and sat quietly. How dare she call me those names. I wanted to scream at her, how could I have been a whore and a prostitute, when I had only ever been with one man, and that was her son!

I was still sobbing and trembling. All I had done was let Dave into my house for a coffee and a chat. I hadn't asked him to knock on my door that night. He was in my living room for half an hour that was all. I had to live with everything that Richard had done with all the other girls, and all the rumours about him. I had to live with those things on a day-to-day basis and was expected to accept them — how did that compare to this innocent incident, which had been misinterpreted by Richard and his mother, without any attempt to listen to what I had to say about what had actually happened?

Richard and Lee went back off to work at the 'Bus Inn'. Lola sat silently in my living room watching me for the rest of the evening. Deborah had fallen asleep on my knee, so I carried her upstairs and put her in her bed.

About two hours later the phone rang and I picked it up. It was Dave.

I started to cry and told him that he shouldn't have run off like he did. He asked if I was okay and I told him that I wasn't and that Richard had hit me across the face. Dave was furious and said that he wasn't leaving me there any longer and he was coming back for us straight away. He said he loved me over and over again and that I was to trust him and things would work out. I went upstairs and started to pack a few belongings for Deborah and myself.

When Dave arrived, I was ready. I had a black bin bag with some of our clothes in. With Deborah in my arms, all wrapped up in her favourite blanket, we left. Dave loaded us into his car and we drove away.

I was sobbing my heart out, as he drove round and round in circles. We drove for miles it seemed. He listened as I cried and told him everything that I had been going through with Richard. I had an awful lot to put up with: the affair with J, all the rumours and the stress from the divorce proceedings. And to top all that, Richard had hit me. Dave then suggested that he take me to his friend's house. It was getting really late.

As we drove, there was a very strong smell of burning. Unconcerned, and carrying on driving, Dave reached across and opened the glove compartment. Something inside there was smouldering, and I could see flames! I was shocked and thought the car was going to blow up! Dave said don't worry and pulled at some wires under there and the flames went out.

We drove a little further and I started to recognise where we were. It was the same area that Maureen was living in with Josie. To my horror, we pulled up outside the very same house. I couldn't believe it. "How come we are here?" I asked him. Dave told me that Josie was a friend of his and she helps people out sometimes and lets them stay there when they've nowhere else to go. I told Dave that I already knew Josie and that Maureen had been staying with her. When we went in, we all chatted for a while and Josie was kind enough to let me stay there with Deborah. It was very late; I had no choice but to stay there. Josie went on to say that Maureen wasn't staying there that night and that she was with her friends. I presumed she would be with her new boyfriend.

Josie went off to her bed, leaving Dave and I in the living room. Before long Deborah had fallen asleep on Josie's settee. Dave and I lay down, on a single bed, which was at the side of the room. We talked and he was saying that he wanted to stay with me. We kissed. I remembered the first time he had kissed me in that dark room at the 'Rec' and how wonderful he had made me feel way back then. There we were, six years later, he was making me experience that same wonderful feeling I had had way back then. Everything he was saying seemed right and so loving and romantic. I wanted him. Before long I was in his arms and we were making love. It was over so quickly. I cried. I just couldn't believe I had had sex with another man. He made me feel loved and cared for, but only for that moment. All the sweet juvenile feelings and the puppy love that I had had for him, when I was younger, came flooding back. I felt like that teenager again. However, I was not that sweet and innocent teenager any more. I was a woman and a mother.

Afterwards, we lay there together, he lit up a cigarette and smoked it slowly in the dark. He then said that he had to go home. I was so upset that he had to leave but I accepted that he had to get back. He promised me that he would come back the day after and with that we kissed and he left.

The morning came and I waited. All that day I waited. All that night I waited too. Dave didn't show. I realised I had been used and that he was never going to show. I didn't want to stay at Josie's any longer. The house was grubby and cold, not at all like the lovely warm home I had with Richard. I wanted to be home. I wanted to be warm. I wanted my child to have a warm home again.

Josie's house was so noisy with all the children running around. She was bringing all those children up alone and things were hard for her. She didn't seem to have any help from any of their fathers at all. Despite this, they all looked so happy with what they had, and I felt the children were clearly loved so much by Josie.

I remember one of Josie's children, she was about seven years old, she was such a bubbly charming little girl and named Maggie too. She had beautiful, naturally curly red hair that hung in ringlets down her back. It would glisten in the sun's rays.

I was getting to like Josie; she was nice to me. I felt she didn't need to have any more mouths to feed, at that time, so that Saturday morning I telephoned my dad and explained what had happened with Richard and asked him if I could come to live with him for a while. I left Josie's that day and tried to forget what had happened with Dave. I realised and accepted that I would probably not see him again. I had been used. I was heartbroken. I was a fool.

Having experienced the way that Josie was living, as a single parent, I became really scared at the thought. What would happen to me? I was actually starting my life as a single parent too? I didn't know what to do. I had no money at all. How would I feed Deborah? I knew I couldn't go back to Richard. I didn't want to go back to him. I didn't want to live like that any longer. I didn't want to be a single parent either. I didn't want to live in the poverty that Josie had. She loved all of her children; however, it was clear that she had nothing and she had suffered. It didn't seem as if there was any sort of financial help from the fathers either. I felt sorry for the way she had to live with the struggle that she had to make ends meet. I realised I couldn't stay there any longer, I couldn't take any of what she had offered, and I couldn't contribute either.

I went back to live with Dad. Deborah and I had to share a bedroom with Laura. We both slept in a single bed at the side of Laura. That night, I held onto Deborah so tightly and I cried myself to sleep. She slept soundly, snuggled into my chest, unaware of the huge mistake and mess I had made of our lives. She was my whole life and I knew I had to sort our lives out fast. I had to find a way to care for and protect my daughter and make a new life for us both. I knew I didn't want to stay at Dad's house, I knew in my heart we shouldn't be there. I didn't want my daughter to hear his raised voice or see his anger. Nor did I want her to know the fear that we knew so well as children, and as adults too. Dad didn't ask any questions about Richard, he just accepted that we had left him and let us get on with things.

Moving back in with Dad, once again, was not how I wanted my life to be. Alone again with my thoughts, I recalled the good times with Richard, the laughter and the happiness that we had shared. I wanted the happiness that Richard had promised. I wanted my home; I wanted my family. My life was going backwards it seemed. I did want Richard. I loved him more than I had loved anyone. He was so right for me. Why did I have to ruin things? It was all over. He had hit me. He raised his hand and struck me. I wouldn't stay with him after that, I couldn't stay with him ever again. It was over. I never dreamed he would ever hit me like that. I was in shock. It was too late; the damage had been done. I had ruined everything. I had Deborah, and she was so precious. I couldn't allow her to have the childhood that I had had. I had to protect her from all that. She was my daughter and she was depending on me to provide for her and give her a good life. I had to rescue her from the traumas of my childhood and keep her safe. I was not sure why I turned to Dad for help. I had no one else. I was desperate and Dad was there for us then. I had no money or any means of support for Deborah. I had received no word from Richard at all, but I didn't presume that he would ever come knocking on Dad's door, because Dad would scare him off, I was sure. I felt that protection. Maybe that was the reason I turned to Dad.

Dad had been re-housed into a smaller home on Cameron Street in Astley Bridge. The house had two bedrooms and was more suitable for him and Laura. Previously, they had lived in a huge four bedroomed house on Montserrat Road; this was where we had all lived. All the horrors and memories of that house still haunted me. The years had done nothing to diminish the dreadful traumas that had occurred there. That house would still hold them and would do so forever. The new house knew nothing of those past traumas. A new home for Dad and Laura, and a whole new start, an end to the traumatic past, and the start of a new beginning.

The new house was just around the corner from Dad's brother, our Uncle Don. Don lived there with his wife Andrea. Andrea was our auntie and their house was on Mackenzie Street. All of us had been quite close to our aunt and uncle, and our cousins, it would be great to have them all so nearby.

Dad worked for a whiskey company, at that time, delivering boxes of whiskey and other spirits to different stores and supermarkets. The Saturday afternoon, after I had moved into Dad's house, there was a knock at the front door. There were three men who showed Dad their cards and said that they were the Criminal Investigation Department (CID). They told Dad that they had received a warrant from the court to search the house for some boxes of whiskey. These had gone missing from the firm. The men were everywhere, searching through the cupboards and wardrobes. They even went outside and searched the sheds and then in Dad's budgie sheds! During their searching, Dad was sitting in his armchair, beside the fire, smoking his pipe with his feet up against the mantelpiece. His tobacco smoke stench filling the room.

I had never before been in a situation where the police had entered our house like that and searched for stolen property. I was scared. I thought Dad was a criminal and they would be arresting him. I was sitting rigid on the settee with Deborah. I clutched her closely and held her on my knee. I looked at Dad; he didn't look at all concerned that there were policemen in plain clothing looking through our belongings! He then looked towards me and winked. I didn't understand what that meant. After a while the officers came back into our living room and spoke to Dad. Then they left. I didn't think they had found what they were looking for. When they had driven away, Dad got up from his armchair and lifted up the shelf at the side of the fire and deep inside there were two boxes of whiskey. Dad had his feet propped up on there all that time. The police didn't think of looking in there! I knew, at that point, what the wink meant.

After a few days, Dad wasn't working with that firm any more and was looking for another job.

When I turned to Dad for help, the day I left Josie's house, I certainly didn't expect him to put a roof over our heads at all. I thought he would turn round and say, "You have made your bed, now you can lie in it." I was homeless. Deborah needed me to keep her safe and warm, just as I had promised her the day she was born. That same day she had made me the happiest woman in the world just by being in my arms. I was desperate not to break my promise to her, no matter what.

My promise to Deborah meant that I had to put aside the traumas and nightmares of my childhood in Dad's house and think what was best for Deborah. It was my responsibility to put a roof over her head quickly. She needed my love and protection then more than ever. As her mummy I had to make sure she wasn't going to be affected by any of the past traumas that had affected my life so badly.

As soon as I had placed my bin bag, containing our belongings, on the floor in that tiny bedroom, that tiny bedroom was the place that I had to share with my little sister, I realised that it was another huge mistake, moving back into Dad's house. The room was far too small for the three of us. I kept telling myself that it was temporary, it was for the best, and I had to think of Deborah. I cried myself to sleep that night.

I must have walked down every street in Astley Bridge that Sunday morning. I was with Deborah in her pram, looking in estate agent's windows. We also looked in the windows of newsagents. We searched for flats to rent. It was impossible, there was nothing anywhere for us to rent. I wasn't working and I had a small child. The places we saw wanted working people to rent their properties. All the notices, in the newspapers, said, 'NO DSS.' I was in a desperate situation.

At the end of that Sunday, I realised I couldn't stay at dads. I lay in bed, huddled up close to Deborah as she slept. I was hungry. I hadn't eaten all day. I didn't want to eat. I somehow drifted off to sleep.

We woke the next day to the sound of the front door slamming. We had slept soundly. Laura had got up for school and Dad had gone to work. The sun was shining so brightly, through the gap in the curtains. After a cup of tea and a slice of toast we were heading on the bus to visit my mum.

It was a lovely sunny day. I had dressed Deborah in a red flowery summer dress and red sandals. The bus ride from Bolton to Blackrod was so long and hot, yet the views through the windows were so beautiful. As we approached Blackrod, with its green fields and meadows, the scenic views seemed to go on for miles. With the sun beaming through the windows, it made us both feel quite sleepy.

Deborah had placed her head on my lap and closed her eyes. I stared at her face as she slept and smiled, she was so beautiful, and I was so blessed to have her.

Before long we were walking along Ainse Road to where Mum lived with Jack, her new man. Mum was gardening. When she saw us coming down the road, she placed her pruning shears on the wall and came towards us. She lifted a happily squealing Deborah up high in the air and carried her into the garden. Mum went inside to make a pot of tea while we sat ourselves at the garden table in the warm sunshine. I felt a huge relief to be at Mum's house, away from the tensions at dads. I took a deep breath, of what seemed like clean country air, compared to the smog of Astley Bridge. Deborah was eager to go exploring around the garden. She played happily on the lawn and picked daisies. Mum returned with a tray of tea and biscuits. She also had a tartan blanket that she lay on the lawn for Deborah to play on in the sunshine. She spoke of the man in her life, 'her prince' as she called him. It was clear that she had found the man of her dreams and she was so happy.

"He'll be home from work soon," she said.

Mum and I talked for most of the afternoon. I told her of my break-up with Richard. As I predicted, Mum seemed relieved and pleased that I had finally left him. She repeated exactly what she thought of him. I didn't want to hear it. I still loved him, and wanted to be back in our home again, and be a happy family again.

I was dreaming! Dreaming of the good times, despite the fact that there weren't many amongst all the problems that we had.

I gave myself a shake and brought myself back to reality. How could I go back to him now? He'd hit me. And I had been with another man. He would never, ever forgive me for that!

I had got to face the facts; I was on my own with Deborah. I had got to get our lives back on track. I watched as Deborah played around Mum's garden, she was so happy. She didn't seem happy at Dad's house. She didn't play with her toys, she seemed clingy and just wanted to sit on my knee the whole time. Perhaps she could sense the tensions there. I was tense and on edge all the time. I didn't want Dad to get angry if Deborah made too much noise or cried too much. I didn't want to be there. I didn't want my child to be there either. Mum could see I was close to tears as we talked over endless cups of tea.

The next thing I knew, we were all in the car pulling up outside Dad's house. Jack had come home from work and Mum had told him of our situation and it was agreed that we should both live with them. We were bundled into his car and he drove straight to Dad's house to collect our belongings. Dad's car wasn't parked outside the house so we assumed that he was probably still at work. I left Deborah, sitting with her nanna, and Jack, in the car. I went in and collected the two black bin bags holding our few possessions. I left the front door key on the sideboard, with a note for Dad to thank him for letting us stay and to tell him that we had gone to live at Mum's house and would see him soon. With a huge sigh of relief, the front door was firmly shut behind me.

I got in Jack's car at the side of my daughter in the back seat, I kissed her on the cheek as Jack slowly pulled away from Dad's house. I never looked back.

CHAPTER FIFTY-TWO
Moving On?

The first few days of moving into Mum's house were so busy. It was agreed that this would be a temporary arrangement. I visited the social security office and discovered that I qualified for an allowance each week to care for myself and my daughter. I also visited our local council office to ask if I could be allocated a council house. After a very long interview, in a very hot office, I was considered by them to be homeless so was accepted by them and then placed on their list to be re-housed. I was over the moon. It wasn't going to take long before we had a home of our own and the beginning of a brand-new life for us both. I wondered what our new house would be like as we walked through Bolton precinct towards our bus stop. I imagined the beautiful bedroom I would create for Deborah; her very own bedroom. Passing the huge furniture stores on the precinct, I stopped to gaze through the windows at the beautiful corner units and oak table and chairs. My eyes widened at the price tags. Disheartened, I carried on walking, a worrying thought going through my mind; how would I ever be able to furnish a new house? There was so much I needed; we had absolutely nothing at all!

While in town, trying to put my life on track, I plucked up the courage to call in to see Richard, at the newspaper office on Knowsley Street. I hadn't seen him for nearly a week. I had to ask him if he could help me financially. Deborah would need some new shoes soon. We had nothing. Most of our belongings had been left behind at home when I left on that dreadful night. I needed to arrange with him to collect all the rest of our belongings from his house. Deborah needed her toys; she missed her teddy.

I was not sure of the reception I would receive from him. I was sure it wouldn't be a very comfortable one. At that point I felt guilty for what had happened. It was not until much later that I realised that I was so wrong to feel guilty and the fault was Richard's. I was sure he would be pleased to see Deborah. I headed up the staircase to his office carrying

Deborah in my arms. I made my way through the heavy door and into the hustle and bustle of the busy newspaper office.

It was a huge room with lots of smartly dressed people, all talking at once it seemed. I was approached by a young lad wearing a very smart shirt and tie who asked if I needed help. I thanked him and was shown to Richards's office, on the other side of the room. Richard was sitting at a huge desk with paperwork all around him. He looked up and glared at us as we entered the room. He then stood up. He smiled at Deborah and rushed over and took her from my arms, then lifted her high in the air; he knew she liked that. He sat back in his chair with her on his knee. He gave her a pen to draw with and a big sheet of paper that was in front of him. She was scribbling happily while we talked.

Leaving his office, I breathed a sigh of relief, that we had managed to talk without an argument. He had given me £20 and an arrangement to call to collect our stuff from Glynne Street. I also suggested that he could call to see Deborah that weekend at Mum's house.

It was a lovely sunny Saturday morning when he called to see Deborah. Her little face lit up when she saw him, she was a daddy's girl. I left them both sitting at the garden table together while I went into the house to make a cup of tea.

Over our cups of tea in the sunshine, Richard started to tell me that he had had a letter confirming that the blood tests, which he had taken to prove the paternity of Matthew, had all come back. The tests had been taken a while back and did indeed establish that he was the father. Richard hadn't wasted any time and had been to visit Matthew the previous day. His wife was living with Matthew at her parent's house in Halliwell. He told me how lovely his little three-year-old son was, and how he was sitting at the kitchen table eating cake. Apparently, Matthew had asked his mum if 'Daddy' was having cake too. Richard said he was shocked to be instantly called 'Daddy,' until his wife said with a chuckle that he called everyone 'Daddy'. Richard commented on how well they all got on with each other, and he had been invited back the next day to see Matthew again. I was happy for them all, and so glad that it had worked out well for Richard, he seemed so happy. I knew Richard had always wanted a son; a blue eyed, blond-haired son he used to say. He was sure I was going to have a boy when I became pregnant. When

Deborah came along, I knew he was happy about that too, although deep down I was sure he would have preferred a boy.

I wasn't expecting to see him that Sunday morning, so when his car pulled up outside Mum's house, I was surprised. He came into the garden and sat on the side wall. We talked over another cup of tea. He seemed nervous and anxious, it looked like he intended to ask me something. Meanwhile he continued to fuss around Deborah.

"What's wrong?" I asked him.

He told me that nothing was wrong but he just needed to ask me whether he could take Deborah with him to see Matthew that day. He said it would be better if he saw both children at once and that his wife would like to see Deborah too. He promised to look after her and bring her back to me in a few hours. After some persuasion I agreed.

I wasn't happy when they drove off down the street. I felt as if my right arm had been taken off. Deborah filled my whole life; I was lost without her. It was the first time I had been without her since she was born. I hadn't realised that I would feel so empty without her.

I looked around the garden; her toys lay on the lawn idly waiting. The sound of her laughter was gone, and there was an ache in my tummy for my daughter. I spent the whole afternoon doing the ironing, for the whole household as I attempted to fill the emptiness.

It was around tea time when they returned. I hugged Deborah so tight I had missed her so much. We sat around the garden table talking about their day. Richard was saying how well they had all got on. They were talking of cancelling their divorce and getting back together again. Despite all their problems, which they had experienced in the past, they were going to try to put all that behind them and make a go of it again for the sake of Matthew. My stomach did a somersault at the thought. What about Deborah? I thought to myself.

I felt such a fool in believing we could ever get back together. I still loved him and I hoped that one day he would forgive me for sleeping with Dave and we would get back together. I had to accept that a reconciliation was never going to happen. I had to smile and pretend to be pleased for him, for them both. I had to wish him well and hope that they would both be happy again. In reality I was devastated. I had to get used to the idea that I would be a single parent. The thought horrified me.

He drove off that evening, leaving me in despair.

That day seemed to be the first day of the rest of my life. I felt alone. I had nothing. I didn't know where I was heading or what was out there, in that big wide world, for me and Deborah. I remember crying myself to sleep again, in that little camp bed, in the dining room at Mum's house. I was comfortably snuggled up to my baby girl who was sleeping soundly beside me. For Deborah, whose smile filled my heart every day, I had to be strong.

Over the next couple of weeks, Richard's visits were few and far between. He was unpredictable and would turn up at times when Deborah was in bed. I would protest against this but he would peep in at her and then disappear again into the night. His visits were short and erratic, he rarely stayed for more than a couple of hours, with Deborah, before he had to rush off. I figured he could be busy getting back together with his wife.

Richard didn't talk about that subject any more. I didn't really want to hear anything about their relationship either or hear about how happy they all were. My main concern was Deborah and to make sure she was safe and happy. It was important to me that she had contact with her daddy, and more importantly that she always knew who her father was, although we weren't together.

It was great to see my mum so happy again. It was lovely to hear Jack calling Mum his princess, and he, her prince. Everything seemed to be going right for Mum and Jack, they were even talking about getting married, after they both received their divorces from their former spouses.

Mum and Jack were very friendly with their next-door neighbours. They were called Peter and Barbara. The four of them would go out together to the local pubs. The Red Lion and The Black Horse, in Blackrod, were favourites. The four of them would go there at least a couple of times a week and especially on a Saturday night.

I would be tucked up in bed, fast asleep when they returned. I would stir sometimes; hearing happy voices and hushed laughter. They were all considerate and tried hard not to wake my Deborah. It was such a contrast, to times not so long ago, when night time in my dad's house, following a night out, would be filled with noise, thuds, screams and crying.

It was a lovely Sunday morning and we are all up early and enjoying the sunshine in the garden. Jack was in his greenhouse potting and watering. Mum was cooking breakfast for everyone. Deborah was riding her little trike, up and down the sloped driveway, chatting away to herself. Mum appeared from the kitchen, carrying a tray, which she placed on the garden table. We all tucked into poached eggs on toast in the sun.

Barbara and Peter appeared from their house next door. They said that they had to go to the train station to pick up their nephew, who was coming to stay for the holidays. When they arrived back, and parked up on their driveway, I was surprised to see a grown man getting out of their car. I was expecting a young schoolboy for some reason. Peter and Barbara introduced him to us as Scott.

I think I blushed slightly; he was quite cute. He was very tall, had dark hair and was very smartly dressed. I liked him, he looked nice. After taking his large suitcase indoors, he came back outside and chatted to us over the garden wall. He had a very strong Irish accent, quite difficult to understand. I sat and listened, while he spoke to Jack, about football. In return Jack talked to him about his work down the pit.

Scott told us that he was twenty-two and he was learning to be a carpenter. He was very charming and smiled a lot. It wasn't long before Jack had agreed to take him to the pub for a pint or two.

Over the course of the week Scott seemed to be a regular visitor to our house. He would jump over the wall like an athlete and come knocking on our door with some excuse or another. When Friday arrived, I was playing with Deborah in the garden. Scott shouted to me from over the wall, "Fancy coming out with me tonight for a drink Maggie?" I instantly blushed. "Please, pretty please," he said.

"Sorry, I can't. I don't go out, and I've got Deborah." I pointed to her and told him I would need a babysitter, but I couldn't possibly leave her.

Mum was bringing in the washing, off the line in the back garden. She had heard our conversation.

"You go out with Scott and enjoy yourself, I will look after Deborah," she said, stuffing the pegs in the peg bag. I was embarrassed.

I provided one excuse after another but finally I agreed to go out with him. "Okay I will pick you up at 7.30," he said. He then rushed off and went back next door.

While I was getting ready, Mum said, "He seems to like you, so enjoy yourself and have a good time." I told Mum that the thought of going out with another man scared me. I didn't want to be taken in by him, or any other man ever again. I convinced myself that it would be just a few drinks and it might just do me good to get out of the house for a while.

I had decided to wear a simple tee-shirt and jeans, and just a little makeup. My hands were shaking so badly that it was so difficult to apply the mascara without smudging it. I was so nervous. While I was getting ready, there was a knock on the door; it was only 7 o'clock. He was early, I thought and I wasn't quite ready. Mum knocked on the bathroom door and said that Richard was there to see Deborah. I was shocked. I couldn't believe he had turned up at that time, of all times, when I was being taken out by another man. He was not going to like that. He would be livid.

Mum had invited him in and he was sitting on the sofa with Deborah, when I finally came out of the bathroom.

"Oh, you look nice," he said, "where are you off to?" I stared at his face and his piercing blue eyes. His eyes were sad. I couldn't speak.

At that point, Scott walked into the hallway. He asked me if I was ready. Mum then turned to Richard and said, "She's going for a drink with Scott to the local pub around the corner. It will do her good, and I will be babysitting so all's fine." I kissed Deborah on the cheek and told her to be a good girl for nanna. Richard asked if he could stay with Deborah for half an hour, Mum agreed and made him a cup of tea.

I had a lovely night out with Scott, in the Black Horse pub. We played pool and drank beer. We laughed and chatted for most of the evening. He was charming and funny, and such a gentleman too, and pleasant company. The evening ended so quickly and he walked me home straight to the door. Once inside I snuggled next to my sleeping daughter and drifted off to sleep.

Scott and I spent some lovely time together through the following week. I didn't have any romantic feelings for him; however, he had become a truly lovely friend. I thought, after making the biggest mistake of my life, when I slept with Dave, on that awful night, that I would not experience romantic feelings again for some time. That fateful evening had happened because I had traumatically split up with Richard.

I knew I would miss Scott after he had left that following weekend. When the weekend arrived, it was a very sad and emotional farewell. All of us were emotional as we waved him off for his journey back to Ireland. We had exchanged addresses and promised that we would write. He had filled quite a lot of my time, during his holiday in Blackrod. It was going to be so quiet without him to talk to.

On the Sunday morning I was awoken with the aroma of bacon and toast wafting through the dining room. Mum was up and cooking in the kitchen. Before long we were all up and sitting in the garden having breakfast.

The sun had reached high up in the sky and it was getting quite hot. Deborah had taken off her sun hat for what must have been the fifth time. I was beginning to get a little cross with her. I really wanted her to leave it on as the sun was hot. I had to chase her around the garden to get it back on her head.

After a while Deborah was getting tired and tetchy so we went inside away from the sun. I tried to settle her down for a nap. As I was sitting, rocking her to sleep on my knee, I hummed to her gently. At that point, I glanced out through the window and saw Richard's car pulling up outside. I was just about to wake Deborah, to tell her that daddy was outside, when I realised that Richard wasn't alone in that car. As I looked closely, I realised it was Maureen in the passenger seat. I stood, with Deborah in my arms. I stared through the window in disbelief at what I was seeing. Richard got out of the car, confidently holding Louise in his arms, he kissed her on the cheek. I looked on for a moment, I couldn't believe what my eyes were seeing. My stomach did somersaults. Louise was wearing a little light blue and white striped cotton dress with little white socks. They all appeared to be dressed in their Sunday best.

I didn't wait for them to walk down the driveway together or wait to ask questions as to what the father of my child was doing with my sister and her child. It was obvious to me what they were doing. I wasn't going to stay in that house any longer, I had to go. I felt sick to my stomach. I had to run.

With Deborah in my arms, I made my way through to the back of the house. I climbed over the fence and into Barbara's back garden and frantically knocked on her back door. When Barbara opened her back door, I collapsed into her arms. I was absolutely distraught. I felt as if I was going to faint. I couldn't breathe. Barbara quickly held on to me and led me into her lounge, where she sat me on her sofa. She was begging me to tell her what was wrong, but I couldn't speak. Tears were streaming down my face; I still couldn't breathe. Her arms were so tightly around me; I was sobbing my heart out onto her shoulder.

After a few minutes, that seemed like hours, she released me from her closeness and wiped my tears with her hands. I took a big breath and began to tell her what was wrong.

"What? Richard and Maureen?" she shouted. "The bastard!" Barbara stood up, she moved to the window and looked at Richard's car, which was parked outside mums. Deborah clung onto me so tightly, she did not understand what was happening. I looked into her big brown eyes and thought to myself, how are we ever going to survive this? How will I ever be able to explain that her daddy is with my sister?

As I rocked Deborah gently, her eyes began to close and she drifted off to sleep. I placed her on the settee and covered her with her shawl. I looked out of the window at Richards's car. He was inside my mum's house with my sister. All the rumours of those two being together, which I had heard about for nearly two years, must have been true. Everything he told me had been lies. How could he do that to me? It was not right. She was my sister. I was shaking. I couldn't believe it. The tears started again. When would they stop?

Barbara guided me away from the window and into the kitchen. She sat me down at the table. "Let's have a cuppa," she said, putting the kettle on the stove. Deborah was sleeping soundly, as we drank tea and talked. I was shaking like a leaf. It was difficult to hold my cup properly. Barbara suggested that I needed a Valium to help with the shock. She reached into her little pill box and handed me a little white pill. "Take that with your tea," she said.

I stayed at Barbara's for the rest of the afternoon. The tears stopped. However, inside I was broken. That afternoon, Barbara had heard everything concerning my life with Richard and what he had put me through. The lies, the cheating, and a year of unpleasant rumours that he had pretended were not true. I had been listening to him, I had believed him and I had trusted him. How could I have been so naïve? How could I have been such a fool? My thoughts then turned to my mum. How could she let him into her house, knowing what he had done to me? Mum was always calling him 'not fit to burn.' She had tried to tell me that he was seeing other women, that he was a womaniser and a sweet-talking guy. Why didn't I believe her? Did she know that Richard had been seeing Maureen all that time?

No doubt he was sitting on her settee, having a cup of tea, with my sister. Why had she let him in? I couldn't believe what was happening. It was only a few weeks earlier that he was telling me he was getting back with his wife, what had happened to her?

When we finally went back to Mum's house, after Richard and Maureen had left, the only answer I got for my questions from Mum was, "She is my daughter too, and Louise is my granddaughter, and today was her first birthday so Richard had brought them to see me." She continued to tell me that Maureen had been given a council house and Richard had been helping her to get settled in.

I was confused. My thoughts, and unanswered questions, were going round and round in my head. It seemed that Mum didn't want to discuss that with me any longer so I walked off into the kitchen. Could she not see how distraught I was? Was she supporting the fact that they might be together? Couldn't she see how wrong that could be? She seemed to be supporting them, as if all her loyalty was with them. She definitely had no support for me, when Richard and I were together, with all the names she used to call him. I knew I couldn't stay at Mum's house any longer, I had to leave as soon as I could. I couldn't wait around for their next cosy little visit. Deborah and I had to leave soon. I felt isolated, betrayed and desperately alone.

The week that followed were tense. Mum was quiet and seemed impatient at times. It felt as if Deborah and I were in the way. It was beginning to look as if she didn't want us to stay there any longer. I started to remember the time in the past where Mum had kicked me out. I saw the same expressions on her face and started to fear that history was about to repeat itself. This caused me great concern because I now had to think about Deborah as well as myself. Mum had a good life with Jack, at that time, and the fall out within the family was hard to deal with, she needed to be happy.

I kept out of her way to the best of my ability. With Deborah in her pushchair; we would go for long walks, even in the rain. We would wander through the streets, checking the adverts in the shop windows for accommodation. This process was pointless as the adverts all made it clear that the properties in question would accept no children and no DSS. With the rain on my face no one could see my tears.

Late that Thursday night the telephone rang. It was the hospital. I had just got Deborah off to sleep and I was sitting reading beside her. Mum shouted my name from the living room and I rushed in to see what was wrong. She told me that Richard was in the hospital and we needed to go down to pick him up. I asked her what was wrong with him. They hadn't told her what was wrong, they just stated that we needed to go to the hospital to collect him. I asked Barbara, from next door, if she would sit with Deborah while we went to the hospital.

When we got there, we were directed to a cubicle where Richard was. He was lying on a hospital trolley with his eyes closed. He stirred when we walked in and we asked him what had happened. The nurse told us that he had taken some pills and had a fall in his bathroom. The fall had caused him to bump his head, but he was okay, by that stage, and was indeed ready to be taken home. The nurse helped him to his feet and we took him home. On arriving at his front door, he searched his coat pockets for his door key. He realised that his key had been left behind when the ambulance had come for him. He said that the back door would probably be open. It was pitch black, as we made our way around to the back of his house, down the back street. The large, wooden back gate was padlocked on the inside. Richard suggested that he would have to climb over. He was over that gate in no time at all like a cat climbing a tree. Luckily the back door was open and he was back in his house. It was late, so we left him alone in his house and returned home.

On our way home, Jack commented on how well Richard had climbed over the gate, considering he looked on death's door when we had arrived at the hospital. He did appear to have made a quick recovery. We all chuckled and realised what a good actor he was. Surely, this was an attempt to seek attention and sympathy from us. Would it not have been more appropriate for him to have contacted his own mother in circumstances of that nature?

The next day, I telephoned him at home to see if he was okay. He answered straight away and began to tell me what had happened the night before. He told me that he was at home with a banging headache. He had taken some aspirins and then gone into the bathroom where he had collapsed. This was in fact just what the nurse at the hospital had told us. I then asked a question that had been puzzling me.

"Where was Maureen, and why didn't you contact her instead of us?" He said, "Why should I contact her? I am not with her Maggie! She is with Jimmy. I caught them snogging in her kitchen, during her birthday party!" Jimmy was in fact the married man that I had heard she had been involved with. He took a breath and continued to say that he brought her to my mums to make me jealous because I had made him jealous when I went out with Scott. He said that he hadn't liked it so it was a plan to get a reaction from me. He said that he wasn't seeing Maureen at all. "I never have!" he said. "She is with Jimmy and has been for a while. It's you I want! It's you I'm in love with not her! Never has been and never will be!"

I couldn't speak. I slammed the phone down. I didn't want to listen to any more of his lies. My head was spinning. I didn't believe him. I knew what I saw when they both arrived at Mum's the previous week. Was that my imagination? Was it the paranoia that Richard was always referring to when I challenged his behaviour? Nothing made any sense at all.

His words were whirling around in my mind. I couldn't eat. I couldn't sleep. He said he was still in love with me! I thought he would never, ever forgive me for leaving him on that awful night in May. We had not been together for nearly two months and here he was, saying he was still in love with me. Was he lying?

I still loved him. I did want my life back with him. I didn't want to be a single parent. I wanted my daughter to wake up in her own bed. I wanted to iron his shirts and cook his meals and clean his house. I loved my life with him and our daughter, despite all the problems. I began to think to myself. I started to wonder how it might be possible to go back to the life that we had experienced before all those horrid rumours that had separated us? I also considered the reality that the affair with J was real; that was no rumour.

While our daughter was being born, he was having an affair with her. How could I forgive him for that? How could I trust him again? I knew in my head it would never happen. I could never trust him to keep away the pain and the torments that destroyed our previous life together. I had to face the fact that we could never be together again. My heart still ached to be by his side. My heart ached for the love that we once shared. I had to move on from all those thoughts that had shattered all my dreams. Deborah and I had to begin our new life together. We had nothing, but we had each other, that was all the happiness I needed. No one would ever take that away from me. I looked at Deborah, while she was sitting, watching her favourite Bugs Bunny cartoon on television.

We had to create new dreams and make new memories along the way. As Gloria Gaynor had said, in her single which had gone to number one, just a few months previously. 'I will survive!' I didn't know how at that point, but I knew I had to, for Deborah.

With a jolt I was awakened. My heart was beating so fast in my chest, that I could almost hear it. I was startled and I sat up in bed sharply. For a moment I didn't know where I was. I rubbed my eyes and realised that I was still at Mum's house with my precious daughter sleeping beside me. I had awakened from a bad dream that seemed so real.

In my dream, I was in a strange empty house, a house that was my new house. I was excitedly running, holding Deborah's hand, in and out of empty rooms. I could see the walls and the bare floorboards of every room. Deborah was laughing and giggling; she was running around her chosen bedroom. I could see the long kitchen and the white kitchen cupboards along with the shiny new draining board. There was a big brown rusty key on the kitchen counter. I picked it up and looked at it as I wondered which lock it opened. Looking around the house, I noticed the back door had a similar sized keyhole. I tried it in the lock and it seemed to fit. I turned the key and with a loud click, I opened the huge back door. I looked out at the overgrown back garden. I was imagining Deborah playing in a sand pit or on a swing, swinging high in the sunshine. I looked up towards the sky; the sun's rays beamed down through the clouds. I could feel the sun on my face. I looked further down the garden and across the garden of another house on the next street. I noticed Maureen standing in the doorway opposite. I stood and stared in disbelief; she glanced towards me, turned and went into the house and shut the door. With a flash I woke up and realised it was just a dream.

The thought of living near to Maureen was not what I would want at all. I knew she hated me; she always had done. I preferred to be as far away from her as I could be. I was so relieved that it was only a bad dream. A bad dream I wouldn't ever want to come true.

The next couple of weeks were increasingly difficult within our household. Mum clearly wanted us to move out as soon as possible. She wanted her home back and to get rid of the disruption we caused. Her dining room, which was taken up with the little camp bed that Deborah and I shared, was in the corner. This was not very suitable as a bedroom for us at all. Deborah's toys were everywhere, in every room. Richard had been making regular visits to see Deborah and this added to the bad atmosphere around the place. Mum was always making snide remarks and making him feel unwelcome and so uncomfortable. I refused to allow Richard to take Deborah off in his car alone, as I wasn't sure where he was taking her. Instead, we spent quite a lot of time in each other's company, down the park or he would take us off to visit family or friends, mostly Richard's family and friends. It was inevitable that we were becoming close again. Before long I was walking back through the front door of the house we once shared together.

Pressure was coming from both sides at that time. From Mum who wanted us to move out as soon as possible and from Richard who wanted us to move back in, as soon as possible. I knew I loved Richard and I wanted to be with him but I didn't want to rush into moving back in with him. I thought that rushing things might mean that I would have to settle for the same horrible routine that existed before. I wanted to wait and take time to decide if it was truly what I wanted for the rest of my life.

Richard's estranged wife had advised him that he needed to sell the house so she could have a divorce and the settlement. I knew that if it was sold, we could all be homeless again. I didn't want to take that risk; I wasn't sure whether I wanted to move back into Glynne Street at all.

On returning home to Blackrod, after Deborah and I had spent the night with Richard at Glynne Street, Mum was so angry. She said that we both should move back in with Richard instead of to-ing and fro-ing. She was shouting and calling him names, she was horrible. Mum had thrown me out on the streets before and it looked like she wanted to do it again, with Deborah.

The next day, Deborah and I went down to the council to inform them that we were about to become homeless. Maybe they would be able to find us somewhere else to live. Anywhere would suffice: a room, a flat, homeless accommodation or anything else. I didn't care what, just as long as I had a roof over my daughter's head. I had been on the council waiting list for a few weeks now. I couldn't be homeless, or on the streets with my daughter. She would have been taken into care for sure if that was to happen. I knew that being taken into care would be better for her than living on the streets, but I could never be that desperate as to allow that to happen to her.

After about two hours of endless form filling, and signing my name over and over again, I was handed a set of keys for a property. It was a two bedroomed house on Padbury Way. I wasn't sure where it was but I thought it sounded really nice. I took the keys straight away. I was in shock. I just couldn't believe it, a house to call our own, our new home. I was given decorating vouchers and vouchers for some pieces of furniture that I would need. I had to go to a certain store to choose the items. I then had to wait at the new property the following day to take delivery.

Bright and early the next day, we were on our way, with our few belongings to see our new place. When I found the property and walked down the front path, I was alarmed to see all the wooden boards were still up at the windows. This was to stop possible vandals from smashing the windows, while the house was empty. The house looked nice enough, with a front and back garden, which was big enough for Deborah to run around in. I couldn't wait to turn the key in that lock and explore. Our voices and the noises from our footsteps, on the wooden floorboards, echoed around that empty dark house that was to be our new home.

With a flick of a switch, in the meter cupboard, the electricity was connected; we had lights! The kitchen was long and narrow with white units. All at once I started to experience a feeling of déjà vu; just as my dreams had portrayed things, I thought. There was a new sink unit and a shiny new draining board. I recalled a flashback to the horrible dream that I had experienced the previous week. Unlike my dream, however, the back-door key wasn't on the counter in the kitchen, it was with the set of keys that the council had given to me.

I turned the key and swung open the back door. Deborah went running out towards the back of the very untidy and overgrown back garden; the grass was up to her waist. I was so relieved to see that there were no properties at the back of our new home. There was just waste land and tall bushes, there was no sign of Maureen at all. I breathed a sigh of relief. I collected my daughter from the long grass and came back into the house and closed the door. I shook off that nasty dream from my mind.

Soon there was a knock at the door. The delivery men had arrived and were delivering our items of furniture. We had beds, a settee, a table, chairs and a cooker. There was so much more that we needed, but this second-hand furniture, from the community help centre, was a start. The house would soon look like a home. I was so happy, Deborah was very happy too. I knew that Richard would be happy for us as well. It had crossed my mind that we could possibly have a future together here in this house. A fresh start! A new beginning?

As the delivery van pulled away. I stood at our front door, looking over the street and our new surroundings. To the right, down at the bottom of the street, were a row of shops and a post office. To the left, were rows of houses just like ours. They reached up an incline in the distance as far as the eye could see. I looked across at the house opposite and through the back garden of a house on the next street. Instantly my stomach did a somersault and I felt sick. There in that back garden was Maureen pegging out washing on her line. My dreams of future happiness in that house shattered right in front of me. I couldn't believe what I was seeing. That was my horrible dream, the one I had experienced the other night. In my dream, I was allocated a house near her, and the reality was the same, the dream had come true. In my bad dream, from the back door, I could see her front door. In reality from my front door, I could see her back door. That nightmare had come true but in reverse!

I came back indoors and cried. I was trembling. I didn't want to go back out there. I didn't want to stay in that house. I wanted to pack up my things and get out of there as fast as I could. How could we possibly be happy in that house? How could all that be happening?

Deborah had fallen asleep on the settee. She was unaware of my tears and the situation that I had landed us in. I felt there would never be a happy outcome. When the tears stopped, I realised that we had no choice but to stay in that house and live our lives the best we could. I knew the council wouldn't offer us another house as we had a perfectly good roof over our heads.

When the tears stopped inside, I felt broken and alone. Deborah stirred from her nap and climbed on my knee and gave me such a tight squeeze. "Mummy I love you! she said. "How much?" I asked looking in her big brown eyes. "All the world, and all the pennies. All the salt in the sea and all the tea in China," she said, chuckling and hugging me again so tightly.

My heart was overflowing with love for that little girl, my daughter. She made everything all right again.

Later that day, after being alone in our new house for most of the time, we were still unable to look out the windows because the wooden boards remained nailed up. I decided I didn't want to stay there overnight, so I got Deborah ready, packed some overnight things and went off into the night. We caught the first bus into town and arrived at Moor Lane Bus Station. We then caught another bus all the way to Farnworth and made our way to Richards's house.

The heat from the gas fire, in his living room, was so inviting so we both huddled together on the rug rubbing our hands. I hadn't realised how cold I was. Deborah had been warm and cosy, under a blanket in her pram, while we walked all the way up from Moses Gate.

Richard was surprised to see us and even more surprised when I told him we had been given a new house by the council. It came as a shock to him to hear that Maureen lived only a stone's throw away from my front door. He listened while I poured my heart out, telling him of my dreams for that house and our future together as a family. The tears flowed; I couldn't contain my devastation. He held me and wiped my tears with his hands. I looked up at him and he kissed me.

"Everything will be okay," he said. His words didn't seem to be fixing things. But then he said, "I don't care that she lives there, all I care about is you and our future together." He continued and said that it would be a new start for us if that's what we wanted. Maureen would never spoil our happiness. He then said that there was an old saying. 'Keep your friends close and your enemies closer.' I didn't feel I could agree with that. I didn't feel I could keep her close, after what she had done while Richard and I were together. She hated me so why would she want to be close to me? I began to feel better by thinking and hoping that maybe she wouldn't want that either, when she found out that we would be living so close to her. Possibly, she would leave us alone, and get on with her own life.

Looking back on the first three months, after moving into Padbury Way, I came to think that the times were mostly good times. I lived in that house for two whole weeks before the council took the boards down from our windows. It was quite scary at times, when there was banging on the boards all around the house. This happened in the middle of the night and the sounds of people running in and out of the gardens could be heard. I didn't dare go out and tell them to clear off. I would lie in bed petrified if Richard wasn't with me. The shouting through the letterbox was scary too. It felt like I was being terrorised. I would hold my hands over my ears and squeeze my eyes tightly shut. I hoped I would fall asleep again. To my relief it all stopped when the boards were taken down.

Shortly after moving in, Richard helped me to hang curtains at the windows. He helped me to decorate some of the rooms and he had carpets fitted throughout the whole house. Richard and I were getting very close again and we spent quite a lot of time together initially. It was clear that he adored our daughter and hated being apart from her. She would cry every time he left her; it would break my heart.

After a while, Richard would stay over some nights and I would stay at his house at times too. I began to hate being away from him at night. If we weren't together, I would miss him so much. It was only a matter of time before we realised that we were meant to be living together as a family again. I was ready to be a family again. We even talked about having another baby. I was getting broodier every day.

439

I didn't want to stay at Padbury Way. I was never comfortable with living so close to Maureen, although it seemed at times that we were becoming sisterly to each other. I did think that it was good to spend time with her and my little niece Louise. I still couldn't trust her entirely, as the hurt that she had caused was still on my mind. I still could not work out the reasons for her past bad behaviour. I never had any answers from her, on that subject, nor did I expect that I ever would. I really believed I knew the reason why; it was because she hated me. She always had done; she didn't seem to ever want to see me happy. I didn't think she wanted me to be with Richard. Richard would say that she was jealous of what we had. I didn't think that was true, she could have had her choice of lads, she certainly had many chasing her.

It had crossed my mind that she hated me because I had taken her across that main road when we were little. We were knocked down and found ourselves in hospital. I was supposed to have been looking after her. We could have died that day. We were never close after that awful time.

I particularly remember an incident, when we were sleeping in the living room at home. We both had a leg in a full plaster cast, this meant we could not get upstairs and so we had to sleep in a single bed in the living room.

One memorable evening, I turned over in bed. We were top and tail and when I moved, the pot leg made contact with the boil on Maureen's backside. This caused the boil to burst and Maureen to expel a hideous and demonic scream. Our dad charged down stairs and shouted to us to shut up.

From that point on I don't think Maureen liked me very much.

Padbury Way was quite nice; however, the area had a bad reputation for lots of crime and drug dealing. I didn't want my child to grow up there. I yearned to be back in Farnworth. I loved it there: the shops, the market and the general atmosphere of the place was most agreeable. It was such a friendly place; everyone seemed to know each other and look out for one another. I didn't have my washing stolen from the line, as had been the case in Padbury Way.

I would hang Richard's washing on my line. This would include his sweaters and sweatshirts; these would promptly be stolen from the line in broad daylight. I would see lads walking around the street, as bold as brass, wearing the very same items a few days later. They were friends of Maureen. I had seen them in her house, smoking cigarettes, rough looking and dodgy so I didn't have the nerve to approach them. I stopped hanging my washing out on the line, unless I was sitting out in the garden. This was only possible in particularly good weather. In my heart, I hoped that one day we would all be back home in Glynne Street where we belonged.

We celebrated Deborah's second birthday at Richards's house. We had friends and cousins, from Richards's side of the family, who all noticed that she was growing up so fast. I was imagining her having a little brother or a sister; I even started looking at all the tiny baby clothes in Mothercare. The time was right, I wanted another baby before Deborah got too used to being an only child. Richard and I were spending every night together.

Three weeks after Deborah's birthday, it was my twenty-first birthday. Richard bought me a gold Sekonda watch and invited a few friends to my house for a party. Richard also brought his mum, Lola, to visit too. It was so nice to see her, despite her rude words to me the last time that I had seen her. I hadn't had any contact with her since I left Richard's house on that cold May evening, almost six months previously.

My best friend Mandy came with her new man, he was called Carl. He was a jeweller and looked so nice. It was obvious that he thought the world of Mandy and Craig. I was so happy for her. We partied into the night.

Over the next couple of weekends, I invited Lola for Sunday tea. It had become a tradition, in my house, to sit around the table together for Sunday lunch. My cooking was improving. I was becoming quite a good cook in fact. Sunday dinners were my specialty. I enjoyed every minute that I spent in the kitchen cooking on a Sunday. Maureen had become a regular visitor to my house.

Her visits were mostly brief, it was very rare that she would spend more than an hour in my company. One Sunday afternoon, after tea, she called round and had accepted our offer of a cup of tea. Richard and I had some news that we were bursting to reveal, we couldn't wait any longer! "We are pregnant again," we both said at the same time. Lola jumped up from her seat and hugged us both saying how delighted she was. Deborah was playfully jumping up and down and clapping her hands together with excitement. However, when I looked across at Maureen her face was like thunder. She didn't look at all happy for us, nor did she come over to congratulate us. She drank her tea and made an excuse that she had to go and was out through the door in a flash. I quickly realised that our news was not what she wanted to hear because of all the pregnancies that she had lost recently. I began to think that we had been insensitive and should have been more sympathetic towards her. We shouldn't have shared our news with her like that, we should have waited until a more appropriate time.

Two days later there was a knock on the door. Two official looking women were on my doorstep waiting for me to answer. They told me that they were from the council office. I invited them in and during their visit they asked questions regarding my relationship with Richard. They had been informed that he was living at my property and in fact that I was at that time, pregnant by him again. How on earth did they find out I was pregnant? They also said that because he owned another property he was not allowed to stay in my house. They recommended that I leave the property, they also stated that I could be evicted if he was staying with me in that house. I was happy to be leaving. I wanted to be out of there as soon as I could.

Within the week we were all packed up and had handed the keys back to the council. That was the end of living on Padbury Way.

The end of 1979 was the start of our new beginning, back where we all belonged in the house, I had always called home. It was the start of our new life together as a family again. Most exciting of all was the start of the brand-new life that was growing inside me.

CHAPTER FIFTY-THREE
1980 Nichola

As the new year began, Richard and I were talking about getting married as soon as his divorce came through. I was beginning to wish I hadn't ever heard the word divorce. I was sick of thinking about it. It was taking so long. I wanted to marry Richard as soon as I could. Our new baby would be due in September, surely the divorce would be granted before then?

We were both in awe of Bolton Parish Church since our visit there on Christmas Eve. We had attended Midnight Holy Communion, so all our previous plans of getting married in Gretna Green had fizzled away, we wanted to get married there. Bolton Parish Church was very large and so beautiful. It stood in the centre of Bolton, on the edge of the valley in which it was possible to overlook St Peter's Way. Its tower stood tall and proudly overlooked the whole of Bolton. While we listened to the choir singing Christmas carols, we looked wide eyed at the beautiful Victorian Gothic architecture. We were reminded of our visit to Paris, a few years previously, where this architectural style was prevalent. Instantly, we fell in love with that church that was right there in our hometown. We thought it was just as beautiful as the Cathedral of Notre Dame, although not as vast or as old. We were just as impressed with the beauty as we were in Paris.

Our new hopes and dreams, of walking down the aisle of Bolton Parish Church, began. Richard would look amazing in a top hat and tails. I imagined myself in ivory and lace. We would exchange our vows together in the presence of God and the congregation. This dream was dependent on whether we would be allowed to marry in a church due to Richard being a divorced man. Some churches did not allow a divorced person to remarry.

Richard was sure and kept on reassuring me that the divorce would be complete that year. His wife was moving on with her life at that time too. She had a new man and was expecting another baby, she was happy.

Richard would tell me that she wanted the divorce just as quickly as he did.

Richard had only seen his son, Matthew, a couple of times. Despite this, he had suddenly decided not to see him again as he felt it was too upsetting and confusing for Matthew. Richard believed he (Matthew) may struggle with the idea that he had two father figures in his life and this was causing some disruption for him. Richard would say that his wife wasn't happy about him going to see Matthew, as it was creating an atmosphere for her and her new partner every time Richard would visit. I was not at all happy with his decision and was hoping I would get to meet Matthew one day. I was also hoping that our children would get to know Matthew as well.

Richard spoke of Matthew so much and about how lovely he was. I thought he had genuinely got attached to him and loved him. I knew Richard had wanted a son so much and I thought he was so pleased when the blood test proved that he was indeed Matthew's father. Due to this, the decision to stop seeing him surprised me. I didn't think that it seemed to be the right decision at all.

Richard was adamant that our new baby was going to be a boy, he would say that he would soon have another son who he could be a proper father to. I was secretly hoping we would have a boy too. A little brother for Deborah, and not a replacement for Matthew. In my eyes, Matthew would always be the big brother of my children. I hoped with all my heart that one day they would meet and grow together and know that they were each other's family.

It had been six months since I had moved back to Glynne Street with Richard. It had been a happy and contented six months for me. It had gone by so quickly with lots of changes and surprises, some good and some not so good. Our talks, concerning our wedding, were still at the front of our minds. I think we were both as excited as each other, particularly as Richard believed that his divorce was imminent.

Mandy and her new man Carl were seriously considering buying a house together. Being a family, they too had marriage plans. They were so happy together. I was so pleased for my best friend. She had found someone else after all the upset of the pregnancy, which had been particularly stressful as she had been alone. She had a new life with her new man and I thought that he would be a great father for her son. Alan, our lodger, had moved out a few months previously and gone to live with Josie, his new love. Josie was a single parent. She was the one, with all those lovely children, who had allowed me to stay overnight at her house on that awful night. That was the dreadful night, the previous May, when I had left Richard. Josie had done the same for Maureen before she was allocated her council house. At this point, Josie was pregnant with Alan's baby. The baby was due in December and both seemed so happy. Alan was still working as a DJ with Richard. He had taken over most of the work at the Bus Inn. His new DJ name was Lee Brown.

Richard had been concentrating on the mobile discos and his new limited company 'The Danny Sinclair Road Show'. The bookings for his shows were coming in from all over the country. He would load all his equipment in his funny looking little white van, which had caricatures of him holding his microphone, painted on the sides. In big black lettering was the designation, 'The Danny Sinclair Roadshow Mobile Disco'. He would climb into the driver's seat with his roadie. This would usually be his brother Lee. Lee would be in the seat next to him, and off they would go wherever the show happened to be.

As always, I was left at home to enjoy my house and my new kitchen, built for me by Richard. Also provided by Richard was a brand-new automatic washing machine and tumble dryer. I couldn't help but show them off when the neighbours came round for a cuppa; I was as pleased as punch.

My old rusty twin tub washing machine sat in my backyard, waiting to be collected by the scrap man. That twin tub had been pulled out every Monday on wash day. It had meant piles of washing on the floor around the kitchen. In the old machine the white, hot wash was the first to go in, then the dark clothes. It would take most of the day to finish the whole week's washing.

My new automatic washing machine stood proudly in my new kitchen. Not many households had an automatic washing machine, at that time, so I felt very posh and well to do. Getting the washing done was so much easier. I would put a load in with the powder and press a button; that was it, so easy. I would sit for ages looking at all the washing in the machine going round and round. I could not quite believe that all that washing would come out clean within an hour or so. I had a lot more time on my hands to spend on other chores around the house. Life was good and so much easier and we were happy. While he worked, I didn't feel lonely or alone, I was content. It was exactly where I wanted to be.

Shortly after the new year, we were talking about getting a dog. Richard said that he had always wanted a dog but was never allowed to have one when he was growing up. My family always had dogs around when we were growing up. I thought it would be good for Deborah to have one, at some point in her childhood. We talked about it quite a lot. Richard would say he wanted a guard dog to protect our property. I wanted a smallish dog that wouldn't be aggressive or bark a lot.

I had fallen in love with my dad's new dog, which he had bought the previous year, she was a Cavalier King Charles Spaniel called Floppy. I don't think Richard was that keen on her though. She was a pretty little pedigree with floppy ears and such big brown eyes. I thought she was gorgeous but came with a big price tag. She was far too expensive for us to buy.

After Spring, we decided to go and have a look at the local dogs' home on Vernon Street. After a few visits, we saw an Alsatian cross, called Shandy. She was lovely, fully grown and house trained. She had been brought into the kennels, a few days earlier, after the owner had died. When we met her, she came straight to us and seemed to like us. Deborah gave her a big hug around her neck. Shandy turned and licked her on her face. We knew this was the dog for us. She settled into our little family quickly, she even got on with our cat Tiggles. It was as if we were meant to find her and she was meant to be with us.

It was turning out to be quite a happy and surprising year, not just for us and my best friend Mandy, but for my sister Andrea too. She had finally left the hospital in Northampton, where she was admitted after she self-harmed, a few years previously. This had been the time when I was pregnant with Deborah. Richard and I had travelled down on the train a few times to see her while she was a patient there. She always seemed so fragile when we visited and would always get really upset when it was our time to leave. It was awful to have to leave her there, but the place was lovely with large beautiful gardens with lots of space to wander around. Andrea seemed to have been looked after very well despite the high walls and locked doors.

Early that year, Andrea was released from the hospital. It was deemed that she was fit and well. She had met a lad called Adrian, from Northampton. They were experiencing a whirlwind romance. Surprisingly they had got married that March and she was expecting a baby, which was due around the same time as mine. I was so pleased to hear this news. I was so pleased to hear that she had recovered and she was happy and putting all her past issues behind her. The fact that she was going to be a mummy too! My little sister was having a baby! It was hard for me to imagine her all grown up, married and pregnant. She had always seemed so small and had needed to be looked after, however, she was now a married woman with a baby on the way!

At the same time as being so pleased for her, I couldn't help but be a little envious and disappointed that my baby sister had married before me. Her child would not have the label of being illegitimate, as my children would have. It made my heart sink and feel angry once again that Richard's divorce was taking so long to come through. We were expecting our second baby; another child of mine to be born out of wedlock. I felt ashamed and embarrassed. I was sure that Richard could sense my feelings of disappointment. He could see the unshed tears in my eyes. He hugged me so tightly when I shared this news with him. "I love you so much Maggie, everything will work out for us soon, I promise," he whispered softly in my ear.

His words didn't take away the shame I felt for my innocent child, that I had brought into this world. I had another one on the way that would also be illegitimate. I was powerless, and hopeless. I couldn't do anything about the way things were except hope and pray that one day the divorce would come through. At that point Richard and I would be married. I didn't care where it was. It could be in a church or a registry office, just as long as we got married soon. I loved my man and I realised that I had got to stand by his side for as long as it would take.

Before long, Andrea and her new husband, moved from Northampton to Bolton. I was delighted to have my little sister back in my life again, although she was not so little any more. She was as tall as me; so beautiful, all grown up, married and blooming with a child. She was so different from the child that she once was.

The haunting image, which I would see many times throughout my life, was that of her at seven years old being punished with that stick because she had ripped her dress. The tears would still fill my eyes. However, I looked at her at that time, I could see the love that she had been waiting for, for so long. This was the love that they both shared for one another.

Adrian and Andrea moved into a little temporary one roomed flat in a hostel in Farnworth. It was slightly higher up the road from where we lived in Glynne Street. Money was short for them for a while, but they were happy with their new life in Bolton. I got to see and to know my little sister, as the woman she had become. Adrian was getting to know the new family that he had married into.

Richard got on really well with Adrian and liked him so much, he soon offered him a job with the discos as a roadie. He also taught him some of the art of being a DJ. Adrian had experience in the building trade and, just like Richard, he was also very good with a hammer and screwdriver. He came in handy with some of the home improvements, which Richard was always doing around the house. With a crowbar and a sledgehammer, he helped Richard remove our old-fashioned tiled fireplace in the front room. He also helped to design and build a new stone fireplace, which stretched across the width of the lounge. On top of the stone work, Richard laid some Welsh slates. When the slates were varnished, the effect was amazing, bringing out the beautiful colours within the slate. Adrian plastered the walls of the chimney breasts and alcoves, in a featured modern design. The remaining walls were stripped of their nicotine-stained wallpaper, which must have been on those walls for over twenty years it seemed, the horrid bright orange painted walls were gone too. New carpets and a new three-piece suite finished off our new cosy front room. It was certainly a vast improvement to the room it once was. I was so proud of my man, and the home he had created for us.

While Adrian was out with Richard at a show, Andrea would be at my house waiting on their return. We spent the night drinking tea, chatting and watching television. Andrea was soon addicted to the television programme 'Dallas,' just as much as I was. We had been particularly engrossed in the episode, which included the shooting of JR

Ewing! The programme had ended before we could see who it was that had shot him! It ended with the mystery of who shot JR.?

Everywhere we went we would hear people talking about Dallas, and who shot JR Ewing. My theory was that Cliff Barns had shot him. I thought this because they had hated each other for years. Despite this, I was conscious that JR's wife, Sue Ellen, knew she was being cheated on. She had a motive, so it could have been her.

I didn't like JR Ewing. I thought he was an evil villain and a cheater. He hurt a lot of people around him so he deserved to be shot. There were so many suspects who could have shot him. It was an exciting plot in my favourite TV programme. The plot was so engaging that everyone was talking about it and engrossed in the mystery. I started seeing tee-shirts, on sale in the stores in the town centre, with the logo printed on the front, 'WHO SHOT JR?' Lots of people were wearing them. I didn't although the suspense of the show was so addictive, I couldn't wait for the outcome when we would finally find out who had shot JR Ewing!

Richard still worked for the newspaper and had worked hard on an advertising campaign promoting the local Odeon cinema. He created a full-page advert, which did really well for the company. That being the case, he was presented with a few free tickets for family and friends to see a newly released film called 'Kramer vs Kramer.' Excited and dressed in a brand-new maternity dress, I proudly showed off my very swollen tummy and we took our seats at the cinema. Alan and Josie were given tickets so they too came to see the film. We all sat together on the same row.

The film starred Dustin Hoffman and Meryl Streep and a little boy actor called Justin Henry. It told the story of a couple's divorce after the wife, Meryl Streep, had left the house, her husband, Dustin Hoffman, and her very young son Billy. They gradually learned to cope and develop a strong bond as father and son. After a year away from the family home, the wife returned for Billy. A bitter custody battle ensued. The court decided that it was in the child's best interest, to be raised by the mother. On the day that she returned to collect Billy, she realised that the best place for her son was with his father. That being the case, she couldn't bear to take custody of him. I cried buckets. It was such a great film with a happy ending.

I thought it was an awful thing for her to walk out on her child. I couldn't ever imagine walking out on my child. My child was a part of me, my whole life would be encompassed by her. I couldn't ever imagine not being a mummy. My children would be my whole life. The father in the film developed a really strong bond with his son. This bond would have been so damaged, if it had been lost by his mother taking him away. I thought the mother did what she knew was going to be the best thing for her son — leaving him living with his father.

Richard was a good father to my child. They had a strong bond. However, I would never leave my child. The traumas of my childhood still haunted me, until I looked into the little face of my child and saw the love in her eyes. She needed me, she needed my love, she needed me to show her the love and devotion that I had known nothing about throughout my childhood.

August arrived with some really warm sunshine. With only around five weeks left of my pregnancy, I was feeling fat and hot all day and night. It was difficult to sleep. I would wake up at times with cramps in my legs. I would have to jump out of bed and dance around the bedroom on my tip toes until the pain went. At times, Richard would rub my legs, easing the pain. Then we would drift back to sleep in each other's arms.

The hot weather brought swarms of wasps everywhere. They would come into the house, despite the amount of fly spray I used to kill them — I hated wasps! I was so afraid of Deborah getting stung one day, as she played in the sunshine. I watched her, playing with her dolly and pram. Shandy was by her side keeping a watchful eye over her, or was it that biscuit in her hand that Shandy was after? Deborah was chatting away to herself, in our backyard, while I watched proudly from my kitchen window doing the washing up. All of a sudden three angry looking wasps appeared on the window in front of me. I jumped with fright and grabbed my wet soapy dish cloth. I collected all three in the cloth and left them to die on the window sill. I would dispose of them later when they would surely have died.

Hours later, after I had been distracted by other chores and the wasps were a distant memory, I picked up my dishcloth from the window sill and instantly felt sharp stinging sensations in my hand. I had been stung three times! I screamed my head off. The pain in my hand was

450

horrendous! I didn't realise it would hurt so badly. I'd forgotten all about those horrid wasps, I thought they would surely have died underneath that soapy dish cloth. I got so worried about my baby and whether the poison from the wasp stings would affect my pregnancy. I was frantic. My hand was slowly beginning to swell like a balloon. Richard decided to ring the maternity unit for advice. He asked them whether it would cause any problem for my pregnancy. After being reassured by the midwives at the hospital, I was advised to use TCP or vinegar on the area. I began to relax, and to my relief the swelling around my hand began to go down after a few hours.

Two days later, I was awakened by the sound of Richard's alarm clock ringing in my ears. I rolled over and tried to get back to sleep, I didn't want to get up just that minute. Richard was up and getting ready for work. Just as I was nodding off again, I heard Shandy barking downstairs. I had no choice, I had to get up and let her out into the backyard. By the time I had arrived downstairs, Shandy was scratching at the back door. She was wagging her tail frantically when she saw me, she was looking very eager to get outside. I opened the door and out she shot like a bullet. She must have been bursting for a wee, I thought to myself. I stood waiting for her to finish and come back inside. My back ached, and I felt so tired, I just wanted to get back in bed. Shandy started sniffing at the back gate and pacing up and down the yard, making weird whining sounds. I called out to her and tried to bribe her with a biscuit to come in but she seemed to be ignoring me. All at once she ran towards the back gate and jumped right over it. It was almost five feet high.

She was gone. I was so shocked; she had never done that before. I rushed to put my shoes on. I called out to Richard that Shandy had run off and I was going to look for her. Dressed only in my nightdress and dressing gown, I rushed out into the yard and down the cobbled back street. I couldn't see her anywhere. Then I heard her bark, at the other side of the park, at the bottom of the street. She knew her way to the park as we regularly walked her down there. I didn't want to go chasing her all the way down there in my dressing gown, so I went back home.

Richard was up and making a brew. He said that she would come back if we just left the gate open for her. He was right, within half an hour she was back with her tail between her legs looking very guilty. She lay down in her bed sheepishly, as if waiting to be told what a naughty girl she had been.

The idea of going back to bed soon left my mind, particularly when I heard Deborah getting out of her bed. As I walked down the stairs with Deborah, my back ached and I experienced a sharp pain; a twinge in my tummy. It soon went away so I ignored it. My baby wasn't due for another two weeks so I put it down to wind or one of those 'Braxton Hicks.' Such things are usually experienced for a few weeks before the baby is born.

While I was making Deborah's breakfast, I had another twinge that stopped me in my tracks. It seemed stronger than the last one, but once again I ignored it.

A few minutes later, just as Richard was leaving for work, another twinge arrived and I had to hold onto Richard for a moment. He asked me what was wrong. I couldn't speak. The twinge went away and I began to tell him I had experienced a few of these twinges but they had gone.

Before he could get through the door, I had another twinge. Richard then said that we'd better ring the hospital. I started to watch the clock to start timing the twinges to see if they could be labour pains. The timing was nine to ten minutes.

Deborah had finished her breakfast. Richard started to get her dressed just in case we had to rush off to the hospital. Inside, I was slowly beginning to panic, I wasn't due for another two weeks. The pains were regular but not intense. I wasn't sure whether they were labour pains or not. The midwives at the hospital suggested that I could possibly be in labour and to arrange an ambulance to take us to the maternity unit. The time then was ten minutes past nine.

As arranged, Richard had to take Deborah to Brenda's house. She was Richard's sister-in-law. She had agreed to look after Deborah when the time came. Alone in my house, I was scared. I began to shake with fear and became very anxious.

As another pain arrived, so did my tears. I kept thinking that there was something wrong. I wasn't due for two more weeks, was there something wrong? I couldn't get it out of my mind. It was nine-thirty, where was Richard? Brenda only lived at the bottom of the street. What was taking him so long?

The pains were strong at that point. I began to pace up and down my living room to get me through the pain. From one side of the room to the other, I paced. I tried to concentrate on counting, until the pain went away. Then as soon as it went there was another pain following on immediately after. At nine-forty, Richard arrived back home.

"I think you'd better phone for an ambulance now, this baby is on its way!" I told him this just as I had started to pace up and down my lounge once more.

At ten to ten the ambulance still hadn't arrived. The pain was so strong that I was beginning to feel the urge to push. Richard then suggested that we didn't wait for the ambulance any longer and guided me out to his car. He drove at a speed up Plodder Lane to the hospital. During the short journey the urge to push was really strong. It felt like the baby was about to be born right there in Richard's car. I lifted the lever, at the side of the seat, to lower the back so I could lie down. I kept saying to Richard, "Hurry up the baby's coming!"

Richard kept flashing his lights as he sped up the road towards the Princess Anne Maternity Unit. Within five minutes we had arrived. He pulled up abruptly outside the main entrance of the maternity unit. Grabbing his keys, from the ignition, he got out of the car and helped me out. He left his car doors wide open and we made our way into the unit. I could hardly walk as we struggled through to the corridor that led to the delivery suite. This baby was on its way!

A porter appeared from nowhere with a wheelchair and asked me to sit in it and he would quickly wheel me round. My protests were ignored and I was placed in the chair and off we went. It felt as if I was sitting on my baby's head, I was so uncomfortable.

To my relief we were greeted by three midwives who directed me into a delivery suite. At that point Richard went to move his car into a more suitable parking space. I frantically kept telling the midwives, "My baby's coming, it's coming! I'm not due for two more weeks, something's wrong, what's wrong? I'm pushing." The urge to push was so strong. I was so scared and shaking, the tears rolled down my cheeks as the midwives tried to reassure me. At the same time, they helped me to get undressed. It took all three of the midwives to lift my dress over my head and get me into a gown and onto the bed. Richard arrived in the room just in time. With one more big enormous push my baby arrived.

It was ten o'clock in the morning on Tuesday 19th August 1980 and my baby was born.

"It's a girl," the midwives said. They wrapped her up in a towel and placed her in my arms. She was so beautiful and the image of Deborah when she was born. I counted all her fingers and toes. She was perfect in every way. Richard was by my side, nestled in close to me, as we inspected our new little bundle. The midwife then asked us what we were going to call her. Richard looked at me. Neither of us knew what to say. We hadn't settled on a girl's name. Richard was adamant that we were going to have a boy this time. I wanted a boy too, for Richard's sake. We both wanted to call him Nicholas, which was Richard's middle name. We hadn't chosen a girl's name.

We had a conversation a few months previously. We thought that we should decide on a girl's name too. Richard just kept saying, "It will be a boy this time."

So, he wouldn't choose a girl's name but came up with a suggestion that I didn't like at all. Richard mentioned that his mum had lost a baby when he was around two years old; a stillborn baby girl. She called the baby Lyndsey. He went on to say that if we named our child after her it would make his mum very happy. I wasn't happy that he could suggest such a thing. I was horrified. I didn't want to name my daughter after his dead sister. I felt sorry for his mum, for having lost her baby girl, but there was just no way I could ever do that.

Richard had a blank expression on his face but I could tell what he was thinking. Before he could make that same suggestion again, I said to him, "What about Nichola?" Richard raised his eyebrows in approval.

"Yes," he said. "Nichola."

Within half an hour after Nichola was born, Richard was kissing us both goodbye and was heading through the door and going back to work. I didn't want him to go quite so soon. I tried to plead with him to stay just a bit longer, but he said he was busy at work and he had to leave. He said that everything had happened so quickly that morning that he hadn't even rung into work, to let them know that he wouldn't be in, so he needed to go. I took his explanation and he left.

As I held my precious second little baby daughter in my arms, I couldn't believe how lucky I was to have two perfect children. I was a mum of two. I was unbelievably happy. I did wish that my mum was here.

It was ten forty-five and I was ready to be taken upstairs onto the postnatal ward. The same porter, who had brought me onto the delivery suite, came to my room with a wheelchair to take me up to the ward.

"Hello again," he said, "you don't mess about do you?" I smiled and shook my head.

I became settled in my hospital bed, on the postnatal ward. I began to feel desperately alone, despite the other three mums in the same bay. Richard had left too early. Why did he have to leave so soon? He could have stayed just a little bit longer. I knew he was disappointed that I didn't have a boy. I could sense his disappointment. I could see it in his eyes. I was disappointed. I wanted a son too, a brother for Deborah. She had a sister instead. I am the mother of two prefect little daughters and I was elated. I intended to have two more children in the future, that was my dream, so maybe next time we would have a little boy.

I was missing Deborah. I gazed at my new baby, sleeping soundly in her cot at my side. I loved Deborah so much. The love I had inside had always been just for her. Where was I ever going to find the same love, I needed for my new baby daughter? My love was overflowing for Deborah. Tears filled my eyes once more as Nichola stirred in her cot and woke for a feed. She was hungry. She needed her mummy. As I held her to my breast, she suckled. I was content. She needed me; I was her mummy.

As she suckled, content in my arms, I looked out from my bed at the clear blue sky through the long window that stretched out along the side of the ward. The summer sun was high in the sky and beaming down through the panes. It filled the room with the sweltering heat. I did wish that my mum was there.

I was suddenly interrupted from my daydreaming by a loud familiar voice. I turned towards the doorway and there stood Andrea. She was dressed in a nightdress and dressing gown. Frowning in disbelief, I asked her what she was doing there. I wanted to jump off that bed and hug her so tightly, but I was confined to my bed for another few hours. My eyes began to fill as I held out my arm towards her. The isolation and sadness that I was feeling disappeared as we hugged each other. She began to tell me that she had been brought into the hospital because she had high blood pressure. A nurse had just told her that there was a woman down the corridor that looked just like her so she came to investigate. Andrea smiled and said that she couldn't believe that I had given birth before her, when she was due before me. Andrea sat with me, cooing over Nichola, and getting more and more excited about her imminent arrival. Andrea's blood pressure had now gone back to normal, so she was allowed to go home, when Adrian arrived to collect her.

The next day I was allowed to go home with Nichola. I was ready and waiting and very eager to get home to Deborah. It wasn't long before Richard arrived. I'd missed Deborah so much; I couldn't wait to see her.

The house was filled with visitors over the next few days, even my dad came to see his new granddaughter, Nichola. With him, came Laura, now ten years old and growing up fast.

I remembered the time when Laura was born. It seemed just like yesterday when I first saw her lying in her carry-cot at the side of the fire in the front room of Shackleton Grove. She had a mass of jet-black hair and chubby cheeks. I still remembered how she smelt of talcum powder when I held her. Today Laura was cuddling my new baby daughter, Nichola, in her arms just as I had done all those years ago with Laura.

Andrea and Adrian were regular visitors also. Andrea was preparing herself for the birth of her baby. She grew more fed up with waiting every time I saw her. I would distract her, from her impatience, with some useful baby practice. I allowed her to change Nichola's nappy and I showed her how to fasten up a Babygro.

At almost nineteen years old, Andrea did seem a little immature at times, possibly because of everything that she had been through in life from a very young age. I was sure that Adrian was the strength behind their relationship and would be there for her if she was to face any of the problems she had experienced when she was younger. Together, I believed that the two of them would make great parents and be a happy family.

I did wish that my mum had taken the time to come and visit us. I had been home with my new baby for just over a week when Richard came back from work and informed me that he had been to the Births,

Deaths and Marriages Department, at the town hall in Bolton, and registered Nichola's birth. I was quite upset that he hadn't taken me along with him. I felt that I should have been there to register my child; I was her mother! I could not believe that the office allowed him to register Nichola's birth without me being there. I was her mother and we weren't married so I could not believe he was allowed to do that.

We had words. He said that he didn't need to have me there and didn't want me to have all the stress of getting two children ready and dragging them all the way down to the town centre, so he saved me a job. When he showed me the new birth certificate, for our daughter, I was horrified. He had named our daughter Nichola Lyndsey, against my wishes. I was distraught. I couldn't believe he had given her that name. I didn't want his dead sister's name to be given to my daughter at all, not even as a middle name. I thought it would be a bad omen. We had discussed it many times but he had totally gone against my wishes. He had also given Nichola his surname. This also shocked me, as I had given Deborah my surname. I thought it best to have both children's' names the same as mine, until we were actually married. I questioned his reasons for that decision, and he continued to tell me that we would soon be getting married so we would all have the same name. This way we would only have to apply for a new birth certificate for Deborah and have her name changed. I did not like the fact that he had done that without telling me. He had not taken any notice at all of what I had wanted, and what indeed we had discussed. I was so angry with him, but once again I took his explanation in the hope of it coming true, soon.

One day, during a visit from Adrian and Andrea, Adrian mentioned to Richard that there was an issue that he had been reading about in the newspaper, that had been really bothering him. He started to mention that a laboratory in Cambridge was performing cruel experiments on animals. There was a large group of people protesting about what the laboratory was doing to a lot of defenceless creatures. Adrian felt that he had to do something to support their cause. Richard listened as Adrian began to tell him of the vivisectionists and the suffering that these poor animals had to endure. There were all sorts of cruel experiments that were performed on them. Some animals had soap and shampoo and other products placed in their eyes. Some animals had a mask attached to their faces which forced them to breathe cigarette smoke. Some animals were injected with different diseases to see what happened to them. There were mice, hamsters, cats, dogs, monkeys, and even sheep that were being held in cages in these laboratories to be experimented on by those evil vivisection scientists. The fate of most of these poor animals was death, or at least brain damage, all in the name of science!

Within a couple of days, Richard had arranged to join the anti-vivisection protest march in Cambridge. He had help from some friends, including my brother Paul, who was out of the army and had married Sylvia. They had a young baby at that time. The twelve men hired a minibus and travelled through the night to Cambridge. They planned to take part in the protests and it was their intention to make an early morning raid on the laboratory. Their intention was to free the animals from their cages and from the cruelty of those scientists. They were due back home later that night.

While they were away, Andrea stayed at my house. She was very heavily pregnant and could have given birth at any time. The whole day went by so quickly, with no word at all from our men down in Cambridge. Andrea and I spent the evening watching television. We watched 'Coronation Street,' 'Sale of the Century' and then my favourite, an episode of 'Dallas.' I was addicted to watching Dallas, even more so since JR had been shot, it was still a mystery as to who it was that had actually shot him.

We expected our men back late that night but they didn't arrive, so we went to bed in the hope that we would be woken by them on their return.

The morning arrived with no sign of Richard or Adrian. We hadn't been worried the previous night, when we went to bed, but we had started to wonder where they were by the time it was morning. We hadn't had any phone calls or any contact whatsoever with them since they had left. We started to worry about whether they'd had an accident on the motorway. We convinced ourselves that it was a long way down there and that they might have managed to get some sleep before they travelled back.

Later that afternoon, all the men had returned and were sitting in my front room drinking tea. They had horrendous stories of what they had encountered in the laboratory after the protesters had forced their way in. There were hundreds of people at the protest, from all over the country. They all had one aim and that was to make their way into the laboratory and free the animals. Hundreds of poor defenceless animals in cages were stacked high in clinical rooms waiting for the next cruel experiment to be performed on them. Most of the cages were opened and some of the animals were freed. Then the place was full of police and lots of protesters, including our men, were arrested as they made their way out of the grounds. They were kept in the cells overnight and released that morning.

When they had left the police station, people from the press were waiting to interview them and to take photographs of the protesters for their newspapers. Some photographs, showing all twelve of the anti-vivisectionists from Bolton, made their way into the Bolton Evening News. Richard, Adrian, Paul and the rest, had been clearly disturbed and seemed traumatised for weeks by what they had seen down there that day.

Later that evening, when Adrian was taking Andrea back home to their house, her waters broke and she went into labour. It was August 28th 1980 and Andrea gave birth to a healthy baby boy; she called him Kevin. The love they both had for him was clearly displayed right from the start. He was adorable.

When Nichola was just four weeks old, I became increasingly worried that there was something wrong with her. Kevin, her little baby cousin, was getting chubbier. Nichola didn't seem to be putting on any weight at all. I was beginning to notice a big difference between them both.

I was breastfeeding Nichola and also Andrea was breastfeeding Kevin too. It was nature's way. We had been advised of this all the way through our pregnancies, it was better for the baby than the powdered milk. It was instinct, so nothing could go wrong we thought. Kevin seemed to be gaining lots of weight and seemed to be hungry all the time. He also cried quite a lot to be fed regularly; whereas Nichola seemed to sleep quite a lot, she seemed pale and lethargic, and didn't seem to cry at all. My breast seemed swollen with milk, so I knew I was producing milk for her, and they would leak too, all the time. My milk would pour out

459

and squirt everywhere when I was in the shower. It would be so embarrassing sometimes. If I was in a supermarket, I would have to hide the two wet patches on my blouse and hide my embarrassment too. I had no idea how to stop that from happening.

When Nichola was feeding, she would only be on the breast for a few minutes before she would fall fast asleep. Sometimes she would sleep past her feeding times and I would have to wake her to feed her. She didn't seem very interested in feeding at all. In contrast, my little nephew, Kevin seemed to be feeding all the time. Andrea would say he was a greedy boy. I thought maybe, because he was a boy and stronger somehow, that this was the reason. My baby girl was so good and seemed contented after each feed, I didn't feel there was a problem and assumed she was feeding well. Despite this, I decided to take her to the local baby clinic in Farnworth to have her weighed and ask the nurses to check her over, to put my mind at rest.

At the clinic, I was shocked to find that Nichola only weighed 5lbs 7ozs. Worse still, the weight measurement included her nappy. Instantly, I was hysterical and had to be taken into another room with my baby. At that point, Nichola was examined by the nurses. Nichola was 6lbs at birth, so it was very clear that she had lost quite a lot of weight since then. Something was wrong with my baby. Despite the nurses being reassuring and telling me not to worry, I was worried. One of the nurses suggested that I feed her there and then in the clinic. After which her weight would be measured again, to see how much she was taking from me during a feed. After a long twenty minutes of feeding my sleepy daughter in the clinic room, she was weighed again. To my horror, there was only half an ounce difference in the measurements. For some unknown reason she wasn't taking enough milk from me, she seemed too exhausted to feed and fell asleep in my arms. This was the way it was each time I would feed her. I thought it was normal. All the books told me it was the most natural way of feeding a baby. The books stated clearly that the process was instinctive. Why was it going wrong for me, I thought to myself? I thought I was a failure and such a bad mother that I didn't realise that she was losing weight.

The nurses then told me that I should take her home and they would arrange for a health visitor to come to my house later that afternoon to

460

check her over. I rushed home in tears. I couldn't understand why this was happening.

By the time the health visitor had arrived, Richard was home from work and had become as worried as I was about our new baby. I sat on the edge of my settee and watched the nurse undress Nichola and examine her. She then weighed my baby again. The nurse obtained the same weight as the clinic had done. Nichola didn't seem to have any energy at all while the nurse was checking her. She didn't cry or make any sound. The nurse seemed quiet. I was trembling. I knew there was something wrong. Then the health visitor broke the awful silence.

"I think we should get this little lady to the hospital, just to be on the safe side. Can I use your phone please, to ring the hospital?" She stood and lifted the receiver and dialled the number. I became hysterical, I was trembling. Richard came to hold me but I pushed him away. I didn't want his comfort; I didn't want him near me.

"It's all your fault!" I screamed at him. "I told you we shouldn't have called her Lyndsey! My daughter is ill because of you!" The bad omen had come back to take my child, is what I thought at that time!

Tears streamed down my face. I was inconsolable as I held my baby in my arms. The health visitor left after giving us her notes and instructions for the hospital. I was too distraught to listen. I was too distraught to speak. I thought that my baby was going to die, just like Richard's mum's baby Lyndsey.

At the hospital, we were directed to the children's ward. Nichola was placed in a huge metal cot that looked more like a cage than a baby's cot. She looked so tiny and so fragile lying there. I was sitting at her side stroking her hair. Before long the doctors arrived to examine her again. Nichola slept through it all and seemed too weak to even open her eyes. The doctors asked me lots of questions about my breastfeeding and whether I thought I had enough milk. I couldn't answer their questions about my milk supply but told them what it was like for me and of the times when I would leak everywhere. It was difficult for me to tell just how much milk she was taking at one feed. I did feel that she had taken enough when she would fall asleep in my arms. I thought I had enough milk by the embarrassing way it would leak out all the time.

The doctors then said that they thought that maybe she hadn't been getting enough milk from me and suggested that some mums find it difficult to breastfeed for one reason or another. This usually applied to busy mums, like me, who were running around after another child as well.

I was a busy mum. I needed to be in a routine. It was important for me to keep the house clean and to make sure Richard's shirts were washed, ironed and hung on coat hangers in his wardrobe. He had to have his meal on the table when he came home, which wasn't always possible, but he never protested either. I was tired, but I felt he was working hard with two jobs to provide for me and our children. I felt it was my duty to look after him and our family. I loved him, and the family home he had created for us. I thought at that time that I was being a good wife and mother. However, I realised I was a failure at breastfeeding my baby. I was not feeding my baby enough. I became inconsolable again when I realised, I could have lost my baby. I believed it would have been my fault. No fault of any bad omen, it was down to me, I was a bad mother.

As my tiny daughter lay sleeping in the huge cot I cried. I kept telling her I was sorry, but sorry didn't seem to be enough, to make things better for her. I was emotional and instantly filled with so much love for her, I didn't realise it was inside me. I prayed to God to help me to make her better so I could take her home, I wanted my baby well again. I felt exhausted.

A baby bottle was prepared for Nichola, with two ounces of baby milk. She drank the lot, and a couple of hours later Nichola woke and cried for another feed. It was strange to hear her cry as she'd hardly ever cried. When the nurse told me that she possibly didn't have the energy to cry, I cried. Why didn't I realise?

After a few days in hospital, with Nichola being fed with baby milk, she had gained weight and we were allowed home. Nichola seemed like a different baby; she was alert and lively and getting noisier as the hours went by. As I got her ready, in her little pink frilly dress and pink pram suit, to take her home, she looked at me and smiled. It was her first smile; my heart exploded in my chest. I cried again with warming tears of joy.

With the regular weight checks, at the baby clinic, and to my relief, my daughter was thriving.

At the end of September that year we were shocked to discover that

Shandy was pregnant. I initially thought she was getting too fat and needed to go on a diet. But late one night she had climbed up on the settee, beside me, when the house was so quiet and Richard was out. She rested her head on my lap and drifted off to sleep. I watched her sleeping while I stroked her body. I noticed her tummy was very swollen. I placed my hand over her tummy and after a while thought I felt a little kick. I soon became distracted, from my episode of Dallas, and watched her swollen tummy, in amazement. She was pregnant and I could see and feel those babies wriggling around inside her. We had kept a close eye on her since the time she jumped over the gate on that morning when I went into labour with Nichola. Richard had made the gate higher so she couldn't jump over it again. Whenever we took her out, it was on her lead, so she didn't have any opportunity to run away. That must have been the very same morning that she had become pregnant! I realised that it wouldn't be much longer before the pups would arrive.

I had to make some plans for Deborah's third birthday, which would come about in the next few days. I had been down the road and visited Farnworth library in search of a recipe book. I had wanted to make a birthday cake for Deborah that year to save some money. This would be instead of having one made at the local bakery. My neighbour, Diane, had previously given me a couple of recipes for rock buns, scones and little buns that had jam in the middle. After spending the whole afternoon baking one day, and following Diane's recipe instructions, the rock buns were so heavy, they really did look and feel like rocks! I was sure they would break some teeth if we ate them, and the scones refused to rise for me at all. I wasn't sure what I was doing wrong. Nonetheless, I was adamant I was going to keep trying to bake a birthday cake for my little girl.

As Deborah's birthday approached, I followed all the instructions from the recipe book step by step. I even sat by my oven, watching the clock on the wall, and trying to time it to perfection. I was tempted to peek in the oven a couple of times just to check to see if it was rising, but I resisted the temptation. To my relief, the cake had risen well and smelled delicious. That night, when Deborah was tucked up in her bed fast asleep, I made a topping of icing and spread it over the top and sides with a pallet knife. It had soon set so I was able to place the iced lettering, reading 'HAPPY BIRTHDAY Deborah,' in a circle all the way around the top of the cake. I finished my design with three iced flowers and three candles in the middle. I was quite pleased with myself at my first attempt at making a birthday cake. I thought it looked good. I hoped that Deborah would like it too.

On Monday the 6th of October 1980 my first-born daughter was three years old. Those years had gone by so quickly. It just seemed like yesterday when I was bringing her home from the hospital. So much had happened since then. I was a mum of two daughters. I was so happy with my little family and the man that I loved so much. I had so much to be thankful for.

At two o'clock in the afternoon, Deborah's birthday guests started to arrive. Mandy was the first with her son Craig; Diane came with little Stuart; my sister Andrea arrived with her chunky four-week-old baby Kevin in her arms; my cousin Julie came too with her very talkative little boy Mark. Mark and Stuart rushed straight through the house and out into the back yard. There they played with their pretend swords in that rare October sunshine.

Richard was surprised to see both his brothers, Lee and Keith, arrive as he hadn't seen Keith for a while. Keith had a new girlfriend called Pat. It was lovely to finally meet her and her three children Beth, Anthony and Robbie. They were so polite, well-mannered and friendly. I thought what lovely children they were. They were all warmly introduced to their new six-week-old niece, Nichola, who then received lots of cuddles from them all. This came as a welcome hands-free relief to me. Lola, Richard's mum, came too. My mum had also been invited. I really hoped that I would not be disappointed by her not responding to my invitation.

The house was full of friends and family, enjoying the birthday buffet of sausage rolls, egg sandwiches, cheese and little pickled onions on cocktail sticks. I had spent some considerable time preparing this food for them all. The birthday cake was, of course, the star food attraction. After the candles had been lit, we all sang Happy Birthday to Deborah. She then made the first supervised cut with a knife into the cake and it was shared around to all her guests to devour. There were lots of approving nods afterwards. It was hard to hide my disappointment when my mum didn't share in our daughter's celebrations. Despite this, the huge smiles from Deborah lifted my spirits and filled my heart with the joys of motherhood that I was sure my mum would realise, if only she had attended.

Towards the end of October Shandy went into labour. She was restless and had not eaten for a whole day. I had prepared a space under the stairs for her to give birth when the time came. I filled it with some old blankets and newspapers as bedding. Shandy seemed to like being under the stairs; it was her safe hideaway where it was dark and quiet, away from noisy children.

The last couple of days of her pregnancy were spent resting in her new bed, only emerging to feed or to visit the garden. At times we would hear her scratching, tugging and rearranging the bedding, to make herself more comfortable it seemed. We knew her time was near.

The house was so quiet. Both my babies were fast asleep upstairs. Richard was out at work as the DJ at the Bus Inn, in Bolton. I busied myself with the huge pile of ironing in the kitchen and at the same time, I kept a close eye on Shandy.

It was late as I reached for the last of Richards' shirts to iron; it was the blue and white striped one with a white collar. I hated ironing that particular shirt, I always saved it until the very last. It would always make me feel so dizzy when I ironed it. I wasn't sure why?

I had been listening to Shandy while I was ironing. She was panting more it seemed and becoming more restless. I looked at her lying there in the nest that she had created for her babies. She was panting very quickly. It was obvious to me that she was in pain. Her eyes were wide and looked at me as if to plead with me to help her. I felt useless. I placed a bowl of water at her side and without even standing to her feet she stretched her head towards the bowl and began to lap the water.

It was very late. I was tired and needed to go to bed but I didn't want to leave Shandy. I decided to sit with her for a while. I thought it would reassure her in some way that everything was going to be fine if she knew I was near to her. I didn't want to get too close or interfere, just in case she protested in some way. I helplessly watched her fidgeting and she appeared to be in so much pain. I yawned; my eyelids were beginning to feel so heavy. I was so tired. All at once she raised her tummy and stretched out her back legs and made a sort of whining noise. She then relaxed and kept looking at her back end. It seemed as if she was trying to push those pups out. I was sure she was having contractions. Shandy was about to give birth I thought.

Ten long minutes later there was a gush of fluid from Shandy's behind. After a few pushes the first pup was born. Within the hour there were four little pups born.

Richard arrived home just in time. With a huge smile, he watched wide eyed as the last puppy arrived safe and sound. We had to drag ourselves away from their side to go off to bed. We left Shandy alone, happy and content, as she tended to her brood. It had been a very long day.

A few days later, on the morning of my twenty-second birthday, Richard woke up and snuggled into me and kissed me on my cheek. He whispered, "Happy birthday Maggie," in my ear. Still exhausted and sleepy, I stiffened and hoped that he wouldn't start to feel amorous and want to make love before he left for work. I kept my eyes tightly shut, I didn't want to be woken up, and I certainly didn't want to be making love that morning, birthday or no birthday! I was warm and cosy, my babies were still fast asleep; I didn't want to get up. I drifted back off to sleep.

When I woke to the sound of my children, Richard had left for work. The cup of tea on the bedside cabinet was a lovely surprise. The tea had gone cold but I felt all warm inside and smiled. I thought to myself what a lovely thing for him to do, he was so thoughtful at times.

Despite it being my birthday, there was no change to my day, it was just another day. Richard and I had made no plans for going out for that evening to celebrate. I wasn't happy about leaving the children with a babysitter. I would have spent the whole time worrying about them while I was away from them, so it was easier to stay at home.

I was busy with my usual morning routine with the children. I also paid attention to the pups, at just over a week old they were getting noisier and more active around their bed. They were so cute; it was fascinating to sit and watch them. Everyday there was a change in them; they were growing so fast; it wouldn't be long before they crawled out of their bed under the stairs.

Early that afternoon Richard arrived home for his lunch. He was carrying a large flat cardboard box.

"This is your birthday present," he said, as he laid the box on the coffee table in front of me. I had just finished feeding Nichola and she had fallen asleep in my arms. I laid her on the settee at the side of me and stared wide eyed and excitedly at the box that contained my birthday gift. Deborah was at my side eagerly waiting to see what was inside.

I lifted the lid. Inside was a large brass wall clock. I frowned slightly and then smiled. Richard removed the framed picture, which was hanging on the chimney breast wall above the fireplace. He then lifted the clock out of the box and hung it in the place of the picture.

"Do you like it?" he asked. I smiled at him and nodded my approval. I told him that it was a lovely present and so perfect for our chimney breast.

Later that evening, my daughters, having had their bath, were ready for bed. We snuggled together in the armchair in front of the fireplace. Nichola was in my arms, having her bottle, Deborah was at my side listening intently to her favourite bedtime story. Richard had been upstairs getting ready for his DJ work at the Bus Inn. Before he left, he leaned over and kissed me and said, "See you later." He kissed his two tired little daughters and walked out through the door. I sighed.

With my two dozing babies in my arms, I looked up at that brass clock and thought, what a load of cobblers, what a stupid present. It was a daft present for a young twenty-two-year-old woman like me. I was puzzled with his choice of gift. I thought only retired people received brass clocks! It was nice enough and just perfect for the place it was hanging. I did feel a little disappointed when I opened the box earlier that day. I didn't expect a bloody clock!

I would have preferred some nice lingerie, a new dress or chocolates! I would have loved a new dress. I was still wearing my maternity dresses despite Nichola being nearly three months old. It was about time I put them away until the next pregnancy. I sighed a big sigh again and said to myself, 'Happy birthday Maggie.'

Towards the end of November, and after eight long months of waiting, all the world finally found out who shot JR. I was shocked to find out that it was Kirstin who had shot him! Kirstin was Sue Ellen's sister, and JR's mistress! JR had been having an affair with his wife's sister! I knew she played a scheming witch in her role as Kirstin and she had obviously crossed the line by having an affair with her sister's husband. I didn't suspect that it was her who had pulled the trigger. I thought it was Cliff Barnes; he hated JR. Despite this, I had thought that if Sue Ellen had shot JR, I could have understood her anger and the reason why, if she had found out he was having an affair with her own sister. Sue Ellen might have wanted to shoot Kirstin as well for her betrayal. Kirstin framed Sue Ellen and tried to get her out of the way, so she could have JR to herself. Sue Ellen soon realised the game Kirsten had played and went back to Southfork to confront her.

At that point Kirsten had moved in with JR. Kirstin then confessed to shooting JR. As JR was attempting to phone the police, to have her arrested, she revealed that she was pregnant with his baby, and continued to say that it would cause a scandal, if a Ewing child was born in prison. That turned out to be another lie on the part of Kirstin; the plot continued. I was sitting on the edge of my settee throughout the whole episode, it was so exciting.

At the end of November, my sister Andrea's husband Adrian was offered a job back in his home town of Northampton. That being the case, they gave up their house and most of their possessions to move back down there. I was devastated that my sister was leaving to live so far away. I was going to miss her and my little nephew Kevin, so much! In fact, they went to live with Adrian's parents, until they were allocated a council house. We promised each other that we would keep in touch and try to visit regularly.

During the second week of December, I woke up and switched on the television. I was shocked to hear the awful news that John Lennon had been shot and was dead. He had been shot five times outside the Dakota Building in New York, the place where he lived with his wife and little son. I couldn't believe anyone would want to shoot John Lennon — why? It didn't seem to make any sense at all to me at that time. He was married and had a little boy. He was a really good singer and used to be a member of the Beatles before they split up. He went on to be a successful solo singer, as did other members of the Beatles. Why would anyone want to kill a singer? I just couldn't understand it. The police arrested Mark Chapman, the man who shot him, and he was taken to jail.

John Lennon was all over the news. The story was on television, on the radio and in every newspaper for over a week. The whole world was devastated by his death. Other musicians appeared on television expressing the devastation and shock at what had happened. John Lennon's music and that of the Beatles was on every radio channel and I knew then that John would be deeply missed by all the world. I knew in my heart that his music would live on forever. Just like Elvis, John Lennon died before his time, they both left a legacy, namely their music, to be enjoyed by future generations forever.

Just before our Christmas celebrations had begun that year, we had to say goodbye to our lovely puppies. At just over eight weeks old, they were ready to be rehomed. It wasn't difficult to find homes for all of them, they were very cute puppies, but they looked as if they would grow to be quite big dogs. We thought that the pups were most likely to be Labrador and Alsatian crossed.

Richard had placed an advert in his newspaper and we had lots of people calling to come to see them. To my surprise, Mum and Jack visited at that time, unaware that we had puppies. When Jack saw the pups, running around in our backyard, he took a shine to the black and tan pup. It ran straight to him and tugged on his laces. Jack picked him up and said that he wanted him. Mum didn't need any persuading. Before long they were driving home with the new addition to their family. They called him Benny. It would be good to be able to keep in touch with him and watch him grow.

Within a couple of days all the pups were rehomed. Deborah cried when the last puppy left our house as she wanted to keep all of them. I cried too. They had become hard work, so I was relieved that we had found good homes for all of them. Even so I would miss them. When the last pup was taken, the new owner wanted to take Shandy too. After thinking it over for a few days, we agreed that Shandy would be better off with the new family. They took her to live on their farm with plenty of fields to run around in. It was sad to see her go.

I thought at that Christmas, that one of John Lennon's hits would be released, after his death, and go straight in the chart at number one for Christmas. Instead, it was a song called, 'There's no one quite like Grandma,' sung by children from St. Winifred's School choir. I loved it. It was a lovely record that cheered everyone up when they looked into the little faces of all those lovely singing children.

It was surely a blessing to hear the children's choir singing at Christmas time and after what must have been such a dreadful start to December for the family of John Lennon. I was sure that they wouldn't want to be celebrating Christmas at all without him.

Our Christmas was spent at Richard's mum's house in Kearsley. I was beginning to get to know Lola and develop a trust in her again, despite the harsh words that she had once said to me. She was getting to know me and things were better between us.

The table was set, the members of our family took their seats around her huge table to enjoy turkey and all the trimmings. Lola had excelled herself; the food was delicious, everything was perfect. It was the best Christmas ever, there were even some silver coins hidden inside the Christmas pudding.

CHAPTER FIFTY-FOUR
The Truth Finally Revealed

At the start of the previous year, the dreams of our wedding day were at the forefront of our minds. All throughout the year, we hoped that the divorce would finally come through so that we could at last be married once and for all. Despite these thoughts, all we had was a year of disappointment. Towards the end of last year, I was disheartened. I had given up dreaming. I didn't speak of it any more. For me the disappointment was too much to deal with. I refused to spend another year waiting for that same disappointment, a disappointment that I had felt for the past few years. The start of 1981 brought on a New Year's Resolution. Specifically, I, Maggie Gallagher would not allow myself to dream of the freedom that the divorce would bring for Richard. This would bring about an end to all the impatient distress, that I had tried so hard to hide inside me for over five years. I didn't want it to interfere with my life any more. I was a busy mother and housewife. I needed to fill my life caring for Richard and my children. I wanted to fill my life with the joy and happiness of being a mummy, it was far easier than waiting for disappointment year after year. I would never be disappointed with my children. Every day was a joy. They filled my life; they were my life.

Despite not wearing Richard's wedding ring, I knew I was his 'wife to be,' Richard would tell me so. He would call me his 'wife' all the time. I knew our marriage would happen one day in the future, unfortunately, the future seemed a long way off at that time; the wait was endless. Richard was worth the wait, and deserved my patience, I thought.

Being a mum was the most important thing I ever wanted to be. I didn't want to be a teacher or a lawyer, just a mum. The thought of not being able to have children scared me a lot while I was growing up. I would hear lots of stories from friends who had been trying to get pregnant for years. They had given up trying, living their lives without any children to raise. There was also my sister Maureen who had been trying to get pregnant, despite not having a husband or the means of supporting the child that she already had. There were many stories of her miscarriages and whether her stories were true or not, things must have been hard for her. I didn't feel I would have been strong enough to cope with those situations.

I would have preferred to have had Richard's wedding ring on my finger before becoming the mother of his children, but that was not to be. It seemed at that time that my life was back to front. I knew I had to wait to wear Richard's ring.

Looking back over my life, I considered becoming a mother, to be my greatest achievement. It was the best thing I had ever done. I seemed to be a natural mother, I was overflowing with love and devotion for my children. I didn't know where it all came from, or who taught me to love my children unconditionally like that. I know for a fact that it didn't come from my parents.

After I had Nichola, I began to want to be able to do more with my life. I didn't want to just be a housewife and mother, stuck in the house all day, every day. I had left school with no qualifications; I couldn't wait to get out of the place. I walked straight into a factory and worked as a machinist. I was taught a lasting trade and I was quite good at it. I had only been fifteen years old. However, in my mind, all I wanted to be was a wife and mother. I didn't feel I needed any qualifications for that job, only love.

When I became a mother, I knew I was the best mother to my children I could have been. I excelled at being a mother. As a 'wife' to Richard, I knew I had several issues to deal with. I wasn't a good enough 'wife' to stop his cheating. At that time, I believed that I didn't excel in the bedroom, nor did I have any expectation that I should have enjoyed intimacy better myself. It was not until much later that I realised that the fault was with Richard and it was him who could not fulfil me. He would comment on this and call me names, time after time, and those issues must have contributed to his cheating ways.

When I was in primary school, I auditioned for every school play and would take part in every activity after school, mostly because I didn't want to go back to the house, we all called home. I would have preferred to have stayed at school all day and every day. I was very studious, always drawing and I had a vivid imagination. I was quite good at English, so my teacher would tell me. I could write little poems and stories, just like Enid Blyton. I read lots of her books and loved the way her books would take me to another exciting world that I could lose myself in.

At one point our class was given a project. We were asked to create a newspaper and fill it with stories and articles to resemble a real newspaper. The class had to write or draw something to be added to the newspaper. I wrote a story about a house fire that had happened in the area where we lived. I also drew pictures of what I imagined a photograph of the event would have looked like. The flames blazed from the windows. My story and illustrations were placed on the front page of the class newspaper. There was a bold black headline, just like the ones that would appear in the real Bolton Evening News.

That memory of my early school days must have been what first inspired my earliest dreams to become a reporter or a writer. From then on, I always seemed to be either sitting quietly reading or I had a pen in my hand scribbling something down on paper. I was not sure how I came to own a typewriter, but I thought it could possibly have belonged to my older sister Ann. At some point she must have passed it on to me. Another option was that Mum had bought it at a jumble sale at our local church. Despite hating the typing class at secondary school, I loved that typewriter. The typewriters at school were so different from my little blue 'Petite' typewriter. They were so much bigger, and electric, it took a long time to get used to them. I didn't like how some of the actions were quite fast and would make me jump. I remember pressing a button and the paper shot out at the top. It scared me to death. All you could hear in the class was the noise of the keys and the constant pinging from all the typewriters.

Mrs Hayworth, our typing teacher, was horrible. She had bad breath and I didn't like her at all. I spent more time outside the class, sent out for talking, than I did inside trying to type using all my fingers and thumbs. The expectation was to do this without looking at the letters on the keys. I could only use one finger from each hand to type a word. I could never look away from the keys when I typed.

When I was in my teens, I would pretend to be a famous writer just like Enid Blyton or Agatha Christie. I think they were the only two authors that I had heard of at that time. The exception being William Shakespeare. His work was confusing to read. I couldn't understand the words he used, it seemed to be a different language.

Typing on that little blue Petite typewriter, and sitting at a makeshift desk, in my bedroom, I started writing a children's story. It took months to write. When it was finished, it was hidden away at the back of my cupboard. I didn't have the confidence to do anything with it or allow anyone else to read it back then. Despite this, I kept it in the hope of reading it to my children one day.

Life took over and my writing continued briefly throughout my life: letters, poems, and I kept a diary too whenever possible. I seemed to be able to find the words to write down on paper, far more easily than being able to express my issues verbally. It didn't help to solve any problems but it did help to stop certain issues from clouding my mind. I found a little time each day to write or draw in the silence of my bedroom, isolated, away from the rest of the world and the thoughts of yesterday, creating my dreams for all the tomorrows I had in front of me. I was a dreamer. It was hard to find the time and the solitary, silent space to write once I had become a mother. I had more important pleasing distractions that needed all my attention.

When I had become a mother of two at twenty-one years old, I began to want more from the life I had to live. I felt I needed to achieve qualifications to make my children proud of me in the future. I was content with being a 'stay at home mummy' with my children but despite my contentment at being a mummy, my new goal was to go to college one day and to create a better me. I didn't think that Richard would approve of this as he disapproved of me working and insisted, as much as he could, that I stay at home as a housewife.

Being a 'stay at home mummy' meant I was always on hand to look after other people's children. Diane, my neighbour, started working and would ask me to look after her son Stuart for a few hours a couple of times a week. He was a joy to look after. The opportunity also came along to look after another little girl, throughout the week, so our house became filled with the sound of children's laughter and the noise of children running around. It was hard work and hectic at times having four children to care for each day, however, I was rewarded by their happy faces. I seemed to enjoy the everyday routine, and the money did come in handy with some household bills, although some days it was hard to even get out of the house to do some shopping. It was difficult to take all the children to the shops, this was particularly the case when the weather was bad.

I would imagine how much easier life would be if I was able to drive. I would watch other mums at the supermarkets. They would be loading their cars with all the shopping, their children and pushchairs too! Their lives seemed so much easier than mine. I was having to carry bags of heavy shopping all the way home, through the wind and the rain, as well as pushing a heavy pram and holding onto my child's hand so tightly. At that time my trip to the shops consisted of a sleeping baby in the pram, a child clipped on a pram seat on top of the pram, and a three-year-old child walking at my side holding my hand. The chrome wire tray under the pram would be full to overflowing with the weekly groceries. It was hard work. I just wanted to be like those other mums. If only I was brave enough to learn how to drive our lives would be so much easier.

My sister Ann had passed her test; however, my friend Mandy had failed and had given up driving altogether, saying it was too hard. Richard's mum, Lola, had taken five attempts to pass her driving test. Finally, she managed to pass on the sixth attempt.

A few years previously, I had experienced a little drive of Jack's car on Southport beach, while on a day out with Mum. I wasn't very good. I remember being so nervous, at one point I pressed the accelerator too hard, the car shot forward. Jack shouted, "Brake!" I pressed that brake so hard, we both jolted forward as the car came to a stop. It scared me to death. I had visions of driving right into the sea, despite it being so far away. I didn't think that I would ever be brave enough to get behind a steering wheel again.

Now, almost two years later, I was a mum of two, I was determined to make our lives easier. I had been struggling for long enough, learning to drive was the beginning of my aim for a better future.

Three weeks later my provisional driving licence came through the post. Immediately, I was on the telephone to Mr Brian Hilldrop, the local driving instructor, arranging to have driving lessons. He was the same driving instructor who had taught Richard how to drive. Richard had passed his test the first time and so had his brother. Mr Hilldrop had taught Richard's mum, and other family members, so throughout those years he had become a close friend to all of the family.

On a sunny Wednesday afternoon at the end of April, the afternoon of my very first driving lesson arrived. I was so very nervous. I had been since I had booked the lessons. My stomach had been doing somersaults and I was so close to cancelling the lessons altogether. I was encouraged by Richard who was there once more with those little reminders as to why I wanted to learn to drive. His reassuring words helped me to fight back my fears and made me stronger.

Mr Hilldrop pulled up outside our house in his blue Datsun. Richard was home for lunch, as agreed, as he would be looking after the children each week while I was on my driving lesson.

During my first lesson I was a bag of nerves. Mr Hilldrop had driven us to a quiet side road which was clear of any traffic. He explained some techniques of driving as we made our way there. Then we exchanged seats. I sat behind the steering wheel, listening to all the techniques once more. Mr Hilldrop spoke in a soft voice and his whole face seemed to smile as he spoke. He was calm and very patient as he waited for me to turn the key in the ignition. There was so much to do before I would be able to get the car to move: check that the gears were neutral, handbrake off, mirrors set correctly and signal before moving. He also mentioned the clutch, the brake and the accelerator all before I moved off in the car. How would I ever be able to remember to do all that before driving off? It all seemed so complicated, I thought to myself. I wasn't at all confident that I would even get the car away from the kerb that day. I couldn't even remember anything that he had just told me; his instructions went clean out of my head, my hands were shaking and sweating. I felt so hot, dizzy and clammy.

With the gear in the neutral position and the handbrake on, I turned the key in the ignition. The engine was ready. Then with some more gentle instructions from Mr Hilldrop, I took the handbrake off and the car began to edge slowly forward.

I let out a screech and looked at Mr Hilldrop. I couldn't believe it; I was actually making the car move. I edged slowly forward at a snail's pace. I was in first gear, driving along the long, quiet, tree lined side road. With more instructions from my instructor, I was able to stop the car, then drive around a corner, and continue along the road until we reached another left turn. We finally ended up back where we had started. I had driven in a circle. It seemed to take forever but I had done it. I was driving. I drove around the same route twice more and eventually managed to get in second gear. I was also driving a little faster.

We exchanged seats again and I relaxed once again in the safety of the passenger seat while my instructor drove me back home. The hour lesson was over. I was so very nervous but that nervousness slowly turned to excitement every Wednesday afternoon when it was time for my driving lesson.

As the weeks went by, my driving progressed from quiet little side roads to major roads, with lots of traffic. The more major routes included Plodder Lane and St Peter's Way. I also went beyond Bolton driving into Salford and Strangeways in Manchester. I had never been into those areas before. I was driving on long dual carriageways, with very heavy traffic. I experienced cars overtaking me very fast. There were also buses and huge great big trucks that looked so fierce as they approached and overtook me. I wanted to squeeze my eyes shut tight when I saw them approaching in my mirror, my hands would grip the steering wheel so tightly until my knuckles went white and I felt shaky inside. I was sure Mr Hilldrop could sense my fear. He would say in a calm quiet voice, "Look straight ahead." I knew he was always ready to grab that steering wheel if I strayed out of my lane, as he had done so many times.

On Wednesday 29th July 1981, I had to cancel a driving lesson. It was the wedding day of Prince Charles and Lady Diana Spencer. The wedding took place in St. Paul's Cathedral. It was declared a public holiday and millions of people around the world were watching that special event on the BBC and ITV. There were hundreds of thousands of people lining the streets of London. They all hoped to catch a glimpse of the royal couple. We were fixated on the television for the whole day.

At the end of October, Mr Hilldrop started to prepare me for my test. I was competent at the emergency stop, and the three-point turn, however, when it came to the reversing of the car, it took months for me to be able to do it without the wheels touching the kerb, I just couldn't get it right.

I remember a week before my test date, I was having a lesson but I couldn't seem to get anything right that day. Everything was going wrong. I was hitting the kerbs, I wasn't indicating when I should, I almost went down a one-way street. I even forgot my left from my right at one point and I almost knocked a man off his bike! The more I got things wrong the more stressed and scared I became. I tried to listen carefully to the instructor's comments, but I just wanted to stop the car and run all the way home. Mr Hilldrop raised his voice slightly and said, "I don't know how you are going to be able to pass your test next week!" He told me to pull the car to the side of the road and stop. I burst into tears.

After five minutes, with his calming words, I was able to finish my hour lesson and drive back home. I was not at all confident about passing my driving test the following week. After telling Richard of my performance in the car that afternoon he agreed with me that it was unlikely that I would pass the test. He did advise me not to give up and to carry on until I had passed. The way I felt at that time, I would definitely not want to have any more lessons if I failed that test, I would give up learning to drive once and for all.

The night before my test, my nerves started to appear. I read my highway code booklet from front to back, about four times. Richard had been testing me on all the street and road signs, and I was confidently answering each one and getting them right. Despite this, my mind was full of the problems I had experienced in the previous week's driving. I remembered how upset I had been that day, and how upset the man was when I nearly knocked him off his bike!

I was worried that the following day, I was going to be sitting next to a strange man, who I didn't know, and I would have to drive around in a strange area too. I was scared. The calming voice of Mr Hilldrop wouldn't be there to keep me relaxed if I became nervous. My tutor, who I had trusted for all those months, wouldn't be there at my side. I was sure my nerves would keep me awake that night.

It was Wednesday 16th December 1981, the day of my driving test. I hadn't slept very well, symbols and road signs were flashing through my mind, and my tummy was doing somersaults all night long.

At eleven o'clock, Mr Hilldrop pulled up outside my house. My test was at twelve o'clock, I was to have an hour driving tuition first then my test. I was shaking like a leaf, as Richard hugged me so tightly, before I left the house. Mr Hilldrop smiled as he greeted me in his car. He could tell I was so very nervous, however, as I drove, the nerves seemed to be disappearing. Not only that but with Mr Hilldrop's instructions, I began to drive confidently all the way to Salford and on to the test centre. We drove around the side streets of that area, practising all the manoeuvre s that he had taught me over the last seven months. Finally, it was time for my test.

I pulled into the test centre car park with ease. I didn't expect Mr Hilldrop to ask me to reverse the car into a bay just outside the office. I tutted to myself as I began the manoeuvre. Slowly and to my surprise I did it right, I parked between the two white lines in the bay. Mr Hilldrop said, 'Well done,' and smiled. I smiled back and breathed a sigh of relief.

We left the car and went into the centre. I was introduced to the examiner. I shook his hand and said, "Hello sir." I didn't know what else to say. He was a stern looking gentleman with glasses resting on the end of his nose and bushy eyebrows. He was dressed in a grey suit with a maroon-coloured tie. He wore a waistcoat that seemed too small to stretch around his swollen tummy, the buttons were almost popping open. He had a gold watch on a chain, tucked inside a little pocket, and he was clutching onto a clipboard which he held under his arm. He pulled the watch from his pocket and said, "Shall we go?"

I could feel my nerves coming back to me, my tummy also began to churn with fear. I took a deep breath as I was led outside to start my test. I looked over at Mr Hilldrop as he stood outside the centre, I waved to him and got into the driver's seat. The examiner made himself comfortable in the passenger seat and placed the clipboard on his knee. He took a pen out of the inside pocket of his jacket. Following his instructions, I drove out of the car park, and onward through the streets as directed. I had been driving for around ten minutes, sitting in silence, listening to his instructions carefully. All at once I realised, I hadn't put my seatbelt on. I asked him if I could pull over and put it on, I didn't feel safe without it. He said, "As you wish," and scribbled something down on his clipboard in front of him.

I concentrated on the routine that I had been taught. I pulled the car up at the side of the kerb and fastened my seatbelt. I was confident with that task and hoped I had done everything correctly. I turned the key in the ignition and began to get ready to set off again. To my horror, the car stalled. I was horrified. I began the manoeuvre again, and the car stalled again. I felt my hands begin to tremble as I tried to start again. After the third time that the car had stalled, I realised I must have failed my test after stalling the car three times on the trot. I was shocked and disappointed. I sighed and started the engine again for the fourth time. To my relief, I was on my way. I knew I could have failed my test already but somehow; I didn't feel nervous any more. In fact, I felt slightly angry at myself for stalling the car.

I just wanted to get through the rest of the test as quickly as I could and get back home. The rest of the examination was a blur, but another thing that I did remember was that when I performed the reversing manoeuvre, I didn't touch the kerb at all, it was something I had not been able to do correctly very often during my lessons. Soon I was pulling into the test centre car park once more and parked the car in a bay.

Throughout the examination, I had watched the examiner scribbling on his clipboard, as I drove. I was sitting silently, for what seemed like ages, as he continued writing on that paper. I was imagining him writing 'failed' in huge letters all across the paperwork. I knew I had failed. He turned the pages over on his clipboard and started to show me symbols and pictures of road signs. He asked me what they were. I answered each one correctly. I had studied them all at home for ages, I was confident I knew them all. Then he asked me different questions about driving conditions and what precautions I would take while driving in fog, I answered correctly. The questions seemed to be too easy as I knew all the answers.

The examiner said, "Well, I am pleased to tell you, you have passed." He passed me a sheet of paper, turned quickly and got out of the car. I was ecstatic as I read the large black letters on that sheet of paper that read 'PASSED,' not the word FAILED as I had expected. My heart was beating so fast. I couldn't believe it. I was sure I had failed. I started to shake like a leaf. I was so excited and happy. I couldn't wait to get home to tell Richard. I knew he would be just as pleased as I was. I got out of the car and wanted to jump up and down with excitement. That day felt like the best day of my life. I saw Mr Hilldrop coming towards me, smiling. I wanted to run to him and hug him so tightly, but I just stood there, overwhelmed with emotion, I was so unbelievably happy. He put his arms around me as tears of joy were streaming down my face.

Mr Hilldrop drove back to Farnworth after the test, I would have been too excited to drive after all that emotional excitement. I don't remember much about that journey home, except that I had wanted to get back to Richard, to see his face light up when I told him that I had passed.

When Mr Hilldrop parked his car outside my house, I saw Richard at the window looking out for me. He came to the front door to greet me as I got out of the car.

Mr Hilldrop and I had agreed to have a little joke with him, when I got home. I was to appear sad so he would think that I hadn't passed my test. It worked a treat. I got out of the car with my head down looking sad.

Richard came to me and hugged me and started to tell me that he was sorry, and never mind, at the next test I would pass it. Then I couldn't bear it any longer, as tears filled my eyes again, I showed him the paper and told him I had indeed passed my driving test. His whole face seemed to light up with a beaming smile. He suddenly grabbed hold of me and hugged me and lifted me high off my feet. I knew he was so pleased.

For the last eight months I had been learning to drive. Every Wednesday afternoon I had been devoted to this task. I had been driving through the hot summer weather, the rain and wind of autumn, and in the frost and snow as we approached the winter. Driving through the snow in December was particularly scary.

"Good experience," Mr Hilldrop would say.

Passing my driving test, just before Christmas, was the best Christmas present ever. Richard had hinted that I would be needing a car as I had passed my test.

Secretly, I was hoping that my Christmas present from him that year, wouldn't fit in any cardboard box.

CHAPTER FIFTY-FIVE
Christmas 1981

Since Christmas of the previous year, time had gone by so fast. It seemed to have been a wonderful year for Richard and I. Maybe our best year up to that time. It was as if we were both fitting together with our daily routines, like a pair of old shoes, that were so comfy and wanted to be worn all the time. Richard was busy with the discos and doing really well. Financially, things seemed to be improving. He seemed happy and content with the life we were living. There was, as usual, no news of the divorce, which I had refused to even think about, for the whole of the year.

With the childminding everyday through the week, I was kept busy doing what I loved. In and around the house, my life was filled with the children every day, except on Wednesday when I would escape that routine for just an hour to see some of the outside world. By passing my test, it meant I could dream bigger dreams, like driving my children to the supermarket to do our weekly shopping, or to the countryside, or to the seaside for a picnic on the beach. I would be able to escape from the confines of my four walls at home, and breathe some fresh air, depending on whether my secret wish for Christmas came true.

That year it seemed it was a year for pregnancies. First of all, a neighbour announced that she was having twins! My brother Paul had got married in June of the previous year. He announced that they were having their second baby, the baby was due in early February of the following year. My sister Andrea had become pregnant again. Even my dad's dog Floppy was pregnant.

Richard and I had visited Andrea and all the family during summer. After Andrea had given birth to the baby in September, we couldn't wait to visit again to see our new nephew. He was another beautiful baby boy. They had called him Jason. They were happily living in a rented house in Northampton. In fact, the house was near to Adrian's family. Andrea seemed happy with her life, although the self-harming issues stayed with her for the whole of her marriage and affected her badly throughout her life. Despite this, she had lots of support from Adrian's family and especially from her sister-in-law Gail. I was so proud of the beautiful strong woman that she had become. It did appear to me, at that time, that the traumas of her past were staying in the past where they belonged. However, that wasn't the case for Andrea, she was still secretly struggling with those demons.

The mother of the little girl that I looked after, also announced too, that she was pregnant again. At the end of the summer, I had to say an emotional farewell to the little girl that I had minded for over a year. The family emigrated to the other side of the world. I loved and missed that little three-year-old girl as if she were my own child, my home seemed empty without her.

However, Nichola, at fourteen months old, had just started walking and was running all over the place before I knew it. In addition to Nichola, I had a lively four-year-old in Deborah. She danced around the house and chatted non -stop. I did have my hands full!

It had been a tense and stressful time leading up to my driving test. I had needed to pass so badly, so my dreams could begin. Failing that driving test would have meant that I was a failure, I would have been so embarrassed. I would have let my children down, and my instructor. I wouldn't have had the confidence to carry on with more lessons. Nothing could spoil the overwhelming elation I felt on that special day when the driving examiner told me I had actually passed.

With the test behind me, we could concentrate on Christmas. It was only a couple of weeks away. We had managed to buy most of the Christmas gifts, for our children, from the toy store on Bolton precinct, a few weeks previously. We just had a main present for Deborah to find. While shopping for gifts, we saw the most beautiful white Christmas tree I had ever seen. It was gorgeous! We both liked it straight away, so we bought it. On the twelfth day before Christmas, as our tradition, and while our babies were asleep in their beds, we started to decorate our house and the handsome tree that we had purchased. Lastly, an angel with a long flowing white gown and a glowing halo, was placed right at the top of the tree. It outshone the gold tinsel, baubles and white lights that adorned the tree. We stood back and admired its beauty.

When she came downstairs the next morning, Deborah's eyes were like saucers as she gazed at the tree and all the brightly coloured presents that she believed Santa had placed underneath. Nichola was wriggling around in my arms, wanting me to put her down so that she could cause some mischief with all those fascinating dangling baubles.

At only four years old, Deborah had a really good understanding of who Santa was, and believed that he was going to be bringing her lots of presents on Christmas Day. I remembered the Christmas of the year before, when we took her to the market hall in Bolton, to see Father Christmas. She sat on his knee and had her photograph taken, despite being too shy to talk to him, she still tried to pull his beard off. Richard and I had decided to buy Deborah a Wendy house, as her main Christmas present. Lola offered to baby-sit, while we went into town to buy it. It was wrapped in fancy paper and placed under the tree with all the others.

Floppy, my dad's Cavalier King Charles Spaniel, had given birth to a little boy pup on the same day as my birthday. We had visited him almost every week since he was born. I was besotted with him. When he was eight weeks old, Dad said that we could have him. The children and I absolutely adored him. We had missed having a dog around, since we let Shandy go to his new home. We welcomed our new addition to our family and named him Timmy.

With just a week to go before Christmas, I was feeling excited and looking forward to all the festivities. Lola, and Richard's brother Lee, would be sharing Christmas with us that year. I worried about everything at that point. I hoped and prayed that my cooking wouldn't be a disappointment to Lola. I was particularly concerned after the beautiful Christmas dinner that she had provided for us the previous year.

In that week before Christmas, I had a visit from my friend Mandy. She came to drop off some Christmas gifts for Deborah and Nichola. She also wanted to meet the new addition to the family, namely Timmy our little Cavalier King Charles Spaniel. Mandy had been in town earlier that day, shopping with Carl and had stated that she had seen Maureen in Woolworth's. Mandy began to tell me that she had experienced a strange conversation with Maureen. Maureen had told Mandy that Richard had bought her daughter, Louise, a Christmas present. The Christmas present was a Wendy house. Puzzled, Mandy asked me why Richard would be buying a gift for Maureen's child, why had it not been from the both of us, particularly since Louise was my niece? I didn't know anything about Richard buying anything for my niece at all, and I agreed with Mandy, it should have been from both of us. Louise, however, was not our only niece, we had nephews too and it was impossible for us to buy them all presents. We wouldn't have bought for one and not the others. More confusing still, we had agreed that we didn't have the money to buy presents for anyone else that year, except for our own children. I was feeling confused. My stomach did a somersault and I felt sick.

I had felt so happy over the last few days, and so pleased with myself after passing my driving test. However, I began to fear that trouble was returning to ruin that happiness and spoil our Christmas. How many more years would trouble be rearing its ugly head for us. I had experienced enough, I wanted it to stop. I needed some answers to a few questions. The lies just had to stop. I felt I couldn't carry on dealing with all these issues year after year! I didn't want to put up with it any more, I wanted it to stop.

We had bought Deborah a Wendy house only a couple of days previously, how could Maureen have known that? I hadn't, at that time, had the opportunity to tell anyone of the Christmas gift we had bought for our child. I hadn't seen or heard anything about Maureen for over a year. Nor had I heard that there were any nastier rumours being spread around about Richard.

Until that day, there had been nothing like this. The absence of such things had contributed to the year being such a pleasant one. I had been so wrapped up with my own children, I had been too busy to even think of anything else at that time.

My initial thought was that she was lying, to cause trouble for us. However, I felt that it was more than just a coincidence that time. She might have been telling the truth this time. I tried to stay calm, but my hands started to shake and I could feel myself getting upset and angry. I had experienced enough of all that trouble making, it was time I had some truth, not lies!

I wanted to know how Maureen could have known about our gift for Deborah, and be able to invent the story, so soon. This had led her to being able to tell my friend, knowing full well that those lies would come straight back to me, as they always had. This would inevitably cause upset between Richard and I.

As far as I knew she wasn't telepathic, nor did she own a crystal ball. I thought that Richard must have told her, he was the only one that knew, and she was then able to make up another fantasy. Or, was she telling the truth?!

When Richard came home from work that evening, I asked him whether he had seen Maureen at the Bus Inn, or anywhere over the last few days? He said he hadn't. I then told him what Maureen had been saying to my friend.

"Not this again," he said sharply. "Take no notice, she's lying again."
"So, you haven't bought Louise a Wendy house then?" I asked him again.

"No, I bloody haven't!! We agreed that we weren't buying presents for anyone this year!" he said angrily.

I was angry. Richard's words sounded truthful, I wanted him to be telling the truth. I could feel the anger building up inside me. I didn't know who was lying to me. Was it Maureen? She had been constantly lying, according to Richard, and was jealous of our relationship, according to Richard! Spreading rumours and trying to split us up, according to Richard! This had been the case since our first baby was born.

Was it Richard? He sounded so sincere and swore his love for me every day and was giving me such a good life and a lovely home, the best life I could ever have wished for. He had cooked for me, cleaned the house with me, fed our children and changed a few nappies. He was a good 'husband,' despite all the issues we were having from the outside world. He had lived for years, continually denying all the rumours and allegations that had been said about him.

My head was spinning, I didn't know who to believe. I wanted to believe Richard, he was my man and I loved him, but I wanted all the lies to stop, I wanted us to be left alone. I had experienced enough! I needed to find out once and for all and put an end to all the lies!

I picked up the phone and rang Maureen. I wanted to find out why she had told Mandy those lies.

"You are wasting your time ringing her, all you will get from her is more lies!" Richard said. I took no notice and dialled her number.

"Hello," she said when she answered. "Maureen, it's me," I said.

"What do you want?" she replied angrily. Shocked by her aggressive tone I continued, "I want to know why you have told my friend that Richard has bought Louise a Wendy House for Christmas, when it's just not true?" After a slight pause she said, "Coz it's true and why shouldn't he!? Why shouldn't he buy her a present, she's his fucking kid!! And if you have anything else to fucking say, fucking come up here and say it to my fucking face!!!" With that she slammed the phone down.

Her child, my niece, was almost three and a half years old. Maureen had never admitted to me in all that time that Richard was her father. Instantly I believed her. My whole world exploded. I felt sick and dizzy. I collapsed to my knees with the receiver still in my hand. I was shaking and crying hysterically. I couldn't believe what I had just heard from Maureen, with my own ears. How could she do that to me, she was my sister! How could she sleep with Richard behind my back? How could Richard sleep with my sister? Why?

Richard stood behind me. He had heard the shouts from Maureen as she revealed her betrayal, he saw the devastation that she had created. I turned and looked at him. He looked pale and gaunt.

"Why?" I pleaded with him to tell me why he had done that. He came towards me to console me. I lashed out and pushed him away. I screamed at him to get away from me.

"She told me Louise is yours!"

"She's lying, she's lying!" he said, trying to reach out to me to stop my screams. "You bought her a Christmas present! Why would she say that if it wasn't true?" "It's all lies!" he said "Don't believe her, that kid is not mine! She's lying!"

"All this time you've lied to me. You said you would never hurt me, you said you loved me, and you've been shagging her behind my back all this time and J too. Don't forget about her, I've not forgotten about her! Have you got her pregnant too?"

"It's all lies," he said.

"Yes!" I said, "Your lies! You are the one who has been lying to me all this time!"

How could I stay with a man who had slept with my own sister, and had a child with her? That child was my niece and cousin to my children.

How could she be their half-sister too? Why did my sister think it was okay to get pregnant with my fiancé? Why did my man think it was okay to have sex with my sister? He had been lying to me for years, I would never trust him again. I had to leave him!

"It's over now Richard," I cried. "I am not staying with you any longer! I have had enough. I will move out as soon as I have found somewhere else to go, I am not staying with you any longer, me and the children will be leaving. It's over!"

My children looking on, silent, not understanding what was being said.

I was exhausted with my thoughts. So many questions were going through my mind. How long had it been going on? Had she been the one who was in my bed while I was in hospital giving birth to our first daughter Deborah!? Then, ironically, nine months later she gave birth to Louise? Were those her tights that had been hidden in my bed, left there on purpose, for me to find?

I was confused, my head was whirling. Richard was having an affair with J around the time I was having Deborah. I believed that it had gone on for months. How could he have been seeing Maureen too? How did he find the time to see all these girls at the same time, plus be with me and our daughter? He came home for lunch every day; he was always home at teatime too. He was always in my bed at night, every night. He never ever stayed out all night. It seemed impossible. I believed Richard when he would say, "When do I have the time, I'm always with you!"

Maureen had professed to having been pregnant on many occasions but had always lost the babies. At least this is what she had said. I had questioned this at the time but did it mean that she had multiple attempts to get pregnant with Richard when this was going on? The thought appalled me but I just couldn't dismiss it. Why would she want to try to get pregnant with my man? Was Richard the one who was trying to get her pregnant? Why would he want to get my sister pregnant, when he was with me?

I remember how careful he was at the beginning of our relationship. He didn't want a child. He would say that he 'always got out at Moses Gate'! He didn't get me pregnant until we had planned to. We planned Deborah and Nichola too. I was his fiancée. We had planned that we would have four children, in time.

I knew that our sex life wasn't very good, that was the reason he cheated. I understood that, however, why with my sister, when he had lots of women chasing him, why did he choose to betray me with her? To purposely get her pregnant, while he was in a relationship with me, just didn't make any sense at all. Why did he call her the nasty names like 'tart' and 'whore'? Why did he say he wouldn't touch her with a bargepole, when he clearly was involved with her, all that time?

I had believed his every word; he knew that too. He knew I had trusted him. I loved him so much, he knew that. I made a life out of loving him while he was betraying me with multiple women, although he tried to hide this, he must have known the hurt that would ultimately be caused. Did he simply not love me — despite constantly saying that he did and building a life with me — or was he amoral or just inadequate? I struggled with all these thoughts. If he had lied to me throughout our relationship then I asked myself if I had been a naïve fool. I just couldn't believe that it could be that simple, nor could I believe that he could have maintained such long-term deceit. Why would he want to, didn't he love our daughters?

Mum's words echoed through my mind; she had warned me that he was a smooth talker who would hurt me. Although the words resonated, I again thought that this was just too simplistic a view of what had happened. If I had known that he was betraying me with her, I would have left him instantly. I would have thought the idea of raising a family with him abhorrent. Surely, he must have known that once I found out our relationship would be over!

I knew that this treachery was not one sided, she had been part of this and my contempt for her would now know no bounds. Did they expect to keep it a secret forever? Maureen was not as naïve as I was, she was very streetwise, she knew I was with Richard, she knew we had two babies together, she knew how much I loved him, and she knew how happy we were together. She had listened to my dreams of marrying him and had chosen to destroy them.

The memory of her visits to the hospital, when I had just given birth to Deborah, flashed through my mind. She did seem like a proud aunty, she sat next to me, cooing over my baby. At the same time, she revealed the fact that she was pregnant too. Was it the case that her envy was such that she had to seek attention for herself in this way?

Was she sleeping with the father of my new born baby at that time? I went cold inside at the horrid thought of her in my bed, with him, while I was in the hospital. Was he intentionally trying to get her pregnant and if so why? How could they create such a cruel and calculating betrayal? Why was he always saying he loved me, and wanted me? Why did he want me to have his children? Why did he say he wanted to stay with me forever? Why had he given me a lovely home and provided everything I would ever need? I was being what he wanted me to be.

Why didn't he tell me to leave, if he wanted somebody else? He had found that easy to do when he went back to his wife, all those years ago.

Richard left the room and went upstairs; his begging and pleading fell on deaf ears. I couldn't stand to hear his voice any longer. I sat on the sofa and held my children so closely. Deborah stroked my face and wiped away a tear that fell slowly down my cheek.

"Don't cry mummy?" she whispered.

Richard sat himself at the table, alone, for the meal I had prepared for him, earlier that day, before I had heard the devastating news that destroyed my whole world. It would be the last meal that I would ever prepare for him, I thought to myself. I didn't want to do anything for him again. I had learned my lesson; he had broken my heart. It was a lesson that had taken me such a long time to learn.

Afterwards he went to his work as a DJ at the nightclub, as usual. I slept in my daughter's room that night. When he finally returned home, he slept alone. He would never, ever touch me again, with the hands that had been all over my sister!

Over the next few days, I refused to speak to Richard at all. I couldn't stand to be in the same room as him. I didn't even want to hear his voice any more. I had heard enough of what came out of that mouth! It seemed that I had totally shut down towards him, and he knew it. I had so many questions that I wanted to ask him; however, I didn't feel that I would ever get truthful answers from him, only more lies. He still denied the affair with J, and he was denying ever going with my sister and having a baby with her! In my heart, I wanted to believe him, as I had done for the last five years, for the sake of my children, however, my head was telling me that he was a compulsive liar and he didn't deserve my trust and devotion any longer. I felt at that time, that he hadn't ever loved me at all. This thought was tearing my heart out. Had I been living a lie for all those years? I was in his life, thinking I belonged there. We were building a home together. I thought we were strong. I was a fool.

Despite all the Christmas decorations, which had made our home look and feel festive, the Christmas joy had gone. In its place, understandably, was a tense atmosphere, especially when Richard was around. I wanted to leave. But I knew to leave the home I had loved for over five years was going to be heart breaking.

I was trying to be strong in front of my children, who were oblivious to the future that we had to face. I didn't know what the future held for us. I was scared for their future. I couldn't allow my children to feel my fear. My life with Richard was over, I knew it and he knew it too. There was no going back to him this time, I had to face the future alone with my children.

My life as a sister to Maureen was over too. If everything she had been saying about Richard was true. Why did she do it? Why did she flirt with him? Why did she cross that line when she knew he was in a relationship with me? She came to my house, saw us together, I had his babies, why did she do this to me? I would never, ever forgive her or speak to her again, for what she had done to me. She had smashed my family to pieces. She was not my sister any more.

When we were children, I loved her just as much as I loved my other sisters, and my big brother. We all had needed to look out for one another. I would dream of us all finding love and happiness when we all grew up. A love that would take us far away, from that childhood home we grew up in. Paul had found love with Sylvia, Andrea had with Adrian and Ann had found happiness in her vocation as a paediatrician in a far-off land. She later married a lovely Scottish man and became a mother herself. I was lucky too; I had found love and happiness with Richard. I did feel his love, he was what I wanted, just for that short while, until the betrayal.

I always knew Maureen didn't like me much when we were growing up. I felt she hated me. I was the big sister that took her across that main road when we were kids and we got knocked down on Moss Bank Way. She had suffered pain in her knee ever since. I didn't know exactly how much she hated me until she had decided to throw herself at my fiancé! I could never forgive her. I knew that she was my sister, but at that moment in time, I didn't think I would ever be able to think of one nice thing to say about her ever again.

Life went on for Richard that week. He went to his office as normal each day and worked at the club in the evening. For me, alone with my thoughts and my shattered dreams, I would cry. I couldn't eat. I couldn't sleep. I was broken and devastated. Somehow, I had to get through that Christmas, without my babies noticing any more tears that were hiding behind my smiles.

Christmas morning arrived, the house was dark and quiet. I crept out of the bedroom, which I had shared with my sleeping daughters, and made my way down the stairs. I felt the chill as it had been a frosty night. I switched the gas fire on full to take away the chill. It was six o'clock in the morning, my babies wouldn't be awake for another hour or so.

The turkey was slowly cooking in the oven and all the vegetables were peeled and ready to be cooked. I was organised and prepared for that special day. I was trying so hard to block the last few days from my mind and to concentrate on the Christmas celebrations for my children. It was supposed to be a day filled with the joys and happiness of Christmas. I had intended to enjoy that with my family. With the trauma slowly fading from my mind, I started to feel a little excited as I sat on the sofa with a second cup of tea. I began to look forward to having a good day. I looked at all their presents under the Christmas tree. I couldn't wait to see their little faces when their gifts were revealed.

I didn't think that feeling was meant to last, when all of a sudden, the front door opened and in walked Richard! It was six-thirty in the morning, he had stayed out all night! I glared at him as he walked in, his eyes were firmly fixed on the floor. He walked past me and straight upstairs to his room, without saying a word or providing an explanation as to where he had been all night. I was in shock. I couldn't believe he had stayed out all night. He had never done that before, ever. I wanted to shout at him, "Where the hell have you been?" I had presumed he was fast asleep in his bed that morning, while I was in the kitchen preparing the vegetables for our Christmas dinner. My stomach was doing somersaults again as I realised, he could have been in the bed of some other girl, or worse still, my sister. In my mind that was where he had been. My hands began to shake. I thought my head was going to explode. I went cold and cringed at the horrid thought of him being in my sister's bed. I couldn't hold onto my tears any longer.

For me Christmas was ruined. Somehow, just for that day, I had to pretend that everything was normal for my children and for Richard's family who were coming to share Christmas with us later that day. They were unaware of the situation we were in, although I was sure that Lola would be able to sense the bad atmosphere as soon as she walked in. I then thought that she was likely to proceed and start asking questions. How would I ever be able to explain to Lola that I was leaving her son and taking her granddaughters away?

It was a long and tense day. Richard stayed in his bed until after eleven. He missed seeing the joy on the faces of our children, as they opened their presents that morning. I believed that he didn't give a damn about our daughters, if he had, he wouldn't have done what he had done. Surely, he would have known that I would leave him and take my daughters with me. I was convinced he didn't care. I was sure he wasn't afraid to lose us.

Lola and Lee arrived at around twelve o'clock. They had a huge bag of presents for my baby girls. We all sat and watched as they opened each and every one of them. Richard had busied himself putting the Wendy house together, and I kept myself busy in the kitchen. Lola was in her element playing with the children all afternoon.

Dinner was served around our borrowed table at around two thirty. We all took our seats. Lola sat herself in a seat next to Nichola's highchair. Lee placed himself next to Deborah. Although she would have preferred to sit on Lees' knee throughout her meal, I insisted she sat on her own chair. The seat next to Richard was where I reluctantly had to sit. He had been trying to make small talk during that morning and throughout dinner, however, as much as I tried, I just couldn't bring myself to look him in the eye. I was sure I would have broken down in floods of tears in front of everyone. I felt as if I had a volcano inside me, ready to erupt at any minute.

When the Christmas crackers were pulled, I couldn't help but giggle, as we all sat there looking silly wearing our badly fitting, brightly coloured paper hats. Despite the long silences, our Christmas dinner did not disappoint. I couldn't seem to eat very much. I didn't have much of an appetite that day, but I felt it was one of the best meals I had ever made. Richard tucked in and commented on how lovely it was. I was sure he would miss my cooking when I was gone. I wanted to cry.

After Christmas pudding and brandy sauce had been served, there was nothing left to do except the washing up. I held back the tears, as they complimented me on the lovely Christmas dinner. It meant so much coming from Lola, I could never compete with her cooking.

Saying goodbye to Lola, as she left that evening was so hard. I had become quite fond of the lady that I thought would be my future mother-in-law. She was quirky and witty and made me smile at times when she would knock on my front door and say that she was just passing and could she have a glass of water. I would say 'of course' and invite her in. She would then stay for hours, chatting away, one subject, then another. She could talk for hours. With being one of the founder members of the Women's Institute she always had lots of interesting topics to talk about.

When I first met Lola, I didn't think we could ever be friends, but as the years went on, we became quite close friends. She clearly loved her granddaughters, and they loved her. I appreciated and encouraged every moment she spent with them. When I started to get to know Lola, she and I would sit for hours reminiscing. We would talk in depth about our childhoods. Her childhood was so different to mine. She talked of the war years and of the soldiers, rationing and the loss of loved ones. She cried, hearing the traumas of my childhood, the fear, the nightmares and the hunger.

I spoke of the many happy school days and my dreams for my future, becoming a mother and a writer one day. Those dreams for the future kept the painful memories of the past hidden away deep in my mind. We had begun to know each other very well over the years. During this time, I had mentioned to Lola that I had written a little children's story, when I was fifteen. She instantly began to persuade me to allow her to read it.

At the bottom of my wardrobe, upstairs was my little old tatty suitcase, which had once belonged to my granddad. He had owned it for a very long time. Mum gave it to me when we were staying at her house a few years previously. That old suitcase was the place I kept my keepsakes and that story that I had written all those years ago. It was safely placed at the bottom of my wardrobe. It was my suitcase of memories that I treasured always.

I shyly showed Lola the story. It was in its own large, brown padded envelope. Lola read the first page. She then asked if she could take it away with her to read that night when she went to bed. After she had promised to keep it safe, I reluctantly agreed. Over the years of living with Richard that followed, I didn't see that story again.

As I hugged Lola so tightly on my doorstep, that evening, the story I had written all those years ago was far from my mind. I had assumed I would never see it again. I held back my tears as I said goodbye. I didn't know when I would be seeing her again, it might have been the last time I would ever be able to hug her. It might have been the last time I saw her. I had an ache in my chest for her as I held back the tears. I watched her drive down Glynne Street, until her little blue Ford Escort disappeared in the distance.

I returned to my living room and to my two exhausted children. Richard had left them alone with their toys and gone upstairs to his bedroom. As I was getting my children ready for bed, Richard came downstairs. He had changed his clothes. He lit up a cigarette and sat himself on the settee watching 'Top of The Pops' on the television. I glared at him, with a nappy pin sticking out from the side of my mouth, as I changed Nichola's nappy. I stayed silent.

I could feel myself getting angrier and angrier inside when I realised that Richard appeared as if he was going out. I knew that the Bus Inn wasn't open that night so he had no work to go to. I instantly presumed he would be going to the same place he had been to the previous night. That place I believed to have been the bed of another woman. I got up and lay Nichola on the settee with her bottle of warm Ovaltine.

"I suppose you are going out, again, are you?" I said sharply. I looked at him. He ignored me, his eyes never leaving the television.

"Are you going to be staying out all night again?" I was getting angrier with his silence.

"You're going to leave your two babies on Christmas night to go and screw some girl are you!?"

I received no answers to the questions I was asking.

I needed answers, I wanted him to tell me the truth. I didn't want him to leave us that night! We needed to talk! I wanted him to admit to me that he had engaged in an affair with J, when our first daughter was being born, if indeed that was the truth. I also wanted him to admit that he had been having sex with my sister, behind my back, for all these years. I wanted to know. I still had doubts in my mind after believing Richard's lies for so long.

The visions of the betrayal of the man that I had loved, and his silence tore out my heart. I couldn't take it any more. I saw red! The volcano inside me erupted!

I picked up the first thing I could grab and that was Nichola's wash bowl. I threw it at him. He jumped up from his seat, and pushed me backwards into my chair.

"You're a bastard!" I screamed at him, as he stormed out into the kitchen. I was in tears, and so angry. My heart was beating so fast, and I was shaking all over. To my horror, Richard came back into the room carrying the washing up bowl from the kitchen sink. He had filled it with water and before I knew it, he had thrown it all over me. He stormed out of the house, slamming the door behind him. It was freezing cold water. It took my breath away; it was so cold. I sat there in the chair so shocked, I couldn't move. I just could not believe he had done that. I was drenched and shivering. The chair was drenched. My children looked on. What had I done to deserve all this?

I didn't see or hear from Richard for three whole days.

On Monday evening, he walked in, went straight upstairs and collected some clothes from his wardrobe. He then came back downstairs, carrying his suit and a couple of shirts over his arm. As he was making his way through the vestibule door, I said, "Aren't you going to tell me where you're staying?"

"At my mum's if you must know," he snapped and rushed through the door.

I didn't believe that for a minute, I felt it was just another lie. He had walked back into our home, bold as brass, after three days, without any regard for our children, who he hadn't seen since Christmas Day. He hadn't even looked at them, not once! All he needed was his change of clothes!

The next evening, he was back. He made himself a brew and sat on the settee. When I had put the children to bed, I came downstairs wondering whether we would be able to talk things over or end up arguing. Richard had reclined full length on the settee and was asleep! Timmy had been sleeping curled up at the bottom of the settee next to his feet. The dog woke up, crawled up onto Richard's tummy and suddenly puked all over him. Richard abruptly pushed Timmy off his chest and snarled, "You can take that mutt with you when you go!" I lifted Timmy up and put him outside in the yard. Richard went upstairs to change while I cleaned the mess that Timmy had made, Richard came downstairs and went through the front door. I was angry and exhausted. I couldn't cry any more.

I began to realise that he had walked out on me and the children. I was living in his house; he could come along and throw us out on the streets at any time. I needed to get some help and housing advice quickly, before I found myself on the street with my children.

The following day, the children and I were walking into the Housing Department. After explaining the situation that we had been put into by Richard, I was placed on the urgent accommodation register.

On the afternoon of New Year's Eve, my brother Paul came to visit. It was lovely to see Paul again, I hadn't seen him for a while, he had been so busy working since he had left the army. He had a family of his own to look after, a wife and two lovely children Darren and Jackie. He did some work for Richard as a DJ at times too, so it was very rare that he had the time to visit.

"I was passing so I thought I would come and see how you are," he said, "and to wish you a Happy New Year! Are you putting the kettle on?" giving me such a tight squeeze.

As I made the tea, the children were showing him all their new toys until they got distracted with the cartoons on the television.

"So," he said, as we sipped his tea, "how've you been?"

My eyes filled with tears when he looked at me. "Richard's left me," I said, holding back the tears.

I began to tell Paul of the events of the last couple of weeks. He listened intently. It felt good to talk to Paul, I had been living through the nightmare alone with my children, for most of the week, it was good to talk to someone.

"He said he's staying at his mother's but I don't really believe that; I don't know where he is. I've not seen him since Monday".

"He's not at his mother's," Paul said, "I know exactly where he is!"

I knew by the tone of his voice that what he was about to say would enlighten me.

"I don't want to upset you any more than you already are," he added, "but his car has been seen outside Maureen's for the last few days!" That was all the proof I needed. He was with my sister!

A few days later as I was watching Crossroads Richard walked in again. He walked straight into the bathroom through the kitchen and had a shower. I knew I needed to confront him with what I had been told. Inside I was fuming. The tears had turned to anger at the revelation of all the lies he had told me over the last five years.

While my daughters watched television in the living room, I went into the kitchen to have it out with him.

"So, is it true then?" I asked. "Is what true?" he replied. "You are with Maureen?"

"Well, you don't want me, do you?" he continued as he ran up the stairs to his room. He collected his clothes from the wardrobe and left without saying another word. I expected him to turn round and tell me that my brother had lied too, however, he confirmed it. He was with my sister!

I was taken by the fact that his eyes could not meet mine as he confirmed this revelation. It seemed that he felt awkward about his situation when he had to confront me. He avoided my direct questions and busied himself collecting his things. It appeared to me that he must have gone straight to her after I had told him I was leaving him. Why? Was he so afraid of being alone?

The next day he came again, carrying a white carrier bag of what looked like his dirty washing, he walked straight through into the bathroom and had a shower again. When I walked into the kitchen, I noticed that he had placed the carrier bag in front of the washing machine. When I looked closer, I saw dirty nappies, and other soiled items, which obviously didn't belong to Richard.

The hard-faced bloody cow, I thought to myself, how dare he fetch her dirty smelly washing into my house! I was livid! I picked up that bag of shite, opened the front door and threw it out into the middle of Glynne Street. It was strewn across the road and run over by a bus, a lorry and three cars within seconds. After another argument he stormed out of the house.

After the weekend was over, I felt I needed to get advice from a solicitor. I was living in Richard's house; the arguments continued every time he called. I didn't want him to keep coming to the house, it would be better if he kept away. I was living with the fear of him coming back and kicking us out onto the streets. I didn't want to wait for that to happen. I needed to find out what rights I had, if any. I made an appointment to see a solicitor at a Citizens' Advice Bureau. I was given lots of advice. In essence, I was advised the best was to leave the house, with my children, before we were put out on the streets. I was also given advice that worried me so much. I would have to go to court to get custody of my own children, if I didn't, it meant that Richard could take the children away and not bring them back to me. I would then have to take him to court to get them back. I was also informed that the court would offer custody to whichever parent could provide the best for my children.

I was horrified! I broke down and cried. I couldn't believe what I was hearing. There was no way I was going to lose my children. I was hysterical. She had taken my man, there was no way she was going to take my children too! The lady behind the desk looked on and offered me a tissue from the box on her desk.

"You will need to pull yourself together, if you are ever going to be able to fight this, try to control your emotions!" She advised me in the following terms. "The courts won't look favourably if you are too emotional!" I had nothing. No money, no means of support for my children, no home to call my own. I was emotional! My children were my life! Without my children I was nothing! I would have to fight for my own children! How would I ever be able to fight the courts, if that was where we were heading?

Since Christmas, Richard had left me with no financial support. The cupboards were beginning to look bare. I was trying to manage with just a few basic supplies; however, they too were beginning to run out.

It wasn't long before all the street had realised what had been going on. Ann had visited and I had to tell her what had happened. Dad then found out too. My friend Mandy and her boyfriend Carl had come to see me and I informed them what had been happening through Christmas and the New Year. One bit of advice, which I had received from the solicitor, was to try to speak to Richard's estranged wife, to see if she could help in some way. She did, at that time, want Richard to sell the Glynne Street house, so that she could have her settlement in the divorce. With her help, I could possibly leave the premises.

Carl and Mandy drove us to Richard's estranged wife's house and she agreed to speak to me. I spoke of Richard's behaviour and of the fear that I could be made homeless with my two babies very soon. I knew that Richard could kick us out. I asked her if she could speak to her solicitor to ask him if he would write to the council to say that she needed me to leave the property as soon as possible, as she needed it to be sold. I told her it could help me in terms of council house allocation, as I would then be classed as homeless. To my relief she agreed and promised that she would speak to her solicitor the following day.

Within the next few days, I had a phone call from the Housing Department, I was advised that a letter had been received by the council from Richard's estranged wife's solicitor. I was to call in to see them on Monday morning to discuss it.

During the visit, they informed me that I had been allocated a two bedroomed flat in Hunger Hill, but it wouldn't be ready for another two weeks. I had a good idea of where the property was located. It was far enough away from where Maureen was living in Breightmet, and far from the house I had shared with Richard in Farnworth. I accepted the property straight away. I was given a card with the details of the property and when I would be able to pick up the keys. I was so excited. I had to try to believe that Richard was not going to kick us out on the streets, as he had promised, and just try to get through the following two weeks. I had decided that I had to keep the housing offer a secret from everybody and prepare myself for leaving the house that I'd loved for over five years.

Richard had been back to the house a couple of times over the last couple of weeks. He had collected his mail and picked up more clean clothes. His visits were brief and we hardly spoke to each other. He hadn't dared to bring any more of her dirty smelly washing into my house, it would have ended up in the same place on the road under a wagon. I was just so pleased that I was offered a property, I didn't care what Richard was doing or with whom. I just had to bide my time for another two weeks, and I could be free of him once and for all.

On Monday of that week, Richard had called as usual for his mail and we managed to have a conversation without raised voices. As we were standing at the door, when he was leaving, I gathered the courage to ask him for some money. I was getting desperate, I needed to ask him for some money for food. To my surprise he took some money out of his wallet. I took it from his hand. He then said that he would try and get some more cash for me through the week. I was relieved that I could buy some food. My eyes filled with tears as I thanked him and nodded in appreciation. My children would be able to eat a decent meal that night, I thought to myself.

Before he left my doorstep, he turned to me, looked me right in the eye and said softly, "We can get married if you let me come back!" I couldn't believe what I was hearing. Anger rose inside me once more. How dare he say that to me after what he had put me through over Christmas.

"I wouldn't touch you with a barge pole now that I know where you have been!" I said. He turned sharply, got into his car and sped away.

All those years I had waited to become Richard's wife. All those years of disappointment that I went through when his divorce hadn't come through. I would have given anything to have been married to Richard in those days. However, I had to face it. I had lived a lie with Richard for over five years; he was a womaniser, a liar and a cheat, it was all over. He would never feel my love and devotion ever again.

When Mandy and Carl paid their usual Wednesday night visit, I told them what Richard had said to me a few days previously. Mandy laughed and said he was a cheeky sod. I had to agree with her.

Later that evening, Carl was at my kitchen sink and happened to glance up, out of the window, at the backyard. He shouted to Mandy and I that he had just seen Richard peering in over the back gate. Mandy and I shot upstairs to get a look at the back street, through the back bedroom window. We saw Richard's car disappearing at the end of the street. For the rest of the evening, we were puzzled as to the reason why Richard had been spying on us. The only conclusion we came up with was that Carl had parked his new car outside at the front of my house. Richard must have been driving by and not recognising the car, thought he would come to spy on us to see who was in his house that night. I thought it was so strange, he could have knocked on his own front door, or just walked in like he usually did. It later struck me that he may have thought that I was with another man, judging me by his own standards.

The next day, our local free paper had been posted through the letter box. Deborah went to fetch it. Richard had left 'the Bolton Evening News' earlier in the year and had started working with another newspaper, The Bolton Chronicle. It was a free paper that was delivered to every house in Bolton. As she pulled it from the letterbox, she noticed the photo on the front page. She stood looking at the picture for a few minutes and then brought it to me.

"Daddy's on the paper!" she said, pointing to the image on the front page. I looked at the photo in disbelief. I was horrified at what I saw.

On the front page of The Bolton Chronicle was a photo of Richard and Maureen; it was their wedding photo. I stared at the photo, not quite believing what I was seeing. As I looked at the photo and read their names underneath, my heart began to beat so fast, my hands were shaking. I had to sit down. I was absolutely astonished by this as Richard had only just proposed to me a few days previously. How could this be, surely the register office needed notice of a wedding and they must have had Maureen's details on record and Maureen must have attended the pre-wedding meeting at least a couple of weeks before the actual wedding. No one in the family was aware of this, if they had been, I would unquestionably have become aware of it. My experience of Maureen was such that I knew she would not have kept a planned wedding with Richard quiet, so the arrangements for it really must have been last minute. For this to happen, Richard must have been in receipt of his Decree Nisi and his Decree Absolute, which I knew would have arrived six weeks later. I had never been told that either of these legal documents had arrived. This made me think that he had strung Maureen along as a second choice, being prepared to marry her if I had rejected his proposal, as I did. At that point, Diane walked in clutching the same newspaper.

"Have you seen it?" she said. Following Diane was Sue, my next-door neighbour and Edith from up the street. They had all had the paper delivered through their doors and had come to see if I was all right. I wasn't all right. I was devastated at what the father of my children had done. With my own sister! However, there were no more tears, I had cried a river over Richard, I couldn't cry any more.

All at once, I heard Gloria Gaynor singing on the radio, I jumped up quickly and turned the volume up higher. I had heard it so many times on the radio over the last few weeks. I was sure it was a sign and the words of the song seemed to be helping to keep me strong. Her song started to play again just when I needed to hear her words once more. The tears began to fall from my eyes again and drenched my cheeks. Holding onto my daughters' hands, we danced around the room, to, 'I Will Survive!'

The very next day, Richard turned up at the house and again walked on through without looking at me or his children. I could feel the anger building up inside me again. I hadn't slept a wink since the previous day. Every time I closed my eyes to try to sleep, I could see the image in the newspaper flashing through my mind. I was exhausted and angry.

I followed him into the kitchen. I needed some answers to my questions and I wanted the truth. Each question I asked, I got the same denials. Our voices were getting louder as we argued. I told him that his daughter had pulled the newspaper from the letterbox and wondered why her father was on the front page with Aunty Maureen!

"How are you ever going to explain that?" I asked him. "It's not right. "Why did you have to marry her? How could you do that to me? She's my sister for God's sake! Why couldn't you wait until I had moved out before you did this?"

Did he even realise that our whole family's lives would be shattered beyond repair by their betrayal?

He kept saying that I didn't want him, so he had the next best thing! I told him he was disgusting and accused him of being a womaniser, with the gift of the gab, all the way through our relationship, and whoever offered it to him on a plate would have their offer quickly accepted. He turned around to me and said, "Yeah, there were lots of women who would offer it on a plate. Lots of them!" he repeated. I was horrified at what he had just revealed.

"Oh, you think you're God's gift to women don't ya?" I said, feeling disgusted with myself, for ever being with him in the first place, when he was probably screwing lots of women when he was working as a DJ.

"Well," he said, "why don't you ask your Ann. I've been through her as well!"

I was horrified! How dare he say that about Ann, I didn't believe it. I accused him of lying again. I knew my sister Ann wouldn't go anywhere near Richard. Why was Richard saying all these horrible things?

"Ask her," he said.

I picked up the phone and rang Dad's number. Ann answered. I was hysterical down the phone. I told her what Richard had been saying. It wasn't true, he was a liar. Dad had overheard the conversation on the phone with Ann and me, I could hear him shouting. Ann put the phone down.

Richard left the kitchen and went upstairs. I sat with my children in the living room watching television. Nichola climbed on my knee, she was so tired. I gave her a dummy and she nestled into my chest and closed her eyes. I slowly rocked her to help her fall asleep.

All of a sudden, the front door opened and in stormed my dad! His face was like thunder. He was raging.

"Where is he?" he said so angrily.

"He's upstairs!" I said, startled by him barging through the door.

Dad ran upstairs and into the front bedroom. I could hear the horrendous battle upstairs, as Dad attacked Richard. Dad was shouting so loudly. I shook with fear and froze to the spot.

All the sounds I was hearing became so familiar to me. I recalled the traumatic memories of when Dad was beating my brother, my mum and then my step-mum. I could hear the thuds and the banging. It had to stop before Dad killed Richard. I ran upstairs and opened the bedroom door. Dad was in a raging frenzy rolling around on the floor, with Richard. He looked as if he wanted to kill him. He was punching Richard in the ribs. Richard had blood coming from a wound on his head. He was trying to protect himself from Dad's punches.

"Dad stop please," I said. I wished I had been able to tell Dad to stop when he was beating my siblings and our mothers. I was a child filled with fear at that time. That fear still remained.

Dad suddenly released his hold on Richard and stood to his feet and followed me down the stairs. Just then Ann walked in with Laura. Dad was ranting and raving about what a waste of space Richard was and how I would be better off without him.

Richard came down the stairs holding a towel over the wound on his head. Dad turned to Richard and warned him not to cause any more trouble for his family, or he would be back. He started to shout at Richard for what he had done to me and told him he should be giving me money to feed my girls, not swanning off with every woman in Bolton, leaving me destitute. Richard turned to Dad and told him that he always gave me money, every week without fail. He walked towards the fireplace and stated that he always put the money underneath a particular ornament. He picked up my favourite ornament and banged it back down on the slate mantle so hard that it broke.

I told Dad that what Richard had claimed just wasn't true. Richard was lying, I had not had any money from him since Christmas except a small amount a few days ago. He only needed to look in the kitchen cupboard to realise that Richard's statement was just another lie. Dad warned Richard again saying he would be back if he heard any more about him and left. Ann and Laura followed. Richard left shortly after without saying another word.

Later that evening Dad, at nearly sixty years of age, was taken into hospital with a suspected heart attack. He was later diagnosed with severe angina and had to have a triple heart bypass a few months later.

I didn't see or hear from Richard again for days. I would go cold and cringe when I thought of the two of them together. I had got to try to forget about them and concentrate on my children and how I was going to be able to provide for them when we finally left that house.

During the following week, I had decided to have a clear out and sort out all our belongings ready for the move to the new flat. I didn't have much, only our clothes and the toys. Almost everything in the house belonged to Richard. I would have to start from scratch with nothing. When I was gathering all my belongings, ready to pack into bags and boxes, I had to go into the bedroom that I once shared with Richard. I could still smell the stench of his sweaty socks; I knew I was never going to miss that smell.

I collected a few items from the wardrobe, items that belonged to me. My new coat, that I had bought, using my last week's wages, had been hanging on the back of the bedroom door, since I had bought it. I hadn't had an opportunity to wear it. When I went to lift it from the door, I noticed there was blood smeared all over it. It looked as if Richard had purposely wiped the blood from his head wound, that was caused when Dad had attacked him, all over the back of my new coat. I hung the coat back on the hook and left it there.

At the end of the week, Richard arrived just after lunchtime. He totally ignored me once again and walked around the house carrying clothes that he had come to collect. During this visit Richard seemed to be taking longer in the house, walking from room to room, looking in cupboards and just idly standing around. I couldn't understand what he was doing. He came into the front room, sat himself in the chair and started watching television at one point. Deborah, as usual, went straight to his side, chattering away to him. I watched as this daddy, who had once doted on his daughter, stared into her little face. He was looking at her but I didn't really think he was listening to her. I wondered what he was thinking of. It was as if his mind was elsewhere, as if he was killing time, before he had to rush off again.

After a few minutes he got up and went into the kitchen. Deborah followed him, I could hear her chattering away to him, asking him questions, such as 'Where are you going daddy?' 'When are you coming back daddy?' His replies always got a 'Why daddy?' from Deborah.

As I listened, I held Nichola in my arms. Deborah sounded so sad when she was talking to him. I thought she was possibly going to cry when he left her that day. All at once everything went quiet. I couldn't hear Deborah's chattering any more, or Richard's responses. Suddenly a bad feeling rushed over me. I shot out of the chair, with Nichola held tightly in my arms, and rushed into the kitchen. I was convinced I was going to find the kitchen empty and both of them gone! To my relief, Richard was bent down in front of Deborah whispering something to her.

Deborah was standing beside him, listening to what he was saying to her. I had no idea what he could have been saying to her, I didn't care either. At that very moment, I thought he had taken her. I thought he had picked her up and vanished with her through the back door! I was in a state and crying my eyes out. I screamed hysterically at Richard, "I thought you'd taken her!" He stood to his feet and came towards me and held my arm.

"I would never do that to you!" he whispered.

I pulled away from him and composed myself. He could feel my coldness. I knew then that I would never be able to trust Richard. It would have been so easy for him to pick Deborah up, and take her out through the back door, and keep her. He knew what my children meant to me. I wouldn't put it past him to try to take my kids, to get back at me for ending our relationship, and leaving him. I would have to keep a closer eye on my children from that point.

As he was leaving that day, he turned to me and said, "We are moving back into the house on Monday, but don't worry, I'm not going to throw you out on the street coz you've got my kids!"

I was stunned. I had a feeling that since Dad attacked him, he would be kicking us out before long. I was confused. Richard didn't say that he wanted us to leave before they moved in. He rushed off before I could ask him. Then a horrible thought rushed through my mind. Was he expecting me to stay there with my children, and live with them, like one big happy family? Maybe he still wanted to use me to cook and clean for them? That just couldn't happen, it would never happen. I had to leave that house. I knew that I would have been bullied and intimidated by her until I had left or they would have locked me out of the house at their earliest opportunity, just to get me away from my children.

I had received the confirmation that I was to be moving into a new flat, in two weeks. I panicked, where would I go until then? I had no choice but to ring Dad and ask him if we could stay at his house for a week or so. Straight away, Dad agreed, and offered to come with his work's van as soon as he could, to pick us up and all our belongings.

Ann and Laura came along to help. The neighbours who had become loyal friends, at that point, came into my home to lend a hand too.

When Dad turned up later that day, everyone agreed we should take everything we could get our hands on in a hurry. I had my two children from that relationship that was all I had and all I needed, but I agreed with everyone that I should take more. I was to be moving into a flat with nothing, no furniture or anything, so we set to work clearing everything from the house. Dad took the fridge freezer, washing machine and tumble dryer and other larger items, as much as he could fit in his van. He stored it all in a garage where he worked, for safekeeping. In the meantime, the neighbours were taking everything out of the house and placing it all in their garages, down the back street. We filled Ann's car with pots and pans, bedding and towels. All our clothes were placed in black bin bags. We took the toys too, all in their boxes.

Before we left the house that I had shared with Richard, which was by then, emptied of all its furniture, Ann thought that she had better mop the floor in the kitchen before we left. It was a large kitchen and there were so many muddy footprints all over the very hard to clean floor. It used to take me hours, scrubbing, on my hands and knees, to get it clean. Ann took the mop, immersed it in the stagnant putrid water in the mop bucket, and went to the little garden at the top of the yard and plunged and saturated the mop in the muddy soil. She brought it back to the kitchen and started to mop the whole floor area, not forgetting, all the way into the bathroom! After she was satisfied that it was all covered nicely, we stood back and admired her handywork. At that point we all climbed into Ann's car and drove away!

CHAPTER FIFTY-SIX
1982 Our New House

I slowly opened the green door of number fifty-one as wide as it would go. My daughters and I peered inside at the concrete staircase in front of us. It looked dark and creepy. The stairway and half way up the wall had been painted with black gloss paint, that was flaking off and chipped with age. Running down the centre of the staircase was a red patterned carpet that had been glued to the concrete. Our eyes followed the staircase right to the top. We then looked at each other. My daughters hesitated, waiting for me to say it was fine to go in.

"Shall we go in then?" I smiled at their apprehensive little faces. I held their hands tightly all the way to the top.

At the top were two doorways on either side of the staircase. They led into cold, empty bedrooms, with bare floorboards, and large wide windows. Further along the landing there were three other doorways, one led into a long large living room on the left, with an old tiled open fireplace and nicotine-stained walls. The small kitchen had just one single sink unit under a long narrow window, and a pantry in the corner, just like the one we used to have in our kitchen when we were kids. The bathroom was on the right next to the kitchen. It was small with an old-fashioned, deep wrought iron roll top bath, resting on four little feet underneath. The four little feet looked like the paws of a lion.

With the noises of our footsteps and our voices echoing around the empty rooms, we began to explore what was to become our new home. With no furniture to fill those large rooms it was so hard to imagine how I could turn it into a lovely home for my children.

As we locked the door to the property that day, when we were leaving, we were greeted by an elderly gentleman who told us that he lived in the flat underneath ours. I initially thought he was about to complain about the noise from my children's footsteps, on the bare floorboards, as we explored every room that day. Instead, he introduced himself as Henry, and offered me a cup of tea, and a drink of juice for the children. I was delighted and accepted.

We drank tea over the boundary fence, between his flagged and pebbled front garden, and my flagged footpath. Henry seemed to be a pleasant elderly gentleman, He told me that he had lived in his flat for over fifteen years, since his wife had died. He then talked about the area and the neighbours. It did seem to be a quiet little street, away from a noisy main road which I was so pleased about.

I remarked to Henry that I would have loved to have a garden for my children to play in, but we were desperate, so we had to take a flat. I was astonished when Henry told me that we did indeed have a garden. He came out of his garden and onto the path that led to my flat. We were then directed past my front door, and further along the flagged path that led around the back of his flat.

"This is your garden!" he said. To my amazement, in front of us was a huge grassed back garden with two little steps that led down into it. Privet surrounded the boundary. A washing line stretched the full length of the garden. The children's faces lit up, and excitedly they began running right down to the end of the garden. To my relief they didn't slip on the damp grass. I was ecstatic!

I was imagining my children playing on a swing and in a sand pit. I was imagining my washing hanging from the line, blowing in the wind. I imagined sitting in the sunshine on a summer's day, watching my children running around with Timmy, our little Cavalier King Charles Spaniel. We could have some rabbits, I thought to myself. We would have to buy a lawnmower too.

A week later, we moved into our new flat. Dad was working at the hospital so he was able to get his hands on three old hospital beds that were being disposed of and two little bedside cabinets. They were suitable for us, for the time being, they were hard and uncomfortable but they had to do until we could afford to buy new beds. I planned to buy bunk beds for my girls, when I had saved enough money. My daughters had been sharing a bed with me, while we were at Dad's house, so it was nice for them to sleep in their own beds for a change.

Mandy and Carl were amazing. They had been at the flat stripping wallpaper, painting and helping with the cleaning on most evenings until late. Carl's mum, Enid, came to the flat with a big food hamper, which she had put together for us. It was full of necessities and some extra treats for the children too. She also said that she had been sorting out her cupboards and found us some curtains, bedding and towels. Carl's dad also turned up in a van one evening, with a black vinyl settee and two chairs and a wall unit for the lounge. I cried. I couldn't get over the generosity of Carl's parents, when we had only met them a couple of times. I would be eternally grateful for everything that they had done for us. It crossed my mind, that in a world where I had recently experienced such extreme unpleasantness, Carl's parents, near complete strangers to me, had demonstrated the best and most positive side of human nature. This had altogether made me have a more positive outlook on the future that I faced with my two children.

My house was beginning to look like a home, and it was all thanks to them. With my agreement, Dad had sold the large fridge freezer, the washing machine and the tumble dryer, taken from Richard's house. By doing this, my dad had raised enough money to enable me to purchase carpets for each of the rooms. I was also able to buy a small fridge freezer and a twin tub washing machine. I did think my days of using a twin tub washing machine were over, when Richard had bought the automatic washing machine for me. I smiled to myself, as I recalled the memories of the piles of washing that would be in my kitchen on wash days.

I wheeled the washer into its place in the kitchen. As a child, I had been brought up with a twin tub washing machine in our house. I had fond memories of using it.

One of my early life experiences was when I was bathed in the washing machine. My siblings also waited their turns to be bathed in the machine as well. We must have been very young and tiny but nevertheless, I do have a very clear memory. I convinced myself that the automatic washing machine was a luxury that we could do without at this time.

From the second-hand store, I also managed to buy a gas cooker, however, after we had moved in, it was to take the whole week before the gas was switched on. We were living on Weetabix, sandwiches and jam butties until it was connected. We were burning rubbish in the open fireplace, to keep the fire going just to keep warm.

It was such a delight for all of us, when Mandy and Carl arrived, just after we had moved in. They unexpectedly brought Kentucky fried chicken for all of us. I could have cried; I was so hungry. My girls were sitting in front of the fire tucking into their chicken, chips and baked beans. I watched them and smiled. Their smiley faces all rosy and illuminated from the flames in the fireplace; their little fingers, greasy from the chicken. They tucked in and filled their tummies. It was the first hot meal they had eaten for a while.

Nichola didn't seem well a few days later. I could tell she was coming down with something. She hadn't eaten much or slept and she coughed all through the night. She was clingy and wanted to be sitting on my knee all the time. I thought it was just a cold coming on.

After a few days she became worse. She had a high temperature and developed an awful cough. The weather had been dreadful for days. I felt she needed a doctor, but I couldn't risk taking her out in all that wind and rain. I hadn't got any money for bus fares, or to make a telephone call at a phone box. I had never taken my children to the doctors at all before. They had never been ill, and at that point, we hadn't had time to re-register at another surgery in our new area. I was in despair; I didn't know what to do. I felt isolated and cut off from the outside world.

Just then there was a knock on the door; it was Henry from downstairs. He was standing at my door with an umbrella in one hand, and a plate pie in the other.

"I've been baking," he said, "and I thought you might like this. It's cheese and onion!" I invited him in for a cup of tea. Nichola had been asleep on the settee under a blanket. She woke coughing and started to cry. I rushed to her side to hold her. Henry could tell that she wasn't well at all.

"She needs a doctor," I said, "but I can't leave her, we haven't got a doctor yet, and I've no money for a phone call. I cried. Henry felt her head. "She is hot! I've got a phone; I could ring a doctor for you."

Within half an hour a doctor arrived. I was so worried as he listened to Nichola's chest. She cried and coughed all the way through the examination.

"She has got bronchitis," he said, writing out a prescription for antibiotics. He also prescribed junior aspirin to bring her temperature down. "Can you bring her to my surgery, after she has finished the medication?" I agreed and took the prescription. Without any hesitation, Henry took the prescription from me and left.

He was back before long with the medication. He was a godsend. Nichola was back to her usual self a few days later.

I was heartbroken when I left Richard's house. I didn't think I would ever be able to stop the tears. It was difficult to show any emotion in front of Dad, after we had moved in with him. I had to be strong and hide all my feelings away. At times, I felt I just had to get out of the house, when my emotions got the better of me. I would go for a walk in Astley Bridge Park, in the rain. No one could see my tears that way. All my hopes and dreams had been shattered. I was finding it so hard to imagine what our lives were going to be like with me as a single parent. I couldn't see our future; I couldn't dream any more. I prayed for the day to arrive when I could pick up the keys to our new flat and be out of Dad's house with my children and begin our new life, without Richard. I didn't have long to wait.

After all those years of falling for his lies, the love for him was slowly disappearing. I had my beautiful children from him, and for that I would be eternally grateful. However, at that time I knew I had to protect them from him. I didn't want him to see them, I didn't want him anywhere near them. I didn't want my sister near them either.

How would I ever be able to explain to them that their daddy was with my sister? I was damaged and disturbed by the actions of Richard and Maureen. I was convinced my children would be too, if they were old enough to understand the truth of what their daddy and their aunt had done. I wasn't prepared to let them hurt my children, the way they had hurt me.

I believed, that he had got what he had wanted, and it wasn't us. It was not likely that he would want to see our babies either, with the way he had behaved when he left his property on Christmas Day. He would come back time and again showing no concern whatsoever for our children at all, during any of that time. I had to ask him at one point for money so I could feed them. He also had no consideration for Matthew, his child with his estranged wife. He was by now, five years old. He stopped seeing him altogether after just a couple of visits.

Deborah understood that we were leaving her daddy, and we were starting a new life without him. At that point, I had to tell her that her daddy had gone to live with another family and we wouldn't ever be living with him again. It would have been easier to deal with, if he had just run off with another woman who was not related to me! My children would possibly not be affected or disturbed by that. Deborah seemed to accept what I had said to her. She would always ask "Why?" to every question but I could never answer. If Deborah was to find out what Richard had done with my sister, at some point in the future, it would be hard for her to comprehend. I felt that Nichola was far too young to know what had gone on and could possibly not be affected. However, Deborah had a close bond with her daddy for the first four years of her life, until he left the house. She did remember him, I had to hope that there wouldn't be any lasting damage. I was concerned that Nichola may become aware of the truth at some later date and I didn't know what the consequences of that may be for her. I had to prepare myself and find a way to deal with those issues if they ever arose.

The words of the lady, at the Citizens' Advice Bureau, echoed through my head, "He could come along and take them!" Richard said he would never take my children; I wasn't sure whether that was another lie or that he meant that he would never hurt me in that way. However, I wouldn't put it past my sister to try to take them as she hated me. She had taken Richard; she might try to come back for our kids too! Just to twist the knife in my back a bit more.

When my children played in the garden, I was there to watch them. As they played with their friends in the street, I stood at my gate watching over them. I never left their side. No one was ever going to try to take my kids!

For the whole of February, it seemed as if I was hitting rock bottom. I cried a lot during that month, over everything, usually when I was alone in my bed. I worried about my girls so much. I felt inadequate, I didn't think I could cope being a single parent. Money was short, I had very little communication with the outside world and Nichola had been ill. This illness had left her with a bad chest. I blamed myself because the house was cold. I had been used to a much better life with Richard, it was such a pity that I had been so fundamentally let down. I blamed myself for everything. I couldn't see how things could get any better for us. I thought we would have to live that way forever.

On Valentine's Day, I missed Richard so much. If we still had been together, if I hadn't found out about him and my sister and the others, I would be happily waiting for a lovely surprise to come my way from Richard. Usually this was a beautiful bouquet of flowers, delivered to my door, with lovely words on the card. Richard's birthday followed on the twenty-sixth. I had to hold back my tears on that day. I would have planned a lovely romantic meal for us both or some other lovely birthday treat. I would wonder at those times, if he missed me as much as I missed him. I wondered whether he would hear me when she spoke his name, or whether he would be reminded of me, when he looked in her face.

I stayed strong and things did slowly begin to improve for us. Over the next few weeks, we had a phone connected and I had managed to save enough to buy brand-new bunk beds for my girls. They were a bargain! The horrible hospital beds that my dad had obtained for us had to go. I had a little gas wall heater connected in my girl's bedroom. This was on HP from the Gas Board. They could play with their toys in their nice warm and cosy bedroom. Gradually, I began to feel better and more confident that we weren't just surviving, we were thriving too. My children were happy, and I was beginning to smile again.

No one else knew where we were; I didn't want anyone knowing where we lived. I couldn't trust my own family. I had to hide away from them to protect my children. If Richard found out, I didn't think he would come to get my babies, unless Maureen was telling him to, however, I did believe she would be doing just that!

At the end of April, Dad arrived with an invitation from my brother. It was to attend the christening of their new daughter Jackie. It was a lovely gesture, however, I felt I had to decline the invitation. I didn't realise until I had received that invitation, that I would never be able to attend any of my family's functions, or special occasions ever again. That situation applied to birthdays, weddings, Christenings and even something as simple as just going round to their house for a cup of tea. I wouldn't be able to do that any more in case Richard and Maureen were there. How would I ever be able to attend and celebrate with the families of my brother or sisters, when the two of them would be there?

Would they expect me to smile and be happy in their company, pretending that they hadn't destroyed my whole life? I would never be happy in their company; I would never forgive either of them for what they had done to me and my family. I didn't even want to be in the same room as her! I had to isolate myself from the rest of my siblings, and that was tearing me apart.

My little sister, Laura, would surely get married one day but I wouldn't be able to attend her wedding, as they would probably be there too. That would break my heart. I couldn't be a part of the family that I had grown up with. I couldn't expect the rest of my family not to be around her, just because she had hurt me. She hadn't hurt them by her actions, she hadn't totally destroyed their lives. I felt segregated, like the black sheep of the family because I left the father of my children, after I found out he and my sister had been having sex, behind my back. What was I supposed to do? Should I have stayed with him and turned a blind eye and allowed it to carry on? I didn't think anyone should have to live with such an evil betrayal as that.

I hadn't spoken to my brother since New Year's Eve. That was when he provided me with the proof, I needed that finally made me believe that Richard had been cheating on me with Maureen.

I rang my brother to explain. Paul listened to my reasons, as to why I couldn't attend. He said that he understood my situation and informed me that Richard and Maureen would not be there, as they had not been invited. Paul continued to say that he wanted me to attend because they wanted to ask me to be a Godmother for Jackie. I felt honoured. I told Paul, I would be at the christening, if he was sure that Richard and Maureen would not be there. I had his word.

A few weeks later, Mandy and Carl kindly offered to drop us off outside the church to attend Jackie's christening. I was nervous, and very cautious. I was experiencing difficulty with trust. I was uncomfortable for most of the ceremony and kept looking over my shoulder to see if they were coming through the huge wooden doors behind me. My children were glued to my side. I didn't let them out of my sight.

After the ceremony, Paul said that we were welcome to join them at their house for meat and potato pie and a buffet. Paul, noticing my nervousness, kept reassuring me that Richard and Maureen would not be there. I accepted.

Despite my anxiety, we had a lovely afternoon. My girls spent some time playing with their cousins. It was wonderful to spend some time with my brother and his wife and their children, and after endless cups of tea I began to relax. I laughed at my brother's awful jokes and told him a few of mine.

All at once, I glanced through the window towards the street and saw Richards' car pull up outside. I stiffened and started to shake. My stomach did somersaults. My children were at my side, unconcerned and unaware of the arrival of Richard's car. I turned to Paul and said sharply, "I thought you said they weren't invited!"

"They weren't!" Paul said angrily. I watched as Maureen got out of Richard's car and came down the path and walked straight into Paul's house. They stood in the doorway to the lounge and spoke to Sylvia.

I stiffened. I didn't even want to look at her. I certainly didn't want her to look at my children. Paul got up out of his chair and stood in front of me, blocking my view of her until she left. I couldn't believe what a hard-faced cow she was, to just walk in like that uninvited; uninvited for a reason, because we were there. She had no intention of staying away! She had got what she wanted, why didn't she leave me alone? Could she actually be wanting my kids? At that moment I realised it was a huge mistake attending that christening. I might have known that she would find an excuse just to turn up and stand right in front of me, to rub my nose into the fact that she had finally managed to win my man. My stomach was churning, my hands were shaking. I couldn't stand the way she affected me. She was an intimidating bully. She made me feel like I felt when I was a child. I was reminded of the times when I would be laying in my bed at night and listening to Dad beat Mary. I would tremble with fear then too. I didn't ever want her in my life ever again. I just wished she would get on with her life and leave us alone.

I was just a woman, who was trying to be a good mum and raise my children without any more emotionally disturbing situations. It became obvious to me that I would never be able to visit my family ever again.

After another cup of tea, it was getting late. I needed to be getting home. Paul kindly offered to drive us home in his car. However, it was imperative that no one else found out where I was living. I didn't want Richard to come and try to get my kids! I refused his kind offer and told him my reasons.

"You can trust me," he said, "I won't tell anyone where you live." After a little persuasion, I agreed to a lift home. I put my trust in my brother to take me home and to keep our secret.

Just after breakfast, the following day, my friend Mandy and her son Craig, arrived to spend the day with us. We were looking forward to a trip to the park later that day. Our kids played happily on the rug in front of the fire with their Duplo bricks while watching their favourite cartoons on the small black and white portable television set in the corner that someone had kindly given to us. Mandy and I were sitting at the table by the window with a cup of tea. I spoke of the christening the previous day and how good it was to see my brother and his family again.

I just happened to glance out of the window, through my net curtains, at the street below and Richard's car was parked outside my house! I gasped in horror at the sight of him. Instantly, I got to my feet and began to shake uncontrollably. Mandy saw my distress and looked to see what I'd seen. We both stood there, unseen behind the net curtain, watching him, without saying a word.

It was nine o'clock in the morning, what the hell was he doing outside my house? He was sitting in his car, alone, smoking a cigarette, with his window wound down. He was looking all around and up at the windows of my flat.

It appeared to me that he had found out where we were living and he was looking for us. After about five minutes, he drove off. I was in tears and still shaking. I rushed into the kitchen before my girls noticed my distress. Mandy followed.

"How the heck has he found out where you live?" she gasped, as she put her arms around my shoulders.

"I don't know," I said tearfully. "What if he comes to take my girls?" I said.

"Well," she said, "he would have a fight on his hands, coz he would have to get through me and Carl too! He will never get your girls!".

Shortly after, we all got ready and went to the park. While the children played on the swings, Mandy and I talked about Richard, and how he had found out where we lived. I told Mandy that I thought it was strange that I went to the family christening, Paul drove me home afterwards and the very next morning Richard was outside my house! Paul must have told him. Paul had promised me that he wouldn't tell him. I trusted him! I became so upset and angry. I shouldn't have trusted my own brother. Why would he tell Richard where we were living? He knew exactly why I didn't want anyone knowing where we lived. I couldn't understand it.

Later that evening, the children were all sitting around the table in the kitchen eating their tea. Mandy and I were in the living room watching Crossroads. I suddenly heard a car outside. I jumped up to look. There he was again, parked up outside my house! Mandy and I watched from behind the net curtains. We noticed he wasn't alone this time. Maureen was in the passenger seat. In the back seat was Lola, his mother, with Louise sitting beside her. I was so angry. Why were they all doing this? Why were they hounding me?

Mandy said that I should go out and find out once and for all what they wanted. She told me not to be scared and to face up to the situation. She said that I needed to confront him to avoid him keep coming back. Mandy kept a close eye on the children while I gathered the courage to go outside.

I walked up my path and stood at the front gate trembling with my arms folded. He saw me.

"What do you want?" I shouted towards him as he turned to face me. I was shocked by his response.

"I've come to find out where you live! I know now! I can send you a summons now!" He then drove, at speed, off my street.

Once again, he had a total disregard for our children. He hadn't seen them for almost four months and he didn't even ask how they were. He didn't come back into my street again. I later spoke to my brother who swore to me that neither he nor his family had told Richard where we lived. The only conclusion I had was that Richard had followed Paul's car, as he drove me home from his house after the christening. I hadn't thought to look out from the back windscreen to check we weren't being followed.

A few weeks later a summons did indeed arrive. I was to appear in front of the magistrates, in Bolton Magistrates Court. His case was to be heard three months on from the date the summons was served. He was taking me to court for access to our children. Richard hadn't seen our children for almost five months. He hadn't once knocked on my door to ask how they were during all that time.

When the betrayal began, my family was smashed to pieces. Maureen had taken my man. As I had suspected, she wanted my kids too. How could my own sister do that to me? I wasn't going to give up my kids for anyone and especially not to her! This was the start of a bitter family feud.

After a long telephone conversation with a firm of solicitors, I was offered a solicitor who was an expert in family law. He would represent me in court. I had to travel to Manchester to his office, to speak to him in person beforehand, to discuss the case. I broke down sobbing when I had to relive my whole life with Richard, to my solicitor. I told him everything from start to finish. The solicitor listened intently, scribbling notes on the pad in front of him as I spoke.

The day of the hearing arrived. I was nervous, scared and shaking like a leaf. I walked into that court building alone and met with my solicitor in the foyer. He took me to an office at the side of the courtroom to discuss what I could expect when we went into the court. My heart was beating so fast in my chest, I was near to tears. I was trying so hard to hide my emotions. I wanted so much to appear strong and composed, when inside I was so fragile and weak. I had never been in a courtroom before. Here I was fighting for my own children. I shouldn't have been there. I felt like a criminal when my only crime was being the mother of his children.

When we entered the courtroom, Richard was sitting facing forward, at one side of a long table. I was seated at the other end, next to my solicitor. I couldn't bear to look at him. The door at the end of the room opened and we all had to stand as the magistrates entered the court. They took their seats at a long table in front of us. The magistrates then address the court. We were then seated.

Richards' solicitor stood to speak. He presented to the court the points that Richard wanted the magistrates to address. Specifically, Richard wanted access to the girls and argued that I was preventing him from having such access. He stated that Richard hadn't seen his children for months and that I had refused to let him see them. He didn't mention the fact that he had married my sister!

It was then my solicitor's turn to address the court. My solicitor said that it wasn't in the children's best interest to see their father. He identified a collection of reasons why I hadn't allowed Richard access to the children. The magistrates wrote notes and whispered to each other. Finally, they rose, having stated that they would retire from the courtroom to consider the circumstances that had been presented to them. We all stood as they left the room.

When the magistrates returned, my heart was beating so fast and hard, I could almost hear it. The middle magistrate spoke to Richard's solicitor. He used a lot of legal vocabulary that was somewhat lost on me initially. It basically meant that they weren't prepared to hear the case and they referred it to the Crown Court in Manchester. He turned to me and my solicitor and articulated more legalistic jargon. Turning to me he said that the court had awarded me full custody of my own children. This had been another of the matters that required legal resolution. In theory there could have been joint custody applied but thankfully that was not the outcome. My heart almost exploded. I had been holding my breath as the magistrate had been speaking. I almost fainted as I realised what he had said. I had to hold myself together. I was so elated but I couldn't show it. We stood once more as the magistrates left the court. Then Richard left.

I sat back in the chair as my solicitor explained everything that had just happened in the courtroom that day. I couldn't stop smiling. I had been awarded full custody. This was a huge relief to me. It meant that neither Richard, nor anyone else, could come along and take my children away from me. They could be free to play outside without me watching over them every five minutes. I wasn't living with that fear any more. Richard hadn't been given any custodial right to my children at all and no access arrangements either at this stage.

After the court hearing, I had to catch a bus to Horwich. Mandy had been looking after my children while I was at the court. When I got there, the children were happily playing in Mandy's mum's back garden in the sunshine. Mandy had filled the paddling pool for them to play in. They were having so much fun they hadn't noticed that I had arrived. Mandy made a cup of tea and we watched the children playing through the window. I told Mandy of the decision of the court. She was as happy as I was. Mandy began to tell me that Nichola had been a handful that morning.

As I listened intently, Mandy said that she had needed to visit a friend who lived on Chorley New Road, near the Beehive Pub. She continued to say that they were all in the front garden of her friend's house, the children happily running around. Mandy said that she turned her back for two seconds and when she looked back, she couldn't see Nichola. Mandy frantically looked all around for her but she had disappeared. She noticed the front gate was ajar slightly. Rushing out onto the main road, Mandy went to see if she could see Nichola.

To her horror Nichola had crossed the road and was running around on the big roundabout opposite the Beehive Pub. Mandy screamed and ran to her as fast as she could, shouting to her, as the traffic was slowing down and stopping, aware of the small child loose on the road and the dangerous situation that she was in. Nichola was laughing and running around as Mandy chased her. Nichola probably thought it was a game. Mandy finally managed to catch her pick her up and hold on to her tightly. She had then brought her back to the safety of her mum's back garden.

I was horrified to hear this from Mandy. My stomach did somersaults. I couldn't believe it had happened. I couldn't believe Nichola had run straight across that busy main road without being killed. She was not even two years old and I could have lost her, while I was in court, fighting to protect her welfare.

Just after the hearing at the Magistrates Court, my solicitor had arranged to have Nichola's name changed by deed pole. She then became Nichola Wendy Gallagher. Nichola also celebrated her second birthday that August. I had expected a card at least from Richard for her birthday, but there was no word at all from him.

Deborah started school that September and looked so smart in her summer dress and brand-new Patent leather shoes. I left her in the classroom. Leaving her there all day, broke my heart. I had never been apart from her at all since the day she was born. Nichola wanted to stay at school with her sister so she cried her heart out when I had to drag her away. She didn't understand why she couldn't stay at school too. That

October Deborah turned five years old. Once again there was no card or gift from Richard.

The court date arrived for Manchester Crown Court. I was called to attend at the end of November when the matter was adjourned until after the New Year.

The memories of last Christmas had been at the forefront of my mind as I began to prepare for our first Christmas without Richard. I was adamant that our first Christmas would be extra special for my children.

I focused all my energy and thoughts towards providing the best Christmas ever. My preparations started in July. By December, we had everything we needed. My children had to do without their daddy. I made sure they didn't miss out on anything else. Presents were wrapped and placed under the tree, with a few extra special ones hidden away, until Santa arrived. When my children went to bed that Christmas Eve night, they hung their empty stockings on their beds, waiting for Santa. I looked around our home that night, and realised how well I had done, after worrying so much, for months, about Christmas. I felt so proud; we had everything we needed. The flat looked very Christmassy: lots of presents under the tree, the fridge was full of food, the cupboards were full. My children were warm and cosy in their beds, wearing their new pyjamas and very excited about what Santa would bring them that following morning. I sneaked into their room, while they slept, and quietly filled those stockings with lots of little gifts and treats.

I had two little excited daughters when Christmas morning arrived. With eyes as big as saucers they unwrapped their gifts. They were thrilled when they saw their new baby dolls and prams. My girls were very happy and the house was filled with their laughter all day. It was the best Christmas ever.

As predicted, there were no Christmas gifts from Richard. The thoughts of Christmas the previous year were a distant memory for the whole day. Seeing my children so happy became a brand-new memory that I would treasure forever.

On Boxing Day, we were invited to Mandy and Carl's house for another Christmas dinner and yet more presents to open.

Three months into the new year, the court date arrived. Again, during this hearing, no access arrangements were made for Richard either. At that time the court ordered that we were both to be interviewed by the Children's Social Services Department of Bolton. A court welfare officer was allocated to us, to decide what was in the best interest of the children.

The children and I had shared our second wonderful Christmas and New Year before the social workers and the court welfare officer had interviewed us and made their reports for the court. We were then back in court, to hear the judge's decisions. A decision was made by the court that Richard was to have supervised access to Deborah and Nichola, initially in the offices of the Court Welfare Officer. This arrangement was to last for a period of two months.

Deborah was now six years old and was in year two at school. She had settled down well with all the school activities and was a studious child. She had learned to read quite quickly and from then on always had her nose in a book. Her first school report stated that she was a pleasure to teach, and a bright and gifted pupil. I was so proud of her.

She would often say that she wanted to be a dancer when she grew up, so I arranged that she could join a ballet class. This was to be on Saturday mornings with The Penny Hartley ballet class. She loved the lessons. She was a happy and cheerful little girl who would dance around the house so elegantly, when we had the music on. I thought she was so talented, I encouraged her in everything she wanted to do. She was also having swimming lessons and loved going to the swimming baths. It was important to me that my daughters learned to swim at an early age. Nichola would be joining the same swimming class when she was a little older. I felt, as a mother, I not only needed to protect them and keep them from harm, I also needed them to realise that learning to swim was a skill that they had to achieve. It would open their world and could possibly save their lives one day. Nichola seemed to have recovered well, from the earlier bouts of bronchitis. This was a condition that had made her so ill eighteen months previously. Now she was a very energetic and mischievous three-year-old. She was very talkative and so funny at times.

One day a council plumber came to fix the toilet. Nichola stood there asking him all sorts of questions, while he worked. She would ask him what this tool and then that tool was for. She watched his every move. After he had gone, Nichola said, that when she grew up, she wanted to be a toilet fixer! Furthermore, when she saw a loud punk rock band on television, she wanted to be a punk rocker too!

My children were clearly developing their own little interesting characters. Although, Nichola wanting to become a punk rocker worried me slightly! Deborah was a quiet, studious and creative child, serious and sometimes seeming to be older than her years. At times she would be a mother hen to her little sister. Nichola was mischievous, funny, noisy and could be very hyperactive at times. They were both so loving, gentle and polite children, it was just a blessing to be their mummy. I loved my beautiful children with all my heart; they were my whole life. I adored them. I had worried so much about becoming a single parent, however, I had found it to be the most rewarding experience I had ever had. We were managing, and we were happy.

I was horrified a few years previously, at seeing the way Josie had lived as a single parent with all those lovely children, she didn't deserve to live like that. I had experienced nightmares at that time, I was hugely concerned about becoming a single parent, and living a life just like hers. That thought petrified me.

Money had always been short, especially when there was a huge utility bill to pay. There were many times I missed meals to put a meal on the table for my children. Deborah would always comment, "Where's yours, mummy?" I would lie and tell her that I had eaten mine before. My children had everything they needed: a clean house, clean clothes and decent good quality shoes on their feet. They had a nice warm bed and plenty of food in their tummies. Most of all they had all my overwhelming love and devotion.

It had been just over two years since Richard had last seen my daughters. During this time, he hadn't sent birthday cards or Christmas cards to them at all. I hadn't heard from him. It was as if he thought that they didn't exist. For my children, he didn't exist at all in Nichola's memory as she had been too young to develop a memory of him. Deborah didn't ask about him ever. I was sure he had slowly disappeared from her mind. Surely, if he cared for our children he would have, at least found out if they were all right.

Despite having no contact with them in over two years, the many solicitors' letters, appointments and court summonses still arrived.

On rare occasions when family members visited, they would always be eager to inform me of any gossip or drama, within the family. Richard and Maureen were usually the topic of conversation. I hated hearing about them. Most of what I would hear was unsettling. I was very sensitive and emotional at that time. It was said that Maureen planned to get custody of my children, as I was unfit to look after them. She would call me awful names and say untruths about my character.

I was told that Richard and Maureen had moved into a large house in Farnworth. They had bedrooms with bunk beds, ready and waiting for my children, with the names of my daughters, on their bedroom doors. Hearing this both infuriated me and scared me at the same time. I would feel inadequate and insecure, and very emotional.

Any knowledge of my household would go straight back to them, in the same way, I was sure. I could trust no one, at that time, especially my own family members.

When I lived with Richard for all those years, I had to endure the constant rumours from Maureen, that ruined our relationship. I thought I had escaped all that when I left him. I had a more worrying dilemma to contend with after that point. Maureen and Richard were coming after my children, they were out to get custody, not access. My children were my whole world. If I lost my children, I had no reason to live. My life would be over. Richard was aware of my devotion to my daughters, and what taking them away from me would mean to me. I was sure that Maureen was the one who was loading his gun for him to fire.

I fought for over five years to keep hold of my relationship with Richard; I failed. I had experienced an even bigger fight since then. That fight was to keep hold of my own babies. It would be the hardest emotional fight I would ever have to endure. I had to do that alone. I had no family to turn to; my family was their family too!

When they married in 1982, I expected her to get pregnant straight away, then they would have left my children alone to live their lives without him. However, she hadn't become pregnant in the two years since they had got married. Maybe she was infertile and that was the reason for her wanting to take my children, as well as my man!

The day of the first visitation came. The visit was to take place in the Bolton offices in the presence of a welfare officer. This was the individual who had been appointed to supervise the access between

Richard and my children. I was to take my children there to spend an hour with their father.

After I had picked Deborah up from school, I had to speak to her about what we had to do that day. We caught the bus into town and chatted about her daddy. She seemed to accept the arrangement that had been made for them. The entrance to the office was down a back street that led off from Knowsley Street in Bolton. We had to climb the narrow staircase to the second floor. The door to Mrs Burns' office was open and she greeted us. I had met her previously when she was preparing her reports for the court, and my children were familiar with her.

I was nervous and visibly shaking as we took a seat in the office. I didn't know how my girls would react when they met their daddy again after such a long time. I was scared that they would be affected badly, but there was nothing I could do to stop that. It seemed that the welfare officer was unconcerned with whether my children would be affected by the meeting or not. She appeared to be more in favour of their father having contact with them. I was just a normal mother of two small children, living as a single parent, in a two bedroomed flat struggling to survive on benefits. He was the hardworking man who had married my sister, living as a family in a large detached house. I felt inadequate, the thought of losing my children was always on my mind.

We all chatted for a while, then another lady walked into the room and asked if I would like to go upstairs with her to look at a selection of donated children's clothing. I said, "No thank you, my children don't wear second-hand clothes!" The welfare officer suggested that I go with the lady so she could get the meeting underway. She wanted me out of the way before Richard arrived to see Deborah and Nichola. I stood up to walk out of the room and my children came to my side to leave with me. I had to ask them to stay there with Mrs Burns, while I went with the lady. I told them I would be back soon. They reluctantly agreed.

The room I was taken to was up another flight of stairs, at the top of the building. It smelt of stale mothballs and was full of racks of second-hand clothes and black bags full of more clothes. These were on the floor waiting to be hung on the rails. I sat myself on one of the chairs, at the Formica topped table, at the edge of the room. I had no intention of looking at what was on offer on any of those racks.

The wait was endless. I had an ache in my tummy for my children. Inside I was screaming. I didn't know what would be happening to them in that office downstairs. My hands trembled. I waited and sat quietly composed.

When the wait was over, I was taken back downstairs to the office where my children were. I greeted them with a huge smile. They both ran to me. I hugged them so tightly. Deborah's face was flushed and rosy as if she had been crying. She grabbed her coat and wanted to leave right at that minute. Mrs Burns stood and began to speak of the meeting my children had experienced with their father. She said they had had a good time, and instantly ran to their father calling him daddy. I didn't believe that for one minute. Nichola wouldn't have known him at all. He was a stranger to her. I thought, at that time, it was possible for Deborah to have reacted like that, it was just possible that she did remember him. I couldn't wait to get out of that office and get my children home. I did feel that the woman had been wrapped around Richard's little finger. I was becoming a nobody. When we walked to the bus stop, Deborah started to say, "Where did you go mummy? That lady locked the door and wouldn't let me out, I was crying for you! I don't want to go there again mummy!" She continued to say that her daddy had given her a present, it was a 'pop up' book and she liked it, but he took it back off her, when he went!

My daughter was six years old; how could she understand all that. My eyes filled with tears at the thought of my children being locked in that room, and the emotional distress that had been caused to my daughter. I hugged her so hard, I didn't know what to say to her to console her. There was no mention of any of that at all that afternoon, from that welfare officer.

That night Deborah woke up screaming and wanted to sleep in my bed. The nightmares happened again for the second night, and the third. My daughter seemed exhausted and didn't want to leave my side. She always liked school but at that time she would cry every morning and was reluctant to go in.

After a week the school began to be concerned, because she would be upset in her classroom. I was called into school to have a chat with her teacher. I spoke to the teacher about the meeting with the welfare officer and the fact that Deborah had said that she had been locked in a room. I thought that such an experience could have affected her badly. They agreed and thought that if it continued, she might have to have counselling. I was angry inside and it was breaking my heart that my child would have to go through that trauma.

To my horror I received a letter from Mrs Burns saying that after the successful visitation between Richard and my daughters, she had made a further appointment for him to have another visit with my girls. I did not feel that the meeting was a successful one at all. Specifically, after that meeting, I had a little girl who had been traumatised and possibly would need counselling!

When I telephoned Mrs Burns, to speak to her of my concerns for my child she informed me that it was understandable that my child was upset, because she was picking up on the bitterness I felt for Richard. She said that I was the one who was causing her to be upset! She said that it would be in her report to the court! I couldn't believe what I was hearing.

I was heartbroken by the way I had split from Richard, and I didn't ever want him or my sister, in my life again. I was happy to have escaped from under his spell. I was thankful that I hadn't wasted any more of my time, love and devotion on him. What they did to me was not normal, I was glad that I had broken free when I did. Their behaviour, at that time, had started a family feud because she wanted to take my kids away from me, and at that point I began to hate her. How could I ever be expected to accept that?

I was living a happy life alone with my children. My children were happy too, until that day in Mrs Burns' office when everything changed. I didn't feel I had any support whatsoever from the children's welfare officer. I felt I was manipulated and that all her concern was for Richard and my sister. I just thought that she would eventually help them to gain custody of my children.

Despite all the problems I was facing with my child, and against my wishes, a second visitation was to take place. I was told that if I was to refuse or hinder the arrangement in any way it could affect the custody case and I could lose custody. Mrs Burns said that she would recommend that it was in the best interest of my children to have regular contact with Richard and eventually Maureen too.

I was powerless. I had to agree to everything that they wanted. The fear of losing my children was too much to bear. Mrs Burns told me that the next meeting would take place at my flat. I was to allow Richard to come into my flat to see the children! I was horrified to be forced into agreeing to that. I felt alone, vulnerable, intimidated and bullied. I didn't want him in my home. I had no choice.

The meeting took place, supervised by Mrs Burns. I stayed in my home and watched and waited until it was over. I didn't want to speak to Richard, I didn't want to make him a cup of tea or be pleasant to him in any way, I just wanted him out of our home as soon as possible. My concern was for my children and making sure they were happy during that meeting. I made sure that I was there if they needed me, and not locked in any more rooms.

Mrs Burns had written a report, following that meeting in my home, she stated that it was a successful meeting between Richard and his children, however, I had been 'hostile' to Richard. She recommended that Richard be allowed to take the children to his home for any further access visits. Once again, I had to agree to further access visits, or there was the stated threat of losing my children.

Richard had now got what he wanted. He was from then on, after only two supervised visits, on the say so of the court welfare officer Mrs Burns, allowed unsupervised access. That was not what the courts had specified but I wasn't courageous enough to complain.

Within a couple of weeks, Richard was collecting our daughters every Sunday morning at ten o'clock and bringing them back home later that day for five o'clock. It wasn't long before we were back in court again.

I had been sent another summons so that Richard could ask the court to allow him more access to my girls. The court allowed him access for Sunday only.

At the end of March, we were woken by a loud knocking at our front door. With bleary eyes, I went down to answer the front door. It was Richard, he had come to collect the girls for his access visit.

"You are early!" I said, looking at my clock which was showing nine o'clock.

"It's ten o'clock," he said sharply.

"Have you not turned your clocks forward?" he asked. The girls came running down the stairs in their pyjamas. "I will take them as they are," he said.

"You won't!" I responded, "they haven't had their breakfast and they aren't washed and dressed yet, so you will have to wait!"

He walked away from my doorstep and went to sit in his car.

Within fifteen minutes there was another knock on my door. My children were half way through their cereal and still weren't dressed. Richard's impatience annoyed me. When I went to the door, I was shocked to find a police woman standing there. She explained that Richard had used his car phone to telephone the police because I was going against the court order and refusing him access to his daughters! I told her that I disagreed with that and explained the situation. She then asked if she could come in and have a chat. As my children finished off their cereal in the kitchen, I offered the policewoman a cup of tea. We sat in the living room discussing the events of that morning. I began to tell her a brief history of what had happened between Richard and me.

"Your sister!! That must have been a shock! Is there any more tea in that pot?" she continued and settled herself into the armchair.

"I don't think Richard will mind if we keep him waiting a bit longer will he.!" At twenty past eleven, my girls were ready to be collected.

The policewoman made it clear to Richard that the children had to be back at the usual time of five o'clock.

When Richard gained more Legal Aid, he appealed against the last court's decision and we were back in court once more. That court case gained him one overnight stay once a month. The Sunday access visits were changed to a Saturday, as we attended church on Sundays.

As there were no offers of financial help from Richard for his two daughters, since we had split, I was advised to take him to court for maintenance. The court case was held in Manchester Crown Court. I was disgusted and insulted to hear that my children had been awarded a total sum of five pence per year — each!

Richard claimed he was out of work and unable to support my children. I couldn't understand how he could claim he wasn't working. He had just bought a brand-new detached property in Farnworth. I also couldn't understand how he could get these official people to believe every word he was saying. I felt he was conning his own children.

During the next three years, Maureen had two more children. When their own children came along, I thought that access to my children would cease. Despite their new babies, I was still taken back to court several times. Richard wanted more access each time. He also wanted the court to decide whether he could take them on holiday! Because of the spiralling problems that would occur during the time of the access visits, I would never agree to the access being increased or ever allow him holiday access. I didn't think Maureen approved of Richard coming to my house to pick up our girls, I was sure she would have preferred it if he didn't have any contact with me at all.

Around this time, I enrolled in Bolton Art College on a three-year course in the history of art. I had also been re-housed at that time, into a three-bedroomed house. We hadn't moved far, it was just across the road, in the same street. The house felt so huge compared to the two bedroomed flat which we had called home for the last couple of years.

My daughters loved the new house. The back garden was enormous, and the front garden was lovely. We had tidy borders with evergreen bushes all around. Deborah and Nichola each had a bedroom, with their own choice of colour scheme. They were in their element. They had new divan beds and new bedding. Their names and their favourite cartoon characters were painted on their bedroom doors. We were a lot better off in that house. It was less likely that Richard would turn around and say in court that I had unsuitable accommodation for my girls. He had tried to use that against me when we lived in the flat, saying that his house was a far more suitable place for my children to live.

The courts at that time agreed with me that the arrangements stayed as they were. It was never the end though. A posh car would regularly pull up outside my house. Two big men, smartly dressed in black suits, would get out, and walk down my path. I would answer the door and be handed a large brown envelope containing another affidavit and a court summons. The whole court process would be starting again, time after time.

The last affidavit was delivered in the same way, at eight o'clock in the morning. My daughters were upstairs getting ready for school. I opened the envelope and started to read the affidavit. As always, it seemed to be line after line of a process that attempted to blacken my character. He said I was volatile, and I had undertaken an affair when we were together. If I had experienced a relationship with a man, it was wrong. If I went to church, that was wrong too. He would state what a loving bond he and Maureen had with my daughters and how it was in the children's best interest to see more of him. His words sounded so believable, just like they had when we lived together. I believed his every word then. I was sure the courts were going to believe him too. I feared that I would lose custody of my children.

The emotional anguish was building up inside as I read every line. He was ripping my heart out with these words.

How could he say such things? He used to say he loved me!

As I sat reading those words, I couldn't stop the tears. At this point, Deborah walked into the living room.

"What's wrong mummy?" she said, as she wrapped her arms around me. "Nothing's wrong," I said, forcing a fake smile and looking directly into her eyes.

"I am crying coz' I'm happy, coz' I've got the most beautiful daughters in the world and I love you both so much."

One sunny Saturday morning, Richard picked the girls up as usual. I had busied myself with my usual routine of cleaning the house and cooking. I was also recharging my batteries, ready for another week with the children that I expected to be difficult. At times the children were so unruly and bad mannered, when they came back from their dad's. It would take me all week to get them back to their normal selves and calm them down, only to have to endure the same again the following week, after another day at their dad's. Week after week was the same. It was spoiling our lives. We didn't seem to have any fun as we used to do before the access visits. I was not having any joy at all in raising my own children, I was always telling them off for their bad manners, when they became very cheeky. I became the bad parent who had to discipline them all the time. Richard and Maureen were the good guys who spoiled them with too many sweets and let them do exactly what they liked, at their house. It was particularly hurtful to hear Nichola say things like, "When we go living at Dad's house, we can have coco-pops for breakfast!"

It was clear to me that my children were being told things like that by Richard and Maureen and made to believe that they would soon be living with them!

After three years I had had enough, I couldn't cope with it any more. I wished it would all end and they didn't have to go there any more. I wished that my little girls would become the well behaved happy little children that they were, before Richard and Maureen had access to them. I wished Deborah and Nichola would say that they didn't want to go there any more.

My best friend Mandy had come to visit for the day. She was staying for dinner which had been cooked and we were waiting for my girls to be brought back home at five o'clock. Five o'clock arrived and my children hadn't arrived home. When they hadn't arrived home at six, I began to panic a little. I had tried to telephone him at home, but there was no answer. I hadn't received a telephone call to say that they would be late or stuck in traffic. When six-thirty arrived, I decided to drive over to Richard's house. Mandy stayed at my house, just in case they arrived back while I was away looking for them.

For the last few months, I had been driving my sister's silver Vauxhall Nova. Ann was working as a nurse abroad, so she had loaned me her car until she came back to England. Before I drove it, I had to get the insurance in my name and have safety harnesses fitted on the back seat for my girls.

When I drove into Richard's street, I noticed his car wasn't on his driveway, and all the curtains were shut. As I turned my car around outside his house, I noticed that there was a note attached to the door. I parked the car and went to see what was on the note. It read:

"NO MILK UNTIL FURTHER NOTICE."

My stomach was doing somersaults. My heart was beating so fast, I was filled with such dread in the pit of my stomach. I got back in my car and drove to Richard's mum's house in Kearsley. She wasn't in either.

It was seven o'clock in the evening. I called at a telephone box to ring my house number to see whether they had arrived home. Mandy said that they hadn't returned home. Sitting in my car I was distraught. I didn't know what to do. I was imagining all sorts. Had he kidnapped my kids? Had he fled the country with them?

I drove around to all the relatives that I could think of. No one had seen them. Still there was no sign of them at home. It was after eight o'clock. Richard should have had them home for five o'clock. My hands were shaking and my head was hurting. I wanted to cry. I felt sick. I then thought that they could have had a car accident. My stomach turned over again.

As I drove back onto my estate, it was almost eight-thirty. I turned the corner onto Knutshaw Crescent and Richard's car was just pulling up outside my house.

As well as the relief of seeing them there, I had got myself into such a state, I was distraught. I saw my girls get out of his car and run into the house to their Aunty Mandy. I pulled up and parked my car behind his and got out. I saw red and flipped. I had had enough. That was the last straw. There was no apology from him for being late, no words of concern that I had been scouring the streets looking for him. I then told him that he wasn't having the kids any more.

"Take me back to court!" I shouted, as I walked up my path to see my children. I didn't know where I had received the courage to say those things to him. I had been too soft and manipulated for far too long. He had walked all over me for long enough. I had been bullied and threatened into allowing Richard all the access to my girls that he demanded. Only for him to take advantage and not follow the agreement. They didn't care that I had spent the last four hours going out of my mind with worry for my children. It needed to be stopped.

As I walked up my path, Maureen got out of Richard's car and shouted that she would see me in court, if I was not too busy showing off driving around in Ann's car!

I turned and gave her a look of complete disgust. She didn't deserve a reply.

I closed the front door behind me. I fell to my knees and cried my eyes out. I was so relieved that my children were back home safely, where they belonged, I held them so tightly.

CHAPTER FIFTY-SEVEN
A Little Miracle and Big Changes

The next day I woke exhausted. I had hardly slept. I knew that I would have to appear in a courtroom with Richard to fight for my girls again. I also knew that Mrs Burns had told me many times, if I hindered the access arrangements in any way, I could lose custody of my children. I had gone against those arrangements and stopped him seeing my girls! I must have cried myself to sleep that night. I didn't think I would cope with yet another court case. The thought of being taken back to court and losing my babies petrified me.

It had been windy all through the night, and that morning the rain was lashing down. My girls were wearing their big yellow raincoats and wellies and splashing in every puddle they could see, as we walked to the bus stop. I was trying so hard to hold onto my umbrella in the wind, as I watched my children having fun in the rain, I tried to smile. I was surely going to lose my children, I thought at that time, as I had gone against Richard's wishes.

As we waited at the top of the hill, for our bus to take us to church that rainy Sunday morning, I was in despair. I was trying to imagine what my life would be like without my children. They were my life; without them I would have no reason to live. I seemed to be sinking into a deep depression. My hands were shaking and I wanted to cry. I wished that I could run away with my girls and hide, and never, ever be found. I looked up to the dull sky. The cold rain hit my face and disguised my tears. I looked downwards towards the road, the stream of water that the rain was creating, was rushing past in the gutter. As I stared into the swirling water, I saw a green and white piece of paper floating by. I looked closer and pulled it from the water. It was a pound note! I showed it to my girls and told them that we could have a nice treat when we left church later that day. Their little faces lit up with huge smiles to match mine.

In my pocket that day, I had enough money for the bus fare to church, and back home again. That was all I had. There was never any money for the church collection each week. There wasn't usually much left over from the benefits, to pay for treats for my girls either. We had to do without a lot of things as we needed to pay bills. It felt like a miracle finding that pound note! I could do a lot with that. It couldn't have come at a much more needed time. My depression lifted as I looked towards the heavens, smiled and said, 'Thank you!' My heart filled with hope. For the first time in a long time, I was instantly filled with a feeling that everything was going to be okay!

The following weekend I was relieved when Richard didn't turn up at my house to pick up the kids. I knew that within a few weeks I would have another summons from Richard to appear in court. When the summons arrived, it was to appear at Bolton Crown Court. Bolton had received a new building, containing both Crown and County Courts, hence I did not have to travel to Manchester as had been the case previously.

As Deborah had experienced a few emotional issues at school, during the time of the access visits, we had been appointed a school child guidance counsellor called Pat Powell. When the access stopped, the change in my nine-year-old was remarkable, thanks to Mrs Powell. That lady became a special person in our lives. Deborah liked her; she grew in confidence every time she counselled her. I could see a change in Deborah straight away. She was becoming that happy, joyful little girl I once knew. Pat became close to both my children and became a trusted friend to me.

When I knew I was to be taken to court again, Pat offered to come along to support me. She had completed the report on the counselling sessions that she had done with Deborah and Nichola. They were available to the courts if required. When the court date arrived, I met with Mrs Powell and my solicitor early in the foyer. Pat and I were taken through two big, double, wooden doors to one of the court rooms. We all discussed the case until it was almost time to go into court. Pat went back to the waiting area, and I sat waiting with my solicitor until we were called in.

When we were beckoned into the courtroom, Richard was sitting at a long table with his solicitor. He had about two dozen photographs strewn across the table in front of him. We took our place at the top of the table and stood for the magistrates as they entered.

The middle magistrate spoke to the court, then Richard's solicitor stood to speak to him. After a while it was my solicitor's time to speak. Then the magistrates left the court. Sometime later they returned and spoke to the court again. I didn't quite understand what was being said. We had to stand again as they left the room. I didn't understand it. Was it over so soon? It ended so quickly. I hadn't even said one word in that courtroom that day. My solicitor then took my arm and we hurriedly left the courtroom. I didn't know what had happened. With my solicitor still holding onto my arm, we rushed through the double doors into the waiting room, and out through the foyer to the outside.

We stood together on the steps of the court entrance. As we walked through the waiting room, I glanced across at Maureen, she was sitting with a couple of women who all looked in my direction as I left the court. I turned my head from them quickly, I didn't want to look at the woman, who was trying to wreck my whole life. As we walked through the waiting room, two large security men were rushing past us. They went into the courtroom that we had just left. I could hear shouting. I didn't know what was happening. I was so scared.

We stood on the steps of the court for a few seconds. My solicitor began to explain to me what had happened in the courtroom. He told me that basically, Richard had not been given any access to my children. He said that the court heard enough reasonable evidence to stop the previous access arrangements and recommended that Richard apply to Manchester Crown Court for a further hearing if he wished.

Pat came and stood by us. She told me that as we walked out from court, she heard my sister saying to the other women, "We've won, I can tell by her face!" I started to cry, "It just shows you," I said, "it's all a game to her! She's playing a game and my children are the pawns!"

All at once the doors to the court flung open. Richard and his party were being escorted out of the building by the security men. As they passed us, Maureen shouted at the top of her voice, from the steps of the court, in front of everyone.

"It won't be access we are going for next time; it will be CUSTODY! Those kids hate your guts!"

I couldn't believe it was my sister's voice, saying all those hateful things. How could my own sister behave like that? I knew all along that she wanted to take my girls from me. Not because she loved them, it was purely because she hated me! I wasn't being paranoid, or irrational. I had just heard it from her own mouth. She said those nasty words to hurt me. Everything she had done was to hurt me. Her words were full of hatred and spite. She was full of hate. I saw hatred in her face that day, as I had seen so many times before. I also saw the angry face of my father staring back at me. It was clear that she was indeed her father's daughter.

Three months later, the expected summons arrived for Manchester Crown Court. My solicitor, a barrister and myself waited around in the long corridor outside the courtroom for over an hour. Richard did not attend. The case was adjourned for some time later. Richard didn't show up for that court case either. My solicitor then informed me that Richard had claimed Legal Aid for all the court cases. He wouldn't be able to claim any longer because he hadn't attended the last two cases. This meant it was all over. The end of all the court cases. No more solicitor's appointments. No more affidavits. No more summonses. After over five years, the long, hard, stressful, emotional fight to keep hold of my children was all over. I didn't lose my whole world. I didn't lose my most precious jewels — my babies.

Travelling back home, on the long bus ride from Manchester that day, I was elated. I felt that it was the happiest day of my life, after the births of my beloved babies. That day seemed like the beginning of the rest of my life. I looked out through the window at the clouds in the dull sky. All at once the clouds parted and the sun shone brightly through, warming my face. I just knew that everything was going to be just fine.

Three months later, Deborah was dancing on stage at Bolton's Albert Halls with Jim Bowen. He was hosting a wedding event. Twelve ballerinas, all dressed in beautiful white tutus, from The Penny Hartley School of Dancing, were chosen to dance on stage throughout the show. They danced so gracefully around the models dressed in such elegant wedding gowns. Deborah loved her ballet class and had passed most of her ballet exams with distinction. However, before the conclusion of the court case with Richard, Deborah would not have had the confidence to perform that routine on a huge stage, as she had been so shy and withdrawn. At that time, she seemed to be a different little girl. She was so happy and full of life. Her confidence had grown so much in that short time.

Nichola and I sat ourselves on the red velvet seats and watched her performance in awe. Nichola didn't take her eyes off the stage throughout the whole show. I feared she wouldn't be able to sit herself still, as usual, however, to my surprise she behaved like an angel. The pride in my children was clearly apparent.

A year later there was another big change in our lives. We left Bolton. We moved from the house on Knutshaw Crescent. I was happy there for a time. However, I felt, after all we had been through in Bolton, that we needed a fresh start. I had been thinking about it for a while. I wanted to raise my children away from Bolton, in the fresh air of the countryside. At that time, Mum had moved with her husband Jack, and had bought a lovely property in a little village called Coppull, near Chorley. Since the end of all the access arrangements, we had spent quite a lot of time at Mum's house in the country.

They had a huge back garden, full of their home-grown vegetables, different types of flowers and shrubs. Jack had a vegetable plot at the bottom where he planted lettuce, onions, green beans, and many more different vegetables. He had a huge greenhouse, where he grew his many varieties of tomatoes and peppers. Whenever we travelled over on the bus to Coppull, we would always find them both sitting in their back garden. Jack would be in the greenhouse and Mum would be sitting at the table under a parasol doing a crossword puzzle. Mum loved her garden, she was surrounded by roses of every colour: black eyed suzies, sasha daisies, and primroses. Climbing vines and huge clematis were weaving around the wooden pergola. I remember the garden filled with butterflies and bees, gathering the nectar from each bud. The girls loved it when the butterflies would fly onto their shoulders and sit for ages as if they were trying to whisper in their ears.

Before long, we were moving to Coppull. We shared Mum's house on Chapel Lane for a little while, then managed to secure a temporary rented property in Blackrod for three months. We were then re-housed into a council property on Longfield Avenue near to Mum's house. Coppull was a beautiful little village with scenic country parks and lots of trees. Deborah and Nichola had enrolled in a new school, called

Chapel Lane County Primary Church School. They settled in really well in their new class; Deborah was one of the oldest in year five and Nichola one of the youngest in year four. It was a tiny village school in a beautiful old building that was built in 1847. There were only twelve pupils in Deborah's class, so different from the thirty pupils in their old school of St. Mary's in Bolton. They both made lots of friends and loved living in Coppull. It seemed so different from the hustle and bustle of Bolton. The local shops and amenities were within walking distance and seemed to be right on our doorstep. We walked everywhere. Rain or shine, the walk to school every morning was lovely.

Dad had been looking after Timmy, our little Cavalier King Charles Spaniel, since we left Knutshaw Crescent. We had settled in our new house so we were able to collect him from Dad's house and he came to live with us again. Every morning he joined us on that walk to school. He was so handsome, he received lots of attention from all the children on the playground. He seemed to love being the centre of attention with all the children. If he found a discarded baby's dummy on the ground, he would pick it up, hold it in his mouth and suck it like a baby would. This would make everyone laugh on the playground. We were amazed later that year, when we entered him into a pet show during Coppull Carnival, and he won 'Best In Show'.

Coppull was a friendly happy place. Everyone seemed to know everyone, or they were related in some way. The neighbours on the avenue, where we lived were friendly too, and we all soon became very good friends. During that summer, when the sun was high in the sky, we would all come together outside in the open space outside our houses. We would sit on the walls, or our sun loungers, drinking tea and watching our children playing on their bikes or roller skates, in the sunshine.

Some days we would go for long walks with Timmy. We would go down to Birkacre, a country park, or sit in the Wheatsheaf's beer garden, having a cool glass of beer. The children would sip a coca cola from a glass with a straw. We all became very close and good friends. We were happy at that time, without a care in the world. Life was normal. Life was good.

At the end of that lovely hot summer, all the children were back at school beginning a new school year. My girls seemed to be growing up so fast. I would gaze at my children and think back on the years in Bolton, our lives had been so different at that time. We weren't happy. It was impossible to live a normal life, with the stresses and torments that we had to deal with during that time.

Our lives in Coppull became as normal as they could be. My children seemed so happy, and healthy. They thrived. I felt blessed to be their mummy. I was so proud of the beautiful, well-mannered and polite little girls I was raising. It became a joy, just to wake up with them every morning.

CHAPTER FIFTY-EIGHT
1988 Repeated History

My dream had always been to have four children one day. I was broody and cooed over any of the neighbour's new babies, whenever I had the opportunity. I would have loved to have two more children, at that happy time, in my life. At twenty-nine years old, I was thinking that time might be running out for me, and I would have to settle with being a mother of two forever. I found it hard to trust another man after the trauma that Richard had put me through. I couldn't see myself ever getting pregnant again.

When I lived in Bolton, I did try to trust a man again. I was invited for a night out with friends to a nightclub called Scamps in Bolton. I met a man there and exchanged telephone numbers with him. Initially, I thought he was nice enough. We dated for six months; however, he would turn up at my house very late at night drunk as a skunk, and I would refuse to let him in. I didn't want that sort of behaviour around my girls.

Another man I dated was lovely too, I thought. He would turn up at my house dressed in a soldier's uniform. All the neighbours would look and stare whenever he arrived at my house. He was tall, blond and so handsome and he would march down the street looking immaculate and proud, wearing his green army uniform. I loved listening to the army stories he would tell.

As the weeks progressed, and every time he turned up, his uniform looked brand new. I began to question whether he ever got the uniform dirty at all! I became suspicious. I later found out that he was not in the army at all, he just liked to dress up! I had been lied to for ages, and I had fallen for the lies again.

I felt I wouldn't ever be able to trust another man as long as I lived. I couldn't tell whether they were telling the truth. I believed that I was a magnet for the wrong sort of men; the liars and the cheaters.

The only way I could tell when Richard was lying was to see if his lips were moving, it seemed. I gave up looking for a new boyfriend and settled down with no worries, as a normal happy, single parent with my two children. I couldn't bear to listen to lies again. I had to give up on the dream of ever having two more children.

A group of friends and I was having a night out in the Wheatsheaf one Friday night. During the evening, I began to be distracted by a man who was playing darts. He was on his own in front of us. I didn't think he was any good at it because none of the darts were hitting the dart board as they should. Most of them fell on the floor in front of him. I tried to join in the conversation with my friends. However, his dart throwing became an amusing distraction. Every time I looked towards him, I noticed he was looking at me. I looked away shyly. It wasn't my imagination. As he turned from the dartboard, after collecting the few darts that had stuck in the board, he would stare straight at me, and try to smile. My cheeks glowed; he was cute. I was embarrassed and tried not to watch him. I would smile and tut to myself as another dart hit the deck.

When I got up to go to the bar, I had to pass him as he threw a dart. Once again it hit the board upside down and dropped to the floor. I stopped and looked at the dart on the floor.

"That's a funny place to have a dart board!" I said to him amused and pointing to the dart. He smiled and went to retrieve it. I walked away and went to join the queue at the bar. As I waited to be served at the bar, from the corner of my eye I could see him approaching. He stood right next to me.

"Can I buy you a drink?" he said as the barman came over to serve me. I accepted with a smile as my face glowed bright red. He then turned to the barman and ordered the drinks. He was so handsome, I thought to myself. I was struck silent. All I could manage to say was 'thank you.' He looked right into my eyes. Then he broke the silence and said, "You have beautiful eyes!" I blushed again, smiled and lowered my head. I picked up my drink, said "thank you" and went to sit back with my friends. To my surprise he followed and sat himself at the next table to ours. It became clear to my friends, possibly by my rosy cheeks every time he tried to talk to me, that he was trying to chat me up, so they invited him to join us at our table. He introduced himself as Stuart. When I heard his name my eyes widened, and he got my attention. With tears in my eyes, my thoughts drifted off to the place where I once knew a little boy called Stuart; I adored him. He was the little son of Diane, a neighbour, and a special dear friend from Glynne Street. She became an inspiration and meant so much to me back then. I missed them both so much. I would always say that when I had a little boy of my own, I would name him Stuart. I had to hold back the tears. I was wearing mascara!

I then introduced my friends to him and told him I was called Maggie. He then almost choked on his beer as I said my name. He chuckled to himself and said, "That was my mother's name!" I didn't believe him for a minute and told him so. He laughed and said that it was true. His mother was indeed called Margaret.

As the drinks flowed, we all became relaxed in his company, he seemed like a really nice guy. We chatted for the rest of the evening, and at the end of the night he asked for my telephone number.

The next day he rang me and asked me out on a date. I didn't hesitate to accept. We spoke on the telephone several times throughout the week. He would tell me about his life, and his work. He also told me that he had split from his girlfriend of two years, a few months previously, he had lived alone in his own house since then. He wasn't telling me anything that worried me about his life. There was no wife hiding anywhere nor were there any vicious ex-girlfriends to worry about. He was just an ordinary handsome single man. Best of all he told me that he liked kids so that was an added bonus. I started to look forward to our date and became quite excited. When Friday arrived, I was nervous.

Josie and John, my friends and neighbours from across the way, offered to look after my girls. They had three daughters of their own, called Emma, Kirsty, and Kate. Emma and Kirsty were the same age as my two daughters, and had become good friends with my daughters, as soon as we had moved onto Longfield Avenue. Kate, the younger daughter, was nearly three years old and so adorable.

I spent hours getting ready for my date. I couldn't settle on an outfit. I finally decided, with help from Deborah, my little fashion advisor.

"Yes, mummy wear that!" she said, choosing my brightly coloured blouse.

When Stuart knocked on the door, I was full of nervous excitement. Nichola rushed to answer the door and invited him in. As he walked into my living room, Josie, John and all the children looked on with smiley faces.

During that week I had been trying to describe him and hoped I wouldn't have forgotten what he looked like. However, he was just as I remembered him. He was so handsome. Stuart then strangely held out a bottle of milk and said, "Do you need some milk?" I laughed and took it from him and put it in the fridge.

John then said to Stuart that that was the first time he had ever seen a man give a bottle of milk to his date, usually she would get roses! We all laughed together. Then Stuart said, "I will bring flowers next time!"

Over the next few weeks, I saw Stuart many times, and I did get flowers too. He would call at my house often and invite me to his house on Hurstbrook too. The more I saw him, the more I was beginning to like him, lots. Despite being in awe of Stuart, at that time, I was holding back my feelings. I had trust issue, and they showed. I didn't want to be hurt again. However, the more I got to know Stuart, the more I realised that he was not like Richard at all, and he would never hurt me in that way ever. I was falling in love with this man who was hard working, charming, funny, honest and decent.

On Thursday 3rd November, it was my thirtieth birthday and I had planned a night out with my friends at the local pub. Josie was coming along too so Stuart kindly offered to look after my girls while we went on our night out. Stuart bought me a lovely birthday card and a Robert Palmer's 'Simply Irresistible' album. He was so sweet.

After the night out, I was tipsy when I got home, and quite sad, in a way, to have turned thirty. It had always seemed such an old age when I was younger, it had seemed so far away. This birthday represented that age and it made me feel old.

I reflected on the life that I had encountered previously, I felt a little down. I wanted to cry. I didn't want Stuart to leave. I didn't want to be alone. I asked him to stay over. I told him I loved him and we made love. We fell asleep in each other's arms.

The next morning, he was up early for his work. He kissed me on my forehead as I dozed, crept downstairs and left the house. I drifted off to sleep again with the thoughts of our night together so clear in my mind. I was so happy with no regrets.

My happiness was short lived. A few days later, Stuart rang me and told me that he needed to talk. He sounded quiet and sad. Instantly, after hearing his tone of voice, I thought, it was not going to be what I wanted to hear.

"I've had a letter from my ex-girlfriend," he said. I listened so intently. He continued, "She's six months pregnant!"

I listened in shock at the familiar words that I had heard before. I was horrified. It was history repeating itself. I couldn't believe it. I didn't know whether to cry or to congratulate him. He had respected me enough to come and speak to me in person, and I thanked him for that. I knew in my heart that he was a decent man, who would do the right thing and be with her, and I also knew he was ending our relationship. Despite our brief relationship, I had a great deal of respect for Stuart, it had been a pleasure to have known him.

Stuart then said that he hadn't wanted to leave his girlfriend, he loved her. She had left him. She didn't realise she was pregnant. As soon as she found out she had to let him know.

As we talked a little while longer, I suddenly remembered we had made love, and I wasn't on the pill. The thought of a possible pregnancy without the father's support filled me with dread. I could feel my heart beating fast in my chest. I turned to Stuart and said, "What if I'm pregnant too?" He shook his head and held my hand.

"That would put the cat amongst the pigeons, wouldn't it?" I said, dismissing the thought completely from my mind.

It took Richard and I two whole months to conceive our girls. I didn't think for one minute that I could be pregnant after making love to Stuart on just one occasion. I wished him well and congratulated him. We parted as friends. I wasn't sad or hurt. I was honoured to have known such a lovely gentleman and to have loved him. His girlfriend was a lucky woman. He was going to make a wonderful father for her child. I would remember the way I felt at that time forever. However, I did cry myself to sleep that night, with the thoughts of what could have been.

Two weeks later my period was due. It didn't show. I thought I couldn't possibly be pregnant and put it down to the emotions I had when Stuart and I ended our relationship. I thought I hadn't been eating properly, I had lost my appetite, and I had been rushing around so much and worrying about Christmas for my children. All those little worries convinced me that this was the reason why my period was late. I also thought that because I was so broody at that time, it could have been a phantom pregnancy. At the end of November, I still hadn't seen my period. I was beginning to wonder. After another couple of weeks, and still no sign, I began to worry. I hadn't told anyone that I could have been pregnant, I kept it to myself. In one way I was so happy at the thought of being pregnant. In another way I was shocked and worried about what people would say because I already had two children, wasn't married and claiming benefits. I thought I should go to a chemist and have a pregnancy test. I handed my sample in over the counter. I paid the £3 and was asked to ring for the result in a few hours.

I called at my friend's house to ask if I could use her phone. I had to confide in Kath about the reason I needed to use her telephone. She had been a trusted friend and I could rely on her to keep my secret.

At 2pm I dialled the chemist's number for my results.

"The result is positive," the pharmacist said, "are congratulations in order?"

"Yes! Thank you!" I said and put the receiver down. I looked at Kath, she had been standing next to me waiting to hear the news. I burst into tears. She held me and sat me down at her kitchen table.

"How am I ever going to cope?" I said as she put the kettle on.

"Just like you've always done!" she said. "You are a fantastic mother and your girls are a credit to you!"

After we had drunk a cup of tea, I began to calm down a little and I got used to the idea that I was once again pregnant. I asked Kath whether I could possibly use her phone once more. I needed to speak to Stuart.

I rang Stuart's work number. While I was waiting for him to come to the phone, I looked at the calendar at the side of Kath's phone. It said 16th December. I then realised it was Stuart's birthday.

When he came to the phone, I quickly told him the news. He went quiet. I didn't expect him to go silent, I expected him to put the phone down but he didn't. I interrupted his silence to say that I was happy and keeping the baby. I also reassured him that I was never going to rock any boats for him and his girlfriend, and that I didn't want anything from him. What had happened had happened and I would raise the child, alone if necessary. I repeated again, that I was keeping the baby. I then asked him if everything was all right with his girlfriend and her pregnancy. He then broke his silence and said, "Yes, everything is fine. We are having a little girl." I then congratulated him and wished him 'Happy Birthday' too I said bye and hung up the phone.

Over that Christmas, I kept my pregnancy a secret from everyone. Kath kept my secret too. Mandy, Carl and Craig visited over Christmas and Mandy spoke of the problems they had been having conceiving. They had married earlier in the year and had been trying for a baby ever since but nothing was happening. Mandy was very concerned as she had wanted another baby so badly. My heart sank. I went quiet. How could I tell them that I was pregnant?! It would break Mandy's heart. I turned to her and said, "When the time is right you will conceive!"

I didn't know what I was saying. Was it the right time for me to be pregnant, in my situation? They had everything to offer another child. However, I had nothing, except my love and devotion. I loved my unborn baby already. How was I ever going to reveal my secret to Mandy, my best friend, in the whole world, and not upset her?

My secret was revealed to Mandy and Carl in the new year just after I had told my daughters. My girls were elated and couldn't wait to tell everyone. Mandy was quite upset, although she tried not to show it. I knew her too well. I could see she was trying to look pleased for me. However, I could see the sadness in her eyes.

After I had told her she didn't seem to want to visit as often as she used to. I understood why. It wasn't long before all the family found out that I was pregnant; my mum had spread the gossip.

On the 26th February 1989 Stuart's girlfriend had her baby. They named her Emma. That date too was Richard's birthday, and my sister Lorraine's. I wouldn't forget that date in a hurry!

Early that year, I found out through the grapevine that Richard and Maureen had split up. She had had three more children with him but now she was divorcing him. Their marriage didn't last long. I didn't want to know the reasons why. I still didn't want anything to do with either of them. They had both tried to wreck my whole life and shattered my whole family. They tried to take my children away from me! I could never forgive them for that, I would never be able to forget.

I had a new life in Coppull. I was succeeding in putting all my past life with him behind me. I had a life that didn't involve or include them. I was glad they were divorcing. I would be even more happy if they stayed a million miles away from me and my children. It was beginning to look like it could be a great year!

CHAPTER FIFTY-NINE
1989 Stuart Born

It was such a beautiful spring and summer with lots of sunshine that year. My tummy was growing and at sixteen weeks, all the morning sickness had stopped. I was blooming and looked so healthy.

At twenty-two weeks I had a baby scan. I was ecstatic when the nurses informed me that I was having a boy. I was so happy. My children were so happy. From then on, I was knitting with blue wool. It was like a dream. I was living a dream.

Arlene, a friend and neighbour, came across to my house with a huge bag. It was full of baby clothes. There was everything I needed for my baby in that bag. Some were brand new, and the rest immaculate and hardly ever worn. I was so grateful to her. My baby boy didn't need anything else at all. Arlene also gave me some beautiful maternity dresses. I didn't have the money to buy myself new clothes. My priority was my children and the new baby, I didn't like to spend money on myself. I was getting fed up with dressing in cheap baggy tee-shirts and leggings, they weren't very flattering to my pregnancy. When I wore the dresses, I felt radiant and proud. I was complimented on how lovely I looked.

My baby's pram and cot were bought from a second — hand shop in Chorley, both excellent bargains. The only expense was the Visivent mattresses. I was fussy and needed new ones. Despite worrying about how I was going to cope having another baby I realised I was actually doing okay. Money was short, it always had been, but we managed. My baby didn't want for anything, I had everything I would need all ready and waiting for my new baby to arrive.

At Coppull Carnival that year I got to meet Stuart's girlfriend. She was nice. I said 'Hello' and smiled as she walked past me. She returned the smile and said 'Hello' too. She was pushing her baby girl in her pram. Emma was sitting up in her pram and looked as pretty as a picture wearing a white frilly sunhat. She was a beautiful baby. I was heavily pregnant. As I walked away from her, I looked down and rubbed my tummy. I knew my baby would be beautiful too.

During my antenatal visits I had to inform the midwives regarding the past history of my pregnancies, and the fact that I had two quick deliveries. I told them I was concerned because I lived quite a distance from Sharoe Green Hospital and I may give birth before I got there. After a long consultation with the doctors and midwives it was agreed that I would have to go into hospital to be induced and stay at the hospital until I had delivered.

The visits from Mandy and Carl were few and far between since I'd told them that I was pregnant. When they did visit, Mandy would be distant. She had no interest at all in my pregnancy. She wouldn't even look at the baby clothes I'd collected or the little knitted cardigans I'd made. It was as if she was pretending or ignoring the fact that I was having a baby. I knew why she was behaving like that and sympathised with her. However, towards the end of my pregnancy, during their visit, Mandy sat herself next to me. My baby had been wriggling around inside for most of the evening and we had all been sitting, watching the movements over my tummy. It was like he was playing football inside me. Mandy then placed her hand on my bump and left it there for ages, feeling the kicks and the wriggles for herself. She rested her head on my shoulder and smiled. Carl looked on. He looked at me and smiled.

On the 27th July, 1989, I was admitted into Sharoe Green Maternity Hospital. At around seven in the evening, I was given the pessary to start me off. I went to bed shortly afterwards and slept through the whole night. I expected to be awoken with labour pains, through the night, but I had none.

The next morning, I was given another pessary and after a few hours I was taken up to the delivery suite. The midwives attached me to a monitor and said that I was in labour. I hadn't felt a thing.

At 1.30 in the afternoon, I was lying on a delivery bed bored to tears. I kept looking out of the window at the glorious sunshine outside, and wishing I was out there sunning myself instead of stuck in that bed. I nodded off. I was woken up by a doctor at 2 o'clock, who had come into the room to examine me, and specifically to break my waters. The midwives were still saying I was in labour. I hadn't felt a thing!

At 2.20 I began to feel some pains. The midwives were around my bed waiting. My baby was on its way. At 2.38pm on Friday 28th July my son was born. The midwife wrapped him in a towel and placed him in my arms. He was the most beautiful baby boy I had ever seen. His skin was like velvet. He was perfect. I looked into his face and all I could see was Stuart's face looking back at me; he was the image of his daddy. "What are you going to name him?" the midwife asked.

"Stuart Ryan Lloyd Gallagher," I said.

"Awww, yes," she said, "he looks like a Stuart." The midwife then took him out of my arms and weighed him and checked him over. He weighed 7lbs 1oz. They placed his identity tags around his wrist and ankle then he was back in my arms again.

A midwife popped her head around the door and said, "You have visitors, can they come in?"

"Yes of course," I said. It was three o'clock and I had just given birth and Josie and her mum walked into the room. I was elated.

"Look at him Josie! Just look at him! He's perfect, he's beautiful." Josie rushed to my side; her whole face lit up with a huge smile. I offered my baby to her to hold. She gladly took him from my arms and gazed into his face in awe.

Later that evening I was allowed to go home. Josie and her mum drove me home. I had to promise that I would go straight to bed and rest for the next twenty-four hours. I was so glad to be going home to my daughters. They sat with me on the bed and couldn't take their eyes off baby Stuart, taking it in turns to hold him.

The next day Mandy and Carl came to visit. Mandy came into my bedroom and sat herself on the bed next to me, while I was feeding Stuart.

"He's beautiful," she said.

Before long she had him in her arms and couldn't take her eyes off him. Mandy looked so happy that day. I hadn't seen her smile like that for a long time. All at once she turned to me, looked me straight in the eyes and said, "I think I'm pregnant!"

That really was a lovely surprise. What an amazing year it was turning out to be.

A week later, Deborah was playing out with her friends, climbing her favourite tree on Pear Tree Avenue. She fell out of it, breaking her arm in three places. She had to go into hospital overnight to have the bones fixed back together. Her arm was in plaster right up to her shoulder. She started year seven at Southlands High School, with her arm in plaster.

Two weeks later, we were all settling down to watch Coronation Street on television and there was a knock at the door. I was feeding Stuart, so Deborah went to the door. To my horror I heard a familiar voice. It was Richard's! Deborah let him in, and he walked straight through the hallway and into the lounge where we were all sitting. I couldn't believe my eyes. He was not alone. He had walked in with another one of my sister's, Jane, and her two little children. I couldn't speak! How dare he?

"I heard about Deborah breaking her arm and I have come to see if she's okay," he claimed. "And I've brought Jane to see you too! She heard you'd had another baby."

Jane had been sent away, when she was about ten years old, to a children's home in Hastings, which was run by nuns. She then left the social services care, when she was old enough, and went to live in Manchester. Before long she became pregnant. She didn't have a very good life when she became a mother either. She had two baby boys that she wasn't allowed to keep, because of the life that she was living at that time. The social services took them and they were adopted. Richard and I had visited her in the hospital, just after she had given birth to her second little boy, who she named Steven. He was born with an extra little finger on his left hand. The doctors had tied a suture around it to cut off the blood supply and wrapped his tiny hand in a bandage. The finger then slowly turned black and shrivelled up and fell off on its own.

Jane had told us at that time that the social workers were coming to the hospital to take him away. I remember being so devastated for my sister, way back then. She had always wanted children. She told Richard and I that she would keep having babies until the social services allowed her to keep one.

The memories of her traumatic childhood were still vivid in my mind. One sunny afternoon, when my big sister and I returned home from our aunt and uncle's house, we discovered Jane standing silhouetted in the hallway. She was wearing her nightdress. She had been punished. The bruises clearly visible through her nighty. She was seven years old.

Around ten years later, Jane was sitting in a hospital bed after giving birth to her second child. She was waiting for the social workers to take him away, just like they had taken her away, all those years ago.

This was the last I had heard of Jane, until that day when she walked into my house with Richard. I thought she looked so grown up, and so beautiful. She reminded me of Kylie Minogue. She had had two more cute little boys. I presumed she had sorted her life out and had kept these two little boys. I didn't like to ask her any questions, just in case it upset her, speaking of the two that she had lost. It was so lovely to see Jane again and talk a little of what had been happening to her since her awful childhood. I started to get a strange feeling in my tummy. I became a little puzzled as to why Richard was in the company of yet another one of my sisters. What on earth was Jane doing with Richard?!

CHAPTER SIXTY
Living Happily Ever After

Richard must have obtained a quick divorce from Maureen. His other divorce took years; who knows what story I would have been telling if things had been different. His marriage to Maureen lasted about seven years! They both went on to marry again shortly afterwards. After all those years, I still didn't want anything to do with Maureen. Just because she was divorced from the father of my children, and we were related, didn't mean I had to have her in my life. I still didn't want to be anywhere near her. I could never forgive her for trying to take my children away! To save me from the life I had with Richard, I could forgive her but not for trying to take my kids! Maureen was in Farnworth and I was in Coppull, a far enough distance away from each other.

In May 1990, my beautiful children were all christened together in Coppull Parish Church. It was one of the best days of my life. We created lots of special memories that day, memories that I will treasure forever. Mum was there for the whole day, and her husband Jack videoed the whole church service on his new video camera. Mandy and Carl and Josie and John, all became godparents to all three of my children and remained close in the years that followed. The sun shone all day long. It was a beautiful day. I felt so happy and extremely proud of my little family.

In 1991, I got to meet the woman who had become Richard's third wife, another woman to bear his children. She was beautiful and such a lovely lady. They had three children together over the next few years.

I was so relieved to find out that she was not related to me in any way!

My daughters, as teenagers, were old enough to make their own decision as to whether they wanted their father in their lives. They did choose to see him now and again. I didn't stand in their way. He was no threat to me any more, he couldn't take my children away from me, or interfere with my life in any way.

I had met a lovely gentleman called Michael, and we were happily living together, despite the continuing trust issues that I had, he was understanding and patient.

He took on my three children as his own. His family was almost as big as mine. They were all so lovely and welcomed me and my children into their close family.

In 1991, Timmy, our handsome Cavalier King Charles, died. He was thirteen years old. He was one of the family; we were all devastated and missed him so much. The house seemed empty without him.

Two years later, Michael surprised me with another Cavalier King Charles, she was a beautiful eight-week-old tri-colour, who we called her Pippa.

Jack, Mum's husband, retired from working down the pit in around 1990. They both had plans to move to Southport and enjoy the rest of their lives out there. However, Jack became ill, and didn't have a chance to enjoy his retirement. He got cancer and died in April a year later. Mum's world was completely shattered, and after a while she moved to Bolton to be near her loving sisters, Noreen and Florence.

Three years after Stuart was born, I became pregnant again. I gave birth to another son in 1993. We named him Dean Michael Brandon. My dream was to have four children; two girls and two boys. I got what I wanted. Life had become normal.

We were a normal family, at long last. I was living my dream.

Unfortunately, the relationship ended a few years later. However, we remained close friends. I was once again a single parent. I was happy and enjoying living the normal life that we had strived so hard for, for so long.

In 1995 I missed my mum. I felt alone at times, with no other family members around us in Coppull. I decided to move back to Bolton to be near Mum. A decision I was later to regret. Michael and I became close again despite the fact that we were better at being friends than lovers.

There was a near reconciliation within the family, and almost an end to the family feud that had developed in 1982. Just after Mum moved back to Bolton, I followed a few years later. It wasn't long before Maureen moved onto the same estate. It was hard to avoid each other. We began to acknowledge each other, and act sisterly again, in the hope of time being a great healer. However, as we tried to get along, I discovered that certain aspects of Maureen's life reminded me of the trauma that she put me through all those years ago. It seemed she was amusing herself in the same way with another poor girl's life at that time. After I had taken the same amusement for over ten years, there was too much bad water under the bridge. I could not forget what she had done or forgive her. I did try to forgive, although I didn't feel as if she was remorseful or sorry at all. I didn't think she even cared who she hurt along the way. I couldn't become a friend of hers, let alone be a sister to her again.

The childhood of my daughters had suffered because of their betrayal. They didn't have the mother's attention that they deserved when they were growing up. My children must have been affected by the constant emotional torment I was under with the fear of losing them. The pressure to keep tight hold of my children was unbearable. I did cry a lot at times and had sleeping problems when a court date was imminent. I was not able to be the mother I wanted to be. I failed to protect them from the emotional traumas at that time. I could not get that time back.

So, there was no reconciliation, I didn't want to know the person she had become, let alone be a sister to her again.

Shortly after moving back to Bolton, we discovered, Lola, Richard's mum was very ill with cancer. Her youngest son Lee, and his then wife, were caring for her in their home, and looked after her until the day she died. My daughters and I had been able to see her and spend some time with her before she died. She passed away on the 8th May 1995.

On the morning of the funeral, there was a police car at the front and the rear, escorting the long procession of cars into Overdale. The traffic was stopped during the whole journey from Kearsley to Bolton. The crematorium was packed as people had come from all over to attend. I was sure if Lola could have been looking down on us all that day, she would have been loving every minute and approving with her proud smile. She would have felt like a VIP.

One haunting image that stayed in my mind of that day was when we all left the house that Lola had spent her last days in. All Lola's grandchildren, most of them Richard's children, of all different ages and sizes, came running excitedly across the front lawn and climbed into a huge black limousine just for them. I couldn't contain my tears at that point.

To my surprise, a few months later, I had a visit from Lee, Lola's youngest son. He had been sorting through Lola's belongings in her house and came across a large brown padded envelope that contained the pages of the story I had written when I was fifteen.

Lola had taken it away all those years ago to read it. I never saw it again; I didn't think I ever would. She had kept it all that time. Lola had promised to read it and to keep it safe. She also promised to get it back to me after she had read it. She had finally kept her promise.

Keith, Richard, and Lee, Lola's sons, were featured on Granada Reports on television, when they had decided to scatter their mother's ashes on Kearsley roundabout.

One morning, at the beginning of 2002, the phone rang. It was a lady from a television company called September Films, she said that she was doing a documentary for ITV, and she had come into contact with Richard. He, at that time, had taken part in a couple of television appearances on various chat shows, regarding certain issues. One in particular I recall was of Richard on a chat show, with a hypnotist, who had hypnotised him on stage, in front of television viewers.

She explained that Richard had approached her and spoke of his story and how he had become involved with the two sisters. He also told them that he had caused the rift in our family and he wanted to try to put it right with a public apology. I went along with the plan, although I didn't think an apology would do any good at all, at that point. Too late for any apologies. The damage had been done.

The filming started. Film crews went to his house and came to my house. They got the footage they needed and within a few months it was on ITV. It was called 'Love Cheats from Hell'. We took part in the documentary, which included four stories of women that had been betrayed by their husbands or partners.

Deirdre from Coronation Street (Anne Kirkbride) also appeared on the programme discussing the role she had played a few months earlier, where she was jailed for fraud after the man that she had married conned her and got her into serious trouble. She talked of the plot in the programme and how she was affected by playing the part of a woman taken in by lies and deceit. At the time, the plot caused outrage all over England despite the fact it was a fictional storyline of a programme. It was in all the newspapers and there was campaigning to free Deirdre.

Before it appeared on the television, our story went in various magazines, and in our local newspaper, the Bolton Evening News. On the morning of the programme, Richard and Maureen also appeared on GMTV. At one point, Maureen stated that she didn't know I was in a relationship with Richard. Richard ended the interview saying that I was adventurous in the kitchen and Maureen was adventurous in the bedroom!

I didn't hear any apology from either of them during the filming. Richard almost appeared pleased with himself that he had managed to have all those children with all those different women, and two sisters. The family feud continued.

A few weeks later we all had one final attempt to be friends again. We were all sitting in a room and discussing everything once again. Richard claimed he didn't remember most of our life together and wouldn't admit to any of it in front of Maureen. And Maureen too denied her part in the betrayal for all those years, with the intention of causing the break-up of our relationship.

Nothing was said to ease the pain that I had felt all those years ago. The lies continued that day, with Richard's and Maureen's denials. I was still left with a feeling of the continuing intimidation and resentment, and I couldn't accept all those lies that day.

I did try unsuccessfully to end the feud, but I couldn't accept the lies, and the denials, so it would never be over. They didn't care what they had done to me and my children.

Neither of them accepted that their actions had the consequences that created the bitter family feud and destroyed the happiness that could have been within. They didn't want to ease my pain. That pain almost destroyed me.

After I sought help from a counsellor, I began to write my story, to heal a wound that had been raw for so long.

At the end of that last meeting, Richard and Maureen stated that they didn't do any of it to hurt me.

It was nothing personal!

My invisible scars told another story!

Our father died of lung cancer, on the 30th September 2006. It was said to me, that at the point of Dad's death, in the hospital, that he apologised to Paul. I wondered if that was any consolation to Paul at that time? I felt I needed to be at the funeral to say my own farewell to the man who had brought me into this world. I sat myself at the back of the crematorium, away from my family, who were huddled together at the front. I was sitting with the support of my best friend Mandy at my side. I listened and watched the vicar speak of the life of my father.

All the information had been provided by Maureen and her family. I watched the faces of my mourning sisters. They shed their tears. I think that was expected of them. My tears came with the haunting memories of my brother being beaten, my little six and seven-year-old sister's visible bruises, and the black eyes and swollen face of my mother, and my step-mother.

Although I was not physically beaten, the emotional trauma that I suffered, in witnessing how life had been back then, was extreme.

For my own part, I particularly remembered my father taking my pet rabbits and slaughtering them in front of my very eyes. He did this with the same stick that he used to beat my siblings to a pulp. Then with morbid cruelty, he served up those same rabbits for tea!

Mum died on 3rd April 2012.

Mum and dad ended up at the same crematorium. For Mum, I sat myself with my family, for her send off. A happy memory of my mum was when she would sing 'Ava Maria' at the top of her voice when she was cleaning. We arranged a singer to perform this song at the crematorium. The singer stopped singing and cried, when she saw all six sisters instinctively stand up, holding hands to sing the last verse; it was unrehearsed and unplanned. The congregation of our aunts, uncles, cousins and friends cried. I think Mum would have been proud that day.

As I have lived my life and had children of my own, and created many happy and lasting memories along the way, and achieved the normal life that I strived so hard for. We were, at that time, living the dream.

I have wished that all those earlier memories would disappear, be erased and be forgotten forever.

The imaginary brick walls that I had built around me to stop the hurt, could be seen from the moon at times, and those invisible scars, which are buried so deep inside, have taken the longest time to heal.

Time heals the hurt. Now is the time for the healing to begin.

THE END

If you are suffering domestic abuse in any way, there is help out there. You are not alone.

There are specialist confidential services available that will support you. They will keep you safe and offer emotional and practical support.

If you feel that you are in immediate danger call 999 or 101.

It's not always easy to ask for help. Living with the fear we had as children it was impossible to even think of getting help by talking to teachers or the police. It was behind closed doors and not even discussed until we became adults and realised it was so wrong.

It's important to seek help, to break that chain, to survive, to be happy x